How To Make
A Whole Lot More Than $1,000,000
Writing, Commissioning, Publishing
and Selling "How To" Information

Dr. Jeffrey Lant

Revised Second Edition

Published by JLA Publications
A Division of Jeffrey Lant Associates, Inc.
P.O. Box 38-2767
Cambridge, MA 02238
(617) 547-6372 • fax (617) 547-0061

How To Make
A Whole Lot More Than $1,000,000
Writing, Commissioning, Publishing
and Selling "How To" Information

Dedication

I dedicate this book to the small boy in Hans Andersen's immortal tale "The Emperor's New Clothes," the boy who looked at the naked emperor and, alone, had the brains to say "he has nothing on." This boy somehow knew what we all must learn again, namely that true knowledge begins with a recognition of the obvious, and a willingness to acknowledge and act upon it — whatever anyone else may be thinking or doing. It is altogether fitting and proper that this of all books be dedicated to this hitherto unsung, nameless hero.

Acknowledgements

As always, many people have been generous with their time and specialized knowledge in the preparation of this book. Because they can also be of the utmost assistance to you as you create and market info-products, I'm happy to include complete follow-up information about them in the text. A few, however, deserve extra recognition for all they have done. They include Professor Robert Dobson, Lucille Dube, James Duzak, Esq., Barbara Hagen, John & Lorraine Hamwey, Joseph LaRosa, Dr. Efrem Mallach and Dan Poynter. I am glad to be able to thank them publicly for their assistance.

TABLE OF CONTENTS

A Few Words From The Author
For The Revised Second Edition

Thousands of people worldwide are now using this book to do two things: improve the quality of the how-to information they deliver to their readers and listeners and to make more money. In other words, with *this* resource they are doing well by doing good. I'm delighted.

I wrote this book, as you'll soon see, because I was very, very angry about the ocean of drivel being put out by how-to "authorities" and because I was tired of seeing well-meaning people fail to profit from what they knew . . . because they didn't have an idea how to package and market it properly.

There is still too much how-to drivel being published and too many people are still failing to profit from their knowledge because they approach the creation, packaging and marketing tasks the wrong way. But I am pleased to tell you that these avoidable errors are mostly made by creatures who haven't troubled to study this book.

Indeed, I'm delighted to tell you that over the last few years hundreds of people have contacted me to express their appreciation for this book — and to tell me how well they've done because of it, producing superior audio cassettes, special reports, booklets and books and profiting accordingly. I am pleased, of course, but not surprised. For years I'd perfected these methods with my own books and materials, and it wasn't until I was supremely confident of their value that I offered them to others in this book.

Now I am offering them to *you*, updated so you can profit faster in the difficult decade of the 'nineties. Now more than ever your customers are looking for value. They not only want you to know what you're writing about... they want you to present this information in the most usable format possible. Too, you want to get back not only the money you invest in your products but a substantial profit — and as quickly as possible. In the pages that follow you'll learn precisely how to achieve both objectives.

When, having studied these methods and produced your info-products, your readers and listeners start complimenting *you*; when you start making a steady income from what you've produced, stop a minute and rush me a wee note crowing about your success. And if this note contains a few words of praise for your production and profit mentor, why I shall accept them with humility (but without surprise).

v

What's In This Book, How To Use It, Why I Wrote It

I have written this book, my tenth, with a single objective in mind: to help you make money . . . yes, lots more than $1,000,000 . . . creating, commissioning, publishing and selling problem-solving information in:

- booklets
- books
- Special Reports, and
- audio cassettes.

This is no pipedream, and this book proves it.

From the earliest days of publishing in this country, Americans have had a love affair with how-to information. We want to know how to do everything better . . . and so we have spawned a legion of individuals who spend their time delivering the facts on everything from how to outsmart the stock market, to looking younger as we get older . . . to writing books on how to make money from booklets, books, Special Reports, and audio cassettes!

The problem is, most of these authors and publishers don't make much money with their products. Study after study shows just how few authors and just how few info-products make significant profit, or any profit at all.

Why do so many of these products — and their authors and their publishers — fail? Significant reasons include:

- not knowing the market. Too many info-products are egotistical productions. If you want to make money from such a product, you must direct it squarely at a large and growing market that has a pain you can take away . . . or an aspiration you can help them achieve.

- not delivering useful information. Most how-to books and products are useless . . . they don't provide the *exact* details people need to achieve the promise of the product's title. But why should anyone pay good money for a product that doesn't deliver what they want?

- not producing client-centered marketing materials. If you want to motivate an individual to buy a product, you've got to tell him just what he's getting, all the advantages, benefits you have for him. But most info-producers talk about their products . . . not about client advantages. As a result, most of the marketing communications produced by info-entrepreneurs end up where they belong . . . in the trash.

- not hammering home these benefits in an organized, efficient, relentless way. If you want to make money in the information business, you cannot be vague or obscure about the advantages you've got for your targeted market . . . you must be direct, pointed, persistent.

- not updating products, selling them for years. Most information publishers take a product out of circulation after a year, two at the most. Smart ones pinpoint a market in need, produce a valuable problem-solving product, and resolve to sell their product so long as this market has this problem. Updating is therefore inevitable.

- not creating a line of problem-solving information products. Information entrepreneurs who become rich do so because they don't put all their eggs in one basket . . . or one product. They diversify, not only updating all products but regularly adding new products . . . both those they create themselves and those they get others to create.

To solve these, and a host of related problems, I have written this book, which I guarantee will help you crack them . . . and so launch you on your way to becoming America's next millionaire information producer.

What You'll Find In This Book

This volume is divided into thirteen chapters. Briefly, I'd like to introduce them to you.

In *Chapter 1,* you get the 23 leading reasons why most information entrepreneurs fail to make money. These are the mistakes you must understand and guard against. The rest of this book gives you the information you need so that you need never make these errors yourself . . . and will prosper accordingly.

When you finish with *Chapter 2,* you know how to do the necessary market research that enables you to select the correct subject for your info-product. Too many authors and publishers think and create egotistically . . . for themselves. If you want to be an information millionaire, you must create with a market — or several markets — in mind. This chapter tells you how to do that . . . so you create and publish a product that you can profit from for your lifetime, or until the problem the product addresses has been solved.

In *Chapter 3,* you get step-by-step guidelines on how to create your product. Never again wonder how to develop a client-centered problem-solving product. Here are the details you need.

Chapter 4 extends this discussion by telling you what you need to do to produce valuable booklets, special reports, and audio cassettes, thereby enabling you to create a line of profit-making information products.

Chapter 5 tells you how to create an end-of-product catalog so you can start making money not only from the information products you produce but also those produced by other entrepreneurs. There's no reason why, within a very short time, you cannot be selling dozens, even scores of information products . . . profiting from them all. This chapter tells you how.

Creating products, however, won't do you much good unless you can produce them efficiently and inexpensively. That's why in *Chapter 6* you get the information you need on how to produce your booklets and books in the most economical, least frustrating way.

Chapter 7 takes up the question of how to integrate the personal computer into your business, making it at once more efficient and economical . . . and broadening your reach to new, profit-making markets. Most information producers haven't begun to understand or use the computer to their advantage. After reading this information, you will . . . because you'll know exactly what it takes to turn the computer into your most effective business management and marketing tool, both saving and making you tens of thousands of dollars.

Because you want to create the broadest possible line of how-to products, you will need to enlist the support of other specialists, turning their expertise into information gold. *Chapter 8* tells you how to do this . . . where to find the specialists you need and how to get from them what you must have to develop your information empire and create new sources of profit.

By the time you've finished the first eight chapters, you'll be well on your well to creating a mighty line of information products. Now you must learn how to sell them . . . as fast as possible. *Chapter 9,* therefore, provides the information you need to think and act like a marketer . . . like a person, that is, whose chief desire is helping others by selling them information products that assist them . . . and motivating them to buy as quickly as possible.

Chapter 10 takes up the subject of how to sell your products through free publicity in print publications and through electronic media. You learn exactly what you have to do to get continuing free space and time . . . and to use it to make money by selling your info-products. Never again will you wonder what you have to do to use these means to sell your products. You'll know . . . and be able to profit accordingly.

Chapter 11 provides the guidance you need on how to sell your info-products through direct response marketing. Here, you'll learn exactly what you need to know to bring your product line directly to the attention of your customers . . . and what it takes to get them to buy NOW . . . not tomorrow! To become an information millionaire, you must master direct response marketing. This chapter shows you how.

The marketing details you need are continued in *Chapter 12*. Here you learn just what you need to profit from workshops and talk programs, creating your own dealer network, sales to libraries and bookstores, selling at trade shows, and the sale of foreign rights. This chapter contains an avalanche of specific selling information!

Finally, in *Chapter 13,* you learn how to establish the right form for your burgeoning information empire, how to develop and maintain your growing wealth and so achieve financial independence, and how to manage your time so that you do all that needs to be done to create and market the products on which all your prosperity is based.

How To Get Your Money's Worth From This Book

Like all the books I've written, you should not merely read this one once and put it aside. I am your consultant, and this book constitutes an active conversation between two people . . . between you, who wants to become a millionaire information producer . . . and me, who has presented certain crucial information that will enable you to achieve this goal.

Unlike other books in this general subject area, this one is dense with practical information . . . and my very direct opinions on what to (and what not to) do. As a result, you may find that it takes you some time to read this book . . . and that, from time to time, you find yourself getting irritated with me. Let me tell you why I'm not worried about these things.

If you really want to become a millionaire information producer, there's lots you must know and master. This is not a subject that can be understood in an afternoon of cocktails at Cannes. This is a business that demands technical expertise and continuing supervision. Get used to it.

Moreover, if, now and again, you find yourself getting irritated with me either because of what I'm telling you . . . or the way I'm telling it to you . . . I beg you to consider that the mark of a good consultant, a consultant who's really worth his money, is his ability to tell you the truth, the truth that may well make you uncomfortable. If this bothers you, I'm sorry, but it cannot be helped. Try to pay attention to the point I'm making, why I'm making it, and how I'm making it. In short, reserve judgment until you're finished.

As for my critics, who delight in commenting on my (often idiosyncratic) literary style, diction, and presentation, I have this to say: tell your readers about my ideas and about my crusade to turn all how-to products into truly useful entities. Remember, my job is to present my ideas in the most forceful way using just the right words. I am not interested in the "objective" presentation of information; I am interested in motivating people to do what they need to do to achieve some desired result . . . and, having motivated them, to give them just what they need to achieve this result. As a result, this book isn't dry and dull. It's alive! Pulsating! Catalytic!

Yes, if you let it, it will change your life . . . and make you a multi-millionaire.

A Few Words About Who I Am And My Role In Your Life

I am, by profession, a consultant. Unlike my more traditionally minded colleagues, I don't believe I need be physically present to assist people. I am perfectly happy to do my consulting in person, of course, but I am equally content to work with my clients through my Sure-Fire Business Success Column (now reaching over 1.5 million people monthly in over 200 publications and electronic data bases), and through my books, Special Reports, audio cassettes, workshops and talk programs.

Over the last fourteen years, using these means, I have myself become an information millionaire. What's more, when I started I had only the slenderest of resources . . . slender, that is, except in my unquenchable desire for success and a willingness to do whatever necessary, go wherever necessary to reach my objective.

Year after year, therefore, I have worked hard to create the information products that have not only made my fortune but the fortunes of many others . . . and which have, at last, become the basis for this book. These products include:

- THE CONSULTANT'S KIT: ESTABLISHING AND OPERATING YOUR SUCCESSFUL CONSULTING BUSINESS. Here's what you need to break into the consulting business and begin to make money from your problem-solving expertise.

- HOW TO MAKE *AT LEAST* $100,000 EVERY YEAR AS A SUCCESSFUL CONSULTANT IN YOUR OWN FIELD. When you want to make over $100,000 every year from your consulting practice, this book has the detailed guidelines you need to do so.

- THE UNABASHED SELF-PROMOTER'S GUIDE: WHAT EVERY MAN, WOMAN, CHILD, AND ORGANIZATION IN AMERICA NEEDS TO KNOW ABOUT GETTING AHEAD BY EXPLOITING THE MEDIA. Never pay for space in print media and time on electronic media. Now learn how to get them for free . . . to sell your products and services.

- MONEY TALKS: THE COMPLETE GUIDE TO CREATING A PROFITABLE WORKSHOP OR SEMINAR IN ANY FIELD. Learn just what it takes to make thousands of dollars daily delivering talk programs based on your problem-solving expertise.

- MONEY MAKING MARKETING: FINDING THE PEOPLE WHO NEED WHAT YOU'RE SELLING AND MAKING SURE THEY BUY IT. Here are the details you need to create a marketing plan and implement it using every kind of marketing technique there is. (By the way, this book is also available on 18 hours of audio cassettes.)

- CASH COPY: HOW TO OFFER YOUR PRODUCTS AND SERVICES SO YOUR PROSPECTS BUY THEM . . . NOW! Here's where you learn how to create marketing communications — flyers, cover letters, ads, brochures, annual reports, proposals — that get your prospects to buy NOW! (Also available in an audio cassette package).

- NO MORE COLD CALLS: THE COMPLETE GUIDE TO GENERATING — AND CLOSING — ALL THE PROSPECTS YOU NEED TO BECOME A MULTI-MILLIONAIRE BY SELLING YOUR SERVICE. If you're running a service business and want to get rich, here's precisely what you need — in 680 unrelenting pages!

- DEVELOPMENT TODAY: A FUND RAISING GUIDE FOR NON-PROFIT ORGANIZATIONS. Follow the guidelines in this volume, and raise the money you need for your nonprofit organization from individuals, corporations, and foundations.

And now there's HOW TO MAKE A WHOLE LOT MORE THAN $1,000,000, WRITING, COMMISSIONING, PUBLISHING AND SELLING "HOW-TO" INFORMATION.

In this book, like everything I create, I invite you to stay in touch with me. This book is not set in cement; it's organic, changing. The techniques that I recommend today to help us both in the development of our information empires will necessarily be augmented tomorrow by the inauguration of new, better processes. I intend to know and use them . . . and I intend to share them with you.

I invite you, therefore, to stay in touch with me. If you got this book through any other source than directly from me, you are probably not on my mailing list. If you'd like to receive a free year's subscription to my quarterly Sure-Fire Business Success Catalog (a copy of which appears in the back of this book), you need to contact me. More, if you'd like me to assist you in creating and marketing your info-products, developing your info-empire, you must let me know. Call me at (617) 547-6372 or fax (617) 547-0061. I answer my own phone and am ordinarily ready to get started immediately helping you. However, I think it's only fair to advise you that if the answer to your question is in any of my books, special reports or audio cassettes, I'll tell you to find it there first, and buy it if necessary. Fair enough?

Final Words

After you've had the chance not only to read this volume but to begin implementing it, after you've had some success, I hope you'll contact me to let me know how you're doing. You see, if I've felt the exhilaration of this business and garnered my share of the financial benefits, I've also experienced its characteristic frustrations and irritations. I know what you're going through and for that reason as you succeed, I want to know . . . and want the opportunity to congratulate you, for you have much to be congratulated for.

Implementing the procedures in this book, you see, will not merely benefit you . . . important though that is . . . it will also benefit the people who will be better off using the information you sell them. I want to congratulate you not just for what you've achieved for yourself, but for what you've achieved for them.

Write me soon! I love to hear good news . . . especially when I may have contributed to creating it.

Your information friend,

Jeffrey

Cambridge, Massachusetts
May, 1993

Twenty-Three Reasons Why Most People Fail To Make Money From The Booklets, Books, Special Reports And Audio Cassettes They Produce Or Commission . . . Why You'll Lose Money, Too . . . Unless You Use This Book

It is not merely my contention, it is, instead, well known fact that the vast majority of people producing or commissioning booklets, books, special reports, and audio cassettes either lose money outright on them . . . or, considering the hours they spend producing and marketing them, have a trifling, insignificant return. I do not intend to let you be one of them. I intend your efforts to be crowned with every success . . . not just so you're better off (delightful though that circumstance is) . . . but so more people — *your* customers — are better off, too.

These are the twin goals that inform this book: to help others and so help yourself. Now it is time to begin to achieve them!

This chapter sets forth the mistakes . . . standard and predictable errors . . . most information product sellers make. These are the faults which when solved result in the maximum number of individuals being helped by the information product you have available . . . and so ensure that you achieve your personal and financial goals as well.

These are the mistakes which when solved lead to the sure feeling that you are doing the greatest possible good for the greatest possible number (including yourself) . . . and ensure that you do

1

not experience the corrosive anger, irritation, frustration and bitterness that are the lot of all too many information product sellers. *They* invest   their time, treasure and talent in projects which, because unknown, are useless to others . . . and fruitless to themselves.

Fortunately, you can take steps to ensure that what you do is both a productive use of your time, of value to the largest number of others, and propels you to the realization of your furthest desires. You will not be like most people selling most information products who consult only their own desires . . . with entirely predictable results. Having satisfied themselves, they succeed in satisfying no one else. In short order, *they* end up the victims of an entirely avoidable cosmic despair.

But, now, this cannot happen to you! For with this chapter, which you need to read pen in hand, I ask you to enter into a compact with yourself so that you will never make these errors — or never make them again. Either way, your success is ensured.

This is not just a chapter, then; when you have finished, it will constitute a written pledge you make to yourself. With it you promise to do all that is necessary to both create and market information products that do succeed in helping both you and the people who need your useful information. You vow to forego both the selfishness and the waste of creating products without general value and appeal as well as the slack and passive attitudes that preclude your active participation in making them known to the audiences who need them. No longer will you be content merely to satisfy yourself or to rely supinely on others for the necessary marketing that must be done to make your products successful. You are a necessary and crucial part of the process, and you cannot abdicate this responsibility to anyone else.

This chapter focuses on errors that must be known and avoided. The rest of the book follows as a matter of course, for it presents the techniques you must use to avoid these errors and reach your objectives. When you finish this chapter, you'll know what not to do, and you'll have pledged not to do it ever again. When you finish the rest of the book, you'll know just what to do, and you'll be ready to begin doing it. Fair enough?

The 23 errors that follow are divided into nine linked but distinct types of mistakes. These nine include serious mistakes of:

- vision
- failure to understand the business you're in
- planning
- positioning
- conceptualization and creation

- product tone and presentation
- marketing
- organization, and
- personal habit.

Remember, you must not merely understand these nine major error clusters and the 23 mistakes grouped therein; you must solve these problems. The success of your info-empire depends upon it.

VISION MISTAKES

Avoidable Error #1.
You don't want to change the life styles, ideas and procedures of the maximum number of people . . . so you don't do what's necessary to reach them.

People who succeed in creating, commissioning and selling information products have the zealous outlook that has always characterized any missionary. They — I might say we for I am certainly one myself — cannot rest content knowing that someone, somewhere who could be better off using the information we have available does not yet have the product that contains it . . . and that what stands between their betterment (and our own advancement) is merely our own inertia. This fact gnaws at us incessantly, until we are moved to connect with that individual. The more successful we are (or wish to be), the less time we allow between the gnawing sensation that something must be done and the moment we do it.

Personally, I find I am incomplete, dissatisfied until I have finished the task that I know must be done to reach out to even one more person who could profit from my information products. I postpone all things, every creature comfort, life's more compelling distractions, until such time as I have done what I can to connect with my prospect. *You must do the same.*

If you fail to live your life in this fashion, your vision is at fault. For if you truly cared that there were people in need of you . . . people whose lives you could improve if you would but do what was necessary . . . you could not rest until you had done that necessary thing. Doing every necessary thing to connect with his market(s) is what differentiates the sure-to-be-successful info-entrepreneur from his lamer brethren.

Not surprisingly, true info-entrepreneurs are a relentless breed. We want to reach as many people as possible . . . change as many lives as possible. If this occasionally makes us less than restful to be around . . . it ensures that we will do whatever is necessary to reach our prospects . . . the people we can help . . . and that we'll spend however much time is necessary to do the job properly.

Recently, I talked to one of the quintessentially foolish authors who abound in my neighborhood and are typical of the breed. "I write for myself," he drawled, underscoring the fact that he couldn't publish, wouldn't publish, hadn't published . . . and that what he wrote was utterly unsuitable for publication, although it satisfied him. Shame on this selfish "artist!" Shame on his unbounded egotism! Shame on him . . . and a warning to you: avoid these paragons of self-absorption at all cost.

Never forget! *You* are now the kind of producer who creates for others . . . to persuade them, to motivate them, to change their lives, to improve their circumstances. *You* won't ever say something as fatuous as "I write for myself," because you don't create for yourself: you create for others!

Henceforth, your vision is clear. You will think of how you can fashion what you know and can discover . . . and what your authors know and discover . . . so that it is of value to the greatest number of those you have chosen to help. You will never again merely write for yourself; such an objective you must regard as insignificant, ignoble. *You* will think and work hard to ensure that the greatest number that can be advantaged by you will be so advantaged thanks to your commitment to producing a product of the utmost quality and to marketing it unrelentingly.

The mistake, you see, is thinking that pleasing yourself is somehow sufficient in the information business. It only can be, of course, if you care only about that immodest audience of one, yourself. The minute you care about the good you can do for others is the moment your vision must change, enlarge. Then you must embark on an entirely different journey . . . a journey that begins in commitment to general improvement of the audiences you can help and never ends until such time as all have been aided to the furthest extent of the knowledge which you both have and can find for their betterment. In short, when you begin to create information products . . . whatever they are . . . you have started a quest. It is at once thrilling, noble, strenuous and draining . . . as every great quest has ever been. It demands the best of you . . . and scorns any attempt to get by with less.

A vision of communal helpfulness informs the work of the significant info-entrepreneurs. We are not just creating a product, however valuable; our aim is far more significant than that. We aim to transform a life and add, if only a little, to its improvement. Unless you are prepared to make this commitment, to prepare a product that embodies it and to create a marketing plan worthy of such a product, do not even begin.

Those who are committed to the mere creation and selling of products instead of to the transformation and improvement of lives have embarked upon a trivial path and are certain, sooner or later, to confront the insignificance of what they are doing. To sell without wishing to improve and without truly offering the means for improvement is a shabby, abject thing that certainly leads to a sense of estrangement and despair.

But this cannot happen to you! For from this moment, you are committed not just to creating a product and selling it but to creating a meaningful *solution* and to bringing it strenuously to the attention of *all* whose lives will be improved because of it.

Whereas before you may have suffered from lack of vision and from an egotistical preoccupation, that is no longer so. The debilitation of myopia and pettiness that may have caused you in the past to think more on the triumph of what you created rather than the exhilaration brought on by the regeneration and improvement of the maximum number of lives is now gratefully history. Your focus now is grander . . . your perception broader . . . your quest universal: you stand not just for the selling of a product, but for the beneficial change of lives. With this as your creed, you will not just see farther, you will always find the energy and spirit you need to extend yourself to the most distant reaches, wherever a single person waits in need of you and the product that embodies your problem-solving wisdom. Live and create by this creed, and you must be successful.

Now commit yourself!
Check this box if you are willing to do what it takes to be successful.

☐　Whatever I may have done in the past, henceforward I vow to focus on helping the largest number of people who can benefit from what I know and can discover. I pledge that my vision will be as broad as possible, designed to touch as many lives as the information I have and can discover can improve. From this day, I shake off as beneath me the insular, the provincial, the narrow and confining. I paint from this day on a broader, more expansive canvas.

Avoidable Error #2.
You don't want to improve your own lifestyle substantially.

I know many people who produce information products. All too many them lead a rather hand-to-mouth existence. Obviously, this must content them. But don't let it content you.

In this business you must want two things, and you must want them badly. They are interconnected and must always be considered together; you must want to help the greatest possible number of people. And you must want to improve the circumstances of your own life. If you do just the first, you will simply be a missionary; a grand eleemosynary character, to be sure, but no inevitably ascending entrepreneur. And if you do the second only, you will be grotesquely selfish and unadmirable, a moral reprobate.

I would like to say a word about what kind of improvements I think you should consider. As the circumstances of your life are bettered, you can devote your new prosperity to the acquisition of things . . . or to the enhancement of self and creation of a self-sustaining and nurturing environment. The thrust of our society is in the first direction: we are bombarded with blatantly consumerist advertisements that tell us to acquire things. Indeed, they scream that you cannot be a complete person if you do not acquire things. But this, I think, is entirely wrong.

People who direct their lives towards the acquisition of things are, by definition, bound to be disappointed. Whatever they have acquired, they will soon be stimulated to feel they cannot possibly be happy until they have acquired something else. As this process is never ending, so their personal happiness and sense of confident well being must always be a mirage.

Consider a recent article about financial author and guru Charles J. Givens by the admittedly pedestrian *Boston Globe* columnist Marian Christy. It reads like an auction catalog: "Givens owns a Sabreliner jet, an oceangoing yacht, and a fleet of cars including a $200,000 stretch limousine." Far from being impressed by this rendition of privilege, I was saddened by the fact that the man was defined (had defined himself?), not in relation to his thought and his ability to help others (neither of which was discussed in the article) but the things he felt obliged to tick off. In this article at least, Givens existed solely as a reflection of his possessions, nothing more. What could one feel for him but sadness, and a pinch of contempt?

That is why you should set your sights on the attainment of your own personal freedom, your ability to do what you wish, when you wish to do it. For this, there can be no doubt that ample financial means are required. Capital is necessary. This is why one of your first objectives, however small your information empire, should be to create an investment program for yourself. I shall have more to say about this later.

You need to be in control of your own time in an environment that is entirely conducive to your work and supportive of it. You must move to the beat of your own drummer, not someone else's. This means you must be free . . . and have the means to sustain this freedom.

You move towards this vital goal as you are successful in touching more and still more people and convincing them that you have something to improve their lives. Your great aspirations can only be realized by touching the lives of a great many others. So, launch your touching plan.

Later, I shall tell you how to create this plan. Now, vow to have it. To succeed as an info-entrepreneur is to identify the largest number of people who can benefit from what you know and can discover . . . and to visualize (and then plan for) the lifestyle that you must have so you have the energy, discipline, resources and enthusiasm you need to reach them — and so nurture yourself and continue your own growth process. This is the very definition of success.

Now commit!

☐ I fully intend to improve my lifestyle, not just to acquire things, which are likely to disappoint, but to craft a situation which nurtures and reinforces and so enables me to reach out to an ever greater number of people who can benefit from what I know and can discover.

THE "YOU DON'T KNOW WHAT BUSINESS YOU'RE IN" MISTAKE

Avoidable Error #3.
You run your enterprise wrongly focusing on production, not marketing.

All people in the information product business *say* they are interested in selling products. But I truly wonder about this. If this were so, why do so many producers create products without giving a second thought to their market . . . until such time as they have mounds of their favored creation, and neither a plan nor means to sell it? In fact, it is my earnest conviction that the great majority of product sellers are far more interested in the production process (as somehow fittingly creative) than in the marketing process (necessarily mercantile and commercial, hence somehow tainted). This is, of course, rubbish.

From this moment, the focus of your enterprise should not be on production, but on marketing. You must get away from the notion that production is somehow the end of the process. It is only the end of the first and least significant part of the production and distribution process. If you are not prepared to turn yourself into a marketer and your enterprise into a market-driven operation, don't even begin.

Remember what your objectives are: to transform the lives of the maximum number of people you can, to uplift them, motivate them, improve them, enthuse them. These can only be accomplished through marketing . . . because it is only through marketing that you reach them.

Production, of course, must not be an afterthought; but it must not be your forethought. Yet, here's how most of our colleagues think:

1. I want to write a book (booklet, Special Report, audio cassette, *etc*). I have something interesting to say, to report, to confirm, to preserve.

2. I will write that thing.

3. (a little later) I have written that thing.

4. I must produce the thing.

5. (a little later) I must now seek to sell the thing. *How do I do that?*

Curtain falls, crushing protagonist . . . and all his dreams.

Without doubt, most of the information product creators I have known think like this. This is not only wrong. It's worse than wrong: it's stupid.

As you will see throughout this book, *your* focus must be different. Yours must be a market-driven, not a production-driven enterprise. Thus, you must follow *these* sensible steps instead of the foolish ones listed above:

1. I have identified a substantial (hopefully growing) market with a pressing want and the means to fill it.

2. I have ascertained what other people are selling to fill this want.

3. I have researched the means available to bring any solution I may create to the attention of this market. I am certain I can control the marketing process that results in my targeted market(s) becoming aware of the benefits I have for them.

4. As a result of this research, I have created the right product . . . namely, the product that will sell.

5. I have dedicated myself to doing all the marketing that is necessary, marketing that will cause my targeted prospects to be aware of the benefits I have for them . . . and which will, in the process, ensure my own success.

See the differences between these two five-step processes?

In the first process, the producer concentrates on his own needs. In the second, the producer concentrates on the wants of the people who will ultimately buy, use and benefit from the product being created. Of course, if you only wish to satisfy your own needs, then there is no reason to consider your market. Your objectives will be fully satisfied merely by creating your product.

Unfortunately, while many producers *say* they will be entirely happy merely to bring their product into existence, in fact, when that product does exist they become morose if it doesn't achieve a substantial measure of popular success and resulting profit.

On the other hand, the producer who concentrates on his market anticipates profit. He expects it . . . and has a right to feel confident about getting it. After all, he gathers his data carefully, assesses them thoroughly, and acts accordingly. His profit follows as a matter of course . . . and so does his celebrity standing, for he is known to be a problem solver for a large number of grateful people . . . known to be the repository of useful information which all his targeted buyers can profit from. The wise marketer develops a simple message of buyer benefit and drives it home again and again and again until even the dimmest prospect cannot but know that this producer has what he needs: not a product, but a solution to his (the prospect's) problem.

Now commit yourself!

☐ Never again will I engage in that self-immolating act of egotism, namely producing my product without considering its audience(s) in advance. From now on, I shall rigorously focus on markets and contain the pestering presence of my own overweening self.

PLANNING & POSITIONING MISTAKES

Avoidable Error #4.
You don't know if your market is big enough to sustain your income objectives and haven't planned how to reach it.

Most of the product creators I know start by focusing on what they want to do, namely creating a product. They then confidently assert that "I'll make a lot of money with this product," but never do the necessary research to determine if that assertion has any plausibility whatsoever.

Consider, for instance, a young friend of mine from Florida. A bright and attractive fellow, he conceived the idea of writing a how-to book for aspiring bartenders, particularly those who wanted a lucrative part-time job. Once he'd conceived the notion, deducing that it would make him a sizable fortune was only too easy. Just how this blessed result was to occur, the producer had no idea at all. But that was the merest trifle. The magical wealth-producing product *had* to be created.

He dragooned the usual minions into his operation: the loving girl friend, adoring mother, and long-suffering, sure-to-help-him friends and associates. In due course the product emerged: a slim volume of slimmer wisdom on the subject of succeeding in part-time bartending. The hopeful young man sank a sizable chunk of his meager savings into this project, sure that these dollars, like fecund rabbits, would prove astonishingly fertile.

However, he'd forgotten one crucial step: making sure that there was a market for this book and that this market could easily be reached; in short, that he could easily identify, approach and reapproach real prospects with marketing communications that would motivate them to respond immediately.

But consider! There is no extant mailing list of aspiring bartenders. There is no association where they congregate. There is no publication dedicated to their improvement and interests. There is, in short, no easy means of either identifying or reaching them. And so what was once an entirely negligible matter, the matter of the market and how to reach its members, became in short order an insurmountable burden.

This increasingly frustrated info-entrepreneur, his dreams of significant wealth inexorably receding, began to approach media sources. He did do the odd radio show; did run the odd book excerpt. Most times someone responded . . . one or two, perhaps as many as three or four. But never more. And often no one responded at all. The game was not worth the candle.

Now what happened? Our aspiring millionaire alternated between a fierce optimism seizing on every response, however insignificant, as a straw in the trade wind . . . and black despair, certain there was no light at the end of this tunnel. What should he do? "Cut your losses," I said. "Learn from this mistake. Stop creating products that seem delightful to you, and start serving markets that have coherent wants, the resources to satisfy them, and ways of getting to them." The entrepreneur greeted this advice glumly, but it was better than his tattered hope. After all, "Hope makes a good breakfast, but a poor dinner."

As this contemporary tale of an info-entrepreneur gone amuck clearly indicates, if you want to be a success with problem-solving information, identify the market *first*. You cannot have a success as an info-entrepreneur unless you remember this rule: there is no market unless that market is easily identified, easily reached and easily reached on a continuing basis. Thus, before creating or commissioning any problem-solving product, identify the market(s) who want and need it. And remember, that between "want" and "need," "want" is infinitely more potent. As Americans constantly demonstrate, people are far morely likely to acquire because they *want,* whatever their *needs* may be.

Here are the questions you must thoroughly answer *before* you create anything:

1. What is the market I am trying to reach? The more specific you are the better.

2. What problem(s) is this market trying to solve that I can help with? How do I know?

3. Does this market have the means to solve this problem (*e.g.*, buy my solution)? How do I know?

4. What organized means exist for me to connect with this market to let its members know I have created the solution they need?

Have I gathered:

— the names of specific publications
— available mailing lists
— specific organizations and associations
— catalogs which market products to this group
— bookstore and library distributors?

How do I know any of these people would be interested in assisting me to bring information about what I wish to create to the attention of my prospects?

I shall harp throughout this book on the need for planning. It is perfectly obvious to me when I talk to most information sellers that they are enamored of their idea . . .. and of the products they have created. It is also perfectly obvious they haven't spent a quarter of an hour doing any market research. Over and over I encounter these hopeful, if deluded, individuals . . .

• The man from Texas with a book about New England foliage;

• the Massachusetts man who created an audio cassette on improving your tennis game;

• the woman from Florida with a regional cookbook.

Each complained to me about their poor sales but none had bothered to ascertain what his market was or how he'd reach it. None knew the most elementary conditions of marketing; each had only the most rudimentary understanding of the channels available to market his product. Yet each had been seized by the fervent expectation that his product was a certain winner; only to have this fond hope rudely dashed to the ground in the face of mounting evidence of poor planning, baseless optimism, and self-defeating unpreparedness.

Let me say this as strongly as I can:

You are now in the marketing business, thus your interests and wishes are unimportant. It doesn't matter that you are interested in fall foliage or tennis or regional cookery. It only matters that your prospects are interested in them . . . and that these prospects can be reached in an organized fashion . . . over and over again . . . with a set of simple, cogent client-centered benefits that you are determined to hammer home.

Remember! What the prospect wants is infinitely more important than what you want.

Remember! When the prospect wishes to achieve this is infinitely more important than when you want to achieve it.

Remember! Reaching this prospect is infinitely more important than creating the product.

Remember! Approaching this prospect a series of times is profoundly more important than approaching him just once.

Now commit yourself!

☐   In the future, I shall not just focus on my product, but rather on my market. I shall make certain that there are enough people in that market to give me the objectives I want to achieve, that these people have the means to purchase what I am selling, that I can reach them over and over again and so control the marketing process, and that I won't give way to the egotism of thinking that just because I have produced something it must be successful (no matter how galling it is for me to give up this cherished nostrum).

Avoidable Error #5.
You're selling products, not Ultimate Benefits.

People who make lots of money as info-entrepreneurs do many things right, of course, but one of the most important is having a clear recognition that the

Ultimate Benefit they consistently sell is far more important than any individual product. What does this mean?

Ultimate Benefits are the abiding objectives of most, if not all, humans. These are the goals people strive for generation after generation. They constitute an essential part of what it means to be human and how we spend our time and resources. Such benefits include, but are certainly not limited to:

- getting or keeping financial security
- being attractive sexually
- getting or staying healthy
- living well
- having prestige and arousing envy
- cutting expenses and saving money
- protecting home and family
- achieving inner serenity
- making the world a better place
- having excitement
- gaining acceptance from one's peers.

Ultimate Benefits are what people *really* want. The products that help them achieve these crucial objectives are of distinctly secondary importance. Thus, the wise info-entrepreneur bases his business not merely on products (which are necessarily ephemeral) but on an Ultimate Benefit (or related series of Ultimate Benefits) which are eternal and which he consistently, simply and believably lets his prospects know they can get from him.

The Ultimate Benefit is the theme, if you will, that links all that the info-entrepreneur does. It is the thing he truly sells and must become known for. It is why prospects do business with him over and over again . . . to get that Ultimate Benefit. People, you see, don't really want a book . . . or booklet . . . or Special Report. They want salvation . . . to live well . . . to have prestige and financial security. And if it takes using books, booklets, and Special Reports to achieve these objectives, why, then, they'll use them.

Ultimate Benefits endure. They are the reason a prospect buys once and why, always assuming he remains interested in achieving (or sustaining) that objective, he buys again.

Individual products should never be the focus of an enterprise, because these products necessarily come and go. That's why dedication to a product is bound to be futile. A product is only valuable insofar as it represents and embodies the Ultimate Benefit. And a product that does embody this benefit is useful not only as a means of generating profit but also because it reinforces in a prospect's mind the fact that you can deliver that Ultimate Benefit, now and later. Thus, when he again wishes to make progress towards achieving that Ultimate Benefit he *must* return to you, its renowned source.

When you focus on your prospects, the crucial significance of the Ultimate Benefit becomes immediately apparent. You are not only willing to admit, you must admit that that benefit is what the prospect wishes to achieve and that your product is only useful insofar as it assists him to do so. Thus, focusing on the Ultimate Benefit — and how your product helps people achieve it — immediately becomes your objective and the basis for all your marketing.

It is otherwise for people who are product-centered. They care less about what the prospect wishes to achieve than about the wondrous aspects of what they have created. Because this product is so significant to them, they are determined it will be equally significant to others, never considering that prospects are not motivated by products . . . but by the prospect of getting Ultimate Benefits as embodied in products.

Not surprisingly, you know at once which info-product producers are focused on helping the prospect achieve the desired Ultimate Benefit and which are product-centered, interested only in what is being sold and not why the prospect wants to buy. Why? Because those selling Ultimate Benefits lead with these benefits and only follow with the features of what they're selling, while those who are product-centered lead with that product and never care that its features are translated into motivating buyer benefits. In that case, producing the product is obviously its own reward . . . since the focus is on the producer's ego not the buyer's benefit.

What You Do After Selecting Your Ultimate Benefit

The successful info-entrepreneur does not stop once he has selected an Ultimate Benefit. By no means! Now he must do one of two things:

1. He can come up with a series of potential problem-solving products that embody this Ultimate Benefit. For each potential product, he must then research the available markets to see how big they are and how easily they can be reached. Analyzing his results (and not forgetting that competitive info-products may exist), he then makes a considered choice about which product to produce. Only then does he produce it.

2. Alternatively, he can research the largest markets available which can easily be reached and then create the appropriate problem-solving product.

Either way the end result is the same: the creation of an info-product that embodies an Ultimate Benefit and is directed at either one or a series of markets that can easily be reached on a continuing basis.

This is the ideal way of proceeding. In practice, of course, you may not be able to approach the matter of product creation quite so scientifically. Why? Because you must take into consideration:

- your own field of expertise
- how easily you can find and package information, and
- what you really want to do.

Notwithstanding these considerations, you here's what you should do:

- Select an Ultimate Benefit.

- Select the specific market(s) you feel most comfortable assisting.

- Make sure these markets are as broadly defined as possible.

- Make certain you can reach them on a continuing basis.

- Then define your product so that it embodies the Ultimate Benefit and is directed to the broadest possible market(s) you are capable of assisting.

This is the basis for a successful info-product.

Now commit!

☐ I'll never focus on necessarily ephemeral products again but on an Ultimate Benefit for which I'll aim to become known. All my products will be secondary to the one Ultimate Benefit (or related Ultimate Benefits) which is the crucial axis of my operations. I intend to become known for delivering that Ultimate Benefit and will ensure that all I do necessarily supports and promotes that fact.

Avoidable Error #6.
You have not assessed your competition . . . and outpositioned them.

If we're honest, all of us in the info-business sincerely hope to make the Great Score. We want to be the first to identify a new market, virgin territory, of unsurpassed size; to ascertain what that market wants to achieve and to give it to them before anyone else finds out what's going on . . . and as a result stimulate a satisfying avalanche of soul-refreshing lucre.

Oh, yes, we all want that.

But you can't run a business this way.

It's better to suppose that one has competitors. And that these competitors are doing what competitors have always done: scheming to create ways that diminish our market share and increase their own.

Thus, our job is clear. We need to do all we can to:

- identify our competitors

- understand what they are offering, and

- outposition them so that our prospects do the only sensible thing: buying from us.

Remember, a competitor is a person taking dollars from you and not so secretly wishing you'd fall down and go boom. Which is just what you've got to help him do.

You won't hear this kind of straight talk from most people creating and selling info-products. Most of them are the products of educations in the liberal arts and profess the virtues of cooperation, group effort, and collective sharing. I don't.

Despite having had that same liberal arts education (and indeed more of it than most of my info-peers), I recognize this: the markets you are selling to have limited resources, including time, money and the inclination to master the kind of information you have available. If they buy what one of your competitors is selling, they are less likely (unless compulsively enthusiastic on the subject) to buy what you are selling. Thus, it is to your competitors' advantage to preach a gospel of cooperation and sharing while less publicly pursuing a strategy of competitive advantage and decimation.

Let me give you an example of what I mean. As you know, I sell a resource (CASH COPY) that helps people create persuasive marketing communications. If a person buys another resource on this topic, he is less likely to want mine. He may reason that:

- the product he has already purchased will meet his needs;

- he shouldn't spend any more of his money until he has found out, and

- there probably isn't that much difference between similar products on the same subject.

All of these thoughts help him put off a purchase decision on my product. What's worse, he is probably one of the majority of info-product buyers who get materials and then never use them. Since this is his characteristic *modus operandi* as regards improvement products, he may reason that there's no point buying something else he won't use since he already has something on the subject. Hence, the purchase decision is postponed into infinity. To my direct loss. Either I don't get the money soon . . . or I don't get it at all. Either way I'm disadvantaged.

Thus, you've got to do whatever is necessary to get your prospect to buy what you're selling first.

This means engaging in a very focused, very strenuous, entirely serious race with your competitors so you get your prospects to buy from you before they expend their limited resources on anything comparable produced by anyone else.

Perhaps you think that given your slender means this is a game you cannot play . . . that the big guys have all the advantages here and that whatever you do is doomed to failure.

Rubbish.

Let me tell you one provocative little story.

Years ago, when I was young and green in the info-publishing world, a major publisher wanted to buy the rights to my book, THE CONSULTANT'S KIT. This was tempting because I always thought that both my social standing and wealth were predicated on my publishing with a leading house, a notion both my agent and the publisher's representative went out of their way to reinforce.

The publisher's argument went something like this: several other major publishers have produced books on consulting. We also want one. You've got one. Sell the rights to us, he said, and we'll go head to head with the others, raising your reputation, filling your coffers.

It all sounded reasonable enough . . . until I looked at the numbers.

They'd sell my book (which I was selling myself for $30) for about $18. I'd get standard 10% royalties on the net which would generally be less than $1.80 per book. They anticipated sales of about 25,000 copies over three years: maximum profit to me about $45,000. There was then every possibility my beloved book would die a natural death as its sales diminished.

Then I looked at my current situation. I was selling the book for $30; 80% of sales were direct at full price. There were, to be sure, the production and marketing costs. But these I coolly assessed from an investment viewpoint, just as I would the purchase of stocks or real estate. Selling just 2,000 copies a year at $30, I would make more in twelve months than the major publisher could promise in three years. What's more I'd be able directly to promote my consulting practice through the book (which the major publisher wouldn't allow) and other products, too . . . thereby stimulating other significant revenue. Moreover, I could ensure the book — with all its marketing magic — would never go out of circulation, thereby continuing to be that golden egg-laying goose. No, selling the rights just didn't make sense.

Was this the right decision? Well, as expected my book on consulting isn't the best selling volume of all time on the subject. Two of the major publishers that that year released titles on the subject still have them in print; one claims to have printed over 100,000; the other probably has sold many fewer. I'd guess that the author of the 100,000+ seller has probably brought home nearly $200,000 in royalties over the last eight years or so. Not an insignificant sum by any means. But my book *profit* in the same period is over twice that . . . and continuing. Moreover, this number doesn't include:

- the speaker fees and consulting assignments directly generated from the book;
- the sales emanating from the catalog in the back of every volume of the book;
- my ability to use this book to promote the many other volumes in the series.

Remember, these are all things the major publisher would not allow. Taking these factors into account, I reckon that agreeing to the seductive contract of the major publisher would have cost me, admittedly over several years, at least $1,000,000.

Think! Neither of my consulting author competitors has such a symbiotic system. They are therefore left to sell a single product rather than reap the benefits from a cluster of related products and services. Moreover, they are totally at the mercy of their publisher and his whims. They do not control the wealth-producing process, nor can they derive maximum benefit from it because of the publisher's demands. My actual sales of the book *per se* may be less . . . but my profit, from the book itself and from the cluster of related products and services, is far, far greater than either can boast. And this is only *one* of a series of related products in the series! Each of the others functions in exactly the same way . . . with exactly the same substantial results.

In short, it would have been a disastrous miscalculation to allow that major, oh-so-prestigous publisher to acquire the rights to my short but potent volume. (By the way, have you acquired your CONSULTANT'S KIT yet?)

Are there lessons here for you? Decidedly so!

1. By focusing on benefits, not products, you can position yourself in any marketplace so that you're competitive against any larger player.

2. Price is not the sole reason why people buy products . . . they buy to acquire perceived benefits. Remember, my CONSULTANT'S KIT has always been higher priced than competitive volumes.

3. By creating fewer info-products (but doing your marketing homework in advance of production) you acquire certain advantages. You do not have to spread yourself too thin. You can tailor your marketing (in ways we'll discuss) and devote more time to ensuring that it's successful. Moreover, because you operate a smaller, less expensive entity, you do not have the immediate need for profit that larger companies have. Guerrilla marketers of info-products are leaner, more inventive, and can subsist for longer on less than larger publishers. So long as we've done our marketing homework, identifying a market that needs what we're selling and keep bringing the benefits of our product to its attention, we will get sales . . . long after larger companies have already decided their product is a failure.

4. Units of products sold are not the bottom line. Selling lots of products isn't necessarily telling. It's not how many you sell . . . it's how much money you get . . . both from the product itself and all the other products and services you can market with and through it.

Remember, no one will ever be as interested in marketing your products as you are. The other two consulting authors are essentially passive. They've produced their products and, through their publishers, put them into the market place to sink or swim. Except for updating the volumes when they go back to press, their involvement with their product is limited to cashing their twice annual royalty checks . . . that is to say waiting until the publisher gets around to giving them their money; (I get mine, of course, as sales are made and can put it to work at once).

This system is fine so far as it goes, but it leaves these people very vulnerable. These authors have essentially said, "I've created my products. They'll have a certain life span during which I'll profit. Then they'll die, and I'll stop making money from the product. In any event, it's not in my hands."

I find this kind of attitude provoking and foolish. Moreover, I know this: such an attitude will at some point result in the death of the product, the cessation of all income from it and the abandonment of the market of individuals who still need this information. Of course, as their competitor this is the moment I wait for with avid interest. Because as their products, so passively marketed, wane, an opening must be created for me . . . so long as the market and the means of connecting with it continue to exist. Expect this moment. It will happen because publishers are in the business of producing books . . . not attending to the perceived needs of defined markets.

Remember, the objective of the info-entrepreneur is to do what is necessary so that *each* of his products makes a profit *every* year. Of course, we'd all like the Great Score . . . the avalanche of really serious dollars. But remember, this situation can be very risky to the small company. When it happens, you may have to add overhead expenses like new help, bigger quarters, *etc.* And then there is always the possibility that if you work through traditional distribution sources, your product may be returned . . . causing you serious financial difficulties. I received a call from such a producer in distress while I was writing this chapter.

I have always run my business on this principle: that a solid yearly income from each product with minimal risk and minimum product returns makes the most sense. Living by this principle has enabled me to keep my overhead costs to the barest minimum and to achieve maximum profit with the least conceivable risk. Which is just the way I want to keep it.

There's another thing that's important to point out about competitors.

While it is true that major competitors usually devote more marketing dollars than you have to launching a product (which admittedly can be rather discouraging to you), their dollars don't necessarily make them better marketers.

Keep in mind that more info-producers are interested in products than buyer benefits. More of them, therefore, attempt to sell their products by focusing on the product and its features than on the buyer and his wants. This is true of even the largest and supposedly most savvy info-producers, as the barest look at their marketing materials confirms.

Consider, for instance, this typical write-up from the John Wiley & Sons Winter, 1988 book catalog:

"Strategic Planning Workbook
K. Hellebust/J. Krallinger

A total business planning guide, this is a 'why' and 'how-to' workbook. Without any experience, the reader will be capable of preparing a strategic plan, business plan, and budget in presentable form. This is also an analysis workbook — new and powerful methods of analysis convering internal operations and external competition are presented for the first time in one place. Uses the case study method, supported by illustrations. This book is straightforward and practical, based on the authors' over 80 years' combined experience as directors, business managers, and business advisors."

This is a major info-product producer, with more money for skilled marketing help than you or I probably have . . . and yet what they've produced makes a host of marketing mistakes.

This write-up concentrates on features (like "business planning guide," "workbook," "strategic plan," *etc.*) not benefits.

Where are the prospect benefits in this write-up? Don't bother to look too far, because there aren't any. There's only steak in this write-up. No sizzle. What this write-up says is "We'll show you how to work, work, work," but we won't show you the advantages you get when you do. That you have to figure out on your own.

This is ridiculous!

Now I ask you. Do you think most people want to work, work, work? Or do you think they want to be enticed by the advantages of working, dazzled with their opportunities and what they get by working? After being hooked by the benefits, *then* they're ready to learn precisely what they have to do to achieve the advantages. It's obvious, isn't it? But not to the critters who wrote this weak marketing copy.

Moreover, there's lots of Assertion Marketing in this write-up, from the unproven words "new and powerful methods" to "straightforward and practical." None of this is proven. What Wiley is saying is this, "Trust me. Get the book, and you'll find benefits there. Believe you me."

But why should anyone believe that?

When I read this kind of jejune, unsophisticated marketing I'm both happy and sad. I'm happy because I know that being big and having access to talent and money doesn't necessarily mean any better marketing will result. If I were producing a book on strategic planning I wouldn't worry about this book as competition. Even the title is wrong: it doesn't indicate a market and doesn't promise any Ultimate Benefit. That makes me happy.

But this also saddens me . . . because this kind of poor marketing is going to sabotage the chances of this book — written by authors with over 80 years of experience. They have, in short, wasted their time, and their ultimate irritation, disillusion and bitterness are predictable. Even now they're probably irking their friends by their constant denunciations of the paltry marketing of John Wiley & Sons.

In the early days of my info-publishing business, I'd open up periodicals gingerly, fearing that I'd find another resource dealing with a subject I had either just dealt with, was dealing with, or wanted to deal with. If I did, I cringed thinking my chances had just been ruined.

I don't do that any more.

When I see a review of a competitive info-product in a publication, I look to see if it carries follow-up information . . . an address or phone number. If it doesn't, I'm pleased, because I know this competitor has failed.

When I see a competitive info-product in a bookstore, but it carries no information on how to buy the author's consulting talents and carries no catalog of additional, related products, I exult. Because I know this competitor has failed to take maximum advantage of the situation and has exhibited his limitations.

When I receive a flyer about a competitive info-product in the mail, and it focuses on the features of this product and not its benefits. When it fails to make an offer that induces an immediate response. When it provides no motivating testimonials, when, in short, it fails as a marketing piece, I'm delighted. Because this competitor is throwing his money away and weakening himself.

When this same competitor sends me only one flyer and makes no attempt to connect with me again in this or any other way, I know he is expecting too great a return from too little marketing, and I'm pleased because I know he doesn't understand and live by the Rule of Seven and that he isn't getting maximum benefit from his marketing dollars. Therefore he cannot be a significant challenger . . . whatever prestigious name adorns his stationery.

When I see a competitor creating non-symbiotic products with different Ultimate Benefits and appealing to widely disparate markets, I'm content. He is not focusing his resources and is trying to succeed by living a "hit or miss" marketing strategy; a strategy that ensures that large numbers of his products . . . including, perhaps, the one directly competitive with mine . . . will fail.

Recently, on KXL Radio in Portland, Oregon, commentator Bill Gallant asked me what would happen if everyone followed my marketing advice. Wouldn't competition get much more intense and the response rate on individual marketing communications fall? Yes, I acknowledged that might well happen. But I wasn't worried.

The information, you see, already exists (made available in part by me) to ensure a higher response rate. But most info-product producers continue to follow their own whims and opinions to the detriment of their profit. And so it is always likely to be.

We humans are an egotistical breed. We regularly ignore specialists who could help, and we're expert in making cunning excuses for our self-destructive behavior. Why should it be any different in marketing?

I see no reason, therefore, to be sad when I see my so-called competitors. Most of them, you see, like most marketers generally, are embarked on a futile and self-destructive course which will leave their products unprofitable and under-utilized . . . just like more than 90% of such products are today.

Thus, you should enjoy your competitors for several reasons:

1. Their products (both content and name) become the standards you can outdistance.

2. Their success shows you where to spend your money; their failures show you what to avoid.

3. Their marketing communications give you clear indications how you can outmaneuver them.

4. And, lastly, their failure is a happy indication of just how much further you have gone and how much more successful you are. Without outdistanced competitors, your own success could never be as sweet.

Now commit!

☐ The mere existence of a competitor, of many competitors, will not discourage me. Instead, I shall use such competitors as a mobile repository of crucial information that will help me assess markets and discover where to put my slender resources. I shall scrutinize my competitors closely both to see what they do correctly and what, more likely, they do poorly. Yes, I shall use their successful methods to my advantage and shall eschew the unsuccessful with delight, knowing that what I have gleaned from their failure will help me at the same time that it weakens them.

CONCEPTUALIZATION AND CREATION ERRORS

Avoidable Error #7.
The content of your products is not timeless.

Larger information publishers have advantages that we smaller types do not possess. One of the most significant is their ability to promote and distribute a product faster than we can. This is scarcely surprising. With greater financial resources, an in-place sales force, and years of experience, they know what to do to put a product into circulation faster. If this is what you need to do, you just can't beat a major publisher . . . if they make a major commitment to your product.

If you want to get a lot of marketing attention all at once and make your money in the shortest possible time, a major publisher is probably the route you have to take. But be warned: the minute the publisher diverts his marketing attention to something else (which is bound to happen), your product will begin to languish and soon die. Most books, after all, only last about a year. Then (from a commercial standpoint) they are as dead as doornails.

That's why we info-producers need to approach the whole business of product content in a different way. It's pointless for us to print a book on the mass suicides in Jonestown, Guyana, for instance, when mass market publishers can do this job so much more effectively . . . getting it into people's hands while media interest in the subject is still white hot. Instead, we need to select a subject of long-term interest (like what you have to do to succeed in your own consulting practice), with at least stable and optimally growing numbers of prospects, and create a product based on information that doesn't easily date and can easily be updated. In short, you need to think perennial, not annual.

Thus, instead of creating a booklet on the Bush inauguration festivities (unless you have official standing to produce and distribute it), it makes more sense to develop a guidebook on presidential Washington. See the difference? One is severely time-bound. Unless you have assured marketing and distribution channels, the first of these could prove a financial disaster; by contrast, the other could sell forever, needing only periodic updating as opening times, prices, *etc.,* change.

My rule of thumb is that it takes about one year for an info-product to become established . . . for you to have created a niche for your product, secured sufficient free publicity to launch it, for distributors to be aware of it, for enough of your promotional material to be sent to your prospects so that they finally know it exists and are motivated to buy . . . and for the critical mass of word of mouth marketing to take effect. Yet this is just the moment when mainline publishers are actually stopping their marketing and downgrading their interest in most of their products! Thus, if we were to follow the system of larger publishers, after just 12 months on the market we'd be withdrawing from circulation a product that was just about to become a profit-making perennial. This is ridiculous!

Your objective must be to create products from which you can draw income year after year . . . with only continuing updates in your material as necessary and as you return to production.

We have a fixation with the new and different in this nation. Things that are newly available get attention; old standbys generally are ignored. But from old standbys should come continuing new money . . . if the products are properly promoted and continually brought to the attention of the right markets. These markets don't care if something is new or not. They care if what you are selling works. Thus, the booklet about curtailing Dutch elm disease is as saleable today as it was five years ago . . . so long as the methods are current, and you focus on customer benefits in your marketing, not product features.

Your goal is to package information that works . . . to make sure you are on top of developments in the field so that the information is always current and always produces results . . . and to keep bringing it to the attention of people who have the problem in such a way that they feel they must have this information to solve it. This must be your creed as an info-entrepreneur, not slavish devotion to bringing forth something "new" merely because it is new. The savvy info-entrepreneur, after all, focuses not on products but on markets with problems. Thus, his concern must always be more on problems than on products, for so long as these problems exist there must be a need for his problem-solving information.

Let this be your formula:

1. Seize an Ultimate Benefit.

2. Focus on a market or series of markets that are growing, have the means to acquire products embodying this Ultimate Benefit, and wish to achieve it.

3. Then create problem-solving products for your targeted markets. These products should be on subjects that interest your market now and will interest your market for years to come. They must not be written for today but for deep into the future.

4. Then devote your attention to two things (in this order): transforming your product into buyer benefits and hammering these benefits home

and, only secondarily, keeping your product up-to-date by noting developments in your problem-solving methods.

This is a formula to conjure with.

Now commit!

☐ My objective is not now nor ever will be merely to produce a product. I want to seize a problem that concerns a sizable, hopefully growing market (that I can reach over and over again) that has the means to solve it. This problem (therefore prospect interest in solving it) must be one that will exist for a substantial period. I aim to create a problem-solving product that brings useful information to members of the designated market. As new methods of solving the problem become available, I shall include them, too, thereby making my old product new again. Deriving money from my problem-solving product for years is my objective . . . not at all merely creating a product now, no matter how ego-satisfying that may at first seem.

Avoidable Error #8.
Your information isn't easy to get and easy to update.

This error is directly related to the one above, but I wanted to draw your particular attention to it.

When you start thinking of regular, ongoing profit and not a quick kill, you must inevitably give your attention to the matter of updating your materials. You not only wish to be known as the ultimate place for the Ultimate Benefit you deliver but also for making available the most up-to-date and accurate information on how to achieve it. This is, fortunately, not so difficult to do, which is why it's unfortunate so many info-producers don't do it.

I think for instance of that valuable resource the *Oxbridge Directory of Newsletters.* It's a truly helpful piece of work listing as it does tens of thousands of newsletters. It is clear that a good deal of work went into producing it. But not into reproducing it. In the 1993 Edition, the latest as I write, there are hundreds of entries for newsletters which no longer exist or for which basic entry information (like editor, address, phone number) is incorrect. And I don't just mean by a few months, either. I know for a certain fact that several dozen of the publications they cite as still current either went out of business three or even four years ago . . . or more . . . or moved from the addresses given! This is slovenly, indeed, in a publication brought out as frequently as this one.

Don't let this happen to you! Resolve that the products you create will always have the most up-to-date information posssible . . . and that each time you return to production you update it accordingly.

This is an area where all too many information products fall sadly short, thereby weakening them with another acute structural problem. All how-to products — not just books either — should be stuffed with the names, addresses, telephone numbers and other pertinent information about subjects relevant to the achievement of the topic.

Thus, if you are going to tell people how to curtail Dutch elm disease and you recommend a product, you need to include complete details on how people can get that product. Or the telephone numbers of experts who are available to do the work. Or the names and addresses of other resources on the topic. In short, whatever you present should be *complete* so that the reader can actually *solve* the problem he's interested in. You must dedicate yourself to providing the precise "how to" details people need, not the general "what-to-do" information that suffices for most authors.

Certainly over time these specifics will change. When they do you can do one of two things:

- In the short term, insert an *erratum* slip in the product updating crucial information. This is the course to take when the new information is needed by the customer to achieve the desired result and when you are not expecting to update your product soon.

- Otherwise, simply make relevant changes when the product is re-produced.

Sadly, most entrepreneurs don't follow this process.

To begin with, they treat a product like it's set in cement. "Here is what I've written," they seem to say, "take it or leave it." But when you're dealing in the how-to area, you're necessarily dealing with a fluid situation, and you've got to plan your work accordingly.

Authors, however, are a "creative" breed: updating bores most of them. For many info-entrepreneurs, updating an existing product is distinctly less exciting than creating something entirely new and different.

But think! It's infinitely easier to update a product and make it timely than it is to create something new and launch it. Still, what would you rather do? Update a profitable booklet on eradicating Dutch Elm disease or create a new booklet on dealing with diseases that destroy tomatoes?

Actually, it should be obvious: you've got to do *both*. The trick to succeeding as an info-entrepreneur is to produce products that will bring you a lifetime income and will sustain you while you create new products that are necessarily untried and therefore risky. Thus, while you must always be working on new products (how else will you diversify your firm and make it recession proof, a necessary objective?), you must always strive to create products that are easy to update.

This probably doesn't sound romantic to you. So what! It is the route to certain profit. Your objective is not to impress your friends and neighbors with how intelligent you are, how creative, how artistic, how different and special. That's sophomoric.

Instead, your goal should be to create solid information products aimed directly at the broadest possible spectrum of your market . . . people who need good, practical, immediately useful information to achieve their goals; goals they know you can help them achieve. This is a perception every product you produce reinforces. Thus, your objective must be to arrange your enterprise so that your material offers this kind of information. This means:

- selecting subjects that people are interested in now and will be interested in in the future;

- including up-to-the-minute information in your products that can easily be changed and updated as circumstances warrant (or, which is more practical, each time you go back to create another run of your products), and

- having this information on computer so that the update process can easily be accomplished.

Of these, of course, selecting a subject that people are interested in now and will be interested in in the future is the most important. Your objective is to become known as *the* place to go for information on this subject.

But it is equally important to let people know they can get up-to-date information from you. Why? Obviously, because people want things to be current when they buy a product; they want to be immediately able to solve the problem you deal with. But equally so because you actually *want* your products — but not the *subject* — to become outmoded.

What???

Consider: if you write a dandy book on how to get major gifts for your nonprofit organization through tax-related strategies but do not include information like:

- current IRS tax tables

- formulas for computing gifts, or even

- the consultants who can help you if you don't want to do things yourself.

Why, then, not only is your book less useful when new . . . but it doesn't age as rapidly.

But think! Most info-producers sell a single copy of what they produce to a single individual. That's it! An individual who buys your book on deciding which franchise to purchase is probably not going to buy too many others for his own personal use; thus you must always be looking for new customers, an exhausting business.

However, an individual who is interested in tax-related giving and who needs current IRS tables to get major gifts cannot use a book with outdated information to achieve his objective. Thus, he must get your latest production on the subject . . . so he can achieve his objectives (the Ultimate Benefit). Most info-producers don't think this way. However, the real goal of business is not to make a single sale to a single customer but to so arrange matters that you transform all your buyers into continuing buyers . . . both of products you produce yourself and of related products produced by others. You must, of course, take several steps to arrive at this place.

To begin with, you have to stop looking for the "great killing" and arrange matters for long-term, certain profit. In this regard, I remember two of my friends from Harvard days. We all belonged to the literary club, the Signet Society, where every young person with publishing aspirations could be found. All were bright; most pretentious; many bombastic. And two particularly so. They promised to burst on to the literary scene *à la* F. Scott Fitzgerald, fame and fortune assured while barely post-pubescent.

I was a gullible boy, and I believed them. Indeed, just being around them and their surgent confidence depressed me. But here it is more than twenty years later and not only has neither creature left a mark in the literary world (or a dent in some publisher's wallet) . . . neither has published a single book of any kind. I have. And publishing well, as the Irish might have said, is the best revenge.

Which is just what you want.

The trick to succeeding in the info-publishing business is to add at least one new major product each year while drawing income from *all* the previous products you have produced, letting each promote the rest and investing a portion of your revenues in both approaching new markets and in developing your capital.

This way you are certain to become rich.

Is this hard to do? By no means. But it does mean taking a very long view and assessing each project coolly . . . always with an eye on the market . . . keeping a firm hold on your ego and personal reasons for attempting the project. And learning how to organize your time most effectively.

Now commit!

☐ I promise to create products that solve problems that exist now and will exist for years to come and to pack them with the most relevant, helpful, and up-to-date information. I promise that this information will be precise . . . leaving out nothing that can benefit the prospect. And I promise to keep this information up-to-date as I regularly bring forth new editions and as regularly make past editions obsolete . . . thus forcing my customers to buy from me again . . . for their benefit and my own!

Avoidable Error #9.
You publish disconnected items.

Have you ever noticed the lists of products published by large numbers of info-product producers? You'll find an oriental cookbook, a pet book, an audio cassette on tennis, and a biography of a long-dead worthy. Is it any wonder these people have serious marketing problems and that the overwhelming percentage of what they produce lives ignominiously and dies abruptly?

This situation is fatal to info-marketers for these reasons:

- You have no linking Ultimate Benefit. Instead of selling one Ultimate Benefit (or logically linked Ultimate Benefits) and hitting it again and again and again until even the dullest prospect understands what you have available, you are forced to stress divergent, competing, and incompatible Ultimate Benefits that necessarily pull you in different, weakening directions. This is wrong.

- You never become known for one thing, just one thing that people really want. You never achieve brand-name recognition as the place to go to solve a certain type of problem. Thus, much of your marketing, instead of both attracting new prospects and reinforcing your Ultimate Benefit in the minds of those who have heard of you and bought from you before, is wasted. You are trying to be too many things to too many people with predictably unsatisfying results and the demise of far too many products.

• There is no symbiosis between products. To succeed in the info-product business your prospects must be both upgraded through immediate additional sales and reapproached on a regular basis for continuing sales. But consider: do you think the chances of a buyer of an oriental cookbook buying the biography of a long-dead worthy are good? As good, say, as the chances of his being interested in an audio cassette on finding and preparing Cantonese delicacies? What do you think?

Do you think such an example unlikely? Well, consider the letter and marketing communications I received from an info-producer this week who has apparently two products: one is on buying corrugated cardboard packaging and the second is on writing and publishing scientific and technical articles. Do these address the same Ultimate Benefit? Speak to the same audience? Provide symbiosis and focus to his enterprise? I sincerely doubt it.

Thus, instead of creating products that enable him to cut his marketing expenses by putting more offers into the same packaging . . . that reinforce a single Ultimate Benefit (or related series of Ultimate Benefits) in his prospects' minds . . . and identify him as the purveyor of a logically linked set of solutions . . . he is forced to pursue distinct markets offering one product to each and thereby dissipating his slender marketing resources with easily predictable results. Yet no doubt he considers himself an intelligent man!

Percentage-wise, your marketing costs should never be greater than with your first product. Thereafter, because you'll be offering related products to the same audience, the percentage you spend on marketing each product should drop. Moreover, as the product numbers — all directed to the same market, mind — rise, that percentage should drop even more. Perhaps two cannot live as cheaply as one, but at least they can be marketed less expensively.

Remember: your chief objective is to get to as many people as possible who have the problem(s) you can solve and to persuade them to buy (and use) your solutions. Because marketing is your chief commitment, you must consider all ways that will lower the cost of bringing your message to a group of people, transferring the savings (partly) into the creation of new products for this market and (partly) into additional marketing connections with additional prospects.

Most info-publishers have never learned this lesson. That's why most publishers engender no brand loyalty. Traditional publishers merely publish books. These books may or (more usually) may not be successful. But certainly customers don't rush to the local bookstore to get the latest Prentice-Hall or McGraw-Hill release. Instead, they look for subjects that interest them . . . subjects that embody the Ultimate Benefit that motivates them.

This madness may be acceptable to larger publishers (although I can't think why it should be), but it cannot be acceptable to you. Larger publishers play the game of averages; they reckon that if they put out 20 books at least two or three will be sufficiently successful to cover for the 17 or 18 that either break even or lose money outright.

This is a ridiculous way of running any business. You must make the decision, and make it early, to see to it that EVERY product you produce is profitable. This is the rule that I live by and run my business by. I will not create a product, any product, even one of my five-page Special Reports, unless I have a reasonable certainty that it will be profitable and unless I am willing to do what it takes to ensure that profitability; unless it embodies my Ultimate Benefit and reinforces in the minds of my customers that I have other products available that also embody the Ultimate Benefit they have just received.

You should organize your info-business this way, too, because if you do you will succeed in achieving something no major publisher in the world has: making *everything* you create profitable, not just in one year but in every year of your life.

Unlike mainline publishers, you can benefit from what the customer wants by building long-term loyalty so long as your company is synonymous with a certain kind (or kinds) of problem-solving information. If you are known as the latest repository of useful information on creating a garden, then would-be gardeners will be loyal to your company because their interests are coincident with yours. Thus, you must stop creating disconnected items and make sure that all items are related and reinforce each other . . . that each item can be legitimately used to promote all the others and that above all, each embodies and reinforces the Ultimate Benefit that you must become known for . . . the Ultimate Benefit that constitutes the real reason people buy from you.

Now commit!

☐ I promise to create items that reinforce each other, that allow me to live and work symbiotically . . . not dividing my time and other resources and weakening my efforts. I promise that each thing I create will not only represent the Ultimate Benefit I have selected but will promote other, related products and services I offer so that I derive maximum benefit from each product and turn each product into a means for promoting all products, and my overarching, linking Ultimate Benefit.

Avoidable Error #10.
The information content of what you produce is too thin
. . . people can't use it to get the results promised by your title.

This is a book about making money. Make no bones about that. But it's also a book about how to create products that are worth putting your name on. Later I'll share with you tricks of the trade for producing dense, valuable problem-solving information. Now let me say this: if the information you produce isn't useful to your prospects, won't help them deliver the promise of your title, then you won't make money, because you won't develop that intense customer loyalty that ensures that they will send you their checks year after year . . . as soon as you produce something new.

Let me give you an illustration of how *not* to write. This paragraph is taken from the book *Cashing In On The Consulting Boom* by Gregory and Patricia Kishel (John Wiley & Sons, 1985). Remember as you read this paragraph the authors are presenting themselves as specialists in the subject and that they presumably want you to be able to follow their advice to be able to achieve the significant objectives they say consulting can deliver.

In the chapter "Promoting the Business", there's a section (there always is in these kinds of books) on "Speeches and Seminars." Here is that section:

"Attending a speech or seminar enables you to accomplish two things at once: to gain additional information and make new contacts. Taking this one step further, though, why not give speeches or conduct seminars yourself? This can be a extremely effective tool for promoting your consulting services and enhancing your reputation as an expert in your field. To achieve the best results, try to determine which topics hold the greatest interest for the people you want to reach. And whenever you give a speech or conduct a seminar, make it a point to get the names and addresses of those in attendance. In addition, by notifying the press of a upcoming speaking engagement or seminar, you should be able to obtain media coverage as well."

Now, let me say this immediately. The people who wrote this paragraph, purporting to be experts, should be ashamed of themselves. They no doubt think what they've offered is intelligent and helpful. I find it infuriatingly superficial and useless. Why? Because they tell you *what* to do without providing any of the essential *how-to-do-it* information that you need to be able to accomplish it successfully. In my uncompromising view, this is downright immoral.

Develop your information empire not merely by telling your customers what to do . . . but by giving them the essential, step-by-step information that will enable them to achieve it. First of all, this is the honorable thing to do. If you are writing a how-to book, then, by God, provide the necessary how-to information. You owe it to your customers. Second, by providing this kind of information, you absolve yourself of all moral responsibility if your customer fails to achieve success. If you give your customers the "what to" information but not the "how to", then you can fairly be blamed when they fail to achieve success. Do you really want their failure on your conscience? I certainly do not. And neither should you.

If you have told your customers *exactly* what they need to do . . . *exactly* when to do it . . . *exactly* how to do it, then if they fail to achieve success, it's their problem. Not yours. Your good night's sleep needn't be disturbed . . .as it most assuredly ought to be if you haven't provided this necessary information, for without this information your customers can't possibly achieve the objectives you are writing about.

Finally, when you provide the detailed how-to information your customers need, they'll be grateful to you. They'll give you dandy testimonials; (though admittedly you sometimes have to prod them a bit. Stay tuned). And they'll both refer other people to you and buy more of your products themselves.

On the other hand, if they don't like what you're selling and consider it a rip-off, they'll throw your cherished product back in your face. Consider this story. The late Joe Karbo wrote a well-known book entitled *The Lazy Man's Way To Riches*. It cost only $10, yet one report I read stated that between 25-50% of its purchasers took advantage of the thirty-day money-back guarantee to get a refund. I was horrified when I read these numbers but not surprised when I saw the book. Indeed, only human lethargy and sloth can account for the fact that even more were not returned. True, the book made money . . . but in the worst conceivable way: large numbers of those receiving it thought it was a rip-off. And Karbo's name is never mentioned among authors who truly helped their readers. Is this what you want?

In my own case, after more than a decade in business, selling tens of thousands of books, well under 200 people have returned my products. What's more, in virtually every instance they have accompanied the item with a personal note explaining why they were doing so; usually this was because of a change in their own plans or because they had ordered the wrong book. In short, their reasons had nothing to do with the product's quality. I defy any company in America to say their record is better than this one, and I attribute this success both to the fairness of the marketing (what people get is what they expected to get . . . or more) and the substantial value of the product (if used properly it will help customers achieve their objectives). This is the standard you must aim for as well.

On this basis, let's take a detailed look at the Kishels' handiwork. Start with the sentence, "Why not give speeches or conduct seminars yourself?" Now, virtually every book on marketing a professional practice (and that, of course, includes consulting) contains this advice. It's hardly original. What would make it original and useful is the degree to which the authorities you've consulted help you achieve your goals through this means.

1. "Try to determine which topics hold the greatest interest for the people you want to reach." The Kishels treat this like the end of the road, but it is most assuredly the beginning. To make this advice worth reading, we need the "how" information. *How* do we determine which topics hold the greatest interest? Precise steps are necessary here.

2. "Make it a point to get the names and addresses of those in attendance." The Kishels make it sound like this is easy. But what if you're giving a speech to 1500 consulting dieticians as I was recently and the association makes it perfectly plain they don't keep lists of those in attendance and cannot be of assistance to you? What then? In other words, we need the help of these self-proclaimed authorities. They need to examine each different kind of speech or workshop and advise you how to get the names; how to deal with situations where the sponsor won't help you; how to deal with especially large groups, *etc.* In short, they need to think through the situations their readers will find themselves in and provide the helpful information that will enable these people to deal with them successfully.

3. "By notifying the press of an upcoming speaking engagement or seminar, you should be able to obtain media coverage as well." What kinds of media should you notify? How should you get in touch? When should you get in touch? What kinds of follow-up should be made? What do media sources need from you? In short, these authors don't bother to provide *any* of the information the reader really needs. Outrageous!

Now let me say this: lest you think I looked for this example for weeks and weeks and had difficulty finding it, think again. I simply walked over to my well-stocked bookshelves and chose a "how-to" volume at random. This illustration is typical of the way most information is presented nowadays. In truth, these authors (I can't bear to call them specialists) are no better and certainly not much worse than what you can easily find and which most information providers sell to an unsuspecting public. They have opted to create a product that purports to solve certain problems instead of creating something that really does solve these problems. Perhaps they achieved their own objectives with this book, but even that I doubt.

I am familiar with the literature in the consulting field, and I never saw this book promoted in publications where it ought to have been; I didn't find it in my neighborhood book stores (and the stores hereabouts are quite good by industry standards). I cannot believe the authors made much money or that they generated much business for themselves from this book; (how could they when there was no way of knowing what consulting work they themselves do and how to contact them?) In short, the project was probably not worth doing and probably didn't help the Kishels realize their fondest desires.

Don't you be this way. In the chapter on presenting information I shall, of course, return to this topic. But here let me say this: what people want from you is not "what" information, not the "what you should do"; they want the "how you should do it" information, precise, step-by-step, detailed and up-to-date. They also want to know what works and why, and what doesn't work and why.

I have thought long and hard about how to present information to people and have been fighting a lonely war over the last decade against "specialists" like the Kishels who may well know what to do but sure as blazes aren't telling their customers. How-to information, you see, is infinitely expandable. You can't just tell a person to promote his seminar via the free media. You've got to tell him:

- what media to approach and why;
- who to approach at each media source;
- when to approach them;
- what you need to be able to approach them successfully;
- what happens when they don't respond to your approach;
- what happens when they do.

And all the other things that lead to your getting promotion for your seminar via the free media. The Kishels make this process sound like a piece of cake; they simply present the idea, you get the publicity you desire. Hey presto! But it isn't a piece of cake. It isn't inevitable. Implementing this *one* idea may involve hours of effort . . . even days . . . lots of frustration and dead ends. And, yes, in the end, there might be no beneficial result whatsoever. Or, a bonanza. Your customers need to be told all this . . . and they need to be told all this in the greatest possible detail that you can muster. Authors who don't provide this information are either lazy or stupid or both . . . but never worth bothering with.

Now commit!

☐ I promise to provide my customers with real, practical, detailed, complete how-to information. I shall avoid the "what to" and always focus on the "how to". I want to provide my customers with the detailed road map they need and want so that they can reach their objective . . . and solve their problem. I will look long and hard at what I produce and scrutinize it closely to make sure I have provided my customers step-by-step guidelines. And if I haven't . . . I'll go back to the drawing board, back to the library, back to wherever . . . until I get the *specific* information they need and which I can be proud to present.

TONE & PRESENTATION MISTAKES

Avoidable Error 11.
You don't make everything you do interactive and intimate.

The unwise marketer essentially throws the information to the prospect and says in effect, "Here it is. You figure out what to do with it." This can't be you.

If you want to succeed in the information business, you've seriously got to consider your tone and presentation. You've got to consider not only the quality of the information (how useful is it to your prospect) but how that information is presented . . . and, by the same token, how you are presented.

What you should be aiming for is this: a conversation between you and your prospect, a friendly conversation between a knowledgeable individual and someone who's eager to get and apply that information so he can achieve his own objectives.

This is precisely how most information these days is *not* presented. Most information is presented impersonally. It's written as if it were Holy Writ that comes from a deity and is meant to be received without question and with profound gratitude by untutored followers.

But this isn't right! Think of what you're trying to achieve:

- you want to develop a relationship with your prospect;
- you want the prospect to like you;
- you want the prospect to feel that you care about what happens to him;
- you want the prospect to feel he's in a conversation with you, a friend;
- you want to be in a position not just to impart information to the prospect, but to use the full range of human emotions with him . . . including exhortation, urgency, demand, anger, love, empathy.

Problem-solving literature today suffers from many flaws. It is thin in content, and it is also detached from reality. In reality most people, however needy, don't simply follow the good advice they're given. They need more than information; they need encouragement and continuing understanding. You have to provide the information *and* the encouragement. What's more, by providing both, you develop the relationship that will truly help your prospect achieve his objectives . . . and ensure that you reach yours!

Intimacy, then, is a prerequisite of the kind of how-to information you must create.

Interactivity is the second.

What does this mean?

Recently I read a business book entitled *A Funny Thing Happened On The Way To The Boardroom* by self-described humor consultant Michael Iapoce (John Wiley, 1988). It's an excellent book, full of insightful material on how to win a business audience with humor, including a lucid description of how to create your own material. As a result of reading this book, I felt sure Iapoce knew what he was talking about and that he would be a good speaker or creator of material for others. But then he blew it by writing this:

"If you *really* feel you must work with a /humor/ writer, call me — I'll be in the San Francisco or Marin County (California) telephone directory."

Now, consider this situation. Iapoce is a humor consultant. What he does for a living is, I imagine, help other people create material and deliver his own presentations to business groups. For either purpose, his book is a superb prospecting device. But it's a device that he misused.

His entire book is about how to break down walls between people . . . how to make yourself appreciated and listened to by an audience. Then, he himself creates barriers. What if you'd want to contact him. You'd have to:

- make a long-distance call to California telephone information (cost at least 50 cents). If you find the number, you must hope that Mr. Iapoce has an answering machine;

- hope that if he does and isn't home, he'll call you back;

- hope that if he is home and does take the call, he can do the thing you want him to do (because, after all, he never says).

What a lot of effort this supposedly client-centered man has forced you to go through. It's just no laughing matter.

Iapoce's approach to his reader and future customer isn't helpful. It isn't client-centered. Why, then, did he do it?

I suspect that the otherwise knowledgeable Iapoce is like most specialists. They are so afraid of the public that they put a series of obstacles between the people who need them and themselves. They do this because:

• they wish to be perceived as important;
• they are afraid of the interruptions they might get;
• they fear kook calls.

But let me tell you something:

Truly important people have no need to try to impress you. Their self-image isn't a product of how you feel about them. Their confidence and self-assurance come from within. They have no need for the trappings of office and visible marks of success. They can indeed "reach out and touch someone."

As far as interruptions are concerned, you don't have to take every call the minute it's made. You can either tell the person when you'll call him back or ask the person to call you back. The important thing is to be in control, know what you're doing, and do what you say you're going to do.

There probably isn't another person in America who gives his direct-dial telephone number to as many people as I do. I give it on national media programs; I send it out on millions of postcards; it's printed in my books and all my articles; it goes monthly to the over 1.5 million people who read my business column. In short, I am ACCESSIBLE. And I know this: if anyone would get annoying interruptions, I'd get them. If anyone would get kook calls, I'd get them.

And I don't.

I control the sequence of incoming calls, either by:

1. dealing with the call the minute it's made;

2. taking a message and telling the caller exactly when I'll call back;

3. arranging with the caller exactly when he should call back.

This arrangement has served me very well for the last decade, and I expect it to last out my lifetime. What's more, it's a system that functions virtually without abuse. Why?

1. Because I'm not afraid to deal with a person's business. I am not afraid to say "yes,", "no,", or "I need more time to consider your offer."

2. I don't play games with people.

3. I let them know I won't welcome their games either.

Some people have found this directness and candor disconcerting. They are used to telephone lies, where they say and are told "I'll get back to you," when they have utterly no intention of doing so;

I think human time is far too valuable for these kinds of lies. If I'm interested, I'll say so; if I'm not, I'll say so. If it's your responsibility to do something, I say that; if it's mine, I unhesitatingly say that, too.

Doesn't this make sense?

That's what makes interactivity work. In all my information products (including this one), I invite serious people to contact me for my help. I warn those who are merely curious or just unprepared not to bother, since I don't feel at all compelled to be nice to them. After all, they haven't considered my feelings in coming to me unprepared.

It is your job to establish this kind of relationship with your customers, to:

- talk to them directly;
- invite them to stay in touch with you;
- set forth your rules;
- adhere to them, cordially but strictly.

Now you are that most important of people: the sincere and earnestly honest friend. I pity those poor souls who don't have this necessary being in their lives, for this person makes it a point of honor to tell the truth, even when telling the truth pains the listener.

Now commit!

☐   I resolve that I shall not merely create a product and disseminate information. I resolve to enter into a relationship with my customer . . . to look upon each product as an extended conversation between someone with helpful information (me!) and someone who needs not only this information but my continuing care and concern to help him use it and reach his objective. Though I may never physically see my customer, I shall treat him like a friend with whom I'm having a friendly conversation . . . and shall use every human device to motivate him to achieve what he wants. After all, that's what a real friend would do, and I am that friend!

MARKETING ERRORS

Avoidable Error #12.
You think marketing is beneath you.

There's a curious (and deeply snobbish) notion present among authors and information developers — I see it all the time — namely that authorship is a superior field that precludes commerce. What nonsense! Don't let this fatuous notion infect you. Commerce — the selling of information products and so touching lives — is the most important part of product production, not the least. Your job is not merely to create gilded thoughts and then take the world's homage from your silken divan. That may be satisfying to the lesser side of your ego, but it will change very few lives. First, make a commitment to problem-solving information marketing. Then to problem-solving information production and packaging. Then, at the very end of the day, recline on those pillows and take the obeisance of your swelling throng.

If you are truly dedicated to improving the lot of other people, and not just in showing them how important you are, you'll do whatever is necessary:

- to produce a truly superior product, a product that will help the conscientious customer achieve the result he wishes to achieve, and

- to get information about this product and what it can do into the hands of the largest possible number of people who can benefit from it.

You will not seek to throw the burden of marketing onto someone else. No one will ever take the interest that you do in your crusade to change lives through your products. Why should they? Their rewards — both psychic and material — are secondary to the ones you'll derive. You are the only one who truly understands the importance of what you have created and just how much better off your prospects will be when they use it. Know this now and act accordingly. Berating others because they do not share your dream is a futile waste of time. Assume responsibility for doing everything you can to bring your helpful solutions to those who can benefit from them.

I have a local acquaintance who writes a book almost every year. Although always published by reputable presses, they are, to a book, failures in that they do not succeed either in making him any money or in building his consulting practice. His, in short, is an exercise in near futility. But then, how could it be otherwise when he:

- refuses to help his publishers write client-centered marketing materials about his books;

- refuses to inquire into their marketing plans before a contract is signed;

- refuses to work with them in pre-publication marketing efforts;

- refuses to work with them in marketing the book once it is published;

- refuses to do what is necessary to incorporate his latest book into the workshops and seminars he gives;

- refuses to contact media outlets to promote his book.

And on and on.

How can one possibly have any compassion for this dolt? All that he does (and fails to do) proclaims that his single interest is creating products; he has no interest in *selling* products. Therefore, I say this to you: he has no interest in changing lives. For if he were committed to making the lives of his prospects better, then he would feel ashamed of his own lack of energetic support for bringing his product to their attention in such a way that motivates them to acquire it.

Now commit!

☐ I promise to stop thinking of marketing as somehow beneath me, as something that others will do, whilst I indulge in blissful ignorance about the selling process. I accept the primacy of product marketing between the two crucial steps of product creation and product marketing and will give to this necessary activity the time, attention and seriousness it deserves.

Avoidable Error #13.
You don't create client-centered marketing communications.

Client-centered marketing communications heap benefits on the buyer; advantages they get when they use the product. They also provide an incentive that motivates the prospect to acquire the product NOW, the *only* important marketing moment. Let's look at some illustrations of information product marketing materials. Then you tell me: do these marketing communications entice you with desireable benefits? Or do they merely tell you that a product is available that has stuff in it? *Attendez!*

Here are excerpts from a sales flyer produced by Continuing Education Publications, Portland State University, Oregon:

"Your Proposal Is A Valuable Fund Raising Tool.

Give It An Edge"

This is the opening panel. This is the section the prospect will see first; thus, it's the most important section . . . the place where the strongest sales argument should appear.

Does this panel speak to you? Does it motivate you to act . . . to spend money NOW? Does it give any indication that the writer knows what you want to accomplish and when you want to accomplish it? Sadly, no.

Now, I ask you. What does a fund raising proposal writer want? Why, to have that proposal funded! To get the money!

But where is that sentiment on this crucial opening panel? It isn't there. So, sadly, we look inside:

(across two panels)

"Third Edition

GETTING FUNDED

A Complete Guide To Proposal Writing

Mary Hall

Sixteen years in print. An Indispensable Reference For Experienced and First-Time Grant Writers Alike.

Formerly: DEVELOPING SKILLS IN PROPOSAL WRITING"

We have now read three panels and still haven't been told this book will help us get the money we need.

This isn't client-centered marketing; it's marketer-centered marketing. Its focus is on the person who has written the book and is selling it . . . *not* on the person who needs to raise money and doesn't care anything about a book *per se* but only about getting the money he needs for his projects.

The focus of this all-too-common information-product mailing piece is entirely misguided. The writer, be he author or publisher or both, hasn't asked himself what the customer wants to achieve and why he will shell out his hard-earned money on a book. A book . . . something which suggests he must invest his time and attention doing work!

Instead, the marketer is saying in effect: "Hey, we've published a book. Aren't you glad! I don't know what you want to achieve with it or won't tell you. But you need it anyway!"

Astonishingly, this passes for marketing with most information providers.

Look at this example:

This is a flyer produced by Entrepreneur's Information Center, Boulder, Colorado, for an audio cassette program entitled "Effective Marketing For Service Businesses and Professional Practices."

Now, before you consider what this company has sent out as its best effort to induce sales, consider this: do you think service businesses and professional practices want to spent their time marketing? Or do you think they are more often forced to do it? We both know, don't we?

The only reason these people market is to get money. If they could forego marketing and still get the business, they most probably would. Thus, the stress in the Center's marketing should be on the money the buyer can make . . . not on the marketer's product.

"Excellent New Program Introduced

Every once in a while a 'new' product comes along that is really worth paying attention to! We've just discovered one.

The Entrepreneur's Information Center (EIC) in Boulder, Colorado has introduced an audio cassette program entitled Effective Marketing For Service Businesses and Professional Practices. This program is different from others because it features successful business people in a news interview format, rather than one 'authority' or seminar salesman pitching and preaching. Fifteen people who have built successful firms in law, research, consulting, insurance, brokerage, financial planning and others talk openly and candidly about what has worked for them, what hasn't and why."

Now, read this again. How many benefits are there in this paragraph? How many specific advantages that you want to achieve? Don't look too hard, because *there isn't a single one.*

After reading this paragraph, your correct response is "So what?". What does any of this have to do with me? What do I get when I pay my hard-earned money for your product? What difference does it make if it's "new?" If it's "different?" I'm not interested in "new" for the sale of new! In "different" for the sake of difference! I'm interested in what will get me more clients and hence more profits.

And where is this crucial sentiment addressed in this flyer?

It's not!

Later, I shall go into great detail on the pivotal question of how to create marketing communications that appeal to your customers and get them to respond NOW. For the moment, however, it's enough to say this: my colleagues in the information industry are wasting millions of dollars because they persist in being enamored of what they are producing. They long to tell their prospects about the glories of their books, cassettes, Special Reports . . . and all their other information products.

I say this: none of these things is important. The only thing that matters is the advantage the product brings to the customer who uses it conscientiously. Thus, the fact that you have written a Special Report is of no importance; is of purely personal interest. What matters is what your customers get when they use it.

You must move as quickly as possible away from the idea that the product you produce as a product is valuable to anyone else but you. It isn't. *Results are all that matter.*

Therefore, you must focus on these results. Hit the specific results that people will achieve when they use (not buy) your products . . . and how much worse off they'll be if they don't use (not buy) your products.

Your marketing materials (as you'll see when we discuss this in more detail) should say in effect:

Get this benefit.

And this benefit.

And this benefit.

When you use this product.

Don't take my word for this. See for yourself. Start collecting the flyers, brochures, letters, and other marketing communications produced by publishers and information product producers of every kind. You'll be staggered at just how selfish they are; just how little the interests of the would-be buyer are consulted.

You must not be this way . . . or you cannot realize your own objectives. Chances are your enterprise is still small. Thus, you cannot afford to waste any of your precious resources. That's why I tell you this: if you want to increase the chances for your own profit, you'll write every marketing communication from the vantage point of your customer. You'll stop talking about yourself, focusing only on what the customer gets. And you'll do what is necesary to induce him to get it NOW!

Now commit!

☐ I pledge to create marketing communications . . . everything I use from a flyer to a four-color catalog . . . from the vantage point of the buyer. That is, I'll focus on buyer benefits and on whatever the buyer gets . . . and forego the selfish pleasures of focusing on my product (which admittedly excites me). From now on, I shall stop talking about what I have . . . and never cease talking about what my buyers get . . . all the things they get . . . in glorious detail. I know this is the way to get them to buy my info-products . . . and make me rich!

Avoidable Error #14.
You don't stimulate your buyers to take immediate action.

When you are approaching a market of prospects and buyers, you want these people to act NOW. I know you do. Then, why don't you stimulate them to do so? Your buyers aren't sitting in a white room without windows and doors with nothing to do but wait for your marketing materials to arrive. But yet you treat them as if they were. When you consider the subject of marketing, you must consider that your prospects:

- are bombarded with possibilities . . . not just in your area, but in all areas;

- have limited time and desire to consider these possibilities;

- have even more limited money to acquire these possibilities.

That's why you've got to realize you're in a war . . . a war with anything that competes for your prospect's time, attention, and resources. If you don't approach this matter like a war, you have lost before you even make the approach . . . just like most people who think they are marketing their *products*.

Thus, if you want your prospects to act NOW, you must give them a reason to act NOW. Look at any marketing materials you use now . . . whatever your business . . . whether you work for yourself or someone else. Have you hit your prospect over the head again and again with all the *specific* benefits he gets from you? And have you given him a reason to act NOW?

I bet the answer is "no" to both questions! If it is, shame on you!!!

Instead of using "Now" to induce immediate sales, most information sellers make these two fatal mistakes:

• They simply say what they have to say and let the prospect decide when to act.

This is what Ventana Press, Chapel Hill, North Carolina, did in a flyer featuring authors Daniel Fishman and Elliot King. Ventana developed this particular flyer for print and broadcast interview sources which might be interested in their new volume *The Book Of Fax*. Purportedly, it wanted to influence these sources to interview their authors and so sell more books.

But who would know it? This is Ventana's anemic headline: "Daniel Fishman and Elliot King have some interesting things to say about new fax technology." Who cares? Interview sources want stories, news, controversy, a reason for interviewing the source. "Interesting things" sounds like a tea party. What's worse, there's no indication until the last three sentences what Ventana Press is trying to accomplish with this flyer ("Either or both authors are available for print or broadcast interviews") or any incentive for the reader to call NOW. Thus, Ventana Press is saying in effect, "We say our story is important, but it's insufficiently important for us to motivate you to take immediate action. Thus, you are perfectly justified in ignoring us and in interviewing someone else. It doesn't matter to us when you act. And we certainly don't want to influence you to do it now." On this basis, how could such a marketing communication be anything other than an expensive failure?

• Or, they have an offer, but bury it at the end of their copy. This is what McGraw-Hill (a company that really ought to know better) did in a recent advertisement for its book *The Small Business Guide To Borrowing Money*. I've reproduced their advertisement (as it appeared in a card deck) on the next page. Can you find the offer that will induce the maximum number of people to respond the fastest? Why, it's the paragraph beginning "Send me this book for 15 days' free examination." This is the motivational offer, the quintessentially American offer of something (a 15 days' examination) for nothing.

Get the capital you need at the best terms possible!

Whether you need capital to start a new venture or expand your present operations, this book can give you a clear edge over other borrowers. It reveals every major source of financing now available, inside and outside regular channels, both private and public. Above all, it shows you the techniques necessary to tap these sources of capital – from how to prepare a loan application to ways to cut through red tape and get your loan approved in record time.

THE SMALL BUSINESS GUIDE TO BORROWING MONEY

Richard L. Rubin &
Philip Goldberg   265 pp., $36.95

03-K181-6200-3

054198-1

Send me this book for 15 days' free examination. After that time I will remit the full price plus local tax, postage, and handling or return the book without obligation. I understand if I remit in full, plus local tax, with this order McGraw-Hill will pay all regular postage and handling and that refund privileges still apply.

Name _____

Address/Apt. _____
No PO Boxes please

City/State/Zip _____
This order subject to acceptance by McGraw-Hill.   03-K181-6200-3
Offer good in the U.S

COMPLETE THIS CARD AND MAIL TODAY • 15-DAY FREE EXAMINATION!

Look where McGraw-Hill has placed this offer . . . towards the very end. And look how they've treated it. Not a *single* word in the offer is emphasized in any way. Thus, the prospect is right to say to himself, "Well, if McGraw-Hill doesn't think this is such a great offer, why should I?"

Not only must an offer be present . . . but it must be treated like something important. Now, I ask you this . . . do you think people want a 15-day examination (even if it's free), or do they want to know how to borrow money through techniques they can get from a free 15-day examination of this resource? See the difference? McGraw-Hill is offering a feature (a 15-day examination), and offering it in the most pale and uninteresting way possible. What they should be doing is stimulating the qualified prospect to take action to acquire the product that will, for 15 days, give them free access to secrets that will get them the money they need.

What McGraw-Hill has forgotten is that people don't want to read another book (reading is work, after all). They *do* want to know the secrets of borrowing money which they can use for their own projects. That's essential to people who need this money (McGraw-Hill's prospects). So, lead from strength . . . sell the sizzle (the borrowed money), not the steak (the book).

McGraw-Hill is speculating, of course, that those who get the book will either value it so greatly or be so greatly disorganized that they won't return it and will pay the accompanying invoice. What's important to point out, however, is that McGraw-Hill has buried its offer. It is attempting to sell a book . . . not benefits from the book . . . and not the supreme benefit of action NOW! This is a very common, very costly, very stupid problem made by the vast majority of info-entrepreneurs.

Looking Even More Closely At These Scenarios

In the first instance, the marketer's position is this: "My customer is a rational person. If I present my information in a rational and reasonable way, my customer will see that I've got something for him and will take action accordingly. I don't need to motivate him to take action now."

THIS IS WRONG. Your prospect may be a perfectly rational person (though I've seen enough humans in my lifetime to doubt it). But he also has a lot of other things on his mind and too few dollars to satisfy his many wants. Thus, you've got to motivate him to take immediate action to get the advantages you've got . . . before someone else motivates him to acquire another set of advantages that drain him of the money and incentive to buy yours.

In the second instance, the marketer's position is, "My customer will read everything I send him and will, bit by bit, work his way to my offer. Since he's going to do that anyway, there's no need for me to motivate him by accentuating that offer. He'll get to it in his own good time."

I ask you . . . do you read this way? Do you start at the top of a page and read through it systematically, considering each fact, assessing each statement, being patient enought to wade through all the words to get to the point? If you do, you should be in the Smithsonian Institution, because you are truly a museum exhibit.

THIS ISN'T HOW PEOPLE READ. Real people, the kinds of people you must persuade in large numbers to give you their time, attention, and resources, immediately want to know, "What's in this for me?" And if you can't tell them, right away, they are right to dismiss you! These people don't have endless time and patience to wade through your marketing communications, even if you have taken weeks to create them. What's that to them? They want to know NOW the benefits you can deliver . . . and only after they've been persuaded by the benefits and the need to take immediate action to acquire them should they be bothered with the procedural matters of how to acquire the product.

In the light of what I've just said, does either of these positions make sense? Not at all. Yet, I assure you, most information providers sell their products in just this way. They say, in effect: here's information about a product. This product is of the utmost interest to me . . . but I can't be bothered to tell you the specific advantages you'll get when you use it. And I certainly don't want to intrude on your life to the extent of motivating you to act now (though I could certainly use your business now). So, I'll throw it at you and hope against hope that you respond.

Or, I know you're busy and that you need motivation to respond, but it's really important for you to read everything I've written. So, I'll create an offer . . . but I'll bury it. I worked hard to create these marketing communications. You should at least do me the favor of wading through and carefully considering them. After you've done that . . . *then* you can take advantage of my offer. It's there all right, but not highlighted. You'll find it . . . if you look hard enough!

Stop "marketing" this way. I beg you!!!

Think! Whatever kinds of info-products you're selling, you're going to have to create a host of marketing communications. These include (but are certainly not limited to):

> ads
> flyers/package stuffers
> media kits
> letters
> brochures
> catalogs
> ready-to-print articles and reviews

And many more.

Let's be clear about why you're doing this. The purpose is not to flatter your ego by having your name and products featured in print or on the air. Any fool with a checkbook can purchase media space (as oh so many do!) or "become known," for as long as he's willing to pay for the privilege of being a known entity.

No, the only purpose of marketing is to motivate a seller, your prospect, to take *immediate* action . . . either to acquire what you're selling NOW or to take the next logical step NOW (calling for information, *etc.*) so you can continue the motivational process that will result in the fastest possible sale. Nothing else matters. Nothing.

Now commit!

☐   I shall never again create a marketing communication — any marketing communication — that doesn't contain at least one inducement to motivate the prospect to act immediately to acquire the benefits I have for him. It matters to me . . . and it's important to the prospect . . . just when the sale is made. I need the money now . . . and my targeted prospect needs the information that I have for him so he can get what he wants. Thus, I intend to do *everything* I possibly can to motivate the prospect to take immediate action . . . and I shall prominently place the client-centered inducement I create so that the prospect sees it quickly . . . and can therefore take fast action to get it.

Avoidable Error #15.
You don't know and apply the Rule of Seven.

To motivate the greatest number of your prospects to respond, one "coat" of your market is quite insufficient. To my continuing astonishment, I meet information seller after information seller who maintains the fatuous notion that you can approach a prospect one time and, because that prospect is in need, sell him your product right away. But the truth is, people, even the neediest, rarely do what what's in their own best interest when told about it *once*.

The other day, an information-selling colleague called me from Florida to give me some media leads; places that could run my Sure-Fire Business Success Column or review my books. As he turned over this crucial information, he complained to me that he had offered similar valuable leads to other friends in the field, but that no one had followed them up. He was hurt, irritated, perhaps incredulous. But why?

Since when have people ever done even those things that are manifestly in their own best interest the first time they were told about them? It doesn't happen too often. (By the way, my own letters to those media sources, like all the leads I get, were sent that very day. This is the only way to stay ahead.)

If you are to succeed as an information seller and make the truly appealing sums that you can, you must arrange your activities by these assumptions:

- no one will respond to your first offer, no matter what its advantages to the prospect;

- you are responsible for any and all follow-up and project progress, whatever the advantages to the prospect;

- you must do your homework about the prospect and his circumstances, you must understand his interests better than he does himself, and you must be willing to do whatever is necessary to fulfill his interests for him . . . as well as your own interests for yourself;

- you will never give up on this advantageous prospect project so long as there are equal advantages to you, whatever the level of myopia, disorganization or plain stupidity on the part of that prospect.

Consider Today's Flood Of Marketing Materials

To begin with, these days information products are a dime a dozen, or less. If you're like me, you're inundated with new releases for every kind of information product. Yet, how often do you hear about these products more than once? I've been doing an informal survey over the course of several years to determine just how often information providers send me more than a single notice about their product. So far, under 5% of the information providers, selling a host of problem-solving products, bother to contact me more than once. 95% not only think I will answer their first communication, but are staking the success of their business on my doing so.

THIS IS ABSURD!

That's where the Rule of Seven comes in.

There are two aspects to the Rule of Seven: the number of times you must connect with your prospect with a focused client-centered message packed with advantages to him. And the time period in which you must make these connections.

As to the first point, you must direct clear-cut client-centered messages to your targeted prospect a *minimum* of seven times before there's a reasonable likelihood he has really focused on your message and understands what you've got for him.

As to the second point, these connections must take place in a time period never longer than 18 months and perhaps considerably shorter given certain key variables such as: what your competitors are doing, a time period dictated either by the product or by other circumstances connected with the product, or by your own desire to motivate a faster response.

Since you expect to make money with your problem-solving information, here are the important steps you must adhere to:

1. Select the specific potential market(s).
2. Research the pressing problems this market wants to solve.

3. Ascertain the ability of this market to pay for what you are selling.

4. Research the means of reaching this market ensuring that you can get continuing access to your prospects *à la* the Rule of Seven.

5. Draft the budget requirements you need for this continuing access using these variables:

   product price
   number of pieces of direct mail
   color vs. black/white printing
   follow up mailing pieces
   postage
   telephone calls
   paid ads (classified and space)

6. Create your first problem-solving information product.

7. Implement your marketing plan for this product.

8. Expand into related problem-solving information products.

Some Key Comments

• If you are not prepared to connect with your targeted prospect a minimum of seven times in a maximum of 18 months, don't even begin to market to the audience. Odds are, your worst marketing return will come from your initial marketing gambit to a specific audience, notwithstanding the fact that you have created a client-centered message, piling prospect benefit on prospect benefit, and that you have given that prospect an incentive to take immediate action.

• If you use the Rule of Seven conscientiously but fail to approach a market that has the problem your product can solve or has the means to acquire that solution, then the Rule of Seven cannot save you. You will still be wasting your money.

• If you use the Rule of Seven with the right market but fail to create an advantageous client-centered message, piling prospect benefit on prospect benefit, and failing to create an incentive for immediate action, you are still crippling your marketing effort.

In short, four crucial elements must be present:

• you must be targeting a specific marketing group that has the problem you can solve with your info-product, knows it has the problem, and has the means to acquire the product that offers them the solution;

- you must pack all communications to this targeted group with client-specific advantages that are both believable to the prospect and advantages they wish to have;

- you must spur immediate action by the prospect by making an offer that gets him to act NOW;

- you must continue to approach the same targeted group of prospects over and over again, at least seven times, in not more than 18 months.

Only if you follow *each* of these steps can you possibly hope to make money selling information-based products. If you don't, your failure is predictable.

Creating Seven-Step Processes That Won't Bankrupt You

I shall share something with you now that probably all information product sellers know, but sadly few live by: the object of marketing is not to spend money on marketing. *It is to make more sales faster.* Thus, the goal of marketing should be to make the maximum number of sales for the least conceivable investment. Seems obvious, doesn't it? Why, then, do most people fail to arrange matters so soundly? I shall attempt to tell you:

- Untutored marketers believe the world runs by rules. That if Company X says it sells so much ad space for so many dollars, then that, indeed, is the way things are. So, reasons this "marketer" if I want that space, I must pay that price.

It should go without saying (but doesn't) that the Savvy Marketer doesn't think this way at all. His objective, remember, is to make the maximum number of sales for the minimum conceivable price. The money he saves he may consider either profit or capital to be invested in reaching still more buyers. Thus, it is his bounden duty to search for ways of broadening his coverage while minimizing his costs. Is there a way of getting more catalogs for less money? He will not feel comfortable within himself until he finds out. Can he get that ad — or a bigger one — promoting his latest product for less money? He *must* find out. Can he cut the discount he pays to have an organization market his books? He fidgets until he discovers.

The Savvy Marketer, you see, is not an accepting soul, does not do well with standard limits and traditional business practices. He has only this objective: selling more for less. All other standards, practices and procedures pale into insignificance before this bedrock principle, and if there are those who cannot accept this way of doing business (and there most assuredly will be many), why, then, their pique must just be reckoned a necessary part of doing business and so many milestones on the way to your handsome fortune.

- Untutored marketers are afraid they will be perceived by the people they do business with as sordid deal makers, or worse. They are afraid to test the limits of their suppliers, to ask for things that others do not get, to risk being turned down.

Well, I am an hereditary Scotman in very good standing; parsimonious to a degree, niggardly, delighting to find new ways to reach more people for less cost, ecstatic when I can shave a penny here, a nickel there to achieve the same result, or even better. (How else can you explain my unending search for book boxes behind the Harvard Square bookstores? I call this "dumpstering", and have been known to take my elegant friends and colleagues straight from a tasty repast out into the dumpsters, to their unfeigned embarrassment. But, mind, I am a Scot and little brings the happy roses to my cheeks like saving money. If this sometimes occurs at the cost of horrifying my friends and colleagues, so be it.)

- Untutored marketers tend (even when they have precious little capital) to prefer expensive marketing alternatives to inexpensive ones. That is, they will buy an ad instead of ascertaining how to get free publicity in the same source. Why? Partly because expensive alternatives are more comfortable to arrange. It is always easier to plunk your money down to purchase an expensive alternative. It usually takes less time, means less negotiation, and takes place with fewer problems. Usually, but not always. Secondly, paying seems to reinforce their self-esteem. "Real businesses have the money to buy marketing," so they reason. "So if I'm to be a real business, I must pay, too."

I utterly reject this kind of reasoning. Your objective must always be how to reach the greatest number of prospects the greatest number of times for the least possible cost. Nothing else matters. Thus you need to:

- ensure you can reach a targeted group of prospects over and over again with a benefit-rich message for the least possible cost;
- find out the real cost of any marketing gambit so that you can make its presenter a profitable alternative, if not the published or public one. I shall have more to say about this later. But your job is to find out how much a card in a card deck costs . . . not merely how much its publisher charges the general public. Once you know *his* cost, then you can dicker accordingly with a very good likelihood that your offer will be accepted.
- structure your Rule of Seven sequence so that you take advantage of the greatest number of least expensive processes over their costlier alternatives.
- ask yourself before you use any marketing gambit, "Have I done all I could to lower the cost of this activity? Either by getting my message to more

people for the same cost? Or cutting the cost of reaching this number? Have I dickered, wheedled, thundered and pleaded to achieve the one thing I must achieve: the greatest conceivable outreach for least conceivable expense?" If you don't feel sure that you have achieved this objective, this may be a marketing activity you need to reconsider.

Now commit!

☐   I shall never again expect my prospects to respond the very first time they hear about the advantages I have for them. I shall structure my marketing activities so that I am not only certain about the targeted prospects I'll be addressing, but shall arrange matters so that they hear about the advantages I have for them over and over and over again. If I am not willing to so connect with them so often, then I shall not even begin a marketing gambit, for such gambits are necessarily unprofitable.

Avoidable Error #16.
Your price is too low.

I read many periodicals where books and reports and audio cassettes are sold. Many of them are ad-sheets where products sell for a very few dollars. Why do the "marketers" bother? You can't make any money this way.

Here's a letter the publisher of such an ad sheet recently sent me: "My publication is probably the most successful of any new publication of this year . . . *It is not making me any money or even covering my expenses* [my emphasis] but in this field the most important thing is getting your NAME known."

Examine this statement from a well-meaning information seller. Getting your name known is important, admittedly; but making money is the *sine qua non* of business success. My colleague clearly hasn't priced either her product or the ads therein at the proper rate to make money. My prediction: unless this situation gets turned around rapidly, "the most successful new publication of the year" won't even be in existence a year from now.

Hence, some rules on pricing:

*   The products you develop must be directed towards the most affluent section of your market — the people who have the problem you can solve (or a desire they want to achieve) and the means of solving or achieving it. Both parts of this crucial equation must be present. Importantly, it doesn't matter if there are millions of people who have the problem you can solve . . . if millions of people are without the means of buying that solution/achievement.

- The product must be priced according to the value of the end result the customer can achieve using the information. Thus, you must know — and use as an inducement to get the prospect to buy — just how much benefit your product can deliver.

- The product must be priced so that with direct response sales you break even at .5% response after you have taken into account the cost of creating a mailing piece, renting names, printing the mailing piece(s), postage, product cost, *etc.*

Significantly, you cannot price your product in a vacuum. You must also consider your competitors. In setting a price there is always tension between what you need to make a profit . . . and the others in the field who have already set a price as low as they can to make money and to discourage you from entering the competition. Nonetheless, you must know who has something comparable to what you have and what they charge.

- What can your market get from your competitor(s)?

- What can they get from you?

- How well known is that competitor . . . that is, what kind of awareness is your market likely to have of the benefit he can offer versus awareness of the benefit you can offer?

By the same token, you must consider the kind of marketing you'll be doing. The price of the product must sustain that marketing and must sustain it alone, unless you are offering other info-products.

Ingenue info-product marketers look more at the production cost of their baby than the value it offers the buyer. To be sure, the cost of production is an important variable — for you — because you have to pay it. But is not important because of its relation to ultimate price. Price should be related to perceived *value*, not production cost. Let's not make any bones about what we're doing.

The product seller's goal is to get rich and have an enhanced life. We need remind no one other than ourselves of this fact, but there it is. Our goal is to test the outermost limits of price, which means pushing the concept of perceived value. How high we can go is a function of several variables:

- the need of our prospect for this information;
- the other ways he can get it;
- how strongly he perceives the value of the information;
- his ability to pay ever greater prices.

We must consider all these variables.

If we wish to increase price, we must increase perceived value. Focusing on the product itself, instead of its substantiated value, is certain to limit how much we can charge for it. Thus, your job is to set the price as high as you can and to institute a marketing campaign that is so focused on value that prospects gladly pay a higher price. This is what I have done, and I can testify to its effectiveness.

Now commit!

☐   From now on, before I price any of my info-products, I shall work hard to determine just what kinds of specific benefits my prospects will get when they use these products. I shall determine product price by comparing these benefits to the prices my competitors charge for comparable products. The price I set will be designed to create maximum profit and fastest sale.

Avoidable Error #17.
You don't sell your products from the earliest possible moment . . . before they even exist.

Whatever anyone says to the contrary, the goal of business is to get as much money as early as possible . . . and to delay your payables for as long as possible. When you're selling information products, this means selling them before they physically exist. To be able to do this successfully, certain conditions apply:

- You need either to be a known entity with other products to your credit, have your own house mailing list, and/or have established relations with marketing sources who know your material and trust your reliability.

- You have to be certain you can produce the product on time. This is not just for the good of your client relations, but because if products are late the federal government gets involved (through the Federal Trade Commission). Thus, give yourself maximum time and flexibility.

If you meet these conditions, however, you should start selling your products as early as possible . . . from the very minute you have a title.

Reasons? To begin with, printers and product producers operate on relatively slender profit margins. Moreover, they have materials and labor to pay for promptly. Thus, they require their money promptly. You will find, for instance, that many such producers require a significant amount of money in advance with the rest often required immediately upon completion of the job. You therefore have significant bills to pay at a time before your marketing effort has produced any significant income.

Secondly, because of the Rule of Seven, you want prospects in your various markets to be told about your products as often as possible. Making pre-publication offers gives you a perfectly justifiable reason to approach any media source and, if they know you and your work, the chances are good you get the publicity you want . . . and the advance sales you need.

Why are these advance sales so important? Well, consider the alternative. If you fail to use all the pre-publication techniques I'll be discussing, you will probably have to pay for the full cost of production and printing within about 60 days. This can be a very significant expense. Thus, whether you are known or not, you have every reason to start your sales process before you actually have products in hand. What you can do, however, is largely limited by who you are, who knows you, your reputation, and resources. Let's look at both situations, when you have a lot going for you, and when you have less.

When You Have A Lot Going For You

Let me begin by saying, I'm not necessarily talking about money here. Rather, I'm talking about things you can leverage like reputation, existing marketing linkages, a house mailing list, *etc.* Sadly, all too many information product producers only start their marketing efforts when they have their product physically in hand. This is a mistake. Instead you should create a pre-publication plan. Consider the following parts.

Use Free Media

If you have followed the suggestions in this and my other books, you will develop good working relationships with many media sources, particularly print publications. Now is the time to derive yet another advantage from this relationship.

- Develop a media release announcing the fact you are creating a new product and announcing when it will be ready. Provide readers of the publication with a special discount (25-30% off the eventual retail price will do nicely) if they act by a certain date (about 30 days before your product will actually be ready). Make sure to announce what the eventual retail price will be and how much prospects save by acting promptly . . . as well as the advantages they'll derive from using the product itself.

Send this release to all publications with which you have worked, which know your work, or have favorably reviewed it in the past. Where necessary, accompany the release with a short personal note reminding the editor of your previous association ("you favorably reviewed my last audio cassette, (name), on (date)."). Send your releases about 90 (but not more than 120) days before your product will actually be available. If there is the slightest uncertainty about just when that will be, be very conservative in the date you promise delivery.

- Carve excerpts from your material so that you have a series of articles available for printing. These articles should include a Resource Box (discussed in greater detail later) providing the name of your product, one or two benefits of using it, and complete order details, including when any special pre-publication offer expires. You should create at least three or four such articles of between 500 and 2000 words apiece.

Why so many? Again, because of the Rule of Seven. You must look at the marketing process of an information product as divided into several distinct but related stages. Certain things should happen before the product is available . . . others when the product is newly available . . . still others when the product has entered maturity and become a staple. It is the Rule of Seven that connects all these stages and informs all approaches to your various markets.

In this case, tell all the editors/publishers you're approaching exactly what articles you have available. Provide them with a brief, descriptive list detailing titles and benefits readers (who are also, of course, your customers) will derive from your information. As I shall reemphasize later, it is a mistake merely to offer an editor a single article about which he must make either a "thumbs up" or "thumbs down" decision. What if he decides not to print some or all of the only thing you've offered? Why, your marketing program has been adversely affected. Therefore, offer these print media decision makers a variety of possibilities; they know what they are trying to do with their publication. Give them several possibilities and the likelihood is greater you can be part of their plans.

Note: not only do I suggest that you give media decision makers several articles to select from but give them several article lengths as well. Indicate these lengths on your list of available articles. By the way, standard practice is to offer length in number of words, not pages.

Further note: these days it is very much to your advantage to make these articles available on IBM-compatible diskette in ASCII code. Give your editors the choice of what format they'd like: hard copy, on diskette, or both. By the way, virtually all editors who wish to have articles on diskette want them to be IBM-compatible.

Your articles should be timed so that in each publication one article appears in each of the three months preceding the physical existence of your product *and* in the actual month the product is available. At that point, you can send a review copy of the product to the publication and begin to benefit from editorial endorsements (reviews).

Before leaving this subject, I wish to say a few more words. You will notice that I have laid considerable stress on your producing anything the media source needs to promote your product . . . you write the media release from which he will draw information about the benefits of your product and when it will be available. You write the excerpts and articles. You create whatever wording needs to be created.

In my dealings with media sources, I attribute my success in large measure to my willingness to do *whatever* work needs to be done. Ordinarily, I leave only one thing to the media source: connecting me with his audience. That is something only he can do and is therefore necessarily left to him. But nothing else.

Whatever you want from a media source, you are best advised to do it yourself, for these are busy people who are beset with a host of production problems and cannot generally be bothered with accommodating you and your wishes. Thus, accommodate them yourself. Resolve to write whatever you wish to have printed . . . or, for that matter, broadcast. On this basis, you will be much more welcome to media sources and so ensure that your message is delivered as you wish it to be.

Use Your House Mailing List

Offer people on your house mailing list a special offer on unproduced items. Four months before the actual date products will be physically available, start selling them. I again emphasize: to make this gambit work, customers must be familiar with your work or at least trusting in your ability to deliver a quality product. Their trust linked with a meaningful discount will help spur sales. I now have a sizable group of people who buy in advance everything I create. They get what they want for a nice discount; I get the money in early. Everyone's happy. I rely on these advance sales to pay at least 50% of the production costs of any new product. This is vastly different from the way most information product marketers work.

Look for ways to beef up this offer:

- Let people know they are getting the problem solving information as quickly as it's available. The lure of getting things fast and before others has always been strong. My policy is to send the early buyers their materials within three days of when they are actually available. This is faster than anyone else I know. How is this possible?

Labels are physically produced the day the customer orders his product. The accompanying upgrade letter, personally addressed to each buyer, (I'll be discussing this later) is produced weeks in advance, as soon as we know which month books will be delivered in. (This letter is dated with a month only, not a month and day). The day before the products are delivered, I begin to fill out the UPS shipping book with the names and addresses of customers. Thus, when the products themselves actually arrive, all we have to do is bundle the book, upgrade letter, and any additional insert pieces and staple the package. That's it. UPS takes those packages the same day. Buyers within New York and New England actually have their product the next day . . . within 24 hours of when I myself first see it. People on the West Coast have them just five days later. That's awfully good.

- Autograph suitable products. You must always seek ways of building the perceived value of what you produce. One easy way of doing this is to autograph your books and booklets for pre-publication buyers and to offer this autograph as part of the reason for early action. Our countrymen value things that are scarce, and they also respect and admire authorship. Take full advantage of this. Tell your pre-publication buyers that you will autograph and date their product, which after all is not only something new, but a First Edition. Don't make the mistake of those few information providers who do autograph but who only sign their names. Make sure you date the autograph. Collectors like things that are scarce and a date indicates a precise moment in time, hence scarcity.

But who are you, you may say, that you should be autographing anything? If this is what you are thinking, shame on you. True, your autograph may not, just now, have the intrinsic worth of, say, Napoleon's at Austerlitz, but you must act as if it might. Perceptions as much as realities motivate people to act. It is your job to add to the perceived value of what you're selling . . . and here a dated autograph certainly helps.

- Date the offer. All offers must be dated to be meaningful. Your special discount offer should expire about a month before you firmly expect to have your products in your possession. Be very conservative about this figure, since there are almost always production and delivery problems. Still, if you expect to have products by the end of October, then promote October 1 as the end of your prepublication offer. You see, you're allowed 30 days by federal regulations to ship your merchandise, and while it is certainly true your customers want their merchandise as quickly as possible, you may well need the extra time.

- Provide a special premium for pre-publication buyers only. Exclusivity has always been a potent motivator. Use it to spur early sales of your products.

But, as I always remind you, don't spend too much money. This is where Special Reports come in. Carve out a section of your product as a Special Report and make this available as a pre-publiation buyer premium. Tell your buyers they will get this premium immediately (and make sure it goes out promptly).

This premium, too, should be accompanied by an upgrade letter saying in effect, "Here's your Special Premium that will give you these advantages. Your product will follow in (month, not on date; that's too specific). Now why not get other products you can use immediately." In other words, just because a product isn't physically available doesn't mean you cannot seek to upgrade its buyer with other offers. Remember, anytime you are in touch with a buyer is the moment to upgrade that buyer, and the moment you're delivering a special offer premium is the moment to close on another sale. The items being offered in this upgrade letter, however, should be available for immediate shipment. You shouldn't try a customer's patience too much.

Other Direct Mail Offers

We now come to the most expensive pre-publication marketing technique: direct mail that is not sent to your house list. It is the most expensive because you not only have the cost of producing the mailing piece but the expense of renting the prospect names, too. Nonetheless, I recommend this technique, if and only if you are willing to:

- Research all the available mailing lists to find just the right one(s) on which your best prospects appear. Direct mail offers fail either because the list is wrong, the offer is wrong, and/or because the copy is wrong. You need to be very conservative in your list selection and begin the marketing process with small quantities of names (5000 is generally the minimum) and only rent others when you have ascertained that your initial test is profitable.

- Work hard to create a totally client-centered marketing piece (usually consisting of a cover letter, brochure, and order coupon). As I have already said and as I shall reiterate throughout the course of this volume, the vast majority of marketing communications created by information product sellers are focused on the product, not the buyer. They tell you what you are buying, instead of what it can do for you when you use it. This is worse than wrong; it's unprofitable.

- Break even with a .5% response. What this means is this: you must draw up a full and realistic budget of expenses, including the cost of designing your mailing piece(s), producing them, list rental, affixing the labels and bundling, postage, *etc.* Don't forget the cost of the product itself. Leave nothing out. Now figure what a .5% response would be. Please, note this is not a 5% response, but a response of one-half of one percent!

Now multiply this number by the actual retail cost of your product. If you are not breaking even at this level (or very, very close to it), then either the cost of your product is too low (one distinct possibility), or you have not tried hard enough to lower your costs. However, if you have done these things and feel reasonably comfortable you have done them well, you should just abandon this promotion and go back to the drawing board.

People who deviate from this formula do so at their peril. I recall, for instance, two bright young women who scheduled a meeting with me several months ago. They were in the mail order book selling business (or so they thought), but had just had a terrible experience. They had paid a consultant, whom I regard as most unethical, a great sum of money. He had cooked them up a mailing piece for a $7.95 book (whose rights they did not control and from which they were getting nothing more than a 50% discount), seduced them from their reason with promises of a response of at least 20%, and then abandoned them to their fate. And what was that fate? They paid at least $10,000 in costs and retrieved under $1000. There were tears in both their eyes when they told me their story, which had wiped out their slender capital. As I heard it I was indignant at the mendacity of their consultant and astonished at the foolishness of the entrepreneurs.

I dedicate this section and its formula to them . . . and to the legions like them who have wasted their money when it was perfectly possible to know in advance if money could even be made.

Finally, don't forget the offer. You already know that your printers will want their money quickly until such time as you are established and can beg, wheedle, and plead for better credit terms; (you will learn to do all three, I assure you, or you will have to continue to fork over your money early with all its painful consequences). The offer, remember, is one of the prime reasons why your prospects act NOW to acquire the advantages you have available for them. You neglect it at your peril. Spurring your prospects to send in their money at the earliest possible moment is your objective; your offer helps you achieve it.

If You Don't Have Resources

Sadly, if you haven't cultivated relations with media sources . . . if you don't have a house list you can exploit . . . if your work isn't known, you do have fewer alternatives. Nonetheless, you must explore them, because your problem is the same as any other product producer's: whoever produces your product will want his money pronto. And unless you are quite prepared to hazard your own fortune at the hazardous game of products, you will want to use money from product sales to finance product production. Here, then, is what you must do:

- Create excerpts. Your problem, of course, is that media sources don't know you and have no reason to suppose that you can produce a quality product. They are thus right to be skeptical about you. This skepticism isn't personal, of course; it's just that they have heard so many people promise so many things, they are right to regard anything you say with a grain of salt. What will help change their attitude is the articles you offer them. With them they can judge for themselves.

That's why any publisher creating any problem-solving product, especially books, is crazy if he doesn't create the excerpts/articles/Special Reports based on this product as soon as he can. If you are producing your own material, these formats should be produced simultaneously with the creation of the product; if you are publishing someone else's product, then the information provider (author) should be required by contract to produce these materials and have them available no fewer than 120 days before the product is physically available.

Let me tell you something I hope you never forget: the excerpt/article is not important insofar as it establishes your credibility with the media sources and captures the attention of a targeted prospect. You do not create the article for the sheer joy of disseminating information; leave that to the charitably minded. You create it because people who are attracted to that article, who read and use it are prospects for the product on which it is based. The article, then, must be regarded as a sort of elaborate headline, or hook, a means of capturing the prospect and, because of the value of what he reads, getting him to move closer and closer still to the most important part of the article . . . the Resource Box that includes information (and the special pre-publication offer) on how he can acquire the product that contains even more of what he craves.

Note: once a media source tells you he values your material (it is quite permissible to ask, if this necessary opinion isn't promptly volunteered), then you should suggest the publication of still more articles, including both further pre-publication excerpts and those (along with the source's own review) which will follow physical availability of the product.

Direct Mail

To my astonishment, there are large numbers of publishers who do not maintain a house mailing list. There are several reasons for this lapse. First, there are those publishers who create products in so many areas that whatever mailing list they might produce would not help sell any new title. Thus, they fail to achieve the necessary synergy that cuts costs, creates automatic buyers of new products, and breeds wealth. This is madness.

Other product producers do not have a computer and so lack the technical ability to maintain a substantial mailing list. Still others, even those with an interrelated set of products, fail to capture the names of their buyers. This is especially true if they are selling their products through bookstores, catalogs, libraries, or other marketing avenues.

These product sellers focus not on the relationship they need to build with the buyer but on the single sale. This is an egregious error. Your job is to capture the name of every prospect and every satisfied buyer you can, to technically arrange matters so this information is easily accessible to you and in a form easy to use, and to continue to bring related offers to their attention until you have decided they are no longer good prospects for what you're selling.

If you are determined to succeed by selling information products, you must work hard to build up a house mailing list. This means working hard to capture the names of prospects and buyers. I shall elsewhere go into the means you can use to achieve this necessary end.

If you dedicate yourself to achieving this objective and so building your house list, you need only be without the benefits of such a list when your first product is created, for from that moment you have the means of connecting with buyers and prospects and stimulating them to be in contact with you so you can organize and preserve this crucial information.

Without a house list, you are left with only the most expensive form of direct mail to use. Clearly, you will follow the formula I have listed above to determine if you should use this alternative. What if, having followed this formula, you determine that the venture cannot break even at or near .5% response and that you are therefore likely to lose money. What then?

To come up with an answer, you need to consider several variables. If immediate sales are insufficient for you to break even, what can you do to improve your cash position?

1. You can stimulate people who are not yet ready to buy to get in touch with you. One of the biggest mistakes information product sellers make is forcing their prospects into either a "buy now" or "don't buy now" decision. The truth is, many people are just not ready to buy now whatever the advantages of the product and whatever their need for it. Product sellers must be aware of this and act accordingly. That's why you must always invite people who want more information to call you and must have a box on your response card for those who need more information . . . or who are not ready to act now but would like to be kept abreast of other products you create.

When should you contact these people? The very day they respond to you. Obviously their interest (even if limited) is greatest on the day they return the card to you . . . or call for further information. So, you must strike when the iron's hot. Thus, at the same time you are creating your direct mail materials, you should create the necessary pattern letters for:

- people who need further information to be persuaded;
- people who have bought and can be upgraded to buy something else.

These letters should focus solely on the advantages to be derived by the prospect from acting NOW using the product in question. You need not even mention his initial hesitancy. Go beyond it to stress and restress the benefits he gets when he acts NOW. In short, ignore what is inconvenient about this prospect and focus on what he gets by immediate action.

Next, look around for ways to enhance the value of any particular sale. Especially if you have only a single product to sell (but certainly not restricted to this situation), look around for related products produced by other suppliers. If you cannot upgrade a buyer by selling him something you yourself have produced, then upgrade the buyer by selling him something someone else has produced and taking your percentage of the sale to increase your profits.

Most product producers, to my profound dismay, do nothing more than ship the product that the customer has bought. That is a huge mistake. That customer has made an investment and is quite capable of making another. It is your job to stimulate him to do so . . . at once!

How many of these customers will act? Figure in an additional 5% and the revenue thereby resulting. This is a very conservative figure but a source of constant revenue and little additional cost to you, since generating computer print-out letters is very inexpensive and, unless you are using book rate shipping, you can simply insert the letter into your UPS package without any additional charge. In short, it's found money.

Now commit!

☐ I intend to start my selling program for my info-product the minute I have created my client-centered title for it. The minute I can show my targeted prospects just what I've got for them is the minute I can start making money from them. I realize that I may have fewer ways to sell pre-publication offers when I am just starting off in the information business. Nonetheless, I intend to use them. And as I become better known, I shall implement more and more pre-publication activities, setting as my goal raising at least 50% of the development and production costs of my product.

Avoidable Error #18.
You don't make creative marketing deals with other marketers.

When you run a product-centered company, you are likely to focus on pride and exclusion. Pride because you've conceived of a product and done all the work to bring it into existence . . . and exclusion because anything that you bring into your universe will detract from the pride of place of your baby. Mainline publishers suffer from this syndrome and too many smaller information providers have the same problem. You won't see McGraw-Hill, for instance, selling a John Wiley book. It just doesn't happen.

But real marketers don't think this way. Our objective is to reach as many of our prospects as we can, as inexpensively as we can. Therefore, the old canons of publishing, insular and exclusionary, don't apply. If company A gets to our market, our objective is to attempt to make a deal with them that will enable us to reach that market, too, for the lowest possible price. There are many ways we can use to do so:

- We could make a deal that would permit them to sell our products along with their products. Our products might become their products, too, as it were.

- We could use bounce-back or insert programs . . . creating a flyer (or even a mini-catalog of our products) and getting that company to insert it into their mail and outgoing packages.

- We could create a co-op advertising program, so that our books . . . and theirs . . . would be promoted through ads jointly financed.

In short, we could be creative.

I shall discuss all these alternatives later and in detail. For now, I'd like to stress just one thing: an info-entrepreneur focuses solely on reaching the maximum number of people with benefit rich copy about his problem-solving products. He fights a continuing battle against mindless canons from the past . . . against any kind of trade exclusion that keeps him from the markets who need him and which he needs to reach his income and lifestyle objectives. And he works unceasingly to create mutually beneficial marketing arrangements . . . arrangements which benefit the people who buy the problem-solving products (the end-user consumer); those who promote and market them (distributors), and those who produce them (himself).

Lest you think this is how all information producers work, think again. Recently, an audio cassette manufacturer in England read one of my Special

Reports in a publication and approached me about putting this Report on cassette for the British market. He was willing to pay standard royalties and required nothing from me but permission to go ahead. He didn't even request exclusive distribution rights.

Had the Special Report been written by me I would have accepted this deal in a minute, as soon as I had worked out the details about percentage to be paid me and times when these royalties would be paid.

Unfortunately, the Special Report was based on another specialist's book. When I wrote to him offering to represent him as his agent, and urging his immediate acceptance of this no-risk, found-money deal, I got back instead of his signature, a series of largely superfluous questions that I couldn't answer and that slowed down negotiations to a snail's pace. This was bad enough, but soon things went from bad to worse. The publisher didn't bother to send the audio manufacturer a needed sample of the book. He didn't answer letters. After four months of this idiotic behavior, the audio manufacturer not surprisingly lost interest in dealing with such a firm and the easy money was lost.

When I chastened the publisher for his behavior (as I most certainly did), he said he was merely behaving in a "businesslike" way. I disagreed — and disagree — strongly. I thought he was the textbook definition of a fool.

When a reputable firm is willing to:

- incur all expenses;
- give you access to a new market;
- pay you a regular royalty, and
- move rapidly ahead

your task is plain: agree and urge them to move even faster.

What you want in this situation is clear:

- a marketing message on every cassette that urges the listener to get in touch with you and

- approval over the marketing materials to make sure they adequately represent your product and hit the benefits over and over again, and

- regular payment of the royalty.

If the company will give you these things, you have secured enough . . . and you ought to be very grateful.

That's not what my sluggish publisher thought and that's why his product wasn't made into an audio cassette for the English market. I maintain this was based on a misguided notion of what constitutes professional behavior and overweening pride of product.

No true info-impressario would ever make this mistake.

Now commit!

☐   Henceforward, my focus will not be on exclusively marketing my line of info-products but on making money from targeted markets. I shall do everything I can to identify other information sellers who reach my market and to make constructive deals with them that will enable us both to benefit from selling my products to their markets. By the same token, I shall do everything I can to sell superior, compatible, and non-competing information products to my market . . . and so profit by these sales. No other way of doing business, certainly not the exclusionary practices of most information sellers, makes any sense at all.

Avoidable Error #19.
You don't try to upgrade every buyer . . . to get him to buy more solutions.

The unwise marketer, the stupid info-impressario, sells his prospect what he wants. The wise marketer, the practiced info-impressario, goes much further, seeking to understand what his prospect is attempting to do and going out of his way to sell him more.

Thus, when a prospect has bought a book or other information product on a certain subject, you should be prepared to sell him something more, an extension that will help him either solve either that problem better or a related problem. What do I mean? When someone buys one of my fund raising books, I have a letter offering him the other. When he buys the beginning consulting book, I offer him the sequel — at a discount . . . if only he buys it within the next thirty days. In other words, I:

- thank the buyer for getting product A;

- tell him I have something else available that will also help him solve this problem;

- let him know precisely the kinds of advantages he gets from this product, and

- make him an offer designed to stimulate immediate action, an offer that expires in thirty days.

Do you do this now? Not if you're like most information sellers. They seem to think that just because a person has bought one product that's the end of the road. But most assuredly it is not; it's just the beginning!

Your job is to think sequentially. Your info-products, whether your own or those produced by others that you are selling, must be grouped in clusters. As soon as an individual buys any given product in any given cluster, he must be directed to all the others (the related products that assist him to get what he wants) and encouraged to acquire them.

This, of course, is precisely how most information sellers *don't* think or act. But you will. Because you are not merely interested in selling your prospect a part of a solution. *You* want him to have everything he needs to achieve his objective . . . and *you* want to benefit by selling these things to him . . . fast!

Now commit!

☐   I shall never again merely sell my customer just what he wants. Instead, I shall cluster my info-products together in logical sequence creating packages of several products designed to achieve precise objectives for targeted groups of buyers. When a buyer buys one of these products, my job is to sell him the rest . . . so he has the tools he needs to meet his objective. If this buyer has bought in person, I shall inquire into what he is attempting to do . . . and let him know what else I have available to help him achieve it. If he buys by mail, I shall immediately send an upgrade letter along with his product, giving him full particulars not just of what else I have available but of the benefits he gets from these products. And I shall give him every encouragement to buy NOW . . . so he acts quickly to get what he needs.

Avoidable Error #20.
You Remainder Your Books

The other day a fellow called me. A couple of years ago he had approached me with a book idea on successful interviewing techniques. It was half a humor book, half a book of solid how-to techniques. And it was wholly off the course I was steering for myself. I, therefore, directed him elsewhere in his search for a publisher.

Now he called me again to let me know that due to a "fluke" (his word), the publisher of the book had several *thousand* copies left over which he was offering to the author for about 50 cents each. They were stamped with the retail price of $6.95. Did I think the author should buy them? Before I answered, I paused a moment; I could tell he was positively panting with enthusiasm when he thought of his 50 cent pieces each multiplying in a few short weeks into a return of $6.95 each.

I waited another moment to consider my response. Clearly, the publisher had sold the number of copies he thought he could sell. Equally clearly he had printed too many, and wanted to get back at least his initial investment in the unsold books. Being a traditionally minded company, it decided to sell off remainder copies (you'll see why I disagree with this in a minute) and by contract they probably had to offer the author first refusal on the surplus. Quick as a bunny, the publisher sent a letter to the author with the grand offer.

I'd heard this song before.

Without too much ado, the author, easily able to see his investment growing by about 14 times within a very short time (what a return!), jumped at the chance to acquire them. But even *he* must have had a nagging doubt in the back of his mind that suggested he check this purchase out with some knowledgeable source. And so, wise at least in this, he called me.

Ever cautious, I asked some questions.

- Did the author do regular workshops where he could build in the book and ensure that participants bought it? No!

- Did he have a mailing list of at least 15,000 people who might be interested in interview techniques that he could sell his book to directly? No!

- Had he researched the market to see if there was a catalog company that could sell a book like his and whether they might be interested in carrying it. No!

Having heard this dismal chorus, I told him I certainly wouldn't invest my money in such a sure-fire money-losing project.

He was crushed — and also mightily irritated. (Why do people ask for advice if they plan on lashing out at the person who gives an honest response?)

But, he said, what about bookstores? Couldn't he work to open bookstore accounts himself? Why, I said? He'd have to spend a lot of time opening accounts, most of which would only take a few copies on consignment and pay him many months later 60% of the retail price, or, more likely, return a good many of the copies . . . now even older and probably soiled to boot.

What about a distributor, then? Difficult to find, I said. And you'd probably make only about 33% of the total. Moreover, the distributor would need you to make a significant investment in publicity. Yet, as the author himself confessed, the likely places that would do publicity pieces had already done so; the original publisher had, of course, seen to that. Thus, generating additional publicity would be more difficult . . . and take additional time by the author. Time he obviously didn't relish giving.

What about direct mail, then? Too expensive, I said, given the expected return. Indeed, on a $6.95 item it was highly dubious he would make any money whatsoever.

He was mightily discouraged. And ungrateful, too, I might add.

A Consultant's Lament

It so happened that this fellow (whom I barely remembered, after all) caught me at a moment of the day when I was feeling expansive and kind hearted; (thank God, these moments are rare). He asked me questions. I answered them. I never mentioned any fee at all, may the deity of the consultants forgive me.

Having responded earnestly and thoroughly to all his questions, he then asked me how much I charge for this kind of advice. I told him. He was aghast, "That's way more than I can afford!" And he hastily hung up with nary a word of gratitude. His behavior irked me . . . and then I got irked at myself.

First, I should have followed my own advice and not told him *anything* for free beyond my name, rank and serial number (and, of course, my fee). Sometimes it's downright masochistic having a humanistic side. Second, I wish I'd been given just a minute to tell him how much money I'd saved him if only he'd follow my advice. He was willing to spend several thousand dollars purchasing books most of which were bound to become dust-encrusted and valueless in his garage. *That* he could afford. But when I showed him that he'd be lucky merely to make back his investment . . . and that after a lot of work, he was irked at me (after all, he probably felt I "deprived" him of the money he thought he'd be making) and astonished at my fee. If he had paid for the time and had followed the advice, he'd have been way ahead in the game.

But enough of this jeremiad against an uncouth world. On to my major point: what happens if developments in a field outpace the material in your product? Do you toss your remaining stock away and start again? You'd have to if you were a regular publisher and simply attempting to get sales from traditional sales outlets, like bookstores.

Fortunately we info-entrepreneurs are an entirely different breed. We think differently. We act differently.

First, you'll examine your field. You're supposed to be the expert. Or you're supposed to be working with the specialist who supposedly knows the field. When are the next major developments expected? I publish a book on planned giving, for instance. Planned giving is tax-related giving, and we have to be very conscious about when there will be major changes in the tax laws that invalidate the information in the book. If I didn't think the author who created this book knew this, it would be my fault for having selected such a slack expert. Stand advised.

Second, even if no major changes are expected, never print more than the number of items you feel confident you can sell in a two-year period. That is the longest you should have a product in existence without updating it . . . even if the updating involves nothing more than a touch-up on the cover. I'll give you a piece of advice here: at the beginning of your career as an info-entrepreneur, your enthusiasm will almost certainly outstrip your judgment. As a result, you'll probably create far more products than you'll sell in a two-year period. You'll assume (despite my advice to the contrary) that your market is hungering for what you've got . . . and that your marketing will be more successful than it proves to be.

To be sure, someone reading this book will hit the jackpot with a book or other product that will take off faster and deplete your stock quicker than you thought. Perhaps you will have the perfect timing that comes once in a lifetime and will get a succession of major media interviews and stories that sell your products faster than you can manufacture them. But remember, before you write me a catty letter, such a jackpot in no way invalidates what I'm telling you. Those kinds of events, just like lottery winners, are very, very rare. And you can't run a business this way. (Nonetheless, if the jackpot happens to you, I herewith accept your invitation to an elegant dinner . . . and if I have to eat crow make sure it's presented *flambé au rhum*.)

Third, if you do find yourself with a product that contains outmoded information at a time of sweeping changes in your subject, consider how you can dispose of this merchandise . . . without lowering the price. Here's where a value-added Special Report or pamphlet comes in. Such a Special Report or pamphlet can present crucial up-to-the-minute information, the kind of information that can refine what you've said in the main product . . . pointing out what has changed, why it's changed, the implications for your customer, and how this customer can take advantage of the new circumstances.

Such pamphlets and Special Reports are relatively easy to produce and certainly a lot less expensive than lowering the price of the original product to the ruinous levels of remainder sales.

Let's take my planned giving example above. Say the tax code was changed in some key way that invalidated portions of the book. My first reaction might well be one of despair that Congress had destroyed my product, and I might then think of remaindering the book. But consider, this 424-page book that retails for $50 would probably garner not more than $1-$1.50 when remaindered, far less than the production cost. Thus, it is very much in my interest to see if I can preserve my investment. Hence the pamphlet.

Now, given a number of variables (such as paper, cover quality, graphics, *etc.*), a 6"x 9" pamphlet (this cost-effective standard size is a good one for inserting into most products) of 32 pages printed in a quantity of 1000 will cost approximately $1.25 apiece. Yes, this is an expense. Yes, it is unfortunate that you have to incur it. But consider the alternatives:

1. You could sell your customers outmoded information. However, how can you live with yourself when you sell this kind of inferior merchandise to people you claim as friends and with whom developing a relationship is crucial?

2. You could remainder the book at a deep discount and likely outright loss to yourself. How can you live with yourself when you inflict this kind of avoidable damage on your firm, the good health of which is essential in continuing to produce quality products and bring them to the attention of people who need them?

However, with a Special Report, pamphlet, booklet or other value-added item, you save the maximum amount of your revenue. What's more, producing such an item may actually generate renewed review attention. Why? Because everyone needs to know about the tax law and rule changes . . . not just you! Thus, your old product . . . with this new attachment . . . becomes a means of bringing useful information to your prospects and thereby achieving additional review attention for you. Brilliant! Yet publishers continue to remainder books, either just breaking even or even losing money on that stock. Do you see why I fall so often into near irreparable despair?

Now commit!

☐   I understand that the information in my how-to products may become outdated. Whenever possible, I shall attempt to determine just when this is likely to occur and plan accordingly. If however I find myself with products that are in some way outdated, I shall not immediately rush to remainder them. Instead, I shall attempt to create a new, inexpensive value-added product that will contain new information useful to my prospects. I shall use this product to bring the other product up-to-date, to induce its continuing sale, and to get further helpful publicity. In this way, I shall continue to derive profit from my major product and give my customers the very latest in useful information . . . understanding that I can achieve neither objective through remaindering.

ORGANIZATION MISTAKES

Avoidable Error #21.
You are not a time management master.

Your tasks in creating an info-empire are clear. You must:

- produce new products at regular intervals;

- update these products at regular intervals;

- regularly commission products from other experts;

- continually market all these products to existing customers through all appropriate means;

- regularly research and open new markets.

You must also sleep, eat, and occasionally call your mother. Which brings me to the pivotal subject of time management.

People often ask me — indeed it is one of the queries I get most frequently — how I'm able to do all this without an office staff of any kind . . . *and* still handle the telephone traffic. Time management is the answer, and you must yourself master its essential points. Otherwise, you will either be forced to hire expensive labor that cuts into your profit or simply fall further and further behind in your projects. Neither alternative is acceptable.

What I'm about to say here may not sound particularly original. I don't care. It *is* particularly important. If you don't follow these steps, you'll be sabotaging your progress.

Begin By Writing Down What You Want To Achieve

Every time management expert tells you to write your objectives, and for good reason: it's essential. Over the past decade, I have met many people who have told me they wanted to make a fortune selling information. But very few have. One reason for their failure is that they didn't know precisely where they were going and didn't create a coherent and reasonable plan for getting there.

Don't you be like this. Write down your precise objective and the precise date by which you want to achieve it.

Now prune away all the inessentials of your life that have nothing to do with reaching this objective. You must decide the only thing that's important is achieving the objective you have selected . . . not the hundreds of inconsequential tasks that prevent you from getting there.

Recently, for instance, I met a young chiropractor who told me he wanted to publish a booklet that could be used to promote his practice. Fair enough. But he also confessed he was having trouble getting started, and that so far he'd written nothing. He wondered what was wrong.

Within just a few minutes, I knew. This very social young man kept a calendar of extracurricular activities calculated to derail even the most disciplined writer. With days devoted to his business and the rest of the time spent on socializing, no wonder he didn't get his project finished. As a result, he felt his self-esteem ebbing while his practice remained too small to suit his rather grander ideas.

The true info-imperialist is a profoundly focused individual. He prunes and prunes away the inessentials of his life. Time he reckons like all other resources. It must not be merely squandered; it must be spent with consideration, invested in projects that have a reasonable chance of paying off.

Is this how you live? Allow me to doubt it.

The info-entrepreneur lives a life of constant deliberation and consideration. He ponders: does what I am about to do make sense? Will it lead me in the direction I want to go? Will it reinforce the other things I am doing? Is there an easier, less costly way to achieve the same results? Can I get someone else to do this so I can focus on what really matters: product production and, more importantly, product marketing? Am I truly as efficient as I might be . . . or do I talk about efficiency while remaining ineffectual?

Keep The Tasks Ever Before You That Must Be Done Today

I look upon my allotment of time rather like the ancient Greeks did, as a cord whose length was established at my birth. Each day I have a little less; what there was in the morning being irretrievable at night. If I am to reach my objectives, therefore, I must work a little towards them each day. Process and habit, you see, are more important than inspiration and intention.

Thus, you must make lists . . . until the lists are part of the very fiber of your being, and you find yourself living them. These lists must involve these crucial tasks:

- developing a new product;
- updating existing products;

- commissioning new products;
- marketing all your products.

The Importance Of Lists

Now you know which categories you should be working in daily. With lists, you can direct your attention to the specific tasks that need to be accomplished. As you and I both know, the world is divided into two parts: those who make lists and those who do not. Those of us who do rule the world. The rest are invariably at the mercy of events.

The items that you list should fall into each of the four major categories that organize your work. If you find there are things on this list — or just things that you do — that do not fit into any one of these four categories, you probably shouldn't be doing them. You should spend some time figuring out how to divest yourself of these things, get others to do them, postpone them to a later time, or just abandon them. In other words, you should make sure you stay focused on the four things that you *must* do.

The Role Of Your Computer

Arranging your day — *each* day — in this sensible, process-oriented way cannot take place without a computer. If you are not yet computerized, you'd better deal with this problem immediately. I speak to you now as a former dyed-in-the-wool computerphobe. But I speak to you today with all the zeal of the convert.

If you are not yet computerized, you have probably failed to take this step for one of two reasons: either you don't feel you have the money, or you are afraid of the machine. Candidly, neither excuse makes any sense, as I can attest.

Following the steps in this book, you will find that your efficiency increases so dramatically once you're computerized that the cost is a small investment. Without it, you are limiting your growth significantly . . . and increasing your cost of business, particularly when you begin to produce major information products, like books.

As far as your own aversion to the machine is concerned, this, too, is a problem that can easily be overcome. If you accept my reasoning that the machine will enable you to produce new products faster, update old ones more effectively, and market more intensely, that, in short, it will help you reach more people and so solve their problems, then you owe it as much to your prospects as yourself to computerize at the earliest possible moment. Your aversion thus stands in the way of your ability to help people. This is unacceptable.

And if you don't? Why, then, you are signalling in no uncertain terms that yours will always be a small hobby business where each thing you do will take far longer than it ought and so diminish the time you have available for the crucial subject of marketing. I pity people who make this decision, but they have dictated their own course of events and must bear full responsibility for all that happens — or, more accurately — doesn't happen in their businesses.

What Needs To Be On Your Computer

In creating your information empire, your computer is your best friend. It will maintain all your:

- information products (including the scripts for your audio and video cassettes) on line. Your products are valuable insofar as they are up-to-date. Your computer allows you to keep information readily available and update it easily.

- marketing materials . . . your pattern cover letters, upgrade letters, letters to media sources, letters to disgruntled customers, letters to suppliers, *etc.*

- mailing list data.

In the creation of your information empire, system is crucial, and the computer is the systemizer *par excellence.* It staggers me, therefore, that in this age of comparatively inexpensive personal computers there are still people who don't have one. Moreover, it astonishes me that most of those who do have such computers have not yet understood how significant they can be in augmenting and sustaining a determined marketing program.

With the computer, you can create all the pattern marketing documents you need:

- documents that get you free publicity;
- documents that get you review materials;
- documents that build your product list;
- documents that upgrade your sales;
- documents that get you the money you're owed;
- standard business forms and contracts.

Each task that you do is either routine or unique. If it involves communication and is routine, then you should create a document you can generate by computer. Now. What's more, even if this document doesn't quite meet the circumstances of an individual case, you'll find a few words of personalization usually fill the bill. Only when this fails should you actually create something entirely new.

Now commit!

☐   I promise to stop merely talking about my objectives and to set them . . . to write them down and post them where I can see them daily. Then I promise to review the activities of my life so that I can prune away those that are essential either to producing info-products or to marketing info-products. These are the important things, and I pledge to focus on them, eliminating all others from my life. Finally, I pledge fully to integrate the computer into my business life, to identify routine tasks and treat them routinely. This means creating pattern documents that can be constantly reused.

PERSONAL MISTAKES

Avoidable Error #22.
You're lazy.

One of the great problems I see with so many of info-entrepreneurs and authors is that they're lazy. They feel that many activities are beneath them, are not their responsibility. Thus, they won't:

- identify new problem-solving products;
- research the market to see if these products already exist and where the opening for new products is;
- review these products to ascertain their strengths and weaknesses;
- take the time to produce a superior problem-solving product;
- research all available marketing, promotion and distribution channels;
- develop persuasive marketing materials appropriate for each of these marketing, promotion and distribution channels;
- send these materials and then follow them up.

And follow them up.

And follow them up.

Until the decision maker in each channel is either firmly committed to the promotion of your product. Or has become positively threatening about your pesky presence.

Ask any author, any would be info-entrepreneur, just what he's doing in each of these areas . . . and listen for the specificity of the answer. In too many cases, you will find that these creatures are resting content as author or publisher, publicly fuming because these things are not being done for them . . . but doing precious little to help themselves. I have news for such people . . . for you: these are jobs you must do for yourself. And you must learn to do them well.

Success as an info-entrepreneur means doing thousands of things right over many, many years. It means constantly working to create and upgrade your info-products . . . identifying the markets for them and never resting until your prospects have acquired these products.

This is your job. It takes technical skills, of course, but more than that it takes the right mental attitude and daily diligence. We live in a time when many people talk about these things . . . but too few exhibit them in their daily life. You must and shall. Because unless you do, you cannot be a successful info-entrepreneur.

Now commit!

☐ I promise to assume full responsibility for the success of my info-enterprise. Instead of searching for others to blame, instead of trying to eschew responsibility for my success, I accept the fact that if there is to be success I must work daily to achieve it. I am ready to do so and promise not to put off until tomorrow the necessary product development and product marketing tasks I can do today . . . every day!

Avoidable Error #23.
You don't persist.

In the information business, there are largely three different kinds of people, and you will meet them all. There are:

- product-centered people;
- self-centered people, and
- (hurrah!) market-centered people.

What is the difference?

Product-centered people people feel pride in their information. They feel the need to educate. They are committed more to the integrity of the product than the satisfaction of the wants of their market. Product has primacy over marketing. Such people return phone calls about their products only.

Self-centered people may be selling a product and ostensibly serving a market, but in fact, they are only interested in their own convenience and operating procedures. Such people, whatever they say, have no interest in helping their prospects . . . in bringing helpful information and products to their attention . . . much less knowing how you can help either that market . . . or, indeed, themselves. They regard anything other than catering to their own whims as bothersome . . . you and their public be damned. Such people never return a phone call . . . unless their personal comfort is at stake.

Then there are the market-centered people. These people understand that their task is to connect markets of people with defined wants and needs with the info-product creators and sellers who have what these people need. They are bright, professional . . . eager to be of service, not least because they know that out of this service comes their own profit. They are willing to entertain any idea that helps their market get the information it needs and which will, in the process, benefit both themselves and you. These people return every phone call . . . so long as they understand just how their market benefits, they benefit . . . and you benefit.

Sadly, there are far more people in the first two groups than in the far more useful third category. You must plan accordingly.

Thus, when approaching product-centered and self-centered people (whether those people are book reviewers, catalog buyers, book store owners, *etc.*), it's best to understand the following:

1. These people are less interested than you are (whatever they may say) in helping their audiences get the problem-solving information they need;

2. They have only the slightest grasp of their own interests, so you must be prepared to instruct them;

3. New ways of doing business (despite being manifestly in their own best interest and in the best interests of their customers) are threatening;

4. You will get no response to your initial letter or telephone call. If you want this deal to happen, you must expect to do all the follow-up;

5. Despite the most reasonable proposals from you and constant professional follow-up, you cannot expect these individuals to be responsive. Many are motivated neither by profit nor by customer service; many simply want to avoid new or more work. Therefore, you must resolve to continue . . . until you make the deal that is so much in their interest (as well as your own). Or until they make it plain nothing is going to happen now, in which case (so long as there is money to be made here and service to be rendered), you resolve to come back later.

You see, despite the fact that the product-centered and self-centered will benefit from what you propose, you must assume the full burden of responsibility. Of course, whenever people behave in a responsible and sensible fashion, I am pleased . . . but I never let these episodic encounters with the enlightened change my basic way of doing business, namely assuming that others will not be so self-actualized and sensibly directed.

It is your responsibility to understand the interests of the people you are producing products for and marketing to better than they do. It is your responsibility to work out the benefits you have for them and to hammer these benefits home again and again until they finally take action . . . the thing that was in their own best interest from the very beginning.

So many of the people you have to deal with in this business put so many things before selling products and serving their customers. You'll meet them all: the arrogant, the disorganized, the egotistical, the lazy, the outright stupid. Whatever they say, their actions belie the fact that they're interested in either commerce or service.

Don't be frustrated. Persist. You are an info-entrepreneur. You are committed to making the world a better place, to the improvement of the human condition. You cannot allow the self-defeating, foolish habits of so many of the people you must deal with to deflect you from your far more important task of getting your material into the hands of the consumers who need it. Remember, one of the chief reasons you are working is to improve their lot, and if some human obstacle stands in your way, don't give up, persist until you get through, over or around it. Your own prosperity . . . and the betterment of your audience . . . depends on your doing so.

No matter how eminent you become, how prosperous, you'll continue to meet people who just can't seem to behave in either a responsibly commercial, professional or even decent fashion. I think, for instance, of David Barillari, owner of a new Cambridge bookstore. When his store opened, I approached him in the usual way, with a letter and a catalog, asking for an appointment.

I knew that if he was an efficient and professional store owner (the market-centered individual), he'd respond to my letter to schedule an appointment so I could show him my books. He didn't call. So I called him.

And called him.

And called him.

Until I got him on the telephone, when he claimed he never received the original material (which had, in the interim, been sent a second time). So I sent him a third set of materials.
And called him.

And called him.

Without so much as a peep of a response.

What's the problem? Is this man arrogant? Or disorganized? Or perhaps sadistic? Who can say? But he's certainly not interested in selling books and establishing relationships with people who can help him.

I do know this, however: I not only give you guidelines, I live these guidelines. Thus, as we end this introductory chapter and proceed into the ins and outs of producing info-products, I say this to you. You are about to embark on one of the most exciting journeys of your life. You are about to discover just what you need to do to produce superior info-products, market them and get rich doing so. But never forget that there is one other significant objective for you, too: improving the lives of others through the products you produce.

To achieve this truly essential objective, you must do whatever needs to be done to persuade the all too numerous and short-sighted David Barillaris of the world to do what helps their customers, themselves . . . and you. You must, in short, persist . . . as I intend to persist until this man, and all who are like him, starts to behave in a reasonable, humane and market-centered fashion . . . until, that is, he carries the products which can do so many (including himself) so much good!

You must, you can!, do the same . . . and you will, for your own sake, of course, but also for the sake of the people who need the problem-solving information you write and commission. Thus, you must keep working until you are using all the means of getting to all the people who need you. Because only then can you be sure you have done all you can to get your essential message to the people who need you.

Take heed, David Barillari. This means I haven't given up on you yet . . . nor on any of the others who behave in your so far pointless, self-defeating, incomprehensible fashion. Neither must you, dear reader.

Now commit!

☐   To succeed as an info-entrepreneur, I know I must not only understand my interests but the interests of all the others with whom I must deal. While it would be nice, it is not likely that they shall understand their own interests as well as I understand theirs. Therefore, once I have made sure I do understand their interests, I shall persist until I have made a mutually beneficial deal with them . . . a deal that will enable both them and me to benefit . . . and which will bring my info-products to the attention of their markets. Because bringing these products to these markets is the most essential thing of all, I shall overlook and overcome everything that detracts from it, including the poor business and human practices of the people I must deal with and my own frustration and anger. My job is to keep trying until my markets are learning about my products in every way they can. That is my objective, and I intend to achieve it!

2

Making Sure You Create The Right Product . . . The Product That Will Make You Money On A Continuing Basis

To be an author, a creator, is not the objective of information product creation. No, indeed! Your objective must be to reach the maximum number of people your information can assist, motivating them to acquire it . . . and to make the most money you possibly can. Thinking like an author (that is, a producer) will not help you achieve these two crucial objectives. Thinking like a marketer (that is, a client-centered and intensely motivating seller) will. That's why the focus of this book is, first, on solving the problems of marketing . . . and only second on solving the problems of production.

Sadly, most information product producers wait until they actually have their product in hand to confront, much less solve, their marketing problems. This isn't just wrong; it's idiotic. The crucial work in creating a profitable information product takes place long before that product actually exists, when, indeed, the product is little more than a gleam in your eye . . . just like the crucial work in producing a baby (if you'll excuse me for saying so) takes place long before the cuddly little tyke is available for pictorial exhibition.

Information producers forget this fact all the time. I think, for instance, of the Michigan educator who produced a book on motivating teen-agers . . . a book dealing with building self-esteem and inner confidence and achieving goals.

The subject is an admirable one . . . so admirable that the author gave way to an orgy of enthusiasm about his topic . . . and the certainty of fame and fortune. There are millions of teen-agers in America! Most have terrible esteem problems . . . many are rudderless! Their parents are worried sick about them . . . surely sick enough to buy a book that can help them! Why, if only a million of them . . . even half a million of them . . . buy his book you could call for the self-publishing author on Easy Street faster than you could say "troubled teen-ager."

And so, after this orgy, the inevitable consequence ensued: in due course, The Book was brought forth. Not to hosannahs . . . but to monumental silence.

Why? Why had this happened . . . when there was so much good in the author . . . and so much that was helpful in The Book?

I'll tell you why. This info-producer had forgotten the following rules, rules *you* must never forget. Your information product must be:

- produced for a defined market of prospects . . . a market that provably and incontrovertibly has the problem you can solve;

- produced for a market of prospects that is large . . . and, better, growing;

- an apt representative of your Ultimate Benefit(s) . . . that is, it should reinforce in the buyer's mind the overriding reason he should do business with you now and later . . . because of the benefit he really gets from you;

- positioned (by title and content) so that it speaks directly to the broadest possible spectrum of that market . . . or, if you select a more limited subsection of that market, priced sufficiently highly to justify investment in that smaller market and the marketing costs of reaching it;

- capable of being brought before that market not just once but again and again and again on a continuing basis . . . so you can be sure it knows what benefits your product can provide;

- priced so that various marketing options are opened to you . . . not closed because of their cost;

- aimed directly at the want or need this market possesses and clearly indicating that it is the solution the market must have to reach its objective . . . that is, your information product must be about solutions and not about "information" or "education";

- a perennial, not an annual; that is, it should be something which you can sell year in, year out to make a continuing, not just a short-term, profit;

* created so that the person reading it can *really* do what the subject of the product promises . . . and is packed not only with immediately useable techniques, processes, guidelines, *etc.* . . . but also includes specifically detailed follow-up information for those who need further assistance and refinements.

Memorize these rules . . . Get them into the fiber of your bones. If you learn nothing else from this book but these rules, your investment in these pages will be more than justified. And don't take my word for it either. A bright, young Michigan educator failed to consider these points . . . and now he considers what to do with all his products, products he sadly knows are not as good as they could be and much more difficult to sell than they ought to be. His self-esteem isn't as high as it should be now that he is the author of A Book . . . nor is his bank balance anywhere near as big as he assumed it would be. If you're not prepared to believe me, take it from him and learn these rules. No rules, of course, will always make a profitable product . . . if that were so such rules, like the Ten Commandments, would be on public display in all publishers' offices. Nonetheless, these rules give you a better chance, indeed the likelihood, of making a profit.

Moreover, by following these rules you'll have more confidence in what you're doing . . . and you can do the proper things at the proper times.

No one should strategize about how to market a product after that product exists . . . Michael Dukakis can tell you that. He launched a presidential campaign without a marketing strategy and during the crucial weeks when he should have been implementing that strategy . . . he was still trying to find it. George Herbert Walker Bush waltzed into a mammouth negative in public opinion polls . . . but with a clean, crisp marketing message. Though this wasn't the most clever or profound or even particularly intelligent marketing message we've seen hereabouts . . . it was sufficiently sufficient to win him the most powerful office in the world. Which, therefore, made it good enough.

Learn, reader, learn!

The crucial work in creating a profitable information product takes place *before* that product physically exists. After that product physically exists all you are doing to sell it is following the plan you laboriously created months before. Your creative imagination, therefore, must go into implementing the crucial guidelines above and ensuring you have the right product. Once that product exists, what you do is fairly automatic and entirely process-oriented. I hope you understand this, because if you don't, you are riding for an expensive and entirely unnecessary fall.

Now let us look at each of those crucial positioning points, always remembering that this is where you must give evidence of deductive powers, client-centered thinking, and business hard-headedness.

Producing Your Information Product For A Defined Market Of Prospects

You must not create a product and then search for the market . . . instead, you must identify the market . . . and then create the appropriate (that is, the profitable) product. This is, of course, precisely what most information product sellers don't do . . . but what every successful one always does.

To begin at the beginning, what is a "market"? A market is a defined, coherent, unified group of people. They are people you can describe by noting their common characteristics: age, sex, geography, income, occupation, education *etc.* . . . or, outlook, ideas, point of view, opinions, prejudices, *etc.*

Your information product, be it book or audio cassette or Special Report, must be designed to appeal to the broadest possible market for whom the problem-solving information you possess will do the most good.

Now, virtually without fail, most of the information product producers I have worked with and studied, cannot tell you *who* they are marketing to. Or, more precisely, they can only tell you in the most general terms. Thus, the author of the book on teen-age goals setting might respond, "teen-agers" when asked who his market is. But, of course, this is wrong on two counts:

1. "Teen-agers" as a market is defined far too broadly. The kinds of problems that engage a barely pubescent teen-ager in rural Ohio are hardly likely to be those unsettling a 19-year old minority woman from New York City. They can't be considered to be the same market . . . because they are not the same market. "Teen-agers", then, is not one market; it is dozens, perhaps even hundreds, of markets.

2. For this book it is doubtful if teen-agers are even the market. Personally, I find it hard to believe that a teen-ager when confronted with the chance to spend his money on, say, some fashionable piece of clothing or a goals setting book is going to buy the latter. Rather, parents may be the market . . . or school libraries . . . or community libraries, or school guidance counselors, or organizations serving the teen-age population, *etc.*

Right off the bat you can see a couple of problems:

- Failure correctly to pinpoint your market with mathematical accuracy means you are likely to turn your attention to the wrong people . . . people who

Making Sure You Create The Right Product . . . **91**

can't buy the information product either because they don't want to or don't have the available means to do so. Because you're a marketer with limited resources, you can't possibly afford this kind of misdirected activity.

- Your information product may well be suitable for various markets; that is, there may be various groups of people interested in your problem-solving information (in this case, teen-age goals setting) who are in a position to purchase it . . . despite the fact that the product itself is not created for them. Your job is to identify *all* the appropriate people . . . and see whether they do constitute a unified market to which you can get continuing access and bring perceived advantages to the ultimate beneficiaries of the product.

It is of the utmost importance that you identify the right markets because all your marketing communications (the actual means you use to induce the sale) must speak to that market. And I can tell you right now, the concerns of a school librarian are different from the concerns of a parent . . . are different from the concerns of the various teen-age subgroups.

One of the endemic problems of information marketers is that they keep trying to find the open sesame . . . the one marketing message that will suffice for all their markets. They make this search for any number of reasons:

- They are lazy. All of us (oh, yes, I sadly include myself) are lazier than we ought to be. We're Americans, after all, brought up on the platitudes of the "livin' is easy" school of comfort. Laziness is an American birthright . . . which is why we all love to talk so much about hard work and application. For such people it makes sense that producing one marketing communication is better than producing two . . . even though the markets are oh-so-very different.

- They act as if all people are alike. If we are all equal under the law (I've always doubted this, too, of course), we are all unequal under the laws of marketing. Thus, we must be approached differently. If you are looking for a challenge, try to produce the marketing communication that will induce sales from a home-based sewing business in Iowa with one employee and a software engineering company in Massachusetts with 100 employees . . . and yet both are "small businesses" under the federal definition.

- They proceed on the assumption that because they know what they've got is useful for the prospect, the prospect ought to accept that, too . . . even if the marketing communication they produce only speaks to that prospect in the most general of ways.

In any event, I can tell you right now . . . one marketing communication isn't going to suffice for all your markets. If you want to make money with information products, you've got to target your markets . . . to whittle them down until they have a certain gem-like clarity about them. Generalities just don't work in marketing . . . precision of approach does.

You can't offer this kind of precision — the feeling in everything you produce and communicate that you are talking to that one specific individual (the individual you want to be your next buyer) — unless and until you have a very precise, entirely coherent, thoroughly unified market of prospects . . . people who would recognize a kinship in each other and are grateful to you for recognizing that kinship and speaking to it.

Here are some tricks of the trade to help you discover whether you have made your market as precise as it needs to be to make your marketing (and hence your product) a success:

- Start by writing down who you think your market is. Say, "teen-agers". By this you mean that these are the people who can buy your product . . . the people you mean to be your customers and whom you'll work hard to reach and motivate to purchase your information product.

- Now ask yourself this: "Do I mean *all* teen-agers, everywhere in the world, wherever they are, whatever their circumstances?" The goal of marketing is to induce *just* the people you mean to be your prospects to contact you . . . to know when they see your marketing communications that you have the right solution, the right product for them. When you speak to them, they must know and feel good about the fact you are speaking to them. There must be no hesitation about their response. They must be motivated to say, "He's talking to me. And I need to contact him to get the benefits he's offering." *This* is marketing: the certainty you are communicating with just the right individual and that individual's certainty that what you have is certainly meant for him.

By this reckoning, you certainly don't mean *all* teen-agers, for you don't mean 13-year olds from Lapland, 16-year old Spaniards, or 19-year old teen-agers at the Sorbonne. These are *not* your market.

- Start deducting the people you don't mean to be in your market. You can let them go without a pang. The wise marketer knows that what he's got is *not* for everyone. He's not like the unsophisticated marketers who are reluctant to let even a single dollar get beyond their grasp. The unsophisticated want that dollar . . . even if it costs them five dollars to get it! Experienced marketers let that dollar go . . . and a good many other random dollars . . . so they can concentrate on their chosen market(s): the people they *know* have the problem they can solve, the desire to solve it, the money to solve it, and who can be reached on a continuing basis.

When you have finished with this exercise, you are left with a tentative market; I say "tentative" because you must complete all the steps in the sequence we're discussing before any final decisions are made. Nonetheless, at this point you are ready to:

- define your market . . . who are you marketing to;
- be precise about who's in your market(s) . . . and who isn't.

You are willing to let all those who are not in your markets go without worrying about them. For now, they'll have to be left to the attentions of other marketers . . . with other products. But for those you have selected, you intend to be tenacious.

It is a marketer's clarity about who he is speaking to . . . his knowledge that he has made a conscious decision about his audience . . . that gives him the focus and confidence he needs to create a precise, enthusiastic, client-centered information product . . . and the precise, enthusiastic, client-centered marketing program that inevitably follows. Without this clarity and precision, you are shooting in the dark, and everything you do afterwards shows it.

Now I'll share a secret with you: most information marketers not only think too generally about their markets . . . they don't begin to have the understanding of how many markets are truly open to them . . . that is, how many people they can identify as a coherent market, translate their product into benefits for, and reach on a continuing basis.

I have succeeded to a considerable extent because I have dug deep into the reality of America, constantly seeking the ultra-precise, now small, now tremendous but always coherent markets that exist . . . and which with modern technology you can reach. My goal is always the same: to redefine the problem-solving information I have as a benefit — a highly focused benefit — to any individual group I'm approaching.

You must take it upon yourself to do this; you cannot expect your market to do the work it takes to discover what's in your information that will benefit them. You must tell them . . . in the clearest possible way . . . over and over again.

Of course, this is precisely what most info-marketers don't do. They take the easy path . . . the disastrously easy path: writing a book, recording a tape, commissioning a Special Report and letting the prospect deduce what benefits he gets by using it. THIS IS SINFULLY WRONG. You can make sure you don't make this mistake by strictly adhering to this point . . . namely, clearly defining your market . . . and then constantly researching all the different markets that exist which could benefit from your product. And then bringing the market-specific advantages of that product to their attention in the most enthusiastic, motivational, and client-centered fashion.

Producing For A Market Of Prospects That Is Large . . . And, Better, Growing

All markets are not, of course, equal. Some are more important than others. Given constraints on your time and resources, it makes more sense to set your sights at those markets that are large . . . and, hopefully, growing . . . instead of markets that are small . . . and shrinking. But you can't do this if you have product-centered thinking.

People who are intent on producing information products . . . and not making a fortune from information products . . . say, essentially:

- I know something. I know something by virtue of my education and/or experience and/or research.

- For the sake of my ego, I wish to put what I know before "the public" and so reap the advantages of authorship; (the first benefit, of course, being the reinforcement of my own wobbly ego).

- I do not know and cannot say if what I know will interest anyone . . . but that it must be brought before "the public" I am assured. Why? Because (with every apology to Descartes): "I publish, therefore I am!"

Those who are market-centered think otherwise. They aim to transform what they've been taught, experienced, or learned through research to the benefit of the largest conceivable market . . . for both the advantage of that market and for their own personal advantage. Though today's damp squibs of liberals may disapprove this conjunction, those who do the most good for the greatest number are the only ones entitled to truly significant returns. When this ceases to be a thought of importance, we shall truly have been transformed into a society dedicated to mediocrity and to letting the slothful and passive share fruits to which they are not entitled.

The question here, then, is whether you have done what is necessary to ascertain how large your market is . . . and whether it is a market that will grow or shrink in the years ahead.

And how, pray, do you find out? By research.

The successful information producer is an avid researcher. But, remember, there are two kinds of research: "pure" research (an adjective applied by threadbare but egotistic academicians) and "applied" research, the profitable preserve in which you'll find the upwardly aspiring (like me!).

These are the questions you need answers to for each market you wish to enter and motivate to buy your product:

* How big is your designated and coherent market now?

* How big will it be in a year? In two years? In ten years? In other words, is this a growing market in which you can prosper by virtue of your own application and the market's own growth dynamic? Or is it shrinking, thus forcing you to do more each year to generate the same amount of business?

* Is the market both easily identifiable and easily reached . . . or is it a "market" that you're only guessing is "out there" . . . but cannot reach through a consistent, focused marketing program?

You get the answers to these key questions by constant research.

As I have said before, only when the means of reaching a market exist does the market itself exist. This means that until you have an organized way of consistently reaching a market, that market doesn't exist. Thus, the key to identifying markets is to identify the means of reaching those markets. Here are some of the important means of so identifying markets:

* The Gale *Encyclopedia of Associations*. Associations are groups of people who share common characteristics and can be reached through the means the association itself uses to communicate with its members, namely publications, a house mailing list, regular education program and conventions, *etc*. No information producer worth his salt can afford not to be aware of this cornucopia of marketing information . . . and yet how few actually use it consistently.

Each year — for each product I either produce or re-release — I again read through all the relevant individual entries in Gale's three current volumes. I look at each entry — and there are thousands of them — asking myself one constant question: do I have something that is of substantial benefit to this organized group of people? Can I define what I have so that I can convince officers of the association (such as the newsletter editor or seminar organizer) to give me access to them? Can I then convince the end-user consumers, my actual buyers, to invest in what I'm selling? If the answer to these questions is "yes", then this is a market I *must* approach. In the absence of unlimited time and other resources, of course, it makes good sense to approach the largest associations first and then work your way into the smaller groups.

- The Oxbridge *Directory of Newsletters*. To an information marketer, a newsletter is an indication that a market exists. Readers/suscribers of the newsletter or other publication constitute a unified market. Again, your objective here is the same as with associations: to ascertain those sources that can connect you to your market in an organized, ongoing fashion.

As with the Gale *Encyclopedia of Associations,* each year I read through the small print of the Oxbridge *Directory of Newsletters*. It has thousands of entries and of each one I ask myself: is this a group of people who need the benefits I have available for them?

If the answer is yes, I have two options: either pay to get access to them (advertising or list rental) or think of the more creative, less expensive ways of getting access to them I shall be discussing with you later. Such access makes no sense, however, unless you are absolutely sure you have advantages for this market . . . and you are willing to do what is necessary to fashion these advantages so that your market understands in an instant precisely what you've got and precisely why they should act NOW to acquire it.

- Mailing lists. There are essentially three different kinds of mailing lists: compiled, subscription, and mail order buyers. I have put them in ascending order of importance.

As we shall discuss later, a compiled list is taken from a variety of information sources such as telephone directories, professional lists, *etc*. What's important to remember about this source is that these people have expressed no interest in being contacted and may not be marketing responsive. This is less true, of course, of publication subscribers; they at least have bought something. That is even more true of mail order buyers who have made at least a single purchase of something that's related to what you're selling. Such people usually constitute a prime marketing source . . . which is precisely why their list owners command a premium price when you rent such a list.

What's important to point out here is that you must make it the constant study of your life to sift through and assess all mailing lists. As with associations and publications (both of which have mailing lists, too), what you are asking is this: does this list get me to a coherent, unified group of people whom my information product can benefit? How do I know? Is there another, better place where I should be investing my limited resources?

Later I shall discuss how to use associations . . . newsletters . . . and other mailing lists. For now, I wish you to concentrate on why you are familiarizing yourself with these sources.

My contention, indeed my fixed belief, is that most information product sellers know too little about all the markets that are available to them. Instead, they focus on producing their product as if production somehow stimulated sales. It doesn't. The world is full of information products that have failed miserably, draining their producers of capital . . . and the esprit that distinguishes all successful info-product sellers.

During this planning season, long before you're ready to produce anything, your objective is clear: you are looking for markets . . . as many markets as possible, that have the problem your information (and ultimate product) can solve. You need to know if these markets are growing . . . or shrinking. And (as we'll later discuss) you need to be aware of how you can reach these markets . . . and what it costs.

When you focus on markets in this manner, inevitably you must focus on what these markets want from you. I'll tell you this: they don't want a product. They don't want some information creation that suggests prolonged study and ceaseless application. They don't, in short, want work. THEY WANT BENEFITS.

But which benefits must you give them, for you already know that each market not only wishes but demands to be given its own benefits . . . benefits unique to itself . . . benefits that clearly show them that you understand their situation and are willing to speak solely to their wishes?

Which benefits? Why, this is where your continuing research comes in . . . for as you research markets . . . you must research each individual market's wants . . . needs . . . anxieties . . . and aspirations. For your apt understanding of these . . . and your positioning your information product as necessarily connecting with these . . . is what sells the product. *Not the product itself.*

Thus, at this stage in your marketing planning, here's where you need to be:

You need a clear understanding of which markets have the problem and/or aspiration your tentative product can serve . . . how large this market is . . . and whether it's large, stable or growing (hence worth your prompt effort) . . . or small or shrinking (and hence not worthy of immediate attention.) Marketers, you see, know where to spend their limited time and other resources, which markets should be attended to promptly and energetically to sell their information products and which can safety be left until another time . . . when the major markets have been seen to.

I guarantee you, this is not how most information product marketers think. For reasons which elude me, they tend to regard all markets as equally worthy of their time and attention . . . spending their precious resources (and, yes, I include their time) in pursuit of a market of 2000 people with the same assiduity as a market of 10,000 people . . . or 1,000,000 people. But before I go on, lest you think that size of the market *per se* is the only consideration, think again.

Other factors can be more important . . . like the ability of that market to easily purchase your product because they already have all the information they need to do so.

Let's say a market of 2000 prospects gets complete order details for your product . . . its name, your address, telephone number, product price, *etc.* And that 1,000,000 readers in another market are only given facts about the product without being given any of the necessary follow-up information. In this case, the first market is more important than the second . . . because in the first you get both an editorial endorsement as well as direct response mechanism . . . while in the second you merely get undirected publicity, the prospect having to do all the rest of the work of acquiring the product; work he very likely won't do.

Thus, you cannot merely take *numbers* of readers/contacts into account. You must also consider whether those prospects will be given all that they need to connect with you . . . *immediately.* Markets which allow for this kind of connection are markets that must always have greater priority for you.

An Apt Representative Of Your Prime Benefit

Have you ever heard the old advertising line, "Sell the sizzle, not the steak?" Let's think for a minute what this brilliant line means. Consider what steak is. Steak is simply dead meat, flesh that was once part of a living animal and has been cut off, moved here and there, left to stand in packages, and finally sold to you. It is, in short, nothing more than a piece of an animal's carcass. Sounds inviting, right?

And what is the "sizzle." Sizzle is something warm, desirable, and suggestive. It has something for the eyes (you can see the sizzle); something for the nose (you can certainly smell that crackling, sizzling flavor); something for the mouth (sizzle is savory), and something for our psychic well-being (sizzle conjures up the enjoyment of a pleasant evening with friends taking pleasure in something you want). Thus, sizzle is inviting while, upon analysis, steak is really rather repulsive.

In marketing terms, "sizzle" is benefit, "steak" is feature. Features are items that describe what you're selling; they're about what you're selling . . . about the information product itself. On the other hand, benefits are about the buyer of the product . . . about what he gets . . . and why he buys. Benefits focus on the buyer . . . features focus on the seller. Benefits are "you" (the buyer) oriented; features are "me" (the seller) oriented.

Now, really, which do you think your buyers are interested in?

It's obvious, isn't it. *People buy benefits.*

In a competitive society like ours, products sell because they offer the buyer a competitive advantage over what's being offered by others; this competitive advantage — a comparison in your favor — is what you're really selling.

Thus, your job is to so arrange your product that it is comparatively superior and that it offers superior benefits to your buyers. These benefits include (but are certainly not limited to) helping your prospect be: leaner, healthier, fitter, faster, sexier, friendlier, cleaner, more intelligent, richer, *etc.*

Getting this credible comparative benefit is what makes your prospect buy your product. But of course you have to realize that your competitors and successors are always on the look-out for ways to improve their product in the same way . . . rendering *them* superior and *you* outmoded. Thus, the process of competitive, comparative advantage is never ending, which is why ours (thank God!) is a society in constant motion. What is therefore important to remember is that whatever benefit you offer today, can, will and should be rendered imperfect tomorrow . . . perhaps by your own improvement processes.

Understanding Ultimate Benefits

Each comparative benefit falls under an Ultimate Benefit, the end result the prospect is trying to achieve. Ultimate Benefits include:

- financial stability
- health
- love
- security
- salvation
- self-regard
- community and peer recognition
- independence
- sexual fulfillment
- beauty/desirability/personal attractiveness

And many others.

Benefits are comparative; Ultimate Benefits are absolute.

As an information product seller, what you have to keep in mind is that you must sell both comparative benefits (making your prospect relatively better off in a variety of ways) *and* at least one Ultimate Benefit.

Let's use this book as an example. It will make you comparatively better off financially. In other words, by carefully following the guidelines in this book, you will make more money and so be relatively better off than others who don't follow these guidelines . . . or follow guidelines offered by others in this field. That is its benefit. It is the immediate or short-term reason why people want to acquire and use it.

But the real benefits, long-term and substantial, are the several Ultimate Benefits you get when you use it, including:

- financial security
- autonomy
- community and peer recognition
- self-esteem from the knowledge you are helping others.

These are what you *really* get when you follow the guidelines in this book . . . and, not surprisingly, they are the leitmotif of what you get collectively from *all* the products I create and sell. These Ultimate Benefits are the real reasons people come to me . . . though they achieve them through the comparative benefits offered by each individual information product. See?

Where's the product in all this? Well, in the Lant system of marketing, it's not the first thing you see. Why? Because you must lead with benefits and follow with features. And a book . . . or audio cassette . . . or Special Report is a feature . . . not, *per se,* a benefit.

Now do an experiment. As an information seller, you are probably on lots of mailing lists. For the next few days, check your mail and put aside all the coupons, circulars, catalogs, flyers, *etc.,* that offer an information product. Before reviewing them, reread this section. Then check out each marketing communication. Does what you're reviewing focus on the product . . . or does it focus on you, the prospect . . . on the comparative benefit you wish to achieve . . . and on the Ultimate Benefit you are really working for?

If the marketing communication focuses on the product . . . then you know you are dealing either with a selfish and/or an uninformed marketer. He's trying to get you to buy features . . . when all you're really interested in is acquiring benefits.

Our Michigan author of the teen-age goals-setting book forgot this. His marketing pieces (and I'm including that crucial marketing communication the product cover) focuses on features. The first thing you see when you look at the cover is "A practical success guide for teen-agers." Is this a benefit? Certainly not, because it doesn't give them a benefit; instead, it's a product description, or feature.

This author forgot who his prospect was . . . what comparative benefit he wanted . . . and what Ultimate Benefit. I say "forgot" rather charitably, because in fact I believe he never knew. Certainly he never knew at the crucial planning stage when making this determination is so very important.

Now let me tell you what Ultimate Benefit I really think he's selling: love. I think the primary audience for this book is people who really care for teen-agers (or are forced to say they do), people like: parents, grandparents, school librarians, community librarians, executive directors of non-profit organizations focusing on the concerns of teen-agers, *etc.* These people are both frustrated by teen-age habits and worried, often desperately so, by them. And they do want to help.

So, here comes a bright, attractive, knowledgeable author with lots of practical experience working with teen-agers and helping them along. He offers the comparative benefit of happier, more productive, less angry teen-agers and the Ultimate Benefit of showing their love to people who sincerely want to help troubled teens.

Unfortunately, in the marketing materials I have before me there are no detailed comparative benefits . . . and there isn't an inkling of the true Ultimate Benefit this author offers. Instead, he's selling a book. Now, think of this. A book is something that demands work, application and a sustained time commitment. In this age of MTV, just how many teen-agers do you think are prepared to make that kind of commitment? As every true educator knows and laments, damned few.

But how many concerned parents are willing to commit a little money on the chance that this may help the child they truly love to make an important personal breakthrough? Very, very many. Why? Because they love that child. This is why the author must speak of care, love, concern . . . not about his book.

I hope you see what I'm talking about. It is so very, very important. Because if you sell an information *product*, no matter how fine and worthy, . . . and not a buyer benefit . . . you are on the pathway to destruction. People, remember, don't buy books . . . don't buy information products . . . they buy the comparative benefits and Ultimate Benefits they can only get when they use these products. Never forget this!

Now sit down and list, in as much specific detail as you can, the comparative benefits your prospects will get when they use your information product. BE SPECIFIC! And write down the Ultimate Benefit these prospects — these specific prospects — get when they acquire and/or use your info-product . . . always remembering that the comparative benefits may well be different for *each* of your markets. The Ultimate Benefits, however, must be the same . . . for these Ultimate Benefits are what you are truly selling and what you really want your company and all your products, whether produced by yourself or others, to become known for.

Positioned By Title And Content To Speak Directly To The Broadest Possible Market

It is undoubtedly true that most info-producers sabotage their products by giving them the wrong title . . . and delivering the content in the wrong way. These are two distinct but related problems.

The goal of your title is simple: to get the designated prospect to stop dead in his tracks, say "this is for me", perceive the benefit he gets from the product . . . and so be compelled to take the product in his hands to take a better, more sustained look; (in a retail setting, he doesn't have to buy the product to do this, via mail order he does). The title, then, is the butterfly net; the prospect is the butterfly.

Now it goes without saying that you can't achieve this result with a title that doesn't simultaneously offer the prospect a benefit . . . and a description of what he's really getting. That's why I prefer two-part titles, like the one for most of my books. The first part of the title I call The Grabber . . . it is what attracts the prospect's attention; the second part is The Descriptor . . . it tells the prospect what he's getting. The Grabber is generally a benefit; The Descriptor is a feature.

The title is important because it's directed to the prospect; the prospect knows in an instant if this info-product is for him (or not for him). That's as it should be. A title that focuses on the product itself (or, worse, tries to be clever) leaves the prospect scratching his head, wondering what he gets from it. Take a title like *Rites Of Passage At $100,000+* by placement specialist John Lucht. Where's the benefit in this title? Who's the designated audience? Would the prospect know this book was for him just by reading the title? In other words, does the title market the book . . . or does it retard the marketing process, which is necessarily brisk and focused? I think you know the answer.

As I shall say often enough, a title is a marketing headline. Thus, like all marketing headlines . . . it must speak directly to the prospect. There must therefore be a "you" in it . . . it must express a relationship between a knowledgeable and caring individual (the author) . . . who has beneficial information . . . and an individual who needs that information to solve a problem he has . . . or achieve an objective.

The title simultaneously:

- grabs the attention of the right prospect;

- indicates to that prospect that the info-product is for him;

- shows this prospect what he gets when he uses the product;

- indicates that he is dealing with a client-centered specialist who has information of the utmost value to the prospect.

If the title doesn't do these things, the title is wrong.

Getting a title is necessarily a difficult task. Right now, all you are doing is making a tentative title decision. Soon, as you'll see in the next chapter, you can make it final . . . and thus launch your marketing effort. For as soon as you have a fixed title . . . with a clear definition of benefit(s) available and audience identified . . . you are ready to start making money from your product. Yes, before you've finished a single sentence of the product itself!

Now is not the time to go into all the ins and outs of creating a client-centered product . . . or arranging the information so that your reader/client feels it's all for his benefit . . . and that you're speaking to him. That, too, must be postponed to the next chapter. Now, however, I'd like to make these points for your earliest consideration.

The most important thing about content is that it be client-centered . . . that is, your information must be presented so your reader feels you understand his situation and care about helping him. Content must be utilitarian in substance and empathetic in approach. In fact the degree to which you are empathetic is the degree to which the material is useful.

Here, for instance, is what reviewer Joy Laughter said about my book CASH COPY in *The Crafts Report,* a publication for artists and craftspeople: "Reading the book, it's as if the author is sitting right in front of you, elbows on knees, his face in yours, grabbing your sleeve and shouting. I had to wipe spit off my glasses a couple of times." This is precisely the effect (well, perhaps not the 'shouting') you want to achieve . . . because this is how the reader gains a sense of your care and empathy . . . as well as an indication of what you consider important for him to do to achieve his objectives.

Consider, for instance, the state of the reader, your prospect. He has a need . . . or want. There's something he wants to get rid of . . . or get. He doesn't have the kind of concerned, knowledgeable friend readily at hand that you most assuredly can be. He doesn't just want information . . . he wants a friend who understands what he's going through . . . and gives him both psychological and technical assistance. That friend is you . . . the information doctor . . . who lays comforting, soothing, caressing and motivating hands on the reader with each word and thought you present.

But I say this to you: if your title is wrong, if your title, that is, is about your product . . . how to you expect the product's content to be anything other than purely disembodied information? It can't be done!

If you have decided to speak to the broadest possible spectrum of your market . . . your title (and content) must reflect this decision. Likewise, if you have decided (for whatever reason) to speak to a smaller subsection of a larger market. Either way, both title and content must be focused on the buyer and the benefits he gets.

Now I ask you. Does your last information product title do this? Does it talk to the prospect you wish to convince? Does it capture his attention? Does it hammer home a benefit? Does it shout, "Hey, you, this is for you!"? Or does it merely present some leaden feature? Or, worse, words that (as in the illustration above) mean nothing at all to no one at all? Be honest! Why? Because if you're not . . . you lose.

The wrong title . . . the wrong content . . . effectively kills an information product whatever value there may be in it, no matter how keenly the market(s) need it. That is why, now, during the planning session, you should brainstorm with three or four friends, getting down as many title possibilities as you can. Later, when you evaluate them, you can see if they meet the title criteria stated above. If they don't, you are planning to fail . . . planning, that is, to deprive the market of your product and all its benefits. Is this really what you want?

For now, however, after you brainstorm for title possibilities, make a tentative selection of title. Evaluate it closely. Does it speak directly to your prospect? Does it convince him you have a benefit he wants and a believable process he can follow to get it? Or have you selected some vague, meaningless title that forces the reader to figure out what you've got for him . . . and thereby limits the likelihood he'll do anything at all, much less buy your product?

As a consultant to many authors and publishers, I have seen just how often these almost universally intelligent and creative people have destroyed their own aspirations and thrown away their money by selecting either the wrong title, by waiting too long to deal with the issue of title, or by hoping that a good title would save a bad book . . . thus introducing an avoidable tension into the title-content equation.

Don't make this mistake! Get a client-centered title as soon as you can. *Then* create the client-centered product that reinforces this title and works with it to convince the prospect that you are offering him empathetic and compelling benefits.

Capable of Being Brought Before Your Designated Market(s) Not Just Once But Again And Again On A Continuing Basis

As I write there is a fatuous debate going on in the independent (a euphemism for "small") publishing world about whether book reviews sell books. This debate, like the Gypsy Moth, recurs at regular cycles and is as pointless (if not as destructive) as the insect. Anyone familiar with marketing knows that for small publishers reviews *per se* do not sell many books. How could they?

Most such reviews and informational articles/broadcasts (especially in larger, mass media sources) don't offer any follow-up information. They provide general information about the product to be sure . . . but not the means necessary for the prospect to follow up (name of publisher, his address, telephone, product price, *etc.*) This places the full responsibility for follow-up on the prospect which is, of course, a prescription for non-action.

Mainline media people think they are doing their job, of course, merely by providing such information as they do give. The fact that what they have provided is woefully incomplete and that they have therefore inconvenienced any number of their readers/listeners is of no concern to them.

In this connection, I remember a sanctimonious *Boston Globe* columnist named Alex Beam taking great delight in telling me how he had informed the subject of one of his articles that it would be "inappropriate" for him to list the name of her publisher and that it was impertinent of her to ask him to do so!

I took strong exception to this opinion and pointed out all the inconvenience that necessarily ensued from his obstinate decision. "But the readers could always call me to get her address," he said in self-defense. Then there was a pause . . . "But, of course, I never told them that," he concluded in what I can only hope was a moment of epiphany for an arrogant man who hadn't the slightest idea what being in the communications business is all about.

No, friend, articles — be they reviews or other kinds of pieces such as interviews, *etc.*, featuring your information products — don't work for small publishers unless complete follow-up information is included, and it is up to every one of us strongly to point out to people in the media just how myopic their current operating procedures are . . . and how generally unhelpful.

Which brings me to my major point: during the planning process, you must focus on identifying those markets that can be reached on an ongoing basis. This is the equation:

Clear Market Focus + Motivating, Advantageous Client-Centered Benefits + Immediate Reason For Action + Continuing "Coats" Of Your Target Market(s) = Continuing Sales

Sadly, most information product sellers, focused on their products and certain of their own inevitable prosperity, don't bother to consider just how they will reach their market(s) . . . and what it will cost them to do so. You can't make this mistake.

If you've been following my suggestions so far, you now have a targeted market . . . or series of markets . . . and a tentative market-centered title and content descriptor. If you're like most ingenue information product sellers, that is to say the greenest of the green, you're probably thinking that all you have to do now is whip up your product and wait magically for it to appear in bookstores, in catalogs, in media sources . . . all without too much effort from you. Don't tell me you you don't think this way. I've seen this all too often. You may know you shouldn't think this way, but think this way you do . . . because your product is an extension of yourself . . . and this is how you think you are entitled to be treated. It just isn't going to happen, however. That's why you need to remember the formula above . . . and live by it.

To make money selling information products, you must be ruthless about the market(s) you select . . . both about which markets you'll work with (because they are likely to make money for you) and those you won't . . . and crystal clear about the benefits you have for the people in them. Moreover, you must be prepared to hit these people again and again and again with both these benefits, a reason for acquiring them NOW!, and complete details on how they can do so.

Unfortunately, when an article about your information product appears in a mass circulation newspaper but doesn't include any follow-up information, you're not going to make much money . . . even if your product is in every bookstore in the metropolitan area (unlikely, by the way). Why? Because the average bookstore only carries three or four copies (if that) of most titles.

In all fairness, I admit that a big story without follow-up information may well sell the vast majority of *these* books. But how are you going to sell the re-orders? Through expensive paid ads? Unlikely. They are just too costly to justify this kind of investment. That's why most mainline publishers think this way: print 5000 copies of a book; get one story in 50-75 daily newspapers resulting in sales of at least half these books; place a significant percentage of the remainder in the same stores (reorders); get other stores to carry one or two copies each of the book and hope for random sales or one good national story; sell the remainder of the copies through library sales (which is why a *Booklist* review is so important). Then after eleven months let this title die a natural death . . . keep whatever profits one has made . . . and go on to repeat the process with another book . . . another author . . . and another marginal profit.

Read this, dear colleague, and weep!

And know that you can't handle your business this way!

Instead, identify the markets you can return to on a cost effective basis again and again and again making continuing sales from your information product . . . year after year.

Thus, which marketing alternative do you think is more important? A major newspaper like the *Boston Globe,* by far the largest in the six New England states, or a newsletter like *Enterprise,* published by the Consultants and Entrepreneurs Group of the Boston Computer Society, with about 5,000 subscribers?

Before you started this book, I'd lay odds you would have selected the former. After all, it's got a daily circulation of nearly 700,000, about 140 times the monthly circulation of *Enterprise.* Being in the *Boston Globe* would impress your friends, wouldn't it, and reflect your own sense of who you are and where you ought to be? Problem is, it just wouldn't sell your products on a continuing basis . . . because it's too expensive for regular use.

Enterprise, however, enables you to hit a designated market of consultants and entrepreneurs (one of my prime markets) over and over again with continuing results and, because of some marketing suggestions I'll share with you later, at trifling cost.

Each month *Enterprise* enables me to provide my prospects with my name, address, telephone, credit card information and a listing of several products and their benefits. It also gives me the opportunity to tell my prospects how to get a year's free subscription to my Sure-Fire Business Success Catalog. At the same time, it runs my column, which enhances my perceived image to my target audience. As a result, they *want* to get in touch with me. The bottom line?

Enterprise has always provided me with an income stream that the more majestic *Boston Globe,* with a circulation 140 times greater, cannot begin to compete with.

Here's the key to this result:

- You must know who you are talking to;

- You must have precise benefits for them;

- You must know you can reach them again and again and again and so get the benefits of synergy and The Rule of Seven;

- You must know you can reach them for the least conceivable outlay of money, thereby making more of your return profit;

- You must do everything possible to safeguard your relationship with such a source, truly a goose that goes on laying golden eggs.

This is the kind of thinking that should distinguish your approach to any marketing device, be it publication, talk program, mailing list, *etc.* As you consider each of these alternatives, you need to know:

- whether the market you have selected can be reached again;

- the means that exist for reaching it again;

- the frequency with which this market can be reached;

- the cost of the various alternatives;

- whether there are less expensive alternatives that you can use, or whether you have to use costlier ones only.

By this sensible standard, smaller publishers shouldn't waste their limited time and money on so-called major media sources . . . ordinarily, the return just isn't there for us. By the same token, of course, it doesn't pay to ignore them altogether either. Insofar as you have *extra* time, energy and money, you can devote some of it to contacting these publicity sources. Why? For three reasons really: publicity there *can* generate *some* sales, if your product is available at retail outlets; such publicity can be leveraged (we'll talk about this later) to get still more — and more profitable — publicity elsewhere, and it *is* good for your ego. So long as you don't let this last consideration overwhelm all the rest of what I'm saying, there really is nothing wrong with some pleasant ego gratification, is there?

Priced So That Various Marketing Options Are Open To You . . . Not Closed Because Of Their Cost

Just what you can do in your marketing will be determined to a considerable extent by the price of your products. The other day an ingenue author-publisher (but established dentist) from Racine, Wisconsin, called to discuss his new book. It deals with the eradication of headache pain through some new technique. Fair enough. He told me 40,000,000 Americans have headache pain and thought sure he had a sufficiently large market to make him oodles of money. Whoa, boy, not so fast!

Needless to say he didn't have a bookstore distributor . . . a library distributor . . . any catalog distribution . . . and, of course, no marketing documents, either. He had no clear conception of market and nary a trace of a marketing plan. What he did have, however, was a price. I think it was $10.95.

Predictably, I was aghast.

He had priced the book before considering the marketing alternatives. Instead, the proper way of handling this matter is to scrutinize the marketing alternatives open to you and see how much you need to charge for the product to make a profit after you've paid for production and marketing. Or, the reverse of what the good doctor was doing.

If the world were truly perfect for marketers (all of whom long for a monopolistic idyll), we'd identify the largest possible markets needing what we have . . . draw up a dazzling list of benefits, thus exciting the market . . . and then price the product according to the benefits. Competition in such an ideal world wouldn't exist and wouldn't be a problem, and we'd soak up money from our markets as efficiently as a sponge soaks up water.

In our flawed universe, however, we must cast a cool eye at our competitors and the price they are charging. What we do will inevitably be influenced by their existence. Here's what we must consider:

- What is the cost of reaching our designated market(s) on a continuing basis?

- Given these costs, the costs of production and general business overhead, what must we charge to make a profit (the goal of all this work)? (Write down a tentative price at this point.)

- Once we have a tentative price, we must look at what others are charging for their competitive products;

- We must also look at the benefits they promise and their approach. Are our competitors focusing on features (which is very likely given the slack marketing of most info-producers), or are they truly concentrating on benefits (which make them dangerous and truly competitors);

- Taking all these data into account, now we are truly ready to set a product price.

Remember, you lower your price only in response to competitors and external marketing factors and, more precisely, only in response to competitors who are focusing on delivering *benefits* to the same group of prospects as you are and are using the same kinds of marketing means. If they're not doing this, they aren't truly competitors.

Lest this procedure seem a little difficult and confusing to you, let me try another tack. Essentially, there are two ways of marketing information products: through retail stores (books and some audio cassettes) and through direct response marketing (books and everything else). When you are settling the matter of price, you are really deciding in large measure which of these two general marketing strategies you'll use.

If you intend to sell your products primarily through direct response marketing, they must ordinarily be higher priced than is usually suitable for retail stores. In other words, while a $10.95 paperback is well within the boundaries for a retail price, it is far too low for direct response marketing.

The real trick is setting a price that will enable you to make money via direct response marketing and yet not lose the retail bookstore trade. My paperback books at between $24.95 and $35 test, I think, the upper limits of price for on-the-shelf retail establishments. They are, however, just right for the more expensive direct response alternatives. But remember this: your objective must be to find a price that doesn't sacrifice either market and that gets you maximum continuing profit from each. This is what distinguishes the shrewdest info-marketers.

I know many info-marketers who have abandoned the retail marketing alternative and selected direct response marketing as their chief mode of getting income. And that's fair enough . . . as far as it goes. These people tend to charge substantial prices (that is, prices over $24.95) for their products.

I know many other info-marketers who have, probably by default, abandoned the direct response marketing alternative to concentrate on the retail marketing alternative. Their products almost without exception sell for under $25, and most for under $20 each. They are speculating on larger sales at a smaller net profit on each item.

By comparison, I know very few marketers who have managed the difficult, challenging, and necessary feat of drawing revenue from *both* marketing spheres. My point to you is this: don't abandon either market unless you are forced to. Do try to make money from *both* types of marketing activity. The goal is plain: to raise your price as high as you can in each area but only to raise your price as you are prepared to focus even further on client-centered benefits. It is the clear rendition and constant repetition of these benefits to your targeted market(s) that justifies the price they are willing to pay and which you always wish to raise . . . as you pound home the benefits your prospects get by using your product.

Last Words About Price

Before moving on to another point, I wish to add a little more about price.

The first time you produce an info-product your inclination may well be to price it low. You may reckon the price as some variable of production costs and reason that if the product has only cost you $2, you should probably only charge $8 or $10. STOP RIGHT THERE!

Price should *never* be a function of production costs; it should always be a function of benefits the prospect derives . . . set against prices charged by competitors and solid benefits offered by them. Benefits, then, not cost should be your prime consideration.

Equally, new info-product producers always assume that they'll get a higher rate of return from their marketing activities than ordinarily occurs. A new information producer exploring, say, the possibilities of paying $2000 to participate in a card pack mailing 100,000 cards may well reckon his return on a 1% basis; (most people seem erroneously to think that all direct mail generates about a 1% response). 1% of 100,000 is 1,000 sales, he reasons, or $10,950 in revenue (using our dentist's original price). Even figuring production costs, shipping and handling, overtime and office time, it's a bonanza — far better than you could do with a certificate of deposit . . . and so much more ego gratifying.

Whoa again!

This is where the lure of "certain" money (cleverly manipulated by a clever salesperson) overcomes common sense and experience, for as seasoned card deck advertisers know, if you're selling your product direct (that is, asking for the sale immediately) you'll probably get a response of about 1/10 of 1%, or about $1000 in gross sales. That's a net *loss* of about $1000, a very different kettle of fish. And you'd have to get about twice the average return to break even. These are odds only a sucker could love. Facts like this suggest several other courses of action:

- raising the price by making the client-centered benefits most truly attractive;
- abandoning the direct sale and instead asking for an inquiry, sending out follow-up sales literature packed with more benefits;
- seeing how you can cut the cost of the advertising vehicle you have selected (the card).

Another thing you must remember is this: despite all the exalted direct mail claims, you should break even at .5% response.

That means that if you're using the mail to make sales (and I hope you intend to), you must first draw up your budget with its cost items of:

- mailing piece production and printing
- list rental and fulfillment house charges
- postage
- product cost
- packing charges.

Taking all these costs into consideration, you must break even with a .5% return. If you don't, your product price is certainly too low. Later, I'll go into more detail on the subjects of direct response marketing and free publicity marketing.

The truth is, I've rarely seen a candid . . . and never a complete and accurate . . . discussion of these subjects in the age of ferocious competition and rising costs. But for now, it is enough to say this:

Because you want so much to believe that your product will be profitable . . . that it will be your ticket to Easy Street . . . you are less inclined to be truly skeptical and completely to scrutinize each marketing activity. Yet you must do so. You must be conservative about predicting response, must do everything you can to get your customer to identify himself to you so that you control the marketing process (and not him), must build in sufficient margin into your cost so that you can bear the cost of repeated thumps on the prospect's thick skull, and must remember that price is related to benefits (and benefits offered by competitors), not to production costs.

Aimed Directly At The Want Or Need This Market Possesses . . . Letting This Market Clearly Know You Have The Necessary Solution.

One of the great problems with the range of "how-to" products is that they're didactic. They mean to give people an education, to tutor them, instruct them, and generally teach them. But outside of the increasingly irrelevant ranks of educators themselves, this goal is of value to almost no one. That is, all people really want to do is get what they want. They'll do what's necessary to get it . . . but they want what they want as quickly and painlessly as possible . . . as fully and completely as necessary.. and with as few obstacles as may be imagined.

As you'll see in the next chapter, the perfect how-to info-product is built with this kind of structure:

* you hurt (or you want);
* here's how badly you hurt (or you want);
* here's exactly what you've got to get rid of the hurt (or get what you want);
* conclusion: get out there and do it.

This formula looks easy enough, doesn't it? Why, then, do so many authorities fail to get it right?

The reason, I think, it that they're in love with information for the sake of information. This is a peculiarly academic trait where those of us in the academy (remember, I was once an inmate myself) are evaluated not by the intelligence of our approach (must less by the results we achieve) but by the sheer volume of what we discover. Thus, information *per se* takes on an importance in such circles that it has absolutely nowhere else.

Not surprisingly, such educated people are disproportionately represented among writers and publishers. Most of these people don't feel they have done their job unless they've given you every last drop of theory going back to the opening discussion of the subject a millenium ago . . . and peppered their findings with erudite quotations, footnotes and arcane references. Why, just the other day I read a book about credit improvement and repair (a hot topic in debt-ridden America) that contained a (thankfully brief) history of credit . . . when all readers want to know is how to get credit and get it fast. (Not surprisingly, the author prominently featured his academic credentials.) SUCH IDIOCY MUST STOP!!!

Instead, you must keep in mind just two words: problem and solution. Or, a variation: desire and achievement.

That is, people either have a problem and want it solved.

Or they have a desire they want to achieve.

If you remember these two mini-formulas, you may approach your work with every expectation of success. Thus:

- If you want to convince a targeted market of people with a problem to buy what you're selling, you've got to paint their problem in truly graphic terms. You've got to make them feel the pain of their problem . . . and thus want to get the solution you can give them. "Here's your problem," you say, "here then is what you must do to solve it."

- Or, paint what they want to achieve (their desire) in the most glowing of colors . . . (remember, the sizzle, not the steak) . . . and tell them what they've got to do to achieve it.

Now, in the crucial planning stages for your sure-to-be-successful info-product, it's time to decide which product you're creating: one that deals with a painful problem that you can solve . . . or one that deals with achieving a desire by following certain steps. But I'll tell you a little secret: products that deal with pain or with avoiding loss do better on the whole than those about achieving something you want. Avoiding loss, removing pain, is more powerful than achieving gain. Remember that. This is because people know the pain they're in . . . and want to get rid of it, or know what they have and fear losing it, while they can only imagine even their fondest desire. Reality, thus, sells better than imagination.

Knowing this, it's time for you to decide which product you're creating and to make sure you are positioning it properly for your market. At this point you may well need to rethink your title. Most people, creating most info-products, create what I call "soft" products; they are based on their personal feelings that the world is a kind and beneficial place, a place where good people listen to good advice and follow it, working steadily to achieve their goals. As you might gather, I don't believe this.

If you remember your college philosophy, you'll remember the potent seventeenth century English philosopher Thomas Hobbes. He believed that men were lazy and essentially irresponsible; that they only acted when they needed to act and lived for today, ignoring tomorrow. As you won't be surprised to learn, I think Hobbes was right.

This infuriates my more liberal brethren who breathe a kind of insipid sweetness and light about the human condition which I find not only irritating but entirely unsupported by reality. They wish to believe such bromides are true despite everything they see to the contrary. I don't. Inevitably this view of the world colors the advice I'm giving you.

If you want to motivate people to act (and I assure you, you do), you must both create and position your info-products so that they speak to their fears and anxieties. If you want to motivate a person in pain to act, remind him he's in pain . . . and that if he acts he can get rid of that pain. This is much more sensible and powerful than merely telling him about some information on the subject of pain removal . . . or giving him an historical overview of his particular malady. What you know must be focused on the prospect . . . must speak to him . . . must remind him of his problem (or his aspiration) and let him know you can help him remove (or achieve) it.

Is this the product you're thinking of producing? Probably not, because your mind has been addled by seeing "The Wizard Of Oz" too many times. But in real life witches don't melt when little girls accidentally spill water on them, whatever you wish to believe to the contrary. Remember that and act accordingly. During the planning process, state the problem as pungently as possible that your info-product is designed to solve. Speak directly to your designated market(s). If you can't state the problem precisely and painfully or draw a vivid and precise picture of the aspiration, you can help that prospect achieve, you are about to create the wrong product . . . with the wrong headline, the wrong content, and the wrong marketing plan. How, then, can you possibly expect this product to make money for you, except for reasons of the most ludicrous egotism? Which is, of course, just what most info-producers do expect.

A Perennial

The other day when going through my bookshelves in hot pursuit of a good read before bed, I came across an excellent volume I had read a year or two before by Evan Connell entitled *Son of The Morning Star*. If you haven't read it, you should: it's the story of the demise of the preening George Amstrong Custer and the kind of mindless arrogance that always gets people into trouble . . . including lots of innocent ones. As I looked at it I thought of all the good publicity the book got, the fact it probably had good sales and made money . . . and thought sadly that it's dead as a doornail today for all its superior virtues. This is why you must not produce this kind of book.

As I've said before, you must aim to produce a perennial, something that you can profitably keep in print for the rest of your life. Why? Not because you're arrogant and wish to do so out of egotism, but because the information you present is valuable to your designated markets . . . markets that are large and growing . . . or which at least give you a suitable return on your investment.

Our aim as marketers must be to fill a niche . . . to sell info-products as Kellogg's sells cornflakes . . . not for a momentary sensation . . . but for certain income year after year.

Is this the project you have in mind? Is this the kind of commitment you're prepared to make? Now is the moment to answer these questions . . . honestly.

What do you really know about your market? How do you know people will be interested in your product even just three or four years from now . . . or that there will be sufficient numbers of them . . . easily, consistently and economically reached, to make your endeavor a profitable one?

If you know this, have you then positioned your product to appeal to these people in the years ahead? Does it promise them a benefit they'll want today . . . and want tomorrow? Or are you so focused on the present that you are dooming your product to a premature death tomorrow?

The goal, remember, is not to produce a product; it's to produce a profitable product . . . and not just a profitable product for now, either; but a profitable product for the rest of your life.

Can you honestly say the info-product you've just created . . . or are thinking of creating, will do this? If not, it's the wrong product.

As you contemplate the information product you are about to produce ask yourself these questions:

- Is the audience of prospects I am creating this for likely to grow in the next decade? How do I know?

- Is this audience likely to have the problem that I am solving with this product? How do I know?

- Is something about to happen in this field that will make what I'm about to write about obsolete and render my product futile? Is something like this likely to happen five years from now? Ten years from now? How do I know?

- If developments in my field make part of the information in this product obsolete, is the benefit I'm offering . . . and the Ultimate Benefit of this product . . . still something my prospects will want?

- If the audience is at least stable (and hopefully growing), if my prospects will want my benefit and Ultimate Benefit five or more years from now, if developments in my field will not make my (regularly updated) product obsolete, do I then have the will and commitment to keep my product up-to-date and pertinent for my prospects? Am I the kind of person who's likely to abandon the tried, true and profitable just because I know about it . . . or can I make a commitment to my product and my market that ensures I get maximum benefit myself from what I'm about to create?

If all info-entrepreneurs asked these questions of themselves and their products before creating them, they'd abandon most of their projects as certain to be unsuccessful.

Our strength as smaller info-producers and marketers is our clear grasp of our market(s), the development of products that will have an extraordinarily long life, the development of products that each reinforce each other and the Ultimate Benefit we are really in business to deliver, and our plodding persistence, the persistence that ensures constant profit from our products . . . long after other, more glamorous, products are forgotten. We are not meteors, you see, brilliant explosions of light in the nighttime sky but fast gone; we are constellations, regularly seen, always present, perhaps momentarily dimmer than a meteor . . . but, over time, casting a longer, more certain glow.

Created So That The Reader/Client Can Really Do What The Product Promises . . . And Packed With Not Only Immediately Usable Techniques, Processes, And Guidelines . . . But Also Including Specific Detailed Follow-Up Information For Those Who Need Further Assistance And Refinements

Let's say you weren't feeling very well and went to a doctor for assistance. At the end of your expensive and time-consuming consultation, the physician said, "Oh, yes, you're ill. I know what you've got, but I won't tell you. And I won't tell you what you've got to do to get better." How would you feel? Angry and frustrated, to be sure, and, of course, cheated. Well, then, can there be any wonder that readers of most "how-to" materials feel this way when they can't use what you produce to get the benefits promised in your title, subtitle and marketing materials?

You see, when you sit down to create a how-to info-product you become a doctor, an advisor. It is your job to know precisely who you're talking to (just as a doctor knows which patient he's treating), precisely what his situation is, precisely what he wishes to achieve, precisely when he wants to achieve it, and precisely what he has to do to get there. It also helps if you know the kinds of obstacles (both external and internal) he'll face along the way . . . and what he can do to overcome them and achieve either the obliteration of pain or the achievement of the objective he wants.

Sadly, most "how-to" writers act like writers, not like advisors. As a result, they write materials with huge, gaping holes . . . holes that literally make it impossible for the reader/prospect to do what's required to achieve what the product's title promises. It's as if they told a traveler in London that all he needed to do to get to New York was cross the Atlantic . . . but neglected to tell him *how* to do that. Providing the detailed information is what makes a how-to author work attending to.

Now, I ask you. For the project you are now considering . . . for the project you have just created . . . do you (did you?) really have and provide the kind of detailed how-to-do-it information that enables your reader/prospect to achieve the objective you've promised? Or have you promised results, and delivered pap?

If you have just created some info-product, look at it. Have you written step-by-step guidelines? Have you included just what your prospect needs to know? Does he feel that you not only know what you're talking about but have walked along with him hand in hand, urging, exhorting, chiding, persuading him so that he, too, can achieve what you have achieved? Or do you simply *think* you've done that?

If you're about to create your info-product, think! Do you really have the information you need . . . and are you willing to give it, all of it, to your reader?

What happens if you don't do this? Why, only, this:

• Your prospects feel cheated when they read or listen to what you've produced. Some, of course, will return what they've purchased for a refund. Others will either dispose of what they've purchased . . . or thrust it onto their shelves, never to be looked at again . . . or looked at as an exhibition of their own poor judgment. Your product becomes a lingering indictment of you and your slovenly work habits.

• Your prospects won't refer you to their friends. There will be no favorable, indeed indispensable, word of mouth publicity, because you haven't done what's necessary — in terms of the authenticity and value of the product — to stimulate it. How sad for you! I can attest to the power of this kind of marketing, because each day I make money, every single day, from people who have been told, often commanded, by their friends and associates to contact me. If you don't turn your customers into marketers for your product, you are dying by slow strangulation.

• Your prospects, having bought one item in a series and been disappointed with it, will not buy other items in that series . . . whatever offer you make them. Thus, your products will not succeed, as they ought, in selling other products.

- Your prospects won't buy your subsequent products even before they're produced. Do you think people will buy from you again when they've been unhappy with what they've already bought? Think again!

- Your prospects won't accept your recommendations about other products that you sell. Hence more revenue will be lost.

- And your prospects certainly won't hire you as a consultant to assist them personally when they've been so disappointed with the extent, quality and usefulness of the information you've sold them.

Just look at the consequences of producing a product that doesn't meet the bona fide wants and needs of your prospects! Can the mere fact of producing an info-product, any info-product, in any way mean so much to you that you'd be prepared to put poor quality on the market merely for the sake of having a product . . . when you know that such a product actively sabotages you in so many ways?

As I look through my bulging bookshelves, now sprawling over three rooms in my home-based office, I see information product after information product. I doubt that anyone has seen so many as I have! Most of their authors created a single product, burst forth upon the world, and were gone again in the flickering of a cynical eyelash, to spend the rest of their lives posturing as authors, but to know nothing of the reality of true creativity and the benefits that derive from it: profit, of course, and the joys of creating a product that truly made a difference in another person's life.

Don't let this be you!

In a moment I shall move on to the practical matters of how to create such products. But for now, let me remind you of this: it is your job to give your reader/prospects the precise details they need to do what you have promised in the title. If, by following your advice, they cannot do what you have urged them to do, then what you have written is incomplete. If there is more to tell than can reasonably be presented in what you are creating, but which does exist elsewhere, it is your responsibility to provide all the necessary follow-up details. This is what communication is all about, and this is what the best info-products are all about.

I wish to stress just how difficult this is to do. For years now I have worked with many authors. All are specialists in their fields. Yet almost none of them when asked to write real "how-to" prose could do so, despite my giving them precise guidelines and actual samples. And these were all published authors some of whose names you would certainly recognize . . . and all of whom had a certain standing in their field! No, I do not underestimate the difficulty of writing the kind of prose that must be the hallmark of your info-product.

But it can be done!

Part of the problem could well be solved by those about to create such products asking themselves if they really knew or had or could discover the precise information their reader/client needed. It is a critical part of the planning process that this be done . . . and plans made accordingly.

Personally, I would like every would-be how-to product creator to be forced, by presidential order, to submit one page of prose to me from his forthcoming opus . . . be it book, audio cassette, or Special Report. I would know immediately if what was being created was a true roadmap for the reader . . . or a piece of Swiss cheese with holes big enough for Cinderella's carriage.

The moment for you to do this is before you make any final decision to proceed with your project. If what you write is not a roadmap, is "what to," not "how to," now is the time to know . . . and do what's necessary.

- Perhaps you don't know enough to create the product yet. That's no sin. It is a sin to produce something inferior . . . something that will damage your reputation . . . and not help others. It is no sin to admit that you need to know more. And then go about learning it.

- Perhaps you haven't thought through the advice you're giving. Of course, *you* know what to do. But that doesn't mean you've presented it in such a fashion that others will know what to do and can easily do it. (I wish writers of computer manuals would all have this sentence tattooed on their foreheads.)

- Perhaps you think you've written this kind of precise information. Why, then, show it to two or three of your prospects and ask them to do *exactly* what you've said. If they can't . . . or if doing it doesn't get them the objective you've promised in your title . . . why then you're not finished, are you?

But perhaps you *do* have the kind of dense, practical, client-centered, results-oriented information that your reader/client needs. Perhaps you have written a page of problem-solving prose that they *can* use and profit from and that nothing, absolutely nothing, is wanting — except the necessary spirit, enthusiasm and commitment the reader/client must bring to the task — to achieve what you've promised they can achieve.

If — I say if — this is the case, then you are ready to go on to the next chapter and launch the production process. Your planning process is finished, and you have the reasonable assurity that you will produce an information product that your reader/client can use profitably . . . and which will, in due course, bring you all the many benefits that do ensue from the production and marketing of such a superior product.

Your Step-By-Step Creation Process

3

How-to products, remember, are created either to help remove your prospect's pain or preserve something he's afraid of losing . . . or to help him achieve some desired objective.

I have already stressed that before you write you must be clear about:

- the audience you are creating for;
- the pain they have and wish to get rid of;
- what they have they're afraid of losing;
- the desire they wish to achieve.

Gathering The Material You Need

Gathering material for a "how-to" product is straightforward, once you understand what you're looking for. Remembering the structure of your product assists you in getting what you must have. That structure has these three parts:

(where pain or loss is concerned)

- conjuring up the prospect's pain and reminding him how much he hurts (or how much he'll lose if he does lose what he's trying to protect);

- giving him the exact steps he needs to remove the pain . . . or preserve himself from loss;

- giving him the necessary push to go out and get started.

(or, where achievement of a desired objective is concerned)

- conjuring up the desired objective, in the most persuasive and attractive way;
- giving him the exact steps he needs to achieve it;
- giving him the necessary push to go out and get started.

If you remember this structure, the process you follow to get your material follows as a matter of course.

First Step: The General Outline For Your Info-Product

There are two ways of getting someplace . . . either setting out aimlessly and hoping for the best. Or using a roadmap. The second tends to make more sense. This is why in creating an info-product you need a client-centered outline. This outline makes clear exactly what you are trying to accomplish and exactly what modules you need to complete to reach your objective.

The best "how-to" products follow this kind of general outline:

- Client-centered introduction. This introduction lets the prospect know that he is in the right place, that what follows is for him, establishes that you understand his situation and provides him with an overview of what he'll find in the product . . . and the benefits he'll get by using it. It also invites him to make contact with you if you have other products and services he can benefit from, and gives him the necessary information so that he can do so easily. This introduction (which I prefer in the form of a letter to the reader, for reasons I'll shortly discuss), though short, constitutes the first complete section of your product.

- The second section is made up of direct how-to-do-it advice and information organized by "what next?" thinking. That is, the first chapter deals with the *first thing* the prospect must do to achieve his objective. You are the specialist, you know what he must do first; here's where you tell him what that thing is and show him exactly how to do it. Subsequent chapters follow in rigidly logical order . . . one following the other as night follows day. The second major section of any how-to product is composed of these logically developed chapters each dealing with a necessary, but separate, series of logically connected steps the prospect must follow if he is to get what he wants.

- The third section of any info-product is made up of what I term the "marching orders." This section reminds the reader not only of what he wants to achieve but his current situation. It reminds him of what he has now learned . . . of what he now has available to help him achieve his objective . . . and gives him a final, uplifting, and motivational message to go out there and get started. This is also a good place again to invite the reader/prospect to contact you for personal assistance, always providing you make such assistance available. (And, if not, why not?)

- The fourth section of your info-product may or may not be necessary depending on your subject. Here you include necessary forms, samples, documents, technical specifications and such other material as is necessary for the reader/prospect to achieve his objective and which fits more conveniently here than in the text, where it may impede the reader.

- The fifth section contains information about you and your other products and services. Whereas both the introduction and conclusion (sections one and three above) contain an invitation for your reader to contact you, this section contains the exact information the prospect needs about what you do and provide. The shrewd info-product producer aims to establish a relationship with his reader. Once this relationship is established, it must have somewhere to go; that's why this section exists. Here you provide specific information about other solutions you have available . . . both the products and services you produce yourself . . . and those of other people that are offered by you. Unlike our feebler info-brethren, we know the relationship doesn't end with this product. It's something that is of mutual benefit for our prospect's life . . . and our own. We aim to develop that relationship right now, when the prospect has our first problem-solving product in his hands and is grateful for the help we've already given him.

Step Two: From Macro To Micro Outline

Once you have finished creating your general (macro) outline, you'll know if:

- your product is complete and covers the subject in sufficient detail so your prospect can achieve his objective. From this outline, you'll know immediately if you have left anything out that your prospect needs to achieve his objective. If you aren't sure, you can be certain you have. Your info-product must be a detailed road map taking the prospect from where he now is (and doesn't want to be) to where he wishes to be. Will the product you've outlined do that?

- your product is logically arranged. Your outline should tell you if you're about to approach your subject logically . . . that is, if you're following "what next?" thinking. Look at your outline. Have you laid out, in precise, logical order, the *exact* steps your prospect must follow to achieve his objectives? Be sure! Your prospects want to reach their objectives in the most expeditious and time-effective way possible, and won't forgive you if you misdirect them, take them on a wild goose chase, or don't approach your task logically.

- you have the information you need to create the various chapters and sections you've laid out. Even the most general outlines show you where you have information gaps that need your attention.

Once you've created your general outline, it's time to create specific (micro) outlines for *each* logical section of your product: your introduction, individual chapters, your samples section and end-of-product catalog.

Smart info-product producers not only create a detailed general outline of their overall project . . . but individual outlines for *each* section. Like the general outline, these individual outlines indicate if this particular section is complete and logically arranged and if you have all the information you need. It's important that you know these things as early as possible . . . after all you may well discover you need to get further information that may involve contacting others (who procrastinate) or doing (time-consuming) research.

An Example

Let me show you what I mean. And remember, you use this procedure for *any* how-to product, be it a book, booklet, audio cassette, or Special Report.

Say you wanted to create a 60-minute audio cassette on how to get an interview on a radio or television station and use it to get your prospects to buy what you're selling. (By the way, don't do this subject in this format. I already have!)

Your outline might look this this:

Introduction

- the high cost of advertising

- its uncertain response

- your need to make sales with limited dollars

- your frustration at how many of these dollars you've wasted

- the fact there is a solution available for you

- statement that you've come to the right place to get it

- list of contents of the cassette . . . benefits you get by using this information.

Chapter 1 (Yes, even audio cassettes can have chapters . . . for organizational purposes!). Mastering The Planning Process

- determining who your audience is
- deciding which problems they want to solve, which aspirations they want to achieve, so you can position your product or service as what they need
- researching which radio and television stations reach your audience
- how to get the names of the personnel you need to contact . . . and their addresses and phone numbers.

Chapter 2. Creating The Materials You Need To Persuade Radio & Television Personnel To Put You On The Air

- creating the materials you need to convince radio and television personnel to put you on the air
- a look at some specific formats: cover letter, brochure, media kit

Chapter 3. Knowing Who To Send Your Materials To And How To Follow Them Up

- how to find out who to send these materials to
- knowing how to follow up by telephone, in person, by letter
- what to do when your prospect says no
- what to do when you can't make contact at all
- what to do when your prospect says yes.

Chapter 4. What To Do To Make Best Use Of Your Free Air Time

- how to prepare for your interview
- how to get the station to broadcast your telephone number and address
- how to get interested prospects in your audience to identify themselves to you
- how to handle a loquacious interviewer who won't let you have your say
- how to handle an interviewer who gets off the track
- how to give out follow-up information when the interviewer doesn't

- how to handle a hostile interviewer
- what to say at the end of the program.

Chapter 5. Interview Follow-Up

- how to thank your interviewer and producer so you get invited back.

Chapter 6. When You Need More Help

- how to get in touch with me and what I can do to help you achieve your objectives.

Here's what you should notice about this outline:

- it provides a complete structure for both you, the creator, (you now know where you're going and what you need to get there), and for your listener/prospect.
- each section can itself be outlined for further ease of creation
- the outline is logical. You know right away if something is out of place.
- the outline indicates places where you may need further information . . . so you can arrange your research accordingly, gathering the data you need long before you need it.

Gathering Your Material

Once you've written your outline, you now know what additional material you need to create the product. The most accomplished how-to product creators are also expert at:

- knowing the information they need;
- knowing when they'll need it;
- doing what's necessary to get it so that their production process isn't retarded by not having it;
- knowing how to write around a specific section while they get information they didn't previously think they'd need . . . or work to find.

In other words, people who create a line of info-products develop a process both for creating their products and for gathering the material they need to create them. Importantly, these two processes can and should go on simultaneously.

Thus, even before you've finished Project I, you should be outlining Project II. Since you can't write or create products all day (it's just too mentally draining), you will have time, even in the midst of a very demanding project, to outline your next project. As soon as your detailed micro outline is complete, it's time to began gathering the information you need for your next project. Your objective is plain: to complete the creative work on Project I and move without a hiatus into a new project. This is what being a professional info-product producer is all about.

The only time you won't be able to do this is during your first project. It's undeniably the case that the reason a first project takes so much longer than any other is because you don't understand the creative process, don't understand what you need, what you don't need, when you need it, how to get it quickly, and how to craft a product . . . instead of attempting to dazzle the world with your intelligence and all the information you've gathered. In short, you won't have mastered the true creative process. Mastering that process is one of the very significant benefits you get when you complete your first info-product, which is why it's very much to your benefit to start another as soon as you can . . . to see if you've really learned all that you need to.

The Letter Templates You Need For Gathering Information

Gathering information, like all other parts of creating a solid information product, should be routinized as much as possible. This means thinking through the different kinds of letters you're going to need and creating them before you need them . . . so that when you need them you can quickly create them.

Here are four template letters you're going to need:

- letter to other info-producers and information sources requesting permission to quote from a given document, article, book, *etc.*

- letter to other information producers requesting a review copy of material (audio cassette, Special Report, magazine article, book, booklet, *etc.*) that you are thinking about citing in a Resource Box in your product;

- letter to information source requesting specific data on a given subject relevant to your product;

- letter to information product producer requesting permission to sell their product through your product and requesting a review copy, discount and drop shipping or warehousing terms.

Let's look at the components of each of these letters.

Letter To Other Info-Producers Requesting Permission To Quote

As Ecclesiastes well knew, authors throughout the ages have always used bits and pieces of other people's work to create their own. You're likely to do the same. If you're going to quote just a few words or lines of someone else's material you don't have to write for permission to quote. Simply give the citation and complete follow-up information including name and address of the source so that your readers can easily follow up.

If, however, you want to quote something longer, or use a document, form, chart, *etc.*, developed by someone else, it's a good idea to secure the permission of the copyright holder before you use it. The letter you develop should:

• inform the copyright holder or his representative (his publisher, for instance) what kind of product you are creating;

• include a copy of the exact thing you wish to use;

• request permission to use it;

• inform the copyright holder how you intend to attribute the information (namely with his name, address, telephone number, or other pertinent follow up information);

• include some biographical information about you to show that you are a reputable individual;

• (in the case of Special Reports, booklets, and other inexpensive products) indicate you'll be sending a copy of the material when it's produced.

For the copyright holder's ease and your own, simply include a line at the bottom of your letter saying, "I agree to your use of the above cited material and how you intend to give credit for it." Include a line for the copyright holder's signature and the date. Along with this letter, send a stamped self-addressed envelope so the signed permission can be returned to you promptly. If the copyright holder doesn't agree, he'll simply use this envelope to write you back, and you can then work out the necessary details.

Letter To Information Product Producer Requesting Review Copy

When you become a true information fanatic and understand that you *always* need to be working on a product, designing a new product, and gathering material to update existing products, you'll be:

• clipping notices of information sources;

- getting yourself on as many mailing lists of information providers as possible;

- requesting catalogs;

- reading relevant trade publications like *Publisher's Weekly,* and the newsletters produced by the National Association of Independent Publishers, COSMEP, and Publishers Marketing Association;

- gathering publication reviews;

- culling through bookstores;

- reviewing the bibliographies and sources cited in other publications, *etc., etc., etc.*

Your quest for information sources is never ending, and you must be voracious in your search . . . and knowledgeable about how to see what you may need for your own products and wish to bring to your readers' attention. This is where the second letter template comes in.

I should probably tell you this before giving you the format: when you're new and unknown in the info-publishing world, you're going to have less luck in getting free information from other producers. They don't know you. They get lots of requests from lots of people for free copies. All publishers are subject to emotionally charged outbursts against the freebie seekers who prey on all of us. Your letter, then, will not always elicit the response you might like . . . but at the very least you can get the promotional information about the product and decide if you should take further steps to acquire it.

Here is what this letter must contain:

- inform the publisher of the scope, nature, and kind of your product;

- let him know that from what you've heard about his (specific) product you think you could cite it in your product;

- let him know you intend to include complete follow-up details on this product, including its name, his address and phone number;

- inform him that if he cannot give you a perfect copy of this product, you will be happy to review a damaged copy. (Your goal, after all, is to get information . . . not to get a free product.)

- if even this is not possible, perhaps the publisher would kindly send you information about the product.

- let him know when your product is expected to be available for sale;

- to indicate your bona fides, provide the publisher with biographical details about you so he knows you're a reputable person;

- before concluding, invite the publisher to send you information about any other of his products or services that may be of interest to those who use what you're producing.

Note: if the publisher will not send you an actual copy of what you want to see, either request your local library to acquire it . . . or offer the publisher 50% of the retail price plus shipping costs ($2 usually does it). This is a discount virtually all publishers use at some point, and as they can still make money from this sale, it's worth suggesting . . . especially if the product you want to see seems likely to strengthen what you're creating and be useful as follow-up information for your prospects.

Letter To Information Source Requesting Specific Data

Those of us producing information products have all found ourselves in the situation of needing a fact . . . some additional data . . . verification of a quotation, *etc*. It's the nature of this business. Since this kind of thing happens all the time, prepare for it by creating a letter template that enables you to get your request out quickly.

This letter should:

- outline the project you have in hand, what kind of project it is and what is the subject;

- indicate the specific nature of your query . . . what do you need from the person you're writing to;

- ask if the person has any further information on the topic you're seeking or can refer you elsewhere;

- indicate when your project will be completed and, if you can, indicate that you'll be happy to send a copy to this source when it's available.

Include a stamped, self-addressed envelope with this letter so your corespondent can get back to you as quickly as possible. Of course, all of us needing this kind of information, need it yesterday.

Letter To Information Product Producers Requesting Permission To Sell Their Product

Later, I shall have more to say about the entire business of creating a profitable catalog that you can bind into your larger information products like booklets and books. Here I'd simply like to indicate what your letter to information product producers should say. This letter should:

- request permission to sell the particular item you're interested in;

- ask for their drop-ship discount terms (that is, where you don't warehouse but ship the names of your customers to the producer with your check, the order to be fulfilled by him);

- indicate that you give first choice to producers giving you a discount of at least 50% off the retail price;

- ask how much shipping for each individual order should be added to the retail price;

- ask if the publisher intends to have stock available for *at least* the next year. Remember, people tend to order from back-of-product catalogs for years, especially when the products themselves are available in libraries.

Here there is no necessary reason for you to tell the product source how you'll be promoting his product. But you can if you wish to.

In concluding this letter, ask if the product source sells anything else of particular interest to your designated market(s). He may well do so.

Sorting And Organizing Your Material

When I was a college student, I had a mentor who was a Pulitzer Prize winning historian. He wrote his books in a summer house on the grounds of his rambling villa overlooking the Pacific Ocean. One day while visiting him when he was in the throes of a book, I was given a most eye-opening experience. In his writing space, there were papers everywhere, thrown hither and yon. It looked more like the scene of vandalism than the work place of a distinguished scholar. I was astonished. What was the relationship between this "system" and the end result: the most limpid and graceful prose I had ever encountered . . . and still, twenty years later, have never seen surpassed? I don't know. But I do know this: unless you're certain you can produce this superior result, don't try either to duplicate such a "filing" system or justify your own disorganization!

Instead, you need a system for organizing the significant amounts of material which you'll undoubtedly need for your projects. Here's the one I suggest:

- Get a series of accordion filing envelopes, the ones which expand. Make sure you have at least one for each individual chapter and your samples section and catalog. Always make sure you have a few extra. Lengthy chapters may require you to review significant amounts of material and should, therefore, be divided into subsections as required.

• Duplicate your micro outline for each chapter or section and tape it on the outside of your file folder. Make sure each file folder is clearly marked with the chapter or section name. You want to see at a glance just what's supposed to go into this folder. Do not staple or paste your micro outline. Regular cellophane tape will do nicely, thank you. The reason? It's quite likely your outline will change, and you may wish to revise it and use a new one. Therefore, you've got to be able to remove the old outline easily.

• Now file your folders in a single drawer of a filing cabinet or stand them end to end on a book shelf. The important thing is that they are in logical order and that you can get easy access to them. Remember, you'll be filing things in them for months!

Once your files are arranged, it's time to create a Research Work Plan that ensures you'll have all the material you need . . . when you need it.

Your Research Work Plan

As you can see, creating an info-project is a labor of lists. Now you need another one: the Research Work Plan.

When you've become an info-product producer *par excellence*, your day will take on a natural rhythm. For me, this means writing in the morning when I'm freshest; creative work, as anyone knows who does it regularly, is the most draining work of all. Writing takes about half my day. The rest is spent doing a variety of tasks, including tracking down the data I need for my next project, including both the next new product and the next update of an existing product. Thus, for me, the afternoon is the right time to pursue my Research Work Plan.

How-to products, as I hope you now see, are composed of modules. Each is distinct and logically follows the one preceding. Linked together, these modules enable your reader/client to achieve what you've promised in your title. Your Research Work Plan enables you to stay on track, so that you have the material you need when you need it; thus, there need be no delays in creating your product.

The time to begin working on your Research Work Plan is the minute you've finished both your macro and micro product outlines, in other words the minute you know what kind of product you'll be producing, what it's to be composed of, and what kind of information you need. You're now ready to gather all the data you need.

You have already duplicated micro outlines and taped them to your accordion files. Now you need to place your complete outlines in a three-hole binder marked "Research Work Plan" and the name of this project. Your macro outline should appear first in this binder. It gives you an overview of what you're attempting to do. Then you should have a section for each part of your project, opened by its micro outline. After each micro outline should follow several pages of lined paper for your task notes and comments.

Note: you're probably already getting the very strong message that producing an info-product is infinitely easier if you're working on a personal computer. That's certainly true. Here's another place where that becomes clear. If you're working on computer, you can simply open a work plan file for each separate section of your project and input your task notes and comments each day.

If your chapter micro outlines are complete, what happens next is much, much easier for you. If they are, you'll know what work has to be done and can set about doing it. If they're not, you won't be clear on what you need until you need it . . . and this will inevitably retard your progress.

If we analyze a particular micro outline, you'll see how to create your own Research Work Plan. Let's take a "chapter" from the sixty-minute audio casette about securing free time on radio and television and how to use it to sell your products and services. This section deals with mastering the planning process and includes the following components:

- determining who your audience is;

- deciding which problems they want to solve, which aspirations they want to achieve so you can position your product or service as what they need;

- researching which radio and television stations reach your audience;

- how to get the names of the personnel you need to contact . . . and their addresses and phone numbers.

To create your Research Work Plan, you must analyze *each* section of *each* component of your info-product, keeping in mind that you will evaluate it according to these three points:

- This is information I already *have.*

- This is information I must *discover.*

- There is more information I shall *refer* my readers to.

Here's what these lines mean:

I Already Know . . .

If you look at an entry in your outline and can honestly say to yourself, "Because of my experience, education and prior research, I already know precisely how to do this thing and can tell my readers *everything* they need to know to do this," then you need do nothing more with this point until you begin writing.

Naturally, because of the good feelings you entertain about yourself and your level of knowledge of your subject, this may very well be just what you're tempted to say. But wait! You already know that most how-to materials are not precise, not specific, not helpful. Are you sure you really have *all* the material you need to provide precise advice; not just vapid what-to-do advice but step-by-step how-to-do-it guidelines? If you do, fine. If you don't, please don't attempt to delude yourself. You're only hurting your own reputation, the quality of the eventual product, and, of course, your readers.

I Must Discover . . .

Until you have some experience creating real, step-by-step how-to products, I think it likely that when you refer to your micro outline you'll probably have much more to discover. That's no sin. Not knowing something . . . having to do more work to discover just the kind of how-to information you need . . . is not awful. After all, to create my various products, I've been in touch with literally hundreds of specialists who have had the detailed information I needed . . . and that my readers needed to reach their objectives. I am happy to admit my ignorance, my need for other experts, if it helps me create a more perfect product and helps my readers reach their objectives.

No, it's not a sin admitting that your knowledge of any given topic is incomplete. But it *is* a sin — and very much against your own interests — to create an information product that doesn't deliver, in hard, diamond-like detail, *exactly* what you promised in your title, subtitle, and introduction. However, you can't deliver this kind of information unless you're either the ultimate specialist in what you are telling . . . and are prepared to provide the necessary details . . . or unless you have put yourself in touch with other information sources, both inanimate and human, until you're sure you do have the detailed information you need.

If you do not have this information, your job, made clear through your Research Work Plan, is to find it.

I Shall Refer . . .

The goal of all how-to products is to enable the reader/listener to achieve what your title promises. You know that. Thus, each of your products, each section of each of your products, must offer the kind of dense, practical information that enables this to take place. This is your first responsibility.

If this information comes from you, well and good. If more detailed information is available from you, perhaps in other products you create, you are fully entitled to say so. Cynics will say you're only doing this for your own good, but that's quite, quite wrong. True, you do benefit . . . but if you have material that will help your readers, telling them about it is very much in their interest. Don't let the complaints of some flatworm deter you from providing what will be helpful to your targeted market(s)!

If, however, you have benefitted from information and materials provided by other specialists, you must say that, too. Your job is to get and provide as much information as your customer needs to achieve his objective . . . and to make sure you give him the necessary follow-up information he needs to further his knowledge and get in touch with specialists who can provide even more detailed guidance, including the personalized attention he may desire. You can do this in your Resource Box, the place where you can thank those who have helped you and where you can offer them more practical gratitude by referring your interested readers to them for further assistance.

Memorize these three short sentences; they'll help you not only with your Research Work Plan but in structuring each module of your info-products.

Creating Your Research Work Plan

If you are the ultimate authority on *everything* you're writing about, or if you're sure before you start your project that you already have *everything* you need to complete it . . . if, in short, you have all you need, know precisely how to render it for the utmost benefit of your readers, and feel comfortable that you don't need another crumb of data, you can skip this section. Instead of reading it, write me a letter: I wish to worship at your feet, for such a one as you comes but once in a man's lifetime, and I do not want to miss the chance to gaze upon your astonishing countenance.

The rest of us need the Research Work Plan, because we have more work to do, beginning with reviewing each line of each of our micro outlines to see what must be done to get all the detailed information we need. To show you how this review takes place, take the line "determining who your audience is" in Chapter 1 of the sixty-minute audio cassette discussed above.

What you're telling your customer is that determining who his audience is will help him get the free radio and television time he wants. If you leave your advice at this level, you've certainly told him something important; you just haven't told him *how* to go about doing what needs to be done so he achieves the objective he wants. In other words, your job is woefully incomplete.

Since you've sensibly admitted that you are not the ultimate authority on this aspect of getting free radio and television time, it's now up to you to gather research information that will at once provide your reader with the crucial step-by-step information he needs to achieve this goal . . . and directs those who are most interested in this subject to additional resources that provide even more complete information.

Now, turn to your Research Work Plan binder. (Note: your Research Work Plan can, of course, be available on your personal computer. Simply open a file for each section. Title each file something like: 'product section name.plan'.)

Begin by writing down the question you need answered or information you need, thus: "I need information on how someone determines the audience he's trying to reach and what steps he needs to follow to make sure he is connecting with the right people."

Obviously, this is a marketing problem. You need a resource on basic marketing research. Now, it's up to you to find one. Either you'll locate a written source (or sources) . . . or a live authority, who might be willing to provide the information in return for a referral in your product.

Once you know what you need, you must set about finding it. Here a book called *Finding Facts Fast* (published by Ten Speed Press) will help. If you need to use a letter to get the information you need, you can use one of the templates discussed above. Otherwise, you'll use traditional research methods and facilities.

If you have written to someone else for the information you need, you must assume they *won't* answer you. Therefore, it's a very good idea to keep a copy of all your research requests. These can either be filed in the appropriate section file, or kept on diskette. In your Research Work Plan binder, however, you must indicate not only the date you contacted the specialist you're seeking information from, but when you need to follow up. My rule of thumb is that you follow up a first request for information within 10-15 business days; (four weeks is a good idea if your request is somewhat complicated). For this follow up, it's perfectly appropriate either to send a photocopy of your original letter with a short note . . . or to append this note to the foot of your computer-generated letter. There's no need to waste precious time and energy starting from scratch!

Follow these procedures for *each* item of *each* micro outline. Thus, even creating the shortest info-product may involve a good deal of research, letters, telephone calls, and, of course, the inevitable follow-up. Expect this. It's your job.

Now that you know what should be done, you'll know why most how-to writers don't do it. You must not only have a vision of what you want your customers to be able to do . . . must not only outline a roadmap that will enable them to do it . . . but you must gather *all* the information (from out of yourself and others) that will provide them with the detailed guidelines they need. Then you'll either provide this information directly . . . or indicate just how your customers can get it.

Of course, it's easier merely to say, "research which radio and television stations reach your market". It's much more difficult and time-consuming to provide the exact details your listener needs so he can, working all by himself, perhaps thousands of miles away from you, follow your directions as if you were standing over his shoulder whispering them in his ear. But I'll tell you something: you cannot be considered a how-to craftman, cannot conceivably be regarded as the consummate how-to professional, and will not reach the helpful heights to which the best of us in this field aspire unless you do take these pains . . . the pains that not only indicate you know what you're doing . . . but that you care about your prospects enough to give them what they need.

All but your dimmest customers (who will always be with us) will recognize when you have taken these pains . . . and they will know when you haven't. If you do, they reward you:

- not only by reading or listening to your product . . . but by using it, incorporating it into their lives . . . and allowing it to change the way they approach their time on this planet;

- buying other products and services you sell;

- referring you to their friends . . . thereby becoming your most effective marketing agents, and

- by calling, writing and visiting you gratefully to report, in the most direct and congenial way, what a significant difference you have made in their lives.

Are you prepared to throw all these benefits away just because it takes rather more work to create the product that ensures you get them? If you are, you're a fool, and a disgrace to this profession.

Final Note On Gathering The Information You Need

It's very much to your advantage to complete your Research Work Plan as soon as you can and get started finding the information you need. Why? Because:

- it always takes longer to get this information than you think it will;

- you don't always get the precise information you're seeking the first time you request it;

- new information often suggests new research paths that must be followed;

- it's often a good idea to return your rendering of the information you've received to the specialist who provided it to see if you've given it entirely correctly.

Invariably, the first time you seek to create a truly "how-to" how-to product, all these things will take much longer than you've reckoned. Later, as you become proficient in the art of creating these products, you'll be able correctly to access:

- just how much useful how-to information you have on any given topic;

- just what you need to complete the information you need and your readers want;

- just how long it will take to discover the right sources for this information and how many of them you need;

- just how long it will take them to respond to your first, second and, quite possibly, third attempt to get the data you need;

- just how long it will take you to understand what they've sent, mold it into what you need for your product, and, where necessary, check to ensure accuracy.

This is the wisdom that comes when you commit yourself to producing not just one but a series of how-to products and why subsequent products are produced so much more easily, and so much more completely, than any initial effort.

The Write Way

It is now time to begin the actual writing process . . . the process that will produce the first draft of your booklet or book, Special Report or audio-cassette script. Here are the steps that will ensure you produce a complete client-centered draft as expeditiously as possible. The first step is to determine when the project must be finished. Subsequent steps involve where you'll create, when you'll create and how you'll create.

Determining A Completion Date

I have a neighbor who's a writer and journalist. Years ago she signed a contract with a major publisher to produce her first book on a subject involving women's history. At the time the contract was signed, the subject was hot . . . and the publisher anxious to proceed. The publisher made it clear that they expected this writer to finish her book — and deliver it — by a certain date. This date was specified in the contract.

The writer, as writers often so, missed this deadline. And missed it . . . and missed it . . . and missed it. Ultimately, the publisher cancelled her contract and notified her it wanted her (now completely spent) advance back.

The book which was to have been the chief ornament of this journalist's career became instead a weighty albatross . . . draining her energies, destroying her self-confidence, the cause of legal threats and psychic unease. A couple of years ago, when she had only one last chapter to complete, I bet her that I'd write and publish two complete books, not a word of which was then written, before she'd finish (much less publish) that single chapter. With the publication of this book, I win that bet. This is one of the reasons why: I not only know when to start a book . . . I set a fixed date for completing it. I then arrange my life and work so that that inviolable date is reached. You must do the same.

Info-projects must not merely be begun; they must be finished. And finished on schedule. The less experience you have creating these projects, the more uncertain you will be about that completion date. Fair enough. But you must set a date notwithstanding.

In practice, I've found that I need about six months to gather the material for a complete book . . . and six months to create it. I need just a couple of weeks for an audio cassette . . . and two to three days to create the script. Special Reports can take as few as two days to research and write . . . or as much as a week. This gives you some idea how long is takes for an experienced writer to create any given product. At the beginning, it will take you longer.

Even so, before you can begin to write, you need to create a writing calendar. This calendar must contain the following parts:

- the street date you want your product available for sale and shipment;

- a break-down of actual production time. (This will be discussed later.)

- the date the final product will be delivered to your designer for page making and lay out.

- the date the index must be completed;

- the date the editor must complete his work on the typescript;

- the date you will complete the product end pages including samples sections, appendices, and end-of-product catalog;

- the date you will complete the conclusion and introduction;

- completion dates for each individual chapter.

Some Variables You Need To Take Into Account When You Consider Your Creation Schedule

There are a number of variables you need to consider in arranging your creation schedule.

- When you are creating a major info-product like a book and intend to have it sold by a distributor to the retail book trade, you want to have it available in enough time either for the fall selling season or the spring selling season. Thus, you need to complete a book either by the end of summer (for fall) or the end of fall (for spring).

- If you are selling through your own (quarterly) catalog, try to arrange your production schedule so that you have a new lead item at least twice a year. This includes a new product and an updated product. Remember, you can only have one lead item in a catalog. Make sure you space your products so that you can give them the attention they need.

- Once you've created your tentative creation schedule, check it with necessary production people . . . including any design, lay-out and product manufacturers you may wish to use. These people can confuse the best laid plans of mice and men.

- Remember, even when you're experienced, allow generous margins for error. It may take you a lot longer to complete a module . . . or you may just catch the flu and fall behind.

"So How Long Should I Allow Then?"

Each of us creates in a slightly different way. Fair enough. But it is my firm belief that when you set an objective and arrange your life accordingly, you have a far greater chance of reaching that objective than if you meander towards your goal. My poor neighbor is living proof of this; for reasons unknown, she refuses to set a fixed-in-cement date for finishing her book . . . and so the book remains unfinished, though she works on it constantly.

What I'm about to say is admittedly rather arbitrary. It may take you less time to complete a project; more likely, it will take you more. Either way, it's not only important to have fixed completion objectives for both the whole and all individual parts of your project . . . but to keep complete time records so, when you start planning for your next process, you'll be able to make more accurate estimates.

Daily Quota

Set yourself a quota of words you must write before you're finished for the day. This quota can either be in words or (if you're composing on a personal computer) in screens of data. Personally, my quota is writing 16 computer screens daily. This is a substantial amount. Beginners should set their daily production output at at least 500 words, or 3000 words per week; (the Lord rested on Sunday, and we can, too!) Given most how-to books are between about 75,000 to 80,000 words in length, this means you should be able to write the complete draft of a single book in just 160 days. As you become more proficient, raise your quota by modest amounts, until you are producing 750 words per day (Graham Greene's current quota) or even 1000 words a day.

Determining The Length of Chapters And Sections

From your macro outline, you now know how many chapters you intend to have in your product . . . and you know you need an introduction, conclusion and, perhaps, back pages with samples and catalog.

Your chapters should be relatively the same length. Thus, if you are creating a product of 80,000 words, here's how to divide up this amount:

- introduction, 2000 words maximum
- conclusion, 2000 words maximum
- 15 chapters at 5000 words each
- sample section of 15 pages of documents.

Setting Completion Dates For Each Section

From experience, I can tell you that even if your daily quota is just 500 words it's not going to take you four days to write your introduction and conclusion. Of these two, the conclusion is the easier to create, as you'll see from my discussion of how to write it a little later in this chapter. Thus allow for two days for your conclusion . . . three days for your introduction.

More importantly, let's look at how long it takes to write each chapter. For chapters of 5000 words each, I suggest you allow at least two weeks to write them, when you are at the 500 words per day level. Personally, I like to start a chapter on a Monday whenever possible and finish it on a Friday or Saturday. When you're just starting out, allowing yourself two weeks to finish a 5000 word chapter enables you to start on a Monday and finish and revise it over the course of two weeks . . . starting your next chapter a fortnight later. This makes a nice, neat package which I recommend to you.

Factoring In The Imp Of The Uncertain

Particularly when you have little or no experience creating how-to products, I suggest you give yourself a margin of error equal to 50% of the time you expect to produce your product. This means that if you expect to produce 15 chapters in 25 weeks, allow yourself 37 weeks to do so. Set your completion dates accordingly. Unless you have major production or personal problems in this period, this should give you sufficient protection against life's sapping viccisitudes.

A Little Secret You Should Know

One of the things I have learned from the process of writing ten books is that the book you finished, notwithstanding the most complete and polished of outlines, is always rather different from the book you started off thinking you were writing. Indeed, you may be well into your project, thirty or even forty percent into it, before you have a perfectly precise idea of the real book you're writing and where this project is going. This is perfectly natural.

Natural though this is, it nonetheless has consequences. Your outline will probably have to be revised . . . new information may have to be found . . . and, certainly, major changes will have to be made in your early chapters. Don't despair about any of this. Do plan for it.

Unless you are amazingly clear about the project you're creating, about your audience, about what you want to say and how you want to say it, it's very likely you'll have to undergo this recasting process. Fortunately, you've built in a 50% margin of error in the time you need to create your product. This is one of the major reasons why you need it.

Post Your Schedule

My hero Winston Churchill used to say that even if you didn't have the time to read books, it was a good idea to have them around, because of their osmotic effect. You'd be a better person just for having them present in your life. I concur. I also believe in having a production schedule posted . . . even if you may not make every deadline on it. Just by having a production schedule . . . and by having it prominently posted in your writing space . . . and written into your calendar . . . you'll be far likelier to make your deadlines than if you don't do this. Thus after you've computed all your deadlines, create a Deadline Chart. List what you want to finish, and the day and date you expect to finish it, thus: "Chapter 3: Your Step-By-Step Creation Process, Friday, March 24." Post the outline with all these dates where you will ALWAYS see them. By always keeping the next crucial date in your completion process in mind, you stand a far better chance of reaching it . . . just when you needed to.

When You Fall Behind In Your Schedule

One of the reason I think my downstairs neighbor is having such trouble finishing her project is because her self-esteem is so low. She's let herself down on so many occasions, she wonders if she can ever rise to the occasion again. So she lacerates herself . . . and despairs. All right, she *does* deserve twenty lashes with a wet noodle . . . but she also needs to move beyond despair, start setting standards, living up to them and generally behaving in a professional way. She has fallen behind her schedule (way, way behind) . . . but that doesn't mean setting a deadline is wrong. It simply means she needs a new deadline . . . and a renewed dedication to achieving it.

Thus, if you fall behind your schedule (even with its generous allocation of extra time), don't despair. If you've never produced this way before, if you've never tried to create a product through management by objectives procedures, it's very likely you won't meet your deadlines — the first time. If you feel you've been working as productively as you can (be honest!) and have been in your writing place each day plugging away, it's clear your initial estimates were not sufficiently realistic. It's therefore time to revise your outline. Do so now.

If, on the other hand, you've been bogged down in the early chapters of what you're producing, don't automatically assume later chapters will take as long. It always takes longer to get into your production stride than to complete an argument once you know where it's going.

Still, for the sake of your positive mental outlook, it's better to have an outline with realistic completion deadlines than it is to look each day at an outline that shows you falling further and further behind, thereby undermining your confidence. If this is the way you feel, don't wait another minute to revise that outline. DO IT TODAY!

A Few Hints About Using This Deadline Information

As I've already said, you need to post your deadline information prominently. Put it on the wall right behind your computer . . . or in front of your writing desk. Each night before you go to bed remind yourself of the deadline you're currently working on; remind yourself of what your daily quota must be on the morrow. See that deadline . . . imagine that quota. Now picture yourself achieving both.

You may think this foolish . . . possibly beneath your dignity as a renowned specialist and authority in your field. But let me tell you something: I do this and I finish a major new book each year, a couple dozen Special Reports and audio cassettes . . . and still run, single handedly, a catalog and marketing consulting business. My downstairs neighbor, bright, capable, qualified, educated, doesn't do this . . . and won't. And so for the last two years has been fruitlessly mired in just one chapter which is today no more near completion than it was when I made my bet with her.

Now, which course of action do you think makes the most sense for you?

Where & When To Write

Recently, a young writer called me who'd read an article I'd written. Since he knew I was accessible, he called for some advice about his career. Having been a struggling young writer once myself, I used some of my limited store of human kindness to answer questions which he put to me over the course of several weeks.

One of the first things I discovered about this fellow was that he had no special place in which to write. Sometimes he wrote on his computer in his room . . . sometimes in the family garage . . . sometimes (to my horror) he wrote in the living room in front of the television set. But it wasn't just that the places changed; the times also changed. Sometimes he wrote in the morning, sometimes in the afternoon; sometimes in the dead of night until the sun came up (how very romantic).

And he wondered why he couldn't complete a coherent draft!

If you're to succeed as an information product producer, you must train yourself as the Russian scientist Pavlov trained his dogs; that is, you must accustom yourself to moving into a "writing mode" merely by positioning yourself in one place, where, come hell or high water, you *will* write.

You must position yourself in this place at the *same* time *every* day . . . and stay there until a certain time every day. During that time, you may do nothing more than Oscar Wilde said he did on a given day:"In the morning I put in a comma, and in the afternoon I took it out again." Even so, you will be there, ready, willing, and able to create.

During this time, you should remain incommunicado. While in your writing mode, in your writing place, you have only three responsibilities:

- to the material itself. It must be shaped, molded, beaten and kneaded into the kind of step-by-step information your customers are waiting for (even though, right now, they may not know it themselves);

- to those customers. Their future success in eradicating the pain that afflicts them, the loss they do not wish to sustain, or achieving the objective they desire depends solely on the quality of the work you do now, and, of course,

- to yourself. No one is going to stand over you and beat you with a stick so you produce. No one will monitor your daily output. No one will set deadlines for you. And no one will ever care as much as you do whether you — you! — produce a valuable, even crucial, piece of problem-solving prose. You must do all these things for yourself . . . without prompting, without prodding, guided only by your inner voice and by your resolute conviction that what you're doing is important and must be done completely, responsibly.

For these three pivotal reasons:

- ignore your telephone. Your answering machine can take your messages and your orders.

- ignore the mundane interruptions incessantly spawned by our picayune era. They will not help you produce the quality of prose you are now dedicated to creating.

- ignore the dust that is swelling in your corners and is beginning its relentless march across your room . . . ignore the riot of spring flowers erupting within eyeshot (now there is no time to stop and smell them) . . . ignore *whatever* threatens the task which must be done today . . . and which cannot be done by anyone so well as by you. This is your mission . . . dedicate yourself to it! And let all the other things, things which might at other times and places be so significant, let them go, I say . . . until you have met the three responsibilities which are yours alone.

Each Day Confront Your Reader . . . Let His Needs And Wants Be Your Guide

Many writers have privately anguished and publicly lamented the agony with which each day they approach the empty page. I am not one of them, and I'll tell you why. Each day I remember why I am creating . . . and for whom. I am not writing for myself . . . I am writing for a designated individual. An individual in pain . . . an individual who fears loss . . . and individual who wishes to achieve some objective. This individual is looking to me for assistance.

As I begin to write, I *see* this person . . . and write *for* her, *to* her. My day's work is nothing more than an extended, very personal, intensely empathetic, consulting session via computer. My job is to understand what my designated and constantly considered prospect wishes to achieve . . . to understand what she needs from me so she gets what she wants . . . to understand what may inhibit her; where she needs practical, technical advice, where the support and encouragement of a friend.

For this person, though she may not know me yet, is certainly my friend. And I intend to act as her friend . . . from the very first words of this project, its title, right through to the very last. Because I am her friend, the style and presentation of my information follows as a matter of course. How many friends do you speak to in a dull, dry monotone . . . in the third person . . . arrogating a superior place to yourself . . . and permanently relegating them to the status of reverential devotee?

You may be such a person. Your "friends" may be such people. God knows, in my neighborhood in Harvard Square there are stars enough who feel that only they must shine and that any other body in the firmament is a threat to their heavenly position. They have no friends. They have only followers. That this is a problem is now generally apparent. The March, 1989 issue of *Boston Magazine* has as its cover story an article on the death of friendship. Well, how can there possibly be friendship if friends are not willing to truly be friends . . . to delight in their friends, savor them, chide them, argue, scold, cajole, and disagree with them risking the perils of honesty without which there can be no love? Friendship — and all its attendant rewards — dies when we think only in terms of markets . . . and not in terms of what it takes to build a sustaining relationship.

Well, I have news for you. You need to be a friend to your readers . . . you need to tell them the truth, the whole truth, and nothing but the truth. Even if they don't always like it. Even if they sometimes rebel and criticize you for it. Even if they don't appreciate it. You need to tell the truth because they need it; because both they and you yourself need you to be a person of the utmost integrity and authenticity . . . to speak directly, bluntly, forcefully . . . with all your knowledge, enthusiasm, intensity . . . and every last drop of your love and human empathy.

This means you must move beyond creating a product . . . and towards building a relationship through the medium of the product you are creating. To do this, you must:

- visualize your prospect and understand his situation;

- speak directly to him . . . you can't have a relationship with a person when you're using the third-person. Use the second.

- ensure that your product is arranged around benefits. Your title presents the major benefit . . . but *each* chapter, *each* section must promise additional benefits. Just as you cannot continue a meaningful marriage in which the romance is gone . . . so you cannot hope to keep your reader's interest if you do not continue to give him additional benefits . . . and to compel his further interest and commitment to what you're saying.

- keep sentences short and action oriented . . . remembering that your objective and your reader's desire is to move that reader from where he no longer wishes to be to a better, more beneficial place . . . carried there by your on-rushing prose and streamlined delivery.

Keeping these points in mind, I'd like to walk you through the several significant sections from which a how-to product is created, suggesting what should be in them and why. These sections include:

- the introduction
- the how-to chapters
- the conclusion
- the samples section
- the end-of-product catalog

How To Create A Client-Centered Introduction

A client-centered introduction follows naturally from your client-centered title. It sets the stage for the helpful information that follows . . . but it does more. It reinforces the relationship you are beginning with your reader/client.

Your introduction begins by using one of these openings:

- an indication of the reader/listener's pain . . . and how you can help remove it, or

- an indication of the fearful loss the reader/listener could sustain . . . and how you can help prevent it, or

- an indication of the delicious aspiration the reader/listener wishes to achieve . . . and how you can help him get it.

In short, benefits!

Remind your reader/listener of his terrible pain . . . of the loss he fears and wishes to avoid . . . or the aspiration he desires to achieve.

Then let him know he can achieve what he wants to achieve working with you . . . and your product!

This sets up the right structure for your product:

* You hurt. I help.
* You fear. I help.
* You want. I help.

Understand that this is what all info-products are really about.

After you've announced you can help, tell the prospect what he'll find in your product. But be careful. Most people tell you the *features* of their product . . . what that product contains. Yet here again your reader/listener doesn't want features . . . *he wants benefits*. He doesn't want a chapter on how to get on the radio. He wants a chapter on how to get free time on radio and use it to sell more of his products and services so he makes more money for less cost. Make sure you understand the difference.

He doesn't want a chapter on marketing. He wants a chapter on how to write an ad for his Sunday newspaper that will get someone looking for a house to call him . . . and not someone else. Oh, yes, he wants benefits.

How-to product creators often strike me as some of the most obtuse people alive. They think that just because someone's got their product in their hand (just because they may already have bought it) their job of motivating their reader/listener to stay with them is over. THAT'S RIDICULOUS!

Your prospect, be he a purchaser of your product or merely a browser, can put it down at any moment . . . thereby costing you all the substantial benefits that come from his continuing investment in and commitment to your product. Don't let this happen to you! Retain his commitment, rekindle his enthusiasm *every* chance you get . . . by continuing to drive home the benefits he gets . . . if only he stays with you.

Thus, in this section of the introduction your mission is clear: define what your product offers not in terms of features, but in terms of benefits. Go through each chapter and ask yourself, "What's in this section that benefits my reader? How can I mold and present these benefits so they are most starkly and cogently delivered to my reader?" These are the key questions . . . they will always be the key questions . . . and you must learn how to answer them with maximum client-centered impact.

After you've outlined the benefit-contents of your product, including the benefit of both your samples section and end-of-product catalog (which is not just a device to make sales for you, of course, but a means of refining what your reader/listener needs to achieve his objective), provide some details about yourself.

When you're beginning a relationship with someone, it's perfectly natural, indeed expected, that you share some relevant information about yourself. That must happen here, too. But, please, make sure that what you're providing is germane to this product. In other words, people are not looking for the standard biographical information that may be appropriate on a resumé but is certainly out of place here. They don't want to know the year you were born, or your hobbies, or where you went to school or any of these tepid facts . . . unless they are somehow relevant to your standing as a specialist who should be heeded. Thus, it is most pertinent in anything I write about home-based businesses to inform my reader that I run such a business, but it is decidedly beside the point when I set down my fund raising techniques for nonprofit organizations.

Moreover, the facts that you do present must be rendered in such a way that they are pertinent to the prospect; that they speak to him and not just provide information about you. Thus, if you have a certain degree, what possible benefit is that to your reader? If you've been in practice for so many years, why does that matter to your reader? If you're a duck hunter (I'm taking this from the introduction of a how-to book that passed my desk recently!), what does this matter to your reader . . . unless you are writing a book about duck hunting; (sadly, this author wasn't).

In short, *every* fact that you present about yourself must be repositioned so that it is not about you but of value and use to your reader/listener. Remember, this is not an opportunity for you to wax poetic about your stupendous achievements, but to convince your reader that you are the kind of person worthy of his time, trust, and friendship. Have you done this? Or have you merely engaged in the usual kind of egotistical vainglory that characterizes most how-to authors?

Before winding up this short but crucial introduction, invite your reader to stay in touch with you. Tell him how you can be of further assistance, and what he needs to do (hopefully, nothing more than drop you a letter to a specified address, or, better, call you right away) to take more personal advantage of what you know and can do.

Take a minute and leaf through the introductions of any of the how-to materials you happen to have. I defy you to find even one that provides this invitation . . . and the means to take advantage of it. Not even 1% of the how-to products produced in this country have this invitation and this necessary follow-up information. Incredible!

But think! Just this morning, while I was still immersed in my breakfast newspaper, the telephone rang. It was a fellow from the Metro Boston area with a software development firm. He had read one of my articles on CompuServe the day before (Sunday) and couldn't wait to talk to me . . . first to get one of my books and then to become his consultant for some direct response marketing he was creating. I took his credit card information and made the immediate sale . . . and scheduled an consulting appointment for him. I didn't have to persuade him about anything . . . didn't have to establish who I was . . . didn't have to overcome his objections. Didn't have to do anything except act like the helping professional I am.

Why did this happen? Because he responded to my invitation to contact him . . . an invitation that everything I produce carries . . . and which the introduction to your info-product must carry, too.

A Note On Format

Most how-to products open with the standard introduction, that is with a few words from the product's creator about what his reader will find. It reads rather like a proclamation. When I was young and green in the publishing trade, I wrote such introductions myself; I thought this form had been handed down with the Ten Commandments. But in fact, as a client-centered specialist, an empathetic helper, you can do much better.

That's why I suggest you use a letter format for your introduction. Turn your introduction into a friendly letter . . . a letter that speaks directly to your prospect about his pains, fears, and aspirations. About what will happen to him if he does nothing to eradicate those pains, deal with those fears, and achieve those aspirations. Speak to him plainly, bluntly, directly, just as a real friend would. Then tell him how you can help and what to do if he needs more assistance.

End this letter, just as you would a letter to a friend, with a signature. As you can see from the introduction to this book, I simply sign "Jeffrey," the same signature that I use for all my friendly correspondence and which has now become my habitual business signature, too. In short, if you want to appear to be a friend, act like a friend. Don't put barriers between you and your reader/listener. Tear barriers down . . . always remembering that this is not just an important act of humanity . . . but the most sensible way to stimulate your readers to trust and call on you for further assistance.

A Few Last Words About Your Introduction

If you want your reader/listener to trust you — and, yes, like you — you must speak to his situation . . . not yours. He can't be expected to be interested in your personal motives for creating this product . . . how proud you are . . . how proud your spouse is . . . how ecstatic your parents. What he wants to know is: do you understand my situation? Do you know what my pain feels like? Do you understand what it's like to have the kinds of fears that bedevil me? Do you truly know what it's like to be seized by the aspiration that possesses me . . . and not to know how to go about achieving it?

Well, do you know these things . . . or do you only know what the experience of creating this product was like for you?

Thus, if you wish to establish rapport with your reader/listener (and I assure you, you do), you must truly understand his situation. You must gather information about:

- his pain. What is his pain like? What happens because he's in pain . . . both to himself . . . and to others who suffer as a result? How long does the pain last? What happens if it goes untreated? What kind of life does a person with this kind of pain lead?

- his fear of loss. What happens if this reader/listener does lose what he fears losing? What happens to him . . . and to those connected to him? What will he have to do to repair the loss or make it good? What will his situation be if he endures this much feared loss?

- his desire to achieve an objective. What is this objective like? What will having it mean? Both to himself . . . and to those connected to him? What will failing to achieve it mean . . . to himself and to others?

You establish a relationship with someone by projecting yourself into their situation . . . by understanding just what their situation is like. In short, by empathizing. Sadly, the bulk of how-to product producers are more interested in achieving their own objectives than in understanding the reader/client's goals. They are more committed to their information than to their audiences. THIS IS WRONG!

How-to products, *all* how-to products, begin with empathy . . . begin with the creator's understanding of his prospect. But there's more. Not only must the creator understand his prospect . . . but that prospect must know and feel that the product creator understands him. Out of this mutual empathetic knowledge their relationship truly begins.

But my question to you is this: how do you find the kind of information that is necessary to this process . . . the information about the prospect's pain . . . his fears . . . and his aspirations?

Why, dear reader, you work to gather it . . . through your research and your ongoing contacts with the people you say you want to help.

If you are writing to people in pain . . . why, then, you need a Pain File. Into this file goes all the information about their pain you can possibly discover. Include:

- the number of people suffering from this pain;

- projections of the greater number who will suffer in the years ahead;

- descriptions of what the pain feels like;

- descriptions of both those who suffer from the pain, and those who suffer because of the sufferer;

- information on what happens when the pain (or the malady generating it) is not treated.

If you are writing to people who fear loss . . . why, then, you need a Fear File. Into this file place information about:

- the number of people who suffer this loss yearly;

- whether more are projected to suffer it in the years ahead;

- how much this loss costs;

- how people feel when they sustain this loss;

- what people who sustain this loss have to do because of it;

- what this loss does not only to him who sustains it but others who are connected to him;

- what happens when people sustain this loss.

If you are writing to people who want to achieve an aspiration, you need an Aspiration File. Into this file place this kind of information:

- descriptions of what it feels like to achieve this goal;

- how many people are trying to achieve it;

- how few succeed;

- what happens to your life when you achieve this goal . . . both to you and others you love;

- what happens to your life if you fail to achieve this goal.

Sharing A Little Secret

Needless to say there are many places you can find this kind of information. But I'll share a little secret with you: your prospects, the people you are creating your info-product for, give you the very best material. They'll tell you . . . in the most direct, pungent and personal way . . . about their pains, their fear of loss, their galloping aspirations. All you have to do is write down what they say and file it properly for future reference.

Do you?

I bet you don't. Why not? Is it because you don't yet think this information important? Because you are intent on creating a product . . . not entering into an instructive dialogue with an individual who needs you? Because you are so centered on yourself and your own needs . . . on your own product and objectives that you've allowed the key organ in this process to atrophy: your ear. I tell you true: every day I hear my prospects tell me about their pain, their fears, their aspirations. Merely by indicating my receptivity to and interest in what they say they tell me more . . . in fact, they tell me things that make my books and articles, my audio cassettes and Special Reports come alive. They give me the seasoning of reality that enriches my products. Just as they will do to yours . . . because when we hear this authentic voice of our audience we know what we must do and say to help them.

The Importance Of This Material

What you learn about your prospects in this way is important for several reasons. It helps create a direct, client-centered introduction that is just the right beginning for your product. But more than that, this is information you can use in all your marketing efforts to sell this product. This information will improve your ads, your cover letters, your brochures . . . everything you produce in an attempt to motivate your prospect to take immediate action to buy what you're producing. We shall discuss these subjects later, but for now remember this: you are not producing a product. You are entering into a relationship with your reader/listener. This relationship will inform all that you do not simply to create but also to sell your product. The minute you revert merely to producing a product . . . merely to disseminating information . . . merely to showing yourself as a sublime and must-be-heeded authority is the moment you have torpedoed yourself and destroyed the one thing that must emanate from your product: a relationship with your reader/listener from which so many benefits spring.

Your Introduction's Length

And how long should this most-important piece of prose actually be? Not long. In about 2,000-3,000 words you can achieve what you need to achieve and can further the relationship you need to develop. In this short compass, you will have done enough to convince your reader/listener that you are truly a knowledgeable, compassionate, empathetic individual . . . or merely another stuffed-shirt interested only in your own aggrandizement and glorification. In just about 2000 words . . .

The How-To Chapters

What follows your introduction is as many how-to chapters as you have decided are necessary to move your designated prospect from where he is now . . . to where he wants to be; that is, to the benefit promised in your title and introduction. These chapters are composed of:

- benefit headlines

- steps ordered logically by "what next?" thinking to achieve this benefit;

- additional subheadings dividing the material presented and assisting the reader's movement to the next point, and

- Resource Boxes that provide crucial data for those interested in more detailed information and procedural refinements.

Let's look at each of these parts in turn.

Benefit Headlines

If the overall title of your product promises the ultimate benefit that product delivers, so each individal section, each chapter must begin with a headline that promises the benefit your reader/listener derives from it. Again, I ask you, which chapter headline do you think stronger?

1. "Selecting The Best Ads"
2. "Selecting The Best Ads For The Kind Of Job You Want"

The first is a chapter title from a book on getting a job using classified ads. Other chapter titles from this book include: "Job Hunters," "Following-Up," and "Maximizing Time Usage."

Title #2 I just made up.

What's the difference between #1 and #2? Just this: title #1 leaves the prospect scratching his head and saying to himself, "So what? What's in this for me?" In this case, the author is asking a lot of the reader . . . asking him to figure out what's in this chapter and why the prospect should bother to read it. There's no benefit . . . it is, in short, steak, not sizzle.

On the other hand, while title #2 probably won't win any copywriting prizes, it is a client-centered title. It sums up just what the client wants to achieve (the only reason he knows of for reading these ads is to get the job he wants) and lets him know this is where he gets that crucial information. Thus, it is a client- and not a product-centered title.

When you write this kind of title, you get another important structural benefit: arranging your material becomes a whole lot easier and more logical. It naturally follows the headline and moves to deliver the benefit it promises.

Steps Ordered Logically

Take chapter headline #2 "Selecting The Right Ads For The Kind Of Job You Want". To reach this objective means following a finite series of logical steps. You are the empathetic specialist. You know what your reader wants to achieve and precisely how he must go about achieving it. Your headline is the "what the reader wants to achieve"; the chapter itself is the how, divided into logical steps.

Writing this chapter, and all how-to info-product chapters, now follows with relentless logic:

1. state the client-centered benefit this chapter delivers;

2. tell the first thing, the *very first thing*, your reader must do to start achieving this objective.

3. tell the second thing, the thing that logically follows from the first;

4. tell the third thing, *etc., etc., etc.*

Each thing that you tell must be fully supported by your candid and complete:

- guidelines
- steps
- processes

- directions
- techniques
- pointers
- rules
- prescriptions.

By anything, in short, that enables the prospect to achieve the benefit you have promised in this chapter . . . and which therefore assists him in achieving the overall benefit of the product itself.

Let's take a look at a recent how-to book to see if this crucial information was included. The book is *How To Market To Consumers: Ten Ways To Win* by Dr. John A. Quelch, Professor at the Harvard Business School (John Wiley, 1989). In his chapter entitled "Quality Marketing", Quelch has a subsection entitled "The Customer Service Program". It begins:

"The success of the marketing program will depend as much on effective implementation as on sound analysis and research. After reviewing several customer service organizations in a variety of industries, we believe that managers should concentrate on the following seven guidelines for effective program implementation:

1. Educate your customers. Customers must be taught both how to use and how not to use a product. And through appropriate training programs, companies can reduce the chances of calls for highly trained service personnel to solve simple problems . . .

2. Educate your employees. In many organizations, employees view the customer with a problem as an annoyance rather than as a source of information. A marketing program is often needed to change such negative atttitudes and to convince employees not only that customers are the ultimate judge of quality but also that their criticisms should be respected and acted on immediately."

Five other points follow this format.

By now you know enough to realize that this prose, published by one of America's premier publishers, is complete and unadulterated drivel, a parody of what it ought to be.

Let's examine it from the top:

1. The chapter headline "Quality Marketing" is a feature . . . not a benefit. Who is the author speaking to? What does this person want? Does he

want "quality marketing," or does he want the benefit that such marketing supposedly ensures? I think you know, don't you?

2. Take the section headline "The Customer Service Program." This is more of the same! A "program" is a feature, not a benefit. What advantage will the reader derive from both this section and a properly functioning customer service program? Either the author doesn't know . . . or he doesn't say. Either way, it's deplorable.

There's also a subtle, but important problem with the subheadings. Quelch uses nouns, features. On the other hand, strong chapter titles and subtitles often begin with an action verb . . . begin, that is, with an indication of movement . . . that the reader is being helped from Point A to Point B. That's what how-to information is supposed to do.

Instead, Quelch plunks down his headlines like they are set in cement. "Here's this thing," he seems to say, "do with it as you will." That's quite, quite mistaken. The empathetic, forward-looking, always progressive how-to product creator is committed to moving his prospect along . . . not plunking down stuff in front of him and getting him to figure out what's in it for him, as Quelch does.

3. The root of Quelch's problem becomes very clear when we look at the first paragraph following the chapter title. The title indicates that this is a book by one John A. Quelch. But here he introduces the invidious pronoun "we". Now, how many times have you in a personal conversation with a friend used the imperial "we" when you meant "I." I trust, hope and implore that you have never done this pompous thing. Yet this is what Quelch does.

Why doesn't he say, "I?" Why doesn't he speak directly to his prospect? I don't know. But I can guess: because he thinks his is the professional way to speak to someone. Well, it isn't. It's an obstacle . . . a barrier . . . something that hinders true human empathy and communication.

But worse is to come!

4. Read the sections beginning "Educate Your Customers" and "Educate Your Employees." Of course, one again feels as if one were in the majestic presence of a punctilious school master. Educate, indeed! But worse, what follows is straight "what to" writing without a "how-to-do-it" line in the bunch. Our expert says customers must be educated, (though he doesn't tell us the benefits we get if we follow this sage advice, leaving us to deduce them for ourselves). But he doesn't give us the steps we need to educate them. So we're left hanging. All right Herr Professor

Doktor, we accept your *diktat*. But where, oh where is what we need to do this eminently worthwhile and sensible thing? Where, indeed? "That, my good man, is your affair entirely," this author and all his kind seem to say.

And yet . . . a supposedly intelligent and well-meaning author considers this how-to advice;
• his editor considers this how-to advice;
• his publisher considers this how-to advice . . ..

. . . And so do his sisters and his aunts and his cousins reckoned by the dozens. They all, with apologies to Gilbert and Sullivan, consider this how-to advice!!!

But we don't, do we? We consider it as close to how-to advice as were the clothes on the naked emperor to the real threads we're wearing today.

The how-to chapters are the heart of a how-to product. If your introduction establishes rapport and empathy with your reader/listener, the product itself firmly takes that reader/listener in hand and moves him by measured steps from where he no longer wishes to be right through to where he most assuredly wants to be. DO YOU UNDERSTAND THIS?

These chapters have a structure . . . they begin with a benefit, the "where we are going" headline. They then include all the logical steps one needs to take to reach this valued objective. The chapter is not finished, is indeed scarcely begun, if you merely tell what the prospect needs to achieve without giving step-by-step guidelines on getting there. And all your credentials . . . all your degrees, all your years of experience, all your positions of eminence and authority do not, I say, matter a whit in the reckoning if you cannot give the precise guidelines your reader/listener needs.

Subheadings Dividing The Material And Acting As Helpful Directional Signals To Your Reader/Listener

If the chapter headline is the objective of your journey, and the detailed steps you provide constitute the yellow brick road that takes your reader/listener there, the subheadings you use in any individual chapter are the necessary directional signals that make it easier for your reader to know where he is and where he is going.

Think of these signals thus: the title of your product is the overall, the grand benefit your prospect gets by using what you've created. The chapter titles are major benefits the prospect gets. By assembling all these major benefits, your prospect must succeed in achieving the grand objective. And the subheadings are minor benefits which move the prospect to the achievement of the major benefits . . . and thus to the grand benefit.

Properly Using Subheadings

You must break your material regularly . . . both for ease of comprehension and so your reader/listener can stop to think about what he has just read or heard. These breaks should occur at logical intervals.

Say you're writing a book about how to get free time from all media outlets, print and electronic, and you have a chapter about how to get on a radio show and use it to sell your products and services.

As you already know, you need to create an outline for this chapter . . . an outline that presents in logical order the steps your reader must follow to reach this objective and so secure the overall objective of the product.

Each step needs a subheading . . . an indication of the benefit the reader will get in this short section. If he wants that benefit, he'll stay with you; if he doesn't, he'll skip over it. This subheading should alert the reader to the benefits he is getting in this section . . . and also function as a directional signal pointing him ahead to the next subheading and the next benefit section. Thus, by reading the subheadings alone, you'd get a pretty good idea of what the chapter contains and the benefits it offers. Which is just how it ought to be.

Resource Boxes That Provide Crucial Data

When you come to the end of one of your subsections, read it. Have you really supplied step-by-step guidelines, a detailed roadmap to take your reader to where he wants to go? Or have you like Herr Professor Doktor Quelch merely told him where he ought to go . . . and then mosied over to the bar to amuse yourself while he figured out how to get there?

Have you provided everything your reader/listener needs to achieve this objective . . . or are there other details which might also help him? Of course, as many of these details as possible and as are necessary to achieve the objective ought to be in this section. But with the best will in the world, it is often necessary to leave some information out, especially if it is not quite germane to the topic at hand. Thus, if you were presenting material on how to get on radio shows and use them to sell products, a detailed discussion of how to get your own radio show might be out of place because it pertained to many fewer people. Nonetheless, these people, too, are entitled to detailed guidelines and further information. This is why there are Resource Boxes.

A Resource Box gives the interested reader detailed information about where to look for further assistance on any given topic. Such assistance may include printed materials . . . or actual specialists on the topic. Here's where you provide names, addresses, telephone numbers . . . anything that practically directs your reader to further help. Here, too, you can thank specialists who have provided assistance to you . . . and direct your readers to them.

A Resource Box is an indication that the committed reader's learning process is never-ending; that further refinements are necessary for all of us and that there is some particular person, some particular source that can be of the utmost assistance . . . if only the reader has the sense to follow up appropriately.

As for you, the creator, using Resource Boxes establishes you as not only a helpful person . . . but an honest person. Neither you nor I know everything. Why pretend that we do? We all owe debts of gratitude to those who have helped us. Why shouldn't we do what we can for them? This argument seems so compelling to me I never thought I'd ever meet an individual to dispute it. But just recently I did.

I know a fellow in California who's writing a book on buying residential properties about to go into default because of unpaid mortgages. Part of this book involves telling his readers how to create a marketing program to identify clients and close sales, and in this connection he made use of some of my material. Without crediting me. When I brought this to his attention, he was startled . . . and, initially, refused to consider any such acknowledgement. Why?

Perhaps he thought that if he acknowledged a debt to others, he would appear to his readers to be less than the superman of his own aspirations. Or perhaps he was just pulling a fast one. Who can say? But what I can say is this: I find such people ill bred and disgusting . . . the kind of people one feels tainted after dealing with. Is succeeding in this way really worth the moral price one must pay in the hardening of one's soul and the shrinking of one's humanity? It is not. This is why I not only to urge you to provide Resource Boxes as directional signals to your readers for their future betterment, but for your own good, too, as a way of thanking the many, many people who have helped give you the knowledge from which you are now benefitting.

Is Your Chapter Finished?

When you have followed these steps, your chapter ought to be finished. But just before you clap your hands and leap for joy, do take a few minutes to answer these questions:

- Does your chapter headline offer a benefit your reader/listener wants to achieve . . . or just a feature that's about the product itself?

- Is the chapter rigorously arranged in absolutely logical fashion?

- Do you have a client-centered subheading for each logical break in your material to suggest the next benefit your reader is getting?

- Is the information you've presented so ordered that it constitutes a roadmap of explicit guidelines that your reader can follow to reach his objectives?

- And, finally, have you presented in a Resource Box such follow-up guidelines as may be necessary, so interested readers can get the refinements and additional information they truly need to master the subject you're writing about?

If you have, congratulations. You have now entered the elite universe of real how-to product creators . . . people who create not merely for themselves, but for the benefit of their designated prospects. You deserve to feel . . . should feel . . . proud of yourself, for what you have done is rare in this field, deserving of the utmost praise.

But! If upon reviewing your creation you discover gaps, assumptions, presumptions, black holes and loop-holes such as distinguish our federal tax code, you are not finished. Yes, you may be tired. Yes, you may have tried hard. Yes, you may think you've done the best you could do. But I challenge you . . . and I certainly tell you . . . YOU ARE NOT FINISHED. Not until you have produced the kind of detailed, step-by-step guidelines your reader/listener is relying on you to provide. This is your mission. Accomplish it.

Your Samples Section

In considering your product's Samples Section, we move from its heart to the end pages. Now in all fairness to other writers, you may not wish to place all your samples at the end of your product. All right.

My rule of thumb is this: if you need to present only a few samples, by all means place them in the text. But if you have many samples, say a couple of dozen, placing them in the text will disrupt the flow of your narrative. *This cannot be allowed.* When your reader is caught up in your argument, moving nicely along from benefit to benefit, don't stop him to look at a document that he can very well review later. Let him finish your case . . . then he can leaf to the appropriate section and study the necessary sample.

Wherever you put your sample documents is less significant than several other considerations you must keep in mind about them. Your sample documents must:

- provide specific illustrations of forms, formats, documents, *etc.,* that your readers need to reach their objectives;

- be sufficiently explained so that your readers know when and how to use them, and

- have a benefit title, not just a feature description.

Let's look at each of these points in more detail.

Provide Specific Illustrations

It is no good talking about the kind of cover letter an individual ought to write to accompany a fund raising proposal to a corporation or foundation, if the reader has never seen such a letter. In my experience, telling people how to create forms . . . but not providing them with the forms . . . is like showing them how to swim and then just pushing them in the water. Many just don't do it right . . . with rather unfortunate consequences.

That's why if you tell your readers about any given format . . . be it a contract . . . or media kit . . . or brochure . . . whatever . . . you'd better be prepared to give them a sample of that document.

This means that when you do your micro outline for each section, you ought to list the relevant samples for this section. In my experience, it's better to find or create these samples in advance of writing about them. Indeed, I can't think of any other way of doing this, since having the sample in front of you while you're explaining what it is and how to use it enables you to be much more detailed and specific in your remarks. Too, it means that when you've finished any given chapter, you've also finished the corresponding part of your Samples Section . . . so you are really killing two birds with one stone.

Explain Your Documents

You've undoubtedly heard the old saw: catch a fish and a man eats for a day. Teach a man to fish and he eats, for a lifetime. (No one explains, of course, what happens when you know how to fish . . . but there aren't any fish. That, however, is another story.) Well, this is a variation. If you want your readers to use the samples properly, you've got to:

- explain what they get when they use them;
- provide guidelines on how to create them;
- provide instructions on how to use them.

You do this first, of course, in the text itself. You also do it in the Samples Section. Here, you can either use call-outs to draw attention to different parts of the document, explain what it's doing there and why it's important, and give tips on how to create it . . . or use a technique I call "essentials of." These techniques are related, but distinct.

Using Call-Outs

Call-outs enable you to draw the reader's attention to specific sections of a document by using lines, arrows, or other emphasizing devices. "Here," you're saying, "is something really important . . . something you have to know about to achieve the benefit you want!" At the other end of the emphasizing device is a box that explains why this section is important, why it is where it is, tips on creating it, and possibly crucial variations and when to use them. In short, it gives the reader just what he needs to both create this section and understand what he needs to do to create and use it in just the right way. Call-outs are perfect when you want to draw your reader's attention to a specific subject . . . and they necessarily amplify the discussion you've already presented in the text.

Using "Essentials Of"

There's another technique, which I pioneered years ago, I call "essentials of." Here, you place the actual sample document on the right hand side of the page. On the left is your discussion and analysis of the sample. In logical order, using bullets to separate your points, you describe each paragraph, and where necessary each line, telling why it's there, how to use it, and how to alter it as needed. This technique gives your reader an actual document to use . . . but also a complete discussion of why this document is being created so he can use it — or alter it as needed — to achieve the desired result.

Provide A Benefit Title

Like everything else in your how-to product, your samples must be distinguished by a benefit headline (or benefit description) . . . not just a feature statement. Thus, which of these do you think is better . . . which do you think offers your reader a greater benefit and induces him to read the sample?

1. Sample Sales Letter

2. Use this letter to grab your prospect's attention and get him to focus on your offer and reason for responding to it immediately.

It's obvious, isn't it? Your prospects, remember, aren't interested in the sample *per se;* they're interested in the benefit they get when they use it. So provide that benefit . . . as the sample's title or in a brief description preceding the document.

Note: almost no how-to writers use benefit titles and descriptions for their sample documents. I think there are several reasons for this:

- sample documents are usually located deep in the text, or in the appendices. Their very position makes them less likely to get the attention, including the right headings, they deserve from their creators.

- sample documents are almost always an afterthought for the product creator. They are ordinarily created or arranged after the main text is completed. Thus, the author deals with them at a time when his own energy and enthusiasm for his project is probably depleted. The author's own system is screaming "Get this project done!," (especially if he's behind schedule, as is virtually always the case at this point). And so, the samples section suffers.

- Finally, there's this reason: the creator thinks the feature is the benefit . . . that is, that just naming the document makes it perfectly clear just what benefit the reader will get from using it.

But we know that's not true!!! If you want your reader to know what benefit he gets from using any given document, tell him. If you can summarize this benefit in a phrase, that's fine. If you have to use a sentence or two, do so. The important thing is that your reader is in no doubt whatsoever about exactly what benefit he gets from this document. Your accompanying notes will then provide him with what he needs so that he knows how to create the sample himself, how to alter it, and when to use it.

A Few Additional Words About The Importance Of The Samples Section And Doing The Samples Properly

If you're creating a product about how to draft a sales brochure that gets prospects to respond immediately, you undoubtedly think you've got a handle on how to write the copy for that brochure, how to design and lay it out, how to alter it for specific cases, *etc.* You may think all this is clear in your own mind, and perhaps it is. But I have news for you: unless there's both a lucid description of what you mean . . . and a sample . . . it's very unlikely that what you know so very well will be adequately transmitted to your prospect.

For reasons which seem to me to be perfectly egotistical, most how-to product creators *assume* a certain level of knowledge in their readers . . . and also *assume* that these readers will be able to achieve the desired results with written directions only. Having been in this business so long, I adamantly disagree. There is often a world of difference between what you think you've said . . . and what your reader thinks you mean.

Shorten the odds, dear reader. When in the slightest degree of doubt provide a necessary sample.

Your Client-Centered Conclusion

To put our discussion of your client-centered conclusion into perspective, let's look at the conclusion to an otherwise useful book entitled *The Complete Guide To Self-Publishing* (Writer's Digest Books, 1985) by publishing consultants Tom and Marilyn Ross. Their two-page conclusion begins thus, "After reading through this book, if you've chosen to publish one of your own, you know you're in for a challenge — and lots of work — and lots of fun."

Their last two paragraphs of the 8 paragraph conclusion read, "Finally comes The Day. Your books arrive from the printer. The dream has been given form. The Madame Curies and John Glenns have nothing on you. You had a goal and you reached it. And as your publishing venture matures, you'll mastermind techniques you never thought possible. Thousands of people have done it successfully. So can you.

Yes, we've traveled a long way together with this dream. We feel we've become friends through this book. And as with any friend, we offer you encouragement, wish you luck, and hope you will triumph!"

That's it, folks. There's ain't no more.

Do you think this is a suitable conclusion to a how-to product? I certainly don't. It's standard, unimaginative, and useful neither to the reader nor to the authors themselves.

Let's take a moment to look at what the Rosses probably want to achieve with this book. Like most consultants creating how-to products, they no doubt wish to use their product as a prospecting device . . . as a means to get future consulting assignments, more business through direct one-on-one consulting, speaking engagements, *etc.* That's perfectly reasonable.

But having read their conclusion, you'd never know this was their objective. Indeed, you'd come to a very different deduction, namely that the journey they had traveled with you, their reader, was over. That the Rosses were going off their way . . . leaving you to go off your way. Sayonara, baby.

This is, however, wrong, wrong, terribly wrong! As I have stressed through this book — as I shall continue to drive home, since the point is of pivotal importance — with your info-product you have merely *started* a relationship. This relationship must be allowed and encouraged to develop . . . must have objectives it can move toward. Your product, in short, must be a launching pad towards these objectives and must never, never, never be seen as the end of the road . . . as the be all and end all of your relationship with your reader. This is the tragic mistake the Rosses — and virtually all how-to product creators — make.

Now let's consider the situation of the Rosses' reader. Do you honestly think this reader, probably an ingenue in self-publishing (which is a business distinguished by both nasty and expensive pit-falls) got all the inspiration and practical assistance necessary from this single book to both create his product and market it successfully? I doubt it.

With the best will in the world, the Rosses, technically proficient though they are, didn't tell their reader everything he needs to know . . . didn't even tell him everything the Rosses know . . . or that they will discover later which could benefit that reader. In short, the reader will need additional assistance; assistance that the Rosses could either provide themselves or through Independent Contractor relationships with other pertinent specialists.

But where does it say that in the Rosses' conclusion? It doesn't.

These authors, like most how-to product creators, see the product they've created as distinct . . . isolated . . . unconnected to anything else they could offer, any other related problem they could solve.

Either arrogant or just plain ignorant, they say in effect, "If you want us, dear reader, you must figure out what we offer. You must figure out how we could help you. You must figure out how to get in touch with us . . . and how we could help you."

Now, I ask you. Is this neighborly? Is this helpful? Is this client-centered marketing? Is this intelligent in any way? OF COURSE NOT!!!

And yet you find it done all the time . . . with virtually every how-to info-product that exists.

You, however, cannot make this mistake, because you will see your product's conclusion as in fact the commencement of a new, extended relationship with your prospect . . . a relationship that may include (but is certainly not limited to) helping him with other useful products, with workshops and seminars that answer more of his questions and give him the chance to question you directly about his situation, and with a direct one-to-one consulting relationship that enables him to make full benefit of what you know so he can achieve his objectives faster and more completely.

Your "conclusion" is, then, just like a school commencement. While it recognizes that one distinct chapter has ended, it nonetheless points towards all the opportunities that come next in this developing relationship between the two benefitting parties, your reader and yourself.

If you have created a client-centered product . . . if you have truly attempted to speak honestly to your prospect . . . if you have gone the extra mile to give him all the information he needs to reach his objectives . . . I tell you this: your reader wants you to stay in touch with him. Why? Because he knows your value . . . and needs a person of your obvious candor, merit and empathy in his life. Will you, having fostered this feeling in this reader, now turn your back on him, merely offering him, as the Rosses merely offer their readers, nothing more than the stone soup of "encouragement", "luck", and "hope"? Your reader, dear reader, deserves far, far better than this from you . . . deserves it and expects it!

So, give it to him.

Structure your conclusion, or, if you prefer, your commencement, thus:

- Congratulate the prospect on sticking with the material until the end;

- Remind him of the significant things he has learned . . . and the benefits he gets when he starts applying his new knowledge;

- Then invite him to stay in your life . . . invite him to get in touch with you . . . let him know what further benefits you can provide him . . . if only he takes the initiative to get in touch.

- Finally, remind him that you have begun a significant relationship with each other . . . a relationship that will be of the utmost benefit to both of you. Tell him how proud you are to be his friend . . . and how you want him to contact you to tell you, in the most glorious detail possible, just how what he's learned from you has helped. Friends delight in the achievements of others and wish to hear about them. Friends learn from each other. That's why you should invite your new friend to tell you how he's doing . . . and what refinements he's made in your methods. It's what a friend would do.

How many words does it take to do all this? Just two or three pages, at the most. And what is the value to you and your reader? Having cemented the relationship with your reader, you may expect him to contact you . . . not as a prospect . . . but as a friend. Because he'll approach you as a friend, you won't have to work very hard, perhaps not work at all, to persuade him to accept your recommendations. After all, he already knows you're a friend.

Your reader also knows that you are going to be there for him in future, as you've already been there for him throughout the product he's just finished reading or listening to. This bolsters his confidence, puts an extra spring in his step, and helps get him started to achieve what both you and he want him to achieve: namely the ultimate benefit of your book. Frankly, this should make you both feel very, very good, indeed.

Does this kind of client-centered conclusion provide the results I say it does? You bet your life. As I write this book, I am working with a fellow who pays me handsomely each month. He responded to the invitation in one of my books . . . asked me to do some work out of which a mutually lucrative relationship has developed. What's more, I've made a very good friend.

When this fellow calls, I feel better. His sunny demeanor cheers me up on even the most frenzied days. If I hadn't invited him through my books to keep in touch and use me when he needed further assistance, would he have taken the initiative to do so? If he hadn't, I'd be much poorer . . . financially and in spirit. That's why I'm dedicating this chapter to Maryland copywriter Dan McComas, CR, and to the process that produced him for me. While I cannot guarantee you identical results, I do say this: if you don't use this method, if you behave like the run of myopic how-to product producers, you're virtually ensuring it won't happen, and certainly placing lots of unnecessary obstacles in the way.

Is this really what you want?

Your Final Section: The End-of-Product Catalog

Part of developing a relationship means not only giving recommendations on what your reader/listener/prospect should do next, but actually having specific products and services available to help. These products and services — both those created by you and those created by others and offered by you — should be available in an end-of-product catalog.

Later I shall provide you with just the details you need to create this catalog. Now, however, I'd like to address a few key points about it.

What The Nay-Sayers Say

There are still people — many people — who, like Michael Dukakis in his ill-fated presidential campaign, just don't get it. That is, they don't understand how helpful this catalog (or, as I often say, Resource Guide or Resource Directory) is to your reader. Instead, they see it only as some kind of mercenary device, designed only to squeeze more money from the hapless and misguided. This, of course, is rubbish.

Unless you have provided every last drop of technical information and personal inspiration in your product, your reader/listener probably needs more help to achieve his objective. Sometimes he only needs and can afford further information products . . . sometimes he needs and can afford direct personal assistance. It's your job to offer both. And this is just what your Resource Directory does.

Here is where your prospect finds just what he needs on a whole host of subjects that he must master to achieve the objectives he wishes to achieve. Do you really feel that this person, supposedly your friend, should be left to find all these resources on his own? You're meant to be the expert; you're supposed to know what exists . . . both good and necessary and bad and avoidable. You've said you're client-centered. Why, then, deprive him of the help he needs . . . and yourself of the income you've entitled to for all the time and trouble you've taken to become so knowledgeable? It just doesn't make sense.

The touchstone of my system is this: do well by doing good. That is, help yourself by helping others. There's absolutely nothing wrong with that, and don't let any of the mealy-mouthed critics, who are sure to attack any good idea, ever tell you there is.

Instead, follow the guidelines I have given you here to create other info-products your particular clients need. Then offer these through your catalog. Too, use my books THE CONSULTANT'S KIT: ESTABLISHING AND OPERATING YOUR SUCCESSFUL CONSULTING BUSINESS (the beginner's volume) and HOW TO MAKE *AT LEAST* $100,000 EVERY YEAR AS A SUCCESSFUL CONSULTANT IN YOUR OWN FIELD (for those who want to make over $100,000 a year selling problem-solving advice) to create consulting services your reader/listener/prospect needs. Then offer these, too, through your Resource Directory. Finally, build useful and profit-able relationships with providers of other problem-solving products and services, as I'll show you how to do. These, too, must be a part of your end-of-product catalog.

How many products should you have in this catalog? That depends on several factors. Naturally, you can only offer a few suggestions on an audio cassette, maybe just two or three; on the other hand, if you produce an audio cassette album, you can certainly include a catalog. On the other hand, in a major information product like a book, you may offer over 100 . . . or even more. It's all up to you and how assiduous you are about seeking out useful products and services for your designated markets and building relationships with their creators. Whatever anyone may say to the contrary, greed is not the primary motivation for doing all this. Following my methods, you'll soon find yourself living very, very well . . . far better, indeed, that any of your sanctimonious (and very, very jealous) critics. The true reason is far different: it's service.

As a specialist in your field, you know what it takes to achieve the objective your reader/listener wants to achieve. You know how much of the necessary information you've given him in your product . . . or through your in-text Resource Boxes. You must also know how many other products and services he can benefit from . . . and must make it as easy as possible for him both to know about and use them. If you don't, you're making your client's life unnecessarily difficult and asking him to duplicate what you already know and the effort you've already gone through. This isn't a friendly act. Indeed, it's both hostile and unnecessary.

As a true friend, make it easy for your reader/listener. Give him access to as much of what you know as you can . . . and if he has to buy some of that, well, there's nothing — absolutely nothing — wrong with that. After all, as someone who has invested so much of your time and talent to discover this useful information, you really ought to be compensated. It is my firm belief that those who have troubled themselves to gather knowledge ought to be compensated for it. Nothing will ever shake me from this point of view. Adhere to it. Live by it. And create your end-of-product catalog accordingly.

Last Words On Info-Product Creation

Even for me this is a terribly lengthy chapter. I am conscious that it is perhaps unwieldly. And yet it is also supremely important. That is my humble excuse for offering it to you in all its considerable length and detail.

If you follow these guidelines, you will solve one of the crucial problems of the info-product producer: knowing precisely what to do to produce a product than your reader/listener can faithfully follow to achieve the objective he wants. As I have continually stressed, the run of how-to creators don't know how to do this. As a result, their products are inferior, second-rate, laughably inadequate. They offer neither what the prospect needs to achieve his objective . . . nor do they help generate the kind of relationship of trust and respect that ensures future, more lucrative dealings with your prospect. Thus, they fail on all counts.

Moreover, if you do not learn to create your own comprehensive and detailed info-products, you will never be able to assist others create them for you. You are therefore dooming yourself to being and remaining one of the smallest, least profitable problem-solving information product entities in existence. Is this what you want?

Of course it isn't. You want to produce the best, most detailed, most useful products you can . . . and want to get others to produce more of these products for you, too. As you succeed in doing this, your info-empire — and your profits — must grow apace.

In this chapter I have moved you closer to this objective. In later chapters I provide more of the information you need; information on creating other specific info-product formats and getting other specialists to work with you to produce still more products.

But if you not only read this chapter, but soak yourself in its guidelines, I guarantee you you will have at your fingertips the essential information you need to produce superior, masterful, client-centered info-products. Such products emerge because of a resolute focus on the individual you wish to help . . . on your determination both to understand his situation and give him all the specific data he needs to remedy it . . . and achieve what he wishes to achieve. When you follow the guidelines in this chapter, you must give this individual just what he needs and must therefore, if he will only heed you, improve his life. You now have what it takes to do this. Go on! Craft your fine products accordingly!

Note: by the way, even though I've taken some pot shots at some aspects of Tom & Marilyn Ross's book *The Complete Guide To Self-Publishing,* I still want to recommend it to you. It has some very useful information. You can get your copy from Communication Creativity, P.O. Box 909, Buena Vista, CO 81211 (719) 395-8659.

Resource

When you're creating info-products, you need to be alert to basic copyright law, including registration procedures (for your own products) and copyright permission guidelines (when you're using other people's material.) These important subjects are handled in *The Desktop Publisher's Legal Handbook,* a new book by Attorney Daniel Sitarz. This volume also deals with desktop publishing business entities (sole proprietorships, partnerships, limited partnerships and corporations), taxation of a publishing business, publishing contracts, defamation and libel, and invasion of privacy. It concludes with copyright registration forms and a series of other legal forms you'll find helpful. To get a copy, contact Nova Publishing Co., 1103 W. College St., Carbondale, IL 62901 (618) 457-3521.

How To Create Your Booklets, Special Reports, And Audio Cassettes

You now know two major things: what it takes to produce a truly useful problem-solving info-product and how to create a problem-solving book, the apex of the info-product pyramid. Now, it is time to unveil more of the mysteries of what it takes to create valuable and marketable products in this business.

Although I've never seen any research findings on this point, I suspect most how-to writers create only a single book and a few articles. That's their complete lifetime output. If this is anywhere near being true, it means most people who create how-to products cannot make much, if any, money from them.

Perhaps making money isn't an objective for them. Perhaps, like so many misguided authors, they find their wants are satisfied merely by telling what they know and getting their name in print. If any money results, so much the better, but that, they seem to suggest, is a distinctly secondary consideration.

Well, let me tell you something: it isn't a secondary consideration for me . . . and it mustn't be one for you, either. This is why you must learn how to create a *line* of info-products, using a variety of formats.

The Necessary Background To This Chapter

As I've said from the beginning, the objective in this business is not merely to satisfy yourself . . . but to focus on your designated markets and satisfy them. Everyone in these markets doesn't learn the same way. Some people are perfectly happy to commit the time it takes to read through and study a major problem-solving book. Others either don't have the need for all that information or cannot make the commitment to learn it all at once time. These people want shorter treatments of particular subjects.

Moreover, all of your prospects may not wish to commit the money it takes to purchase your major info-products. Sometimes this is because they just don't have the money . . . but, equally often, it's because they don't know you and have no reason to trust you. Even with a money-back guarantee, they'd rather commit just a little money and see if you've got anything worthwhile to say to them. Then, their qualms having been satisfied, they'll be ready to go ahead and buy more.

What I'm telling you, therefore, is this. When you're building your information empire, the focus must be on:

- your prospect, not on yourself;
- how that prospect learns, not just what you've got to say, and
- how he wishes to buy, not just on how you want to sell.

Practically speaking, this means you cannot simply produce one product format . . . of a single length . . . at a single price. If you do, you're both limiting your market and not providing all the options that market needs to be satisfied. You must take into account *all* the different problem-solving information formats that exist . . . and create the right client-centered product at the right price for each. Only in this way are you giving your markets the choices they must have.

Benefits Of Developing A Line Of Products

There are many benefits to developing a line of info-products.

1. Each product can be used to reinforce the Ultimate Benefit your prospects get from buying from you. That is, you can use each product to remind people of the overall benefit they get by doing business with you.

2. Each product can be used, through both your client-centered introduction, conclusion and end of product catalog, to sell your other products and services. You can use each product to sell other products you offer that help your prospects get what they want.

3. When you pro-rate the cost of marketing over an entire line of products, the cost of marketing any individual product drops substantially. Your goal is to bring your problem-solving products to the attention of as many buyers as you can . . . for the least possible cost and greatest conceivable profit. This is more likely to happen when you can reduce the individual marketing costs for each item . . . and raise your response rate because you're appealing to more buyers.

4. Finally, as you can see, you make more money. Whatever plans you have for your info-empire, you're going to need money to realize them. You must therefore be keenly aware of what it takes to cut your costs, increase your reach, and upgrade your return. A line of products is essential in helping you reach these objectives.

Now, let's take a look at some key formats in your future product line.

Creating Booklets

Books, as you know, are major information products. They run in length from about 65,000 words up to about twice as long, the length of several of my (probably too long) products.

Booklets are a distinct, but related genre. They may be anywhere in length from 5,000 words to about 40,000 words with most falling between 10,000-20,000. Just how many pages that is will vary with the booklet size you've selected. 6"x 9", for instance, is a standard size.

I would argue, however, that length is always secondary to purpose. Before writing a booklet of any kind, you've got to ask yourself these questions:

• What am I trying to accomplish with my booklet?

• Whom am I trying to reach?

• How do I want him to feel when he's finished the booklet?

• What do I want him to do when he's finished?

These are the important questions. So, let's take a look at each.

"What Am I Trying To Accomplish With My Booklet?"

By now, you should know the answer to this question. Are you trying merely to disseminate information? Or do you have other motives?

The shrewd info-entrepreneur has several objectives for his booklet. One of them most certainly is *not* to dump information on his prospect. Or to overawe that prospect with how smart he (the creator) is.

Certainly one goal is to give the prospect useful information, information he can follow to achieve the benefit promised by the booklet title. That you must always keep in mind.

Additionally, however, you need to do what's necessary both to get your reader to trust you, to read your booklet (and so increase that trust), and to accept your invitation to develop a relationship, a relationship that involves your further assistance through recommended products and services.

As you can see, therefore, what you wish to achieve with a booklet is the same as what you want to achieve with a book. The problem is, you have less time and space to accomplish this.

"Whom Am I Trying To Reach?"

Booklets are rigorously focused on a specific target population. Because they are shorter than books, your targeting must be even more precise. You must know . . . and ultimately your prospects must instantly know . . . just who you're speaking to . . . and just what benefit you've got for them.

Recently, an insurance salesman from Los Angeles approached me for help with a booklet he'd just finished. He'd given it the title "Revelations Of An Insurance Salesman."

I asked him who was supposed to buy his booklet. "Anyone who wants full coverage but doesn't want to pay full price," he responded. "But how do these people know your booklet is for them when they read your title?" I said. Silence. Of course, they wouldn't know this product was for them . . . because there is no clear benefit in the headline . . . or a clear indication of whom this booklet is for. Deduction: few sales.

Booklets work to the extent you have clearly targeted your market . . . clearly created a benefit-rich product for them . . . and clearly offered them this benefit in your title. There must be no mystery, no confusion . . . only clarity about audience and benefit.

"How Do I Want Him To Feel When He's Finished The Booklet?"

This should be an easy one for you now. This is what your prospect should be saying to himself when he finishes your booklet:

- In this booklet, I found a source that offers me the exact information I need to achieve the limited objective I want to reach;

- This source is interested in me, knowledgeable about the subject, and committed to helping me achieve my objective;

- This source is offering help in this booklet . . . and the possibility of future help through other products and services which I'm glad this booklet has brought to my attention. I can trust the source to deliver further help because of the quality of the assistance he has already rendered me. I'm glad I made this connection!

"What Do I Want Him To Do?"

Another easy one! Here's what you want your prospect to do when he's finished with your booklet:

- be ready to go out and start doing what's necessary to achieve the benefit the booklet title promises;

- either call you (better) or write you (acceptable) for further assistance, both through other products you recommend and sell and your direct one-on-one consulting help.

A Few More Considerations Before You Decide To Go Ahead With Your Booklet

If the booklet you've got in mind meets these criteria, then you're near making a decision to produce it. Now you must consider these points:

- Does this booklet reinforce the Ultimate Benefit offered by your company?

- Does this booklet lend itself to being part of a series?

- Can the information in this booklet be reused in other products?

Let's look at each of these points in more detail.

Your Booklet Must Reinforce The Ultimate Benefit Offered By Your Company

As I hope I've made perfectly plain, every product you both create and offer through your company must be about and reinforce the Ultimate Benefit (or related series of Ultimate Benefits) that constitute the real reason your customers buy from you. These customers come to you to achieve that

Ultimate Benefit and must not be distracted or confused by unrelated Ultimate Benefits. If they are, you are undercutting your own effectiveness.

Thus, if your primary benefit is offering sex appeal and you produce a product offering financial security, you are dividing your message and threatening the clear perception your prospects must have of what you are doing. Thus, make sure the booklet you are considering offers the same Ultimate Benefit as your other products.

Your Booklet Must Lend Itself To Being Part Of A Series Of Related Products

Your goal as an info-entrepreneur is both to help people and make money. You can best achieve this goal by offering products that are related . . . products that naturally lead your prospects from one purchase decision to the next. You can only achieve this goal if you think in terms of series. Thus, you tell me: say you have just produced a booklet about how to grow red roses. Do you think the next booklet in the series should be about yellow roses . . . or about how to grow barley?

One of the greatest problems I've discovered among information producers is that they don't think logically. They don't consider what the buyer of any individual product will want to buy next . . . will in fact consider a "must" acquisition. But this is the marketing problem you must solve. Anyone can create a product. That's not the smart part. The smart part is creating a product that someone will buy . . . and that launches a client-centered series of products that that individual prospect — and all the people like her — will also buy. That's very, very smart.

The Information In This Product Should Be Reused In Other Products

The goal in the information business is not always to find something new and different . . . but to reuse the information you've got, repackaging it, so you can bring it, in a different format, to a new group of prospects.

What do I mean by this?

My books, as you perhaps know by now, are lengthy. They are, in fact, some of the most long and detailed how-to products ever created. I like to be thorough, and I make no apologies for offering my customers more information than most would consider entirely satisfactory. I have my own standards to maintain, after all!

But I am well aware that all people who have the problems I can solve don't want to read through a major book . . . nor do all my prospects need everything in those books. Therefore, my job is to repackage some of the information and offer it in other formats so that others with their different needs can profit from it.

Here's how to consider this process:

• a major information product is composed of modules of problem-solving information. Even *before* the major information product is released, these modules of information should be spun off in many different formats, including highly specialized and focused booklets;

• the major information product should then be released and promoted accordingly;

• thereafter, the major information product should be further broken down into still more highly specialized and focused products (Special Reports and audio cassettes) and sold for further profit. Each product, whenever it is produced, can be used to promote all the related products . . . and thus induce further sales.

Let me give you an example of how this might work in terms of a problem-solving booklet.

Say I was writing a book about how to market a small business. Say that one of the modules in this book dealt with how to create classified and small space ads to get the maximum number of inquiries . . . and then how to respond to these inquiries to get the maximum number of sales. In the major product, this subject might constitute a chapter.

There are people in the world who don't want to read a whole book on marketing (whether they need it, or not). Either they are doing sufficiently well overall that such an investment of their time and resources doesn't make sense . . . or they only have an interest in a certain marketing subject. Either way, they will only acquire what they want.

Your task as a marketer, therefore, is plain: to create another product using this information . . . the only information they will purchase. This product could be:

• a booklet
• a Special Report
• a 60-minute audio cassette.

Or all three. Because in this case, it's perfectly conceivable to me that any and all of these products . . . in addition to the major information product . . . would sell nicely. This is not, of course, always necessarily the case.

As you see, these products can start coming out as soon as you're clear about your market and certain that you have the problem-solving information it must have to reach the benefit promised in your title. If you've got this, why wait to start making money and helping people? This means that booklets mined from your major info-product may very well be available before that product itself.

Your Booklet Look

Just because your booklet will not end up being the Gutenberg Bible doesn't mean it should be sloppily produced. One of the reasons booklets are held in rather bad odor is because so many of them are so poorly designed, laid out and produced. These days, with the advent of desk top publishing, there's absolutely no excuse for this.

As a general rule, your booklet should be produced in such a way that as an object it mirrors the benefit promised by its title. In other words, if you're producing a booklet about money, the booklet's look ought not to shout poverty.

Later, I shall be discussing some production and design considerations. They focus on books but are applicable to booklets, too. Here, let me just say this:

- particular attention should be given to the cover. Even if you are going to sell your booklet principally by mail order, you need a cover that not only promises a client-centered benefit but looks as if the author can deliver it.

- pages should be laid out for ease of reading with sufficient margins at top, bottom and the sides of the pages;

- the printing quality should be sharp. I wince when I see smudged pages when it's so easy these days to get sharply printed ones.

Your Booklet's Price

The reason to be particular about these items is clear: you want your buyer to feel that the price he's paid for the product was worth it, even though the booklet itself might be only 10,000 words. Moreover, you want him to think well of you: that you're not only knowledgeable and client-centered but dedicated to producing a quality product. If he doesn't feel this way about you, it may very well inhibit him from acquiring the other products you'll be offering him.

So what, then, is a fair price for a booklet? This depends entirely on the benefit you're offering your prospects. For instance, how much do you think a booklet entitled "Revelations Of An Insurance Salesman" would be worth *vis-à-vis* one entitled "How To Save Up To $859 On Your Annual Home-Owners And Car Insurance Premiums . . . And Still Get Full Coverage!"

It would be hard setting a price for the first booklet. My client wanted to charge $25 postpaid for it. But where did the title promise at least that much benefit? It didn't. So $25 was most decidedly too much.

And for the second? Well, the real question is whether this booklet's prospect can be convinced that paying $25 would realistically save him up to $859 . . . and, of course, what competitive products to which he was being exposed were charging for similar information. After considering these two factors, $25 might well emerge as the sensible price to pay . . . the price the buyer would consider a bargain. Which is just how you want him to feel.

Booklets And Benefits

Here, then, we return to where you must *always* start with *any* info-product . . . to the benefits your prospect gets from using it. For booklets, as for all the other products you want to create, these benefits must be:

- in the title. The designated prospect must know instantly that this booklet is for him . . . and give him a meaningful benefit . . . something he wants;

- in your booklet introduction. Booklets lend themselves nicely to introductions in letter form. This letter should clearly point out just what benefits the reader gets from you . . . and how else you can help him.

- in the chapter or section titles. Each section of your booklet must promise — and then deliver — benefit information. Not just data . . . but guidelines that enable the reader to achieve the subsidiary benefit promised in the chapter title . . . and thus the overall benefit promised by the product title.

- in the conclusion. You must remind your reader, again a letter format works well, about the benefits he'll get when he starts using the information he now has . . . and just how you can help him in other ways.

- in the samples section. Yes, even in booklets there can be samples.

- And, of course, in the end-of-product catalog. You'll want to scale this catalog down, of course, given the smaller size of a booklet. But even here, it's your responsibility to tell your reader what he needs to succeed . . . and how to get the products and services he needs . . . from you!

Creating Special Reports

Having reviewed booklets, we are now ready to assess the benefits of Special Reports, how they fit into your info-empire, and what you need to do to create them.

There are so many benefits to Special Reports I scarcely know where to begin providing them. These reports:

- meet the need of contemporary people for highly specific, immediately usable information. There's no chaff in these reports. They constitute the real "down and dirty" information source. Your prospects don't have to spend much time reading them and, if the reports are properly prepared, come away with a real feeling that they have learned something, are better off, and can go out and make progress in achieving a desired objective.

- have the substantial benefit that you can sell them . . . before they physically exist! As you have already seen, while it is certainly true that to a certain extent you *can* sell major information products before they exist, the bulk of the selling takes place after you've made your substantial investment in them. This is most decidedly not true with Special Reports. While you must invest your time, attention and enthusiasm to create them, as you'll see, you don't actually have to *produce* them until you have the customer's money in hand. Thus, with the Special Report you've solved one of the most important publishing problems . . . how to diminish your investment and produce absolutely the correct number of products that your market wants to buy. With Special Reports, in short, you'll have never invested in stock that doesn't sell.

- tend to be bought in bunches. Before I produced my always-being-augmented series of Special Reports, I wondered just how many of them people would buy. My anxiety, of course, was that they'd only buy one . . . and that the marketing cost of bringing my catalog to their attention would quickly overwhelm any profits I'd make from individual sales. As my experience has demonstrated, however, this fear is groundless. No doubt in large measure because of my current special three-for-$14 offer, my customers tend to buy in lots of three. Indeed, it is the rare customer who buys just one or two reports . . . and it is commonplace to have people buying 3, 6, 9 . . . or more. Indeed, I even get customers who buy every Special Report being offered!

- Special Reports are *very* profitable. Because people tend to buy in multiples of three, Special Reports have become a very important profit center for me. No wonder. Consider the cost. Direct costs include the value of my time in creating them (which may mean recycling material from other sources) or, as you'll see in another chapter, getting other specialists to create them for me. Thereafter, the only costs are the laser printer paper I use to print them on (I can print about 1000 reports from a box of paper costing $22; the cost of toner (about $145 for 20,000 sheets), the manila envelopes I ship them in (about 9 cents each), the shipping label, and, of course, first-class postage — my single biggest expense in this production process.

Still, despite all these expenses, Special Reports pay for themselves in two ways:

1. Directly. Factoring in all expenses, including postage, the individual Special Report costs about 45 cents to produce. I sell them for $6 without any problem. The *per* report cost dips, of course, when people buy multiple reports, as they generally do. The profit rises accordingly. If a single report costs about 45 cents to produce and ship, three reports cost only about twice as much.

2. Indirectly. As you will not be surprised to learn, each Special Report concludes with at least one Resource Box. This box includes information about related products and services offered by me that will be of value to the reader of this particular Report. If the Special Report is based on the work of another specialist (see next chapter), it concludes with *two* Resource Boxes . . . one about materials produced by this specialist (and available through me); the other offering my products and services. Special Reports thus become sophisticated marketing materials . . . like all the how-to products you produce. Why? Think how you handle your marketing materials . . . brochures you get, letters, ads, *etc.* Do you actually read them? Keep them around? For the most part, you certainly don't. You throw them away immediately.

But people do keep Special Reports. Why? Because they've paid for them . . . because the density of information is high . . . and because they've probably marked essential points they want to remember. Significantly, when they keep the Special Report . . . they keep your Resource Boxes, too. This is very good news for you since it means they're *keeping* your ads!

More Special Report Benefits

With this impressive list of benefits, we still have by no means exhausted the advantages of Special Reports. There are at least four more that are worth sharing:

• Special Reports can be printed as articles so that you derive more general marketing and promotional benefits from them. Let me share a secret with you. Special Reports actually have two names. I call them Special Reports when I sell them to individual buyers. And I call them articles when I offer them *without charge* to editors and publishers for immediate publication.

Nothing else is different; you need make no changes in the actual title or content for the different markets. Thus, this format offers extraordinary versatility. Later, I shall be sharing with you how to create your own self-syndicated column bringing you an avalanche of superb publicity and specific, client-centered ads. These Special Reports, in their article incarnation, are the basis for this column and all the benefits that stem from it.

- Special Reports are easily produced. You can produce your Special Reports with a personal computer and letter-quality printer. Indeed, here, as elsewhere in the information business, a word processor and printer are absolutely essential. As people buy your reports, you print them. *C'est tout!* It goes without saying that you can also use desk-top publishing equipment to produce a more finished look to your reports, but, frankly, (and to the occasionally criticism of zealous desk-top publishing consultants) I prefer a more "rough and ready" look; this makes it look like I've just written my material and am rushing it to this customer so he can profit from it right away. For this reason — and for speed in production — I personally produce my Special Reports in printer draft mode.

- Each Special Report should be personalized with the name of the purchaser, thus: "Special for Jane Customer." In true Dale Carnegie fashion, the very first thing that your customer sees is her own favorite thing: her name. I head *each* Special Report with the customer's name . . . although on days when you're exceptionally busy, you could get away with only personalizing the first page.

Personally, I don't separate the different reports in any individual customer's order. Instead of separating the pages, I use the customer's name and report title at the top of the page as dividing devices showing where a new report begins. I find that keeping all the reports together like this makes it easier to ship them. Inevitably, of course, some man did once write in to complain that he had to tear the reports apart himself! It figures. (I felt fully justified in writing back and asking whether he'd gotten up on the wrong side of the bed.)

- Finally, Special Reports are easy to update. After you've typeset a booklet or book . . . or recorded an audio cassette . . . there's a certain finality about it. Both psychologically and in fact because it *is* more difficult to make changes in these products. But that's not true at all with Special Reports. Here changes are as easy as updating any other computer text file. Product prices change? No problem. Crucial laws and regulations just altered? Again, easily dealt with. In short, Special Reports are ALWAYS up-to-date. This is what gives them their special place in your info-empire, and why your object must be to seize a series of related subjects, and let your prospects know that you'll ALWAYS have the up-to-the-minute information on them. You must not only let them know this, however. You must mean it, arranging your research and work habits accordingly.

So, Why Don't More Info-Entrepreneurs Have Special Reports?

With all these benefits and no major drawbacks, why don't more info-entrepreneurs have Special Reports? I think there are several reasons:

1. snobbery. Books are "real". Books give you a place in literature's pompous pantheon. Special Reports, the reckoning goes, do not. This, of course, is rubbish. As I keep saying, shift the focus from yourself . . . from your objectives . . . and put it squarely where it belongs: on your prospect. Special Reports meet a want in their lives. And the smart entrepreneur, as every schoolboy knows, succeeds by finding wants and filling them. You do the same.

2. computer and marketing illiteracy. One reason Special Reports are so wonderful is that they give you inexpensive products easily produced, products which are also in themselves marketing vehicles for other products and services you produce. There is thus a captivating elegance about them that must make any info-entrepereneur's heart sing. Unfortunately, too few people understand how to use the computer to create these products (which is a sin in this day and age) while also failing to see the connection between these Special Reports and both the profit deriving from them and as a means of generating further sales of other products and services. In short, they understand neither the technology nor the marketing advantages.

3. lack of knowledge of how to gather the necessary information and create the product. In part this problem should have been largely solved in our last chapter. The rest of what you need is here. But let me say this: your Special Reports succeed to the extent that you focus on a very specific problem your reader wishes to solve, or opportunity he wants to profit from, and that you give him the step-by-step information he needs to meet his objectives. If you do this, your reader must be grateful to you . . . and must admit that the trifling investment he has made in this report was very well worth it and that the lack of fancy packaging matters not a whit.

How To Craft Your Special Reports

Now that you know the benefits of this very special format, it's time to learn more about how to create it. As you consider this section, remember what you've already learned about creating valuable, persuasive info-products. And remember that a Special Report reflects the genre generally.

This is the structure of a Special Report:

- Benefit Title. Like all info-products, a Special Report opens with a title that offers the reader a benefit he wants to achieve. In other words, you must tell the reader exactly what he'll get by reading and using your Special Report.

- Immediate focus on your reader. If the title of a Special Report promises the benefit you can deliver, the opening paragraph hits the reader right between the eyes. It's a zap ray, riveting the client's attention by saying, either:

  - You hurt bad.
  - You fear loss.
  - You want something important.

Most Special Report writers act like they're writing an academic term paper, thinking their opening doesn't matter. Well, it does matter. Your reader is most interested in himself. He's reading your Special Report because you've promised him something in the title . . . and now you want to capture his interest for long enough so that he actually gets into the meat of the text. You can't do that with a dull, dry, and uninteresting opening.

- Then let him know that he'll get what he wants thanks to what you're about to tell him. In other words, once you've hit his pain nerve, reminded him of his loss anxiety, and thrown up the grandeur of his great aspiration, it's time to let him know he gets what he wants right here. That'll keep him reading!

- Now provide the step-by-step details he needs to make progress towards getting what he wants. Again, the key phrase here is "step-by-step". Special Reports work to the extent they're detailed. This means telling things like they really are. A Special Report is no place to mince words. To establish the kind of relationship you really want with your reader/client, tell him the truth. The whole truth. And nothing but the truth, limited only by how much truth you know and how much space you have to tell it. Tell him what he's got to do, how to do it, when to do it, when not to do it. And give him the names, addresses, telephone numbers, and follow-up details he needs that will also help him do it. This is your responsibility!

- Conclude your Special Report by reminding him of what happens when he doesn't follow the guidelines you've just provided . . . and what he gets when he does.

- Then, in your Resource Box, let him know how else you can help him. Make sure this is a client-centered Resource Box, focusing on what your reader wants . . . not what you can do. What's the difference? Take a look at something lawyer Jeffrey Babener just used:

"Jeffrey A. Babener is a partner in the law firm of Joseph, Babener & Carpenter (address). Mr. Babener is a graduate of the University of Southern California Law School and a member of both the California and Oregon State Bars." And it goes on through 16 more lines of this egotistical prose.

Now, I ask you, after reading this what do you think: that Babener is interested in you, his reader and, he no doubt hopes, his future client? Or in himself? Obvious, isn't it? The man comes across as a credentialated ego-maniac without a gram of empathy or client concern. And yet he no doubt thinks he's a real swell guy!

Resource Boxes give you the chance to inform your reader, whom you must also regard and treat as a prospective client, what else you can do for him. Remember, if you've provided him with useful information, information he feels can help him and is worth the price, he's quite prepared to believe well of you and to buy from you again. Therefore, focus on client benefits . . . not author features. That is, tell him what he'll get when he works with you . . . not just egotistical biographical details about yourself.

Thus, transform everything in your Resource Box to a client-centered phrase. Let's go back to the self-centered Babener. He's a partner in a law firm . . . what benefit does this offer his prospective client? He's a graduate of a certain law school. What benefit is this to his client? He's on the editorial review board of a certain publication. What benefit is this?

In fact, what you'll discover when you look at your Resource Box in this way that most of what you might be tempted to use just doesn't fit. Babener's clients don't care where he went to school . . . they care what he can do for them. And it's his responsibility to tell them.

In the case of one of my Resource Boxes, this doesn't mean I tell people I went to Harvard and was a Woodrow Wilson Fellow. Why do they care about that? But it does mean that I tell them I can write their brochures so they make more sales and spend less money producing them. If that's what they want . . . and they trust my ability to assist them (based on the relationship we've already begun developing) . . . then they're prepared to buy my further help. It's as simple as that! And, apparently, as difficult. Take my word for it, though my argument about client-centered Resource Boxes is, I think, irresistible, the next time you pick up somebody's Special Report or how-to article, the odds are overwhelmingly that it'll end with self-centered biographical details about the writer . . . despite the fact that in virtually all cases the writer also sells additional products and services he wants his readers to acquire. Don't tell me the "Me Generation" is dead. I see too much self-defeating evidence every day that it is flourishing.

Hints About Writing Your Special Report

Here are a few more tips for writing effective, client-centered Special Reports:

- Speak directly to your reader. Always use "you" language. Never write in the third person or with the imperial "we."

- Keep sentences and paragraphs as short as possible. Make sure that each helps move your reader closer to his objective. Special Reports, like all info-products, are alive with movement. Your reader must feel that, with your help, he's making step-by-step progress towards his goal and that, at the conclusion of your report, he is discernibly closer to achieving it.

- Divide sections of your report with benefit subheadings, just like you do in major info-products.

- Be human. That is, use the full range of human emotions . . . from laughter to tough-love sternness. Remember, you're a physician. You have both the right and the responsibility to do *whatever is necessary* to motivate your prospect to do *whatever is necessary* to achieve his goals.

- Always end by inviting those who want further help to contact you. Give your reader your address and telephone number. The illusion of intimacy you have created with your reader through a Special Report can be destroyed instantly if you don't give your reader what he needs to continue the relationship you have now worked so hard to begin. Don't get him all dressed up and leave him with no place to go.

Some Technical Considerations

As with all info-products, there are some technical considerations involved in producing Special Reports. Here they are:

- Input your Special Report into your own personal computer. This gives you the ability to both produce and update it easily and allows you to commit the fewest possible dollars to producing it. And, of course, if you are planning on using desk-top publishing to lay out the report and print it, this course is essential.

If you don't have your own computer, first write your report; then take it to one of the commercial desk-top publishing establishments to have the text input and laid out so camera ready art can be produced. Then have your reports printed accordingly. This means you're tying up some of your capital in a report you as yet may not be certain will sell . . . but at least this method still allows you to produce Special Reports.

- Produce two text files for a single Special Report. One should contain the document you'll print and should include underlinings, italics, bold, and other emphasizing devices. This is fine for you but this text file will produce problems when imported into foreign systems that don't share your software. Thus, create a second text file in ASCII of your Special Report. This is particularly important when you're making your Special Reports available as articles to time-pressed editors and to electronic data base publishers who need material on diskette but without your embedded software commands.

- Keep your Special Reports the same length. Why? For uniformity of format. I have selected five single-spaced pages as the length of my reports, because this is the exact length you can ship for the cost of a single first-class postage stamp, an important consideration when you recall that postage is the largest expense involved in producing and shipping these reports. This length is also important because it's sufficiently long to enable you to give your customer a good grasp of what to do to solve an individual problem . . . and yet short enough to be read in just a few minutes . . . which is just what most people want to do. It's also absolutely as long as most editors want for articles.

Last Words On Producing Your Own Special Reports

As the amount of available information continues to grow apace, the importance of Special Reports will grow, too. Why? Because each of us must know ever more to achieve our objectives . . . and yet each of us continues to have the same, very slender body of time in which to master this burgeoning body of crucial information. From this tension emerges the need for Special Reports . . . and the reason why they'll be a substantial profit center for you.

Your opportunity and responsibility thus are clear: to give your prospects the essential information they need in a form they can readily take in and use. Insofar as you give it to them, they will reward you, as I can personally attest. Since I began to create Special Reports . . . which I now do at a brisk, measured pace that yields between 24-28 a year . . . my gross product sales have risen substantially.

More than that, I have solved yet another problem of *every* small business: how to get my client-centered marketing message to ever greater numbers of people while keeping the cost of doing so in check. With Special Reports, my prospects not only pay for information they can immediately use but for information on how I can help them further . . . with other products and services. It's a very neat system, and one that ought to be an essential part of your info-empire.

Creating Audio Cassettes

Throughout this book, I have stressed the need to produce products that not only provide detailed guidance but do so in a way that fosters a warm, intimate relationship with your customer. Both factors are essential.

Most how-to writers, for reasons which should now be plain to you, find it difficult to establish this tone of authoritative empathy. They write in a professional patois that is stilted, dry, arcane, condescending, rambling, and verbose. Who wants a friend like this? Nonetheless, all how-to writers, working with nothing more than words, must make the empathetic connection with their readers.

The same problem exists when it comes to audio cassettes, only here you have a great advantage: the words will be spoken. By their very nature, audio programs have the potential to be warmer, more intimate, much more "reach out and touch" oriented. This, of course, is due to the human voice that transmits the message.

Just as this voice is the great benefit of this format, so it can be the greatest single drawback as well — if it doesn't do what's necessary to reach beyond the sound track and captivate your listener-prospect. That's why in creating an audio cassette, you must always keep two key factors in mind: the quality of the detailed information you provide in your script and the way in which this information is delivered to the listener.

Let's look first at the script.

Producing Your Audio-Cassette Script

Whether you are producing a 60-minute audio cassette (a sort of Special Report on tape) or a multi-cassette album, you need a script . . . that is, a controlled piece of client-centered, directive prose. Personally, I do not approve and cannot recommend that you record your programs live (for instance at a workshop session) and sell these cassettes. In live situations, there are too many interruptions and extraneous noises which even the best editing rarely removes entirely; moreover, you seldom have the kind of complete control which is the hallmark of scripted audio cassettes.

I think this kind of control is essential . . . so that you achieve with your cassette what you need to achieve, namely:

- the establishment and development of a friendly authority-client relationship with your listener;

- moving this client from a place he no longer wishes to be to somewhere he wants to be via your detailed step-by-step information;

- convincing him that you are both knowledgeable and empathetic;

- not only giving an invitation for him to follow up . . . but making it easy for him to do so.

This is what you want . . . and what you can achieve with your script.

Producing The Client-Centered Audio Script

Since a script is written, you should now feel comfortable producing it. After all, it's merely another kind of written how-to product. What I'm telling you, therefore, should come as no surprise.

Good scripts, like all good how-to products, start with a client-centered title. Again, this title must offer the listener a clear-cut, specific, enticing benefit. Say you wanted to do a cassette on how to use your newsletter to sell additional products and services. Which title do you think would be more attractive for your listener:

1. "Building Newsletter Sales Power", or

2. "How To Use Your Newsletter To Get Your Readers To Buy Your Other Products And Services"?

The first title I took from a recent article in *The Watkins Report*, a newsletter on consultants' marketing strategies. It's boring, unspecific, even confusing . . . and wouldn't do very well as the title for a client-centered audio cassette; (it doesn't work as the title of an article, either!).

The second title promises your customer a benefit. If he has a newsletter (market identifier) and if he wants to make money by selling more of his products or services (benefit he wants to achieve), and if he believes you, the specialist, can deliver what he needs to know at a price he feels fair, then he wants your audio cassette more than he wants the money it takes to buy it. Your title is an essential part of what gets him to make this crucial buy decision.

The Guts Of Your Audio Cassette

After you've got your title, the rest of your audio cassette will fall nicely into place. First, introduce yourself and your subject thus:

"Hello, this is Jeffrey Lant and during the next hour I'm going to share some very important information with you about selling your products and services by getting free time on television and radio."

Now continue basing your remarks on one of these three points:

- the pain your listener is in;
- the loss he fears will occur;
- the benefit he wants to achieve.

My illustration above, of course, the one on using your newsletter to sell more products and services, is about a benefit the listener wants to achieve. So start off by dazzling him with just how much of a benefit it is. How much can a newsletter proprietor make by selling his readers more? Give some numbers, some illustrations from successful newsletter publishers, in short entice your listener.

Only if he's truly excited by the benefits he can get by doing what you're about to tell him will he actually want to do it; that is, will he actually be engaged with you and your information. As I keep stressing, he must be engaged with both you and your information . . . or else you won't derive the additional benefits stemming from your listener's involvement with this cassette.

By the same token, if you're opening with pain . . . remind him of just how painful his situation is . . . or how much he would suffer if the loss he is anxious about actually takes place.

These openings are hooks. They are designed, along with the client-centered benefit title, to rivet your listener's attention . . . to focus him on your cassette . . . and to get him to make the necessary commitment to listen to it. Remember, at any time this listener can switch you off . . . dismissing you from his life and consciousness. This, of course, is disastrous for you . . . since you want him to take the necessary steps to further your embryonic relationship. You must always keep the possibility of this tragedy in mind (a tragedy for both you who has the problem-solving information and the listener who needs it) and work to make sure it doesn't occur.

Setting a rigorously client-centered title is one thing that makes sure this doesn't happen.

Crafting an introduction that focuses on your listener's situation is another thing that makes sure this doesn't happen.

And letting him know that he can get what he wants by following the detailed information you're giving him is yet another way of making sure this disaster doesn't happen.

So, give him that information.

The Heart Of Your Audio-Cassette

The heart of your audio-cassette, like all info-products, is the detailed information you provide your client . . . information designed to push, prod, motivate, activate, wheedle, cajole, humor, shame, and excite him into staying with you . . . hearing what you have to say . . . and following your explicit directions so he can achieve his objective.

Here, as elsewhere in your info-products, you'll use "What Next?" thinking to structure your information. You must lead with the first thing your listener needs to do and follow in logical order with all the other things he needs to do . . . keeping only in mind that the format you have selected, be it a 60-minute cassette or an 18-hour series (like my MONEY MAKING MARKETING audio program), will mean certain things must be deleted. Thus, focus on the most important things your listener must do.

As you create your script, remember . . . you are actually writing your side of a two-sided conversation. You must always remember that you are only one of the two participants. You must regard this individual as an active and engaged participant in the conversation you are structuring. This is why it is in your interest to write the script as if it were for a particular person . . . a real, live person; perhaps someone you know, perhaps a representative composite of your targeted market. Write for . . . or, better yet, talk to this pivotal person.

I'm sure at some point in your life, you've had a long conversation with a friend or associate in which you talked for an hour or more with only the most minimal conversational responses from your listener. Yet if the listener was interested in what you were saying . . . and if you received the necessary body language reinforcements, the lack of a verbal response wasn't troubling.

In this situation, you must do what's necessary to stimulate this kind of engaged, but non-verbal, response. How?

• Put in involvement asides. End certain key sentences or paragraphs with phrases like these: "Haven't you felt this way?". Or (with a laugh) "Remember the last time this happened to you?". Or (sternly) "You know you feel this way. Now don't you?" Or even, "You know what I mean." You want your invisible but still very much present listener to nod her head . . . chuckle with you . . . unite her experience with yours and come to the conclusion, "Here's a person I like and can trust. What a relief!"

• Share secrets. When you're talking to a friend and feel a sense of rapport, you often share important things . . . things you just don't tell everybody. So it should be here. As a battle-scarred professional, you know what your listeners *really* have to do to achieve the promise in your title; what to do, and what to avoid. So, tell them. Preface an important line, as I have learned to do, by saying, "I'll tell you a secret." Or, "here's something I've kept just for you." Or "I don't usually mention this, but . . ." See? If you want your listener to feel special, treat him special. Don't only give him the detailed low-down on what he needs to do . . . do let him know what you're telling is only meant for him.

- Reach out and touch your listener using the full range of communication options. The other day I was listening to some audio cassettes on time management, a subject that is of increasing interest to me every year as I have more things to juggle. The speaker's approach was dry and academic. He was a college professor, and he acted like I was a freshman who should be grateful for the opportunity to sit at his feet and learn.

During the time I was listening to the tapes, the phone rang three times . . . a neighbor came by to borrow a tomato for a salad . . . my own dinner-in-preparation demanded my constant attention. The professor simply droned on oblivious to the realities of contemporary life . . . and thus dispensed advice that, while no doubt well intentioned, was unconnected to how I was living.

There was no humor . . . no empathy . . . no seeming understanding of how contemporary people like me live. I finished the first of the 16 cassettes . . . closed the package . . . and put them on the shelf, never to use them again. I don't remember the name of the speaker . . . and certainly wouldn't consider calling him for any personal assistance. For me, he's history. Why? Because this speaker, with all that he knew, didn't speak *to* me, merely *at* me.

These days more than ever before in human history, people need a kind, knowledgeable, empathetic friend in their lives . . . a person who understands them and can help them.

They don't simply want to enroll for a course where some egregiously egotistical and disconnected-to-their-reality creature lectures to them. They want helpful information . . . but they also want the invigoration of touch and concern that a truly empathetic professional can provide.

Think of the endearing, ever-memorable pictures of Norman Rockwell, an American classic if ever there was one. Consider, for instance, his doctors. We trust them with our very lives because they radiate both humanity and profound candor. We instinctively feel these people pull no punches . . . they tell us just what we need to know (no matter how jolting it is) . . . while at the same time they're ready to comfort us, every man, woman, and child of us, offering utter, unquestioning, unwavering support.

This, my friend, is the person you must both be and remain for your listener.

And this is why you must not merely dispense information like my irrelevant time-management professor did. You must reach out . . . right through the packaging of your cassettes . . . through their plastic boxes . . . through each individual reel . . . right into the situation of each listener.

If this takes pleading, plead.

If this takes shaming, shame.

If this takes anger, be angry.

If this takes an upsurge of compelling rhetoric, deliver it.

Your job, as I will never stop stressing, is not merely to give people information. Any computer can do that. Your job, your unique and thoroughly creditable mission, is to help transform people . . . to motivate and change them . . . providing them, at each step along the way, with both the actual data they need to achieve their objective . . . and the psychic support they must have from you, their true friend.

Concluding Your Audio Script

At the conclusion of your audio script, you must include an invitation for your listener to be in touch with you. Again, you must stress a benefit they get when they do so . . . not a feature. In other words, don't ask them to be in touch to learn about the fund raising consultation you provide for nonprofit organizations; ask them to be in touch to find out how you can help them get corporations and foundations to provide the money they need for their important services. "Fund raising" is a feature; "money for their important services" is a benefit. *You must see the difference.*

As always, make sure you give your listener the information he needs to make getting in touch with you easier . . . your address and telephone number. If he needs to prepare for your call (and so become a qualified prospect), tell him just what he needs to do. By now, if you've given him useful information and truly spoken to his situation, this listener is quite prepared to follow your advice.

Technical Matters Pertaining To Writing Your Audio Script

Now that you know the structure of your audio cassette script, here are a few technical details that will also help you:

- Your audio script should be 19 single-spaced pages long (acceptable) or 38 double-spaced pages (better) for a 60-minute cassette. Of course, everyone's rate of delivery is different so the length of your script will vary slightly. One thing must not vary, however: giving people a full hour's worth of detailed information, if you've advertised a 60-minute cassette.

Sadly, I know of several people, purportedly reputable, who tape 45 minutes of (often flaccid) information and advertise it as a 60-minute program. This is immoral. I'm a tight-fisted New Englander, and when I buy an hour's program, I expect it to be fully 60 minutes long. Anything else cheats your customer.

- Keep your sentences and paragraphs as short as you can. Your listener doesn't want — and won't pay attention to — long, complicated, rambling sentences and interminable paragraphs. Sentences should be no longer than two lines; paragraphs no longer than 6 to 8 lines.

- Annotate your script as you would any marketing copy. Too many people in the how-to business treat all words as if they're equal. That's simply not true. The objective of any how-to product is to move a person . . . to motivate him . . . and excite him . . . as well as instruct. Thus, it's up to you to indicate which things are more important. These things should be marked in your script with such emphasizing devices as capital letters, underlined words, and phrases in bold type. Your script isn't finished until you've indicated just what is important . . . so you'll know what to stress when you're reading it.

Preparing To Tape

A lot of nonsense has been written about creating audio cassettes. You need a studio, one authority writes. You must have shimmering music in the background, says another. You just have to be introduced by A Voice, admonishes a third. Not surprisingly, most of these comments come from the professional producers who stand to benefit by your doing what they want you to do.

However, as you would expect from a man who in his pre-computer phase wrote a couple of books on the back of used pieces of paper, I suspected there must be an entirely acceptable, much less expensive way of doing things. And so there is.

To begin with, while music and a professional announcer and all these other things are no doubt nice to have when money is no object, they are the tail, not the dog. The "dog" is the solid, step-by-step transformational information you have . . . and the empathy with which you deliver it. Never forget this. Thus, before you tape, the really important thing to consider is whether you are covered on both these points. Thus:

Read over your script. Have you promised a benefit in your title and does your script deliver the information your listener needs to achieve this benefit? In other words, have you created a detailed road map? Using this tape, can your listener *really* achieve what he wants to achieve? Have you given him specific follow-up information so he can make even more progress towards his objective? Or have you let him down, providing only general, disappointing "what to" information?

Also, have you spoken as directly and personally as you can to your listener? Will he feel that you are *really* speaking to him? Will he feel that you both understand his situation and can help him move beyond it? Or will he sense that you are only going through the motions . . . creating this product merely to make money, and that you don't care much if he reaches his objective or not? Are you, in short, a friend?

If, after considering these questions and the script you have created, you are satisfied that you have not only done your best . . . but that your listener will be grateful for both the detailed information you've gathered . . . and your client-centered, empathetic approach, you are ready to move on to rehearsal!

Rehearsing Your Script

Unless you're a trained actor or superb speaker, you're not going to move from a finished script to a finished cassette in one step. You need to practice. You need to practice for two reasons, to:

1. see if your script is the right length for the cassette you want, and

2. make sure you put just the right spin on every word in the script, to ensure, that is, that the listener hears the precise message you want him to.

You'll realize the first of these objectives by timing your reading. Remember, cassettes are divided into two sides. In a 60-minute cassette, each side should be about 29.5 minutes in length. Moreover, side one should conclude, whenever possible, at the end of one of your points, not in the middle. And it should never, never, never end in the middle of a sentence.

Only by timing your reading, will you be certain just where you want to end the first side of your cassette. At this point, you simply add the words, "Now turn to side 2 to get (whatever benefit comes next)."

While timing is easy and straightforward, speaking your script is more difficult. Most people are afraid of any kind of speaking activity, afraid of being judged and found wanting. Well, I can assure you of this: if you deliver your message in a strained, stilted, and condescending fashion, you will be judged, found wanting . . . and dismissed.

Remember what you are aiming for: to be perceived as a knowledgeable friend, as someone who knows what he's talking about . . . and exists to serve. Not slavishly but responsibly. Your voice should convey concern, warmth, and authenticity. Here are some techniques that will help you achieve this:

• Speak in an amiable, conversational tone of voice. This is a "fireside chat" between two friends, after you. Why should you shout? Your listener very much wants to hear what you have to say.

• Stress key words. Remember, you've already annotated your script. You've marked the key words and phrases you want to emphasize. Now, do emphasize them with your voice. You can't deliver a truly client-centered message in a monotone, and you can't condescend when delivering such a message either. But you can — and must — stress the words and concepts you feel are most important. I've found that to convey the importance of these words and concepts, I tend to lean closer to the microphone when I say them, just as I do when I write — actually thrusting with my body just as I intend to thrust with my words and the intonation of my voice.

• Repeat key sentences. The objective of your tapes, remember, is to persuade an individual to do things. You can't expect him to understand and absorb everything you say the first time . . . not even the most important things. So repeat them. Verbatim. Or with slight variations. Orators throughout the ages have done this. You do it, too. This will signal the listener that what you're saying is truly important.

• Modulate your voice. While it's perfectly all right to deliver most of your script in a friendly, conversational way, don't overlook the power that comes when you change your voice modulation. If you want to indicate that something is most important . . . raise your voice. And if you want to force the listener to pay even closer attention, drop your volume a little and make him move closer and stop doing anything else.

These skills will come with practice . . . you're not going to be perfect all at once. Don't worry about that. Just do the best you can. But do make sure you read your script at least three times aloud . . . just as you intend to deliver it on tape. (Note: if you need to, do a practice taping and listen to yourself. Have you achieved what you wanted to achieve?)

Work Alone

For your own peace of mind, make sure no one is around while you're practicing. Put yourself in the room where you intend to tape, in the chair where you'll be sitting, and read your script aloud. As you read ask yourself:

- Do I truly sound friendly?

- Do I sound light, confident, as if I know what I'm talking about . . . and eager to be of assistance?

- Is there a welcoming tone in my voice?

- Am I modulating my voice so that what *is* important *sounds* important?

When you feel confident in your answers, you're ready to tape.

Setting Up Your In-Home Or Office Taping Studio

Contrary to what you may have heard from audio professionals, you don't need to invest in a studio, a professional voice, music, *etc.* Particularly for 60-minute audio cassettes, you can easily set up your own "studio" at home, or in your office. Here's what you need:

- a tape recorder
- a 60-minute audio tape
- your script
- a glass of room-temperature water
- a desk and chair.

As far as a tape recorder is concerned, any of today's models will probably do nicely. Personally, I use an inexpensive Panasonic model no. RQ-320, and it's perfectly acceptable.

For tapes, I recommend either Maxell or Scotch C-60s, although others will quite rightly recommend other top-quality brand names. Don't stint here. You are producing master tapes, after all.

Once you have these items, select a time when you are least likely to be disturbed (I recommend Sunday afternoons). Remember, even when you're really good at this, you'll need about twice as much time as its final length to tape your script. Now, unplug the telephone, close the door to your "studio", sit down at your desk . . . and begin taping.

Until you've got the hang of creating your master tapes, you'll probably make some mistakes. Don't worry about them. If you've misspoken, dropped a line, or made some other minor error, simply go back and record over what you've done. With my machine, you don't even hear a click indicating starts and stops. That's what you want. You want the final product, no matter how many tape overs you've done in production, to be a seamless garment. That way you won't need any editing . . . which is exactly what you want.

One of the benefits of recording in this way is that your costs are kept to the absolute minimum. Still, your first product may be rather uneven. To avoid professional editing, you may have to record your program again. If this is the case, I suggest you start with a fresh tape. Under the circumstances, it's a very small cost.

Last Words About 60-Minute Audio Cassettes

Using these methods, you can produce 60-minute audio cassette master tapes in record time. When you're more expert, you can literally produce your script in one day and have your finished master tape the next. What then?

When you've finished your master, it's time to send it off for production. There are many places that duplicate tapes these days. One souce of leads is Dottie Walter's lively publication *Sharing Ideas Among Professional Speakers,* Royal Publishing, P.O. Box 1120, Glendora, CA 91740 (818) 335-8069. Since so many professional speakers need tape duplication services, this is a good place to look for them.

Personally, I recommend Larry Adams at Dove Enterprises. Here, you get your tapes duplicated, a label printed and affixed (typesetting charges not included), and a box . . . all for about 90 cents per cassette (as of this writing). Contact Larry at Dove Enterprises, 907 Portage Trail, Cuyahoga Falls, OH 44221; (800) 233-DOVE. (Note: remember to put a "P" and a "C" and the date on your label; this is for copyright protection.)

How many cassettes should you produce? Most novices recklessly over order. Unless you are *certain* you have both a market and a means of regularly reaching it, your initial order should be about 100-150 copies per cassette. Don't print too many!

When You Want To Do Multi-Cassette Packages

At some point, you're going to want to do multi-cassette packages. You can, of course, follow the directions above and do them yourself. Then, you'll only have to worry about packaging. For this, you can either use Larry Adams or Bill Guthy (see below), or do it all yourself.

You can get the vinyl albums you need by checking the Yellow Pages under "looseleaf" or "book and catalog covers" or through the following suppliers:

American Thermoplastics
622 Second Avenue
Pittsburgh, PA 15219
(412) 261-6657

Blackbourn, Inc.
10150 Crosstown Circle
Eden Prairie, MN 55344
(612) 949-2155

Dilley Manufacturing Company
211 East 3rd Street
Des Moines, IA 50309
(515) 288-7289

Sealtronics
8633 Sorensen
Santa Fe Springs, CA 90670-2680
(213) 945-7655

For cassette labels, try:

Audico, Inc.
219 Crossen
Elk Grove, IL 60007
(312) 640-1030

(available in white and colored stock)

Avery International
150 N. Orange Grove Blvd.
Pasadena, CA 91103
(818) 304-2000

(available in white labels only, 15 per sheet)

But what if you don't want to do things yourself? First, I recommend you read the chapter in my book MONEY TALKS dealing with professional audio cassette production. After you've finished, you've got to find a competent firm that will give you the professional assistance you require. I suggest you contact my friend Bill Guthy at Cassette Productions. To begin with, you can ask for his free, helpful booklet "How To Produce A Cassette Program And Never Leave Your Office" (a good booklet illustration, by the way). If it induces you to use Bill's services, so much the better; he is well-known in the audio field and well thought of. You can reach him at Cassette Productions, 5796 Martin Rd., Irwindale, CA 91706-6299; (818) 969-6881.

Last Details About Audio Cassettes, Including How To Price Them And Use Them To Induce Other Sales

One of the questions you need to settle is how much to charge for your cassettes. Here, as elsewhere, you won't be surprised to hear me say you should charge according to the benefits the listener receives and what your competition is doing . . . not merely some multiple of the production charge. This is yet another reason to focus on just what your listener can get from you if he follows your step-by-step guidance.

In practice, I have found that while audio cassette prices vary widely, you should be able to charge about 17 times your production costs . . . or about $16 per single 60-minute audio cassette. The per-cassette charge drops when you start selling multiple cassette packages. With these, consider charging about $16 for your first cassette and $8 for each additional cassette. For 90-minute cassettes charge about 25% more for each cassette. Remember, these figures are for your guidance only! What's important is that you always focus on the benefits your listeners get . . . and just how much your competitors are charging. The specific benefits you offer enable you to charge more . . . your competitors, of course, may force you to lower your price.

Once you have your audio cassettes and have priced them, it's time to start using them in the following ways:

1. as a profit center. Of course, you want to make money from them in their own right. Now you can!

2. as a premium. Audio cassettes are some of the best premiums going. Why? They have a real price. When you give your customers an audio cassette as a premium for having bought other things, you've giving them something of value. But beyond their retail price, they have a more substantial value because of the information they offer. You must stress this when you use your audio cassette as a premium. Thus: "A $14 retail value, your *free* audio cassette gives you the information you need to (get whatever benefit it offers)." An audio cassette used as a premium offers you two ways, you see, of motivating your customers to do what you want them to do: both because of its actual retail value . . . and because of what they get when they use it.

3. to generate additional sales. Audio cassettes, like all how-to products, are the best brochures going. Because they have a real value, your customers are not going to throw them away. Thus, they'll retain your add-on message . . . the message that lets your customer know what else you can do for them. Every time they listen to the audio cassette — every time, that is they want to achieve the objective it promises — they'll hear your client-centered follow-up message, too. This means there's an enhanced likelihood they'll finally figure out what you can do for them . . . and call upon you for further products and services.

4. as a means of generating good publicity for you. Audio cassettes are products, and products can be sent to relevant publications for comment and review. You must not just produce and sell your audio cassettes . . . you must leverage them to secure promotional advantages both for the cassettes themselves and for you and your company. Thus, when I release a new audio cassette, I also send a media release to the appropriate media sources. This release focuses on two things: the new cassette itself and the benefit it delivers to targeted audiences. The "newness" of the cassette is one reason for featuring it; the benefit of its information to designated prospects is another reason. Use both.

Last Words On Audio Cassettes, First (And Only) Words On Video Cassettes

As you can see, I am a believer in audio cassettes, what they can do for you and their role in your info-empire. It took, perhaps, a little longer than it should have for me to reach this point: I am, you see, very much a print person by nature. What's more, my academic background made me perhaps just the slightest bit haughty about the superiority of words in print to words on tape. We all have our crosses to bear.

But that was yesterday. Now I have my 60-minute programs . . . and my 90-minute multi-cassette programs. And there are more in development. Moving in this direction as I am, it is nonetheless clear to me that audio will never replace print as anyone's primary means of gathering information. Instead, it is a helpful ancillary tool . . . just as the audio products themselves will be a helpful addition to your line of how-to products, which will be incomplete without them. I do not feel the same way about video cassettes and am leaving them out of the discussion of this chapter. I feel I ought to tell you why.

While the construction of a video tape very much follows what you already know about how-to products, video tapes demand a much greater financial investment. $10,000 for an hour's program is by no means uncommon, though there are, of course, ways to cut corners. Such an investment might be warranted if how-to video cassettes were more easy to sell. But just now, they aren't. General retail distribution for the kinds of programs people like you and me create is still problematic. This then leaves us with direct mail promotion as our primary means of marketing. In subsequent chapters, you will learn how to use this to your advantage.

Only when you become an expert in direct mail . . . and have the necessary capital to invest in a video program . . . should you even consider moving in this direction. At that point . . . when you have extra capital at your disposal . . . and are expert in direct response marketing . . . only then, I say, does a how-to video make sense.

This moment is still down the road for you. Think how many things you have to do first: create and distribute your own how-to books . . . and booklets . . . Special Reports . . . and audio cassettes. In short, years of effort.

During this time, you will gather many thousands of names and begin to create your in-house mailing list. You'll become a specialist not only in product development but in market identification and in the kinds of persuasion techniques that get people in these markets to buy what you're selling . . . NOW!

Then . . . only then . . . will how-to video cassettes make sense.

So, wait until that moment to consider them. Now, focus on mastering the kinds of production issues that have so far dominated this text. And on the marketing issues which will shortly begin to overtake them.

As soon as you:

- have identified a market for a video cassette;
- have the money to invest in creating it;
- are the master of direct response marketing, and
- have your own catalog of other how-to products that will help offset the cost of marketing both your cassette and everything else . . .

why, then, by all means go ahead and create a video cassette.

Until then, spend time mastering the necessary steps . . . including the next one, creating your own catalog of how-to products.

Resource Box

While creating a video cassette should certainly not be the first thing you do, you should still be snooping around good sources of how-to videos, getting a sense of what successful people are doing in this field. In this connection, I suggest you check out The Crisp Catalog. Produced by my friend Mike Crisp it contains not only top-quality how-to booklets but also audios and videos. You'll find some of his titles listed in my own catalog, but to see everything he's got write to Crisp Publications, 95 First Street, Los Altos, CA 94022-9803. 1-800-442-7477.

How To Develop And Run Your End-Of-Product Catalog

Before we get into the inky depths of booklet and book production, we must discuss how you develop and run your end-of-product catalog. If you've accepted my argument that whatever how-to product you produce is only a step (however necessary) in your developing relationship with your reader/client, then you know just why you need this catalog.

Virtually no how-to product, no matter how thorough, tells your reader/listener/client everything he needs to know to achieve his desired objective. And certainly no such product gives him everything he needs to reach the Ultimate Benefit offered by your company and its products and services. Thus, any how-to product, however complete, is by its very nature merely a component of what your customer needs. He still needs more to get what he wants.

But where does he set about getting it?

The need for your end-of-product catalog begins in your recognition that the run of people don't have your specialized knowledge. As an authority in your field, you know what resources exist . . . and you know where they are. This may be, indeed probably is, the stuff and substance of your everyday life. However I have news for you: your customers don't have this information at *their* fingertips. Thus, when they wish to achieve what you already know so well, they just don't know where to start . . . don't begin to have a clue. This isn't because they're stupid or

209

inadequate, either. It's just because they haven't specialized in getting the kind of knowledge you have. So don't go feeling so superior!

Thus, because your customers need help . . . and because they trust, rely on and like you (all thanks to the way you presented yourself and your information in the actual product) . . . you must include an end-of-product catalog.

A Few Introductory Points About This Catalog

To begin with, while we'll call this listing of resources a "catalog" in this discussion, you needn't actually use this word to describe what you're creating. Let me show you what I mean.

We're all familiar with the word "catalog." It suggests something you get free from a company that's filled with products and services for you to buy. This description, however, immediately suggests several problems:

1. "something you get free." If you're like me, you don't value too much things you get free. Day after day, I get free catalogs in the mail, and they end up in a stack in my office, most completely neglected. I didn't pay for them . . . and so I don't value them much.

2. "filled with products and services for you to buy." We know when we get a catalog that if we want anything in it . . . we're going to have to buy it. And, while everyone likes having, few actually *like* buying, *i.e.,* spending their money to acquire.

My solution to these two problems is to upgrade the perception of your catalog by repositioning it . . . as a Resource Directory or Resource Guide.

Now, which sounds more valuable to you: catalog or Resource Directory? It's obvious, isn't it?

A Resource Directory is a client-centered marketing tool. It suggests that you have available materials that can help your customer achieve what he wants to achieve . . . not just a catalog he can buy from.

At all times, you have only these objectives: to convince the prospect that what you have is necessary for him . . . that with it he gets what he wants . . . and that the mere listing of these materials is valuable for him, hence something he should keep at hand . . . not stack away in a corner or throw away (like he does with the lowlier catalog).

Your Resource Directory meets all these crucial criteria.

A Word About Names

You needn't be slavish about using the words "Resource Directory." Be creative! Try to create a title that suggests both value and a client-centered benefit. Thus, instead of "Catalog of Sales & Marketing Products," how about "Your Guide To Selling More Products And Services."

My point, you see, is this: "catalog" suggests spending money. People get defensive when they're asked to do that . . . no matter that what they're being asked to buy is actually in their own best interest. When, however, people see the benefits they get from something . . . they actually *want* to buy. In fact, demand to buy (we are, after all, Americans and buying is our birthright.) In this case, letting people buy becomes a service you offer and as such is valued by your customer.

Finding The Right Products

If you've made the decision that helping your customer doesn't end with the last word of your how-to product . . . if you've decided to be truly helpful and truly assist your customer by offering him more of what you know . . . if you've decided to build your relationship with him . . . and, not so incidentally, if you've decided to benefit personally because of this relationship by virtue of all the additional products and services you sell . . . why, then, it's time to set out on a contemporary Scavenger Hunt . . . seeking the best in current how-to products.

Imagine! You are about to embark on a gigantic hunt through the storehouse of America's how-to products. Why, in any given year, over 50,000 books alone are published . . . not to mention the booklets . . . the audio cassettes . . . the Special Reports . . . and the avalanche of other things that will help you help your customer.

Where, oh where, do you begin?

You begin, my friend, with a healthy dose of skepticism. Despite all the things that are available, you'll find it difficult to find products that live up to the high standards of this book . . . the high standards I hope you are now committed to running your business by. In short, there's an enormous amount of junk on the market. That's why you should keep these guidelines in mind before you approach anyone to request products, much less make a distribution and sales agreement.

- You always want to offer your own products. This is not for egotistical reasons, either. You should lead with what you've produced for three reasons:

1. Your customers want more of what you yourself have produced. Believing in you as they do now, they want to use more of your helpful materials. Give these to them . . . right away!

2. Because you've followed the guidelines in this book to create these materials, what you're producing will be some of the best products on the market. I guarantee it!

3. You make more money from the sale of your own products than you ever will from anyone else's. Why? Because from what you product yourself, you get 100% of the proceeds . . . while you'll rarely get more than 50% of the proceeds from what other people have produced.

- As soon as you know which products do best in your catalog, you should create your own product offering that benefit and Ultimate Benefit. In other words, you need to use your catalog not only as a sales but also as a prospecting device . . . determining what things your market wants to buy from you. When you know, produce it!

- You must always give first preference to items giving you at least a 50% discount off the retail price. Thus, while you may at first be forced to deal with companies that have more limited discount policies, as your search broadens and you become more familiar with the materials that are available, you should drop the products produced by these companies in preference to those giving you a better discount, always assuming that the quality of information remains constant (a big assumption).

- You must give preference to companies that are client-centered . . . always remembering that in this case the client is *you!* That is, you want to do business with companies that not only give you a good discount but good service. This may involve, but is certainly not limited to companies:

  - sending you information about their products and how to sell them;

  - providing you with sales copy you can use;

  - making available review copies of their materials;

  - shipping your orders promptly and handling customer service problems expeditiously;

  - willing to ship even single orders at a 50% discount and not committing you to buying up large amounts of their merchandise which may not be sold by you . . . or returned to them.

In short, what you are looking for in the companies you do business with is this:

- superior how-to products that really enable your customers to achieve the benefit promised in the title;

- a significant discount of at least 50% off the retail price;

- marketing copy you can use immediately;

- no restrictive practices that force you to get more stock than you can use and also tie up your money;

- responsiveness to such legitimate trade requests as catalogs, merchandise samples, customer service for problems, expedited delivery if they are shipping for you, *etc.*

If you have had no experience in marketing and merchandising, you may think that all companies conform to these criteria. I can assure you, they don't.

In fact, one of the most astonishing things about establishing my own Sure-Fire Business Success Catalog has been the discovery of how few companies actually work this way. For the last several years, I've been at a peep-hole looking in on the things causing the decline of American competitiveness, all the egotistical, selfish, downright stupid trade practices that are destroying us. Be advised.

Nonetheless, you are committed to helping your customers . . . and you want to derive the extra income that comes from helping them . . . so you must make the search for the additional how-to products you need.

Making Sure You're Looking For The Right Things

Before you start your search, check your direction. You will remember our previous discussion about benefits and Ultimate Benefits. Now is the moment to remind you of this.

Your end-of-product catalog must represent your Ultimate Benefit . . . that is, the *real* benefit your customers get by doing business with you. Everything in the catalog must reflect and reinforce this benefit; nothing in it must direct the customer away from this primary advantage. Thus, each product must both mirror the Ultimate Benefit and, in its own right, deliver a benefit leading to this Ultimate Benefit. Catalogs work, you see, because they're tight and coherent . . . everything marching in the same direction. So it must be with yours.

Thus, this is a good time to review the Ultimate Benefit (or Benefits) you're in business to deliver. As you look at any given product or service, you've got to ask yourself: does this reinforce my Ultimate Benefit? If it does, you may consider it. If it doesn't, don't bother. In time, of course, as your perception of your market and its wants becomes crystal clear, you'll know instantly if a product fits or doesn't fit your format . . . that is, whether it helps reinforce the Ultimate Benefit you're delivering . . . or distracts people, confusing them. At the beginning, you may be tempted to take on a product merely because it sounds good. DON'T DO IT! As I've said before, your Ultimate Benefit is more important than any given product . . . and everything in your catalog must reinforce it.

Where To Look

How-to products are everywhere. Here are just a few of the good places to seek them out:

- Search through *Books in Print* (published by R.R. Bowker Co. and available in most bookstores and libraries). Here's where you find a complete list of the books currently available; a companion volume lists forthcoming books . . . another good place to look so you can get the jump on your competitors.

- Scan *Publishers Weekly,* Bowker Magazine Group, Cahners Magazine Division, 249 W. 17th St., New York, NY 10011. Its pages are crammed with ads for books . . . and three times a year it offers a catalog of the new listings of publishers. Also look at *Small Press*, Meckler Corp., 11 Ferry Lane West, Westport, CT 06880-5808. Also check the other *Small Press* periodical published by Henry Berry (P.O. Box 176, Southport, CT 06490). From both, you'll soon know just what publishers produce the kinds of things you're interested in and can ask to be on their mailing lists accordingly.

- Review *Literary Marketplace,* R.R. Bowker, Data Base Publishing Group, 245 W. 17th St., New York, NY 10011. This annual lists the names of all publishers releasing at least three books a year. Again, get their addresses and write for catalogs.

- Read the newsletters of the professional publishing associations. These are particularly useful:

  - *COSMEP Newsletter,* COSMEP, Inc., P.O. Box 420703, San Francisco, CA 94142

  - *PMA,* Publishers Marketing Association, 2401 Pacific Coast Hwy., Suite 102, Hermosa Beach, CA 90254

  - *Publisher's Report,* The National Association of Independent Publishers, P.O. Box 430, Highland City, FL 33846

  - *SPEX,* Marin Self-Publishers Association, Box 1346, Ross, CA 94957.

- Check out *Booklist,* published by the American Library Association, 50 E. Huron St., Chicago, IL 60611. Only about 20% of books received by *Booklist* end up getting a review, and a review there is a "buy" recommendation for America's libraries. This way, you're taking advantage of the review work already done by someone else.

- Read *Sharing Ideas Among Professional Speakers*. Already mentioned, this lists lots of books produced by and for professional speakers.

- Research the Gale *Encyclopedia of Associations*, Book Tower, Detroit, MI 48226. Read the newsletters and publications produced by professional associations in your field; they list lots of books and products. These days many associations produce their own line of products, too.

- Review the Oxbridge *Directory of Newsletters* and *Standard Periodical Directory*, both produced by Oxbridge Communications, 150 Fifth Ave., New York, NY 10011. Between these two sources over 85,000 publications are listed . . . you'll certainly want to be familiar with the ones connecting with your market.

- Read Nigel Maxey's publication *Small Publisher*, Box 1620, Pineville, WV 24874-1620. Also read the catalogs and publications produced by that astonishing book creator and seller Russ von Hoelscher, Profit Ideas, 305 E. Main Street, Goessel, KS 67053. And review the regular book catalog produced by Neal Michaels, Premier Publishers, P.O. Box 330309, Ft. Worth, TX 76163-0309.

- Contact me. If you're selling to businesses, independent professionals and nonprofit organizations, look no further. I'm very much at your service.

Then, of course, you can do what I do:

- Go through the resources and bibliographies of existing books. How-to products that you like will usually lead you to other how-to products you'll like.

- Haunt bookstores. I'm always going through the newest releases in my neighborhood bookstores.

- Read your "junk" mail. I get lots of leads from the circulars people send me as well as from card decks, unsolicited direct mail, flyers, *etc*. So will you.

Another Way To Find The Products You Want

Looking for products this way is all very well and good; it's something you'll always have to do. But it's insufficient. There's another important thing you can do.

Through your researches, you'll soon identify publications that reach the producers of the kinds of how-to products you want in your catalog. These will be the publications of product producers . . . and you need to be aware of all of them. Many I've listed above; others you'll discover as you read these. In any event, about 90 days before your closing deadline for new materials for the catalog you're working on, send a notice like this to these publications.

Lant Seeks New Books For
Sure-Fire Business Success Catalog

Cambridge, MA. Massachusetts author and entrepreneur Dr. Jeffrey Lant is seeking books, booklets, Special Reports and audio cassettes to sell in the summer edition of his Sure-Fire Business Success Catalog. Books must be of particular interest to small businesses, entrepreneurs, independent professionals and others with a product or service to sell.

Usual terms are 50% discount and your ability to drop ship. Selections for the summer catalog must be made by April 15, 1993.

If you haven't seen a copy of this catalog, ask for a sample of the new spring issue which features 350+ profit-making recommendations.

Note: once the circulation of your catalog goes over 20,000 copies, by all means put this fact in your media release. It enhances your standing and makes it more likely you'll receive review materials.

The objective here, of course, is to get people with products to identify themselves to you. What astonishes me, however, is that of all the people who sell how-to materials, I'm one of the few who actually places notices like these. What can the others be thinking of? It's the height of marketing common sense to get out your message to producers you want to do business with and to use someone else's money to do so. But why will the publications print this? For one reason only: because helping their readers sell products and make money is one of the reasons they're in business. Take full advantage of this fact.

Special Note: after you read this book, produce your product and READ MY CATALOG TO SEE WHAT I'M LOOKING FOR, if you think I'd like and could sell what you've got, by all means send me a copy with your promotional materials.

Crawling Before You Walk

Of course, before you get to the point where you're placing these free notices in relevant publications, having products rained on you (as they are rained on me), you need to get started creating relationships with existing product producers . . . and getting them to make merchandise samples available to you. When you're new and green in this business, there's a particular art to this.

As you seek to see merchandise you could sell, keep this in mind about the people you're soliciting: we (for I'm one myself) are inundated with requests for freebies. College professors write requesting them . . . reviewers want them . . . even prisoners (amazingly well organized these days) constantly request free copies of what we produce. They all have the best of reasons . . . and none seems to give a thought to the fact that we are all in business to make money, not merely distinguish ourselves as charitable characters. What's more, we have learned from sad experience that most of the freebies we send out either are not read or used and certainly don't generate new sales.

Not least, most of the people who request free products because they're certain they can sell them are people who have no track record and are simply names on a page. They write . . . they request . . . they get samples . . . they disappear.

Under the circumstances, is it any wonder people like me are very, very cautious about who gets free copies of our products?

If you want to succeed in getting the merchandise that you want, you'll understand this caution, take it into consideration, and act differently from the run of the mill freebie seeker.

Writing For Merchandise Samples

After you've identified someone whose product you think you can sell and that you would like to review for inclusion in your end-of-product catalog, it's time to see it. Before writing for a copy, have you checked your local bookstore outlets or library to see if you can review it on the shelf? In all fairness to you, of course, if the product is widely available, it's probably something you shouldn't consider carrying. The best catalogs, after all, are made up of specialty merchandise you just can't conveniently find and that isn't generally available. Nonetheless, you ought to check the shelves anyway, just in case.

Not having found it, it's time to write a letter to the person who can get you the merchandise. If you're writing to a publisher, your letter should be sent to a person whose title may be director of publicity or, better, director of special sales. Special sales, for your information, are those that are made outside of regular retail channels. In larger companies, there may also be a director of catalog sales. In any event, a call to the publisher's switchboard will usually direct you properly. Get the person's name you want to talk to, her title (it's usually a woman), address and direct telephone number. Keep these on file.

Getting Ready To Compose Your Letter

Before you write your letter, you need to consider a few things:

1. How are you going to promote their product: will you just put it in your catalog and/or will you promote it through your product itself (in a Resource Box) and in a Special Report or article?

2. Are you going to stock merchandise, or do you want the publisher to ship for you, (this is called 'drop-shipping')?

3. Do you have credit references available?

Let's look at these points briefly.

Promoting Their Product

You're more likely to get all the merchandise samples you want, if you indicate just how broadly you'll promote their product. While you may only be printing 1000 copies of your product, hence 1000 back-of-product catalogs . . . you can also help the publisher you're seeking to do business with by indicating you'll be providing complete order information in the text of your product. Moreover, you can always create a Special Report and/or article featuring their product. In other words, it's your responsibility to do what you can to build your credibility and foster this relationship.

Stocking Merchandise Or Drop-Shipping

The debate on stocking merchandise vs drop-shipping will probably go on forever. That's because there's something valid to be said on both sides.

If you stock merchandise, you usually (but not always) get a better discount than if the publisher ships for you. And, of course, you can get your orders out more quickly.

On the other hand, if you stock merchandise, you do have to take up your own space, tie up your dollars . . . and handle all the shipping details. Until you know just how many units you'll be selling, you just can't be sure how many you need . . . so you may either have too few (usually not a problem) . . . or too many (very much a problem). Either way, it's a guessing game. Moreover, as publishers update their products you could be left with outdated merchandise you'd have to mark-down to get rid of.

Drop-shipping is the other side of the coin. On the positive side, you only order what you want . . . when you want it. As you get paid orders, you can order the merchandise you want. Also, you don't need a lot of space to run a drop-shipping business. This is the way I handle most of my business with product producers; I work from a studio condominium in a very high rent area where space is at a decided premium. Warehousing books just isn't a physical (or financial) possibility. I put my extra money into marketing (which is where it should go) not into stock charges and overhead.

On the other hand, with most major publishers, when you use drop-shipping you don't ordinarily get the best discounts. There is also room for lots of confusion; I often think, in fact, that you have to be a certifiable idiot to work in the shipping facilities of most publishers given the kinds of mistakes they make. Also, if a customer doesn't like the product (which will happen), all too often he returns it to the shipper (the publisher) . . . not the seller (you), thereby causing lots of unnecessary aggravation, since that book actually belongs to you if the customer doesn't want it. Finally, if you take purchase order numbers from institutions like I do, you have to advance your money to pay for products that you'll only be reimbursed for later. This can cause you cash-flow problems.

For newcomers to this business, however, I'd suggest beginning on a drop-ship basis and, if you have the space, progressing into the warehousing of small amounts of stock (say 5-10 copies of each title), going slowly, never overordering, making sure you can sell what you stock. If I lived on the steppes of Wyoming with a bunkhouse for my office, this is what I'd do myself.

Getting Credit References

One of the biggest problems in publishing is getting people to pay their bills in a timely fashion . . . or, indeed, at all. Frankly, this is a scandal. That's why I advise you to do as much cash business as possible . . . and both present the best possible credit references to people you want to do business with . . . and live up to them. Your credit references should consist of people who have known you for at least six months and should include the highest amount of credit they've granted you. If you're newly in business, by all means use personal credit sources, such as credit cards.

Now, Compose Your Letter

Your letter to the special sales director or manager of catalog sales should have the following components:

— *What The Publisher Needs*

- an indication of what title(s) you're interested in;
- how you're planning to promote them;

- market you are trying to reach;

- number of people you'll realistically market to;

- credit references about you;

- sample of any previous catalog you may have created or copies of materials in which you have promoted either their products or those produced by others.

— *What You Need*

- copy of the title(s) you're interested in;

- publisher's advertising and marketing copy;

- information about publisher's drop-shipping program, discount rates for both drop-shipping and warehousing, and amount of shipping money publisher wants with individual orders;

- assurance there will be sufficient stock for up to six months after your product comes out;

- recommendations of other titles appropriate to your targeted markets, both those available now and those scheduled for publication;

- getting put on publisher's mailing list.

Letter-Sweeteners

Remember what I said about the cautiousness of most publishers, caution born of constant requests for freebies and equally constant disappointment about the results of their generous actions? Well, here's where you can indicate that you are a true marketer . . . not just a freebie hustler. Indicate that if perfect merchandise samples are not available, you'll be happy to accept slightly cover-damaged stock or else pay the regular wholesale discount price on a single copy.

Take my word for it, the publisher will appreciate this offer . . . and may, out of a sense of deep gratitude (and shock), give you just what you really want! If you do get the imperfect stock or have to pay something for the materials you want, remember: this, too, is only a step on the road to your ultimate success. As you establish your relationship with this producer and begin to sell their products, you can rest assured you'll move beyond this point rapidly. I know.

The Publisher's Response

Most, but certainly not all, publishers will respond promptly to a professional letter like this one. But if you don't get a response within two weeks, either call the person you've written to, or send a copy of your initial letter (a computer makes this very easy) marked "second request" and the date. This should motivate the laggards.

Now it's up to you to evaluate what you've got according to the guidelines I've already given you. As you do so, here are a few refinements to keep in mind:

- While you won't know right away which companies are better to work with (that comes with experience), as you do learn, keep in mind that with the disorganized producers you will either have to stock merchandise . . . or just not do business with them. After your second complaint from a customer of non-delivery of merchandise (or other irritating foul-up), it's time to make this decision.

- It's better to work with an efficient, well-organized company that gives you a rather lower discount (40%, say, instead of the minimum discount of 50% you want) over a company that gives you a bigger discount but constant headaches. As you'll learn, the greater discount isn't worth the greater hassles.

- Smaller companies (those, that is, where the owner can immediately be reached by you) are generally more easy to deal with than larger companies where "customer service" representatives have no vested interest in things going right and keeping you happy.

- Just as you get a good relationship with your account representative at larger companies, she'll be gone. On average, I'd say that 6-9 months is about the length of time you'll deal with any individual in a special sales situation. Then, you often have to start all over again; after all, they don't know you! (By the way, one of the special services you provide in this world is training such people.)

Are you feeling somewhat overwhelmed? No wonder. The minute you've decided to create even the tiniest end-of-product catalog, one perhaps designed just to fill up the two or three empty pages at the end of a signature, you've entered into a merchandising labyrinth. Don't worry about it. Do the best you can, and remember your objectives: to help your customers by recommending additional products they can use to their advantage . . . and to help yourself with the extra income.

Keep one more thing in mind, too: you're learning yet another business, connected but distinct from your own product production and marketing. Personally, I started my catalog with a single back-to-back 8 1/2" x 11" flyer which I used as an insert into my outgoing book packages and mail. That was just a few years ago . . . and now I have one of the largest how-to catalogs in the nation! When I started, I knew next to nothing about merchandising, discounts, drop-shipping, fulfillment . . . or any of the other things you must master. And will — because it's to the advantage of your customers . . . and yourself. *And* because you'll be able to take everything you learn in your dealings with other producers and help yourself . . . as you enter into merchandising relationships with those who want to sell your products, a subject we'll be dealing with later.

Crafting Your Catalog

Through the various ways we've already discussed, you'll soon be getting merchandise to review for possible adoption by your catalog. As you review these materials, always ask yourself if what you are looking at is consonant with your theme, your Ultimate Benefit (priority 1), whether your market wants to get the benefit this product offers (priority 2), whether it's the best conceivable how-to product on the subject (priority 3), whether you're getting the highest possible discount you can get (priority 4), and whether the product producer will be easy to work with (priority 5 which can quickly become priority 4). Once you're sure about these things in relation to any given product, it's a go, something you want for your catalog. You now need to do two things:

1. write the catalog copy you need, and
2. prepare for the orders you're going to get.

Writing Catalog Copy

Later in this book, I shall be discussing how to write copy, so I intend to postpone my major discussion of the subject until then. Moreover, I have written a complete book on this subject which I now recommend to you. If you're really serious about learning how to use words to get people to buy what you're selling, don't just read, religiously follow CASH COPY: HOW TO OFFER YOUR PRODUCTS AND SERVICES SO YOUR PROSPECTS BUY THEM . . . NOW! Immodest though it may be to say so, it's the best book ever written on this pivotal subject and will, if faithfully followed, both save you money . . . and make you a good deal, too.

Here, however, let me simply remind you of a few key points:

- Catalog copy, like all copy, must be centered on client benefits, not product features. In other words, don't write about the product . . . write about what "you" (the customer) get when you *use* the product. This is a completely different thing.

- This copy should be heavy on benefits . . . but also empathetic in tone. Your customer must feel you're really speaking to him . . . advising him . . . urging him . . . taking an interest in what he wants and giving your best advice on how to get it. The best catalog copy is warm copy . . . human, empathetic, entirely client-centered.

- Your copy must be about movement . . . it should be transformational in nature, clearly indicating to the prospect that with the product you're recommending he'll move closer to where he wants to be. The best how-to copy is always about movement . . . about helping a prospect get out of one place and into another . . . thanks to the product he's about to acquire.

- Your copy should be short, action-oriented, spirited, never bland or boring. There's an excitement about the best copy that leads to your customer feeling thrilled about the product itself . . . and stimulates him to acquire it. Remember, your prospects want a reason to buy . . . and they're looking for that reason from you. Give it to them!!!

Points Particularly Pertinent To Catalogs

The heart of your catalog is, of course, the write-ups about the various products. Please note I said "write-ups"; for the kind of end-of-product catalog I am discussing, it is not necessary to have photographs. You should be able to make your point quite nicely with words alone . . . always assuming you are using the right words . . . and a barrage of client-centered benefits. Still, there are some refinements you should know about:

An Introductory Letter

The goal of your how-to product in general . . . and the objective of this catalog are the same. You want immediate sales, of course, but you also want to establish a long-term relationship with the buyer, a relationship that will generate many future sales. This means you have to talk to your prospect . . . and an introductory letter is a perfect place to do this.

- Open with a client-centered salutation. "Dear friend" isn't nearly good enough. Instead, put the benefit you're delivering in the salutation, thus: "Dear Colleague Building A More Profitable Home-Based Business."

- Then tell your prospect exactly what he gets from using your catalog . . . lay heavy stress on the benefits . . . and why he should pay attention to what you've got.

- Follow-up with any special offers that the prospect gets when he buys from the catalog. You always want to give people incentives to buy more . . . "When you invest $150 before (date), here's the benefit you get . . . When you invest at least $200 here's the benefit you get." In short, let people know what they get . . . and what they have to do for it. Do this in your introductory letter.

- Tell those who didn't get the product from you directly (who may be leafing through it in a bookstore or library), they must get in touch with you to learn about other benefits you have available. Understand that all people, even those who need want you're selling, aren't going to act immediately to acquire it. You've therefore got to give them an incentive to contact you . . . even if they're not buying today. After all, it's to your benefit to "capture" the name.

- End your letter with another benefit. "Sincerely yours" is mundane. So how about, "Your constant profit maker"? In other words, let your prospect know what benefit he gets from you . . . and stress this benefit everywhere you can.

- Sign your letter with your first name only. Why? Because your given name is the name you use with friends. Don't make this just a business letter . . . make it a friendly letter between you who has the means to be helpful . . . and your prospect, who wants the help.

Now you've got a great opening letter.

Tricks Of The Trade For Making The Inside Of Your Catalog More Client-Centered

Once you've started out friendly, you must continue friendly. Here's how to do this:

- Put in personal asides and observations. One of the things people keep commenting about in my catalog is how "you are there" it sounds . . . how fresh, immediate, real. This is exactly what you want to achieve. Speak to your customer like the friend you want him to be . . . like the friend you want to be. This kind of authenticity is essential in creating a client-centered catalog.

- Use testimonials that focus on the benefits of certain products . . . and the value of your catalog as a whole. Don't have any such testimonials now? Don't worry. As you start distributing your products, put a short note inside asking people to tell you how they've used your products . . . and what they've gotten as a result. If you like, use self-addressed stamped postcards with this message: "After you've achieved something significant using this (how-to product), please let me know what it was. Please be as specific as you possibly can be." Now leave space for the customer's name, address and telephone number. If you want to stimulate more responses, tell them they'll get a Special Report of their choice when they respond. I guarantee you, this will produce lots of testimonials you can then use in your catalog.

- Remind people about the special offers you've got. Just because you've told your customer once that you've got a special offer for him . . . don't expect him to remember that. If you've got something important for him . . . keep saying so.

(Almost) Last Words About Your End-Of-Product Catalog

There are essentially two ways to approach your end-of-product catalog. Either you can develop your catalog to simply fit any blank pages that may remain in the last signature of your booklet or book. Or you can create it in a standard length. While it is certainly all right to put your toe in the catalog water with the first alternative, it's better for you if you move as soon as you can to the second, that is, to producing a catalog that's a standard size. That way you can work on it while you're producing the product itself.

Just how long this standard size will be will vary, of course, depending on how many products you've found. You'll certainly want it to be 8 pages, perhaps 16.

If you do produce a standard-sized catalog, however, you still may end up with empty pages at the conclusion of the final signature. Fortunately, you can prepare for this by asking the publishers you do business with if they have standard-sized (8 1/2" x 11" or 6" x 9") camera-ready art (often called PMTs or slicks) available into which you can slip your name, address and telephone number. Most large publishers don't have this kind of camera-ready art available . . . lots of smaller independent publishers — like me! — do.

In fact, if you find yourself at the last minute with empty pages, are directing your product to my kind of market, and want to make extra money, you can contact me. Your art work will go out the same day.

Now that you know this, the next time you see blank pages in anyone's book headed with the word "notes", you'll know they were willing to pay for empty pages instead of doing what's necessary to fill those pages with items of use to both their customers and themselves. Astonishingly stupid, no?

A Word About Including Services In Your End-Of-Product Catalog

If you've read my Sure-Fire Business Success Catalog at the back of this book (and if you haven't, you certainly should), you see that in addition to a host of products, I also promote my own consulting services. You should do the same.

As I hope I've made plain, a how-to product enables you to help your reader/ listener/customer in many ways. You help him in the individual product itself.

You help by referring him to other specialists who can help. And, through the end-of-product catalog, you help him by making other useful products available.

Some people, however, will want still more help . . . more direct help from you. You must be prepared to give it to them. Thus, by all means include detailed information about what you can do for your customers in a consulting capacity. Let them know just what benefits you can help deliver . . . and how you work. Do what's necessary to stimulate them to pick up the telephone and call you immediately. Because selling your consulting services is likely to be quite lucrative for you, far more than what you derive from your individual problem-solving products, by all means devote more space in your catalog to these services . . . or develop special full-page ads you can insert at the end of your product.

The important thing is that your customers know what you can do for them individually . . . have some incentive for calling you now . . . and the information they need to connect with you immediately. Doesn't this seem sensible to you? It certainly seems so to me . . . which is why I've been perplexed for many years at just how few how-to writers, so many of whom have consulting services available, include this crucial information in their products. Just what can they be thinking of?

Preparing For The Orders You'll Get

The good marketer not only knows how to stimulate orders . . . he knows how to prepare for the orders that will inevitably arrive because of that stimulation. This means getting prepared for fulfillment . . . even before a single prospect has your end-of-product catalog.

In another chapter, I'll be giving you crucial information on how to integrate your personal computer into your how-to business. You've already seen the importance of this computer in creating your product. Now you'll see how important it is in product fulfillment and customer relations.

Let's start at the beginning: in your end-of-product catalog there either are (or will be) both products created by you and products created by other people. Your goal with these products is simple: you want to get them into the hands of their purchasers as soon as possible . . . and you want to motivate their buyers to buy something else . . . as soon as possible. With the computer, it's easy to do this.

Using The Computer With Products You Create

Your best customers are customers who have already bought from you and are happy with their purchase decision. If they have the money to buy more products . . . and they want to make more progress towards achieving their own objectives, they want to hear how you can help them. That's why you need an Upgrade Letter.

An Upgrade Letter is composed of the following parts:

- a notice in the upper right hand corner that the offer you are making is good for thirty days only and expires thirty days from the date you give them; (using a computer macro key with today's date keeps this function automatic).

- a personal salutation;

- your thanks to the customer for buying this product;

- an indication of precisely how the customer can use this product to get what he wants (remember, just because a customer has your product doesn't mean he won't return it. Therefore, you must always let your customer know precisely what benefits he gets from it.)

- an indication of 1-5 other products you have available that contain benefits you're sure this particular customer (because of his interests) will want to have. Ideally, you've packaged all these products as part of a series . . . thereby making the logic of your recommendation even clearer. Thus, if this customer has bought volume 3 of a 7 volume set (the current number of my own Get-Ahead Series), you can point out the benefits in the other volumes . . . and what the customer gets from them.

- a special price you are making available to this customer on any one of these items . . . or the complete set . . . if only they act in the next thirty days.

  - a postscript where you either point out some particular benefit of acting or stress some other customer benefit. For example, right now on my customer upgrade letters I'm asking the buyer to send a letter of recommendation to his local library about the particular book he's bought, send me a copy and get a free Special Report of his choice. Thus, I get local people recommending my books to the acquisitions librarians of local libraries . . . and making additional sales. Smart, huh?

An order coupon should follow your letter. If you're computerized (and I hope by now you're either committed to getting a computer or using the one you have more effectively), you can put a box before each product you're making available and put an "x" in the one the customer has already bought. All the customer has to do is check the additional products he wants, fill out the shipping information and supply you with credit card details or a check.

Does this work? You bet it does! To begin with, your customer has probably never seen a letter like this before. No wonder! Until now I've probably been the only publisher in America to use it. So, it has the value of novelty. Secondly, it's client-centered . . . giving precise guidelines to your customer about how to move closer to the objective he really wants to achieve. Third, it takes full advantage of the product you've sent. If your product is a solid one, one that delivers the benefits you said it would, then it only stands to reason that your customer will want more of your fine products. Fourth, you're offering a discount. Your customer knows he can get what he wants . . . and save money, too — an irresistible combination. Finally, it's a timed offer. The deadline — the knowledge that the special offer will be lost if he doesn't act — causes the action you want.

And what is your commitment to the process? Writing the initial letter and entering the customer's name and address. Then printing. My three-page letter (two pages of client-centered marketing copy and a one-page response coupon) takes less than a minute to print out in draft mode, which is perfectly suitable for this kind of response. While it's printing, I enter the check in my cash receivables journal for the day. When I'm finished with that, my upgrade letter is done, too . . . and I've created a totally focused client-centered marketing letter. It brings in money regularly . . . and gets more of my products out into the world. In short, this technique:

- makes my buyers know I'm thinking about them and have other means to help them;

- makes additional sales (and so helps my bottom line), and

- gets more of my products into the world (where still more people use and see them.)

Note: when you're selling other people's products, you can use an Upgrade Letter whether you drop-ship or not. If you drop-ship, you can send your Update Letter to the customer letting him know approximately how long it will take them to get what he's ordered (allow at least four weeks for book rate and two weeks for UPS, including the time it takes the shipper to get the order and send it). If he's paid by credit card, include his charge slip . . . then indicate what else you have available to help him reach his objectives. Remember, stress benefits . . . not features! And include an order coupon that leaves minimal work to the customer. Send this letter out the day you receive the order. If you're shipping the order yourself, simply include this letter with the products.

Creating Order Forms

When product manufacturers are shipping for you, you need to develop a form you can send them with the information they need. What you send should be in the form of a letter. It should:

- be sent to your customer service representative;

- indicate which book/product you have sold;

- provide the customer's name and address;

- either indicate that you're including a check for a certain amount (an amount based on the discounted price of the book and the shipping charges they want) or that you're to be billed at their highest discount;

- if this company requires your mailing label for the customer's package, indicate if you've included one.

This is the information they need to fulfill this order.

Now add another section that will help you with your next catalog:

- indicate when your next catalog closing date is;

- ask them to be sure to send you their catalog of products and promotional literature, and

- have them send samples of any additional products they have available for your designated audience (remind them of what that is).

Then, after your signature, leave space for the customer service representative's name, company and address.

When this form is available on computer, all you have to do is add the customer's name and address each time you get an order. Additionally, just keep the price information up to date, and the name of your (ever-changing) customer service representative and . . . *voilà* . . . you now have an easy means of fulfilling your orders and staying current.

Now, simply keep the week's orders in one place and allocate a couple of hours each week to sorting them, writing your checks, creating the package mailing labels for companies requiring them, and getting them out.

More Preparation

Following these guidelines, you'll make rapid progress towards being ready when your orders come in. Here are some other things you need to know about:

— Credit Cards

A wise friend told me years ago, when I only did business in coin of the realm, that taking credit card orders would increase my business significantly. He was right. And so, as early as you can, you must take credit card orders, too.

Depending on where you live, this may be easier said than done. For some reasons, many banks look down on companies that do business without a store front and as a result refuse to open merchant credit card accounts for those of us operating in non-traditional ways. I've never quite understood their point of view, but it seems to go something like this: companies without store fronts are more ephemeral than those with them . . . and placing orders by telephone is more subject to abuse than placing orders in person. Such arguments, of course, are rubbish. Still, when has a reasonable argument ever impressed a banker?

If you're having trouble establishing a Master Card or VISA merchant account, do the following:

1. Go directly to the president of the bank that holds your company account, personal account and/or home mortgage. The fact you are doing other business with the bank should help your cause. If your own bank won't open a merchant credit card account for you despite the fact that you do other business with them, change banks. Don't patronize people who won't help you.

2. Shop around. Not all bankers are myopic. Use your personal and other business accounts as leverage. Make a package deal: "I'll put all my accounts at your bank, if you open a merchant credit card account for me, too." Banks are in the negotiating business, so negotiate.

3. Network with people who already have such accounts who can vouch for you. In one recent case, I was able to get a friend an MC/VISA account by picking up the phone and calling the bank that handles my account. Despite the fact that I am in Cambridge and he is in New Jersey and that the bank is very local, he got the account! My recommendation was the crucial reason, so the vice president handling the business told me. If my friend had applied cold, he wouldn't have succeeded.

Note: Virginia author and publisher John Cali had the usual problems getting a merchant credit account. Fortunately, he solved them using some of these recommendations, and now has written an informative Special Report on the subject, which I advise you to get (it's just $26.95 postpaid). Contact John at Great Western Publishing Co., 778 Manor Ridge Road, Santa Paula, CA 93060-1651 (805) 933-2317.

— Packing Materials

One of the things you have to deal with in this business is packing materials. You need both outer shipping materials and inner packing.

For outer materials, you'll probably use either boxes or jiffy bags. Don't buy either from retail stationers; the price is just too high. Instead, follow the directions in Tod Snodgrass' excellent book *Found Money: The Expense Reduction System,* Lowen Publishing, P.O. Box 6870, Torrance, CA 90504-0870. Check the Yellow Pages in your neighborhood for discount office supply businesses. Depending on how competitive your area is, you should be able to find a good price on jiffy bags by the box (100 pieces) . . . and get delivery, too, as I do. This is most convenient.

As far as boxes and many other packing supplies are concerned, try Robbins Container Corp., 222 Conover St., Brooklyn, NY 11231 (718) 875-3204.

Note: in my neighborhood there are lots of bookstores that throw away thousands of good book boxes. For years, I've simply carried home the ones I wanted and saved lots of money doing so. My physician says I need exercise, and, as a parsimonious Scotsman in good standing, I can't think of a better way of getting it — and saving money — than going "dumpstering" in Harvard Square. Sadly, some of my younger friends, forced to assist me in these post-prandial exertions, find the activity less than compelling. Do you think this is yet another sign of the weakening moral fiber of the next generation?

As far as your inner packing needs are concerned, some people use the non bio-degradable (and greasy feeling) "peanuts". I don't. They're not good for the environment . . . and cost money. I've found that you can use regular garbage bags (bought in bulk from a discount grocery store) and old newspapers. If you need inside packaging (as when you're packing several books in a box, for instance), simply wrap the products in a garbage back and then pack in old newspapers. This works perfectly well (I've sent thousands of packages this way) . . . and costs very, very little. So does the method used by publisher Rich Partain of PF$ Publications, P.O. Box 9852, Bakersfield, CA 93309. He tells me he has an arrangement with a number of local furniture stores and a retailer of spa and jacuzzi equipment. From them, he gets both foam packing sheets and blocks which he uses to pack his books. He merely approached the stores about his needs. They were delighted to help, because they were paying to have this material carted off. He does it for free . . . and gets all the packing material he requires!

— *Shipping Labels*

In addition to boxes and packing materials, you're going to need shipping labels. Many people use labels that look cheap and shoddy; I cannot accept this. For years, I've been using the ones produced by Stationery House. Admittedly, they are not the least expensive ones available, but they do look good . . . and never fall off in transit. You'll need both Fourth Class (book rate) and First Class labels. Ask Stationery House to send you their catalog: 1000 Florida Ave., P.O. Box 1393, Hagerstown, MD 21741.

— *UPS*

As far as shipping your packages are concerned, I wish to state as unequivocally as one can: AVOID THE U.S. POST OFFICE. To be sure, fourth class book rate shipping is the least expensive way of transporting books. It's also hazardous. If books are lost or damaged in transit, you have virtually no recourse, and certainly no meaningful way of getting compensation. Insuring books is too expensive and time-consuming to be practical for your business. So, you are left to hope for the best, not a reassuring way of shipping.

What's more, I find postal employees shockingly lax. Just this morning, I went into the Harvard Square Post Office with 10 large envelopes to mail . . . and, as usual, the clerk complained that it was four more than by regulation he had to weigh and put postage on. Imagine! No doubt the man thinks he's a valuable employee . . . no doubt he feels egregiously underpaid. But I find such snivelling unbelievably petty and inappropriate. No, it's better to avoid the post office whenever you can.

This leaves us with UPS for delivery in the continental United States and southeastern Canada. Yes, you will pay more (including a $5 weekly charge) . . . or rather, since you'll certainly pass this on to your customer, he will pay more. However, your packages will be conveniently picked up at your door, (automatically and daily once you become a regular account). You can develop a relationship with your driver (I bribe mine with seasonal libations) . . . and, importantly, you can trace missing packages.

Now when someone writes to complain about non-delivery, I simply phone UPS, ask for proof of signature . . . and, within just a few days, send it on to the customer with a short note pointing out in the nicest possible way that he already has the product. In the old days when I exclusively used the post office, I would have been left with no recourse but to send a duplicate . . . fuming all the while. UPS is not perfect, but, particularly for our kinds of products, the better alternative has not yet been invented.

When To Contract With A Fulfillment Service

As you become more successful, you're not going to be able to do all this yourself. With the best will in the world, you're going to need help. Personally, I find packing boxes most therapeutic. I always have. No one, no matter how brilliant, can spend all day writing and marketing. It's just too exhausting. Others crochet . . . or drink . . . I pack boxes, which, in my opinion, combines just the right mixture of the practical and the mindless. Still, there will come a time when, as the number of your own products grows, you have just too many packages to get out.

At this point, try to get someone local to help you . . . a high school student, for instance. Those who aren't making a fortune selling crack will probably relish the fact that you can afford to pay rather better than minimum wage for their assistance. There is a benefit to arranging things this way: when you pack your boxes in house and insert an Upgrade Letter in each and ship UPS, in effect your letter (and any additional marketing materials) travel free. Once you contract with a fulfillment service (which most assuredly won't stuff your letters in outgoing packages), you're automatically increasing the cost of connecting with your new customers . . . and upgrading them.

Still, if the number of your orders increases substantially, you'll probably have to find a professional fulfillment service. You can find them listed in *Literary Marketplace,* in the ads in *Publishers Weekly,* and in the other publishers newsletters already cited. Also, use Dan Poynter's excellent Special Report entitled *Book Fulfillment: Order Entry, Picking, Packing And Shipping.* (Get it from Para Publishing, P.O. Box 4232, Santa Barbara, CA 93140-4232.) Fulfillment services are undoubtedly a convenience . . . but just because you use one doesn't mean you can afford to dispense with the Upgrade Letter and other means of regularly connecting with your buyers. Whether you use a fulfillment service or not, it's your job to thank your buyers for what they've already gotten . . . and make sure you present the benefits of related products you have available . . . and give them an immediate incentive for buying them.

Characteristic Problems Of The Catalog Business And How To Deal With Them

Even when you create the tiniest end-of-product catalog, you're opening yourself up to any number of problems. Most can easily be dealt with . . . all take time. And for each you need to know what to do and systematize your response.

— You're Not Sure Your Customer's Check Is Good

Sadly, there are lots of people these days who want what you'll be selling . . . but can't afford it. So what, they reckon, when all they have to do is sign their name to a little colored bit of paper . . . and send it to you? You need to keep a close look-out for these thieves. Here's how:

- If a person uses a post office box, hold the check for 10 business days until it clears. Legitimate companies and individuals doing business this way will be happy to give you a MasterCard or VISA number to guarantee their check, if you ask for one. (Ask for one.)

- If the check features one address and the customer is asking you to ship to another address, hold it until it clears.

- If the check features a low serial number, hold it until it clears.

- If the customer is ordering a disproportionately large number of your products, wait until the check clears. If he is exigent about wishing immediate shipment, ask for a credit card to guarantee the check.

- If the customer's order doesn't make logical sense . . . that is, if he's ordering items that don't seem to fit together . . . hold it until the check clears.

- If the handwriting is illegible, and you can't tell who you're dealing with, hold the check until it clears.

- If there's no printed name, address and telephone number on the check, hold it until it clears.

If you follow these guidelines, you will decidedly minimize your bad check problems. While I have had a few people bounce checks on me in the last year or two, most of the checks looked sufficiently suspicious to me in advance that I only lost the fee the bank charges me when the check bounces (an injustice if there ever was one, by the way).

In such situations, do the following:

- Notify the person who sent the bad check that you've been charged a fee by your bank. Say that if he's a decent person, he'll at least pay that. Then add that if he still wants the merchandise to send a new check (which I need hardly say you'll hold until it clears).

- If you've already sent the merchandise, ask for it either to be paid for or returned. Say that you'll wait 10 business days. That if you don't hear from the individual within that time, you'll assume he meant to steal from you (use this word). Frankly, as the thieves know, there's not much you can do at this point, but what little there is, do it.

Personally, I notify *Bad Guys,* P.O. Box 7600, Newark, DE 19714. It's a unique nationally syndicated column written by Donald Smith. Smith will try to collect the sum owing to you and will report whatever happens . . . including delinquency . . . in his column. Sometimes this gets you your money; sometimes it doesn't. But at least it alerts other people to the creeps who just want to steal from us and have no intention of paying. They ought to be exposed in any way that's available.

- After you've tried these alternatives, write a direct, honest letter to the thief that calls a spade a spade. Say that you're personally distressed and disappointed about being ripped off . . . and that it sickens you there are such people in the world. Practically speaking, a letter like this probably won't do any good in getting you either your money or materials . . . but it does give you the chance to say what you feel and allows you to release the burden of your justifiable rage. Spit it on the thief who soundly deserves it.

— *Your Customer Doesn't Receive His Merchandise*

For situations where you've sent the merchandise, you need two letters: one that will accompany the UPS proof-of-delivery document. The other, for when you're at fault, is an apology for your foul-up . . . and, if you like, tells the customer you're including a free Special Report by way of apology.

If the merchandise was drop-shipped, develop a letter to the publisher. This should include the customer's name, product ordered, and date you received the order. If you have a copy of the check with which you made payment, send this. For just such times, it's a good idea to include on the check the last name of every customer whose order is included in this check.

— *Your Customer Receives The Wrong Item*

If your customer calls and tells you you've sent the wrong item, simply ask him to return it to you, and you'll get the right item out. My advice is not to send the right item until you receive the wrong one back; customers have a way of forgetting what they promised after they get what they wanted.

It's a good idea to ask the customer to pack the item securely . . . and for you to reimburse the shipping money. We all make mistakes, but that's no reason for your customer to pay for them! Alternatively, send a small but useful present like a Special Report. If the customer simply returns the wrong item, send the right one . . . with your present and shipping reimbursement check.

If your drop-shipper sends the wrong item (of course this happens!), send a letter and ask him to send the right one. If the wrong item is something else you sell, have your customer send it to you . . . and send the drop-shipper your usual check. If it's something you don't sell or already have in abundance, have the customer return it directly to the shipper. Again, it's your responsibility to reimburse the customer's shipping costs . . . although (since it's not your error), you should delete them from your next order to the manufacturer. If you are asking the customer to send the item to you, so advise the drop-shipper.

— Your Customer Receives A Packing Slip And Mistakes It For An Invoice

For reasons completely mystifying to me, some large publishers include packing slips with their orders that look like invoices. Naturally, customers are irritated by this, as it looks like they're being asked to pay for their order a second time. Rest assured they will take out their irritation on you!

If a customer calls you about this, of course, you can clear it up in a sentence or two. But for times when customers write, you can either develop a short explanatory note . . . or simply write on the bottom of their letter and return a response instantly.

— Your Customer Wants To Return The Merchandise

This is an item of catalog business that most greenhorns get most agitated about. They wonder just how many people will take advantage of a 30-day money-back guarantee to return what they've bought. The answer is "it depends."

It depends, that is, on how candidly and thoroughly you've described your product . . . and how clearly your customer feels he can benefit from it. If you've represented the product honestly and fairly — and it can do what you say it can do — you're going to have very few returns. On the other hand, if the customer perceives that your description was hyperbolic, your return rate will be significantly higher.

However, even where you've been completely honest, there will always be people who want to see your product for free . . . perhaps even use it . . . or, more charitably, may find it isn't what they wanted after all. But just how many will there be? Personally, I get about one return each month in my business nowadays . . . a trifling percentage.

Here's what you do when you get the merchandise back:

- Refund the customer's money immediately. Even if the product is returned in less than pristine condition (you can, in fact, expect that), refund the money for the product. But don't refund the shipping costs. These are not refundable.

- Send your refund out right away with a short note saying you're sorry the customer didn't like the product . . . and hoping he'll get something else from another catalog. Point out that while you're not refunding the shipping money (mention that that's standard practice in the industry), because of his undoubted inconvenience and disappointment, you'll be happy to extend a 30-day special price for one of your popular items. Mention the price . . . and ask the customer to return his order/payment with this letter. This way you're offering the customer sometime else. Sales made in this way will more than pay for the cost of sending this letter to disappointed customers and will establish you as a very reasonable person.

— The Merchandise Is Back-Ordered

Depend on it, whether you're stocking merchandise or having others drop-ship for you, you'll soon discover that some product supplies are exhausted and products are back-ordered. Sometimes you discover this the bad way when a customer complains about non-delivery and, upon following-up, you discover this; sometimes the good way . . . when a supplier sends you a notice that a product is currently out-of-stock.

Either way, the minute you discover this, you need to send your standard letter notifying the customer that the product he has ordered is not currently available and giving him as much information as you can about when it will be sent.

Note: publishers are notoriously bad about predicting just when stock will be available. My policy is that when a customer complains the third time about non-delivery to offer him his money back automatically and withdraw the order. Keep this customer's name in your "pending" file, however, so that when the merchandise becomes available you can let him know again.

— The Merchandise Is Out-Of-Print

This is a variation on the above. As soon as you know that a product is permanently out-of-print (and you always don't find out as expeditiously as you ought), write your customer and tell him so. Don't automatically include a refund check. Instead, tell him he has a credit available with you, and include a copy of your catalog. By all means offer him the possibility of a refund . . . but also give him the chance to find something else he wants. After all, you don't want to give him back his money unless you absolutely have to!

Last Words On End-Of-Product Catalogs

By following these guidelines you're excellently situated to achieve several important things:

- You'll let your reader/client know there are other ways you can help him . . . other benefits he can get from you.

- You'll open up new sources of profit that can be marketed to your prospects for very little cost.

- And, as later discussion on this point reveals, you'll be admirably poised to jump into the direct mail catalog business . . . for are you not now cognizant of just what it takes to create a catalog . . . and do you not have the basis for creating a truly significant catalog which you can now send out as a free-standing item, further promoting your products and making additional profits accordingly? I say you are and in Chapter 11, I'll give you the further details you need so you can do just that.

P.S. At the very moment I was completing this chapter, I received a telephone call from Barry Millman in Ottawa, Ontario. He had picked up MONEY MAKING MARKETING in the local library and now wanted to buy all the books then in this series. In under three minutes, I sold him not only the five books he thought he wanted but CASH COPY, too . . . for $175. All because of the end-of-product catalog in that book. Oh, yes, I'm a believer! Not least, because when Barry takes MONEY MAKING MARKETING back to the library, it'll be waiting for my next customer to pick it up . . . and buy from it, just like he did.

6

Booklet And Book Production Tips

We're now ready to discuss the often complicated, generally expensive, frequently frustrating business of booklet and book production. Frankly, I didn't want to face this important topic alone, and so persuaded four knowledgeable and helpful sources to share what they know with you, too. Each is intimately acquainted with the details of info-product production and each, because of his or her distinct vantage point, sees the business differently. Our discussions went on for months and were exceptionally candid. Even though we didn't always agree, I am grateful I've had such thorough specialists working with me on this chapter. They are:

- Barbara Hagen. Barb's an account representative for a large book manufacturer — Walsworth Publishing. She's worked for over 20 years in the printing and publishing industry and can guide you from manuscript to the finished book.

- John & Lorraine Hamwey. John is a graphic designer/illustrator and printing broker. He and his associate operate a Desktop Publishing Service Bureau — ABC Publications, Inc. — in Canton, Massachusetts. They have helped me for many years in the production of my books providing design, typesetting and printing.

- Dan Poynter. Dan's a publisher in his own right and well known as a specialist in the creation and production of books.

239

Not surprisingly, each of us approaches the business of booklet and book production rather differently. But what's important to remember is that each of us shares a common objective: creating superior products as smoothly as possible.

It seems to me that the creation of the booklet or book you want divides naturally into five task areas:

- deciding what kind of booklet or book you want;

- finding your desktop publishing service bureau, cover designer, and printer;

- working with your desktop publishing service bureau, cover designer, and printer;

- knowing what to do if you have a problem (particularly with your printer), and

- getting perfect books to you.

Let's take a look at each area.

Deciding What Kind Of Booklet Or Book You Want

The worst thing you can do is to focus exclusively on the content of your product. . . and ignore the way it looks inside and outside. Certainly bookstore and workshop sales demand an attractive, eye-catching product, and it's your responsibility to provide it. Thus, spend some time reviewing products *qua* products. Spend time in your own library, your friends' libraries, and bookstores reviewing:

- cover designs, colors and laminates. Which ones attract you? Whenever possible, get a color photocopy of the covers that you think work.

- booklet and book sizes. It's likely you'll want your product to be a standard trim size, if for no other reason than this costs less to produce. Popular trim sizes include 5" x 7", 6" x 9", and 8 1/2" x 11". Note: pay real close attention to the size you select, for two reasons. 1) Size may determine your printer. Different printers specialize in different sized products, and 2) it's a good idea to produce a series of products in the same size since this makes it easier to pack and ship them.

- paper qualities. You'll find many variations here, but the standard choices are 50#, 55#, and 60# white or natural offset.

- bindings. Certain kinds of binding (like GBC spiral bound) are really not appropriate for bookstores. You need to select a binding that is appropriate for stores and will ship easily (GBC spiral bound, for instance, doesn't stack straight in a box.)

- photograph and illustration quality. First, find illustrations that you like. Then, make sure they can be well produced. These days photographs and illustrations can be scanned directly into your pages (most desktop publishing service bureaus can provide this service). Or, for high quality photo reproductions, your printer should be able to screen and position your photos. Remember: what you give your printer should be clear, sized, cropped and ready for him to shoot from.

Too, look at the way pages are laid out and the kinds of typefaces that are used. You're looking for pages and type that are attractive and easy to read. You're looking for page layout and typefaces that:

- attract a buyer;

- hold a buyer's interest;

- convince the buyer that spending time with this product will be both profitable and enjoyable;

- are able to disseminate information easily, without undue strain to the buyer.

Unless your product succeeds in doing these things, you have failed. . . no matter how useful the information in the booklet or book actually is.

Note: it goes without saying that typefaces must reproduce well on the printed sheet. Thus, you need to ask your printer just what method of printing he uses and what typeface works best with it. For example, as Barb Hagen points out, "Paper plates will not reproduce a light typeface such as Baskerville, Tiffany or any other light type face, especially with very light serifs." Fortunately, most book manufacturers use the negative/plate printing method and will be able to reproduce any typeface well. Smaller printers, however, use paper plates which are a poorer quality and are not good for long printing runs. Ask your printer to be upfront with you about just what he uses and its benefits and drawbacks.

Another Note: by the time you've finished your search, you'll have quite a collection of material. Don't worry if you don't know the correct printing terminology for everything you like. That will come. Do worry that you've found examples that achieve the necessary objectives.

Finding Your Desktop Publishing Service Bureau, Cover Designer, And Printer

In producing your booklet or book, you need the assistance of at least three distinct people and/or companies: a desktop publishing service bureau, cover designer, and printer. If you find and work with technically competent, client-centered individuals, you will get the end product you want in reasonable time, for a reasonable price, with no more than the routine aggravations of this line of work. If you don't. . . But let's see about how you *will* find the right people you need.

— *Your Desktop Publishing Service Bureau*

People constantly ask me why I don't design and lay out the pages of my books. I'll tell you precisely what I tell them and in the same brisk manner: the job of the info-entrepreneur is to create products and sell products, not to engage in technical tasks of product production that are best left to the experts. While it is certainly true that I could learn all that needs to be done to design and format the pages of my products, my time is better utilized doing the necessary product development and marketing tasks that are the basis for building a fortune in this business. I say this unequivocally: I have known some info-entrepreneurs who design and lay out their own pages, but I have never met an info-millionaire who did so. Only the littlest guys think you can do it all. That's why I'm recommending that you find a competent desktop publishing service bureau (sometimes called an "electronic publisher") and strike up a beneficial working relationship with them.

The best of these businesses can work either from your product typescript or from an IBM/compatible or Macintosh diskette. If you're still not computerized (and I know that after reading this book you surely will be), your service bureau needs to have optical character recognition scanning (OCR), that is the ability to scan your copy into a computer so that the typescript need not be manually entered. The copy that's scanned, of course, must be quite clean and error free.

If you are computerized, the service bureau will work from your diskettes. They will be responsible for translating them so that they're compatible with whatever system the service bureau regularly uses. They will also be responsible for formatting the material and having it typeset. Further, it is the desktop publishing service bureau which generates the first proof pages (and subsequent edited proofs) of your product on which you'll make changes.

While it is certainly true that some printing companies can do all this for you, most of these companies do not have these services in-house. Instead, they simply contract with outside providers for them and then mark up their bills . . . by as much as 40% or even 50%! You are therefore better off working with a separate desktop publishing service bureau and printer.

The real question is: how do you find such a bureau? Well, this is a problem only if you fail to accept my recommendation to use John and Lorraine Hamwey of ABC Publications. I've worked with them over many years now and have referred many people who are as happy as I am with their competent work and thoroughness. As I've remarked to them often enough, they are two of the people who work as hard as I do, my supreme compliment. Still, if you want to shop around, look for leads in the following ways:

- Review the *BCS Buying Guide*. This regularly updated booklet lists any number of desktop publishers and publishing services. It's published for members (who get member discounts on services) by the Boston Computer Society, One Center Plaza, Boston, MA 02108 (617) 367-8080.

- Consult a copy of R.R. Bowker's *Literary Marketplace* where you'll find a section devoted to such people.

- Read *MacWorld,* published by Communication, Inc., 503 Second St., San Francisco, CA 94107 (415) 546-7722. Here, as in other publications devoted to the Macintosh, you'll find ads.

- Read the publishing newsletters mentioned throughout this book. Desktop publishing service bureaus regularly advertise in these publications.

- Call any local dealer of Macintosh products. They're likely to be able to refer you.

What You're Looking For

Because there's no licensing procedure to be a desktop publisher, the quality of the services being offered varies tremendously. Recently in fact a friend of mine returned from California where he'd met a "desktop publisher" at a cocktail party, who admitted, under his gentle questioning, that she didn't even have a computer! As a result, you've got to apply some commonsense precepts before deciding to hire the company. Thus:

- Develop a standard letter outlining your project. Include details about its length, your time schedule, the date you want your product on the streets, whether your material is available on diskette or just hard copy, *etc.* The more specific you can be about what you want and what services you need, the better. Ask your correspondents to call you. Note how long it takes for them to get back to you. It's essential that desktop publishers be well organized. If you can't get this kind of letter answered promptly, don't even think of doing business with such a firm.

- When the desktop publisher calls, have a brief telephone conversation in which you get some answers to the questions above. If this person seems competent and well informed, invite him to your office for a meeting. Note: if the desktop publisher won't come to see you now when he supposedly wants your business, you can be certain he won't bother to see you after he's got it. Ask him to bring samples of relevant work with him to the interview. You want to see other booklets and books he's produced recently. Try to schedule at least three such appointments with different publishers. You want to have comparison data about the quality of work, work procedures, and price.

- Run the interview with the desktop publisher the way you run all such interviews: in a focused manner. You want this person to know you're serious, to know that while this may be your first product, you certainly expect to have others, and that you are seeking a long-term, mutually beneficial relationship. Make these points immediately. You want this person to know you're a serious player.

Describe your project in as much detail as you can. Then ask the desktop publisher to describe exactly how he goes about delivering the materials you want. What you're looking for is someone who knows what he's doing, has a system for doing it, and can give you the guidance you need. Frankly, from a marketing standpoint it would be nice if these companies had their operating procedures written down and clearly outlined. I hope this will happen. Still, you need to pay close attention to ensure that what you're hearing makes sense and you're dealing with a competent individual. Ask questions like these:

- Do you pick up and deliver diskettes, page proofs, *etc.?*

- Do you have written text inputting guidelines and procedures that will enable me to give you the material in just the form you want so you won't have to rework any of my material (for additional cost)?

- Do you charge by the hour or the project? What are your rates?

- Can you advise me on ways to keep my expenses on this project to a minimum?

- How do you ensure my deadline will be met?

- What will your schedule be like at the time I need to start working with you?

Finally, ask for the names and telephone numbers of a couple of recent clients so you can find out from others if they were satisfied with the work.

By discussing your project with three different desktop publishers, you should get enough information to make an intelligent selection. What you do after you've made this choice depends where you are in your own product development process and will be discussed momentarily. If you've chosen wisely, however, you've now solved one of the major problems of product production: how to produce perfect mechanicals from which your product can be printed. You thus have the *inside* of your product well in hand. It's now time, therefore, to turn to the *outside*.

Resource

My preference, of course, is that you spend time on creating your product and selling it, not on laying out and formatting pages. Still, if you want to do this, fine. You'll need two books by desktop publishing specialist Roger Parker. Get *Looking Good In Print* and *Desktop Publishing With Word Perfect*. Both are available from Ventana Press, P.O. Box 2468, Chapel Hill, NC 27515.

— *Your Cover Designer*

It's now time to find a cover designer. By now, of course, you should have a file full of covers that work. . . that attract buyers, hold their interest and get you to focus on their telling sales message. It's now time to find the person who can create one of these crucial covers for you.

You cannot, of course, simply throw the matter of the cover onto someone else. There are, after all, things you must both know and do to get the cover you want. Creating the cover breaks down into two major tasks: writing the cover copy and designing the cover art work. Both are obviously important, though art work should always be subservient to copy. To assist your designer, work on the cover copy first. Remember, you have three areas to create copy for:

• the front cover
• the back cover
• the spine.

To get the cover you want, it helps to consider what must be present.

— *On The Cover*

The cover must contain:

• the complete name of your product, both grabber and descriptor

• your name as author

• an indication of the problem the booklet/book solves or the aspiration the product helps deliver.

— On The Back Cover

Too many info-entrepreneurs neglect the back cover. This is a terrible mistake. If this is your only product, use the back cover to provide ancillary reasons (benefits) why the prospect should buy the product NOW. This may include testimonials and very likely a more detailed inventory of contents. . . and benefits to be derived.

If you have other products, use the back cover like a menu. Present these products. . . the benefits targeted prospects can get from them, the number of pages, ISBN number, and price. Turn your back cover into a movable client-centered brochure!

In addition, the back cover must contain:

- the name of the product
- the product's price, and
- (if you expect to have bookstore or retail sales) a bar code.

Just like a jar of mustard, your books need a bar code if you're going to sell them through bookstores. This is a pictorial representation of your ISBN number and price and goes in the lower right hand corner of the book's back cover. It's designed to be read by computer and makes it easy for the bookstores (particularly the chains) to both ring up the price and keep tabs on the stock. Places that provide bar coding regularly advertise in the publishing periodicals I've previously referred you to. However, I'm happy to give you the name and address of the company I use: GGX Associates, ATTN George Goldberg, 11 Middle Neck Road, Great Neck, NY 11021 (516-487-6370).

— On The Spine

The spine of your book is yet another sales area. . . remember, many bookstores (and all too many book exhibitors) will stock merchandise so that only the spine is observable. Thus, make sure your spine contains the *complete* title of your product, the author name, and price.

Getting The Right Designer

Having written the necessary copy, it's time to find the cover designer. What you want is a designer who can provide an eye-catching design that draws attention to the product's title. . . and to the benefits the product delivers. Sadly, all too many designers are disinterested in commerce and prefer to consider themselves "artists." Avoid these people like the plague! Your designer must understand what your product's cover is intended to do. . .

namely attract a prospect and direct his interest to the important marketing copy. If you don't get the sense your designer can do this, drop him. You cannot afford a pictorially beautiful cover if it doesn't work to captivate buyers and motivate them to do what a cover should: get them inside to the text.

Where do you find the right designer? You can gather leads by:

- writing to the various publishing associations asking for referrals;

- reviewing the relevant section of *Literary Marketplace;*

- writing the publishers whose covers you like and asking to be put in touch with the designers;

- calling the local advertising club in your area and asking for suggestions. If you're lucky, your area has a superb directory like ours does. Called *Worksource: New England's Creative Source,* it contains a host of designers and many other creative people. It's published annually by Turnbull & Co., 15 Mt. Auburn St., Cambridge, MA 02138.

- working with designer John Hamwey, like I've done for many years.

As with your desktop publishing service bureau, you're going to need to talk to more than one potential cover designer. Why? Because each has his own style and way of doing business. You need to find someone who's not only good at delivering a compelling cover but whom you'd like to work with. Thus:

- Draft a letter to cover design candidates. Include your product's name and the date you want it on the street. Ask the candidates to call you to schedule an interview at which you can review their portfolios and discuss your project, their operating procedures and price. Ask the candidates to call you. As before, look to see how quickly the designer gets in touch with you. This is a good indication of just how client-centered he is.

- When the designer calls you, spend a few minutes on the telephone explaining your project and getting some preliminary information about the candidate's experience producing book cover designs. You want to work with someone who's familiar with the genre.

- At the interview, review the candidate's portfolio. Do his designs accentuate the copy, drawing the prospect's eye to important selling information on the front and back covers? Or do you see too many designs that do not enhance and emphasize this truly important copy, being instead "designs for design's sake"? Where is your own eye drawn in the design?

- Ask the candidate how he works, when he'll need copy from you, what kinds and how many preliminary designs he'll give you to review, and how he prepares the final design for the printer. Remember: your printer needs camera-ready copy. This means he must have the *final* artwork to shoot from. Thus, the designer needs to know how many colors are involved as well as any screens of ink (percentages of color) or bleeds (that is, when ink extends off the cover). If any of these items are incorporated into the cover design, your designer needs to provide a mechanical with color overlays, rubylith overlays, clearly marked with ink colors and percentages. Registration marks and crop marks are needed to let the printer know the exact alignment and cover size. In short, the designer must not only design, he must provide exact directions for the printer.

Based on what you see — and hear — you should be able to make a decision about your cover designer. You've now got the outside and inside of your product taken care of. It's now time to turn to that all important third selection, your printer.

— Your Printer

In discussing printers, I'd like to share a few observations based on my (occasionally deeply distressing) experience with printers over the last decade. You know I'm a man of strongly felt opinions; these are some of my most abiding.

• Printing prices vary dramatically. It's not at all uncommon to get quotations from one printer on the same job that are double, triple or even higher than another printer's. In this business, it isn't that you get what you pay for . . . it's you get what you search and haggle for. Moreover, the price you pay may not be determined until weeks *after* the job is done, depending on the quality of the product. Indeed, on one memorable occasion, I had actually been selling a book for a couple of months before the printer and I worked out the final price I'd pay for the (rather botched) job. Note: if you send in a job that varies in any way from the one the printer quoted on, ask for a "variance quote" the day he receives your mechanicals. Oftentimes, your job specifications change (for better or worse) from the time you've received your original quotation; upon submission of that job, you therefore need to get the final quotation.

• Despite instructions of the greatest clarity, printers can produce jobs that are mind-bogglingly mediocre. Thus, it is your job to monitor each aspect of every job with every printer. . . or suffer the consequences.

• Printers do not love books the way you and I do. Indeed, some of my most shattering moments have occurred when I realized that printers and their minions could and would do things like: pack books so carelessly the top product in every box was destroyed; throw gum into boxes because no waste basket was handy; bleed on books when packing them rather than take the time to bind a cut; print pages upside down and expect to get away with it . . . and an assortment of other horrors. While printing sales people are almost invariably charming, the charm leaves with them and seldom exists in the printing plant itself, whatever they say to the contrary.

Having said these things, I now welcome you to the wonderful world of printing products. Your first task is to know where to look to get the names and addresses of people who print books and booklets, because you only want to deal with people who have experience producing what you want. Even with them you'll probably experience difficulties. With others, however, things might be even worse!

To find printers, use the following resources:

- John Kremer's *Directory of Book, Catalog, And Magazine Printers*. Kremer tells you how to request a printing quotation and save money on your printing, gives you 20 points to consider when selecting a printer, provides analyses of printers including what other publishers have said about them, tells how to work with overseas printers, and gives you price comparison charts and a helpful glossary of printing terms and a bibliography of resources. John Kremer is a publishing workhorse, and I'm delighted to recommend this superb resource. Get it from Ad-Lib Publications, 51 1/2 W. Adams, P.O. Box 1102, Fairfield, IA 52556-1102.

- Dan Poynter's *Buying Book Printing: Selecting And Working With Printers*. Poynter's booklet was designed to be a shorter treatment of this subject. It deals (though in a less comprehensive way) with many of the topics Kremer tackles, while still containing helpful information including a list of printers from whom you can solicit quotations. It's available from Para Publishing, and you can call Dan at (805) 968-7277.

- Contact Barbara Hagen. If Walsworth Publishing can do the job, ask to work with Barbara. If it can't, I'm sure this most helpful person will be glad to help you with a referral.

Get It In Writing: Developing Your RFQ

Printing quotes are good for between thirty and sixty days (ask each company how long its quotation is good for). Thus, don't start getting quotations until close to the time you're ready to go ahead with your project. So that you get comparable data from the various printers you're considering having print your job, use a Request For Quotation form. The form used in soliciting printing quotes for this book is duplicated below.

REQUEST FOR QUOTATION

Please quote your best price for the following book and provide delivery and printing time.

Identification

Title of book: HOW TO MAKE A WHOLE LOT MORE THAN
                 $1,000,000. . .

Author: Dr. Jeffrey Lant

Specifications

Quantity: Quote on 3000, 5000, and 7000

Number of pages including frontmatter: 580

Trim size: 6" x 9"

Press: Offset Lithography

Copy: Customer furnished camera-ready

Illustrations: Not applicable

Cover: Customer furnished camera-ready mechanical

Paper:
   Text   50# Finch Opaque 606 PPI
   Cover   12 pt C1S

Ink:
   Text   Black ink throughout
   Cover   Covers 1, 4 & spine print 2 PMS with
                 bleeds 3/s plus UV coating

Proofs:
   Text   Complete bluelines
   Cover   Complete bluelines

Binding: Perfect

Packing: Single stack cartons on pallets

Terms: Net 60 days

Deadlines: Please quote by   /   /

Your quote:

3,000 copies: $
Overruns: $
Reprint of 3,000: $

5,000 copies: $
Overruns: $
Reprint of 5,000: $

7,000 copies: $
Overruns: $
Reprint of 7,000: $

100 extra cover copies: $

Price per halftone: Not applicable

Delivery charges: Freight to Cambridge, MA 02138

Discount for prompt payment:

Delivery time:

Other miscellaneous charges:

Remarks:

Signed:

For:

Date:

Quote valid for:

Any item in this RFQ takes precedence over any industry standards. The boards, flats, and all artwork shall be returned to the customer on completion of the job.

Some comments are called for on this Request for Quotation.

Title and author. This identifies your project. If you don't have a title yet, use a number.

Quantity. How many you'll print is a direct reflection of how many you really think you can sell with 5,000 being the high for most first printings. Remember, you want about a two year's supply. As Dan Poynter says, "Ask for two, maybe three, different quantities so you will be able to see what a difference in price the different amounts make."

Number of pages. You should be counting everything (including blank pages) but the covers. Remember, the most economical count is in multiples of 8 (depending on the printer's equipment it can also be 16 or 32) because that's the length of the "signatures" in which books are printed. At this point, you can determine if you'll have any extra end pages that you should be using for sales material. There shouldn't be an empty page at the end of your product! Note: very often you'll be getting a printing quotation before you know the exact number of pages. Don't worry. Give an approximate number. Request a variance quotation upon submission of your mechanicals.

Trim size. I've already mentioned some of the standard trim sizes. Remember, if possible keep all your products one size for ease of shipping and handling.

Text copy. You can supply the printer with pasted-up boards or film. If your film is coming from another printer, add that information here. The quoting printer must provide for restripping or possibly using another printer's film flats. It's not very likely one printer can use another's film flats. Most need to be restripped to the printer's own imposition.

Cover copy. If necessary, once you've approved your cover design, have the designer talk to the printer to make sure he presents what is needed.

Text paper. Remember, most books are printed on 50 or 60 pound white offset book paper. In your search for useful samples, don't forget to consider paper. To save money, ask your printer for his paper samples. You can economize if you use house stocks.

Cover stock. If you're doing what's called a perfect bound book (like this one), the standard cover stock is called 10 pt. Carolina. It's coated on one side, dull on the other. (This would appear as "10 pt C1s" on your specification sheet.)

Cover coating. While you have many choices, here are the two I recommend. You could use an ultra-violet varnish coat, which is a liquid process. This forms a thin transparent protective coating either totally or in selected spots, as you wish. Or, you can go with poly film lamination. This is a thin film of plastic bonded with adhesive and pressure. It offers a smooth lustrous appearance, such as you see on the covers of my books.

Ink, text. Most books are printed with black ink. Other colors cost more.

Ink, cover. You can use anywhere from one to four colors. You can usually do quite nicely by using just two colors, screening one of them to give the effect of additional colors.

Color. If you are using color inside your book, the printer needs to know things like these: Will you be supplying transparencies or reflective art such as photographs? Do you want the printer to handle the color separations or will you supply them? If you're using "spot" color (that is more than one color on a page), you must supply the printer with overlays indicating where each color will be used and what percentage it should be. Too, will the color photos be grouped or spread throughout the text? As you certainly realize, inside color adds significantly to the price.

Binding. There are many different kinds of bindings, including perfect (adhesive) bound with a softcover, case bound (hardcover), saddle stitched (stapled), comb bound (plastic), spiral bound (wire), and the new lay-flat binding especially for computer books, cookbooks, and music books, *etc.* Dan Poynter discusses them all in his book *The Self-Publishing Manual.* You'll be helping yourself if you collect samples of the kinds of bindings you like and present your choice to your printer's sales representative with a request for his recommendation. He'll also be happy to show you such samples.

Jacket. If you're printing a soft cover book like this one, you don't need a dust jacket. If you're doing your book in hardcover, you may. As Dan Poynter points out, "Jackets are normally specified as 80# coated stock with 3.5 inch flaps and a plastic laminate." If you decide to do a hardcase book and don't want the extra expense of a dust jacket, Barb Hagen suggests asking for a quote on a printed cover instead of a jacket featuring 1 to 4 colors. Such covers should always be film laminated for durability.

Bluelines. Once the printer has photographically shot your boards, made negatives and stripped them into flats, he will burn photosensitive paper and fold it into trial signatures. This is the last time you can do any proofreading, although at this point it's most expensive to do so. The book you see now should be *perfect,* exactly the book you're actually going to get.

Packing. If packing isn't done properly, some of your stock is certain to be damaged. I like books to be packed in what is called "single-wall, single stack" fashion, that is just one stack in a box. It certainly helps if there's plastic between the books and their carton to avoid scuffing. Note: cartons should be tightly packed so you can stack them. Poynter is right to advise that "The carton should have slip sheets of cover stock or other heavy material on the top and bottom so that covers will not be sliced if the carton is opened with a razor knife." Most printers quote on packing "bulk pack", but you should always find out what this means. Remember, you should be getting the kind and size of boxes that you can use, when empty, to ship your other products.

Terms: Let me say right away, here's where it pays to negotiate. Most printers want you to pay in thirds: one-third down on contract agreement, one-third on return of the blueline proofs, and one-third on delivery of the books. This is not in your interest for at least two reasons: 1) money is the only leverage you have with a printer. If he's got at least two-thirds of your money, you've lost at least two thirds of your leverage. 2) Even with a well-organized advance sale program, you probably won't have collected too much of what the products cost. You need some time to sell some products and collect the money! Granted, if this is your first info-product, you're probably not going to get the best credit terms, and you may well be asked for some form of credit guarantee. Even so, try to pay "reverse thirds": one third at completion, one third in thirty days and the final third in sixty to ninety days. While this may not be possible immediately, work towards this objective! Recently, yet another printing house salesman approached me to get my business. He told me I'd have to pay the usual thirds equation. I just laughed . . .

Overruns. Convention allows the printer to send you 10 percent over or under what you asked for and consider this an acceptable job! If you get more books than you ordered, however, you should be able to get them for between 50-80% of the price of the rest. Clearly, overruns cost less than the first lot and you should benefit accordingly. Make sure you do. . . by paying less for them!

Reprint price. If you're following the guidelines in this book, you are going to reprint . . . often. You need to plan for this reprinting at the time of the original order. This means finding a printer who prints from negatives and plates . . . not paper plates. Paper plates are disposable and cannot be used for reprints. Negatives (film) are kept in storage for reuse. A reprint cost at a printer using negatives will be less. A reprint cost at a printer using disposable paper plates will not be any different than the first printing cost.

Delivery. The sales representative of the printer you select will be able to tell you how long it will take to get your order delivered, but you should allow between three weeks (for a reprint where the printer needs to do little or no additional work) and six weeks for a new job. The counting begins when the printer gets the bluelines and assumes there are few alterations. Typesetting and hardcover binding take longer. On the whole, most established printers do make their deadline, or close enough.

Shipping. Clearly, the price you want includes printing, binding and shipping. In practice, I have discovered that it is not necessarily cheaper to reprint books close to home where the printer can reuse most of the negatives from a previous job and to use out-of-state printers on new books. You must always shop around and remember that freight charges are a significant pricing variable. Note: printers can, however, review negatives (or flats) made by another company, but they often charge a fee for setting the imposition for their equipment. What's important to point out is that 1) you should not think of shipping books until you have reviewed at least two copies sent by the printer for your analysis, and 2) should only accept (that is, become responsible for) books when they're actually delivered to your warehouse. I learned this the hard way. On one notorious occasion, books were accepted at the printing plant in Virginia. The trucker who took them. . . along with a few tons of ball bearings and the like. . . decided to abandon his job, family. . . and my books. . . somewhere in Ohio! There they sat alongside the interstate for a couple of days before the police found them. . . but never the driver. Since you never know when a teamster is going to have a mid-life crisis, make sure you only accept books when they're safely delivered to wherever you're going to store them! (By the way, in this case, the shipping company said it would have been responsible for the loss had the books not been found.)

Other miscellaneous charges. Such charges will certainly include the cost of shipping bluelines and mechanicals back and forth if you're working out of state. If there are any other charges, this is the moment you want to know about them. If additional charges not on this RFQ are added to your bill, this is the best way of fighting them.

Deadline for quote. Give the printer 10-15 business days (two to three weeks) to respond to your Request for Quotation. If they want the business, they'll honor this reasonable deadline. If you haven't heard from a company which has come highly recommended, do call. But make sure they confirm everything in writing.

"Any item in this RFQ takes precedence over any industry standards." I am grateful to Dan Poynter for this sensible section which offers two benefits: 1) this RFQ is the sole basis for your agreement with the printer (thus you know exactly what you're getting), and 2) at the completion of the job, you'll get everything back. While most printers are happy to return all your materials upon request, some look upon them as their property, not yours. Clarify this matter here so you can get your materials back without a problem.

Note: obviously, once you've done a few RFQs you'll feel more comfortable with the process. . . as well as the language. This probably won't be the case the first time you do one. Ask for help. Fill out as many items in the RFQ as you can. Then make an appointment with a local printer or his sales representative to whom you'll be sending an RFQ. To this meeting, bring the samples you've collected. Ask for the representative's help in filling out the RFQ. No, he won't necessarily like this, knowing as he does that others will be bidding on the job but. . . he wants to bid on it, too, so he should help. At least this way, you benefit from the assistance of someone in the industry when making up your RFQ.

Circulating Your RFQ

When your RFQ is finished, it's time to circulate it. My advice is to select at least six different printers, at least two that are local and several that are out of state. If you're really diligent, send out a dozen the first time. As you get to know the business better, sending out three or four makes sense. Don't expect the printers to keep filling them out indefinitely, however, unless you give them some of your work!

Accompany your RFQ with a brief note pointing out the number of books you're asking them to quote on, your deadline for the quote, and requesting any additional sales materials they have. With the out-of-state printers, ask to have their sales representative call on you if he's in the area. The larger firms maintain regional offices or at least regional representatives, and it helps to chat with this individual to make sure the company can do a job like yours. And if you select this company as your printer, it is very definitely to your advantage to have someone in the company who knows you and will represent your interests.

Deciding Which Printer To Select

In due course, the RFQs will be returned. Now you must review them! Remember what you're looking for: the price for bound books packed and delivered to you. Keep in mind that the printer is making you an offer. You can either accept this offer out of hand, or, better, negotiate to secure something more to your liking. I hope you like bargaining. . . because this is the time you need to do some.

If a local printer has offered you a higher price even though he doesn't have to ship very far (I'm very accustomed to this happening in expensive Massachusetts), show him the RFQs you're getting from out of state that give you what you want. . . including shipping. . . at a lower price. Remember, prices in the printing industry are remarkably fluid; unless your printer knows you for a tough negotiator, you're almost never going to get the best price on Round 1.

So, expect to dicker.

Chances are, your local printer, if he wants the work, will readjust his price, especially if he knows you're serious about getting the best possible price and service. When he lowers his price, take his adjusted quotation back to the most competitive out-of-state printers to see what they can do. Then return your new quotations to the local printer, who will now probably give you the best price he's able to give. . . or take himself out of the running. You should now have a good indication of the price you're going to have to pay for the job. . . if it's perfectly done.

You may not like dickering this way; you may liken the printing industry to a grocery store with set prices. However, it's not at all similar. And when you remember that it's your profits you're really negotiating for, this may keep your spirits up. Anyway, you've just got to do it.

Note: before you make any final decision about which printer to use, contact Publishers Marketing Association to see what they know about this company. (Reach PMA at 2401 Pacific Coast Highway, suite 102, Hermosa Beach, CA 90254; 213-372-2732.) They maintain a Better Business Bureau-type file on printers and can tell you the experiences of others. Remember, price really isn't everything. Lots of low price operations have provided giant publisher headaches. Equally, check John Kremer's evaluation of this printer. John's very conscientious about keeping records about publishers' experiences with various printers.

Another Note: if you'll be printing a number of booklets and books over the next year (or even just one more), see whether you can make a multi-product deal with the printer and so secure an even better price. If you're giving this printer more work, he probably can quote you a better price. In short, it's your job to use everything you've got for negotiating leverage. . . this includes both current work and new work and reprintings.

By following these steps, you will both get a printer and a price you can live with . . . if the printer delivers what he says he will. So, tell him the good news. Call the winning printer or his sales representative to let him know they've won your trust. . . and your business. Say you're counting on them to deliver a product that will make them proud. . . and that will sit proudly in libraries, bookstores and on customers' shelves nationwide. All too often printers forget that you're producing something intellectually significant that can live for ages. Remind them. It's good for their souls. . . and may help deliver the quality product you want! During this conversation, ask how they want the mechanicals delivered. Then wrap these materials carefully and ship insured via UPS second-day air or use an overnight service.

Do not under any circumstances use the U.S. Post Office, which is useless in tracing a package gone astray. What you're sending is the fruit of years of your labor and much work by your desktop publisher and cover designer. Treat it accordingly! [Note: make sure you have a photocopy of everything you send your printer, for two reasons. 1) If your materials are lost, at least you'll have a back-up, although xerox copies don't replace a galley page or mechanical. And 2) you need a copy so you can check your printer's proofs against your original. This eliminates the question about who's responsible for a slipped piece of copy . . . you or the printer.]

Accompany your package with a cover letter that includes the following points:

• your formal acceptance of the offer outlined in your RFQ which they have accepted in a letter of (specific date);

• notification that this letter is accompanied by the boards and any other materials you're sending;

• confirmation of how many copies of the product you want;

• any changes or deviations from the print quote;

• confirmation that you want an additional 100 covers (your bookstore and sales representative will want them);

• an indication of where you want the bluelines sent when available for review.

• your desire to be called when these materials have arrived safely.

Dan Poynter cautions that you should always add this line, too: "Any item in this letter takes precedence over any industry convention."

Working With Your Desktop Publishing Service Bureau, Cover Designer, And Printer

You've now made your decisions about who to work with to handle the inside of your product, the outside and the printing. Now it's time to know when to work with them and how. Here's some advice.

— Working With Your Desktop Publishing Service Bureau

You need to select your desktop publishing bureau before you begin to input text in your computer, or as shortly afterwards as you can. Why? Because each desktop publisher has — or should have — guidelines about how to input text so that the later design and lay out of pages is most economical. If you can handle certain matters expeditiously and efficiently while inputting text (or editing your material), why should you have to pay the desktop publisher to do the task? Thus, an early meeting with this publisher is advisable to get specific instructions for setting up your text files so you can provide "clean" disks — files requiring no changes.

These items might involve:

• being given certain codes to use for such items as bullets;

• knowing how to set columns of figures in order to make the conversion easy;

• using the tab instead of the space bar in selected cases, or

• knowing whether you can leave your embedded commands (for bold, underlining, *etc.*) in the text (because your systems are compatible) or having to remove them from the text file you give the desktop publisher.

As you see, an early conference with your desktop publisher makes the most sense, particularly when you are not using the same kind of computer systems.

Note: make sure the desktop publisher *writes* down his guidelines and text inputting recommendations and explains each one to you thoroughly. If this publisher knows his business, he knows what you need and will give it to you in a clear and easy form you can readily follow. Insist on this.

Many months may pass between your initial conference with the desktop publisher and any subsequent meetings. During this time, you're busy creating the product. As you move towards completing the project, here's what you must do:

• Contact the desktop publisher to let him know where you are in the process. Tell him when you'll be finishing writing and editing the material, when your outside editor will be finished with it, and when you'll be ready to give him diskettes.

• Ask him what his schedule will be like at that time and if he foresees any trouble making the deadline for the camera-ready copy the printer needs. Remind him of that deadline!

On The Need To Edit And Re-Edit

There's one very good reason to factor in the two edits mentioned above, one by you, one by an outside individual. That reason is MONEY. If you wait to edit your material until the desktop publisher has already dealt with it, you'll pay for him to make any corrections you may wish. The easiest and cheapest time to make these changes is before the desktop publisher gets any material at all.

Thus, before handing over your text to the electronic publisher, first print out your complete booklet or book and read it yourself. . . as your readers will read it, making any necessary changes. Reading an info-product is different from creating that product. You want to correct the obvious typographical errors, of course; you also want to review each sentence, every paragraph, to make certain they are not only factually correct but stylistically graceful. One without the other is unthinkable, whatever the fatuous critics think who suggest you can write an information product that contains nothing more than information.

When you've finished this first editing of your work, turn it over either to an editor hired to review the text or use another outside consultant to read it. Personally, over the last several years I've had the inestimable advantage of being helped by my persnickety friend Professor Robert Dobson who has read my text at this point and delighted in bringing howlers to my attention. His payment? During the production of this book, I took him to London for a few days of sybaritic living. Was this expensive? No, the travel tickets were free. . . compliments of Continental Airlines and their mileage producing credit card, the one I previously recommended to you.

Note: if you're thinking of using me to help strengthen your text and make your product more client-centered, *this* is the moment to get me involved, namely after you've given the subject matter your best shot and before you've spent money to format pages. Please keep this in mind!

After you've input any changes, it's time to make duplicte text files of each chapter (unless your software is compatible with the system your electronic publisher is using). You need one text file with your embedded commands and one without. Obviously, you'll be putting the latter onto floppy diskettes for your electronic publisher and printing a hard copy (complete with underlinings, bold, *etc.*) from the former. You turn over this complete package. **Remember, any alternations originating from you from this point, cost you money.**

Now what? You wait. While the desktop publisher is working on the pages, you can take a well-deserved vacation. You deserve a few days off, and now is the time to enjoy them. But don't vegetate. There's lots to do now. . . and more to come. The cover will need your attention, of course, and you can also start drafting your media packet for this product and selecting the places where you'll send the first batch of review copies. It pays to begin selecting the review sources and typing their labels now. After all, the day your new product is ready, all you want to do is drop it in an already prepared and labelled jiffy bag and ship so that all your review sources will have their books within a week of when you first see it yourself!

Correcting The First Page Proofs

Soon your desktop publisher will give you the First Page Proofs. Just how soon depends on many variables including how simple or elaborate the page lay out is. Are there headers, footers, font changes and sizes, rules, tables/charts, spot illustrations or photos, with or without captions? Hopefully, your desktop publisher is both prompt and conscientious. If so, these first page proofs will be relatively clean. What's more, you'll have a fairly good idea at this point just what your booklet/book will look like. It behooves you, however, to spend a good deal of time on these proofs making sure:

- typographical errors are corrected

- words are properly divided

- chapters start on the right

- the margins at the top, bottom and sides of pages are correct

- there is consistency in layout and type, including the headers, footers, bullet items, photo positions, type size and font. Look, too, for consistency with line rules, paragraph indentation, and tabulation. Is there either tight line spacing or excessive space between words? Either way, now's the moment to catch these problems.

It's a good idea to have two people read these first proofs; yourself, of course, and someone who hasn't seen the project before. By this time, you'll be very tired of this project and won't be as sharp picking out errors of both commission and omission. I earnestly advise you to get a person like Bob Dobson to assist you. He loves the dictionary, adores finding errors I make, and generally makes a complete nuisance of himself. . . which, in turn, makes my books much, much better. Over the past several years, he and I have gone head to head over literally hundreds of sometimes microscopic points. I haven't always appreciated what he said, but I do listen. And I am grateful.

Just how long will it take to revise the first page proofs? That depends on the length of the project, of course, your assiduity, and that of the person who assists you. But I'd say that you'll need at least two weeks for a project the length of this book.

Tip I

When you're working on the first page proofs, you'll need both the proofs themselves and the original typescript. You must make absolutely sure no lines have been dropped in transition. You can only know for sure by comparing the proofs against the typescript.

The objective of the first page proofs is to return *one set* of corrections and additions to the desktop publisher. This means you need a master set of proofs on which all final corrections/additions are recorded. Don't destroy your desktop publisher's equilibrium by returning two sets of corrections!

Tip II

If the first page proofs are messy and full of errors, you may now rue the selection of this particular desktop publisher. Still, unless absolutely necessary, it's a good policy not to change horses (or publishers) in mid-stream. In the event of particularly messy proofs, you'll be both angry and disappointed. You can only take out so much of your frustration on the desktop publisher before he starts taking out his own anger on you — and your job. Thus:

• Take out your anger on someone else for the moment. Keep your eye fixed on the main objective, getting this project done expeditiously;

• Schedule an appointment with the desktop publisher to go over the proofs and see what he suggests doing. . . besides your spending days and days of your time cleaning them up;

• Do as much as you can to get this project finished.

If you are really unhappy with your desktop publisher's work, after the project is finished you can withhold part or all of the money still owing on this job (keep in mind that you're going to be asked by the desktop publisher for partial payment at various intervals as your job nears completion, so there will be only a fraction left to pay at this point). Don't say this, of course. Just do it. For now, focus on getting this project finished.

Correcting The Second Page Proofs

Shortly, the dekstop publisher will return the Second Page Proofs to you. These should be, but frequently are not, perfect. It's your job to find out. Oftentimes, your desktop publisher will only return those pages on which you previously made corrections/additions. It's not really necessary for you to see a complete set of proofs at this point, just the places where changes were made. It is, however, necessary for you to make sure each of your suggested changes has been made. I prefer a system where the desktop publisher checks off in red ink each change as he makes it. If he does this, it's easy to make sure all the necessary changes have actually been made.

— Working With Your Cover Designer

If you know when you're going to finish your product and are working along close to your schedule, start making contact with cover designers as soon as you've:

- set the title in concrete (filling out R. R. Bowker's Advanced Book Information form is a good indication of this), and

- finished between one-third and one-half your text (although for a booklet you'll certainly want to act earlier).

Once you've selected your designer, you need an initial planning meeting. At this meeting, you should:

- remind your cover designer about just when your printer needs camera-ready art for this project;

- ask your designer to tell you just when he needs front, back and spine copy from you;

- ask when he'll produce his first rough sketches for you to review.

You can expedite the designer's work by giving him color reproductions of the covers you like and by pointing out things you find exceptionally attractive or eye-catching. Personally, I've always been very involved in the creation and design of my book covers and intend to stay involved. I let the designer know in no uncertain terms that the objective of the cover is to attract prospects to this product as soon as possible, to get them to focus on the important client-centered benefits that appear on the covers, and to get the prospects to open the book and look inside. If the cover does these things, it has been a success, and I don't need any award to confirm this!

Contact With Your Designer

About half-way to the agreed-upon date when the designer is to present his initial cover sketches to you, call to see how things are coming along. A phone call at this point may be just what the doctor ordered! Then about two weeks before the deadline, call to schedule a time when the designer can drop off his sketches.

Personally, I prefer not to have the designer on hand when I review the cover sketches for the first time. Instead, I want to look them over at my leisure and to show them to selected friends and associates. In both cases, I'm looking to see just how the design elements do what I need them to do, namely direct the prospect's eye to the important cover selling copy. . . the title and product benefits. The design works to the extent that it captures the prospect's eye in the first place. . . and directs it to just that spot where you want it. You must keep this in mind as you review these preliminary sketches. Only after you've reviewed the sketches yourself. . . and had a number of others do so. . . is it time to see the designer personally. By this time, you should know whether:

- one design towers above the others;

- you have a great many wonderful designs to select from;

- nothing strikes your fancy but you are impressed with the designer's ability, or

- you're dealing with an uninspired hack who couldn't produce a book cover if his life depended on it.

Not surprisingly, what you'll do at the meeting depends on which of these situations you find yourself in.

Of these four possibilities, the first two are the best. . . and the easiest to deal with. If your designer has produced one truly superior design that meets the necessary marketing criteria and which enthuses you and your associates, exult . . . and have him go back and turn it into camera-ready art. You've been blessed. By the same token, if your designer has produced many fine options for you, use the meeting to solicit his opinion on just which of them makes the strongest visual statement while catching and directing the prospect's eye.

Note: if you have many fine designs to select from, make sure you get color copies of them for your files. It may be that you can use these designs for future info-projects.

The final two alternatives are less convenient and need more comment. If your designer is technically proficient but hasn't yet produced an acceptable design, you need to discover if there's a problem. Is the designer having personal difficulties? Does the project not inspire him? Does he need more time? Now's the moment to find out. If the problem is soluble and the designer feels he can produce the necessary design, by all means encourage him to go back to the drawing board. All creative people have dry spells, after all. The only difficulty here is if you're paying the designer by the hour instead of by the project. Although now is not the moment to raise the issue, if the designer needs more time, you can probably get some adjustment in your bill. By all means discuss the matter before you pay his invoice. Now, however, focus on getting what you need: the compelling product cover.

Note: in this case, keep in close contact with your designer until you're certain he's moving to give you the cover design you need and not just stringing you along. Schedule another meeting in a week or two to go over the next batch of sketches. This time there should be real progress towards the objective.

The last possibility, finding you've retained a hack, is distressing, indeed. Still, it happens. If you're certain that the designs you've seen cannot be improved and feel sure the work is beyond this "designer", simply say so and continue your search for a better artist. If the designs are definitely substandard, wait until your invoice comes in and make a counter-offer on payment. Why should you be penalized when the designer has submitted poor work? Don't however, focus on your disappointment. Instead, go back to the search, so you can find the designer you need for the compelling cover you must have. And, by all means, consider my designer recommendation!

Another Meeting With Your Designer

Once you've selected the cover design you want, the designer goes back to his studio to create the finished design. At your next meeting, he should present it. At this time, the designer should advise you on the necessary colors and flourishes that will complete his design and make it the hook your product needs. As previously suggested, at this point it may well be a good idea for your designer to consult with the printer so that that printer gets just the proper materials he needs to work with.

Working With Your Printer

For the moment, you can breathe easy. A lot of the pressure's off! Of course, you have many other publishing chores to do. . . you can use this period to:

- identify review sources;

- write the cover letter that will go to these sources;

- create your media kit;

- work on getting excerpts from your info-product printed;

- arrange speaking engagements where you can promote your product and sell it, *etc.*

In short, there's much to do. But at least, the production process has gone into another stage. Still, you cannot afford to be completely out of touch. Hence the following advice. I previously recommended befriending a sales rep. from the printing company. In fact, you need to do a little more. In this business, you must anticipate that problems will take place. And when the issue is printing, the problem is certain to be frustrating and time-consuming and probably expensive, too. Thus, find out in advance who's:

- the customer service representative inside the plant;

- in charge of your job at the plant. Contact this person and let him know you're available at any time to take questions. Stress that you need to be kept informed about the progress of the job;

- responsible for quality control. Many printers, whatever they say to the contrary, are very slipshod and are quite capable of palming off a mediocre product if you're prepared to accept it. Instead, identify the quality control supervisor and, again, make contact letting this person know that you expect good work and how he can reach you at all times.

What I'm saying here is exercise due caution. If you're in the neighborhood of your printer, by all means drop by and meet these people. Chances are you'll be working with them again, and a good personal relationship helps. It also helps if your printer takes an interest in your job. The chances for a good printing job the first time around are greater, and it also helps when there is a need to resolve a problem.

Work out a communications schedule with whoever is responsible for your job. This may be the sales representative, this may be the floor supervisor. Either way, keep in close touch so you know:

- when the job will be run;

- when the job will be finished;

- how the job looks when it's finished;

- when bound copies will be sent to you for review prior to general shipment.

Note: keeping this communication system working well when there's no problem isn't difficult. It's when there is a problem that it's got to work. That's why you must stress that you want your calls returned promptly and letters answered efficiently. As I know well from my own experience with printers, they can hide out when there's a problem, not informing you, not acting pro-actively to solve it. Tell them right from the beginning what kinds of management and communications standards you expect from them.

Knowing What To Do If You Have A Problem

As all too many publishers can sadly attest, working with printers is, at best, a chancy business. Therefore it's good to use a defensive strategy with them. . . and to plan for problems. If they never take place, fine. If they do, you're prepared. Here's some advice on how to handle problems:

The first problem that's likely to take place is the lack of responsiveness. You need to have your RFQ completed promptly, acknowledgement that the bluelines and other materials have arrived safely, notification when your job is being run, *etc.* Printers are not trained in communication or in customer relations. Thus, *you're* going to have to do some training! If you don't receive the service you need, don't stew. Say something. And say it in writing. Send a letter to the quality control supervisor and the sales representative at the very least. Be polite but be firm. The way to handle problems is to deal with them when they're small. . . and to work for the professional relationship you have the right to expect. But if you don't say something. . . you probably won't get it!

You probably won't be aware of other problems until you see your book. That's why it's so important for you to get two copies of your bound book as soon as they're available, even before all your books are bound. Only now will you get evidence of other printing and printing machinery failures, including spotty ink application, crooked pages, upside down pages, *etc., etc., etc.* Whatever the problem, your heart will sink. You'll be angry. . . and depressed. In fact, I remember one Christmas Eve with one of my authors when her first book arrived from a very well known printer. She was here when the first boxes were opened and immediately noticed a host of these kinds of problems. She burst into tears. . . and an irremediable blot destroyed the holiday for both of us. It was like a story by O'Henry. Fortunately, I followed the advice I'm giving you now. In time, the printer redid the job so that the author, her fine work, and my interest were well represented.

Unless you're an expert in what is permitted in the printing industry, you may not be fully able to judge if the book you've got in your hand is acceptable by industry standards or not. If you have the slightest doubt, it pays to ask another printer or a printing broker to evaluate the product. He can tell you if what you've got is acceptable, or not. If you know or if your advisor tells you that the product is acceptable, fair enough. If there are things about it that bother you after scrutinizing it carefully, keep a list. You may be able to get some minor form of compensation. . . perhaps an agreement (get it in writing) for more books on your next job. I've been known to do this even with books that were allowable by industry standards but which didn't live up to mine.

On the other hand, if you have more major problems, consider your options:

1. You can accept the book as is and go for financial compensation. If the printer accepts your analysis (and since your evidence is visible to everyone, this isn't too difficult), this is what he'll want. After all, he's already done the job and doesn't want to do it again. He'll take a lower amount rather than incur the greater expense of reprinting at his

expense. You, on the other hand, may not be able to live with the product as it is even with a lower cost. In the Christmas example above, the printer was only too happy to make me a very low offer for the products; I just didn't want them.

2. You can work to get the printer to do the job again . . . and get it right. This many printers will be very reluctant to do, even if the job has been significantly botched. One of my many complaints about book printers involves this point. If a printer knows the job is substandard and if he knows it's his fault, he should, in all fairness, tell the customer this immediately and let him know precisely what he intends to do about it . . . and when the customer can expect to have perfect books. All too often, this is the moment the printer, his quality control supervisor, sales representative, *etc.*, become invisible to you . . . the exact moment you need them most. It is for this most unhappy situation that you need the financial leverage I mentioned above. If you haven't paid for the product, you have control. If you have, you don't. It's as simple as that.

Whether you can accept the spoiled job or not, you're going to have to build a case, that is if you want some financial compensation or new books. If you can live with the job, imperfect though the product is, you'll get more compensation (that is, a lower bill) by detailing just what's wrong with it. Frankly, unless you're a printing expert, I earnestly advise you to turn this over to someone who is and to give him these simple instructions, "Write me a detailed report on exactly what's wrong with these books." You must do the same if you want the job rerun. Again, unless you're a printing specialist, work with someone who is. You could try Jim Spry, U.S. Testing Laboratory, 1415 Park Ave., Hoboken, NJ 07030. Dan Poynter has recommended him.

If you can stay cool and reasonable in the negotiations that now need to take place, once you've got the evidence, arrange a meeting with the sales representative and/or quality control supervisor. If you must send the evidence elsewhere and cannot be physically present, don't send the originals. Use photocopies. Of the various people you may deal with, your sales representative will probably be the most sympathetic; after all, he doesn't want to lose your account! If you feel he can effectively present your case to higher-ups at the company, ask him to do so. If not, go over his head. Indeed, consider bringing in an independent printing broker to represent you. He has no emotional involvement in the case and can act more impartially.

At this point, it's important that you or your representative deal with the decision maker and continually stress your major point: "We want perfect books. Just tell us how you're going to get them to us." Don't let this matter run on indefinitely, not least because you've got a marketing campaign to get on with and because you have advance orders to fulfill. Give the printing company a reasonable time to come up with a proposal to you and hold them to the deadline. In my experience, I'd say three days is enough time for them to consider the case and come up with an offer.

If these tactics don't work, and if you're a member of Publishers Marketing Association (you're beginning to see, I'm sure, that you ought to be), you can bring your case to the Printing Resolution Board which will mediate the publisher-printer conflict. Although I have never used this particular PMA service, I have had to use another of their conflict mediation procedures, and I found it well run and efficient. Too, read Attorney Gary Moselle's *Book Printing Fact Sheet*. Gary's a former PMA president, and his booklet, available through PMA, provides good coverage on printing disputes.

By following these procedures, you will get a resolution. . . especially if you haven't paid all the money the company is owed for the job. This unpaid balance (which should be about a third of what the printer is owed) remains a very potent motivator. . . much more so than the fear of losing your future business. Money they're owed now is always more motivating to a printer than money they may (or may not) get in the future. Note: when you work with a printing broker, you're paying the money you owe for the print job to him. He in turn holds it until you get the perfect books you've got a right to expect. Either way, whether you work alone or with a broker, this money is very important.

Getting Perfect Books To You

Are you now ready to take delivery? Just about. . . if you are certain you can happily live with the product and have taken the steps required so that the merchandise that's delivered is in perfect condition. Both points deserve comment.

If at this point you can "live with" your baby, fine. Get ready to take it over. If you are still not happy, have you tried everything so you can be? Remember, you're the one whose name is on the cover. . . you're the one who has to take the flak for a product that's less than perfect. You get the glory. . . but you also get the complaints. So be prepared. If you can't be enthusiastic about this product, how do you expect anyone else to be? But if you are satisfied, make sure you do what's necessary to get your books to you in the best possible shape. This means:

- selecting the right kind of box. Remember, the box must be appropriate both for shipping to you, for storage, and for shipping to both wholesale and retail customers. As I said above, I've found single-stack boxes do nicely. You want books to fit snugly into the box and not move around inside.

Books that move are books that get damaged. Thus, if you can't get a snug fit into the box, make sure the printer puts cardboard or other packing materials inside. This must be arranged beforehand with your sales representative who will have to oversee the process. Remember, the people actually packing your books are the low men on the totem pole simply paid an hourly rate to stack your products in a box. Without supervision, you can imagine what happens!

- protecting the top of the box. Too many printers use help that's careless about packing. Therefore, you've got particularly to worry about the tops of the boxes. It's very easy to damage the top books in a box unless they're protected with cardboard or another packing material. Too, because boxes are taped, they're often opened with a knife. An unthinking opener can easily run his knife right through the cover of the top book. Protect against this kind of damage!

- considering shrinkwrapping. If you use film lamination on an uncoated stock, your cover will curl in the open air. Thus, try to avoid this process. If you do use it, you should consider shrinkwrapping at least part of your order, though this costs 15-20 cents apiece. This keeps the cover properly in place. It's easier, however, to avoid shrinkwrapping altogether.

- delivering on skids. Make sure the printer puts the books on skids and covers the whole ensemble with plastic wrapping. This wrapping saved me a lot of grief when a large shipment of books was delivered in a rainstorm. I got soaked. The books were fine.

Now you're ready to ship. Again, make sure the price you were quoted in the original RFQ included freight to your destination, and make sure you only accept delivery at that destination. Otherwise, it may be your problem if your teamster chucks it. Make sure your printer lets the shipper know what type of delivery is needed. Do you want them in your garage? Do you need help getting them there? Is there a dock? Do you have a dolly? Charges vary according to what the shipper finds when he's ready to off-load the truck. Also get the shipper's tracking (called "PRO") number from your printer so that you can track down your shipment in case your books don't show up on time.

Note: you've either dragooned friends and family into helping unload your books or hired some brawny helpers. Either way, I advise you to give each of them an autographed copy of your book as a memento and gratuity. When CASH COPY was delivered, one of my helpers was a muscular kid, just graduated from high school and the football team. When we finished our work, I gave him an autographed copy of the book. . . and he stunned everyone by refusing to be paid for helping, saying the book was more than enough. This touched my heart, restored my faith in America's youth. . . and made me glad I took a little time to do some of the physical labor I detest and which I avoid whenever possible.

Now, Do You Really Want To Do All This, Or Why Using A Printer Broker Makes So Much Sense

You now know what you've got to do to produce your product. It's a lot of work, make no mistake about it. And particularly when you're new at it, the chances for error are pretty high. Moreover, this work comes at a time when you are intellectually exhausted (maybe hating the thrall of the booklet/book) and beginning to turn your full attention to the more exciting (and demanding) business of marketing.

Confronting this situation, years ago I decided I needed help, that personally I wasn't either sufficiently interested or knowledgeable about the printing process to handle all these things alone. . . and that my time was best spent on handling the inevitable, and crucial, marketing and distribution chores. Necessity being the mother of invention, at that time I snapped my fingers and, hey presto, conjured up John Hamwey.

John is by training a graphic designer/illustrator. He became a printing broker because he had lots of clients like me, people who needed help interfacing with printers. John talked their language. . . and mine. . . and was further gifted with an easy temperament, something I, at least, occasionally lose. What he does is act as a project coordinator. I hand him my diskettes. He works with his associate Lorraine who formats and runs out or produces the pages. John then handles the tasks above including:

- drawing up and distributing the RFQ
- making a deal with a printer
- overseeing the production of perfect books, and
- seeing to their delivery.

This sounds easy, but it is time consuming and exacting work, and if I have occasionally been less than understanding about his difficulties, I'm here to say that I appreciate them. . . and the way he solves them.

Simultaneously, while dealing with the printer, John deals with me:

- bringing me proofs
- working with me to get the product I want
- developing the cover concept and design.

Why, he's even present at the warehouse when the products are delivered. In fact, it's John who slips (my) money into the hands of the fork lift operator and other helpers, though this is admittedly beyond the terms of his commission!

You can, of course, work with John Hamwey directly. His number appears below. Whether you choose to work with him or not, I advise you to work with an independent printing broker. At the beginning you'll do so because you don't understand the business and need someone on your side who does, including knowing which printers to use and which to avoid. Later, when you do understand what can go wrong (and have your own war stories to prove it), you'll need someone like this because your time is severely limited and it ought to be spent creating products and selling them. . . not producing them.

Having said this, I'm sure you're interested in the answers to two questions: how are printing brokers compensated and how can you find one?

Printing brokers generally charge a percentage of your job as their fee. The percentage, usually between 15-25% of the job's cost, varies depending on the size of the job, the amount of the print run, *etc.* Ordinarily, the broker lowers his percentage on an expensive printing job and will universally raise it on a smaller job. Either way, when he submits an estimate to you for your job it should include his fee. Here's what you've got to decide. Do you want to save the cost of the broker's fee and do everything yourself? There are both risks and benefits to this course. This way, you'll not only save money, but you'll also learn aspects of the publishing business which are useful to you. Of course, you'll also be totally responsible for the project at a time when your knowledge is decidedly limited. Or, do you want the convenience of working with a broker and his technical expertise? This costs more, to be sure, but means you'll have a specialist's help throughout what can be a frustrating process. Only you can decide, but I think you know where I stand on this issue!

To find a printing broker:

- look under this category in the Yellow Pages
- write the publishing associations previously mentioned to ask for referrals
- network with other publishers.

Get the names and phone numbers of several candidates. Send them a letter outlining:

- the job you need help on;
- how many copies you'll be printing, and
- when you need to start.

Be as specific as you can be (reread this chapter) about the services you desire, and ask what the broker does and how he charges for the service. As with an RFQ, ask for a response within 10 days. Since the broker will be local, either ask to schedule a meeting now, or after you have the opportunity to review what he sends you. Remember, you'll be talking to your printing broker regularly; it's important you like this person and get along well with him. He must understand what you're trying to do and must be willing to assist you in getting it. In short, he must care.

Once you hire this person, schedule a meeting to discuss technical aspects of your next project. Show him the samples you've collected and get his opinions on what will work best given what you're trying to achieve. Now, monitor what takes place. Again, if the broker lets you down at any time, say so. Be clear about what you want, and hold the broker's feet to the fire so you get it. The broker is your representative, but you cannot escape your part of the responsibility for producing a superior product. The broker can help. But in the final analysis, this responsibility is and will always be yours.

I hope you have selected your printing broker wisely. If you have your life will be a lot easier. Certainly, I credit both some of my success and the fact I haven't yet died of publishing-induced apoplexy to my relationship with John Hamwey, his associate Lorraine, and the assistance they've given me over the years, and I can wish you no better than that you are served by professionals and friends such as these.

Last Words

In due course, your booklet or book will be printed. . . and in your hand. Congratulations. Now you have truly given birth. Further, you are now a member of an elite body that includes among its members people as diverse as Plato, St. Thomas Aquinas, Queen Victoria, and Albert Einstein. . . people, that is, who have enriched the world with the printed word. You are entitled to feel very, very proud, and I hope you indulge yourself. Only people like us who have created in this way really know what this moment is like. . . the first moment you cradle this printed bundle crackling with ideas, packed with useful information, eternal evidence of your intellect and concern for others. Yes, there is nothing like it!

It's now time to protect your interest in this work. Do so by calling the Library of Congress' Copyright Office Hotline at (202) 707-9100 (or write The Register of Copyrights, Copyright Office, Library of Congress, Washington, DC 20559). Ask them to send you Copyright Form TX and the page of line-by-line instructions for filling it out. You can submit this form with two copies of the work and just $20 as soon as your official publication date has passed. There is some advantage to submitting the necessary paperwork within three months of the work's publication date, but you can submit it anytime. With this registration, you truly belong to the ages.

The Help You Need

I've now given you the guidelines that will help you get the superior info-product you want. I'm grateful to my industrious experts who have assisted me with their technical information, and I am happy to recommend them to you for the times when you need technical assistance, too:

— Barbara Hagen, Account Representative, Walsworth, 1256 Grenada Ave., N. Clearwater, FL 34624 (813) 530-0982/fax: (813) 530-0875. Barbara is personable, knowledgeable, indefatigable, amazingly well organized. . . and likes books. If Walsworth does the kind of product you want to produce, and you work with Barbara, you're a fortunate person indeed. Send her your RFQs.

— John & Lorraine Hamwey, ABC Publications, 770 Dedham Street, Canton, Massachusetts 02021 (617) 575-9915. If their line is busy, it's probably me. After reading this chapter and learning all there is to do, you know why.

— Dan Poynter, Para Publishing, P.O. Box 4232-607, Santa Barbara, CA 93140-4232 (805) 968-7277. Dan has long been recognized as the guru of self-publishers. His work is top-quality and thorough. What's more, like me, he's accessible and genuinely cares that you produce the best book you can and sell as many copies as possible. Get his catalog and stay on his mailing list. I do, and I make money from the things he says. So will you!

Another Resource

Just as I was finishing this book, another very useful resource on book production appeared. Entitled *D. Armstrong's Complete Book Publishing Handbook,* it contains helpful, detailed information on all facets of book production and the management of a publishing company. You'll also find a very extensive section on American book manufacturers and other services publishers will find helpful. You can get it from D. Armstrong Co., Inc., 2000M Governors Circle, Houston, TX 77092 (800) 83-BOOKS.

You, Your Info-Empire And Your Computer

By now you're probably scratching your head at all the work you have to do to make the money you want to make and reach the people you want to reach. And just think, we haven't even begun to discuss all the marketing tasks you must also accomplish!

You need help.

Luckily for you, help is at hand. Very much at hand. In the personal computer.

With any luck (or foresight), you already have a personal computer and word processor and know how to use them. Good. You'll use this chapter to increase your efficiency and learn new ways of integrating the computer into your life . . . so that you can reach more people faster, more economically, with less hesitation about what to do and when to do it.

If, on the other hand, you're one of those people who remains a computerphobe, or just doesn't understand how this mechanized cylops can help you, this chapter has twin objectives: to move you as quickly as possible not merely to an acceptance of the computer . . . but to a bonding with it. And then into a mastery of both the strategic and tactical tasks you must accomplish to reach your overall goals.

Understanding What The Computer Does For You

The computer is important for the following reasons. It:

- stores information
- sorts information
- performs routine tasks rapidly
- enables you to personalize all your marketing materials and emphasizes your client-centered approach to business.

Since you'll be doing all these things every single day you're running an info-empire, you have these choices:

1. you can treat each task that you perform as distinct and unconnected to any other task you perform, and run yourself ragged doing all you need to do;

2. you can hire other people to do what needs to be done and so cut substantially into your profits;

3. you can cut back on the things that need to be done . . . so depriving people who need your information of what you've got . . . and yourself of the profits that come from selling it to them;

4. you can get a computer and use it for a few tasks thinking that that is all you're capable of doing or understanding, or

5. you can understand just what a personal computer fully integrated into your operation can do to help you reach vast numbers of prospects and buyers . . . making you not only more efficient but also richer.

Sadly, of the publishers I know, virtually all fit within the first four categories above. That is, they are either approaching each task as if they had never done it before and will never do it again . . . spending money recklessly on outside help before exploring the considerable savings of complete and thorough computerization . . . reducing their activities because they don't have the time or energy to do more, don't understand computers and can't afford outside help for all that needs to be done . . . or fooling themselves that the little they do with their computers constitutes all that can be done with them.

THIS CAN'T BE YOU!!!

And it won't be after you've mastered this chapter on how to use the computer to build and sustain your info-empire.

To use the computer properly, however, you must understand what it can be used for . . . and why. Essentially, the computer can assist you with each of the following essential tasks of your info-company:

- strategy
- developing your own products
- acquiring products from others
- marketing
- customer relations
- routine management.

The objective in each case is the same: as the brains of your operation, you must think through exactly what you need to accomplish in each of these areas and develop all the appropriate forms and materials to do what you need to do. All these forms, as you'll see in this chapter, must be available on computer . . . so that you can use them instantly when you need either to initiate an action you knew you'd have to take . . . or respond to a situation you knew you'd have to respond to.

The real value of a computer, you see, is that it gives you control. In quieter moments of your day, you can plot out exactly what you need to do . . . exactly when you need to do it . . . exactly how you need to do it. In these same quiet moments working at your computer, you can develop all the forms and formats you need to accomplish what you wish to do.

With all this accomplished, when you must initiate an action that relates either to strategy, product development or acquisition, marketing, customer relations or routine management . . . or respond to someone approaching you in any of these areas . . . you'll be ready and can take *immediate* action.

No other way of running your business makes any sense whatsoever. Yet if this is so, why do so few info-entrepreneurs use these methods? There are, I think, several reasons:

- Many are computerphobes. They hate the machine, don't understand it, and don't understand how their failure to master and integrate it into their businesses is costing them big.

- Some think they can't afford the necessary equipment. However, getting a computer and fully integrating it into your business (two quite distinct things) are essential if you are going to reach the larger markets you must reach to make the larger financial gains you wish to have. No computer. No fortune. It's about as simple as that.

- Some think they are already doing this . . . when they're not. If you have a computer and think you're using it to its fullest potential, pay particular attention to this chapter. If you don't have most of — if not all — the forms and documents on diskette that I'm talking about here and you're not regularly using them, you are not really computerized, whatever you think to the contrary.

- Others fail to see just how much of their business lives is routine . . . and must, therefore, be routinized to ensure maximum efficiently. These people see each task as distinct and unconnected and are, as such, hopelessly labor intensive. The trick to running a profitable info-empire is to make each prospect and customer believe you are truly focusing on him, while relying on standardized documents and operating procedures to do so.

- Finally, most of those who are not fully computerized have lost sight of the big picture. Unless your computer system is fully integrated into each essential facet of your business, you can't reach the greatest number of prospects, can't maintain good relations with them and can't respond to opportunities sufficiently quickly. Each day you fall behind those of us who do have complete computer integration and do understand that it is the essential tool for maximizing your outreach . . . and dramatically increasing your profit. If this is acceptable to you, fine. That's your decision. If it isn't, pay close attention to this chapter, because what I'm about to share with you appears nowhere else and is a crucial part of what it takes for you to become a multi-millionaire information producer and seller.

Resource Note

If you're one of the legions of computerphobes who still exist, I have two things to say to you: GET OVER IT. Then do what it takes to come to terms with the machine. In this connection, I suggest you look at Norma Leone's fine little book *A Mother's Guide To Computers,* Lion Publishers, P.O. Box 92541, Rochester, NY 14692. It's the equivalent of a gentle literary laxative on the subject and will remove much that needs to be out of your system . . . and replace it with good introductory knowledge on the subject of computers.

Beginning At The Beginning: Getting The Right System

When I got my first computer several years ago, like most people I agonized over what to do. In fact, I spent lots more time analyzing computers and shopping for values than I did when I bought my first condominium, as great an admission of seriousness as you're ever likely to find.

Having gone through this process I have several pieces of advice for those of you who have not yet taken the computer plunge:

- The great debate between Apple Macintosh and IBM (or compatible) folk, while heated, is somewhat beside the point. Either system will probably suit you, although I myself give IBM the palm for these reasons:

  - More people have an IBM or compatible machine, so when you're working in this universe the chances are better you can simply send a diskette or file without having it translated. In fact, in all the years I've been computerized I've never dealt with either a publications editor or data base systems operator who couldn't take my IBM-compatible diskette . . . or who wanted me to translate it into Macintosh before being able to send it. Thus, there's more universality and efficiency in having an IBM-compatible system.

  - Much more software is written for the IBM system.

  - I hate the Macintosh mouse.

In all fairness to Macintosh, I think its system does have an advantage in terms of both the uniformity of its user interface across all applications and in desktop design and graphics. However, as you already learned in the previous chapter, I don't think you should spend lots of time doing design yourself. Reason? You have only so much time, and you should be spending it on producing products and marketing them. Leave design to the designers. You may disagree, but you ought to know where I stand.

- Buy your computer hardware locally . . . and your printer by mail order. Why? Because with your computer, you're going to need telephone or on-premise assistance until you become comfortable with your machine. There's nothing more annoying than trying to make the machine do something that it just won't do. Mail order people won't help . . . often, in fact, they just don't understand the equipment. That's why you need a knowledgeable and helpful hardware expert close at hand . . . and the best person to help is the person you bought your machine from. Don't ever consider buying any machine until you ask how the company handles follow-up phone calls.

So, what kind of computer should you get? One thing that's very important is that you get sufficient disk space to hold your books, booklets, Special Reports, audio scripts, and all the various letters and forms we'll be discussing in this chapter. *And* your mailing list. Thus, don't get anything smaller than a 30 megabyte hard disk drive . . . and do consider getting more. You'll be surprised at just how fast you fill this space. When considering the kind of system you'll be getting, make sure it's easy to add more disk space, because I assure you, you'll be needing it.

As far as printers are concerned, don't pay retail prices! Because printers are relatively east to set up and learn and require only routine maintenance, you can afford to buy yours via mail order and pay less. You can find lots of dealers by paying the small annual fee ($39) to join The Boston Computer Society (1 Kendall Square, Building 1400, Cambridge, MA 02139. 617-864-1700.) When you join make sure you get the *BCS Buying Guide* which gives you member discounts.

The kind of printer you need should be a high-quality, fast-printing laser printer. Every reputable laser printer on the market today enables you to produce both labels and envelopes with a quality that you can't come close to with a traditional dot matrix printer. If you're serious about building your empire, you need to be turning out materials that are impeccably professional! You just can't do this with a dot matrix printer. Personally, I use a Hewlett Packard Laser Jet III — and absolutely love it. It has cut down on the amount of time required to print all my documents (which given the vast number of special reports I sell is considerable) . . . and has vastly increased the aesthetic quality over the old dot matrix. However, laser printers, although not expensive, do cost more than dot matrix printers. Don't be penny wise and pound foolish here! Laser printers will cost you only a couple of hundred dollars more and save you lots of time as well as increase the quality. You can get a Hewlett Packard Laser Jet like mine for around $800 now. Note: one way you can save even more money is cutting the cost of your toner cartridges. You'll want to get yours where I get mine: Advanced Laser Products, P.O. Box 1534, Brookline, MA 02146 (617) 278-4344. They have the lowest prices I've found (just $45 per refill, delivery charges included) and the quality is consistently high.

Note: You'll notice I'm steering you away from using a printer from which you can print your own cheshire labels (4 across, 11 down per page). That way worked once but, frankly, it's a lot easier — and your names and addresses will look better — if you use the ink jetting process discussed on page 429; the price is also comparable. However, when you upgrade to a laser printer, keep your old wide-carriage printer as a backup.

- Use off-the-shelf software. Many people have gotten rich lately selling business people more software than they need or have the capacity to use. Don't swell this tide. Personally, I have found myself more than adequately served by dBASE IV software for my data list management and XyWrite for my word-processing program. While you may make other decisions for your software, what you need to keep in mind is this:

  - You need a list management program that easily enables you to input data, sort them by field and print cheshire labels in the wide-carriage format.

- You need a word-processing program that is command- (and not menu-) driven. While a menu of options may be appealing when you're unfamiliar with your software, as soon as you are, they take up a lot of screen space and slow you down. It's a little more painful and time-consuming to learn all the commands at the beginning, but it's well worth it in the long run.

- Ideally, the software you select should have an 800-number for technical assistance. I assure you no matter how well the training and instruction manual is written (and some of them, as we all know, are impenetrable), you're going to need help from a real person. Make sure it's available.

Assembling Your Back-Up Team Of Techie Specialists And Support

One of the most important things I've learned about computerization is how necessary it is to have technical back-up support, how specialized your back-up experts usually are, and how mobile they are . . . often making them difficult to find. In any event, I can assure you that while computerizing increases your efficiency exponentially, it also makes you a lot more vulnerable. In this game, you just can't do everything yourself . . . and shouldn't try. That's why you need a back-up team. This team should include:

- your hardware consultant. This is the person who knows how your machine functions and can often give you tips by telephone on what to do without forcing you to send your machine away. He's also the person who'll be honest with you when you do have to send it for repair.

- your software consultant. This person is an expert in how your software, both list management and word-processing, works and, again, can often give you tips by phone. These consultants often offer classes and one-on-one tutorials. A few of these tutorials usually make excellent sense, especially if you are a fast learner with particular questions. In actual fact, you will probably need a consultant for your data base software and another one for your word-processing software. You will probably need your list management consultant more often than your word-processing consultant.

- your printer maintenance technician. Count on it, your printer is going to need periodic cleaning and repair. Be prepared. Check the yellow pages under "computer wholesale and manufacturers", "computer dealer", or "computer service." You need to know approximately how long companies take to repair a machine, if they will accept your warranty, and if they have a rush fee for faster service.

- a courier service. As I've learned, while UPS is great for shipping books and paper products, I've had very bad luck using them to ship my highly sensitive and, yes, fragile printers where just one thump can make the machine inoperable. Granted, you may not be near enough a printer repair location so that using a courier makes sense, but if you are I strongly suggest you not use the post office or UPS to transport your printer, but get a courier service instead. In large communities, courier services are very competitive and prices vary widely. Before you need one, it pays to call around, check prices and open an account. Remember, courier services will also deliver your printer or computer after business hours for a rush charge, but this can easily be twice as much as their day-time rates.

One Essential Task Your Software Experts Can Help You With As Soon As You Have Your Equipment

Before going on to discuss how to find the specialists you need, I'd like to point out one essential task particularly your software experts can help with: creating your own operations manual.

With generally the best will in the world, the manufacturers of software and hardware can't seem to write a training manual that's fit to be read by literate humans. As the industry becomes even more competitive, I suspect this will change, but for now I have my own suggestion: create your own operations manual.

Because using specialists can get real expensive real fast, it's very much in your interest to take part of your available money and use it either to have certain key tasks explained to you or, better, written out in language you can easily follow. Keep these easy-to-understand step-by-step instructions in a three-hole binder inches away from your machine. Here are some of the items you're going to need and certainly must understand: how to

- create text files in ASCII

- copy text onto a floppy diskette

- use telecommunications software to receive and send text files

- differentiate entries on your mailing list, like people who have purchased certain things at a certain time, those who have not purchased, those who have inquired, *etc.*

- mark names for deletion

- delete names from your main list and remove them to another list

- mail merge

- create macro keys, including automatic date

- back up your hark disk.

A few words about each will, I think, be useful to you.

Creating Text Files In ASCII

ASCII is best understood as a computer language. When you use it, you enable your correspondents to read your text files with their systems. When you use your word-processing program, ASCII is embellished, if you will, by certain commands that appear in your word-processing program, such as commands for underlining and bold. Unless your correspondent is using the same word-processing program as you are, the commands you used will go right along with the text thereby confusing the reader. Thus, you need to learn how to strip all the embedded commands out of your text file . . . so that you can send just the text alone. This takes a series of steps that ought to be in your manual.

Copying A Text File Onto A Diskette

The more computerized you are, the more computerized people you deal with, you'll be copying your text files onto diskettes for immediate shipment. You need to know the steps it takes to get your text out of your computer onto a diskette that can easily be read by your correspondent.

Using Telecommunications Software To Send And Receive Text Files

One of the things you're going to have to acquire is telecommunications software, including a modem. This enables you to send and receive text files. This is particularly useful when you start working with electronic data bases which will post your articles and Special Reports as marketing devices. Thus, you need to have the steps immediately available through which you can transmit and receive data.

Calling Up Relevant Sections Of Your Mailing List

When you start dealing with lots of people, you have to know how to deal with them efficiently. You're going to add prospects daily . . . but you'll want to delete them after some amount of time if they haven't bought. Before deleting them, however, you'll want to let them know they're about to be deleted . . . so they can hurry up and buy something.

By the same token, you'll be adding buyers daily. Some of these will keep buying (which is why your house-list is so valuable); others, for whatever reason, will stop buying and need to get a deletion notice . . . and then, if they still don't buy, actually be deleted. While entering data, once your consultant has established the data fields, is easy, sorting your data can be complicated and requires very precise language. You need to know the steps to take to:

- let certain people who have inquired but not bought up to a certain time know that if they don't buy within a certain time they will be deleted from your list;

- include in this zap notice those buyers who have not bought up to a certain time . . . so that you can print one unified list of all those, inquiries and buyers, who have been marked for deletion.

Because you'll be marking these individuals in a certain way (I use a * * next to their name on the mailing panel), they must all be on one list . . . otherwise you'll pay the mailing house a fee for a separate list, a fee which is entirely avoidable. By the same token, your regular inquiries and buyers will appear on a separate list. In either event, you need to know the steps to follow so you get just the right people on the right list. Not doing this correctly can cause immense problems.

Deleting Names From Your Main House-List And Removing Them To A Separate List

If people (either inquiries or past buyers) don't respond to your zap notice, at the time of your next mailing they must be removed to a separate data base file. Thus, you need to know how to remove them from your major list and copy them onto a separate list with another name. These names, though no longer active, may still have a value. You may well wish to write them another kind of letter offering them some special inducement for returning . . . or the chance to be on your mailing list again, if only they'll fill out a card or call you. Either way, you must handle these people separately, so you need to know just how to get them off your main list and onto a list of their own.

How To Mail Merge

One of the great things about the computer is how easy it is to create powerful, personal letters stuffed with benefits. This is where the mail-merge option comes in. You need to learn — and should include in your own training and operations manual — the steps you must follow to create a data base and set up form letters into which you can insert the personal information you want.

Creating Macro Keys

When you use a macro key (also sometimes called a "glossary entry"), you automatically insert a set series of words — or even today's date — into the document you're creating. Given that most letters and many other documents are made up of standard components, these keys make it fast and easy for you to construct the documents you need with the minimum time.

What you need to do is both learn how to create these keys and then draw up a list of sentences, phrases, paragraphs or even documents that you use over and over again. Then assign each of them a designating number or letter and write these in your operations manual until you memorize them all. Very quickly, you'll see just how fast you can create letters and other documents out of the macro keys you have available.

Of course, it goes without saying that you may well have other standard documents in a text file (including many of those we'll be discussing shortly) into which you need only insert particular names and addresses, *etc.* These need not necessarily be on a macro key since you can easily call them up with their text file name. Instead, macro keys tend to be ideally suited for shorter blocks of text which you use in many different documents.

Backing Up Your Hard Disk

Computers have their problems, perhaps the greatest of which is their susceptibility to information wipe-out from any number of causes. For you, these are terrifying moments when, in an instant, you can lose everything because of a system failure. Because such problems are not uncommon, you must certainly have and daily employ some kind of hard disk back up. Without it you are playing Russian roulette with your products. That's why backing up your hard disk must be a daily task, *never to be skipped or forgotten to your peril.*

Assembling Your Support Team

In practice, all you need to do is find one of the helpers you need, and the Boston Computer Society vendor list is a good place to start. From this single source, you'll quickly get referrals to the rest . . . so long as you ask for them! One of the delightful things I've discovered about the computer world is just how friendly and genuinely helpful these people are . . . it's a lot different from the scholarly world I was used to where manners may be courtly but relations often poisonous.

As you find helpers you can trust, keep good records of their names, addresses and all their telephone numbers. In practice, these people seem to have several!

Final Thought About Your Back-Up Team

For what I'm sharing with you in this chapter, your back-up support team is essential. You will call on its members dozens of times at the strangest of hours. Be nice to them. One thing you can do for each is refer them enthusiastically to your friends. When you do, use your computer to send them a Referral Note. Include the name, address and telephone number of the person you've referred your helper to and a line about just how glad you are to do so . . . because of all the help he's given you. In other words, don't just do the good deed . . . be seen as doing it, too. After all, you'll be sure to need more help. This is one way of getting it promptly . . . and with a smile.

Note: when you need a knowledgeable and sympathetic person to call with questions about your hardware or software, try Russ Walters, the computer witch (yes, it's what he calls himself). Russ operates a unique computer consulting business not far from me. You can call him 24 hours a day (I once called at nearly midnight on a Saturday and he took the call) at (617) 666-2666. (You can also write him at 22 Ashland St., Somerville, MA 02144). He'll work diligently to solve your problem, and he won't charge you a dime. He's also author of a series of well thought of books on how to use your computer more effectively. Ask him for a catalog, and to keep this unique service going, buy something!

The Computer And Your Product Creation And Updating

What I'm about to say should by now come as no surprise to you: all your products should be both developed on computer and kept on computer so they can easily be updated. Thus, you will use your computer to:

- develop your overall product outlines;

- develop outlines for each particular product section or chapter;

- enter and maintain data you wish to include in your how-to products (while also keeping hard-copy back-up files of this material);

- develop each section or chapter;

- update the parts of your product that necessarily change over time, including names, addresses, telephone numbers, prices, *etc.*

Since I've already discussed these subjects in an earlier chapter, there is no need to do so again. Suffice it to say that from the minute you are computerized, you should never again create any of your products in any other way than on computer screen. Please!

Note: the ideal word-processing software to use is one that is not only command-driven but also gives you the ability to flip back and forth between different screens of data; between, for instance, a screen that contains the outline of a particular book . . . and a screen that contains the section of that chapter you are currently working on. XyWrite does have this ability, and I recommend it to you. There's nothing more irritating that being able to call up only one text file at a time. You want to be able to move back and forth between text files and also to tag certain material in one text file, mark it for transfer, and move it to another text file by hitting just one key. That saves you an enormous amount of time and aggravation.

The Computer And Your Syndicated Column

Later I shall be discussing how to develop an internationally-syndicated column based on your Special Reports/articles, a column offering you an incredibly powerful, profitable, and inexpensive marketing tool. Now, however, I would like to advise you on how to use your computer in the development and dissemination of this column.

To start with, remember that, as with all your how-to products, your Special Reports will be created on your computer; uniquely, however, these Reports will also be produced for sale from your printer. Later, as you will soon see, you will increase the number of your Special Reports by discovering other specialists and getting them to add to your series — for free. Thus, when your system is fully operational you'll have the following things to do to create and disseminate your Special Reports:

- You will write some Special Reports yourself.

- You will identify other specialists to write Special Reports for you.

- You will contact these specialists with information about the benefits they get from writing Special Reports for you, how to write these reports, and your next deadline for copy.

- You will write previously uncontacted editors of print publications and system operators of electronic data bases with information about the Special Reports/articles you have available . . . and the benefits they and their readers get when they use these reports/articles.

- You will develop long-standing relationships with editors of print publications and system operators of electronic data bases and will, at regular intervals, inform them about what Special Reports/articles you have available . . . and about other items of interest (such as the publication of new books and booklets and the manufacture of new audio cassettes) they may wish to bring to their readers' attention.

Let's look at what's happening here, since the method is one we'll be following with each category . . . and which you must use to routinize the procedures of your info-empire and know when and how to bring your computer into play.

What we are trying to do is identify the crucial tasks that you need to accomplish to get what you want. In this case, what you want is to reach the maximum number of people who can buy your products and services at the very lowest conceivable cost to you and yet do so in a way that ensures that they pay attention to what you've got . . . and respond to it. This is the game, and it's a very important one to win.

To achieve your objective, you must identify *all* the tasks you need to accomplish . . . and develop the appropriate letters (in this case) that enable you to do them successfully. If each task is one you must successfully accomplish over and over again to achieve your real objective, then you need to accomplish two things. You must create a client-centered document that gets the person you need to convince to do the thing you want him to do . . . but which he must perceive is in his best interest . . . and you must involve the computer in the process so that you can send the client-centered document immediately . . . and so demonstrate your seriousness and control.

In other words, you must use your marketing savvy to creat a client-centered document packed with benefits . . . and your computer savvy to ensure that all the documents you need are available on computer ready to be used the *very instant* you need them. Real marketers don't perform like most people . . . don't wait until tomorrow or next week . . . or next month to do what's necessary. They anticipate what they will have to do . . . create the documents they need *before* they need them . . . and then use their computers to act *immediately*.

Is this what you do? I doubt it. But after this chapter is concluded, this is what you *will* do . . . or consign yourself to the also-rans of the info-business.

The Computer And Your End-Of-Product And Free-Standing Catalog

The process you use to create all your info-products and both develop and disseminate your column is also the one you must follow with your end-of-product and free-standing catalogs. Having read Chapter 5, you should be able to tell me what documents you'll need. In case, you've forgotten here's a list:

To computerize your search for products, create the following documents:

- letter to product suppliers with information about what you're doing, how you can benefit the manufacturer or distributor, and what you want from him;

- follow-up letter to be used when the above letter fails to get a prompt response;

- notice to publications reaching product suppliers with whom you wish to do business about your search for appropriate products for your catalog.

When you are revising your catalog, create the following document:

- letter to product manufacturer or distributor asking for information on projected product availability, price, drop-shipping, postage and handling, *etc.*, with date by which you need this information.

When you are placing orders with product manufacturers or distributors for either drop-shipping or shipment direct by you, create the following documents:

- (when you're shipping product) letter providing your purchase order number, how many products you want, where you want them sent, how you want them sent;

- (when manufacturer or distributor is drop-shipping for you) letter providing customer name, address and telephone and how you intend to pay (either your check is enclosed or you get billed).

For the inevitable customer relations snafus and problems, create the following documents:

- refund letter to customer to accompany your check;

- letter dealing with back-ordered merchandise and projected date it will be available;

- letter dealing with out-of-stock merchandise and what options you are giving your customer for the money he already sent you;

- letter to customer who hasn't paid bill owing for 30 days;

- letter to customer who hasn't paid bill owing for 60 days;

- letter to customer who hasn't paid bill owing for 90 days;

- letter to customer whose account is 120 days in arrears . . . and steps you propose to take to settle this matter forthwith;

- letter to customer who has received the wrong merchandise;

- (when drop-shipping) letter to manufacturer or distributor about customer who has received the wrong merchandise.

Note: it should go without saying that you'll also create your catalog on your computer. Doing so enables you easily to construct the catalog, move items about, make editorial changes, *etc.* When you're finished, if you're not doing the desk-top lay-out yourself (and unless you're awfully good at design, you shouldn't try), simply give a diskette in ASCII to your designer . . . and a hard-copy that indicates your underlining, bold, *etc.* Providing your copy on diskette will make your designer's life easier . . . and save you money.

The Computer And Marketing

Just as you can be more efficient and productive using your computer to create and maintain your info-products, so your (properly used) computer will be your most powerful marketing tool. To make sure it is, let's look at each of the following components of successfully using your computer in your profit-making marketing:

Using Your Computer To Upgrade Current Buyers

Before you even sell one of your products, you must anticipate that someone will buy one. You've done your market research, right? You know who your market is? Where they are? And you've decided how you'll be reaching them? *At least you had better!*

Of course, you can be like most info-sellers; when a buyer buys from you simply send him what he asks for . . . or perhaps stuff a flyer or two in the shipping package and think you've done your job . . . all your job. Or you can use your computer to function — and profit — like a marketer. That's where the Upgrade Letter comes in.

You need a letter for *each* product you create . . . and for *each* product you ship (sadly, other distributors will not include your letters in their packages). Thus, whatever the customer buys, you are ready for him . . . ready, that is, to confirm that he's made the right sale . . . and to start motivating him to acquire the rest of what he needs to reach his objective.

Using Your Computer To Remotivate Lapsed Buyers

Just as you want to upgrade current buyers to buy again . . . so you want to remotivate lapsed buyers to buy from you again. Again, the computer can help you.

Develop a letter that you can send to buyers who are about to be dropped from your mailing list because they haven't bought within a specified period of time. I keep a buyer on my mailing list for 15 months after he buys, sending him quarterly catalogs. One year after he's bought but has not bought again, he gets the deadly zap notice indicating he'll be dropped from the mailing list within three months if he doesn't buy again. If he *still* doesn't buy anything, this poor benighted creature becomes a candidate for this kind of last-ditch personal plea and benefit-rich motivational letter.

Note: in the early days of your info-empire, when your customer base is relatively small, you can use your mail-merge facility to send each lapsed customer a personal letter saying how regretful you are that you haven't heard from him lately . . . and indicating what he's about to lose. Simply call up the names you're about to zap, put them into a separate data file and create the letter.

Later, of course, when your customer base grows into the mega-thousands, you won't be able to send a mail-merge letter anymore; it's just too time-consuming and expensive. But you still can send a post-card with a strong message . . . indicating what the lapsing customer will be missing if he doesn't respond . . . and giving him the opportunity to call to stay on your mailing list. Here you'll use the computer to mark the right names for this effort. You can then run cheshire labels off your printer.

Using Your Computer To (Unabashedly) Get Free Media

While the computer is of immeasurable value to all facets of your operation, bringing order, efficiency and enhanced profitability to all parts of your work, when it comes to unabashed promotion the computer is truly your best friend. You will use it to:

• develop and disseminate all the documents you need to get all the free publicity you want;

• get publicity even before your product is finished or released;

• maintain a running list of review comments and media appearances so that you can use them to motivate other media people to give you the coverage you want.

Let's look at each of these sections in turn, so you'll know what you should be producing to get what you really want: free media attention that brings your products to the attention of your prospects for the least possible cost.

Develop And Disseminate All The Documents You Need To Get All The Free Publicity You Want

It's clear to me, as I suspect by now it is clear to you, that in relation to getting free publicity too few info-producers (and, of course, publishers as a whole) bother to think through:

• what they want to achieve;

• when they want to achieve it;

- how they're going to achieve it;
- what they need to achieve it (in terms of marketing documents, *etc.*).

They are thus left playing both a defensive game and constant, enervating catch-up.

But this won't happen to you! Because you will know:

- what you want to achieve;
- who you need to persuade to take action to help you get what you want;
- what they need from you, and
- the form in which they need it.

Of course, you're going to use your computer to assist you.

The roots of successful unabashed promotion lie in creating the documents you need *before you need them*. These include:

- a media release about *each* product focusing, as you will see later, on the benefits it delivers, not its features;
- a cover letter for individual media sources pointing out the benefits of your info-product and asking if they'd like a review copy;
- a follow-up letter to the above for the (many) times they don't respond to your initial letter;
- a cover letter to accompany each of your products sent to print media sources, pointing out their key benefits and points you'd like cover in any article (including postpaid shipping price and your name, address and telephone number for convenient reader follow-up);
- a follow-up letter to be sent 60-90 days to find out when the (as yet unpublished) review/article will appear;
- a cover letter to be sent to media sources where you could either personally be interviewed (as with local television stations or those in cities where you are traveling) or by telephone (as with radio stations from outside your area);
- a letter to media sources agreeing to interview you confirming the time of the interview, where it is taking place, the telephone number to use for calling you, if you are not going to be physically present, *etc.*;
- a biographical feature story providing interesting information about you;
- a question-and-answer interview with yourself;

- an introduction of yourself suitable to be read on radio and television stations;

- a list of questions you might be asked by media program hosts;

- an announcement suitable to be read by the host of a radio or television show advising his audience how to get in touch with you and giving your address and telephone number.

- finally, a complete list of everything you have available. There's no need to send everything to every media source, but you can let the source know all the things you have available. This form should be in check-list format and include your name, address and telephone number so all the media person has to do is check off what he wants and return it to you . . . or call for faster service.

The documents you create must be able to help you do the following:

- persuade a media person to feature your products . . . and provide his readers/listeners with the follow-up details that will enable them to get in touch with you;

- enable you to put a convincing packet of materials together as fast as possible . . . both when you are initiating contact with the media source . . . and after that source has initiated contact with you.

- influence the content and direction of a print or electronic media interview so that you get your client-centered message to the attention of your buyers . . . and are perceived as the knowledgeable, helpful individual you wish to be.

The computer, of course, cannot help you with the content of these documents; that's strictly a marketing problem. But it can help you with speedy and efficient response . . . and in demonstrating your organization and control.

Get Publicity Even Before Your Product Is Finished Or Released

One of the documents you need to create is a Special Advance Sale Announcement. This announcement is something publications (particularly those that know you and your work) will run about 30-60 days before your product is actually available. The publication runs this announcement because they know you and the quality of your work . . . and both because the subject of your product is of interest to their readers . . . and because they can give these readers a price break they can't get generally, thereby showing these readers just how valuable the publication is.

Your computer gets involved in this process in one of these ways:

• either you both develop a data base of publications editors you wish to contact and a mail-merge letter with the announcement you want run. (Send this about 90 days before your product will be available);

• or, simply develop your announcement, print it on your word-processor, and mail it to your designated editors. (By keeping the document in memory . . . you can use the format again with your next product.)

Maintain A Running List Of Review Comments And Media Appearances So That You Can Use Them To Motivate Other Media People To Give You The Coverage You Want

Contrary to what they like to think about themselves, media people are some of the least creative people you're ever likely to meet. In fact, they have a pack mentality, very much acting and thinking in unison. That's why you need to keep a running list of all the (presumably good) comments people make about your how-to products, and use your automatic date macro key to make sure the list is always perceived as being up-to-date.

Why? Because the favorable comments of other people in the media will influence still other media people to feature your products. What's more, being lazy, these media people will simply use what you send them to create the copy they need. Thus, the more good things you send them, the better the resulting coverage stands to be.

With your computer, you can enter comments in the appropriate text file the day you receive them . . . and send this complete list of comments to every media source you wish to motivate. This list will put you light-years ahead of the others seeking media attention. Oh, sure they may use testimonial quotes. But their documents are virtually certain to be printed and thus cannot have the air of immediacy and up-to-dateness that yours necessarily have.

Note: because review comments are so important, develop a computerized cover letter and a list of people who can give meaningful endorsements to your product. The minute your product is ready to be reviewed, send them the letter, a product sample, and a self-addressed stamped envelope — and a deadline for responding. As their comments come back, add them to your list.

And if you can't get either meaningful endorsements . . . or early media comments? What then? Collect testimonials from people who have actually used your product and achieved substantial results because of it . . . or the methods you're writing about. While media people are more likely to be influenced by the comments of other media people, if you don't have them, use what you've got . . . and can get. Then as you get better comments, drop those which now seem a little anemic.

The Computer And Your Talk Programs

One of the ways people creating how-to products make money is by providing a variety of talk and workshop programs, programs that may range in length from an hour . . . to full-blown institutes going for several days. Of course, you're going to do the same thing. The money's good . . . both from speaker fees, product sales and resulting consulting engagements . . . and the stroking from your adoring fans is a not inconsequential inducement. Here, as elsewhere, your computer can help . . . both before you speak . . . while you're speaking . . . and after you're finished speaking.

Using Your Computer Before You Speak

As I keep saying, you must think through what you want to achieve and how you want to achieve it. Before the program, here's what you want to achieve:

- you want to identify meeting planners and persuade them to hire you as a speaker;

- once they've hired you, you want them to sign your contract;

- you also want them to promote you to participants so that you are perceived as a knowledgeable and empathetic specialist;

Here's how you use your computer to achieve these objectives.

Identifying Meeting Planners And Persuading Them To Hire You As A Speaker

You will use your computer in two ways, to:

- create a data base of individuals who could hire you as a speaker, and

- craft a detailed client-centered description of the benefits your programs offer.

The first objective can be satisfied in your data base program; the second with a text file that outlines all your programs and clearly states the benefits participants get from them.

I suggest that this file also include such information as: special features about your programs, their cost, how you handle expenses, cancellation, *etc.* In other words, you need a file that is directed to people who book speakers. As you'll see in more detail when we discuss this subject, what these people want to know is: what benefit do program participants get from you, how easy are you to work with (from a meeting planner's standpoint) and what are the particulars of your contract.

Your Talk Program Contract

This file is a natural outgrowth of the document presented above. Your standard contract should be available on computer and should strictly parallel the items presented in your meeting planner proposal.

Promoting You To Participants

Most speakers fail to give proper attention to how they are promoted to the people who will be listening to them. If you wish to be perceived as a must-be-listened-to specialist, you must be promoted as one. Therefore, here are the computerized documents you need:

- exact program description and the benefits participants will get from it;

- problem-solving articles you have available for printing in sponsor's news-letter (with resource boxes, of course!) . . . conditions of their use . . . and how the sponsor can get them;

- terms under which the program sponsor can sell your products and how much remuneration he gets;

- terms under which you allow audio reproduction of your program by the sponsor and how much you need to be paid for it;

- media releases on products you have available that are of particular interest to the audience you are addressing (of course you want them reviewed in the sponsor's newsletter both before and after your presentation);

- a biographical feature story providing interesting information about you;

- a question-and-answer interview with yourself suitable for publication in the sponsor's publication;

- finally, a complete list of everything you have available so that the sponsor can pick and choose what's appropriate given his situation.

Using Your Computer The Day You're Speaking

Your computer can be of immense assistance to you, too, the day you speak. Thus, prepare the following:
- an introduction about yourself the presenter can simply read from the podium;

- a client-centered survey that asks people in your audience to tell you what benefits they wish to achieve, problems they want to solve. This is a great way to get your on-the-premises prospects to tell you what they want . . . so you can follow-up appropriately and sell it to them. Run these off your printer, and collect them at the end of your talk. Note: even if people are not checking any items that will lead to immediate sales of your how-to products and services, make sure to have a box reading thus: " ☐ Check here for a free year's subscription to (name of your catalog) offering (kinds of benefits you offer)." Make sure you have a place for their name, address, and phone number.

Using Your Computer After You've Spoken

When you're returned to your office, there is much to do . . . and, as always, your computer can help you do it more efficiently. Thus, you need the following documents:

- thank-you letter to program sponsor, including your request for a written testimonial you can use to induce future sponsors to hire you; indications of how you can continue to work together (they can run your articles, review your products, bring you back to do other specific programs, *etc.*) Don't forget to ask for a copy of the audio cassette of your program!

- mail-merge letter to all those wanting the benefits your products and services deliver . . . with specific information on how they can get them.

- letter to other program sponsors pointing out how successful this program was . . . providing the name, address, and telephone number of the original program sponsor for confirmation and testimonial . . . and telling potential program sponsors you'll be in touch to discuss their hiring you, too.

Do you wait until you get back in your office to write these after-the-program letters? Certainly not! You do it all beforehand . . . before the sponsor is satisfied with you . . . before you know your program is successful or not. You anticipate that all will go well . . . do what you can to ensure that it will . . . and get ready for immediate follow-up the minute you've returned to your trusty computer. This is the way to be awesomely efficient, completely in control.

The Computer And Your Consulting Services

I have long argued against the foolishly strict definition of consulting as something one must do with the other individual physically present. That's nonsense. Consulting is nothing more than the application by a specialist of technical information to a problem which when solved offers a disproportion-ate benefit to the client compared to the fee he pays. It's as simple as that. Under this definition, it's perfectly acceptable — indeed mandatory — to look at all the ways possible of doing consulting . . . in person, by telephone, via computer, in articles, booklets, books, Special Reports, audio cassettes, *etc.* Consultants who don't understand this reduce both their incomes and influence dramatically.

As I've said before, when you craft the right kind of how-to product . . . be it an audio-cassette . . . a Special Report . . . or your *magnum opus* in hundreds of brilliant pages . . . you are simultaneously stimulating your reader/listener/ prospect to contact you . . . so you can do the very thing for him you're talking about. Unlike the foolish how-to authorities whose involvement with their reader/listener stops at the end of the product . . . yours does not . . . not least because your how-to products will contain an invitation for your reader/ listener to connect with you and get the help he desires.

Having impressed this individual with your empathetic authority, having given a warm and persuasive invitation, you had better be prepared to respond when in fact he contacts you . . . as will inevitably happen. That's where your computer comes in. Use it in the following ways:

- develop a client-centered letter thanking your prospect for contacting you and providing him with the information he needs about how you function as a consultant (including operating procedures, fees, *etc.*) and what you need from him. This letter must include information on how you intend to follow up, or whether you'll be leaving follow up to the prospect.

- develop any work sheets the prospect needs to complete that will give you the detailed information you need about his problem, so you can determine whether you can help . . . and if you want to;

- develop your consulting contract and have it available to be sent to your new client immediately.

- for individuals using your services on a prolonged basis (like a retainer client), develop a monthly invoice, and

- for those who pay you slowly, create an overdue invoice form into which you need only insert the particulars of any individual case.

Here, as elsewhere, you think through in advance precisely what you want to happen, what you will need when it happens, and do what's necessary to prepare yourself accordingly. Your clients want you to be knowledgeable, of course, but they also want to be reassured by your thoroughness, control and efficiency. When you're fully computerized, they get what they need . . . because of all you've done in advance.

The Computer And Your Dealer Network

The same principles apply in both creating and serving your how-to product dealers. Later you will see how to recruit potential dealers, what they want from you, and how to maintain good relations with them. Now, you must understand how your computer will help you do what needs to be done. You must develop:

- a letter you will send potential dealers who respond to your advertisements and other promotional activities seeking such dealers;

- a letter you will send to dealers already in the business whom you would like to persuade to carry your products;

- a letter you will use when notifying dealers about changes in prices, new dealer marketing materials, *etc.*,

- a notice you will send to publications read by prospective dealers indicating that you have a dealer information kit with camera-ready materials they can use.

- a dealer-information kit including:

  - instructions on suitable markets for your products;

  - how to develop and where to place classified and small space ads;

  - where to purchase mailing lists;

  - sample sales letters your prospects can use for both direct mail marketing and in response to queries from ads;

  - sample Upgrade Letters your dealers can use when people buy products from them.

The Computer And Data Management

As you have seen, you'll be creating not only many different text files, but also many data base files. These include:

- your main house-list of buyers;

- lapsed buyers of your products;

- media sources who are regularly interested in your products;

- dealers who sell your products;

- editors of publications carrying your column (you should mark those editors and system operators of data bases who want your column on diskette and those who have not used your column lately and need a separate, motivational letter);

- bookstores, catalogs and other retail outlets selling your products;
- libraries who buy your products regularly;
- program planners and others who can hire you as a speaker.

In all fairness, each of these may not actually need a separate data base. You may simply wish to create different categories in your main house-list and tag certain files (as you easily easily do with dBASE) so you can sort as you need to. I can easily see, for instance, how you would both like to able to include dealers, editors, bookstores, libraries, program planners and others in your main house-list and still have the ability to call up these fields separately for specialized mailings. The important thing is to know in advance what you need and to program your computer accordingly . . . to think through just how many different markets of people you'll be dealing with and to ensure that you have the ability to talk to them directly about their quite individual concerns.

Daily Life With Your Computer

These days readers of my how-to products drop by regularly. Cambridge is one of the half dozen places in the world visited by every literate person (and, of course, by all those with pretensions). Because of my accessibility, people like to come by to get acquainted. My products offer an invitation, you see, rather like the line "you come, too" from one of Robert Frost's friendliest poems. They do come. And so, very likely, will you.

When you do this, I'll show you the nerve-center in what I call my International Lair, the place from which my market motivating exhortations go forth. In a small studio apartment high above the Cambridge Common where George Washington took command of the Continental Army, looking down on the road where William Dawes, the little known companion of Paul Revere, galloped by in April, 1775, to warn the colonists the British were coming . . . right here where I'm writing to you today sits a little green box whose incessant hum has become the music to which I choreograph my life.

What happens in this room is simply this: I apply my brain to see how more people can be motivated to do what's necessary to buy my products and services . . . and be better off. And I call upon the little green box to assist me in making it easier to reach these people and so bring my client-centered arguments to their attention.

Once I have decided where I must intervene in these people's lives . . . once I have decided what form an intervention should take . . . then it is time to bring my computer into the process so that I can create the actual means of intervention and make sure that that intervention can take place promptly as needed or as initiated by me.

You must do the same.

This chapter, of course, has not given you the format of each document you need to create; other chapters provide that detail. Here I have been trying to get you to rethink the way you do business . . . to gain an understanding of an essential step you must take: the mandatory and complete integration of your computer into every facet of your how-to business.

When you do — and when you link this integration with the stunning power of client-centered marketing — something splendid will happen in your life. Each day you will sit in a place of your own, your brain engaged with the buzzing box before you. From this place, with these components, you have full control over an empire touching the lives of millions . . . transforming them and making them better because of your assistance. As a result, not only will these lives be better, but so will your life, both materially and psychically.

I guarantee this will happen to you . . . with the daily assistance of your computer and the benefactions of client-centered marketing. You now know and understand the one. After one final chapter on product development, I shall present you with what you need to know about the other. Then you will certainly be ready to triumph grandly.

8

How To Get Other People To Produce How-To Products For You

Remember your Tom Sawyer . . . how clever he was about getting other people to paint the picket fence . . . what a joy he made it seem . . . how exciting and desirable? Well, I dedicate this chapter to Tom Sawyer, one of my heroes, a boy who had the knack of persuasion in the fiber of his bones. I often think of Tom and try to emulate his bright and cheerful . . . but always directed . . . ways as I, too, attempt to get others involved in my info-empire.

Why You Need Other People In Your Empire

With the best will in the world, with constant application, a mighty brain and consummate application, with work habits that are commendable and steel control over your time, you are still not going to be able to produce every single product you need. Partly, this is because knowledge these days — and forever after — is fragmented. There is just too much for any single individual to know. Secondly, there is just so much you can do before you, too, succumb to exhaustion.

Before you reach this point, it's time to think about getting others involved in your enterprise . . . people who have information your markets want and that you can sell to them for the profit of those markets, the individual with the information . . . and yourself!

This chapter is devoted to these crucial points:

• determining which subjects you want to handle;

• finding the specialists you need to produce the products you want;

• understanding what these specialists want from you;

• making sure they can give you what you want;

• developing a meaningful (contractual) relationship;

• making sure you get the product you want;

• maintaining the relationship in good working order.

Let's look at each point.

Determining The Subjects You Want To Handle

At the very beginning of this book, I scotched the notion of producing random products . . . a book on one subject here . . . an audio cassette on something quite unrelated there. This is the way too many information providers run their businesses . . . which is why they never derive the benefits of synergy and benefit recognition. This book is dedicated to a different proposition.

Your task is to dedicate yourself to delivering an Ultimate Benefit to targeted markets . . . to letting these markets know that, first and foremost, you are concerned that they achieve the Ultimate Benefit (or related Benefits) you have selected. And then to selecting and developing a list of how-to products that, in their different ways and different formats, help your designated markets get what they want.

In the early days of your budding info-empire, most of the products you sell will necessarily be other people's. After all, others have been on the scene longer. If they're smart and inventive, they've been using their time wisely to create the products and fill wants for designated markets. When you're new, you can't expect to start where the veterans already are . . . nor be as immediately prosperous as the smartest information providers. But you can expect to craft a plan that will put you where they are . . . faster than they got there thanks to chapters like these and your own greater grasp of what needs to be done.

Essentially what needs to be done is this:

• you must select an Ultimate Benefit or series of related Benefits that you intend to become known for delivering;

- you must research available markets and see what markets are slated to grow . . . or at least not decline . . . in the years ahead;

- you must craft your first how-to product for this market. It must be a product that is targeted broadly . . . delivers benefits your markets ardently want to achieve . . . and confronts a problem that will not be solved immediately. Following these guidelines, you have something you can sell for years . . . a perennial, not an annual . . . and something your targeted market really needs so it gets the Ultimate Benefit it wants.

- you must identify other products that deliver the Ultimate Benefit you are delivering and have targeted the same, or related, markets. Enter into relationships with their producers so you can derive the benefit of selling these products to your market.

As soon as you achieve these objectives, it's time to go to the next plateau:

- keep a running list of all the other subjects your markets want to know about . . . because they deliver the Ultimate Benefit those markets want to achieve.

- now, start your relentless move to national stature and significant profit by yourself creating the necessary products that deal with these subjects . . . and by identifying other specialists who can create these products for you.

There are many information providers working at the first level. There are many fewer of us succeeding at the second. What distinguishes those of us who have gone beyond the first plateau from those of us who either have not yet done so . . . or will never do so . . . is this: a plan.

The plan consists of these crucial parts:

- Ultimate Benefit(s)

- designated markets

- products that need to be developed (or in the short- and intermediate-term, products produced by others which we need to identify and sell).

You already know about selecting an Ultimate Benefit and researching and designating markets. Now you must learn about developing and maintaining a product list.

Here I'll share a little secret with you. I try to map out my work for at least a decade ahead. That is, I can tell you right now which products I'll be working on not just a year from now . . . or five years from now . . . but ten years from now. In short, I have a Master Plan.

Like all plans, this one, too, may change. What now seems an entirely sensible product to create . . . based on current market data . . . may not, in five years, seem nearly as convincing. That's life. Nonetheless, there is a plan. With this plan, I can:

- determine my work;

- begin gathering the information I need for new products long before I need it;

- keep tabs on the competition to see what they are doing with the subjects in which I'm interested;

- gather information on other specialists in the field, specialists I myself may wish to work with;

- keep abreast of who's distributing what . . . so that when I have a product they're interested in, I'll know who to approach . . . and can make the necessary connections far in advance.

This Master Plan is entirely different from the way most information providers work. They stumble from season to season picking products as they would lottery numbers, hoping that at least one will win and so make up for their losses on all the others that fail. I abhor this way of doing business.

As I've said before, I expect *each* of my products to make a profit. I do not accept the traditional reasoning that condones a heavy percentage of product losses as somehow acceptable. I'm a good Scot, remember, and tossing away even one groat is painful, much less regular handfuls of gold.

The mode of operation I have been recommending to you is this: to seize a subject and devote yourself to it for life . . . to become known as the ultimate source for useful information on that subject . . . the source that delivers, in-season and out, the Ultimate Benefit your targeted markets want.

Each thing you offer . . . each thing you create . . . each thing you get others to create for you . . . delivers that Ultimate Benefit by delivering subsidiary benefits on particular subjects. When you run your operation this way, you immediately separate yourself from your lesser information brethren who have not yet discerned and are certainly not operating on this basis . . . as well as distinguishing yourself from the larger publishers in our business. With their smorgasbord approach to publishing, they run their companies in an entirely different way, a way that consigns a significant percentage of what they produce to the scrap-heap and so many authors to frustration and despair.

Not you. Not now.

To achieve a better result, open a file in your computer called "Ideas." Head the document with the words "Ultimate Benefit." Now write down the Ultimate Benefit you're in business to deliver. Then write down your designated markets. Who are you in business to serve . . . and make money from? Are you sure that you have selected these markets wisely? Are they destined to grow in the years ahead? How do you know? Are the means available by which you can reach these designated markets again and again and again . . . until you can establish yourself as The Supreme Specialist . . . the source who must be sought out? Once you have satisfactorily answered these questions, you can go on to the next step.

Start writing down every conceivable question that your designated markets wish to have answered so that they can achieve the Ultimate Benefit you know they want.

Don't be judgmental with yourself. You're brainstorming. Just keep at this as long as you can. This is not a task that you can complete in a day . . . indeed, it is the work of a lifetime.

Let's take an illustration to show you how to do this. Say I wanted to work with nonprofit organizations and that the Ultimate Benefit I wanted to deliver to them was security . . . making them strong in all ways, financially, organizationally, programmatically.

Here are some of the questions nonprofit executive directors (a target market) want answered to achieve these results:

- How can I raise money from individuals from special events?

- How can I raise money from individuals through direct mail?

- How can I raise money from corporations?

- How can I raise money from foundations?

- How can I raise money from fees for service and the development of new products and services?

- How can I get money from government grants?

- How can I set up a friends organization?

- How can I get the Board of Directors to contribute to my organization?

This list, I need hardly say, is only a tiny fraction of what it could be. Still, I hope you get the idea of how to go about creating it. How-to products are the complete answers to important questions your designated markets want answered. If you expect to create meaningful products, you must ask the questions your market is asking . . . and answer them. If you expect to create a complete line of products, you must ask *all* the questions your designated market is asking . . . and answer them completely.

The next task is to group these questions into logical divisions . . . divisions that become, in turn, products you'll either create, commission, or arrange with others who have already created them to sell. Note: some of these questions lend themselves to being answered in complete products . . . other questions must be grouped together to become the basis for products. Thus, you can answer the question "How can I raise money from individuals from special events?" in an audio cassette, article, Special Report, booklet, or even complete book. Or you could answer it as a chapter or section in another product. Ideally, of course, over time you'll both create a separate product answering this single question . . . and answer the question in a chapter in yet another product. That's how you derive maximum advantage from a single body of information.

What To Do Once You've Grouped The Questions

As you look over your list of questions, a list, remember, you're constantly adding to, here's what you need to decide: either you are the expert who can answer this question (or you're willing to do the work to become the expert) . . . or you're not. If you're not (and are not willing to be), then you have to find the appropriate specialist who is.

Projected growth in your info-empire begins when you systematically go through your questions . . . both individual questions you will answer in a single product and those whose answers will be grouped to create a single product . . . indicating those you'll be answering (and giving a preliminary indication of the format you'll use to answer them . . . Special Report . . . booklet . . . audio cassette, *etc.*) and those you want others to answer. (Again, keep in mind that while you ultimately wish to create or commission your own products on these subjects, in the short-term you may answer these questions by finding and selling other people's products to your designated markets.)

As you make your preliminary decisions about these questions, you are in fact moving toward the creation of a plan . . . a plan that will set the direction of your life for many years to come . . . perhaps, indeed, for your whole life. Does this give you an anxiety attack? I hope not. If you have selected an Ultimate Benefit people really want to achieve . . . if you have selected markets that are growing and that you can reach on a continuing basis . . . if you are willing to find, create and commission how-to products . . . particularly create and commission products . . . that deliver that Ultimate Benefit, your success is ensured. Such success is worth committing yourself to.

As you look over your list (preliminary though it is), you may think of all the work you have to do. Yes, there is a lot to do. No one builds an empire without effort. But the great thing is, you don't have to do it all yourself. To gain an independent reputation, you will want to produce some of your info-products yourself. Indeed, until you get the hang of both producing these products and running your business, you may wish to produce them all yourself. This is what I did.

However, if I had it all to do over again, I'd get other specialists involved earlier. It's very taxing trying to both discover and organize vast amounts of problem-solving information, package it into products and market it. I did all this myself, however, to learn every facet of the business . . . and, as it turns out, to write this book. But now that you know how things are really done . . . you can get other specialists involved faster and profit earlier. The trick, of course, is finding the people who have the information you need, the skills it takes to create products, and the desire to work with you to do so.

As you look through your idea file, it should be pretty obvious to you which subjects (no matter how important they are to your market) you don't want to master . . . either because of personal disinclination for the subject or simple lack of time. It doesn't matter which. Still, some of these subjects are sure to be money-makers, subjects you'd like to create products about. But how do you know?

Before running off in hot pursuit of a specialist, try an intermediate step. Search through the information sources previously mentioned in an attempt to discover products already created on the subject you're interested in. Make a sales agreement with the manufacturer following the steps you now know and see how well the product does for you. Once you're clear that this is a subject that is of popular interest, then it's time to see about creating such a product of your own. Now you must find the specialist to produce it.

Finding The Specialists You Need To Produce The Products You Want

Just how you go about finding specialists will vary depending on the kind of product you want to produce. For instance, when you want to produce Special Reports and audio cassettes, book authors are perfectly appropriate. You find these authors by using the same techniques you use to track down their books and booklets. These days to be sure, many publishers are also producing audio cassettes, and you may find that a book author already has a cassette series, existing or planned.

As far as Special Reports are concerned, however, you'll have the field pretty much to yourself. So far as I know, I'm the only person right now who systematically tracks down book authors and asks them to create targeted Special Reports based on their volumes. This field, then, is virgin territory.

As in so many other ways, your computer can help you here, too. If you've decided to commission an audio cassette or Special Report, develop a computer-generated letter you can send to your specialist. This letter should:

- compliment this individual on some aspect of his work;

- indicate that you have a means of helping him sell more of his books and, if he offers his service independently, get additional clients;

- say that you're interested in producing an audio cassette and/or Special Report;

- indicate how many people you will be promoting this product to and in what ways;

- say that, while your format is strict, samples of previous audio cassettes and Special Reports are available as guidelines;

- indicate your next deadline for materials;

- say you'll be getting in touch with the specialist, if you have the means to do so, or

- ask the specialist to get in touch with you, if you don't have his telephone number or the means of getting it.

You'll notice that any business details (read "money") are not included in this letter. For now, all you want is an expression of interest from the specialist.

When you go fishing for a specialist for a booklet or book, it's a little harder. Though unknowingly, people who can create your Special Reports and audio cassettes for you identify themselves regularly . . . each time they publish a book, for instance. Those who may want to write booklets and books are not so easy to find.

One way of finding them is to get yourself included in *Literary Marketplace*. Once you're at the stage of publishing or reprinting at least three titles a year, LMP will publish a listing about your company. Authors looking for publishers often check this publication to see which companies might be interested in what they've got. Obviously, it'll take you a while to work up to three titles a year, though.

Also check *The Reader's Guide To Periodical Literature*. You're looking for a knowledgeable source who can also write. Periodicals are a good place to look. Do the same thing with publications listed in the Oxbridge *Standard Periodical Directory* and Oxbridge *Directory of Newsletters* and the Gale *Encyclopedia of Associations*. Remember, most associations produce newsletters which run articles and cite experts.

You can also approach writers' organizations. Check *Writer's Journal*, P.O. Box 9148, N. St. Paul, MN 55109 or *Writer's Digest*, F & W Publications, 1507 Dana Ave., Cincinnati, OH 45207. Many are listed in their pages. There are, of course, hundreds of writers' organizations in the country. If you're seeking writers on a particular topic, send an announcement to the two listed above . . . as well as the publishing newsletters previously cited (writers often read these, too).

Send an announcement, too, to the newsletters of professional associations whose members may have the kind of information you're looking for. You'll find these newsletters, as previously mentioned, in the Gale *Encyclopedia of Associations* and Oxbridge *Directory of Newsletters*.

Finally, stay on the look-out for upwardly mobile individuals. Frankly, the best kind of person to write a how-to book or booklet is someone who's knowledgeable and ambitious . . . not too well known yet but wanting to be . . . a person who can use a book for career leverage. How do you find such people? It's a mixture of kismet and process.

You have to know what book you want to publish . . . you have to research available professional societies and organizations in that field . . . you have to network like crazy keeping your eye on your main objective: finding the ambitious, not-yet-known, specialist you really want to find. I'd like to tell you there's an easy way to find such people . . . but there isn't.

My own experience with author Debra Ashton is a good case in point. Years ago when I was seeking someone to edit a book on planned giving I'd published, I asked one of the contributors if he wanted to do the job. Unfortunately, he was too busy. Then I asked for a referral. He sent me in Debra's direction. It was an inspired choice. She filled the bill perfectly . . . being supremely knowledgeable and poised for a massive career jump . . . if only she had a nationally visible book.

In the short-term, she did the editing job on the book I needed . . . then, as we both recognized, it was time for her to do her own book. Her COMPLETE GUIDE TO PLANNED GIVING was the result . . . a book that filled (and continues to fill) an important need for nonprofit organizations seeking major gifts . . . and gave Debra so much favorable publicity, her speaking calendar alone shows profitable bookings years ahead. What's more, her book has made her a major figure in the planned giving universe . . . and catapulted her ahead of many envious former peers. If ever there was one, this is a case of perfect timing . . . the right publisher . . . the right author . . . the right subject . . . the right results. Alas, this doesn't happen too often.

Still, in a situation where the fickle finger of fate intervenes, you can organize things to a considerable extent by:

- keeping a list of the subjects you're ready to do projects about;

- publicizing notices about selected subjects in publications that reach knowledgeable individuals;

- cultivating authorities in the field . . . they may be too grand for you now but they are likely to know (as with Debra Ashton) who's up and coming;

- being persistent. So much is at stake here . . . both for you . . . your author . . . and your market . . . that it pays to keep looking.

Perhaps you're wondering at what I've said in this section. You've probably read article after article about the sad plight of American writers (our so often behind-the-times *Boston Globe* publishes them regularly and as regularly I respond to them, without avail). You've probably heard how few publishing opportunities there are for them and that there is despair in the land. This is so much bosh. The real situation is far different . . . though equally sad: it's very hard to find individuals really knowledgeable in a field who can write the densely detailed how-to prose people need to achieve the benefit promised in the product's title. THIS IS THE REAL PROBLEM.

In my role as a publisher, and because I do utilize the author-seeking steps outlined above, I get a steady trickle of would-be how-to authors writing me with ideas and manuscripts; recently, I even had one on how to pick up women in Boston singles bars (a strange manuscript indeed when you consider that women significantly outnumber men in this city). So far, without exception, these manuscripts have been a depressing lot. Consider, for instance, that in the singles bar manuscript, the author began by telling his lusty male readers to take a shower before going out! I thought this was a joke, hipster humor; sadly, the author meant it seriously. (Since the author met his own wife in a singles bar, I take it he showered beforehand, and I pass on this useful piece of advice to you in case you need it.)

No, the sad truth is, when you start looking for people to produce how-to products for you . . . and I don't care what kind of product it is, either — you have entered into a difficult search.

- Genuine authorities on any given topic are rare.

- People who can write detailed how-to prose are rarer still.

- Those willing to work with a publisher — you! — not just to produce a useful product but to sell it are the rarest — and most necessary — of all.

The truth is, many American writers (and would-be writers) *are* in a bad way . . . but to a considerable extent, it's their own fault. Writers must realize that profit-minded publishers seek a particular kind of product. If the writer wishes to be published, he must produce that kind of product . . . or find a publisher who will produce what he wants.

Writers, the most self-indulgent of people, frequently complain about the state of the market . . . about the glaring inadequacies of publishers . . . about the fact that an untutored world is not merely disinterested but outright hostile to their effusions. Well, I say this: as a publisher marooned in a sea of wailing "writers", I spend an enormous amount of my time seeking material fit to publish. The markets exist . . . the means to produce these products exist . . . the distribution system exists . . . but what doesn't exist is the kind of valuable step-by-step information delivered in a highly readable format. And it doesn't exist because we don't have enough of those magical combinations of knowledgeable technician and client-centered writer. Most unfortunately, this will adversely affect your business, too. Thus, when you do find such a person, keep him happy . . . he is an important part of what will make your info-empire great and profitable.

Understanding What These Specialists Want From You . . . And What You Can Give Them

As you undertake your constant search for these client-centered specialists with a gift for language and organizing information, keep in mind what these people want from you . . . and what you can do for them.

As I have stressed before in connection with your own continuing relationship with your reader, the best info-products create and stimulate a relationship between specialist and reader/listener. So it should be with products created by your specialists. What you can do is both foster this relationship and provide the information the reader/listener needs to take action to develop it.

Is this what most publishers give their authors? Certainly not. Take the book *Teamworks: Building Support Groups That Guarantee Success* by Barbara Sher and Annie Gottlieb (Warner Books, 1989). Sher's book jacket blurb merely says she's "a therapist and career counselor with a private practice in New York City, is the founder of Women's Success Teams and the highly acclaimed Success Teams Workshops."

Or how about the book *Tender Power: A Revolutionary Approach To Work And Intimacy* by Sherry Suib Cohen (Addison Wesley Publishing, 1989). All we learn about her is this: she's a "journalist, teacher, lecturer, wife and mother."

Now I ask you: presumably these women want to make more money . . . presumably Barbara Sher would like people to sign-up for her private practice, join her Women's Success Teams and come to her "highly acclaimed" Success Teams Workshops.

By the same token, Sherry Cohen might like to get some extra lecture bookings.

The problem is, the reader just doesn't know how to go about contacting them . . . or even what benefits he can get if he does contact them. In short, these blurbs, despite the usual glowing, gregarious author pictures, are an exercise in futility: no one knows what the authors can do for him. . . and so no one calls to get it. It's as simple — and as stupid — as that.

As an info-entrepreneur interested in building sustaining relationships with knowledgeable authorities, you can do lots better than this. You can do what's necessary to provide readers/listeners with the benefits your authority can provide . . . and complete follow-up details. This can be one of your selling points as you seek to recruit these authorities. Indeed, properly handled it will be a major selling point.

Let's look at some numbers to show you what I mean. Say you're publishing 3000 copies of a book and selling it for $25. Say that you're giving your author standard royalties of 10% of all receipts. Even if you sell every book at full price (you won't, of course), the most — the very most — your author can expect to make on the first print run is $7,500 . . . and it could easily take two or even three years to make even that amount, depending on a number of variables. Given the amount of time it takes to research and write a quality product (or even an inferior one for that matter) . . . and given what professional salaries are these days, the project is probably a net loss for the author . . . if you look at the royalties alone.

But you can't look at just royalties alone . . . you've got to look at the place of a valuable info-product in the development of an individual's career, the development of his national stature . . . and as a means of stimulating other sources of revenue. In short, while the product itself is a revenue stream . . . it is also the faucet you use to get other, more significant, revenue streams.

How? In this way: a how-to info-product contains the step-by-step answers to the problems of a designated market (or markets). Some of these people will be entirely satisfied by the information in the product. Others may not be entirely satisfied but may not have current means to purchase additional solutions. Still another segment may wish to get further assistance from a specialist they know now and trust . . . and may have the means to purchase this assistance. Through the product, these people must be given the means to connect with the authority . . . and you, as publisher, must provide them.

Hitherto, mainline publishers, as with the examples cited above, have not helped in this way. Their job, so they reckon, is publishing books, and that's all. Specialists and writers come to them in part for the (usually non-existent) riches of royalties . . . but also for the ego gratification of seeing their name in print. THIS IS DUMB.

As Samuel Johnson rightly said in 1776, "No man but a blockhead ever wrote, except for money." But there are many ways of getting this money . . . in the form of an advance . . . and, more likely, by working with the publisher to ensure that the writer gets what's necessary to connect him with his market in meaningful ways, ways that will, in the final analysis, help both that market and the writer himself.

One reason you will get authorities to write for you . . . authorities who could go to more "prestigious" places, is because you take the time to understand what the authority really wants . . . and fashion means of giving it to him. Thus:

- Enclose a full page in the product detailing the benefits readers can get from working with the authority. Make this a piece of client-centered cash copy . . . not just a feature-heavy ad. Include a few minutes (three will do nicely) at the end of an audio cassette with the same information;

- Include such crucial follow-up information as address and telephone number; also indicate that readers/listeners can get in touch with the authority directly through you . . . and say how.

- Indicate how the authority can help the reader/listener . . . in workshops and talk programs, through direct one-on-one consultation, *etc.*

- As publisher add your own two cents' worth and say how knowledgeable this authority is . . . and invite readers/listeners to contact him to get more personal attention for their problems.

In short, do what you can to craft the proper client-centered image of your writer . . . and provide both the means and the follow-up information client prospects need.

Who does this now?

Almost no one . . . except me, as you're hardly surprised to discover.

I do it because I understand the role of an info-product in the developing relationship between a reader/listener/prospect and the author/authority/consultant. And so should you.

The publishing business as a whole . . . our how-to subsection as a part . . . is mired in attitudes and habits that are ridiculously outdated. As a result, the authors/authorities suffer because they don't get from their relationship with their publishers and their products the results they have a right to expect. And the readers/listeners suffer because they don't know what to do to connect with the specialists they need in their lives. Yet for reasons that elude me, large numbers of people are willing to go on this way, feeling all the while that what they are doing is right and professional. Is it any wonder that I have dedicated this book to the little boy in "The Emperor's New Clothes"? In a trice, he'd know just how foolish and unprofitable this futile situation really is.

And now you know it, too.

It is your obligation to do what you can do to connect your authors with your readers. Be up-front with your authors: tell them they will likely make more, much, much more, from these contacts . . . from the speeches, workshops, consulting assignments and other beyond-the-product experiences the product stimulates . . . than they'll make from product royalties. That's fine. The idea of the product was to help people and make money. And if this is the method is takes to achieve these objectives, so be it.

If you promise your authorities you will work with them to stimulate this kind of additional income . . . while doing, of course, all you can to sell the products themselves . . . then you have a superb chance of signing authors in the way you want. But before you sign anyone, make sure your authority is really a swan, and not just another ugly duckling.

Making Sure Your Authors Can Give You What You Want

As I'm sure you realize by now, most authorities, no matter how knowledgeable, find it hard to write client-centered, step-by-step directions on how to achieve what their product title promises. The last thing in the world you want, striving as you are to build a useful (as well as profitable) info-empire, is to enter into relationships with people (no matter how technically equipped) who cannot produce the kind of product you need.

To produce a how-to product merely to produce a how-to product strikes me as suicidal. You must produce a how-to product that truly helps your readers/listeners and presents the information in an easy-to-read, easy-to-follow format. In short, your presenter must not only be technically equipped but focused on his client. Ensuring this result is Problem One. Problem Two, equally significant, is making sure the authority can and will assist you with the necessary marketing of the product. Let's look at both of these.

I have now worked with many authorities, almost all of whom had experience as an author, in creating the books and Special Reports I publish. Suffice is to say that almost none of them, despite their experience, knew how to create the kind of dense, step-by-step writing that distinguishes the best how-to products. This is sad . . . but it is true. Thus, the mere fact that one has supposedly been a how-to author before is no proof that one has written how-to material. In fact, the chances are, one hasn't.

So, then, how do you know the individual is capable of writing up to the standard you must insist upon . . . the standard, that is, that will not only assist your reader/listener but establish your reputation as the creator and purveyor of superior products? You ask for just one single chapter of the product . . . or even as few as ten pages of what the authority regards as finished prose, that is, of prose he feels his readers/listeners can follow to achieve what the title of the product promises.

Now read it closely. Can you achieve the thing the writer says you can achieve with what he has written? Or has he produced what you now know as "what to" rather than "how to" prose? Be sure. Be tough. Be professional. And call this spade a spade.

My hunch is that what you'll see is "what to" writing . . . and as such is useless. That was what my friend Debra Ashton produced in her first draft of her book on planned giving. I then sat down with her to explain what needed to be included so the end result really gave the step-by-step guidelines her reader needed . . . and which she had so far not produced. Was she shocked? Probably. Disappointed? Undoubtedly. Yet this is what she said in the acknowledgement section of her book: "The best thing Jeffrey ever did was to send me back with my first draft slashed into bits. I am grateful for his time, patience, and sound advice. Without him, there would have been no book."

This is what your authors should say of you, too. And this is the way you must behave from the very first minute of your relationship with an author-authority.

For remember, you are in a unique situation. You represent the readers who must use the material to achieve their desires. And you represent the better genius of the author, too . . . the genius that wants to produce a truly useful work.

Don't let either side down now. It would be better, despite all the time and effort it took to find this authority, to let him go than to proceed hoping against hope that he'll produce the product you want, despite an inability to produce even the short sample you asked for. If this is what the writer gives you now, your product is doomed . . . and you are dooming your readers to endless frustration trying to make sense out of what both you and the author will be responsible for giving them.

The Author's Role In Marketing

Many authors feel their job is done when they turn in their completed manuscript (or, these days, diskette). Henceforward, they assume, everything is the publisher's responsibility. This, of course, is nonsense.

Publishers and authors must work together to ensure that a how-to product is properly marketed. This means having a proper undertaking of the roles of both author and publisher. It is the publisher's job to:

- advance the money for the project;
- find the right printer and have the books manufactured;
- ship books;
- establish relationships with distributors, including catalog houses, book stores, other book dealers, *etc.*;
- ship review copies to pertinent publications and media sources;
- keep tabs on royalties and pay them at specified intervals, *etc.*

It is the author's responsibility to:

- develop appropriate excerpts and articles based on the book and work with the publisher to find print sources to publish them;
- appear on electronic media programs which can help stimulate interest in the benefits the author has available in his book.
- develop workshop and other talk programs that might incorporate the book as a premium or text . . . or where the book could be sold;
- carry the publisher's sales materials to all programs and distribute them to interested buyers.

Some of these authorial responsibilities you've probably never considered before, so let's look at them in a little more detail. Remember, if your author prospect is not willing to do these things, ask yourself if he's really the best author for the client-centered how-to business you're trying to run.

Develop Appropriate Excerpts And Articles

As you'll soon see in the chapter on unabashed promotion, you must work with print media sources to sell books . . . not just you the publisher, but you the author, too.

Particularly where booklets and books are concerned, authors need to develop a list of excerpts and articles/Special Reports both the author and publisher can place with various publications in order to get publicity. Each excerpt and/or article should end, as you know, with a Resource Box that contains information about how to order the book. If publications are not prepared to give you this Resource Box, ask for ad space . . . or to insert your sales literature in their publication.

Don't expect everyone to give you either the Resource Box, ad space . . . or insert privilege enthusiastically. This is something few authors/publishers get . . . and usually only when they push for it. Most publications, you see, like to keep themselves free from any commercial taint; they're also afraid of what doing this for you will require them to do for others, notwithstanding that they are depriving both their authors and their readers by such a short-sighted and selfish policy.

Appear On Electronic Media Programs

These days, there are very few author tours, and only for the biggest books . . . the ones the publishers have invested heavily in with an advance . . . or that they think will sell lots of copies. How-to books are rarely in this category. Still, there are ways to use the electronic media to sell books, as we'll discuss later.

What you're looking for here is your author's willingness to:

• appear on electronic media programs, both radio and television;

• develop a client-centered, benefit rich media release and appropriate media materials;

• be trained not just to talk about the information in the book . . . but to provide information that will sell copies;

• schedule at least some of his own appointments.

As publisher, particularly of a small enterprise, you have many things to do, and you need help — an author's help — to sell the books via electronic media.

An author should be willing to draft a client-centered, benefit-rich media release that you can send to media source. Who knows more than the author about the benefits of using his book? At least get him to share these benefits with you, so you can include them in the release.

More than this, your author should be willing to spend some time being trained by you in what to say so that people will call and order your book . . . or at least request more information about it. Most authors left to their own devices are perfectly happy to bask in the glow of public adulation . . . but know nothing about how to sell a book. If you think I'm off-base in saying this, pay close attention to the next radio or television author interview you hear. Unless the individual has published the book through his own company, expect the author to conclude without providing an address and phone number where an interested prospect can call to get the book . . . immediately. Most authors think this important activity is beyond their commission. It's not. It is their commission.

Finally, there's no reason why the publisher has to schedule all an author's media interviews. The publisher can:

- brief the author on what programs are appropriate for this subject;

- help in developing the media packet that induces media sources to be interested in the how-to subject . . . and the author's solutions;

- ship books to be reviewed by program directors, and

- yes, even schedule some appearances.

But no one knows — or should know — more than the author about the population the product is aimed at, what their situation is, and what benefit they'll derive from using the product. Why keep this key player, then, off the court, when he's so terribly valuable? It just doesn't make sense.

Develop Workshop And Other Talk Programs

Talk programs are a superb way of selling books . . . as well, of course, of helping the author-authority make extra money. Moreover, if the talk program is scheduled by a professional association or other organization with a publication, these programs become a superb means of promoting a product . . . and thereby inducing additional sales. That's why your author-authority should agree to do them.

Having said this, it is not the publisher's direct responsibility either to find sponsoring organizations . . . or to set up these programs himself. But it is his responsibility to make sure the author is willing to do these programs . . . and then provide readers/listeners with details about how to book the author for such a program. Doing this is in the direct financial interest of the author (it also builds his stature, of course) . . . as well as your own.

Carry The Publisher's Sales Materials

Most authors have the curious notion that all you have to do is say you have a book . . . and audiences will wend their way to the appropriate place . . . and buy it. As any publisher can tell you, nothing is further from the truth. The moment to make a sale is the moment the prospect's interest is at its highest . . . which is the moment he's just finished a positive article about it . . . or heard a superb presentation by the author.

Thus, what you need to know from a prospective author is this: "Will you take sales materials with you wherever you go? Will you distribute them to the audience? Make a (controlled) sales presentation? And pick up the (completed) order forms right away?" If an author won't do this, you've got a serious problem, because then he'll be stimulating audiences without giving them the means of immediately ordering the book. This is wrong.

Note: if authors want to sell products directly to their audiences on their own account, that is acceptable. In this case, authors get your dealer discount and are treated just as you treat your dealers. They also derive their royalties from sales just as they derive royalties from all other dealer sales.

Entering Into A Mutually Beneficial And Clearly Defined Relationship

As Robert Frost once said, "Good fences make good neighbors", and nowhere is that more true than in your relations with your authors. You will need written agreements with them whether you have commissioned a booklet, book, audio cassette or Special Report. But the form of these agreements varies in complexity with the different formats. Let's look at the most complex first, the agreement you need for booklets and books, and can easily modify for audio cassettes.

This agreement deals with both the rights and responsibilities of the author and the publisher. Here are its key points:

— *The Work*

The author guarantees to produce a work of a given length (ordinarily expressed in words) by a given date. He acknowledges that if the work is delivered after the contractual deadline, the publisher may decline to publish it.

The author guarantees that the work is original and has not been printed elsewhere and agrees to hold the publisher blameless in the event of any suits that challenge the originality of the work or the infringement of other individuals' copyrights.

The author agrees to make such reasonable amendments to the material as deemed by the publisher to be necessary to the successful sale of the work or to avoid legal problems.

The author agrees to provide the publisher with certain rights to the material, such as United States rights or world rights. (You want the latter, of course.)

The author agrees to provide all photographs, charts, maps, illustrations, *etc.*, without additional remuneration or having the publisher pay for applicable reproduction fees, unless otherwise agreed.

The author agrees either to provide an index himself or at his expense.

— *The Remuneration*

The publisher agrees to pay the author royalties on sales and to pay them at specified intervals. My suggestion is to pay no advance against sales but to pay your royalties within 10 days of the end of each month. This is significantly different from the way most publishers do business. They pay royalties twice a year, namely by June 30 and December 31 for royalties accummulating up to May 1 and November 1. (During all this time, of course, publishers are using an author's money, getting interest, *etc.*) Additionally, many publishers hold in a reserve fund up to 15% of the royalties due against possible returns.

My recommendation is different. Instead, pay your royalties each month but only on books that have actually been paid for; in other words, as you get paid, your author gets paid. If you have been paid for certain books that are later returned and you have to refund the money, debit your author's account accordingly.

As far as the percentage of royalty to be paid, you, like other publishers, should pay the standard 10% of all sales. If the book does not need substantial (and costly) changes in its second printing or edition, you can raise the royalty paid to 12 1/2%.

Note: you will find in practice that authors are willing to forego an advance if they get a monthly royalty check from you. Giving them a monthly sales report also has the advantage of showing them what's producing sales . . . and, when sales dip, of stimulating them to help with further marketing. This is a real plus.

Specific items:

- Copyright notice. The publisher agrees to print the author's name and the year of publication in the book and to register the book with the Copyright Office of the Library of Congress in the author's name.

- When royalties are not due. The publisher will pay no royalties on copies presented to the author or to the media or for copies destroyed in any way.

- Subsidiary rights. The publisher agrees to give the author all monies derived from any articles or excerpts from the product published by periodicals and related media sources. Note: this is a bit different from standard contracts, where the publisher usually takes at least 10% from the sale of excerpt rights. My personal feeling is the author should get all the money from excerpts; it's usually little enough, but will make him feel good.

- Other Editions. The publisher agrees to share equally (50%-50%) with the author the proceeds from any new edition (including any foreign edition) to be published by another publisher.

- Audio Cassettes And Film Rights. The publisher agrees to share equally (50%-50%) with the author proceeds from any sale of rights and royalties with an audio cassette publisher.

- Author's Copies. The publisher agrees to give the author six free copies of the work.

- Revision. The author agrees to revise the work as necessary and without additional payment from the publisher. Any expenses that are necessary to revising this work are the author's responsibility. If the author neglects to revise the work, or fails to do so, the publisher may procure some other person to edit or revise the work, or supply new material, and may deduct the expense for doing so from the royalties payable to the author.

- Expansion or abridgement. The author may not, without the publisher's express agreement, prepare any work which is an expansion or abridgement of the work or of a nature to affect prejudicially the sales of the work.

- Publisher's default. If the publisher fails to fulfil or comply with any of the provisions of this agreement within one month after written notification from the author of such failure, or if after the work is out of print the publisher has not within four months of a written request from the author issued a new edition, then the work shall be considered the property of the author. If the author wishes to purchase the plates from the publisher for a mutually agreed sum (and so bring out the work himself), he may do so but does not have to.

• Work in print. The work shall not be deemed to have gone "out of print" so long as the publisher continues to have copies of it available for sale and is engaged in marketing it in any way.

• Arbitration. If any difference arises between author and publisher touching the meaning of this agreement or the rights and liberties of the parties, they shall follow the guidelines of the American Arbitration Association to resolve the problem. (You can get these guidelines by writing the Association at 140 W. 51 St., New York, NY 10020-1203 or by calling (212) 484-4000.)

• Signature. Both parties to this agreement should sign and date it, and each should have a copy.

While this agreement is principally used for booklets and books, you can also use the applicable clauses when you draw up a contract with an author for an audio cassette.

Special Reports

Special Reports need to be handled differently, for two major reasons:

1. the author of a Special Report will not derive a royalty from its sale, and

2. you don't need exclusive rights to a Special Report.

A Special Report has these purposes. It's:

• a product for sale

• based on other product(s) that are for sale

• includes sales information about your company and your other products and services

• an article publications can use . . . and so develop your reputation and promote all the products and services it mentions.

Given these purposes, the agreement you enter into with an author for a Special Report is rather different from the full-blown agreement outlined above.

- The author of the Special Report (unless that author is you!) will derive no direct monetary compensation from its sale. These authors get their remuneration from the sale of the product mentioned in the Special Report and made available through the Resource Box. If they are the publisher of the product, they will keep approximately 50% of the product's sale price; if they are the author of a product produced by someone else, they'll get their standard royalty on the sale.

- The author of the Special Report makes available to you non-exclusive reproduction rights. In other words, authors maintain all other rights to the Special Report and may themselves sell it, reprint it, make it available to publications, *etc.* However, in return for this, the author must agree to keep the Special Report *exactly* as it was written for you, that is, to maintain the complete Resource Box.

Note: what if the author of the Special Report agrees to this clause and fails to live up to it, reusing the Special Report/article but deleting your Resource Box? In practice, you're hardly going to sue him for this transgression. All you can do is try to get him to live up to your original agreement. If he doesn't, simply exclude him from your Special Report series . . . expand your column (which, of course, uses these reports as articles) . . . and make him feel real bad.

You may put these clauses . . . along with title, length and due-date . . . in a Letter of Intent that can be signed by both you and the Special Report's author.

Unfortunately, the mere existence of this agreement doesn't ensure that you'll get either the quality of Special Report you want . . . or any Special Report at all! Despite the fact that authors constantly complain about the lack of publicity for their books and other info-products, many take their own sweet time to produce the Special Reports that'll help them.

One author I know whose book fit nicely into my Special Report series said she couldn't be bothered to produce the precise report I wanted . . . yet I never see her book promoted anywhere; others constantly attempt to fob off old articles and chapters on me, despite the fact that these don't fit my format. The problem? Sloth, of course, and stupidity, the besetting sins of all too many authors. So, while you may find an authority, get him to agree to do a Special Report . . . and sign a Letter of Intent, you may still not actually get that report. Which is a pity . . . for the author . . . your targeted markets . . . and you!

Making Sure You Get The Product You Want

As these last comments suggest, finding an authority . . . and getting him to agree to produce a product isn't enough. Every publisher, large and small, has been in the unfortunate position of entering into a contractual relationship with an author . . . and then failing to get the product he needs (and that he's sure his market wants). While there's no way to avoid this problem absolutely, I do have a few suggestions on how you can both work with your authority and oversee his work to make sure you get what you need. Here are the steps to take after the contract is signed:

- set a work plan;
- get regular progress reports;
- see material early;
- return your comments promptly;
- have a vision . . . and stick to it;
- stroke your author.

Let's look at these points.

Set A Work Plan

Too many authors suffer because they don't have a clear idea of what they're supposed to be doing and when they're supposed to be doing it. Thus, they flounder. Don't let this happen to your authors. Instead, set a plan that looks back from the date you want your product available for shipping through each hurdle that must be successfully negotiated to get there. Consider how long it takes to:

- manufacture the product

- review the final proofs

- edit the final proofs

- create the final proofs

- lay out the pages

- translate the diskette into one compatible with your designer's system

- make sure the diskette is in a form the designer can easily work from

- read through the entire product in typescript and make necessary editing changes

- edit each chapter or section

- produce each chapter or section

- outline each chapter or section

- gather the material you need.

These are the essential steps in producing a product, and each step takes time . . . usually a lot more time than you initially allow. Prepare accordingly.

It is the publisher's responsibility — your responsibility! — to oversee the project and make sure it is completed on time and in the way you want. Thus, head your paper with the date by which products must be available and then assign *realistic* dates to each part of the production process, including dates for completing each chapter or section. No other course makes sense. Product production, you see, is a business and must not be subject to the insipid whims of inspiration or other foolish notions.

Both you and the author should have a copy of this work plan. If major changes are necessary in it, you must know about them. Such changes will inevitably influence your marketing plans . . . when you offer pre-publication discounts, for instance, and when you can officially publish the product (that is, three months after it's actually available). These decisions must not be made by authors, who generally have an insufficient understanding of these publishing and marketing mechanics. But to make them intelligently, you must stay on top of the process. That's why you need regular progress reports.

Get Regular Progress Reports

When I was younger and naive, I actually believed people would adhere to deadlines. I believe this no longer. That's why I insist on progress reports. These reports can be given in person or by telephone (letters are far too cumbersome) . . . but they must be given.

In these sessions, you can get a real handle on what the authority is doing . . . how much copy is being produced . . . and how the project is coming along *vis-à-vis* the work plan discussed above.

How often should these mandatory sessions take place? In the case of a major work where timing is of the essence, I'd say every two weeks. This way you keep close tabs on what's happening and should have fewer surprises.

Some authorities, veritable prima donnas, won't like this kind of close oversight. Be understanding . . . but be firm. Those who understand that publishing is a production business should present fewer difficulties.

See Material Early

Virtually without exception, the major mistakes in a product are made early. That's because the creator may not yet fully know just where his product is going . . . may not yet have a clear direction. And may not be entirely focused on his reader/prospect and be providing him with the detailed step-by-step information this person needs. Thus, one hour of early attention is worth ten of later attention. Thus:

- get two or three chapters as soon as you can;

- review them carefully. Is your author providing "what-to" or "how-to" information? Unless this is an authority trained in the techniques of this book (you have given him a copy to consult, haven't you?), it's probably the former. What he's producing, therefore, is wrong.

- be unmercifully thorough. If you don't correct things now, your authority will regard your silence as consent and approval for what he's doing.

Return Your Comments Promptly

In my experience, most authors, particularly new authors, want and need direction. One of the worst things you can do, therefore, is assume that because your authority is an authority he'll produce a superior and valuable piece of work. Nothing could be further from the truth, no matter how well meaning and conscientious he is. Thus, get your comments back to your author as early as possible. Before doing so, schedule one of your oversight and progress conferences. Make it for about forty-eight hours after the author receives the material, in other words after he's calmed down . . . and is prepared to hear . . . really hear . . . what you have to say and not fight you every inch of the way.

Particularly in the early stages of a project, you can expect your author to be defensive. After all, he is the authority, isn't he? And he has put in lots of work on the project so far. Neither of these points matters, however, if the product isn't detailed and client-centered; I don't care if God Himself writes it. If it's vague and has taken three centuries to produce, it's wrong and must be rewritten.

Still, you should empathize with what your author is going through. Start the conversation by telling him what's good about what he's produced. Stretch a little, if you must, but deliver some kind of compliment. Then remind him of what he's supposed to be doing: producing a step-by-step client-centered work that delivers the benefit promised by the title. If you can, help him by working with him to rewrite a page, a paragraph, showing him what you want and how to rework his material (or add to it) so that the end result is valuably dense and thorough.

Note: I cushion the blow of this early (and inevitably disheartening conference) by telling authors *in advance* of just how difficult it is to write a finished piece of how-to prose. I also tell them that in my many years of experience, so far *only one person* has written on the first draft the kind of detailed step-by-step prose that's required . . . and he was a public relations professional who did this kind of writing every day. Everyone else was sent back to the drawing board . . . inevitably disappointed but, I can only hope, inspired by my vision, by the justifiable wants of the market . . . and by a renewed desire to produce a truly superior piece of work. No, these conferences are not always fun . . . but they are always necessary.

Have A Vision . . . And Stick To It

One of the worst things that can happen to an author is for a publisher to change his vision of the book in the middle of the task . . . thereby forcing the author back to the computer terminal to rework what has been done. My neighbor, the one I spoke about previously whose book will probably never be finished, is the victim of this crippling phenomenon. I think it's cruel . . . and unnecessary.

As publisher of how-to materials, you need to have a vision of the product you want to manufacture . . . of what it will do for the people you want to buy it . . . and, therefore, what needs to be in it. This vision needs to be strongly communicated to the author . . . needs to be understood by the author . . . and needs to be adhered to by both of you. Having arrived at this point, don't change horses in midstream.

Granted, when you are new to the info-business, your vision may be weaker than it will become. Still, be precise about what you want . . . about the high standard you wish to achieve . . . about giving readers and listeners the information they must have to achieve the objective of the product. Then stay firm.

So often over the past months, my neighbor has called to tell me yet another individual has seen promise in her book . . . if only she'd change the focus, rework all the chapters, make major changes, *etc.* Why, just this week yet another agent called to tell my friend she was interested in the book . . . but had to regard it as a first draft. A first draft??? DESPITE THE FACT MY FRIEND, A TRAINED JOURNALIST, HAD ALREADY SPENT OVER 9 YEARS WRITING THE BOOK! This agent, of course, is within her rights to say this . . . but think how dispiriting this news is . . . and how avoidable if you as publisher maintain your vision of the product . . . and work regularly, diligently with the author to achieve it.

Stroke Your Author

Authors are different from the run of mankind. We live in considerable (and entirely necessary) isolation for long periods of time . . . then burst on the scene hoping for the unrestrained hurrahs and adoration of millions.

More often than not, what authors get instead of these hurrahs is indifference, apathy . . . and complaints. "Why don't you write a book like Danielle Steel," the particularly unenlightened will say. Or "I don't see how you can stand to be alone all that time." Oh, yes, it is a very curious life. Which is why you as publisher are in the nurturing business.

My very wise friend and first editor Roger Machell of Hamish Hamilton, Ltd., London, knew this. When I was a young author, as yet unknowing of what I'm sharing with you now, he knew what had to be done. And he did it: hand delivering the acceptance for my first book on Christmas Eve (I won't say the year), treating me at intervals to a lavish dinner at London's Garrick Club . . . and to sumptuous literary luncheons in his rooms at the exclusive Albany where his bathroom was papered in book jackets from the projects he'd worked on; (he showed me where mine would go).

It was very heady stuff for an ambitious young man. Of course, there was kindness in all this, but there was more. What was done soothed my ego and made me want to work for that man, to give him a book he could be proud of. I like to think I succeeded (read INSUBSTANTIAL PAGEANT and let me know). He certainly did. And so will you . . . if you remember that you are not merely in the manufacturing and marketing business . . . but in the business of nurturing human talent and lending a hand to molding and perfecting it.

At intervals, then, remember why your author is working so hard . . . and support this work. Call not just to check progress but to reinforce the great expectations that that author, no matter how small the project, is undoubtedly harboring. If you cannot pour the sherry, at least provide it . . . and none of your inferior vintages, either! In short, do what is necessary to help your author through the days of isolation and uncertainty that inevitably attend the creation of a how-to product, or any publishing venture. Why? Because it's the right thing to do. It's also the smart thing to do.

You want this author to produce a superior piece of work for you . . . so that you can bring a superior piece of work to your markets. And you want your author to produce it for you not just now but in the years ahead. You are making an investment in this person and his abilities. Cultivate him accordingly.

Maintaining The Relationship With Your Author In Good Working Order

When INSUBSTANTIAL PAGEANT was published in this country, my American publisher Louis Strick of the Taplinger Publishing Company gave a very extravagant reception in my honor at Boston's Parker House, the same place where Charles Dickens used to stay when he was in Boston more than a century before to do just what I was doing: promote books. At the time, of course, I thought this reception, which was attended by literary notables, media folk, and a gilding of diplomatic personnel, was simply my due. Weren't all books launched with caviar sandwiches and very fine white wines?

Now that I am a publisher myself I realize just how fortunate I was in those days . . . and how long ago they seem now. Indeed, even here in Boston these kinds of festive literary events are now very rare, showing a sad inverse relationship to the number of new books published.

The major reason for this deplorable decline, of course, is cost. The return on investment for these events is not good. That's why (despite my fondness for them) I cannot advise you to build your relationship with an author in the genteel way Louis Strick once did with me. Still, there are many things you can do to build this relationship:

- get a citation from a civic authority in honor of the author and his work;

- get a list of the author's friends and relations and send them information about the work;

- send a copy to the author's parents and spouse with a fulsome note of praise;

- send a media release about the author and his work to places he frequents or is associated with such as a college alumni association, or civic and religious organizations;

- send information about the work to leaders in the author's field or important people in his professional life, such as his employer;

- send the author copies of all the good things said about him.

More needs to be said about these relationship-building devices.

Without a doubt, whatever the product produced, ego-gratification is one reason for producing it. Authors, even of minor works, are accorded at least some measure of the adulation and praise that most people get so rarely. One of the things you as publisher can do for your authors is help stimulate this blessed balm.

Get A Citation From A Civic Authority

As I first pointed out in THE UNABASHED SELF-PROMOTER'S GUIDE, every civic authority in the United States, be it your town, state house of representatives or senate, your governor, or the Congress and President of the United States, has the means available to recognize people who do worthy things. Most people don't know this . . . nor do they know how easy it is to get most of these forms of recognition.

Say you wanted to get a citation from the house of representatives of the state where your author lives. How could you do so? Easy. Just write your author's state representative and request a citation. In this letter:

• say the author is a constituent of the representative;

• tell what notable thing this author has just accomplished (namely, writing a timely and important book that will benefit many people);

• say what you want (a citation from the state house of representatives);

• say when you want it;

• even provide the exact wording you want, and

• give details on when you'll be following up.

Include any back-up materials you have, like review comments, testimonials, a copy of the product, even details about your company, *etc.* Your request must seem as reputable as possible . . . and your author as deserving as possible.

Following this method, the chances of your getting the citation are excellent. Personally, I have only been turned down twice. Once in the early days of Harold Washington's mayoral administration in Chicago when there was a distinctly anti-white bias; second, when a very provincial governor of Florida told a publishing association headquartered in the state that he didn't believe in recognizing the contributions of non-Floridians, a bias by the way that I thought distinctly hilarious given the fact that most Floridians are non-Floridians.

If you can arrange for the author to pick up the citation in person from the state representative, so much the better. The representative ordinarily can arrange for a photographer to be present. Instantly, you have an ego-building presentation ceremony . . . a photo that can be autographed and hung prominently . . . and can be the basis for a dandy media release about your author's achievement. Not to mention one very grateful author . . . who owes it all to you.

Get A List Of The Author's Friends And Relations And Send Them Information About The Book

As you'll remember from your contract, the author only gets six copies of the work. Except in the case of the most anti-social of authors (these, too, exist) this is hardly enough. One genteel thing you can do, therefore, is volunteer to send a letter to all the author's friends and relations (those who cannot be honored with one of the rare free copies), including reviews, testimonials and other ego-gratifying and product-selling devices. Give these people a special price on the product (20% off will suffice) . . . and tell them their copies will come autographed . . . by the person they love.

This way, many of the important people in the author's life will know about his achievement (something the author will like) . . . while simultaneously buying copies (which you will like). This is creative thinking.

Send A Copy To The Author's Parents And Spouse

As you can quickly see, most dedications of books are to parents and spouses. To gratify your author, gratify these people, a variation on the old "love me, love my dog" maxim.

Send a copy with a special note from you (hand-written, if possible) to the author's parents . . . or spouse . . . or children. This letter should point out:

- what an important product their loved one has created;

- its place in the literature;

- how proud they should be;

- how glad you are to have published this, and

- how delighted you are to make this special presentation copy available.

These letters, I need hardly say, will be some of the most cherished correspondence these people will ever get . . . will be read and reread over the years . . . showed to friends and relations . . . treasured. As they rightly should be.

Only you as publisher can send such an important letter . . . if you don't, you're missing a golden opportunity not merely to enhance a relationship, but to become an ever-lasting part of a family's folklore . . . besides showing just how badly bred you are.

Send a Media Release About Your Author To Places With Which He Is Connected

One of your jobs is to discover your author's connections . . . and to acquaint them with his achievement. Thus, develop a (computer-generated, what else?) media release in which you can highlight relevant data about your author . . . where he went to school, where he works, his civic and religious affiliations, *etc.* These people like to print notices about members of their group who have distinguished themselves. You can be certain that in virtually every case this media release will be used (unlike those sent to the general media) . . . further gratifying your author . . . and swelling your sales, for, of course, you include complete details on how to get this useful product.

Send Information About The Author's Work To Leaders In His Field And Important People In His Professional Life

Unless your author is at the very top of life's greasy pole or utterly disinterested in his professional advancement, you can help him by bringing information about his work to the attention of leaders in the field . . . and important professionals in his life, such as his employer.

These letters are of the "FYI" nature, saying in effect "here's information about an important colleague in your field and substantial work he has just completed". Include with this letter the by-now usual reviews, testimonials, endorsements, articles, *etc.* And, almost as an afterthought, an order form (full price here, please). Before sending this letter, ask your author if he intends to change jobs in the near future and, if so, where he may be going. It's perfectly appropriate to dispatch this kind of letter to people your authority may be interviewing with in the months ahead; it helps him establish his expertise and standing in the field and will make his interviews just that much more successful . . . and him just that much more grateful to you, the all-impressive Svengali.

Send The Author Copies Of All The Good Things Said About Him

For years, publisher's have asked media sources to send them two copies of their reviews and articles. One, of course, is for the publisher's use and files; the other goes to the author. You must maintain this sensible tradition.

Whatever is published about your product and author you need to send him . . . particularly if it's good. This is more difficult to do with broadcast material; most shows are not taped and are thus lost. Still, you can ask stations if they happen to have a copy of what has been produced. Sometimes they do. When you know about a program in advance, of course, you can always ask the producer to tape the show . . . or make arrangements to do so yourself.

The objective here is twofold: in the first place, authors are always curious (whatever they may say to the contrary) about what people are saying about them. Despite our inner compass, we still wonder what others think of what we've produced. Secondly, authors need to know the bad things being said about their work. Some of these things may be changed in a later edition or second printing; there is thus a real incentive for getting these in the author's hands. But not, I think, immediately. Send the good things first . . . and as often as you can. Leave the less good for the moment when the work is being redone . . . or when the authority begins another work that could benefit from correcting what you may now see as characteristic problems.

As you see, then, there is much you can do to give your author things that are as important, and in the case of particularly older authors, arguably more important than money itself. These things — esteem, respect, attention, deference, admiration, flattery — are things he almost certainly wants, but which he may well feel diffident about admitting that he wants. You, my publishing colleague, can deliver them . . . again and again and again. In the process you will promote your product and sell it, to be sure, but more than that you will create what is so rare nowadays: a bond of genuine affection and loyalty between publisher and author, a bond that must be of the utmost assistance in developing the universal info-empire that is your fondest aspiration.

Learning To Think . . . And Plan
. . . Like A Marketer

You now have your products . . . your books,
booklets, audio cassettes and Special Reports. You're
no doubt champing at the bit . . . you want to get out
there and sell them, don't you, and bathe in the
kudos of your adoring fans? HOLD IT! *You're not
ready yet.* And you won't be ready until you learn
how to think and plan like a marketer.

Arguably, the information in this chapter is some of
the most significant in this book. Yet it is information
all too many info-entrepreneurs know nothing about
and won't implement, because these seem like extra
steps that stand between them and their stupendous
enrichment.

But I have news for you. These aren't extra steps.
They're crucial steps.

Marketing, you see, is really made up of two distinct
components: planning and execution. Too many
marketers, in their haste to get started, completely
by-pass the planning stage. All aflutter with the
possibilities of their situation, they produce their
product and then dash about telling all and sundry
about it . . . until, all too suddenly, they realize they
haven't got the foggiest notion what they're doing,
where they're going.

This, however, won't be you. As a consummate-
marketer-in-training, you're going to do what needs
to be done so that you launch your info-product
properly. You're going to know where you're going

337

. . . why you're going there . . . what you're going to do when you get there . . . and you're going to profit accordingly.

Understanding Marketing

Marketing is really a very simple thing. Think of marketing as an interchange between just two people. The more important is your prospect. In his pocket he has money. He knows what this money is worth and knows how hard he's had to work for it. Yet he will spend it . . . if he can be persuaded that he'll get something he wants more than the money. The marketer's job, therefore, is clear-cut: persuading the prospect that what he's got is at least as valuable, and hopefully more valuable, than the money the prospect knows he has.

On the other side of this potential exchange, there's you, the marketer. You have a product. This product is a change-agent. When the prospect uses it, he's better off than if he doesn't use it. Your job is simple: you must persuade the prospect that your hand is full — not of product — but of benefits . . . and that all the prospect has to do to get them is give you the money. Then he gets all the advantages you have persuaded him you have readily available . . . in your product.

To make this even simpler, think of yourself with your right hand open to the prospect. Think of this hand heaped full of benefits the prospect gets if only he reaches out with the money in his pocket, money he's going to spend anyway.

Keep this image before you at all times: see your right hand extended. Visualize it heaped with benefits, the most enticing and persuasive at the very top of the stack. Let your prospect see these benefits . . . let him taste, smell and feel them. Let these benefits, in short, motivate him to part with his money, which, because of the wealth of benefits you have in your hand, looks progressively less interesting and valuable than the benefits which he oh-so-clearly wants.

If you keep this image strongly in mind as you consider this chapter, you cannot fail to become a better, stronger, more client-centered marketer.

Unfortunately, this is precisely what most "marketers" don't do. They push products and services, not enticing client benefits.

Do you doubt me? Let's get into the swing of this chapter by looking at some book marketing materials I've received in recent days. Remember, these are real marketing documents. Real people spent good Yankee dollars on these materials . . . on design, lay-out and production, on printing and mailing . . . maybe even on advertising copywriters . . . in a vain attempt to get me (for I am the person they sent these to) to buy their products. Remember this as you consider the following.

Here's the beginning of what they call a newsbrief from Almar Press, Binghamton, New York:

"PUBLISH NEW REPORT ON HOW TO REDUCE BUSINESS CRIME.

A new report designed to help retail business combat the crime that is costing up to $10 Billion a year in inventory shrinkage and losses from bad checks and credit cards has been published. It is entitled 'How To Reduce Business Losses From Employee Theft And Customer Fraud' and reviews the most important methods for eliminating the losses from theft by employees and customers."

Now I ask you: is the person who receives this newsbrief interested in the fact that Almar Press has published a new report . . . or is he interested in knowing how to cut his own losses from employee theft and customer fraud . . . and save money?

Put this way, it's obvious isn't it? Thus, real marketers come to the realization that their prospects are interested first, last and always in themselves. Prospects don't care about products . . . don't care if it's new . . . they only care about what they'll get from the product. Marketers learn to lead with benefits (which are about the prospect) and follow with features (with are about the product). Even more than this, marketers learn to lead with the strongest conceivable benefit first . . . and to make sure this is the benefit the prospect really is interested in having.

Using this yardstick, Almar Press has thrown its money away because they wrote about themselves . . . and not about the prospect receiving their material.

How about this one, the front page of a catalog from University Associates, San Diego, California?

"NEW PRODUCTS

Position yourself on the leading edge of the Human Resource Development industry with the newest products from UA!"

Remember, my illustration above . . . of you with an outstretched hand heaped with client benefits. Now, what do you think would happen if you took away the real benefits and replaced them with words . . . words like:

- great
- big
- world-class
- superior

- tasty
- important, or
- leading edge?

When you use words like these (adjectives and adverbs mostly) . . . instead of solid, substantial, real benefits . . . you're asking your prospects to trust you. But why should they?

There isn't a person alive today who hasn't trusted someone . . . and been badly burned. The next time they're asked to trust . . . they do so less readily. And less readily still the next time . . . until they all become residents of "Show Me" Missouri . . . and demand (Dragnet-like) the hard facts, ma'am, and nothing but the facts. This, of course, retards your marketing . . . unless you lead with the hard, client-centered benefits . . . facts about what the prospect can get from you when he uses your product.

Examining the few lines of characteristic University Associates copy listed above, we find these sad errors:

1. The copy leads with the two words "new products." These words are of no conceivable interest to the prospect. Prospects don't care about products . . . new though they may be . . . they care about benefits. University Associates is guilty of what I call "selfish marketing," of marketing, that is, that focuses on what they're doing . . . not what their prospects want.

2. University Associates asks you to position yourself on the leading edge. Well, I ask you: what benefit will you get when you're on that edge? University Associates either doesn't know . . . or won't say. Either way, it doesn't much matter which, because, you see, their real interest is immediately apparent: "the newest products from UA." As evidenced by its catalog cover, the only thing University Associates cares about is its own products . . . not the benefits you, as prospect, can get from them.

3. Look at the pallid verb in this sentence: "position". People, dear reader, don't want to position themselves . . . they want to get something. They don't want merely to be in a place . . . they want to have . . . to experience . . . to profit from . . . to enjoy. In short, they want what the product can deliver. And what can the University Associates products deliver? Being "positioned on the leading edge", whatever that means. UA is asking its very busy prospects to figure out what benefits University Associates products deliver . . . instead of making those benefits crystal clear. This is very characteristic, very poor marketing copy, indeed.

Here's a look at the catalog of Gower Books, Brookfield, Vermont.

The front page of the catalog says simply "Business Books. Gower. 1989."

Inside, there's a letter from Market Coordinator Susan Mielniczuk that begins:

"It goes without saying that American businesses, both large and small, are affected more and more by international business practices. Every savvy businessman knows the importance of 'thinking global.'

Whether you are an executive concerned with the U.S. Free Trade Agreement with Canada, the CEO of McDonalds with your expansion into a previously untapped Russian market, or the corner hot dog stand owner who is affected by the price of Argentine beef, international business practices affect you and your company."

What's wrong here?

Well, to begin with Gower's cover is surpassingly dull. Is there really any reason to open a catalog that says nothing more than "Business Books, Gower"? I think not. Gower, like all too many info-marketers, is focusing on itself . . . not on the prospect. There's not a single client-centered benefit on the entire color-rich front-cover of this catalog. Instead, Gower relies on you, the prospect, to spend more of your time digging to discover what they've got for you. Does anybody have that much time anymore?

Having wasted the important front cover, Gower then . . . wastes the inside front cover, too.

I read the marketing coordinator's letter in vain for a benefit . . . any real, substantial, meaningful benefit that I'm going to get by delving deeper into this material . . . much less buying a Gower book. It isn't there.

This marketing coordinator isn't marketing . . . she's building a leisurely case in an age when leisure is a luxury that certainly has no place in either business or selling.

Dear reader, hark back to the outstretched hand heaped with benefits, the most wonderful benefit of all on the top, immediately apparent. Then look at the Gower copy. Where's the benefit, any benefit, in the first paragraph? In the second paragraph? Look in vain, because there isn't any.

One of the prime rules of marketing is to get to the point . . . the real client-centered point . . . *immediately.* Not in the fourth paragraph . . . or the third paragraph . . . or the second paragraph . . . but *right away.* Where the eye of the prospect first alights.

When you know the benefit you've got, you have but one job: to hammer it home unrelentingly to the person who can really use it. That's all.

Before leaving the expensive and entirely ineffectual Gower catalog I must draw your attention to its table of contents. It lists the following seven categories: "Management Skills, Financial Management, Marketing, Personnel Management, Gower Training Resources, Index of Titles, Ordering Information."

Now I ask you: are there benefits here . . . or are there features? Does the discussion focus on Gower . . . and what it has available for sale . . . or does it focus on the *prospect* and what he wants to get? Do you honestly think anyone is really interested in "Management Skills", or are they interested in what they get when they have and use these skills? Isn't it obvious?

Marketing, dear friend, is about other people . . . not about you. It's about their wants . . . and their fears; about giving them what they want . . . and protecting them from their fears. *Not about your info-products.*

Avoiding The Marketing Mistakes That Cost Others Big

Fortunately, there are ways you can avoid the characteristic . . . and expensive . . . mistakes other "marketers" make. Here's how:

- Be clear about who you're marketing to.

- Know how badly they hurt . . . also know what they want to achieve.

- Turn every product feature into a buyer benefit.

- Prioritize the benefits by market . . . know which is the most important benefit for any individual market and lead with it.

- Create offers that get people to buy immediately.

- Get client-centered testimonials that reduce prospect fears . . . and stress user benefits.

- Master emphasizing devices that draw your prospect's attention to what's really important.

- Learn the tricks of the trade for writing and using cash copy.

- Develop all the documents you need before you need them.

- Understand and live by The Rule of Seven.

Let's look at each of these.

Be Clear About Who You're Marketing To

One of the things that infuriates me about most of the marketing documents I look at is how tentative they are . . . how vague and nondirected. The best marketing is always resolute, confident, self-assured. Why? Because the best marketers always know precisely who they are marketing to and have done their homework to make sure they give these people what they want.

Let's go back to the Gower Books catalog. Notice that the writer directs her copy to executives concerned with the U.S. Free Trade Agreement with Canada, the CEO of McDonalds and the corner hot dog stand owner. Now I have news for you: while it is certainly true that all these people are in business, each is very different. Do you honestly think, like the Gower person seems to, that the CEO of McDonalds and the corner hot dog stand owner can be approached in the same way with the same product? Very, very dubious.

The objective of marketing is to offer just the right people just the right benefits. To make them believe and know that what you have is meant for them . . . and only for them. Thus, you must be specific.

Ingenue marketers, like the Gower copywriter, try to cast their net too broadly . . . so that no one escapes. But I have news for you: the CEO of a major corporation is an entirely different animal from a small-time operator peddling hot dogs on a lunch cart. They don't think alike . . . and they certainly don't have the same problems, opportunities, needs and wants. They cannot be treated the same way. Or hooked by the same marketing copy.

If you want to be successful selling your info-products, you will create these products with your targeted markets in mind, learn those precise markets inside and out and speak directly to their wants and fears. When you work this way, you will both create and market your products with the utmost confidence . . . a confidence that most info-marketers just don't have.

You see, the people you approach want to know in an instant if what you've got is for them. They don't want you to hem and haw in a suspicious attempt to get their money. They want you to know that what you've got meets their wants. Your ability to tell them . . . directly and honestly . . . builds your credibility and leads to your making this and future sales.

There are many reasons why marketers fail to be this precise.

- Some are afraid that someone who could benefit from their product will get away if it appears the product is for others. Don't worry about this! Your job is to concentrate on the mass of your prospects. If you've done your research homework, you know who they are and where they are; you know how to connect with them over and over again until they understand just what you've got for them and act to acquire it. You will make the bulk of your money by persuading *these* people to act . . . not by wasting your time and effort pursuing the odd sale from disparate groups beyond your focused targets . . . or by writing copy that could attract them but leaves your real prospects scratching their heads.

- Many are afraid to be precise . . . because they don't really understand their prospects. Have you ever listened to people talk about a subject they don't understand or haven't studied? Their remarks are generally unspecific, vague, insipid. Like most info-entrepreneurs' marketing! When you know what you've got to help someone . . . when you know he wants or needs it . . . bring it to your prospect's attention with confidence . . . enthusiasm . . . assurance. Of course, some people will be turned off by your directness; you can't please all the people all the time. Misanthropes through the ages have always found this kind of focused client-centered marketing an affront. What do you think Scrooge would have said about it? But what do you care? So long as the bulk of your market is persuaded that you have benefits available for them . . . and act to acquire them . . . your fortune (and theirs) is entirely secure.

Your job as a marketer is to speak directly to your prospects, to make each prospect feel you are speaking directly to him . . . that you understand his situation and have just the thing he needs to get just the thing he wants. "Only connect," English novelist E.M. Foster said. Only connect, indeed! But you can only connect if you know thy prospect, know what he wants, speak to him directly, and pile one irresistible benefit on another to motivate him to act.

Know How Badly Your Prospect Hurts . . . Also Know What He Wants To Achieve

Those of us who live by our marketing wits know a little secret that most other people don't know: namely, that more people act out of a desire to remove pain . . . or avoid loss . . . than to achieve gain. Read this sentence again. When you think about it, this makes sense. If your prospect is in pain . . . he wants to remove that pain. Why? Because he hurts. By the same token, if he has something . . . he knows what he has . . . and wants to make sure he doesn't lose it.

Pain and the fear of loss are, you see, real.

On the other hand, gain is illusory, deceptive, elusive. Of course, we'd like to make the gains . . . but we know very well that keeping what we've got is more important than speculating to get what we merely want. You must keep these insights in mind as you move towards mastering marketing.

In creating your how-to product you've already spent time collecting information about pain, loss, and aspiration. Now it's time to utilize this material in your marketing.

When you market to people, you've got to remind them :

- just how badly they hurt,
- just how devastating the loss they fear would be, and
- only then, what it would be like to achieve the aspiration they desire.

Your job, then, is clear. Before you market, you must:

- collect pain information. Just how much pain is your prospect in?
- gather loss information. What will happen to the prospect if he loses the thing your product contains guidelines about protecting?
- focus on your prospect's aspiration. What can he do if he achieves the promise outlined in your title? What will his life be like then?

Many people, perhaps even you, will shrink when you read this sequence of ideas; you'd far rather inspire with an aspiration than motivate with pain and fear of loss. You may feel that using a person's pain or fear of loss to motivate him is rather like hitting below the belt, definitely not the Marquess of Queensberry's rules. If this is the way you feel, listen up.

You didn't put your prospect in pain.

You aren't the one that's going to cause him to lose anything.

But you are the one, remember, who has what he needs to overcome his pain . . . avoid his loss.

Keep in mind that as a master marketer, your job is to motivate people. Anything that motivates people to take an action in their own best interest is fair; anything that retards immediate action towards that beneficial objective is not.

By this standard, do these marketing materials work?

Here's what's on the front cover of the Valley of the Sun Audio/Video catalog, Malibu, California:

Under a picture of Dick Sutphen with his arms crossed in front of him (an off-putting image of self-protection) are these words:

"Dick Sutphen's Self-Creation System

What is success? For one person it's wealth, for another it's career satisfaction. Someone else wants recognition and I know people who measure successes by their personal freedom or their level of awareness . . ."

My response to this? GET TO THE POINT, DICK. There's nothing motivational going on here . . . only Dick Sutphen, whoever he may be, showing off . . . with his defensive picture and some bromides about "success."

Dick Sutphen wants us to know he's swell . . . the top banana. And while I feel sure he's most interested in having me, his prospect, act to acquire something in the catalog . . . he does nothing . . . nothing at all . . . to motivate me to read the first page . . . or get inside to the second. And if, by some quirk of fate, I do go beyond the insipid cover . . . here are the first words I find:

"Dick Sutphen is a masterful communicator who has established distinguished careers in advertising, brain/mind technology, publishing, and seminar training, in addition to writing several best-selling books." This all too typical paragraph begins a page of this kind of egotistical information and is situated right next to a picture of the back of an empty chair (I kid you not) overlooking a broad expanse of water. Now think for a minute! The man is a "master communicator" but the image he shows us is the back of an empty chair overlooking a watery void. It's hardly congenial, is it?

Dear friend, learn what our "master communicator" Dick Sutphen has never bothered to learn: when you want to motivate your prospect to take action . . . talk about *him* . . . focus on *him* . . . heap benefits on *him* . . . give *him* an immediate reason to respond. Don't talk about yourself or your info-products and services. As Rhett Butler might have said about such me-first displays, "Frankly, my dear, I don't give a damn!"

Show your prospect you know he hurts . . . and can help him avoid more of his gnawing pain.

Show your prospect you know what he fears losing . . . and can give him the protection he wants.

Show your prospect you understand his aspiration . . . and have the tools available to helping him achieve it.

This is what your prospects want from you. This is what they want today. This is what they'll want tomorrow. This is what they'll always want. NOT SELF-EULOGIES BY DICK SUTPHEN AND HIS MYOPIC ILK.

Turn Every Product Feature Into A Buyer Benefit

As I have said before, you must lead with buyer benefits . . . and only later follow with product features. To do this, you must be able to turn these product features into buyer benefits.

Let's start with features. What are they? A feature is a component of your product. It is a part or aspect of the info-product you've developed. Features in info-products include, but are not limited to:

- size
- number of pages
- date of publication
- number of chapters
- content of individual chapters
- length of the audio cassette
- number of photographs, charts, diagrams, graphs, *etc.*
- content of these photographs, charts, diagrams, graphs, *etc.*
- availability of an index, *etc.*

In short, whatever makes up your info-product is a feature. When considering features it helps to consider that they all point back to the product (or service) . . . that is, to yourself.

Thus, if I tell you that CASH COPY has 480 pages, you are right to say, "So what?" You're right . . . because marketing isn't about my product . . . isn't about me . . . it's about you and what you want to achieve. Thus, all features must be translated into client-centered benefits.

Now, let's say that I have a chapter on how to get on a radio or television show. This chapter is so many pages long and covers so many subjects. If I leave the discussion here, however, I've failed. Why? Because I haven't been able to transform these facts into motivating copy that stimulates you to act and acquire this chapter (and the info-product of which it's a part) NOW!

How can I achieve this? With these two little words: "you get."

If you want to become a champion marketer, you need to remember just a few things . . . and two of these things are the powerful words "you get." Now, write down your feature: "a 32-page chapter with 16 ways on how to get on radio and television shows around the country to promote your product or service for free." These are the facts, ma'am.

Start your client-centered sentence with "you get." Then add the facts, thus: "you get 16 detailed ways in 32 thorough pages about how to promote your info-product or service absolutely free on radio and television stations around the country."

We're moving along . . . but are not quite there yet. Why? Because you must lead with benefits and only then follow with features. So, let's change the emphasis of this sentence so that we lead with the biggest benefit.

"Save up to $5,000 . . . and make up to $50,000 more . . . when you learn to promote your info-products absolutely free on radio and television stations nationwide. In (name of product), you get 16 ways you can use right now in 32 thorough pages!"

This may not be prize-winning copywriting . . . but it is money-making copywriting. And I'll tell you why. It moves the focus of your presentation from the product and its features (the 16 ways, 32 pages, *etc.*) to a focus on what the prospect wants to achieve, namely save money and make money. Only if the prospect really and truly believes he can save and make money by using your product will he pay for it. He won't spend his money merely to acquire another thing. Please remember this!

Now what you've got to do is transform every single feature of your product into a benefit. If you can't write a "you get" sentence about the feature, the feature has no benefit and is therefore worthless from a marketing standpoint. This work takes time. It takes time for a couple of reasons:

- You've probably never focused on your prospects before. Oh, sure, there may be lip-service. But here there must be more. A feature is pointless until it becomes a motivating client benefit. Thus, your mind-set must change, because the only thing about a feature that's important is the extent to which you can use it to motivate a prospect to buy NOW the product of which it is a part.

- While you are probably relatively familiar with the features of your info-products, you probably don't really know what people get when they use them. BUT YOU'VE GOT TO KNOW. You've got to know just what your prospects get when they acquire and use each of the features of each of your products. If you don't know . . . how do you expect your prospects to know, and if they don't know, why should they shell out their hard-earned dollars to find out? FINDING OUT AND TELLING YOUR PROSPECTS IS YOUR RESPONSIBILITY . . . AND ONLY YOUR RESPONSIBILITY. NEVER THEIRS.

• Your benefits will probably be vague and toothless. The real problem with most people's "benefits" is that they aren't real benefits. **Real benefits are specific benefits.** Don't tell your prospects they can go faster. Tell them how much faster they can go. Don't tell them they can be thinner . . . tell them how much thinner they can be. Don't tell them they can borrow money. Tell them how much money they can borrow.

Of course, this means you have to monitor your step-by-step guidelines and find out just what real people can achieve using them. That's where the numbers came from in the illustration above: "save up to $5000 . . . and make up to $50,000 more." These are real numbers. But where did they come from?

Either you worked out these numbers yourself to show the benefits your prospects could make when they use your information . . . or else you've followed the careers of real people who have used your information to achieve these benefits. Note: you are not promising that everyone who uses your info-product will achieve these results. Hence the use of what is called in the trade the "weasel word", in this case "up to". This means that someone has achieved the maximum result but not necessarily that everyone has. It also doesn't mean that this individual prospect will achieve as much . . . but that he *could* achieve this much if he utilized your guidelines assiduously. Practically speaking, the "weasel words" are there to entice the prospect with what he can get . . . but to protect you from complaints by people who fail to achieve this result that you promised they would.

Benefits, remember, are the real reasons people acquire info-products. You must therefore spend time on them, polishing them until they are diamond bright and hard. These benefits:

• go on the cover of your info-product;

• are presented and discussed in your client-centered introduction and conclusion;

• are stressed in *every* single marketing document you create, including cover letters, post cards, ads, upgrade letters, *etc.*

The trick with benefits, you see, is not to be creative . . . it's to be focused on just what any individual market wants and to hammer home these benefits with specific details, vitality, enthusiasm and unflagging persistence. This is what real marketers do. This is what you must do.

Prioritize The Benefits By Market . . . Know Which Is The Most Important Benefit For Any Individual Market And Lead With It

If Art Linkletter knew that people are funny, Jeffrey Lant knows people are different; that they must be treated differently. That's why you must not only transform each of your features into client-centered benefits . . . you must lead each marketing piece with the appropriate major benefit for that individual market.

Astonishingly, though info-marketers themselves demand to be treated as individuals, they persist in running businesses that treat all people as if they were the same. I know this because of the paucity of their marketing materials . . . and how general they are; how else could you conceivably explain Gower's attempt to sell to entrepreneurs exporting into Canada, the CEO of McDonalds and hot dog vendors with a single mailing piece?

For each market you are attempting to motivate to buy from you (each market, I must suppose, you are communicating with), you must lead with the strongest single benefit *for that market*. I think for example of a recent project in which I was involved dealing with insurance brokers. After a nationwide market study it was discovered that brokers over 40 said they were not primarily motivated to buy products because of the commissions they received but rather by the way they were treated, that is service considerations. Brokers under 40, however, were more interested in price and profit issues and gave service second place among factors that determined where they'd buy. Very well. Once you know this kind of information, you can speak to the different markets accordingly, with a far greater likelihood of motivating them to take immediate action.

The real question is: how do you prioritize the benefits by market? Why, you ask prospects, of course. As a consulting marketer, I insist that my clients check any marketing document with the exact kind of people who'll be receiving it . . . before it's been printed! Ideally, it's an excellent idea to check two or three varieties of this document with the same people to see which is the most motivational to them.

Most marketers don't like doing this. It's time consuming and puts off the date when they can disperse their marketing materials . . . and collect their swag. If you don't do this, however, it's at your peril.

One of my chief principles is that you are not your market . . . you are not coincident with it and while it is certainly possible for you to understand it, you should not assume that you have some godlike intuition about it. If you want to know which benefit will motivate most people in your market to act immediately to acquire what you're selling . . . ask people. Test. And test again. Remember, people are funny . . . which is why you can't assume you know what they're going to do. That's why you can't second guess your market . . . but must keep researching its wants.

The end result of this process is that your prospects know immediately that you're talking to them . . . and see immediately the chief benefit you have for them. I must stress and restress that the chief benefit come first. You are not, after all, writing an English essay, leading up to your point. You are trying to motivate an individual to buy something . . . and to buy it NOW! Your prospects don't have infinite time and cannot be expected to wade through all your long-winded copy to get to the point. They have a right to expect the point immediately. And if that immediate benefit doesn't persuade them, you can bet your bottom dollar nothing else you've got will persuade them either. So take your best shot immediately.

Is this what Shamrock Press, San Diego, California has done in this copy on the front inside cover of its catalog?

The page is headed "Required Reading for the SERVICE REVOLUTION.

AT AMERICA'S SERVICE
How Corporations Can Revolutionize The Way they Treat Their Customers

by Karl Albrecht

This practical, action-oriented sequel to **Service America!** shows you how to deal with the issues and overcome the obstacles involved in making your organization a winner in the service revolution. Karl Albrecht explains, in depth, what managers at all levels have to do to create and maintain a service culture in any business."

Dear friend, this is standard book catalog copy and nothing more. It's packed with error after error . . . one looks in vain through it for any hint of a client-centered benefit, much less *the* client-centered benefit that is designed to motivate the designated prospect of this mailing piece to take immediate action to acquire the product (and its benefits).

Here's what's wrong here:

- The headline. How do you feel about the words "required reading"? They bring me uncomfortably back to high school and college classes where I was at the beck and call of sadistic academics. These words are *mal apropos par excellence* and evince no shred of client-centered benefit. And what, pray, is the "service revolution"? Revolution is a word copywriters love; it smacks of the new and exciting. To me it merely means I have to accommodate myself, all unwillingly, to yet another change. Being relatively happy with the way things are and touched by sloth, this unnerves me. Another minus. And no benefit yet either.

- The title of the book. These marketers have created a book about corporations, "their" customers and revolution. Dull and pointless. Where's the "you" so that the right prospect instantly knows this book is for him? Where's the benefit he gets? Why should corporations "revolutionize" their customer service? These people are making their reader/prospect do all the work . . . without giving them the slightest hint what they get when they do it. I'd bet a farthing (and you know I'm not a betting man) that Karl Albrecht and his editors have been teachers . . . they want us to do the "required reading" and do lots of work . . . but they sure don't give us any carrots to make it all seem worthwhile.

- The descriptive copy about the book. The product is "practical" and "action-oriented." These are assertions . . . there isn't a scintilla of proof in this write-up that the book is either of these things. The marketer is asking us to trust him . . . that he knows what he's talking about and that the info-product really delivers these things. But why should we trust him? He's a hired gun . . . his salary depends on writing this kind of ego-gratifying copy for Albrecht and his publisher, and he certainly won't be punished for gilding the lily. Why, indeed, should we trust such a minion?

The debacle goes on . . . the marketer says we can learn how to "deal with the issues and overcome the obstacles involved in making your organization a winner in the service revolution." Well, what do we win??? Dear reader, do you see that there are no benefits here . . . none at all . . . and certainly no lead benefit that screams, "Hey, bub, look at this super great thing right here for you if only you take action NOW!" There's nothing like that here, just the fatuous notion that you can "become a winner in the service revolution," whatever that means.

The publisher of this book and catalog are assuming that the right reader will know this copy is directed to him . . . are assuming that this reader will understand what the benefits are that he gets . . . are assuming that after he does this work he'll order the product. What an abominable lot of assumptions.

Assumptions, dear reader, are antithetical to marketing. In marketing, you don't assume. You know. You know who you are trying to sell to. You know about their pains, their fear of loss, their aspirations. You know the benefits of what your product can do for them . . . and you know which of these benefits will motivate this individual, this very targeted individual, to take immediate action.

YOU DON'T LEAVE IT TO THE DISCRETION OF YOUR PROSPECT TO DISCOVER THESE THINGS. You fill your right hand with benefits for this prospect, one specific, believable, eminently credible benefit on another . . . and then you extend this hand to the prospect saying, "Look, really look, how much I have for you . . . and all you have to do is part with that itty bitty bit of money in your pocket to get ALL THIS!" *This* approach is irresistible. Which is precisely why *this* kind of copy is not: "*At America's Service* sets forth a model for management in the service age." So what! So what! So what! Your prospects don't want a "model of management for the service age" . . . they want benefits . . . and they want to know just which of the many benefits you can offer them is the most important. Because if they don't want that, nothing else you have matters to them either.

Create Offers That Get People To Buy Immediately

Most info-marketers act like it doesn't matter to them when their prospects buy. Buy tomorrow? Okay. Buy next week? Okay. Buy six months from now? Okay.

But I'll tell you something: when my prospect buys matters very much to me. I don't want him to buy six months from now . . . or next week . . . or even tomorrow. I WANT HIM TO BUY NOW! NOW!!!

Yet think of this: your prospects are overwhelmed with other possibilities, not just competing info-products either . . . but everything that absorbs their discretionary dollars. Whatever you may think, most people's expenditures are largely set and predictable, leaving a very limited amount of money left over for discretionary purchases . . . and a world of options. You're competing against everything else that delivers the Ultimate Benefit this person is attempting to get . . . and other Ultimate Benefits he also wants. This is why you need an offer, that is a reason that motivates the prospect to act NOW!

We're all familiar with offers . . . if you've ever bought anything on sale, you've taken advantage of one. In the info-business offers include:

- a lower pre-publication price
- author autograph

- Special Report with product
- special price for package of info-products
- special premium (like an audio cassette) with product or package of products
- consultation with author, *etc.*

The trick to using offers is this: the offer must be something with a real value. In other words, the offer itself should have a retail price and client-centered benefits. Thus, don't say, "Free audio cassette with the purchase of (name of product)." Who needs another audio cassette just because it's free?

No, say something like this: "By acting now, you get a free 60-minute audio cassette packed with 16 ways you can make up to $50,000 selling your product through free radio and television time nationwide. ($14 retail value.) Not available in stores, this cassette is yours absolutely free . . . but only if you're one of the first hundred people who order (name of product)." Now, that's a motivational premium! It's not only free . . . but 1) it gives you the chance to make up to $50,000 by learning how to promote your product on radio and television, and 2) it costs everybody else $14.

Secondly, your offer must be limited, cannot be open-ended. Offers must not only have a real value to your prospect . . . but must have a motivating limit. It is the combination of benefit and limit ("first hundred people who order") that makes a powerful offer.

Even info-entrepreneurs who should know better often forget the offer (practice doesn't necessarily make perfect). The May, 1989 issue of *Sylvia Porter's Personal Finance* magazine features a full-page ad for her new *Active Retirement Newsletter* (an info-product if ever there was one).

The ad begins:

"THE MYTH:

Work hard, save your money, enjoy a worry-free retirement.

THE REALITY:

You may not have enough money to enjoy a worry-free retirement.

THE SOLUTION:

Sylvia Porter's Active Retirement Newsletter: Planning Your Financial Future."

This copy takes up about a third of the page. There is no specific market designation. No specific benefits. And certainly no motivating offer (except for the words "send no money now" buried at the bottom of the page). That is, Sylvia Porter, a large information seller, gives you no compelling reason to buy NOW, instead of buying tomorrow. She thereby sanctions the procrastinating prospect putting off until tomorrow what there is obviously no reason for him to do today. THIS IS RIDICULOUS.

If you are going to market . . . if you are going to create marketing communications . . . you are going to need offers . . . motivational reasons for getting your prospects to act IMMEDIATELY. And you are going to need limits to these offers . . . because it is the limit, as much as the client-centered benefit of the offer itself, that gets your slothful prospect to move his overfed body and take immediate action.

Get Client-Centered Testimonials That Reduce Prospect Fears . . . And Stress User Benefits

Most American buyers are burnt buyers. By that I mean every single one of us has bought something that didn't satisfy us . . . and many of us do this over and over again until we feel we must have been born with a "kick me" sign. We want to buy, of course . . . but as our poor decision-making powers are confirmed, we get most decidedly anxious about doing so. That's where the testimonial comes in.

Testimonials, you see, have two reasons for being:

- they make us less anxious about buying by presenting people either like us or whom we trust telling us that they benefitted from the product, and

- they also include your lead benefit and thus make us want to take action to acquire it.

Is this what the testimonials of most info-entrepreneurs are doing? Well, decide for yourself . . . Here's the lead testimonial used by *Tax Haven Reporter*, Houston, Texas to sell its book *Tax Havens Of The World:*

" 'I was quite satisfied with the content of *Tax Havens Of The World*, it being written in a professional but easily read style. I am quite certain your treatment of the Code will aid our own efforts to render the best possible service to our clients.' David G. Forbes-Jaeger, Esq. (member of a Geneva, Switzerland Law firm — all the principals of which are graduates of the NYU School of Law."

Now, dear reader, let's take a closer look at this testimonial:

- "quite satisfied". First of all, this is an incredibly weak testimonial. The word "quite" undercuts its impact.

- "professional style". What does this mean? This is a description, an assertion; it leaves the prospect scratching his head wondering what it means for him.

- "the Code". What code? Again, it's most unclear.

- "best possible service to our clients." What kind of clients? What do they want . . . what benefits can they get from the product?

- "member of a Geneva, Switzerland law firm". Which one?

- "all the principals of which are graduates of the NYU School of Law." So what?

In short, this testimonial doesn't do what it's supposed to do. It doesn't include the information the prospect needs to make up his mind to buy the product. It doesn't tell him that someone just like him (or someone he can respect) got a benefit from the product . . . a benefit he (the prospect) also wants. This testimonial is just so many words . . . flaccid, vague, pointless . . . without a single motivating benefit.

How much better would have been a testimonial saying, "I was tired of paying high taxes to the U.S. government and wanted to find safe foreign places with minimum tax requirements. Using *Tax Havens of the World,* I did. Last year alone I saved $7,000 — and got a free trip to the Bahamas, too, to inspect my investment."

Here's what this testimonial is saying, "Fed up with paying high taxes? Interested in keeping more of your money? Here's something that can help you do just that. I used it and saved $7,000. If you want this much — or possibly even more — get this book!"

Of course, you need benefit-rich testimonials for each target market you want to motivate. I can think of at least two markets for this book, for instance:

- law and accounting firms advising clients on where to invest for minimum tax;

- individuals tired of paying high U.S. taxes and interested in finding safe overseas tax havens.

It's the publisher's responsibility to gather the testimonials that will motivate the prospects in each market to take immediate action.

So, where do these testimonials come from?

You can gather testimonials in several ways:

- Ask people who use your product to tell you what benefits they get from it. Along with every product you send, include a post script on your upgrade letter asking your buyer to contact you and tell you what results he achieved. Additionally, invite your readers to do so in both the introduction and client-centered conclusion of your product. If you want to find out how your clients have done, just ask them to tell you. Give people a small present (Special Reports are good) when they write to you. Use this premium as an inducement to contact you.

- Prod people. When you meet people who have acquired your product ask them how they're doing with it. You'll hear the most amazing stories about just what your sensible methods helped them achieve. Then either write down what they say on the spot and get their permission to use their words as a testimonial (better) or ask them to send you a letter with a written testimonial (not as good because it puts the burden of responsibilty on them).

- Send out a letter to your readers and ask them to tell you about their specific results and how your info-product helped them. How long should you wait after you've sent the product? That depends on how long it will take to get results. The gardener you sold the flower-growing booklet to can't tell you how good the flowers are . . . until he's seen them!

What's amazing about testimonials is how many good ones every reputable information seller loses because he's just not organized. Not me! Because I have a system for both stimulating and logging testimonials, I'm ready the minute there's either an opening or a new testimonial.

Say someone calls on the phone (as happens daily) with a compliment about one of my books or info-products. Since I'm virtually always at the computer, I simply call up my "testimonial" text file and type in the words of this satisfied customer, his name, city and state. If the grammar is a little wobbly, I merge this text file into a standard letter I have available asking both for permission to use this quote and giving the quoter the opportunity to clean it up a little. This letter goes into the mail instantly.

Doing this every day has left me with lists of wonderful quotations which I use in my catalogs, mailing pieces, *etc.* Why just yesterday one of my dealers wrote and asked me if I had any new testimonials on CASH COPY; I was able to get him a single-spaced three-page list of new material. How long did it take to do this for him? Under a minute. Can you do this?

Of course, the final way to get testimonials is from celebrities in your field. To do this, all you have to do is draw up a list of people you want quotations from, gather their names and addresses, then create a data file and mail-merge letter. Send your product and supporting information as soon as you can. Note: don't just ask for a quote. If you don't prompt the reviewer, you'll probably get the standard "great book" line. Instead, you want an answer to the question " *Why* is this a great book?" If you don't tell your celebrities and authorities this is what you're after, chances are you won't get it. Remember, your prospects want to know what they get from the product . . . not just that some authority thinks its great. Thus, be sure to ask your would-be endorsers to comment on why the product is a good one . . . not just their feelings about it.

Master Emphasizing Devices That Draw Your Prospect's Attention To What's Really Important

Consider the phrase "Your pant leg is on fire." Now, which rendering of this phrase do you think will motivate the prospect to take more immediate action:

1. (pianissimo) "Your pant leg is on fire."
2. (fortissimo) "YOUR PANT LEG IS ON FIRE!!!!"

Obvious, isn't it? Why, then do most info-marketers act as if all words were equal . . . as if it doesn't matter how you bring your message to your prospect's attention.

It matters very much.

If you want your prospect to think something's important, you've got to let him know IN NO UNCERTAIN TERMS that that thing is important.

Consider this news release from Sun Eagle Publishing, Granada Hills, California. It begins thus:

"Sun Eagle Publishing (in bold)

NEWS RELEASE (in pale gray)

FOR IMMEDIATE RELEASE

CAN THE COMMON COLD REALLY BE STOPPED?
New Age Scientific Breakthrough!

A Ten Minute Cure for the Common Cold is the result of ten years of clinical research by a prominent California Chiropractor, Dr. Jim Dorobiala. This 'how to' health book and accompanying videotape gives the reader/viewer clear, precise instruction in the cure and management of one of mankind's oldest pests — the common cold."

There are many problems with this news release, of course. There's not a single client benefit (do you think prospects are interested in knowing if the common cold can really be stopped or that their most provoking and debilitating cold can be wiped out?). You now see this problem as well as I do.

Part of the reason for the lack of emphasizing devices in this copy is that its creator really hasn't made any effort to deduce the benefits . . . that is, to determine which things really would be important to his readers. If he knew what was important to them . . . he could make them seem important to them. Thus, the root of the problem is a failure to understand what his prospects want . . . and to emphasize that he has benefits for them . . . if only they act NOW!

Therefore, when you look at this copy here's what you see:

• The single most emphasized phrase on the page is the name of the publishing company, Sun Eagle Publishing. The marketer put this in the largest-sized type on the page . . . and gave these three words the boldest ink. Why? Because these three words are about him . . . it's his company, his name, his baby. And he wants you to know it. Okay. So we now know it. What difference does it make? Do these three words give us a benefit? Make us an offer we can't refuse? Stimulate us to act? No, they don't. Thus, there's no point to emphasizing them, is there?

• Perhaps the next most emphasized phrase on the page is the question that constitutes this marketer's headline. It's in bold capital letters but a couple of sizes smaller than the name of the company. Again, there's no benefit here . . . just a question.

• Finally, the only thing emphasized in the actual text itself is the name of the product, which is underlined.

End result? The three most prominently marked phrases on the page have:

• no benefit
• no offer
• no fear
• no aspiration
• no motivating aspect whatsoever.

YET SOME DARE CALL THIS MARKETING!

If you want to motivate people to act, you not only need to write benefit-rich, motivational copy. You must also let the prospect know what's important . . . through the use of emphasizing devices. These devices include (but are certainly not limited to):

- arrows
- boxes
- color
- indentations
- bold lettering
- capital letters
- bullets
- italics
- punctuation.

And what things should be emphasized?

Well, to begin with, the item you have selected as your major benefit for this target market should get major emphasis. In this case, what do you suppose that benefit is? Why, not getting knocked out anymore when you get a cold. The real benefit of this book is that if you use it, you can kill colds in ten minutes. If you believe this (and value your cold-free life), you get the product. If you don't, you don't. It's as simple as that. Thus, you must emphasize the primary benefit.

Equally, you must emphasize the offer that motivates the prospect to take immediate action. In this case, given that the marketer is selling both a book and a cassette for a combined price of about $35 postpaid, I'd make the audio cassette (retail value $9.95) the inducement for the immediate sale . . . if the prospect buys within a limited time. This has a couple of advantages:

1. it raises the value of the average sale for the marketer (very important), and

2. it provides an incentive for the prospect to take immediate action . . . instead of waiting to do so until he gets around to it.

There is a third advantage, too: it puts more of your products (with more of your client-centered messages) into the world . . . and thus gives you a better chance of stimulating further business from your products. As matters now stand in the flyer I'm looking at, none of this is happening. It's a product announcement, pure, simple . . . and ineffectual.

No marketing communication . . . be it a flyer, post card or six-page sales letter . . . should ever leave your office without your doing a necessary review to determine if you have really emphasized the things that will get the prospect to take immediate action. Remember what you are trying to do: you want to seize control of your prospect's eyes and mind . . . and, yes, pocketbook, by directing his attention to what you know is valuable and motivating to him. In effect, you're saying, "Look, bub, look at this . . . and this . . . and this . . . this is what you want . . . here's all you have to do to get it!"

What you're really creating with your emphasizing devices, I call the Internal Message. The Internal Message of any marketing communication is composed of those key items that are both the most motivational to the prospect . . . and which the prospect must know and do so that the sale is closed. These include:

- the benefits
- the offer
- the time limit on the offer
- testimonials packed with "I-got-them!" benefits and fear-reducing results
- a telephone number or other immediate response device.

These are what must be emphasized. When you do, you've got a prospect-compelling Internal Message. And what does that do for you? When you read it, read all that's been emphasized, you've really got the whole message, the pith and heart of the client-centered message. Thus, as you write copy, keep this in mind: you're not only writing one marketing message . . . you're actually writing two, the second being borne home to the prospect with the assistance of the wide variety of emphasizing devices that you must use . . . but which most info-entrepreneurs unaccountably do not.

Learn The Tricks Of The Trade For Writing And Using Cash Copy

Just as emphasizing your key points . . . the points that really motivate your prospect to take immediate action . . . will improve the response rate on your marketing communications, so there are other cash copy tricks you need to master, too. You need to master these before you start creating any marketing piece so that the actual act of creation is both controlled and certain. What you are aiming at here is not to be creative . . . but to do those things that work in getting people to buy the products you're selling. Here are some you must keep in mind:

- Put your strongest selling argument where the eye of the prospect first alights.

- Use the upper right hand corner of your marketing piece to present your offer.

- Don't use a standard salutation . . . use one that focuses on the benefit the prospect wants to achieve.

- Hammer home at least six benefits in your letters, flyers, product descriptions, brochures, *etc.*

- Reinforce your benefits with testimonials.

- Never merely assert . . . always prove.

- Repeat your major benefit in a client-centered post-script.

- Keep your sentences short . . . start them with action verbs.

Let's look at each of these briefly.

Put Your Strongest Selling Argument Where The Eye Of The Prospect First Alights

You know your target market, right? You know who should be using your product, right? You know the chief benefit this supremely important person gets from you, right? If you do, then deliver your strongest benefit immediately . . . where the eye of the prospect first alights; in most cases this means on the envelope or mailing panel.

If you have something valuable for your prospect, don't make him wade through heaps of words to find it. GIVE IT TO HIM IMMEDIATELY.

Since this is your lead benefit, you must give it your utmost consideration. After all, if your selected prospect passes on this one, he's less likely to be motivated by your other (less compelling) benefits.

Use The Upper Right Hand Corner Of Your Marketing Piece To Present Your Offer

Because your offer is motivational and is probably the thing that gets your prospect to act immediately, move it to an important place in your marketing communications: the upper right hand corner. As you now know how to do, make this offer client-centered and specific. And emphasize it! Since biblical times (and probably before) the right has been more important than the left. This is where your prospect will look first, so make sure you have given the strongest possible consideration to the client-centered message you'll use there.

Don't Use A Standard Salutation . . . Use One That Focuses On The Benefit The Prospect Wants To Achieve

Not only do most marketing communications look alike . . . they begin alike: "Dear friend," "Dear colleague," "Dear customer." Dull! Dull! Dull! Remember the prime Lant rule: each sentence of each marketing communication either helps motivate an immediate sale . . . or there's absolutely no point to having it. Thus, *use* your salutation; don't just have it.

"Dear Taxpayer Fed Up With Paying Exorbitant U.S. Income Taxes."

"Dear Nonprofit Executive Wanting To Raise More Money From Corporations & Foundations."

"Dear Friend Who's Sick Of Losing Ten Days Every Year Because Of The 'Common' Cold."

Get the idea?

You've never seen salutations like this, have you? And, therefore, you may be a tad squeamish about them. They don't look like everybody else's marketing salutation. THAT'S JUST THE POINT.

Everybody else's salutations get skipped over without a first (much less a second) thought. And everything that's been used to create and disseminate them is therefore wasted. Your job is to drive home the prime benefit you've got for your prospect . . . and your salutation gives you another chance to do so. Use it.

Hammer Home At Least Six Benefits In Your Letters, Flyers, Product Descriptions, Brochures, *etc.*

When I was a college student I had occasion (God knows why) to visit a pig farm. There I was taught a prime rule of marketing. The pig farmer took me to a pen full of porkers and gave me a demonstration in motivation I have never forgotten. "Pigs move," he said. Nothing happened. "PIGS MOVE!," he commanded. Nothing happened. Then he took out a blunt instrument and hit the biggest pig on the snout. That pig moved . . . and all the rest followed. "And that is how you motivate pigs," the farmer said conclusively. Remember this as you act to motivate your prospects.

As you now know, when you create marketing documents you are not presenting facts . . . you're motivating immediate action. That's why you need to assemble your six most telling sales arguments . . . or, if you prefer, client-centered benefits. Then you need to rank them in order of importance. You'll be leading, remember, with the most compelling to the largest number of targeted prospects.

Essentially, your structure goes something like this:

Here's the most compelling client-centered reason for immediate action.

Here's the next most compelling reason.

Here's the next most compelling reason.

Here's the next most compelling reason.

And the next.

And the next.

You get the idea!

Six is the magic number here . . . although that number may be increased if you are using, say, a six-page sales letter. Or reduced . . . if you are using a post card.

Either way, you use as many motivating sales arguments as you can to get immediate action. DON'T JUST TELL. SELL.

Reinforce Your Benefits With Testimonials

For each benefit of each of your info-products, get a testimonial. Use this testimonial to reinforce your benefit. Thus, if your lead benefit is that you need never suffer the miserable drawbacks of a common cold ever again . . . your lead testimonial should confirm that. Thus, the rhythm: "You get this benefit (seller) . . . I got this benefit (user)." Remember, you get . . . I got.

To get these testimonials, you use the methods presented above. To know what testimonials you need, however, you must list and then prioritize the benefits. Then set about getting the testimonials you must have to confirm them. Note: in fact, there is rarely enough space in each marketing document to enable you to put in a testimonial for each benefit . . . but make sure you always have testimonials for your leading benefits. These must be confirmed and reinforced in your prospect's mind.

Never Merely Assert . . . Always Prove

The problem with most marketing communications (pick up virtually any example to confirm this) is that the marketer asserts . . . but never proves. Dear reader, whoever you are . . . however grand . . . however much the apple of your mother's eye . . . no one has any reason to believe you. Thus, you must prove. To do so use testimonials, third-party reviews, lab reports, the confirmation of satisfied customers, *etc.* These proving devices are most important.

That stands to reason, doesn't it? People are rightly cynical about the claims made by most info-producers (or any other marketer). Since these producers stand to benefit through the sale of the item, the prospect reckons he (the producer) will say anything to sell it. Then it's the prospect's problem to make the product work.

Because this is the way most (badly burned) American consumers feel . . . you need to start from a different place. Assume that your prospect will *not* believe you . . . realize he has no reason to trust you. And act accordingly.

If you are going to say something . . . *prove* that something. Don't just throw in a descriptive fluff word that seems to get you off the hook . . . but actually convinces your prospect of nothing.

You know the kinds of words I mean. I've listed some before. Here's a batch of them taken from the ads in a recent issue of *Money* magazine:

- legendary
- elegant
- dazzling
- celebrated
- exceptional
- award-winning
- undeniably
- remarkable
- enriched
- revolutionary
- superb
- merging

I could go on and on. These fluff words — all adjectives and adverbs — are unproven "trust me" words. The marketers — well meaning, honest people mostly — ask their prospects to trust them . . . instead of proving to these prospects that they have a believable, compelling benefit for them. DON'T DO THIS!

Lead with your strongest benefit . . . then confirm it. However you must confirm it. *But confirm it!*

Dear friend, just because you say something doesn't make it so. Yes, the thing you say may be true. Yes, you may be an honorable person. But put yourself in your prospect's shoes. He doesn't know you. Has no reason to trust you. And does need his fears reduced . . . and his reason to act reinforced. This is your task. Don't give your prospect a legitimate reason for not acting immediately . . . build the strongest possible case for immediate action.

Repeat Your Major Benefit In A Client-Centered Post Script

Almost universally, copywriters recognize the importance of the post script. So should you. It's one of the most read sections of any marketing document. Here is your last chance to hammer home your lead benefit . . . the most important reason for your prospect to act NOW! In actual fact, this reason is probably your client-centered offer . . . the reason you're using to motivate your prospect to take immediate action.

By the time your prospect gets to this point, he should already know what that reason is. The post script is not the place to present anything new; it's the place to emphasize the great benefit you've already lead with and discussed. Why do so many info-marketers fail to get this point? Why, that is, do so many present new material — usually their offer (if they have one) — so late in their communication? It's because, I think, they want to lead up to what's important . . . not begin with it.

If you begin with what's important and truly make your best shot . . . you'll use the end of your marketing communication to try once more to make your major point . . . the point that gets your prospect to take immediate action. Don't expect, as so many info-marketers seem to do, that your prospect is going to carefully read all your words. This kind of thinking is what gets these marketers into trouble. Instead, hammer home your lead benefit on the outside of your mailing piece (where the eye of the prospect first alights) . . . in the top right hand corner . . . and in your post script . . . where you get one more chance to make the leading point that will motivate immediate prospect response.

Keep Your Sentences Short . . . Start Them With Action Verbs

Remember what marketing is all about . . . it's about moving a person from a place where he feels uncomfortable and/or incomplete . . . unhappy in some way . . . and transporting him (through your product and the act of both acquiring and using it) to another situation where he's better off. Thus, marketing is about movement.

There must be a throbbing beat in your marketing. You can't just say "here's my product." You must say instead, "Here's how much better off you'll be when you use my product." Saying the first is about non-movement; saying the second is about movement. You must see the difference.

Thus, as you write selling copy, this copy must be pulsating with movement . . . the beat of real life. There must be nothing in the copy that drags . . . that retards a reader . . . that slows down the process of rushing towards what both you and your prospect must regard as the inevitable conclusion: immediate purchase.

What you write must be:

- energetic
- enthusiastic
- directed
- channelled
- action-oriented.

Building your copy with these traits is what gives you copy that motivates real people to take immediate action.

Thus, it is perfectly acceptable to:

- begin sentences with action verbs;

- telegraph benefits . . . using phrases . . . and ellipses;

- put capital letters in the middle of sentences . . . if you have something important to emphasize.

- keep paragraphs to just three or four sentences . . . introduced by client-centered headlines.

Remember what you're doing . . . you're putting a fever in the prospect's blood . . . you're helping pump him up, move him out, increase his pulse rate . . . and move him to action.

Elegant sentences with perfectly turned periods . . . long, turgid prose stuffed with jargon . . . awkward sentences that ramble from paragraph to paragraph . . . sentences with unfamiliar words that confuse a prospect and make him feel stupid . . . sentences, in short, like William F. Buckley writes. All these are anathema and must be avoided.

Think of the almost primitive drum beat you are pounding home: Call now! Send in your coupon now! Buy now! Do it now! NOW! NOW! NOW!

The best marketing communications are carried on these two words: benefit and NOW! If you clearly communicate benefits and clearly communicate the need for immediate action, you are way ahead in this game . . . way ahead of your competitors who are merely presenting the facts about their products in a dull, leaden, unexciting, anti-motivational fashion.

This can't be you. Not now! Because you know what you're doing . . . you know the direction you want to move your prospect . . . and you'll create your marketing communications that get him to go there . . . immediately.

Develop All The Documents You Need Before You Need Them

Now that you know how to write . . . it's time to create all the documents you need so they're ready when you need them. I think by now I don't need to spend much time on this crucial point. I've already pressed home the benefits of using your computer to augment your efficiency. Later chapters present more information about how to fashion the various documents you need.

Here let me simply say this: if you are going to be the consummate marketer, you must think through all the marketing documents you'll need . . . before you need them. And create them as soon as you have the material you need, so that when you need them you can use them . . . immediately.

These days when someone calls me (and during any given month thousands do), I am ready for them . . . whenever they call . . . whatever they want. 99% of the contacts I have with people in my business are routine . . . and can be dealt with in routine fashion. By thinking through in advance just what my prospects and customers are likely to want and just what I must have to satisfy their requests, I can create — long before I actually need to use it — each document I require. Routine tasks, you see, must be treated in the most automated and routine way possible. When you will do tomorrow what you did yesterday, it is time to see if your computer can be of assistance.

Understand And Live By The Rule Of Seven

True marketers understand just how difficult it is to motivate people to do anything . . . particularly the overfed American consumer. While there are no doubt many people in the nation who need what you're selling, for perfectly obvious reasons you can only sell to those who have the means of acquiring your info-product. The vast majority of these people are often sluggish and difficult to motivate . . . precisely because they already have so much. That's where the Rule of Seven comes in.

You must both identify the individuals who have the problem you can solve . . . or the aspiration you can help them achieve, the means of acquiring your product *and* can be reached in an organized way on a continuing basis. Then you must fashion a plan that gets you to them at least seven times in a maximum of 18 months. In the Rule of Seven, the mimimum number of contacts (7) must not vary; the time period (18 months) clearly can, with some info-products having a much shorter window of opportunity than others.

As I discussed in MONEY MAKING MARKETING (a volume I recommend to you if you are determined to succeed in marketing), there are many ways of creating your seven-step plan. You can use:

- free publicity
- paid ads
- direct mail
- workshops and talk programs, *etc.*

What is important, however, is that in each phase of your plan you thrust home with benefits . . . and do everything in your power to capture your prospect's name . . . so that you control all subsequent marketing encounters.

Take a look at almost any marketing gambit you like. Here's a classified ad found in a recent issue of *The National Home Business Report:*

"WORKING AT HOME: Booklet of income ideas for women who can't get out to 'regular' jobs. SASE for details."

What's wrong with this ad? Everything.

It leads with work. Remember television character Maynard G. Krebs and his response to work. "WORK!," the bearded wonder used to shriek . . . and then run away. Of course. No one likes to work. Instead, you must lead with benefits . . . follow with features. If your prospects aren't interested in your benefits . . . they're not going to take the necessary action to acquire them. Too, there are lots of wasted words here. Given that this publication is mostly for women who work at home . . . why waste words targeting this audience? The publication has already done that for you.

Even worse, there's no meaningful attempt to capture prospect names. "SASE for details" is what this marketer uses. But it's anemic. No one wants "details." People want a benefit. And unless you entice with this benefit, you can't get people to send you their names. And unless they send you their names, you don't control the marketing process . . . they do!

Thus, the Rule of Seven is most powerful when you work hard to capture the names of your prospects and then follow up with client-centered, benefit-laden documents replete with action-motivating offers. At least six more times!

Most info-marketers, instinctively understanding the validity of the Rule of Seven, nonetheless don't bother to follow it. Figuring that all the world needs what they've created, instead of targeting precise groups of prospects . . . they fling their marketing materials helter-skelter in a vain attempt to influence someone, anyone to respond. THIS IS WRONG!

The Rule of Seven works when you have targeted just the right groups of prospect for the info-product you're selling . . . have deduced all the benefits for this group from your product's features . . . and are determined to do everything you can to make these benefits enticing for your prospects . . . and to keep hammering them home relentlessly. This is profit-making marketing. This must now be your marketing.

With what you have learned here . . . and the specific tactical information still to come . . . you'll be ready to do what no major publisher has ever done: make every single product you produce profitable. I know. By turning myself into a marketer, I have *never* produced a product that didn't make money . . . and that isn't still making money today. It will be the same for you . . . if only you do what's necessary to become the marketer you need to be. When you're in doubt . . . return here . . . fast!

Selling Through Free Publicity

Every day I start my day by contacting at least five media sources . . . places (be they electronic or print) I have determined could give me the means (on their money!) of reaching my targeted markets . . . and so making sales. Over the course of the last decade, I have done this day in, day out . . . in addition to periodic larger mailings to the media about selected products. No one I know has been as assiduous about cultivating free media. Is it any wonder then that my products are constantly featured or that I have found this such a profitable activity?

You must do the same.

Here as elsewhere, however, info-entrepreneurs have some unfortunate ideas. The objective of working with the media is not to make yourself into a star . . . or to be on some exaggerated ego-trip. You don't need to become a household word in order to become an information multi-millionaire and most of those who have succeeded in this field have low personal name recognition.

Too, the objective is not simply to "promote" your books as an end in itself as so many people in this business seem to think. According to my handy dictionary, promote simply means "advocate actively" or "work in behalf of." But your job as an info-entrepreneur is much more focused than that: it's to sell using, in this case, the free media: radio, television, newspapers, magazines, and newsletters.

This chapter then has a single objective: to give you the details you need so you cut the amount of time and money you spend to get free media attention . . . and to use the free media attention you do get to maximum effect so you sell more of your information products immediately. Merely getting on a radio or television program, therefore, is no achievement . . . whatever your fragile ego thinks. Merely getting your book or product mentioned in a publication is no achievement, either . . . unless the readers have all they need so they can acquire it at once.

In short, when you contemplate the issue of using the free media to your advantage, keep in mind that everything you do in this area is futile and pointless unless your reader or listener can take action to acquire your problem-solving product immediately. Reread this sentence!

By this standard, the following activities make no sense:

- getting on a radio or television show that doesn't tell your listener how to get your product right away;

- getting a review of your book in a publication . . . but not giving the reader follow-up details;

- being featured in an article that doesn't give people the means of connecting with you and acquiring your products.

I trust I make my point.

Having said this, I now advise you to listen to any program featuring an author . . . or read any print publication where information products are discussed or presented. All too often, you'll listen or look in vain for the kind of direct response information which I insist upon. Why? Don't the people whose products are being featured want to sell them as much as you do? Of course they do . . . but they let other considerations get in the way:

- They believe they have no right to suggest what should happen . . . or how their products should be presented.

- They get caught up in the "glamor" and egomania of the media . . . allowing their true interests to be forgotten in the rush to get their mug on the tube . . . or their name in ink.

- They forget their readers . . . and what those readers must go through to get the product.

- They simply don't understand how this business works . . . and what they must do to make the sale they say they want to make.

Fortunately, these sad things won't happen to you . . . if you pay close attention.

To do what you need to do — arrange matters so you entice your prospects and get them to act as soon as possible — here's what you must do:

- understand what the media want from you;
- produce the materials media sources want from you;
- locate the right media sources to promote your products;
- create and implement a plan for approaching the media sources;
- master follow-up so you do get the time and space you want and your products do get featured;
- learn some tricks of the trade for getting what you want from media sources, and
- develop a relationship with productive media sources.

Let's look at each essential component of your media strategy.

Understanding What The Media Want From You

Always keep this mind in mind: media sources are not in business to promote you. Indeed, any assistance that you receive from them is of distinctly secondary importance to media sources. Their *raison d'être* is to keep themselves in business by providing their targeted audiences with information of interest and value to these people and by giving advertisers access to them, for a price.

If you want to get free time and space from a media person, you must show him that you can help him achieve his desires. In return, he'll allow you to get what you really want: the opportunity to bring your problem-solving product for free to the attention of your market, which also happens to be the source's audience.

It astonishes me just how few info-entrepreneurs (and other information providers) get this crucial message. Essentially, they act as if they are doing the media source a favor by making themselves available. These people reckon they're the stars and that everyone in the media should salaam.

Smart info-entrepreneurs think differently. They understand that their job is to create a symbiosis . . . a situation where both the media source's needs and their own can be met. This happens when you understand what the media source needs . . . and sublimate your own needs, to ensure you get them met.

Media sources need two different kinds of information. They need hard news and they need feature material. Hard news is precise, factual and objective (we all know better, but this, at least, is the theory). Feature material, on the other hand, is more personal; it focuses on people's lives and interests and ranges from the very practical to the essentially frivolous.

Which of these kinds of information do media sources look to us information providers to give them? The answer is both. Info-entrepreneurs by the nature of our work are always developing news stories with material of interest to selected media sources. Additionally, we constantly provide feature material, both practical and human interest.

While media sources rely on our supplying both kinds of information, it is important to point out that ordinarily providing only one actually benefits us: feature stories. That is because only with feature stories do we actually have a fair chance of getting included the essential follow-up information our prospects require. This crucial information is almost never included with news stories.

Consider, for instance, the notorious Salman Rushdie case and his book *Satanic Verses*. While the book has been mentioned in thousands, perhaps tens of thousands, of news stories . . . never once have I ever seen any information provided about how to get it; indeed, many stories focused on how you *couldn't* get it . . . the antithesis of what a marketer desires.

In this case, no one at Rushdie's publisher probably cared a whit . . . since this book has become the single most promoted volume of the entire century, and every bookstore rushed to stock and display it prominently.

This probably won't happen to you and your info-products, which is one good reason why you should focus on getting the more beneficial feature stories than the admittedly more dramatic but ordinarily less useful news stories.

If you accept my point and focus on providing media sources with feature material, what the source wants from you is this: information that will help his targeted audience solve a pressing problem . . . or achieve a desired objective.

What the media source wants then is:

- your understanding of his market . . . who is he trying to reach;

- an understanding of his format . . . how is he trying to reach them;

- your attempt to fashion your information in a way that does not ostensibly promote you . . . but does provide his audience with information they can use.

If you do these three things . . . . always assuming you are approaching the right source . . . you have an excellent chance of getting the air time and space you desire . . . and the opportunity to do what you really want to do: sell products.

Producing The Materials Media Sources Want From You

As you will not be surprised to hear me say, you must think through all the materials media sources want from you and produce them before you need them. That way, you're always ready for any media opportunity . . . and can keep farming for possibilities, day in, day out. Here are the materials you need:

— *For Print Media*

- a pre-publication offer in the form of a letter and/or media release;

- a sales letter to induce print sources to review or feature your info-product;

- a basic media release with details about the info-product;

- a list of previous review comments and places the product has already been featured;

- a cover letter that accompanies the product you are sending for review;

- a follow-up letter to be sent after 60-90 days to check the status of the article;

- ready-to-use columns and articles;

- a cover letter to accompany these columns and articles;

- a biographical feature story with information about the author;

- a captioned photograph of the author

- a captioned photograph of the product, and

- a list of everything you have available.

— *For Electronic Media*

- a sales letter to induce electronic sources to put you on the air;

- a follow-up letter to be sent after 30 days to check on the status of your request to be put on the air;

- your on-air introduction;

- the offer you'll use to induce prospects in the audience to contact you;

- follow-up details the announcer can read so people in the audience can contact you.

- sample questions you can be asked to ensure an interesting — and profitable — interview.

Here's how you create and use these crucial materials.

A Pre-publication Offer

Products should be sold before they even exist . . . always presuming that you know what you're doing . . . and that you can meet your deadline for delivering them. If these conditions are met, the first document you should develop is a pre-publication offer that enables certain targeted groups to purchase your product for a special price before it physically exists. The offer may be delivered to selected publications either in a letter and/or media release. Either way it should:

- lead with the benefits your product will deliver;

- mention that this is a special offer for readers of (name of publication);

- stress the special price (a 20-25% discount is usually adequate);

- include a cut-off date when the offer expires (you can use the month your product is actually available);

- include details about who you are . . . and why readers should pay attention to what you've got to say;

- mention other products that you also have available.

The entire release should be no more than 150-200 words in length and should, of course, include your name, address, telephone number and credit card information.

Send this release to publications that both know you and your work (they're more likely to use it) and to selected publications interested in developing more reader benefits. These include smaller specialty publications, including newspapers and newsletters.

Along with this release, either enclose a second sheet of paper asking the publisher if he's interested in getting a review copy of the actual publication (include "sell" copy on the benefits to his readers) when it's available, or develop a tear-off coupon at the base of your letter which the publisher can fill out and return if he's interested in seeing a review copy. This will give you more definite prospects you can ship your product to when it's available.

A Sales Letter To Induce Print Sources To Review Or Feature Your Info-Product

If you've never stopped by the book review office of a publication, you ought to. It's a sickening experience. Piles of books lay stacked everywhere; more arrive daily. At most publications only a tiny fraction are ever used . . . the rest either end up in staffers' hands for lunch-time reading . . . or are sold by venal review editors for their personal profit (which is why you ought to stamp all your review copies: "Review copy. Not for sale."). All in all, it's both a scandal and a tragic waste of money.

You can imagine the profound effect such a situation has on the good Scotsman for whom a penny saved is a profoundly moral act. I value my books too much to give them such an ignominious fate. That's why I instituted the farming system. This system is essentially composed of two parts:

1. I make a decision about which publications (for that's what we're talking about here) will most likely feature or review my products, and

2. those which are less likely to do so.

At any given time, the first group is infinitely smaller than the second, a situation I am always working to change. The first group is made up of publications that I have ongoing relationships with, that publish my articles, have reviewed or featured my books favorably in the last year or two, and which are important in my field . . . places where it is worth risking the usual fate of review copies, because any mention is valuable.

The second group is all other publications which reach people who would benefit from having the product in question.

I shall discuss the first group shortly. Now, I'd like to concentrate on the second, larger, body.

Given the fact that there are probably over 200,000 print media sources in America today, you can't possibly send an unrequested review copy to every single source without knowing there's a very good chance it'll be used. It's just too expensive and time consuming. Standard publishers "solve" this problem by allocating a fixed number of books for review purposes (100-250 in most cases) and sending the bulk of them to the same places . . . whether it's a cookbook . . . or a novel. This idiotic system has resulted in the appalling "system" cited above.

This is where farming comes in.

Farming gives you the opportunity to present your case to a print media source . . . to provide the benefits its readers get from your info-product. And to invite the source to request a copy in order to review or feature it (along with giving complete follow-up information). This way, you only risk the cost of your mailing piece and postage . . . instead of the expense of sending the actual product.

Using this system, you send your info-products to the sources most likely to review them . . . either because they know you and your work . . . or because they've requested a copy and can be dealt with accordingly.

The sales letter you develop needs to include the following:

- a focus on a major benefit the publication you are approaching is in business to deliver to its readers;

- an indication that you have something that will help these people get what they want . . . and so benefit not only them . . . but the publication itself;

- your best sales arguments about why your product is important . . . what it can do for people . . . what they get from it . . . and how much better off they'll be when they use it;

- your offer . . . a free review copy;

- details on precisely what they have to do to get it . . . call or write immediately.

In short, this is a client-centered piece of prose . . . just like any other direct response marketing communication you'll ever write. Just like these, you need to ask yourself before creating it: "What am I trying to accomplish with this letter?" The answer is: to motivate an editor or publisher to pick up the phone immediately to request a review copy of your product. Keeping this objective in mind, ask yourself, as you review what you've written, have you done *everything*, used *every* motivator you possibly could to achieve your objective. If you haven't, the letter must be rewritten.

As with all the marketing communications I'm discussing in this book, this letter needs to be available on your word processing software. Why? Because you should send it out every single day to designated publications. Sometimes you'll have a very limited group of publications you can attempt to motivate . . . sometimes (as with CASH COPY and MONEY MAKING MARKETING) literally thousands of publications. Either way, this letter needs to be immediately available . . . and sent regularly.

Note: unlike mainline publishers, your products don't need to be new to get media attention . . . particularly from specialty publications. My book THE CONSULTANT'S KIT though published several years ago continues to get reviews just like the rest of my books. The acid test is the value of your information. If what you've got to say is important and valuable to a publication's readers, it is in that publication's interest to promote it.

A Basic Media Release With Details About The Info-Product

To add weight and further persuasiveness to your initial contact with the media source, you need to send other materials along with your sales letter. These include the basic media release . . . and a list of testimonials and reviews.

The media release gives hard-pressed journalists the opportunity to run an article about your product . . . only it will be an article you've written! These days this is happening more and more often, and there's a reason why.

With the advent and widespread use of desktop publishing, more and more people are publishing more and more newsletters and periodical publications. Most are staffed by only a few people; many by just a single over-worked individual. As these people will tell you at a moment's notice (I hear this constantly), they simply don't have time to read books . . . much less write intelligent articles about them. Still, they want to bring useful material to their readers' attention.

These people rely on your media release . . . the story about your product as written in the third-person and which, when published, seems to come from the publication . . . not from you.

To give you an idea of what this important piece of promotional material looks like, I'm reproducing on pages 380–381 the media release used for the first printing of my book CASH COPY (in the original, it's 8 1/2" x 11"). It's been printed more or less as you see it by a number of publications.

Publishers can use this exact release merely by making a few changes in the introductory section . . . or by cutting the first few paragraphs out altogether. The story essentially starts with the title of the book . . . and ends at the conclusion of the release at the bottom of the second page. Editors without this much space will still find the exact details they need to entice their readers with the benefits of this product . . . and how these readers can get it . . . immediately. Either way, whether all or just part of the release is used, you benefit.

JLA Publications
A Division of Jeffrey Lant Associates, Inc.
50 Follen St., Suite 507
Cambridge, MA 02138
(617) 547-6372

Publication Date: February, 1989

To: publishers, editors, columnists, reviewers, interviewers, and others who want to help every business, independent professional, entrepreneur, nonprofit organization — and anybody else selling products or services!

Your readers are throwing their money away on flyers, brochures, cover letters, free client newsletters, response cards... and every other kind of marketing communication... that don't get their prospects to buy... and their buyers to buy again.

You can help them! By bringing this crucial new money-making resource to their immediate attention!

HOW TO OFFER YOUR PRODUCTS AND SERVICES SO YOUR PROSPECTS BUY THEM... NOW!!!

by Dr. Jeffrey Lant

The problem with most marketing communications is that they don't work... whether it's a sales letter, a brochure... or a four-color annual report... they don't succeed in motivating the prospect to take *immediate action*... to pick up the phone, ask for an appointment, or buy what's being sold NOW.

Over 98% of marketing communications fail to achieve their purpose... getting a prospect to buy... or a customer to buy again. They're just thrown away.

The cost of this waste is astronomical... mounting up to the billions and billions of dollars each year.

Now this foolishness can stop... because now there's **CASH COPY: How To Offer Your Products And Services So Your Prospects Buy Them... NOW!!!**, the ninth and newest money-making title by internationally-syndicated columnist and marketing specialist Dr. Jeffrey Lant.

CASH COPY is packed with techniques that get prospects to respond... fast!

Here's precisely what your readers need to know to make all their marketing communications profitable... whatever they're using.

Nineteen information-packed chapters in Dr. Lant's characteristically hard-driving style tell your readers how to:

* identify the 21 biggest copywriting errors — and avoid them;
* run a client-centered business — so you can create client-centered marketing communications;
* find out what you need to know about your prospects and buyers... so you can motivate them to take immediate action;
* turn every feature of every single product or service into a benefit that your prospects will act promptly to acquire and use;
* create offers your prospects find irresistible;
* motivate your prospects to act NOW... not later.

There's lots more!

Find out how to:

* get and use testimonials that make people want to buy what you're selling;
* make every marketing communication you create talk directly to the needs and wants of your prospects and buyers;
* make your copy interesting... not dull... keep it focused on the prospect, not yourself.
* outposition your competitors so your prospects buy what you're selling.

There's still more!

You also find out how to:

* master the writing process that enables you to create client-centered marketing communications;

- use lay-out and design to motivate immediate response, and
- find and work with a cash copywriting consultant, if you don't want to do all the work yourself.

Why there's even a chapter on money-making marketing, how to use the cash copy you've created in a marketing plan that will maximize your results!

With **CASH COPY**, you need never again wonder how to create any kind of marketing communication that puts you in touch with your prospects or buyers. You'll have exactly what you need to create flyers, cover letters, media kits, free client newsletters, catalogs, classified and small space ads, response coupons, postcards, fund raising proposals, annual reports, and much, much more!

It's all here... in 480 pages.

You learn how to create the components of cash copy, including envelope teasers, offers, testimonials, headlines, salutations, opening paragraphs, post scripts. You'll find out how to present relevant work experience, resumé information, and biographical facts... so they motivate your prospects to respond.

Even the tiniest business spends thousands of dollars on creating marketing communications that are supposed to generate profit. But until now, most of what's been used has failed to get prospects to respond. Not any more. Not with **CASH COPY!**

Now there's no excuse for failing to produce — time after time — marketing communications that get your prospects to request more information, schedule appointments, walk into your business, send money... or whatever you want... and to do it NOW! It's all here, easy to follow, a resource your readers will use every time they want to motivate their prospects and buyers to take immediate action!

About The Author: Internationally-syndicated columnist and marketing consultant Dr. Jeffrey Lant is well known as a specialist who pulls no punches in providing information that's detailed, timely, and easy to follow. Over 1,500,000 people monthly read his Sure-Fire Business Success columns in nearly 100 publi-

cations and electronic data bases. His eight other titles include **The Consultant's Kit: Establishing and Operating Your Successful Consulting Business.** (the only title the U.S. Small Business Administration recommends to new and aspiring consultants in any field); **The Unabashed Self-Promoter's Guide: What Every Man, Woman, Child and Organization in America Needs to Know About Getting Ahead by Exploiting the Media** (widely regarded as the definitive book on how to use free media to promote anything); **Money Talks: The Complete Guide to Creating a Profitable Workshop or Seminar in Any Field** (*Booklist* calls the 1988 Revised Second Edition of this book "a unique resource"), and **Money Making Marketing: Finding the People Who Need What You're Selling and Making Sure They Buy It** (which *Booklist* also enthusiastically recommended in 1988.)

HOW TO OFFER YOUR PRODUCTS AND SERVICES SO YOUR PROSPECTS BUY THEM... NOW!!!

by Dr. Jeffrey Lant

480 pages/paper/$27.95 postpaid ($24.95 retail)

Publication Date: February, 1989
ISBN 0-940374-14-5

To order your books or request a review copy, please write or call:

> Jeffrey Lant Associates, Inc.
> 50 Follen Street, Suite 507
> Cambridge, MA 02138
> (617) 547-6372

Don't forget to tell your readers they can get a *free year's subscription* to Jeffrey Lant's quarterly Sure-Fire Business Success Catalog, featuring over 100 ways to make their businesses more profitable and better organized.

Note: as you see, in this release I mention the names of some of my other products; this both gives me standing as a specialist . . . and makes more people aware of them. Further, you'll notice this release concludes with information about my Sure-Fire Business Success Catalog. This is yet another attempt to catch the "soft" prospect, the person who is not yet ready to buy. I need a way to motivate him to take immediate action so I can capture his name and control the marketing process. I use the free year's subscription to my catalog to do just that.

A List Of Previous Review Comments And Places Where The Product Has Already Been Featured

Despite what they may think about themselves, media people are usually neither original nor creative. They think and act like herd animals. That's why it's important for you to use every review, feature, and testimonial comment you get about your product . . . to get more.

As you've already seen, you need a text file in your computer where, the day you receive any positive comment about your product, you can record it. At the beginning of your career . . . or when a product is new and you have few good comments about it, it's perfectly acceptable to mix media and consumer endorsements in one file. Later, as you become more adept at this, you'll probably want to have two files: the one filled with media comments you use to motivate media people; the other packed with consumer testimonials you can use in creating your catalog, mailing pieces, *etc.*

Head this file with an enthusiastic headline like "Here's what media people just like you are already saying about (name of product)!" Don't forget to use your automatic date macro key to give this list the impression of immediacy that's so important to people in the media.

Now, send this list along with your sales cover letter and media release. Remember, you can send up to five pages of material for the cost of a first-class postage stamp. What this means is that you can send up to 50 or even more excerpted review comments along with your sales letter. This is very powerful. Remember, the more review comments you have, the more you're likely to generate because media people want to see what's so great about what you've got.

Using this three-part packet consisting of cover letter, media release and testimonial list, scarcely a business day goes by that I don't receive at least one review request.

A Cover Letter That Accompanies The Product You Are Sending For Review

Once the media source has nibbled, it's time to close the sale and enhance your chances of getting reviewed/featured. You therefore need a cover letter to accompany your product.

This letter should:

- thank the media source for his attention and ensure him he's getting a product that will help his readers;

- stress the benefits (starting with the most important, remember) his readers get from your product;

- provide the basic details about the product: its name, number of pages or length, price, and complete order information. Remind the media source just how important it is that he provide this information for his readers and how it inconveniences them if he doesn't;

- provide your telephone number in case the source has questions;

- indicate that a cover photo of the product is available;

- inform the editor you have articles available based on the product which are available to him without cost. Indicate their titles, lengths and how he can get them (call NOW! would do nicely). Don't forget to tell him you have these articles available on diskette and tell him precisely how they're formatted (straight ASCII text on an IBM-compatible diskette is best).

- in a post script indicate any other product you've produced which you feel may also be of interest. Note: don't send two products to an editor. Lots of reviewers just like to collect freebies. My policy is to send one review product at a time. When it's used, I send the next one. If it isn't used, I ask for it back. I don't always get it . . . but I always ask. Why should someone get a free copy of one of my products if he's not going to do anything with it!

Note: whenever possible, send your review copy via UPS. As stated, this enables you to check on its delivery. This is very important with media sources. Why? Because they lose things and then say blithely that they never got them in the first place. In one extreme case, a Los Angeles publicist I was working with sent four copies of one of my books to a major radio station personality who kept telling her he wasn't getting the volumes. She finally hand-delivered it to his desk . . . where she saw two of the copies she'd sent and which he'd been claiming he'd never received! Fortunately, she had the presence of mind to take back all but one. Ultimately, I did get on the show . . .

A Follow-Up Letter To Be Sent After 60-90 Days To Check The Status Of The Article

Journalists are like magpies. They're always requesting new material . . . but only use a small fraction of it. Thus, even though a media source has requested your material, there's an excellent chance it will never be used. You must keep this in mind and do what you can to improve your chances of being featured. This means following up.

Develop a letter you can send between 60 and 90 days after you've shipped the media source a review copy. In this letter:

• remind the source about your product and when you sent it;

• ask if it has already been featured or reviewed, in which case request a copy of the article;

• if it hasn't already been reviewed, ask for the specific date when it will be;

• bring the source up to date on the new review comments and testimonials the product has recently generated (you can simply enclose your current list of review comments with today's date);

• indicate that excerpt articles are available and provide a list of what you've got;

• advise the source that it's perfectly acceptable to you that he write his responses on your letter and return it to you immediately.

Truthfully, only a fraction of journalists are going to answer this letter. Therefore, it's perfectly acceptable to call them and ask the same questions. If you catch the journalist unawares, however, he'll certainly need to be briefed on who you are and what you've sent. Be prepared for that.

Develop Ready-To-Use Columns And Articles

One way you can assist yourself enormously is by requiring all your authors and product developers (including yourself!) to create a series of articles and columns based on their products. There is a reason for this. As you already know, contemporary journalism is very definitely a market-driven, not a copy-driven, enterprise. This means many publishers are far more interested in selling their product and space in it . . . than they are about what goes between their pages. While some may worry about the long-term implications of this trend, marketers can benefit from it by understanding what is happening and moving to take advantage of it.

Your job is to get the best marketing coverage for your info-products by any means you can. If you want to do this, you'll produce articles that any editor or publisher can use exactly as they are without editing . . . even without inputting into his computer system. If you produce this kind of copy, editors will grow to be dependent on you and will use whatever you send them . . . which is precisely what you want.

When you're starting out, here are the kinds of articles you need:

- two or three 500-word problem-solving process articles providing practical information to the publication's readership on how to solve problems in which they're interested. For instance, from this book I could write an article entitled "How to get a radio producer to put you on his show . . . so you can sell your products and services for free."

- a couple of 750-word articles on either the same subjects or (better) different ones.

- two or three 2000-word articles.

This is an acceptable *introductory* inventory; obviously, to keep getting this kind of publicity, you'll have to keep adding to it.

As you won't be surprised to hear me say, each of these articles should:

- speak directly to your prospect (who, remember, is the reader of the publication, not the publisher);

- raise his anxiety level about the problem you can solve;

- indicate a solution is possible, if only he follows certain steps;

- lay out as many steps as you have space;

- conclude with a Resource Box providing complete follow-up details including the name of your product, number of pages or length of broadcast, address, telephone number, and credit card information. Don't forget to include a soft offer (like a free subscription to your catalog) for those who are not yet ready to commit to buying. Your job, remember, is either to get someone to buy NOW or get him to act NOW to get some benefit . . . after which you control the marketing process.

Write A Cover Letter To Accompany These Columns And Articles

Articles and columns are products and as such need a cover letter. This cover letter should:

- indicate what you are sending the source;

- provide complete details on how these articles can be used;

- make clear that complete follow-up details (as provided in the Resource Box) must be included with each article . . . even if the article must be divided into parts because of the publication's space limitations;

- suggest that if the publication does not use your Resource Box, a fee of $100-150 per article will be owing to you;

- ask the publication to put you on its mailing list so you get a copy of each of your articles, and

- indicate what other articles (and products, for that matter) you have available for future reference.

A Biographical Feature Story With Information About The Author

From time to time, a publication will wish to do a feature story about you . . . particularly as your products become more well known and you yourself become an embryonic personality. Be careful! Personality pieces are all very well if you use them to sell your products . . . but they're fatal if you allow them to bloat your ego and obscure the real purpose of such publicity.

Sadly, most authors forget the true objective of a biographical article and happily babble on about the most intimate details of their lives. Not me. And not, I trust, you. I don't care what kind of article format a publication is using . . . a book review, a column or a personality profile . . . my objective is the same: to target prospects who can be better off because of the info-products I have . . . and to motivate them to act. The personal details of my life are just that: personal, and I frankly have no desire to share them with any prying journalist in hot pursuit of a titillating tale. Thus, you must give every consideration to the biographical feature stories you produce about yourself . . . and make sure they promote your true interests . . . and those of your prospects.

A biographical feature story is your story as written in the third person and appearing to be written by an outside source. To write the right story, you must keep the following points in mind:

- the story is actually yet another means of your targeting your designated prospects and motivating them to act;

- the material you use in this story must be material of interest to these prospects;

- as in all media stories, print or electronic, there must be follow-up information and a call to action.

Here's the skeleton of your biographical feature story:

- the headline contains an audience identifier and motivator and your name. Thus an autobiographical feature story about me intended to motivate home-based business owners might read: "The Man Who Helps Home-Based Businesses Make Money . . . Dr. Jeffrey Lant." Note: the headline opens with my market and what that market wants . . . and only then goes on to give my name, the less important part of the headline. In other words, despite the fact that this article is in theory about you, it's really about speaking to and motivating home-based business people to take action . . . and buy what you're selling . . . so they get what they want.

- the opening paragraph deals with your prospects' fears . . . or their aspiration. Fear, remember, is stronger. Thus, "Dr. Jeffrey Lant sits in his office overlooking the Cambridge Common and reels off statistics: 'four out of five new businesses fail within five years . . . most of these within the first year of operation,' he says. 'Of the nation's 8,000,000 home-based businesses, most gross under $15,000 a year.'"

Why am I starting this way? For several reasons: 1) you want an opening that focuses on your prospect. Your best prospect is the one who is motivated by anxiety to take immediate action . . . so he avoids the situation you're talking about. And 2) you want to establish yourself as a client-centered authority instantly . . . as someone who knows what he's talking about . . . and will talk straight to the situation of your prospect.

- Then add a line like this: "The 46-year old Lant knows what he's talking about. He's been running a home-based business himself for the last 11 years . . . and providing advice on how home-based entrepreneurs can avoid the pitfalls and problems that doom so many to quick extinction."

Again, what's happening here is that you're emphasizing both your knowledge and your ability to solve the prospect's problem. As a result of the opening paragraphs (and, yes, the headline) your prospect already knows:

- he is your prospect;

- you are a credible source;

- you can help him solve his real problem . . . staying in business and making money.

- Now you can add some more information that will add to your credibility and begin to motivate the sale you actually want from this article: "Lant's advice is detailed and available in a series of volumes he's labeled his 'Get Ahead' Series. It includes (now provide specific details)." After this paragraph, your reader not only regards you as an expert . . . he knows several ways he can benefit directly from your help (also read "your products").

- Carry on by providing some useful information the prospect can relate to and find of value. "With this wealth of practical experience, what does the Harvard-educated Lant suggest home-based business people should do not merely to stay alive but really make money? (Now list some suggestions)." The suggestions you list should be practical and helpful and should be interspersed with quotations by you, the expert. Thus, "Says Lant enthusiastically, 'The chief problem I find with home-based business people is that they operate their business like a hobby. This is wrong.' Lant suggests each home-based entrepreneur set a yearly financial objective . . . and work out the numbers so he knows just how many widgets he has to sell to achieve it. 'Post this number on the wall right in front of your computer,' Lant recommends. 'You've got to see it every day and use your subconscious mind to help structure your behavior.'"

See what's happening? You're always talking to your targeted prospect . . . and always doing three important things: convincing him that you're his friend, letting him know what you've got available to help him . . . and motivating him to take immediate action to acquire them.

- At the end of the biographical feature story, just the same as with your problem-solving process articles and Special Reports, you need a Resource Box so your readers can follow up. "To put Dr. Jeffrey Lant to work for you, write or call for your FREE year's subscription to his Sure-Fire Business Success Catalog. It's got over 130 ways to help make your business more profitable." Then give your address and telephone number.

Note: each time your name appears in the article, modify it with something that will either build your credibility with your targeted audience . . . or give them further information about your products. Thus, in targeting a home-based business audience, I'd use name enhancers like:

- home-based business owner;

- recent winner of a home-based business owner award;

- author of CASH COPY, a book that tells home-based business owners how to get more customers from all their marketing communications.

You get the picture.

In other words, what you use to describe your name, while certainly about you, is chosen with an eye on your audience . . . on the people this article is really for and whom you're trying to motivate. It doesn't matter how swell you are and what credentials you have; if you can't motivate your targeted audience, you're a loser.

How long should this article be? 500 words, tops; that is, one back-to-back 8 1/2" x 11" page double-spaced.

Given that this article is targeted to a specific group, you won't be surprised to hear me say you should have something similar for *each* group you're marketing to. This marketing communication, like all marketing communications, must be targeted. Thus, if you are targeting home-based entrepreneurs, small businesses, insurance agents, realtors, *etc* . . . you need a separate article for each. Again, once you've computerized your basic document, this is easy to do . . . because all you have to do is change a few audience identifiers and (always assuming your information is equally applicable to your target markets), *voilà*, you have an entirely new, different — and appropriate — article. Aren't computers wonderful . . . now that you know how to use them?

A Captioned Photograph Of The Author

Along with your biographical feature story, you may well need a photograph. Oh, God, I hate these pictures! Having curves and not angles in my body, I am one of the legions of people who say, in all seriousness, "I don't photograph well." Nonetheless, we all need an author picture, so that's that. As I say in THE UNABASHED SELF-PROMOTER'S GUIDE, you really need two such pictures: a head shot and an action shot.

The head shot should be simply that . . . full face with dazzling smile and combed hair. I have only one thing to say about this picture: lean into the camera as you would lean into a conversation with a friend. The prospect must feel you are inclined toward him and looking him full in the face. Thus, make sure you don't put your hand on your head or otherwise obscure your face.

As far as the action shot is concerned, it should deal with some aspect of your info-product. Thus, if you have written that booklet on eradicating Dutch elm disease, your action shot better show you out saving a beleaguered tree.

Both your head and action shots will need captions, and, as with all marketing communications (for that's what captions are), you can't leave these to chance. Personally, I would suggest you caption your photos as needed rather than rely on a stock caption. Thus, your photo caption for a story directed at home-based entrepreneurs might read: "Home-based business owner and author Dr. Jeffrey Lant. His step-by-step books help home-based entrepreneurs make money." That'll get the attention of the right people . . . unless those people are computer consultants, for whose newsletter this photo needs another caption — tailored for them.

A Captioned Photograph Of The Product

Finally, you need a photo of your product . . . and a client-centered caption. These pictures need not be fancy. They must simply show a frontal shot of your product sufficiently closely that the title is easy to read. While you're at it, you might also like to have a group picture taken of all your products . . . or all the logical groupings of your products.

As far as the caption is concerned, it must also focus on the targeted prospect. Thus, "CASH COPY by Dr. Jeffrey Lant" isn't as good a caption as: "CASH COPY by Dr. Jeffrey Lant tells you how to get more prospects and customers to buy faster." Alternatively, you can use a reviewer comment . . . preferably one from the publication in which the photograph will be used. Thus: "'Every marketing-oriented librarian should read CASH COPY.' *Marketing Treasures*." Whichever alternative you use, remember the purpose of the info-product caption: it isn't to discuss the product . . . it's to entice the prospect. If you've done this, you're helping to motivate the prospect to take immediate action. If you haven't, you've wasted yet another opportunity to connect with the all-important prospect.

A List Of Everything You Have Available

You need one last thing to make your materials file for print media complete: a list of everything you have available. Simply draw up a complete list of everything you've created that could be helpful to a print media source (with short explanations as necessary) and include it every time you communicate with an editor or publisher. After all, how are they supposed to know what you've got if you don't tell them?

Remember, your objective is a clear one: it's to make dealing with you so easy, to make incorporating all you've got so simple, that no sane editor will possibly pass you by . . . as they do most info-producers. The fact that even when you've done all this work some editors will still pass on what you've got should not discourage you; it only shows some people are really as dumb as you can imagine.

Gladly, however, when you follow these guidelines you'll get a disproportionate share of print media attention given your size and number of products . . . which is precisely what you want. (Recently, when I complained to a newsletter editor that he hadn't used one of my releases he said, "What do you want, you already get three times as much publicity in the publication as anybody else?", as if that meant anything to me. "I want four times as much," I replied evenly. But I lied. I really want even more . . .)

What You Need For Dealing With Electronic Media Sources

Not surprisingly, much of what you create for print media sources you can use or adapt for electronic sources, radio and television. Here are a few comments about the basic documents you need.

A Sales Letter To Induce Electronic Sources To Put You On The Air

Like print sources, electronic media sources have to be convinced to give you some of their scarce commodity: air time. Make no mistake about it, competition for this time is steep, but hardly insuperable if you go about things in the right way. Thus, in your sales letter make sure to include the following:

- information about why an interview with you will interest the source's audience;

- an indication of why your information is important now;

- details on previous radio and television shows on which you've recently appeared so the producer understands you're a trained performer;

- the availability of a tape of a previous media appearance or speech so the producer can judge your on-air or audience-motivator qualities for himself. (Don't send the tape with this introductory letter under any circumstances. If the producer wants it, he'll ask for it. Interestingly, the fact you've made it available tells the producer you're a pro, and he's therefore much less likely to request it);

- how the producer can get a copy of your product;

- what you may have available to send free to the host's audience. (They like to give their audiences things . . . like a free year's subscription to your catalog, for instance);

- your time availability, in case you want to get booked on an out-of-town program;

- whether you'll call to follow up this letter (better) or wait for them to call you (not so good).

The information in this letter is designed to do three things: 1) convince the program director that your subject is a timely one; 2) that you can handle yourself well on air, and 3) that you have something useful to say to his audience.

Of these three points, the second may appear to be an obstacle to you, especially if you've never done radio or television before. My advice? First, read THE UNABASHED SELF-PROMOTER'S GUIDE and spare yourself a lot of aggravation and frustration. Second, run don't walk to the nearest college radio station in your area or cable television station where it's almost laughably easy to get on the air . . . and practice. True, you won't have much of an audience. But until you've got some experience on a set or behind a mike, you probably won't deserve much of one, either. Like everything else, you need experience. As you get it, make sure you get a tape of your performance, for two reasons: 1) if it's good you can use it with other media people; 2) if it's not, you can watch or listen to it to learn how to make yourself better.

Note: don't forget to send your basic media release and list of testimonials along with this letter. Here's where the media testimonials and endorsements are particularly helpful.

Develop A Follow-Up Letter To Be Sent After 30 Days To Check On The Status Of Your Request To Be Put On The Air

Media people, both print and electronic, are both notoriously disorganized and unbelievably arrogant. Their positions give them power and like all too many people it quickly goes to their heads, even if the individual in question is nothing more than a college intern on a 7 a.m. Saturday talk show. Most of the time I grin and bear it with these people, because, after over a decade dealing with media sources, I know that nearly all will have careers as short as a May fly's and far less useful. In any event, you can count on most media people not responding to your initial letter. Therefore you have a couple of options:

1. Since your first letter is computerized, you can simply send a duplicate copy of it marked SECOND REQUEST in the upper right hand corner. When you're particularly busy, this is acceptable.

2. You can telephone the producer to find out what's happening (you did record his name and the date you sent the letter, didn't you?). Chances are, you'll find out:

   a. this person is an unreachable phantom;

   b. if you do reach him, he's never heard of you or your material (send it again rather than attempt to explain yourself over the phone);

c. he got what you sent but has already lost it (as already stated, send it again).

Whenever possible call these producers directly after a show . . . not before. They are least busy when they've just completed a program, most busy just before going on the air.

If you decide to send a second letter, it should parallel the follow-up letter you use with a print media source.

Craft Your On-Air Introduction

I cannot sufficiently stress the value and importance of persisting with media sources. Frankly, I regard my single-mindedness, my bull-dog intensity and persistence as my greatest assets; many people in the media who have had to deal with me might not agree, but my approach works wonders. And it'll work for you, too. When you persist, you get a disproportionate share of air time and print space. That's why you need to craft your on-air introduction . . . you'll need it!

One of the things that startles me most of all is how few people position themselves before their audience, whether that audience is remote (as in media) or right before them (as with a speech). It's your job to craft a client-centered introduction that speaks directly to the people in the audience you can help and whom you want to motivate to buy your info-products.

Thus, your introduction should:

• have an audience identifier that essentially says, "Hey, bub, this program is for you!";

• indicate why this group is in pain;

• stress that you can help solve their problem;

• mention the product that will help them, and

• urge them to have a pencil handy to get the freebie you're making available or otherwise contact you.

Thus: "Today we have a very special program for anyone running a small business or professional practice. Did you know that national studies show that you're probably wasting 98 cents out of every dollar you spend on your ads, flyers, brochures, cover letters and other marketing communications? If you want to stop throwing your money away, you're in the right place, because today we have the author of the new book CASH COPY with us and during the next thirty minutes cash-copy specialist Dr. Jeffrey Lant will show you how to offer your products and your services so your prospects buy them . . . NOW ! By the way, Dr. Lant has a complimentary gift available for you, so grab a pencil now so you can write down his address in just a few minutes."

Is this introduction long? Yes, a bit. But the trained announcer/personality will say it very quickly; moreover, it has the additional benefit of setting the stage for you so you can come on as the client-centered problem solver you need to be. How many people get introductions like this? Just a handful. Sadly, those who do not think about their introduction as a piece of client-centered marketing copy that's supposed to target an audience and get that audience in the proper frame of mind to believe you and act on what you say, focus on themselves not that audience. The result is introductions that are replete with author credentials . . . not audience motivators. Wrong, wrong, wrong!!! Media, remember, are good for selling products; that's all.

The Offer You'll Use To Induce Prospects In The Audience To Contact You

Audiences, remember, are made up of three kinds of people:

1. people who are interested in the benefits you're offering and will buy your product immediately to acquire them (the smallest part);

2. people who are interested in your benefits but are not yet ready to take action to acquire them (a larger group), and

3. people who are entirely disinterested in your benefits and can never be induced to acquire them (ordinarily, the largest group).

Now, I ask you: does it make sense to treat all these groups the same way . . . are they all equally valuable to you? Put this way, the answer's obvious, isn't it? Why, then, when you listen to a radio or television show do you feel the info-entrepreneur or other promoter is talking equally to everyone? That's not at all in his best interest . . . or the interest of his targeted market. Thus, the info-entrepreneur must develop a strategy for the first two (far more important) groups, his buyers and prospects.

What these people are looking for is:

1. clearly stated benefits, and

2. an inducement for immediate action.

Here I am concerned with the inducement for immediate action. Before you go on a radio or television show, you must think through exactly what inducement you'll give people to contact you NOW, that is either during the program itself (because you'll provide a phone number that connects to an answering machine, answering service or your office staff) or immediately after the program. Here's where mini Special Reports or fact sheets are very helpful:

1. they provide helpful information to people in your audience;

2. they're inexpensive to produce;

3. they enable you to capture the names of prospects and so control the rest of the marketing process;

4. if they're the right length and weight (three pages or under), they enable you to include a sales letter and product sales literature with your response.

There are, of course, literally tens of thousands of informational inducers you could use. Here are a few:

- free test to discover if you are at risk of having a heart attack;

- chart showing how much money you have to make each hour, each day to make $50,000 a year; $100,000 a year; $1,000,000 a year;

- pay-down information on your home mortgage;

- guidelines for getting your kid a well-paying summer job.

I hope you get the idea.

Again, you need to give each of these informational pieces a benefit headline and, on air, talk about the benefits of using this information. In other word, don't push the information . . . push the benefits you get when you have and use it. Thus, saying you have a "free brochure" available or "free information" is pointless. Yet this is precisely what most on-air info-producers say. Note: again, you won't be surprised to hear me say that I use my free one-year subscription to my business resources guide (aka "Sure-Fire Business Success Catalog") to motivate people to respond immediately. People flock to get a free subscription who couldn't be bothered with yet another catalog . . . even if it is free; positioning really is everything.

Draw Up A List of Sample Questions The On-Air Host Can Ask You So That The Interview Is Focused . . . And Profitable

As I'm sure you now see, it is your job to control your time on the media to the maximum extent possible, to make sure that you get out of this interview what you need:

- to clearly identify the market you're attempting to motivate;

- let them know you're the salvation to their problem;

- motivate them to respond to you immediately . . . not later.

To achieve these critical objectives, you need to direct the interview. You can do so by drawing up a list of questions the host can ask you. You need about 20 questions for a half-hour interview; 30-35 for an hour's program. Half these questions should be general. Their purpose is to get you to provide general information about the target market you're attempting to motivate and an indication of the problems they face. Remember, if this market doesn't think it has a problem, chances are it won't feel much of a need for you.

As you answer these questions, you project an air of knowledgeability and expert standing. You are seen as the kind of person the targeted market, your prospects, remember, need to know about . . . and do business with. Thus, for an interview on how to make marketing communications more effective, suitable opening questions could be:

- When a person spends a dollar on marketing, how much of this investment is actually useful in getting his prospect to respond?

- How much is wasted?

- Why do business people waste such a large amount of money?

- Are they aware they're doing it?

- What can they do to stop wasting their money?

The last question above is a transition question. It enables you to start discussing specific steps your targeted audience can take to help themselves. This question and your answer to it are important hooks. You're saying in effect, "Look, you've got a bad problem, a ridiculously bad problem. Fortunately, however, you can do something about it." You then give some useful suggestions about what they can do. If they accept that these suggestions are useful, they'll buy your major suggestion ("Get a copy of CASH COPY"), too.

You'll need questions, however, the host can ask you to elicit information about the product you're there to sell. Thus:

- You've written a book, haven't you, that explains how people can get a better response to all their marketing documents? Tell us about CASH COPY.

- In CASH COPY, you talk about the importance of using testimonials to motivate people to respond to marketing communications. How do you do that?

Get the idea?

You can't just start an interview with information about your product. Your audience isn't prepared yet for several reasons:

- the people you're targeting need to know you're talking to them;

- they need to hear you discuss their problem . . . and need to get a sense of how bad it is;

- they need to feel that you're an authority who can help them;

- they need to hear some useful advice they can use to help themselves;

- they need to know more about the info-product in question . . . and become more familiar with it.

Then, of course, they need precise follow-up details so they can get the problem-solving how-to product you've positioned so enticingly before them.

Follow-Up Details The Announcer Can Read So People In The Audience Can Contact You

An interview or program that you give where follow-up details are not provided is an interview or program that's completely pointless. If you're the producer or author of a book and these details are not given, think what happens:

- interested people write down the name of your product on a scrap of paper;

- at some later time (not immediately), they drive to a local bookstore if there's one near at hand (remember, large areas of the country either don't have them or have only the semblance of a bookstore). Then they try to find a parking place;

- after they do (very difficult in urban areas like mine, by the way), they search the shelves for the book. With even the best stores stocking no more than 10-15% of titles at any given time, chances are very good it's not there.

- the customer approaches a clerk to ask for assistance in finding the product; the clerk has never heard of it and (if the customer is lucky) gives the stock response, "We can order it for you from the publisher. It takes about 6 weeks until you get it. We'll send you a card when the book arrives." If the customer isn't lucky, the clerk says the store doesn't carry it, that he's never heard of it . . . shrugs and goes back to talk to the other clerks about how low their pay is and when they get their next break.

- if the customer buys the book, his interest may be sufficient to wait until the product is available . . . or he may simply not respond to the store's card when the book comes in. If he doesn't, the bookstore returns the product.

Is this what you really want to make your customers do? Do you really want to take the risk that a customer will do all this to get your product? Come on now! This is why you must provide *complete* follow-up information every time you give any kind of media interview . . . including radio and television. Thus, "To get your free year's subscription to the Business Resources Guide and get over 130 recommendations each quarter on how to make your business more profitable, write or call (complete details) now."

If a producer or on-air host won't broadcast this kind of follow-up information for you, the program probably isn't worth doing . . . unless you're absolutely certain your product is available commercially in the broadcast area.

Locate The Right Media Sources To Promote Your Products

Now that you've got the marketing materials you need, it's time to develop a list of your print and electronic media sources. There are essentially two ways to get media source leads:

1. by continually and systematically searching through the wide number of media directories that exist, and

2. by using services to generate leads for you.

Let's look at each.

Continually And Systematically Searching Through Media Directories

I doubt that anyone really knows how many print and electronic media sources there are nowadays, but they number in the many tens of thousands with the vast majority being relatively small and highly specialized. Your task is to keep searching for the ones that will benefit you . . . that is, that will connect you to their audiences, which are also your prospects.

As I talk to info-producers nationwide, several things strike me:

- most are poorly informed about the number of media sources that exist;

- they either don't own or have easy access to the kinds of media directories they need;

- they don't have a daily routine to bring information about their products to the attention of these media sources.

The result is hardly a surprise: they get very little media attention and what they do get is episodic, not continual.

So that this isn't you, familiarize yourself with and regularly use the following sources:

- *Book Marketing Update,* published by John Kremer, Ad-Lib Publications, P.O. Box 1102, Fairfield, IA 52556-1102. This is the best newsletter being published on marketing books. Kremer's research always impresses me with its timeliness and thoroughness. Because of this newsletter — and the many other helpful resources Kremer publishes for independent publishers — it would be a good idea to write to ask to be on his mailing list.

- *Encyclopedia of Associations,* Gale Research Company, Book Tower, Detroit, MI 48226. A multi-volume guide to over 25,000 national and international organizations. You use these volumes to get leads to associations and their publications. Specialized publications are a superb way to get continuing publicity. Gale also publishes the two volume *Directory of Publications,* your guide to America's print publications, and *Computer-Readable Databases,* a giant directory packed with information about electronic databases that can run your articles (on diskette) and use information about your products.

- *Hudson's Subscription Newsletter Directory,* 44 West Market St., P.O. Box 311, Rhinebeck, NY 12572. An excellent listing of subscription newsletters published annually by newsletter guru Howard Penn Hudson.

- Oxbridge *Directory of Newsletters,* Oxbridge Communications, 150 Fifth Ave., New York, NY 10011. Features over 14,000 newsletters, again specialized publications where, if your market overlaps with the publication's, you can keep excellent coverage. Oxbridge also publishes *The Standard Periodical Directory* listing about 65,000 U.S. and Canadian publications.

- Specialized publications for media sources in your area. All the major cities of the United States now have specialized media directories. A call to the reference desk of your library should give you the specific information you need. One company to be aware of is Burrelle's Press Clipping Service, 75 East Northfield Rd., Livingston, NJ 07039. They publish the media directories for New England, New York, New Jersey and Pennsylvania and have other services you may find helpful.

- THE UNABASHED SELF-PROMOTER'S GUIDE. My book contains the most complete listing of media directories I've ever seen. If you're looking for specialized media sources, this is a very good place to start.

How much would a library like this cost? Plan on spending between $500-$750 assembling your media library. Does this seem like a lot? It certainly is, if it isn't used. You can cut your expenses by checking your local library and by asking the acquisitions librarian to purchase the most expensive volumes. Unfortunately, most libraries just don't have the means to acquire each of these resources yearly; that means a percentage of what you'll find is inevitably out of date.

Using Services To Generate Media Leads For You

While you're reviewing the directories mentioned above, you should also be using the services that exist to generate leads for you. These services, using one format or another, make media producers aware of your info-product and give these producers the chance to request further information about what you've got. You can then follow up with a copy of your product and compelling sales copy about why they should feature you. Here are some services to be aware of:

- Bradley Communications, 101 West Baltimore Ave., Lansdowne, PA 19050. My friend Bill Harrison is someone you must connect with. He runs one service *(Radio & TV Interview Report)* that sends information about your book to several hundred electronic media program directors. And he runs another *(Newspaper Feature Report)* that sends a story about your book to about 11,000 newspaper editors. I've used Bill's services for years on a very satisfactory basis.

- Broadcast Interview Source, 2233 Wisconsin Ave., NW, #406, Washington, DC 20007. Mitchell Davis distributes this directory to about 5,000 people in the TV, radio and print media.

- News USA, Inc., 1199 National Press Building, Washington, DC 20045 (202) 682-2400. They also will send your article out as a camera-ready column to a host of weekly newspapers.

- Also try *Spotlight,* a promotional newsletter to radio interviewers which limits those participating to just 19. Contact them at P.O. Box 51103, Seattle, WA 98115. And *Publicity Express,* 2966 Diamond St., Ste 442, San Francisco, CA 94131. It's a big, brassy, glossy (and more expensive) magazine style format.

By reading such previously mentioned publishing trade publications as *Publisher's Report,* PMA, and COSMEP, you'll become aware of the latest services of these and other companies. It's important to keep in mind that these services are only as good as the lists they use, the number of pieces they send out, and the marketing copy either you write or they help you with. Do some comperative shopping to ensure you get the best deal you can.

Creating And Implementing A Plan For Approaching Media Sources

What's wrong about the way most info-entrepreneurs deal with the media is what's wrong about the way they generally run their businesses; it's haphazard. If you want to get free media attention — and I assure you you do — you've got to have a plan and you've got to work that plan daily. This plan must have these two parts:

- a monthly objective for the number of radio and television programs and print media articles you want;

- a daily number of initial letters and follow-up letters and telephone calls you must send and make to stimulate the necessary number of programs and articles.

You must also have a log book where you can note the stations and print sources you've approached and their current status.

There's nothing magical about working with the media. They need programs and articles; you need coverage. It's a perfect marriage. At the beginning, however, you just won't know how many prospecting pieces you need to send out to generate a single lead or how many leads generate a single program or article. That remains to be seen. If it takes a combination of ten introductory letters, follow-up letters and telephone calls to generate a single article or program, and you want one of these each business day, you're going to have to do 200 media connections monthly to achieve your objective.

The important thing here is that you have a considered and written objective and that you keep records so you know just how much effort it takes to achieve it.

A few years ago, my objective was one media story, review, feature or program daily . . . a record many large companies would find enviable. I achieved it by writing the objective, posting it prominently, and by both culling through media directories and using the prospecting services. In fact, I set up my column to help me achieve the objective . . . and in not too long a time I did achieve it, whereupon I upped the ante. Now, I often get four or five media "hits" in a day . . . a fact that in no way makes me complacent. I still farm for more leads and use lead generating services like those mentioned above. Just like brushing my teeth, these activities are a daily part of my life . . . as they must be with you.

Master Follow-Up So You Do Get The Time And Space You Want And Your Products Get Featured

This item is, of course, properly a part of the one above, but follow-up is so important I thought I'd better speak to it specifically. The Rule of Seven works as much in motivating a media source to feature you and your info-product as it does anywhere else. That's why follow-up is so important.

You can't simply expect to send a single media release, or post card or letter to a media source and get the greatest number of bookings and articles. Yes, you will get some; no, you won't get all you can. You'll get time and space because:

- you've taken the time to understand what this media source wants from you;

- you've decided this is the right media source for what you've got, and

- because you persist.

Of these various traits, persistence is, perhaps, the hardest to instill in an individual. Why? Because most of us take no for an answer; most of us take even silence for lack of interest. Not me.

If I have done my homework . . . that is, if I know that I'm approaching the right person with the right story and have the right persuasive materials for this individual, then I reckon it's simply a matter of time until I get what I want . . . and give the source what he wants, too (— even though he may not know it yet).

If the audience the source reaches is an audience who will be better off because of my info-products, I persist — whatever the source may say. Indeed, I let the source know I shall persist . . . and continue to show him just why what I've got is so valuable to his audience . . . and to him.

In this connection, I think of a newspaper publisher who not so long ago told me in no uncertain terms that he didn't want to publish my articles or information about my books. The message, essentially, was "Beat it, kid." I wrote back immediately telling him that he'd made a mistake and explaining why . . . and I said I would continue to bring information to his attention until such time as he saw just how beneficial it was to his audience . . . and how much easier it made his life.

Did his negative bother me? Only to the extent that I thought it unfortunate that both he and I had to spend more time on preliminaries than I like or find useful. But did it discourage me? No, because I was certain that my key criteria were present.

Over about six months, I gradually wore down his opposition and, at last, he ran one of my articles/Special Reports. Then he ran a review. Then he hired me to do a workshop. And nowadays I'm the leading writer getting far more space than anyone else . . . in every issue. Too, he sells my books . . . features them . . . and hires me to do an occasional workshop program . . . at which I sell still more books. Plus, I trade my column for ad space and so get still more promotion.

Does the publisher remember what he said to me initially? Oh, sure. We laugh about it occasionally; now, it's humorous. But it wasn't then. It was a near tragedy, for what if I'd listened to him and slunk away? However, I didn't listen . . . and neither should you when some person who understands his market less well than you do tries to brush you off.

And remember this, too: when you're approaching media sources, you really have twin markets to consider. You must first persuade the producer or on-air personality or editor or publisher that you are a person they want to deal with . . . and then you must persuade their audience (your market) that you have something for them. You must succeed with both items, or you cannot succeed in using the media the way that will benefit you most.

Learn Some Tricks Of The Trade For Getting What You Want From Media Sources

Following these suggestions, you should begin getting air-time and print space very, very soon. You're on the way to selling more of your products and, yes, becoming a star yourself. Don't blow it now. You need to master some tricks of the trade for making the most of media. Use these tips:

- Bring duplicates of all the materials you've sent to the producer, journalist or editor who's doing your print or on-air interview. Don't count on their having anything. That's just too much to hope for.

- In your print media interview, make sure to remind the journalist to provide the complete name of your product.

- Remind him, too, just how important it is for his readers to get complete follow-up information and how unnecessarily difficult it will be if the journalist doesn't give it. Don't expect a journalist to think of this on his own; it rarely happens.

- When dealing with a television producer, ask if your follow-up information can be flashed on the screen during your interview. Don't wait until you get to the station to request this. By then, it's probably too late.

- Always ask the producer of your program how you can get a copy of it. Ask before you arrive at the studio in case you have to bring your own cassettes. Smaller radio stations either require you to bring your own . . . or charge you to make a copy. Video copies of television programs, too, can be purchased.

- Before you go on the air remind the producer or on-air host to provide follow-up information. Don't leave this to chance.

- While you're on the air, always refer to your product by its title, never by a pronoun like "it" or noun like "book." It's your responsibility to hammer home your product's name.

- Try to include the name of your product in as many sentences as you can . . . again to reinforce it in the listeners' minds. Thus: "As I say in MONEY TALKS . . . ", instead of just beginning with the answer to the question.

- If you're doing a call-in show and someone asks you a long or personal question, give that person your office telephone number on the air; you're not only giving it to him, of course, you're repeating it for your whole audience. This also establishes you as a warm and helpful person.

- If the host hasn't provided the follow-up information by the time of the first commercial break, remind him to start the next part of the program by providing it.

- If the host hasn't provided the follow-up information by the end of your program, prompt him on the air. Thus, "Get your pencils ready so you can take down the address and phone number where you can get your free year's subscription . . ."

- After you're off the air, ask the producer to leave your follow-up information with the station's receptionist. People will call to request it.

In short, don't be passive. Don't make the mistake so many info-producers make; namely, that merely being on a program or doing an interview meets their objectives. It doesn't. If there's no clear and easy way for your prospects to get in touch with you and acquire your product, you've failed. Let's not mince any words about this.

Developing A Productive Relationship With Media Sources

As media people will be happy to tell you, they have to deal with a lot of turkeys . . . people who are bad interviews, who ramble, are uninformed, and are just plain dull. Thus, if you prove to be a good interview . . . have something useful to say and develop a rapport with your audience, they want to see you again. So, make it easy for them.

- When your interview is over, thank the journalist, on-air personality or producer for having you on. Send them a written thank-you note, too.

- Give them an indication of the new projects you're working on and see if any of these might be of interest for another article, program.

- Tell producers in the city where you live that you're available at a moment's notice to be a substitute guest. Media guests cancel all the time and back-ups are regularly required. Let them know you'll be happy to stand in (and promote your products!).

- Keep a data base file of the media people who have featured and helped you. Make sure to send them advance information about your next info-product and let them know you're giving them first dibs on an interview or program.

- Keep these media people on your general mailing list. Send them your catalog or other materials. It's a very good idea to keep your name before them.

- If you find out they're leaving their jobs (a very frequent occurrence in the media), send them a note of goodwill and godspeed. You'll be the only person to do so . . . and remind them what a swell person you are (and what a swell guest you were.)

Note: you can't be in your office all the time and after you've done an interview with complete follow-up information, your prospects will call . . . all the time. So be prepared. Program your telephone answering machine with a client-centered message. Don't just give the old "I'm not available right now . . . please leave your number after the beep". Try this instead, "Hi, this is Jeffrey Lant. I'd like to help you sell more of your products and services faster. You can with my book CASH COPY. It's just $38.50 postpaid and comes with a 30-day money-back guarantee. To get your copy, leave your name and address and MasterCard or VISA details after the beep. Don't forget to ask for your free year's subscription to my Sure-Fire Business Success Catalog."

P.S. One day I returned home to find a sputtering message on my machine from some salesman on whom the tables had at last been turned, "It's the first time I ever made a call and got turned into the prospect," he said. Good. This is just what should be happening!

Last Words

For most authors and publishers, getting a review in the *New York Times* remains the summit of their objectives. Not me. I'd rather have one in the newsletter of the International Herb Growers & Marketing Association. Why? Because the first will not supply follow-up information and remains rootedly disinterested in helping their readers get the product. Not the second . . . it's in the business of helping readers. And if that means providing them with complete follow-up details on my info-products, so be it.

These days I take less and less interest in major media and devote my attention to the electronic and print sources that will give me what I want. Apparently lots of other people feel the same way, because the media titans who so dominated the scene just a decade ago are progressively losing their market share as people turn to the exact, specialized media sources they desire. Good.

Maybe someday the big guys will figure out what's going on and why their popularity is on the wane. Not that it matters much to me, however; I intend to keep spending my days locating the publications and electronic media sources that will help me connect with my prospects and give them the exact follow-up details they need to contact me now. These are the media sources which give me the greatest possible return for the least conceivable investment. This approach won't necessarily turn you into a household word. However, it will certainly turn you into a multi-millionaire. Which do you really want?

11

Selling Your Info-Products Through Direct Response Marketing

This chapter has one objective: to show you how to use direct response marketing profitably to sell your info-products. Some people continue to refer to this kind of marketing as "mail order", but I think it's more valuable for you to focus on what you want the customer to do (get your product direct from you) than on the means you're using to stimulate him (mail or something else). Moreover, "mail order" is no longer technically correct, since you will be using other means of connecting with the customer than just using the U.S. mail. Still, I suspect most people will continue to talk about "mail order" when they mean "direct response marketing," and this doesn't bother me at all . . . so long as they follow the right steps to make this kind of marketing profitable.

Before examining the things you need to do to make your direct response marketing profitable, however, I'd like to build a strong case as to why using direct response makes so much sense. I am doing this for a couple of reasons:

1. Despite the fact that direct response marketing techniques are now very well developed, many info-marketers are not using them, and
2. the majority of those who are are not using them thoroughly and conscientiously.

It seems to me there are several reasons for this absurd situation:

- Many people continue to think that unless they have their books in bookstores, they're not a "real" info-publisher. In fact, however, far more books are sold outside of bookstores than in — which means that more of your attention must necessarily be devoted to these means than to getting in a bookstore, important though that may be.

- Too many info-publishers are exclusive. That is, they only want to concentrate on selling their own titles. While they may use direct response marketing for this purpose, they are all too often unwilling to consider how direct response marketing can also help them augment their product line and make more money. As for me, you won't be surprised to hear me say that I am in business to deliver selected Ultimate Benefits to my prospects and make money doing so . . . and if I can do this by selling other people's related products as well as my own, so much the better.

- The vast majority of info-publishers focus on selling their prospects just a single item and therefore do not use the techniques of direct response marketing to gather names and get buyers to buy again soon. This is suicidal. While one object of direct response marketing is certainly to motivate a targeted prospect to buy as soon as possible, another is getting the buyer to buy again . . . as quickly as possible. Direct response marketing can help.

- I should also point out, of course, that many info-publishers are afraid of direct response marketing . . . and for good reason. Almost without exception, the info-entrepreneurs I talk to have been badly burned by direct response marketing. That is, they have invested their money in the development and dissemination of a marketing communication . . . and have had an abysmally low response. Once bitten, twice shy, they have decided direct response marketing is either overrated or won't work for them, and have given it up . . . prematurely.

The fact is, however, you cannot become an info-entrepreneurial megamillionaire, unless you master direct response marketing . . . unless you become sufficiently expert in its techniques so that you can target the right markets for your info-products and using direct response persuade those markets to invest their money NOW! to acquire your products. With few exceptions, bookstores and other traditional marketing outlets will be a subsidiary source of income for you for reasons which will shortly become clear. Only direct response marketing can assure you certain, continuing access to the markets you must be able to motivate and from whose motivation you derive your substantial capital.

For these reasons, I ask you to pay particularly close attention to this chapter and study both the benefits and, yes, the draw-backs of direct response marketing. If you do not master these precepts, you will be forced to fight the unequal war for bookstore space and live with the debilitating vicissitudes of that infuriating business.

Benefits Of Direct Response Marketing

Here are the reasons why direct response marketing makes so much sense:

- You are your own master.
- You select the type of communication.
- You determine exactly who gets your sales message.
- Your prospect gets your message exactly as you want it delivered.
- You determine its timing.
- Your prospect focuses on your message alone.
- You can promote many items for the same (or minimally higher) basic costs as just one item.
- You can use drop-shipping to increase your inventory rapidly.
- It's convenient for your buyer.
- Your buyer can be motivated to act immediately.
- It's convenient for you and enables you to have a more flexible schedule.
- You can develop a base of satisfied customers perfect for repeat sales.
- You can make extra money by renting your mailing list.
- A direct response business needs very few people to run it successfully.
- It lends itself to computerization and computer-based efficiencies.
- It can be run out of a very small space.
- You can determine just how quickly you want your business to grow.
- You can test market with a limited investment.

Let's take a look at each of these reasons.

You Are Your Own Master

One of the frustrating things about the info-product business is just how many people control our destinies. We have to kow-tow to book distributors, book buyers, catalog buyers, media producers and personalities, book reviewers, journalists . . . to anyone in fact who can help us sell our products.

Personally, many of these people disgust me. So often they're loutish, ill-educated, lazy, disorganized, not good about paying the money they owe — definitely not the kinds of people you'd want to invite to dinner. Nonetheless, you have to deal with them . . . or you can't get access to the marketing means they control. So be it.

But do you want to kow-tow your entire life? I certainly didn't . . . and don't. That's why I looked for a means that would give me what I most desire: autonomy, the freedom to be my own master and promote my books in the way I wanted . . . when I wanted . . . to the people I wanted. Without having to give anyone else a second thought. Direct response marketing gives me this essential freedom. It frees me from the vexing circumstances that characterize so much of info-product marketing nowadays and puts me in the driver's seat . . . exactly where I want to be.

This is where you should want to be, too . . . both for your own good and for the good of your products. If you rely on the standard distribution channels alone, you are entirely at the mercy of other people . . . people who can say when and to what extent your product will be marketed. If this is okay with you, so be it. But I'm sorry for you. Because both the big psychic and financial rewards come when you control not only the means of production but also the means of distribution. For us info-entrepreneurs, this inevitably means direct response marketing.

You Select The Type Of Communication

What's important about direct response is the response. That is, the only thing that matters in direct response marketing is getting an immediate response from your prospect. Nothing else counts. Thus, your investment in marketing needs to be no greater than the minimum amount that will generate the all-important response. There is, therefore, no need to use four-color printing if a flyer printed on stock colored paper will achieve the same result. The objective here, remember, is not to present yourself in a particular way but to generate a response.

You must therefore ask yourself which kind of direct response format makes the most sense given the people you're approaching and the info-product you're selling:

- an 8 1/2" x 11" flyer
- a four- or six-page sales letter
- a post card
- a personalized computer-generated letter.

We'll discuss each of these later. What's important is that when you use direct response marketing, you control the format that contains your marketing message. So long as you remember why you are marketing (to generate an immediate response) and so long as you have done what you can to ensure that you achieve the purpose of this marketing, you can use any format you like . . . including the least expensive. This is not true when you work with other people and their forms of marketing. All of them will have their own way of doing things and if you want to participate in what they're doing, you have to do it their way. That is definitely not true with your direct response marketing.

You Determine Exactly Who Gets Your Sales Message

The essence of marketing success is directing just the right message with just the right motivational offer to just the right sales prospects. If you can do this, you will make money. This is precisely what direct response marketing enables you to do.

To do this, you need the services of an intelligent list broker, and a little later I'll advise you how to find this crucial member of your success team. This person can assist you in determining just the right people to get your sales message . . . the people who have the problem your info-product can help them solve . . . or the aspiration the product will help them achieve. The list broker is your consultant. You are the one, however, who makes the final decision . . . the one who controls the entire process.

Think for a moment of the control you have when you make this decision *vis-à-vis* the "control" you have when your products are in a bookstore. In direct response marketing, you make a calculated decision about the people you will be sending your sales message to. You know just where they are, who they are, some crucial characteristics about them . . . and you are (relatively) certain your message will at least get to them.

With a bookstore things are different. There, even if you can sell your product to the buyer (a big if), you have no control about where it'll be placed, just how the store attracts its customers or moves traffic once people come in, how long the products will remain on the shelf or in the window, when they're out of stock and need to be reordered. In short, *all* the crucial decisions are out of your hands . . . as they most assuredly are not with direct response marketing.

Your Prospect Gets Your Message Exactly As You Want It Delivered

I don't know about you, but precision of language is very important to me. When I say something I want the message delivered *exactly* as I crafted it . . . no ifs, ands or buts. I want it expressed in just the way I expressed it . . . designed and laid out just the way I want it . . . and delivered just when I want it.

When you're working with other people, you're just not going to have this kind of control. I think, for instance, of a Resource Box currently running at the end of one of my articles in a professional newsletter. It starts out by saying, "Jeffrey Lant specialized . . ." as if I were dead. Though I've written to them to correct this problem, the mistake remains . . . wrong by just a single letter, a letter that nonetheless completely changes the meaning of the sentence. No, if you want control . . . you need direct response.

When you use direct response, you get to determine precisely what goes into your message . . . exactly what benefits to stress and how they should be stressed. You can lead with what's important . . . and not have to worry that some nitwit somewhere is going to change the order of what you've written because he doesn't like it. Again, you're in control.

This is particularly important as you grow to become a client-centered marketer. Over the last decade, as I've become more knowing about the power of client-centered, benefit-rich marketing and how few people practice this kind of motivational, persuasive selling, I've become even more punctilious in demanding that product sellers marketing my products use my marketing copy exactly as I've written it.

Not surprisingly, it distresses me just how often people who don't know better (but should) make changes without telling me . . . and thereby dilute the effectiveness of my copy. Rest assured this, too, will happen to you . . . except when you institute your own direct response marketing program and control everything yourself. Then and only then can you be assured your client-centered benefits will remain exactly as they ought to to motivate the maximum number of people to buy your offer.

You Determine The Timing

Among the many things you control in direct response marketing, timing is one of the most significant. When you work through other people to sell your products, you must march to the beat of their drummer. They determine when their catalog will be printed and shipped . . . they determine when their publication will go to press . . . they determine, in short, just when your prospects will see your offer. I use these methods, of course (I neglect nothing that can profitably sell my products), but this absence of control bothers me.

With direct response marketing, you determine the timing of your offer. You need work only with the members of your design, production, mailing label and fulfillment team . . . and with these people you can determine the timing. True, when you use the U.S. mails you can't determine just when (or, sometimes, even if) your marketing communication will in fact arrive. That, I admit, is a drawback to this system . . . but you can at least decide when you'll be mailing it and not be dependent on anyone else.

In this regard, I think, for instance, of one post card deck firm, the kind of company that sends a number of post card offers to a selected list of prospects. Only recently they went through a 120-day delay in mailing a post card deck for which I had paid in advance. In their own good time they got around to sending it . . . but only after repeated protests and complaints. If mine had been a dated offer, I would have had a terrible problem. When you control your own direct response marketing program, this can't happen.

Your Prospect Focuses On Your Message Alone

When you go into a bookstore . . . when you read a catalog . . . when you look at a publication, you have many different items to select from. As a consumer, of course, I welcome this selection. When I'm a marketer, however, I detest it. As a consumer, I want to be polygamous; as a marketer, monogamous. However, only direct response marketing can ensure that a single prospect stays focused on your single marketing message.

I want to make sure you understand what the purpose of this message is: your objective is not to be fair. It's not to share your prospect with all manner of men. It's to gather a disproportionate advantage . . . to hold his attention longer than anyone else . . . to hammer home your benefits harder than anyone else . . . to motivate your prospect to take action and buy your info-product faster than he buys anyone else's. *In short, it's to get more than your share.*

Consider how you browse through a bookstore, however. You may walk from section to section . . . from book to book . . . looking at spines or covers . . . even picking up a few . . . before making your selection. When prospects engage in this kind of shopping, most product producers lose.

Your job, therefore, is to capture the attention of your prospect immediately and to do *everything* you possibly can to hold that attention . . . until such time as the prospect has either decided he doesn't want what you've got . . . or until he has made an immediate purchase decision and picked up the telephone to get the benefit you've both brought to his attention and continually stressed.

All's fair in love and war . . . and marketing. And one of the supreme benefits of direct response marketing is its ability to make the prospect stop dead in his tracks and hold his attention against a world of competing possibilities by no means limited to other info-products.

Direct Response Marketing Motivates Your Prospect To Buy Immediately

Once you've captured your prospect's attention, your job is to motivate him to buy immediately. Direct response marketing enables you to do just that. Indeed, one of the most important advantages of direct response marketing is its ability to motivate the prospect to take immediate action.

Remember, the essence of direct response marketing is contained in just two words . . . BENEFIT . . . NOW! Indeed, if you remember the words YOU GET (BENEFIT) NOW!, you can successfully master direct response marketing to your considerable profit.

Most "marketers" approach the business of marketing as if it didn't matter to them when their prospects buy. Look at the way most bookstores do business. Virtually all the titles are stacked on shelves indistinguishable from one another. If there are any sale items at all, they appear on tables unappetizingly marked "marked down merchandise". In short, there's no selling going on . . . no attempt to motivate real people to take instant action.

But true direct response marketing is never passive like this. It's active. It pulsates with life and energy and enthusiasm and motivators that get prospects to take immediate action. It's not about stacking merchandise on shelves . . . it's about motivating people to acquire this merchandise IMMEDIATELY.

Your job in direct response marketing is clear: to focus on the right people . . . to do everything you can to capture their attention . . . to pile benefit upon benefit until the overwhelming weight of these benefits pulverizes the trivial insignificance of the money it takes to acquire them . . . to motivate the prospect to take immediate action . . . and then be entirely prepared for him WHEN-EVER HE TAKES THAT ACTION.

You Can Promote Many Items For The Same (Or Minimally Higher) Basic Costs As Just One Item

Direct response marketing can be used to promote a single item . . . or many items. But one thing you should keep in mind: some of your significant costs will be the same whether you promote one item . . . or hundreds.

Thus, you can promote one item or several *hundred* for the same basic bulk rate postal charge; the weight of the piece, not the number of items is the determining factor. By the same token, the cost of renting your mailing list is the same whether you sell one item or hundreds. Of your major costs only printing will be more substantial; it takes more space and paper to promote 100 items than to promote one, but, of course, you pay less on a per-thousand basis as the amounts you print go up.

For these reasons, it pains me when I see info-producers attempting to make their fortunes with a single $10 or $20 item given all the costs of producing and marketing it. This is the likely way to ruination . . . not easy street.

To make direct response marketing profitable for you, you must either promote a sufficiently highly priced product so that you can break even at .5% response . . . or a group of related products which will, at a .5% response, enable you to break even.

It is important to point out that you can make money in this business both from single-item promotions . . . and from promotions featuring several items. The first promotion must focus exclusively on the benefits of the single info-product. The second must offer info-products that are linked together by a theme . . . by the Ultimate Benefit we discussed earlier.

One of the reasons a marketer's multi-product mailing may fail to be profitable is because the products are not thematically linked . . . that is, there is no necessary reason why the buyer of one should buy yet another; the products are seen as disparate, disconnected and detached. This is a mistake. If you want your prospects to buy multiple products from you, you must show them how they benefit and why acquiring several is so much in their interest. Merely sticking disconnected offers in an envelope — as so many info-producers do — doesn't work.

Recently this was brought home to me in a rather unpleasant way. One of my book dealers used my four-page mini-catalog as a back-up offer to another product he was selling. His main offer and my catalog were not related . . . and he made no attempt to say anything about my products in a cover letter linking the various things he was selling. He simply stuffed my catalog in with his mailing piece and sat back waiting for riches. Instead of money, he received three orders out of 1000 pieces from my mini-catalog . . . and promptly wrote me a truculent letter blaming me for his problem. But this was hardly fair.

This dealer simply dumped information on his prospects . . . information about unconnected products. He made no attempt to motivate his sellers . . . made no attempt to link the things he was selling. Made no attempt, in short, to persuade people that what he was offering made sense for them. The result was predictable, if sad. People need guidance . . . not more paper. And if you're not willing to provide this guidance . . . make the benefits to them clear . . . and motivate them to take immediate action . . . it just doesn't make sense to send them anything at all, much less disconnected offers.

You Can Use Drop-Shipping To Increase Your Inventory Rapidly

Because the per-thousand cost of printing decreases the more marketing communications you produce and the per-item cost of mailing lists and postage remains the same, you'd have to be a ninny not to see the advantages of increasing your (always related) product line as soon as possible and using the advantages of drop-shipping as previously discussed.

Using drop-shipping, a single individual operating from a small space with only a computer for back-up support can develop a product line of several hundred products within a very short time. To make this kind of enterprise work, you need to:

• link all your products with an Ultimate Benefit;

• select reputable suppliers for your product;

• write persuasive client-centered copy, and

• make your business more efficient by integrating the computer into all you do.

There are problems with drop-shipping, of course; your discount is less and suppliers often give less than perfect service. Nonetheless there are advantages for those of us who have limited amounts of space in which to operate.

Sadly, most people who could profit from drop-shipping just don't understand how it works or how to make it more efficient. I think, for instance, of one company I know which has a line of products of interest to non-profit organizations. Instead of using their computer to notify publishers of what they want sent, they have printed up individual order forms for each publisher listing which books they carry and how much to send. What a lot of work! And just think of what happens when the publisher (inevitably) raises his prices. All the forms will have to be hand corrected. What a lot of work! Here's a company, therefore, that's using direct response marketing to create a profitable side-line but is making lots of extra work for itself by not using the computer efficiently. It just doesn't make sense.

You Can Develop A Base Of Satisfied Customers For Repeat Sales

Walk down to your local bookstore and ask them how many people bought products last week . . . what they bought and what their addresses are, and they'll look at you with astonishment. They just don't know. I don't care if you ask this question of the greatest bookstore in America . . . or the very smallest . . . they still don't know. Yet they think they're client-centered!!!

One of the reasons direct response marketing is so powerful is because you can develop a nationwide customer base . . . despite the fact that you may be running your business from a kitchen table personal computer (hold the mayo!). But the key is you've just got to know who bought, what they bought, when they bought, and how much they bought. Otherwise, you just won't know how to process them.

As I have repeatedly stressed throughout this book, you are most likely not going to make your mega-million dollar fortune from a single item. What's more, no single product will ever be as important as the Ultimate Benefit you are in business to deliver and which every single product in your line embodies and reflects.

You must decide your first day in business that you will work hard not merely to get a customer and not merely to get that customer to buy something . . . but to get that customer to buy again as soon as possible. In other words, you are not merely looking for an immediate sale . . . but for ongoing sales from people who trust your judgement and your ability to deliver both the benefits and Ultimate Benefit they desire. This is how you make money.

To do this, you must work hard both to get customers . . . and to keep customers. Take a look in any bookstore at any book, and you'll see just how cavalier most info-producers are about this.

Over 99 books in 100 don't ask you to get in touch with the producer to secure future benefits. Take McGraw-Hill or John Wiley or Prentice-Hall, for instance. All of these large companies currently produce card decks in which they bring a series of their books to potential buyers. Yet not one of these publishers tells you in his books (which you can find in every library and bookstore in this country) where to get in touch to get a free subscription to this service. For reasons I do not understand, these companies make no connection between their various sales activities; they treat them as disconnected. Yet, they could generate tens of thousands of names for their own mailing activities by making just a small alteration in the way they currently do business.

Okay, so the big guys are dumb. That doesn't mean you have to be. Your aim, remember, is to sell your prospect something once . . . and to sell him something again. This means you need his name. You can get it when he buys something from you directly; you can also get it when he buys something of yours in a bookstore . . . or reads it in a library . . . if you stimulate him to contact you.

I COLLECT MY PROSPECT NAMES ANY WAY I CAN . . . AND SO
SHOULD YOU.

Yet consider how many info-producers consider everything they do as somehow separate and unconnected from everything else that they do. This kind of
thinking is just plain suicidal . . . especially when you are selling products that
are linked by an Ultimate Benefit. Here, when a prospect acquires one, he is
telling you that he is interested in the Ultimate Benefit you can deliver . . . and
if this is the case there is a very good chance you can motivate him to acquire
additional products. But not if you don't know who he is . . . or if you are
prepared to allow him to decide when (and whether) to act.

Capture that all-important name however you can and control the marketing
process. This is what makes direct response so powerful.

A Direct Response Business Needs Very Few People To Run Successfully

People often ask me how I'm able to do all the things I do . . . write a book a
year, update the existing titles when they go back to press, write and distribute
an internationally-syndicated column, run a consulting business . . . and a
catalog company. Well, the truth is I:

- am good at time management;
- focus on the things that are really important;
- use my computer efficiently;
- rely on outside support help, and
- run a business that is largely direct response oriented.

A direct response business, you see, is a way of getting maximum outreach with
minimum support staff and hence minimum personnel expense, ordinarily the
largest expense in any business. In my (largely) direct response business the
largest expense is marketing . . . not personnel salaries. To make this kind of
business work, however, you need:

- a copywriter
- a list broker
- a designer
- a printing broker
- a printer
- mailing house personnel
- back-up computer service support.

Now take a look at this list. Not one of these people will be on your pay-roll.
One, indeed, (the list broker) is actually paid not by you . . . but by the list owner

who provides a sales commission. Thus, while you're getting all the help you need, you will not pay expensive salaries . . . and can retain more profit.

What's important to remember about a direct response business is that the focus is always on motivating people to act . . . and only secondarily on getting them what they want. Moreover, neither of these activities needs to be a full time task. That's right . . . you can run a direct response marketing business reaching literally hundreds of thousands of people yearly with only one part-time person . . . you!

I know what I'm talking about: I do it. With my catalogs alone, I reach well over 600,000 people yearly and still spend only about half my day running my direct response business, assisted at periodic intervals of course by my team of service advisors and experts as stated above.

How many more people could I reach before the tidal wave of response overwhelms even my organized system? I'm not sure. I feel like a fly boy testing the envelope . . . probing limits, anxious to see just how much is possible before having to add personnel expenses. I like this challenge . . . and it has taught me one important thing: direct response enables you to contact and motivate truly staggering numbers of people with only a part-time commitment. Moreover, the hours you work are flexible . . . so long as you have in place the means of taking buyer information at all hours. How many businesses can say as much?

It Lends Itself To Computerization And Computer-Based Efficiencies

No one with even half a brain would attempt these days to run a direct response marketing business without a computer. The notion is simply fatuous. Still, there are those about who are trying . . . and failing. To be in direct response marketing means to be in league with the computer. Why? Because the computer can help you:

- store the information you need for your marketing communications;

- draft and edit copy;

- design and lay out copy;

- store data base information;

- generate specialized letters to specific marketing populations;

- process orders;

- handle problems and complaints;

- request products, *etc.*

In short, the computer is essential.

What's important to keep in mind about running a direct response enterprise is that even though the numbers of people you may be contacting are in the many millions, the tasks you need to complete in order to reach and serve them effectively are quite simple and routine. Hence, the importance of the computer.

What astonishes me, however, is how few direct response businesses are any where near being fully automated. When are these businesses going to understand that the focus of a direct response business, or a business relying principally upon direct response marketing to sell its products, is to generate immediate responses from prospects . . . not to spend time and resources creating unique responses to routine situations?

Thus, just yesterday I received correspondence from a woman who's selling her book primarily by direct response. As such, she is dealing with catalog houses on a regular basis . . . or should be. Why then was the letter she sent me personally typed (with personalized errors) . . . meaning that the next letter to a catalog house had to be personally typed, too . . . and thereby feature new errors! It just doesn't make any sense.

The goal of direct response marketing is to motivate an immediate response from a prospect. Your computer can help you do this . . . and handle many of the routine tasks of keeping in touch with your prospects and handling business problems that recur daily. If you don't use the computer in this way, you cannot make your fortune in this business. Case closed.

Your Direct Response Marketing Business Can Be Run From A Very Small Space

When I was a teen-ager, my father told me something very wise that I have never forgotten. He took me to visit a business associate of his who ran his concern from a cubby hole of an office jammed with papers. Perhaps I shrank back in disgust from the rather Dickensian figure I was introduced to and perhaps my father saw it. In any event, after leaving he let me know the man was a millionaire (which really meant something back then) and had nothing to prove to anyone nor any desire to impress. He got the job done . . . and made money. I've never forgotten this . . . and hope that in some way this knowledge explains the fact that I work in the oldest of old clothes . . . in a small office.

One of the things you must keep in mind about direct response is just how little space you really need to run a national business . . . always assuming you are not going to have to warehouse products. You need a computer work station, filing cabinets, an area to store packaging materials and wrap packages, and a typewriter. From such an area you can speak effectively to millions of people.

The money that you save working this way you can devote to twin objectives . . . some must be invested so you develop your capital resources; the rest you can reinvest in marketing activities that connect you with even more people even more effectively. Yes, it is a great game!

What's always important to keep in mind, however, is that your enterprise will be no less national for all that it's operated from a small space . . . nor will it bother your prospects a whit (partly it must be confessed because only the tiniest fraction of them will ever see it). The focus of your enterprise must be on doing all you can to reach ever greater numbers of people . . . and doing all you can to motivate them to take immediate action. Does a large, impressive office do this? Certainly not! Thus, it can be abandoned . . . and all the money saved that that would have cost you.

You Can Test Market With A Limited Investment

What's wonderful about direct response marketing is how quickly and with what a limited investment you can find out if you have an info-product that's profitable. Think, for instance, of how many millions of dollars United Airlines wasted to discover the new name it selected for itself (Allegis, remember?). Or look no further back than the marketing debacle surrounding the introduction of the New Coke to discover that even the giants can make breathtaking miscalculations. By comparison, *we* can find out precisely what we need to know for a drop in the bucket.

Direct response marketing enables you to test market as few as 5,000 pieces (a good test sample) to determine the effectiveness of certain key variables such as:

- market
- offer
- copy.

Certainly none of us likes to lose any money, but it's great to be in a business where you can minimize your losses and keep your shirt even when your thinking is severely flawed. Direct response marketing, in short, is a business where you can take the tiny, tentative steps that produce the directional signals you need, before committing more major donors. This always cheers me up, because, as you might expect, losing a dollar depresses me deeply; losing two, however, is life-threatening.

You Can Determine Just How Quickly You Want Your Business To Grow

I am, in case you've missed the point, a cautious man. I don't buy lottery tickets. I haven't bet on a horse in over twenty years. I make it very clear to those selling commodity options I shall never invest with them. In short, I am, depending on whose fable you're reading, either the ant . . . or the tortoise. That's why I like direct response marketing.

With direct response marketing, you can start small . . . very small . . . with a single 8 1/2" x 11" flyer stuffed into your outgoing packages. If the market is right for your product . . . if you've made an irresistible offer . . . if you've piled buyer benefit on buyer benefit . . . you will make money even from this format. And so be ready to do something grander . . . to reach out to still more people in perhaps more expansive ways . . . such as through a brochure or sales letter. Operating on the pay-as-you-go method, you can move ahead surely . . . if you keep your mind fixed on what direct response marketing is all about: motivating an immediate response . . . and connecting with even more people with the offers that motivate this response.

Many info-entrepreneurs, including many who read this book, will never develop large and profitable direct response enterprises. But this, I am forced to conclude, is their own decision. They won't:

- work hard to discover what their prospects want or fear;

- transform features into benefits;

- pile one benefit on another to make a tantalizing offer;

- provide a reason for the prospect to respond immediately;

- test what they've got with a limited market;

- take what they've learned and make the appropriate alterations, and

- reinvest to bring successful promotions to ever larger audiences.

What, then, do they expect? Miracles, of course. But I am of the school of thought that man makes his own miracles; any others you read about are fairy tales.

You Can Make Extra Money By Renting Your Mailing List

Direct response marketers have a unique way of making money that is not available to other businesses. Indeed, try walking into a hardware store and asking its owner if he is making money by renting the names of his buyers to other people who sell similar or related services. He'll look at you blankly. But *you* can make money from your customers and prospects not just when you sell them a product . . . but when you rent their names to others who want to sell them products.

There is, however, much confusion about mailing list rental. The other day a fellow called me who had read one of my articles on how to succeed in direct response marketing and told me he wanted to sell his list of 300 names. How much did I think he could get for it? I asked him if the list was hard to assemble . . . did it contain the names of people who were otherwise difficult to reach . . . was it, in short an economic commodity? No, the fellow said, it was simply a list of 300 people who had bought his (not so unique) computer product. What was it worth? Not much. Not much at all.

If you're going to make money renting your mailing list, you need lots and lots of names. Otherwise, it's not an economically viable product for the list broker who has the expense of listing and promoting it. How many names? Figure at least 5,000 buyers and 10,000 inquiries as a minimum. And they must be pretty recent, too . . . not more, I'd say, than 18 months old.

What this means, of course, is immediately obvious: you can't dabble in this business if you expect to succeed in getting back-end income from mailing list rental. You've got to institute a serious program of name acquisition using every means you can use to get the names and addresses of buyers and prospects.

Once you've got the minimum number, you should approach your list broker and ask for the names of companies that manage lists. Shop around as the commission rates vary; you should expect to get about 90% of the rental income, however, paid about 90 days following rental by a customer. How much will you get? That entirely depends on how difficult your list was to assemble and how many competing lists there are, but I've found in practice that the $1 a year per-name I was told I'd receive was too high. I'd say half that much is about right.

Still, it's found money in two ways, really. First, because of the outright income you get . . . and second, because you can use your mailing list to trade to get the lists of others. In other words, you can trade with those people who have a list you want and can exchange names on a one-to-one basis, thereby saving the cost of list rental. Or, when you start negotiating with card deck companies (about which I'll be talking shortly), you can barter your mailing list as at least partial payment for card insertion. After all, these companies always need new names . . .

Resource

After you've got the minimum number of names for list rental, you may like to check with the company renting my list, Good Fortune Marketing, 210 Commerce Blvd., Round Rock, TX 78664-2189 (512) 255-6014. Ask for Debbie Moran. Perhaps they'll be interested in your list, too.

The Last Big Reason Why I Love Direct Response Marketing: It's Convenient For Both You And Your Buyer

I'd like to finish my discussion of the benefits of direct response marketing by pointing out one of its major attractions: it's convenient for both you and for your buyers.

The average business opens at certain hours and closes at certain hours. As a business operator, I can certainly see the benefits of that . . . for me! But what about the prospects? When you're truly client-centered, you must be prepared to sell your product whenever your prospect is ready to buy it. This means running a twenty-four hour enterprise.

Running such an enterprise is, of course, absolutely mandatory when you start selling to the entire nation . . . or the entire world. Thus, if you're on the East Coast, you've got to be ready to take your West Coast orders late in the day or early in the evening. Otherwise, you risk both inconveniencing people, losing orders and convincing prospects you're really not as interested in helping them as you say you are.

When you run a direct response marketing business and effectively integrate modern technology like the computer and the telephone answering machine, you're ready to take orders when people are ready to place them. How much money did you make on Christmas Day, New Year's Eve, Memorial Day and other major holidays? Not much, I reckon. But I made money *all* those days . . . because my customers placed orders on *all* those days.

How many times have you been lounging about the house watching your favorite television program and eating that bad-for-you junk food we all love so much and made money? Not many, I'll bet. But I do . . . because my buyers call whenever they want to. All my catalogs say I'll take their order twenty-four hours a day, 365 days a year. And I do . . . either in person . . . or with my trusty answering machine.

If you don't, it's because you're either disorganized, selfish or trying to force your buyers to do things your way. By contrast, I want them to do things the way they want to do them . . . whenever they want to do them . . . so long as they get my products in their hot little hands and pay me. For a client-centered marketer that is all that matters!

By the same token, while the direct response business is convenient for prospects, it's also convenient for you. It's the kind of business that gives you flexible hours. A good portion of the year, you can spend your mornings like I do developing new products. While you're working on the future, you can let your answering machine attend to the present. In the afternoon, you can return calls and deal with orders. You can take a day or two off in the middle of the week; after all, Tuesdays and Wednesdays are the slowest mail days. This means mini mid-week vacations are possible . . . and (if you're willing to postpone handling Monday's mail, the week's heaviest, until Thursday) you can occasionally get a good four-day vacation. This just isn't possible in many, many other businsses . . . or when you work for somebody else.

Obviously, then, there's much to be said for the direct response business . . . if you're willing to do what it takes to build an enterprise sufficiently large to deliver the customers and dollars you need to succeed.

Direct Response Negatives

If all that I've said is true (and it is), why then don't all people in direct response marketing make money? There are, I think, several reasons that need to be discussed. Here they are:

- They have no budget.

- Most (unsophisticated) marketers expect too great a return on their mailings.

- Too many direct response marketers are dabbling . . . not being serious about making money. They therefore don't do what's necessary to succeed.

- You can finance very little of your investment. Direct response marketing is a cash up-front business.

- Direct response marketing is costly . . . and all too many products being sold are too low-priced for the entrepreneur to make any money.

- The post office is often careless about delivering the mail.

- Your marketing communication arrives with many competing marketing communications and is usually not a high priority for the recipient who has other things to attend to.

- Your prospect controls his approach to your marketing communication. You don't. You are thus at your prospect's mercy.

- Your prospect may well feel uncertain about whether your product is as you describe it and may therefore postpone action.

Let's examine each of these in turn.

There's No Budget

The truth is, when you become knowledgeable about direct response marketing you can pretty much predict just how much money any given promotion will make. This knowledge level, of course, involves not only knowing what a reasonable response is for any given mailing but also how to motivate a market and how to find the right mailing lists. Each aspect is crucial. One thing, however, will help: knowing just how much it really costs to connect with your prospects and just how many of them have got to respond for you to break even . . . and make money.

Thus, success in the direct response business begins with a good, solid, honest budget of costs. I'll bet you a dollar, however, that most people in this business don't have such a budget. Instead, they are like gamblers betting their fortunes on yet another mailing, hoping against hope that this time — at last! — they've come up with the right product, the right offer and the right list to make money. THIS ISN'T THE WAY TO DO THINGS!!!

You've got to find out exactly how much it's going to cost you to reach your prospects . . . and motivate them to act.

Most (Unsophisticated) Marketers Expect Too Great A Return On Their Mailings

As soon as you have your budget, start figuring out what your return must be. You already know you should break even with a .5% return. If you can't, you're probably headed for a real problem. And you should never anticipate a response greater than 1.5% . . . unless you have consistently generated a greater response from a comparable list and offer.

This means you can't look at your direct response business as a "get rich quick" scheme. It's not. Consider it, instead, as a cash cow . . . as a means of generating a good, solid income for you, time after time, by following a few simple, easy-to-understand rules.

The real problem with most people's involvement with direct response is that they expect too much too soon from a single product. Failing to get it, they get discouraged or disgusted and drop out . . . losing much of their money.

Your business should be arranged so that you make a consistent profit at about a 1.5% return. If you can do this time after time, you're doing things right . . . and will profit accordingly.

Too Many Direct Response Marketers Are Dabbling

The people who make money in direct response marketing treat it with the seriousness the subject deserves. It is something they work at regularly, always remembering there is really only one question they need to answer correctly: "What does it take to motivate my prospect to act immediately to acquire the benefit I have available for him?"

Sadly, the majority of people who are using direct mail to attempt to motivate people don't treat the subject seriously. How else can you explain the large volume of chain letters and photocopied promotions we all get? These are a complete waste of money. Except for the originator of the scheme (and often not even him), no one makes any money with them. They look cheap and fraudulent . . . as most of them most certainly are.

Like any other serious subject, direct response marketing demands your full attention. You can't expect to become the expert you need to be if you only mail infrequently and are only trying to make a few dollars a year in your spare time. It just won't work.

You Can Finance Very Little Of Your Investment

One of the practical reasons many people dabble, of course, is because direct response marketing demands money. Your two greatest expenses in this business are postage and printing. Postage, of course, you must pay up-front; printing terms can be negotiated, although you're usually better off paying in advance because you can get a somewhat lower rate. Either way, you have precious little flexibility.

Many people are either unable to make this kind of cash commitment . . . or are very, very nervous about doing so. No wonder. If they haven't identified the market, worked hard to translate product features into buyer benefits, haven't created an irresistible offer and motivated the prospect to act NOW, they probably realize they are throwing their money away. They thus mail less . . . and hope more.

I prefer to operate a different kind of business. Whether you're sending 5000 pieces or 5,000,000, you need to go through certain steps . . . the steps that force you to focus on the prospect and do everything you can to motivate him to act immediately.

Skipping over these steps merely because you're investing a small amount of your money makes utterly no sense to me. If you can only mail a few pieces, learn from the experience . . . do what is necessary to motivate these prospects to take immediate action. If you can motivate 1.5% of 5000 people to take action . . . you can motivate 1.5% of 5,000,000 people to take action . . . and you can benefit accordingly.

Moreover, if you are conscientious about both developing your capital resources and reinvesting in your business, you'll soon find that the number of pieces you're sending jumps exponentially. The real question is finding out just how many you can comfortably handle alone . . . or with a two-person operation, *etc.*

What aggravates me is that the smaller direct response marketers are generally so incredibly sloppy. They seem to think their small investment justifies small thinking. It doesn't. All of us started small. Those of us who were smart, however, saw "small" as a staging area . . . a place where we could learn the ins and outs of the business.

Small doesn't mean second-rate; it means learning what needs to be done to motivate people. Look upon the money you spend when you're small not only as an investment to motivate your prospects . . . but also as educational dollars invested to teach you exactly what you should be doing to motivate more people. Unless you think this way, you can scarcely expect to derive full benefit from the early dollars you spend.

Direct Response Marketing Is Costly . . . But Too Many Products Being Sold Via Direct Response Cannot Cover The Costs, Much Less Make A Profit

As the merest glance at a direct response marketing budget confirms, this is a costly way of doing business. Many people give way to galloping optimism, speculating on an unrealistic return with a product that's priced ridiculously low. I think, for instance, of two young women who came to me recently for consultation after having lost about $10,000 (their life savings) on a venture involving a $7 book.

To my disgust, they had hired another direct response marketing consulting who had persuaded them to sell this product and who had charged them a whopping fee to design their mailing piece. They would break even only with something like a 10% return! Not knowing any better (and, deplorably, not being advised any better), they went ahead with this suicidal project. When they came to me both were literally in tears. I think they had grossed about $1000.

This vignette illustrates many points:

1. (Unrealistic) hope is eternal.
2. There are charlatans in our field who prey on the innocent.
3. People keep betting on impossibly stupendous returns.

I have said it before, and I'll say it again: You're not going to make your fortune on a $7 info-product produced by someone else . . . certainly not when you're using direct response as your principal means of marketing. You're not even going to make your fortune on this product when you produce it yourself. The profit margins you need just aren't there when you consider the significant costs.

The Post Office Is Often Careless About Delivering The Mail

Although no one knows just how much mail the post office disposes of illegally or is careless about delivering, the sum total is many billions of pieces annually. It's a national scandal, and all of us in the direct response business suffer accordingly. Conservatively, I think that you can count on between 5-10% of your correctly addressed mail not being delivered. Other reasons, too, lower the percentage of your mail delivered.

- Your prospects have moved. You may count on about 25% of any given list being undeliverable in a twelve-month period. Yes, 1 in 4 people move during the course of the year . . . and bulk-rate (third-class) mail doesn't get forwarded.

- Names and addresses are often difficult to read and therefore data are input incorrectly. Large amounts of the data provided by individuals for mailing list purposes are so difficult to read that even the most conscientious person inputting data is likely to get about 5% of them wrong. I know. The handwriting on the cards and letters returned to me in their thousands is often very, very difficult to decipher despite my pleading to "PLEASE PRINT." I cannot guarantee the accuracy of all these data . . . and neither can anybody else. Moreover, all of us make other inputting mistakes that make delivering the mail difficult, if not impossible.

- Mailing houses are sloppy about affixing labels properly. These people often want their money in advance and then destroy the mailing piece with their poor work. This is why you want to do one of two things: either check with current mailing house clients to see if they have any complaints about how their labels have been cut and affixed . . . or get your names to the mailing house on a magnetic tape for ink jet addressing. The cost should be the same for either process (from roughly $13 per thousand names to $16 per thousand depending on the quantity you're going).

Personally, I prefer ink jetting since this process literally "jets" the name right onto the mailing piece... along with any code and/or marketing message you wish to use. The problem with ink jetting is that your mailing house must get the names in just the right format. Thus, it's to your advantage to make sure you get specific tape formating instructions from the mailing house and give them to the company providing the tape; my mailing house, for instance, has a printed booklet which you can give to the company outputting the name.

Resource: I am happy to recommend Boston Offset which handles my catalogs and ink jets the names on them. If you've received a copy of my catalog in the mail, you'll have a sample of their work! Contact them at 565 University Avenue, Norwood, MA 02062 (617) 551-2900.

Your Marketing Communication Arrives With Many Competing Marketing Communications

To my continuing consternation, many people in direct response marketing act as if their prospect is an information-starved prisoner in an empty room that has no windows or doors; that this person has nothing better to do, in fact, than wait for your marketing communication to arrive. They seem to think that when that communication arrives these poor souls cannot wait to get it . . . dropping everything and everyone else.

Can you see just how stupid this is?

Think how you read your mail. You look for checks and personal letters first. Other items get a distinctly lower priority. Why should it be any different with others?

It is not only a fight to get your mail into your prospect's hands . . . it's a fight to get him to read it. You're not fighting only against other pieces of mail, either. You're fighting against his regular work . . . the telephone . . . interruptions . . . and the fact that you're asking him to make a decision, something he probably doesn't like to do very much. The people who are successful in direct response marketing understand the unendingly competitive nature of the game . . . how they must continually strive to capture their prospect's attention . . . to draw him away from something else and keep him reading what they've sent.

Thus, as one sage in this business said recently, the purpose of the first line in a marketing communication is to get the prospect to read the second line. The purpose of the second line is to get him to read the third line, *etc.* Each of these tasks is a challenge . . . and if you fail this challenge, your mailing piece ends up in the trash — just where most of them do right now. Thus, your investment has been literally thrown away. I don't know about you, but this makes me sick . . . and I'll do whatever is necessary to make sure it doesn't happen to me.

Your Prospect Controls The Approach To Your Marketing Communication

Direct response marketing is a battle . . . a battle generally fought between a piece of paper packed with symbols and one human being. Your interests are represented by that paper, by those symbols. If you're doing things right, so are the prospect's.

In point of fact, however, the prospect is more likely to control things. You're not there, after all. The prospect can determine when he picks up your paper . . . how much of it he reads . . . when he responds . . . in short, he is in a position to determine just what will happen and when it will happen. BUT THIS IS PRECISELY WHAT YOU DON'T WANT.

You want to motivate the prospect . . . you want him to stop dead in his tracks and act NOW . . . you want him to push everything else out of the way and concentrate on what you've got for him. When you succeed in doing this, you succeed; when you don't, you fail *and* the prospect loses the benefits you have for him.

Too many direct response marketers lose because they allow the prospect to determine the course of events. In other words, they let the prospect decide just when things will be done . . . and just how things will be done. BUT NOT YOU! Your job is to fight the battle with that piece of paper and succeed in capturing another human being . . . rendering him oblivious to everything else that's going on and doing what you want him to do when you want him to do it.

Remember: if you consider the relative strength of a human being and a piece of paper, this looks like an unequal battle . . . a battle that you, the sender of the paper, cannot hope to win, especially given all else that you must fight against. But this is just the challenge. Moreover, it's a challenge you must win, or you cannot succeed.

The paper you send . . . the ad you write . . . the card you put in the prospect's hand . . . must be so potent in power and appeal that the unequal struggle is immediately turned to your advantage (which is also, of course, the prospect's real advantage). This is what direct response marketing is all about and why it's such a fun game to play!

Your Prospect May Well Feel Uncertain About Whether The Product Is As You Describe It And May Therefore Postpone Action

Have you ever bought anything by mail and then been disappointed by what you got? Of course you have, and unless the company sending it to you was prompt, courteous and efficient about refunding your money, you probably were far less likely to trust them a second time. Moreover, your sad experience with Company A may well have influenced you in deciding not to buy with Company B, another direct response company. Thus are the innocent condemned with the guilty.

The correct way to deal with this situation, of course, is to assume that your prospect has been burned in the past . . . and to do everything you can to calm him down, meet his reasonable objections, and persuade him to act immediately.

Astonishingly, all too many direct response marketers act as if America is a virgin territory made up of people who were born yesterday and are the kind of yokels that distinguished former times. It's just not true.

Being an American, your prospect wants to buy . . . badly. Money means nothing to us; spending it means everything. But each and every one of us remembers just how we've been taken advantage of . . . how the merchandise didn't match the picture; how glorious the description, how paltry the product. It's your obligation to know this . . . and to reassure your prospect so that he does what he wants to do (buy) and doesn't hang back and do nothing.

There are many ways to provide this reassurance: a money-back guarantee or a notice about how many years you've been in business, for instance. The point is, however, if the prospect has the slightest doubt that you can deliver the benefit he wants . . . or that he'll get stuck with something he doesn't want, it makes perfect sense for him to do nothing . . . thus destroying your chances of success.

If these situations are not dealt with, you're crippling yourself, undermining your own prospects. Fortunately, to a greater or lesser extent each and every one of these problems can be dealt with successfully . . . so you increase the probability of profit.

Making Direct Response Work For You

What follows is a discussion of the things you must do to sell your info-products using direct response marketing. If you succeed in doing these things well, you'll make money, lots and lots of money. If you don't, you'll be left trying to make the present unsatisfactory system of book distribution work for you. Your revenues will be minimized and so will be your reach into your targeted market(s). Pay close attention, therefore. What follows is a blueprint for wealth production.

Developing Data Fields On Your Computer

Right from the start, you need to develop a house mailing list. There are several reasons. You will have your best return with your house mailing list. These are the people who know you best, trust you most, and so respond in greatest numbers to your offers. Moreover, as I've already pointed out, you will profit from these names both by renting them to others . . . and by using them as barter material for people who have names or want them.

Before you set out to acquire your names, however, create your data fields. For mailing list purposes, the data fields you want are:

- last name
- first name
- title
- company name
- address 1
- address 2
- city
- state
- zip

Note: address 1 may well be a post office box; address 2 is a street address. I use the former for mail and the latter for UPS shipping. Both are therefore helpful.

Additionally, you will want to include the following fields to help you sort and delete data:

- inquiry date
- purchase date
- cumulative amount of purchases

For sorting purposes, you may also want categories that indicate which of your info-products the customer bought. Thus, when you have a new edition available or related title, you can bring it to the attention of a very select list.

Picking Your Market(s)

One of the reasons so many people in direct repsonse marketing are so spectacularly unsuccessful is because they are slipshod about market selection; being imprecise about the market means you are necessarily imprecise about the list that connects you to this market. This is disastrous.

We have already discussed selecting markets in connection with creating info-products. You will remember that it is a very good idea to ensure that you can reach your market on a regular basis before you create any product. The availability of rental mailing lists is one thing that makes this possible.

Before renting any list, however, it is a very good idea to check with several list brokers to see what they recommend. There is no fee for their research so take advantage of it. What you are looking for from a list broker is his:

- willingness to hear precisely whom you're trying to reach and understand what you're trying to do;
- specific suggestions about how you can reach these people;
- ability to take your order with a MasterCard or VISA.

A little explanation is necessary.

There are essentially three kinds of lists:

- compiled lists. These are made up of names and addresses usually taken from printed sources like telephone and professional directories. These lists are the least expensive because there's no way of knowing if these people are mail responsive.
- subscription lists. These are the mailing lists of publications. These are mail responsive names interested in a given publication.
- lists of mail order buyers. These people have bought certain products by mail.

I have put these different categories in ascending order of value. Compiled lists are the least expensive but ordinarily the least valuable; lists of mail order buyers are usually the most expensive but, if recent, are the most useful.

What you want to hear from the list broker is which of these different kinds of lists are available and which make the most sense for you. Always remember that the broker works on commission; the more expensive the list he rents you, the more money he makes.

In addition to tips on lists, you want to make sure the company you deal with takes MasterCard or VISA. Why? For two reasons, really: 1) this gives you a month of credit before you have to pay for the lists, and 2) you can get frequent flyer mileage credit for list rental if you are using a card offered by a major airline, such as Continental or United. Wouldn't you like to get a couple of free trips out of renting mailing lists? I have, and I recommend it.

In addition to renting lists, of course, you also want to spare no effort to develop your own house list. To my complete astonishment, most people in direct response marketing are downright retarded about house list development. Not you! Like me, you should give everyone who comes within a country mile of any of your products or direct response communications the opportunity to be on your mailing list . . . and get some benefit. Thus:

- use your products to stimulate people to get in touch with you. Your books, booklets, audio cassettes, Special Reports and articles should all include information on how to get your catalog, *etc.*

- include an inducement on every single one of your mailing pieces (like FREE year's subscription to your quarterly Business Resources Guide) so the prospect gets in touch with you . . . enabling you to capture the name. Remember, everyone isn't going to act immediately to buy your info-products. You still want the name. Don't just ask people to make a "thumbs up, thumbs down" purchase decision. If they're not going to buy now, let them know you still want them to be in touch . . . so that you can keep working to motivate them to buy as soon as possible.

- get lists of all the participants in all your talk programs;

- make sure your authors get lists of all the participants in all their talk programs.

You must learn, too, how to use card deck programs. Card decks are made up of several dozen individual offers presented on post cards. They are mailed as a package to targeted prospects, generally in lots of 100,000. You'll find information about existing card deck programs in *Standard Rate & Data*, 3004 Glenview Rd., Wilmette, IL 60009 (312) 256-6067. Keep in mind, though, that once you're in one deck, you'll be aggressively sought out by other deck managers who'll want you to be in their decks, too.

What's important to keep in mind about card decks is that they work best as a two-step process. First, do everything you can to capture the name. Then, follow up with your sales literature. Selling direct from card deck cuts the response dramatically.

The second rule of successfully using card deck advertising is to negotiate on the price. These days 100,000 post cards in a card deck are publicly advertised at about $3,000-$3,500. Your objective, however, is to pay about $1200 cash for a card with color, that is, at least 60% less. Is this possible? I do this all the time . . . to the consternation of other card deck owners. Indeed, just recently I made a very unusual deal to get 100,000 post cards for $800 . . . but that was a real gift.

The trick to getting this price is to offer the $1200 up front and then stand firm. Make it clear to the account representative who contacts you (or whom you contact directly) that you will pay no more, that you have camera-ready art available, and that you'll send your check with your insertion order. Be polite, but be firm. Nine times out of ten, you'll get what you want.

Or be more creative. Suggest $1000 cash and 5000 of your most recent names. I did this during the writing of this chapter . . . and I got 100,000 post cards. When you make this suggestion, the account representative (who is generally not the decision maker) will probably have to check it out with the deck manager. This person will usually take the offer because 1) once his fixed costs are met whatever he gets is profit even if it's not all he wants, and 2) he can use the names and thereby cut his direct costs.

Note: once you've established a relationship with a card deck company (that is, after your first insertion) ask for standard credit terms, net 30. There's a very good reason for this. The card deck business goes through periods of acute instability and recently there have been many failures in the industry. Inevitably, many people lost money and didn't get the cards they paid for. Protect yourself either by giving the company a credit card and telling them they can charge half at the time of insertion and half when the cards are mailed or by doing the same with checks. When you place your second insertion order, you have the right to be billed . . . and won't have to pay until the cards are sent. I like this best of all!

Once you've made the deal of the century on your card, don't blow it. Make sure you are using the card to do what it's supposed to do: swell your list of targeted prospects. Take a look at the card on page 437. It's the one I've been using for years now. One card deck operator told me I get 10 times the standard industry response with this card, and I can believe it. Why? Because it pushes benefits including a free year's subscription.

The objective of this card is to get as many targeted prospects as possible to let me know they're my market . . . and then follow up with my catalog. I want these names for my own direct response program, of course, but I also want as many as possible because of the rental income I derive from them.

Note: there's another way to use card decks — through a nationwide lead-generator program. You've probably already seen — or maybe even responded to — a card in such a program. Instead of one advertiser buying a card and running his offer, on the lead-generator card the card owner buys the cards and rents space to many advertisers. This card runs in many decks where prospects check off what they like and return the card to the card owner. The prospects are then sorted and sent to the advertiser. Sound promising? Then call *me* at

(617) 547-6372 since I mail out hundreds of thousands of these cards regularly at surprisingly low cost to my advertisers.

Do The Budget

It's now time to do the budget. Your budget should consist of the following items:
• product cost *per* item
• fulfillment/shipping cost *per* item
• lay out and design for mailing piece
• printing cost for mailing piece
• bulk postage cost

- list rental
- list coding
- cost of running your house list
- mailing house costs of list set up, affixing mailing labels, sorting mailing pieces and delivery to post office.

Most of these items are, I think, self-explanatory. List coding may not be. This code, run on the label, enables you to determine which lists are drawing best. A code like "S/01/94" might mean *Savvy* magazine subscribers used in your January, 1994 mailing. This is very important information to maintain so you know where to direct future promotions . . . and where not to.

Remember, you need to break even at about .5% response. Product fulfillment/ shipping costs, of course, will be paid by the buyer. Clearly, you will want to develop a couple of different budgets based on different printing quantities, postage, *etc.* Some costs, like printing, will decline on a per-thousand basis as your order increases.

Only after you have determined and reviewed your budget will you get an idea of whether the project you are considering makes sense. At that time, you'll either go back to the drawing board . . . or proceed with final list rental. Note: before renting your mailing lists, keep in mind that most mailing houses want cheshire labels from you, not pressure sensitive. Cheshire, by the way, refers to the cutting and gluing process that gets the labels on your mailing piece . . . not to a kind of paper. Thus, cheshire labels can and should be printed on wide carriage continuous feed computer paper. This paper comes in at least two thicknesses. While 20-pound will do, see if you can get something heavier.

Checking Key Points In Your Copy

Are you ready to mail now? Not quite. It's a very good idea at this point to make sure that what you're sending is really worth sending . . . that is, that it has a good fighting chance to motivate another human being to pick up the phone . . . or send in a coupon or a check IMMEDIATELY. If it doesn't, you have to go back to the drawing board. This means checking your direct response copy for the following components:

- Benefits. Have you filled your extended right hand with one benefit after another . . . real, believable, specific benefits the prospect wants and which reduce to insignificance the money he has to spend to acquire them?

- Anxieties and aspirations. Have you played either on the prospect's fears (better) or aspirations (less good) . . . reminding him just how bad things are now . . . or how much better they could be . . . if only he'd act immediately? Remember, anxieties stimulate. Aspirations stimulate, too, but not as well.

- Offer. Have you made an irresistible offer your prospect simply cannot refuse? Have you led with this offer . . . placing it prominently and using it to motivate an instant response?

- Testimonials. Have you reinforced the benefits with believable, specific testimonials from real, credible sources?

If these factors are not present, you need to do some more work.

This takes care of the copy . . . now what about the graphic emphasis? Have you directed your prospect's attention to the important things . . . the benefits, the offer? Have you made important words and phrases seem important by the emphasis you've given them? Or have you left it to the prospect to figure out what's really important? If you have, shame on you! You're in the motivation business, remember. You're not writing an English essay.

Selecting The Right Direct Response Format

Once you've written the copy and reviewed it, it's time to decide on the format you'll be using. Will you use a flyer? A cover letter and brochure? A post card? It depends on who you're contacting and what you want them to do. Keep one thing in mind, however: the purpose of whatever you send is not to spend money . . . but to stimulate an immediate response. The objective, in fact, is to spend the minimum amount of money producing the maximum response. Too often, marketers forget this. Sending something to a prospect is never an end in itself.

Let's take a quick look at the major formats you can use:

- flyer
- cover letter and brochure
- post card
- catalog.

I'd like to say a few words about each.

Flyers

A flyer is a single 8 1/2" x 11" piece of paper often folded in half or in thirds. Flyers are superb for mailing to a very targeted group of people . . . people who know you for instance. You might use a flyer when offering a revised second edition of one of your products to people who purchased the first. You don't need to impress these people; they'll buy again if they continue to have the need and if they found the first product useful. With a flyer you can stress benefits and highlight the need for immediate action. Flyers are also useful for pre-publication offers.

Cover Letter And Brochure

This standard two-part package consists of two different kinds of sales documents. In the trade, it is often said that the brochure is the "tell 'em" document and the cover letter is the "sell 'em" document, but I don't believe this any more. Both are "sell 'em" documents, only with a variation.

In a cover letter, you should hammer home the benefits and the immediate reason for action. Your brochure (which can simply be a one-page flyer whole or divided in thirds) tells prospects what they'll find in the product . . . and how they'll benefit by using it. While it is certainly true that the cover letter leads this parade, the brochure should also focus on what the prospect gets. This package is very useful when you're contacting people who don't know you and your work and who need to know more about the product you've got and what it can do for them. I can't think of an info-product being sold by direct response marketing that wouldn't profit from this combination.

Post Card

Here you're asking for an immediate response . . . usually by telephone. The post card is excellent for retrieving people for your mailing list who haven't bought anything in a while. Three to six months after you've zapped someone from your list, send him a post card reminding him of all the benefits you offer . . . and asking him to pick up the telephone and get them again. Post cards are also good for sending information about your product to media people to get them to tell you they want to see a review copy.

Catalog

The catalog is a perfect direct response vehicle because it contains so many possibilities for your prospect. Catalogs also have a perceived value that other forms of direct response marketing do not. Studies consistently show that people are hesitant to throw away catalogs and therefore keep them longer. While you want your prospects to buy immediately, of course, you certainly don't want them to throw your materials away if they don't. With catalogs, there is a good chance they won't.

Last Words About Formats

There's nothing sacred about any of these formats. Each has its purpose. Your task is to think about what you want the prospect to do and consider whether the format you've selected is the least expensive you can use to achieve that result.

What I want to stress is how similar all these formats are. All direct response formats are variants of each other. All are built of the same basic components mentioned above. Variations in space will, of course, determine just how much client-centered copy you can use, but whatever format you use should still feature the basic components of successful copy.

As an info-entrepreneur, your attention must always be centered on the prospect . . . and on discovering just how *little* you can spend to motivate maximum response. That is the magic formula, and each of us must spend some time discovering it. It doesn't take brains to spend money to reach people. American car makers, for instance (some of the stupidest marketers), throw money around wildly without knowing whether what they're doing makes sense. Smart people aim to spend as little as possible . . . to get the best result.

Thus, people like you and me:

- screen one color to give pizzazz to a piece . . . instead of paying for two colors;

- use stock paper colors . . . instead of spending good Yankee dollars for a more exotic shade;

- experiment with less expensive papers instead of using the same quality paper other saps are paying for. (Of course, I worried when I switched from a higher priced paper for my catalog to newsprint. But newsprint enabled me to print tens of thousands more catalogs for the same price. What's more . . . the response actually increased!)

For reasons that absolutely amaze me, the self-image of many info-marketers is bound up in the quality of marketing materials they develop. What rubbish! Do you think you're a better, more superior person because you use four colors instead of three . . . that you use 60-pound off-white stock instead of newsprint? Don't be silly.

The sole purpose of marketing is to motivate immediate prospect response. Your job is to cut your expense in doing so as far as you can as fast as you can . . . until the point where you have incontrovertible evidence that your cheese-paring ways are diminishing your response. Then and only then you'll know you've gone too far. Until that point, your job is clear: keep cutting your expenses.

How Often Should You Mail?

Having said this, I'd like immediately to say that while you should always be studying ways to cut your costs, whether you have to hone your skills as a negotiator to get less expensive card deck rates or your skills as a designer to find out how color screening can enhance the attractiveness and appeal of your marketing communications; having said this, I say, I must add that mailing oftener is better!

If you want to make mega-millions as an info-entrepreneur, you want to cut the cost of all your mailings . . . use less expensive formats in place of more expensive formats . . . and mail oftener.

Face it. Your prospects are like my prospects: they're inundated with offers. They're also slothful, disorganized, forgetful. They need constant prodding with the strongest possible benefits and offers you have available. The key words here are "constant" and "strongest possible."

Remember the Rule of Seven. You not only need to target your market and understand what that market wants. But you've got to hit that market again and again and again and again until even the dimmest among them (and they are so very, very dim) know just what you've got and why it benefits them. In this business that means using:

- pre-publication offers
- an offer following your first big review
- preferred customer offers
- an offer leveraging a whole stack of excellent reviewer and user comments
- an offer when a sequel is available
- new edition offers
- an offer that you make when the audio or video version of your successful product is available
- your quarterly catalog offer
- your birthday offer
- your upgrade offer.

Pre-Publication Offers

Give your market a chance to acquire your (not yet available) product at a special discount. A flyer works perfectly well here.

An Offer Following Your First Big Review

The minute someone important says something useful and good about your product . . . use it to sell that product. Again, a flyer works well here.

Preferred Customer Offers

Tell your preferred customers you value them the most. Then, offer them the chance to buy something . . . or a package of somethings . . . at a special price. A post card or flyer will do nicely.

An Offer Leveraging A Whole Stack Of Excellent Reviewer And User Comments

Have you had a run of excellent media and user comments about your product? Wonderful! Now use them to motivate sales. Send a flyer packed with prospect benefits and reviewer comments and an offer inducing immediate action. Or send a cover letter and brochure that features more of the great stuff people are saying about your superb product. People like to go with a winner . . . few like to be the first into the water. So, use what you've got to sell more.

An Offer When The Sequel Is Available

Send a flyer to the people who bought an initial product when its sequel is available. This could be a pre-publication offer, of course, or it could coincide with actual publication. Either way, target those who are already profiting from your information . . . and let them know just how many more benefits you have for them.

New Edition Offers

Is your product coming out in a brand-new, info-packed, superior edition (it better be!). Then, offer it to people who have already profited from the previous edition. Those who have bought probably only need a flyer; indeed, you might be able to get away with a post card. Those who haven't probably need a cover letter and brochure.

An Offer That You Make When The Audio Or Video Version Of Your Successful Product Is Available

When the new audio and/or video cassette of your successful info-product is available, it's time to sell . . . everything: audio, video, and print product. Sell each part separately . . . and make an especially attractive offer on everything altogether. Again, a flyer will probably do to previous buyers. Send a cover letter and brochure to those who haven't bought yet.

Your Quarterly Catalog Offer

So far the prospect contacts I've suggested have necessarily been episodic . . . they are dependent on something happening, like a new book coming out. Not here. You need to institute a regular quarterly catalog mailing program that brings all your products and, yes, your services to your prospects' attention. Here you use your entire list as opposed to specialized sections of it.

Your Birthday Offer

How about a slightly less serious reason for mailing? Like your birthday! As you know, I strive mightily to establish a personal tone to my business . . . to make what I do person-to-person communication. If I'm happy, I like to spread that joy to my customers. An annual birthday sale is one good way of doing that; a very good excuse for another customer contact. Don't miss it.

Your Upgrade Offer

Your customer has just bought something? Excellent! Sell him something else with an upgrade offer that gives him either more detailed information about the problem he wants to solve . . . or information about a logically related problem. The moment someone has bought something from you, always assuming he has the money to buy more, is the perfect opportunity to sell him something else; after all, you know his interest is hot. Why not take advantage of it . . . and help the prospect, too?

What I'm basically saying here is that you've got to hustle. You must assume your prospect will be distracted by an avalanche of other offers. You've got to assume that even when you've got what he wants, he won't remember. You've got to assume that one connection just won't be enough. And you've got to operate accordingly.

Direct response works when you target carefully and keep hammering home to your prospsect the benefits he gets by acting NOW! These benefits must be hammered home today; they must be hammered home tomorrow. They must be hammered home next week. It's the consistent, persistent hammering, as much as the message itself . . . that ultimately brings about the sale. Sadly, it's this consistent, persistent hammering that most info-entrepreneurs ignore, letting hope instead of a system dictate their operating procedures.

Another Way To Make Money From Direct Response Marketing: Your Package Insert Program

Clearly, one of the biggest expenses in the direct response business is postage. That's why I spend lots of time trying to reach my market without having to pay additional postage costs. This is why a back-of-product catalog makes such good sense. It's also the reason why you must create a package insert program . . . both for your own info-products and for other people's. The theory is this: since you're already communicating with a targeted prospect or buyer it makes sense for you to put additional offers in his hand that may interest him.

You can do this by developing your own 8 1/2" x 11" flyers on particular products. Whether you have a catalog or not, you'll want some of these flyers. Catalogs, after all, are too bulky to go into your outgoing business envelopes . . . yet you want an offer to go out with *every* piece of mail from your office. Remember, you can send five 8 1/2" x 11" sheets for the price of a first-class postage stamp. Don't waste the value of that stamp! Of course, when you don't have a catalog, your flyers are your main marketing materials.

In addition, you need to seek out other info-producers with compatible products to yours and make a distribution deal with them. Depending on where you shop, you can get about 1000 8 1/2" x 11" flyers on a stock colored paper for about $35-$45. You need camera-ready art from the info-producer and his best discount (remember, ideally this is 50%). Note: it's unlikely the info-producer will deliver the actual insert pieces to you with your name and address, but even this happens. If the individual wants to get access to your market badly enough, he'll pay for the insert pieces with your address. Personally, I avoid dealing with people who want all orders generated by your insert program to go to them; I've found in practice that this "honor system" doesn't work very well. I prefer to get the money, deduct my commission, and send on the order and my check to the info-producer for him to ship. This works much better.

By the same token, of course, you want others to put your insert pieces in their outgoing mail. Here you can either exchange 1000 of your flyers for 1000 of his. Or simply make a joint distribution agreement.

Note: I doubt that an insert program will ever be a huge money maker. Why? Because an insert is never the main offer. Still, I make money regularly both from inserts in my outgoing mail and from my inserts in other people's mail . . . and so should you. If the cost of developing the marketing communication and inserting it is less than the money you make, it's worth doing. Your insert program, then, becomes merely another revenue stream.

Another Note: if you're interested either in having your material disseminated in my outgoing mail (what you sell must be compatible with what I sell), or in having my flyers go out with your mail for your further benefit, please let me know. You won't be surprised to learn that I'll be trying to get you to pay for the cost of printing your insert piece with my name and address on it (so be prepared!). But, like most other things in life, this is negotiable . . .

Last Words On Direct Response Marketing

You've already discerned just how enthusiastic I am about direct response marketing. No wonder. It enables me to say what I want to say when I want to say it to the people I want to say it to. I don't have to wait for others . . . or work to convince stupid people to carry my products or worry that I'm being robbed by any of the dishonest product distributors who abound.

Before ending this section, here are some last tips so that you, too, can profit as much as you can from direct response marketing, tips that will make the marketing documents you create truly extraordinary.

• Work not just on being but on being perceived as being honest, candid, genuine and authentic. I think one of the reasons for my successes is that I'm blunt and to the point. If I've got something of value for someone else, I say so candidly. If the customer doesn't agree, I'll take the product back. In an age of hype and misrepresentation, people like this kind of refreshing directness, even if some of them think I'm a trifle eccentric (imagine!).

• Let your character shine forth. These days most enterprises are anonymous. Don't let yours be one of them. Stand for something. Be a person your customers can trust. Don't try to be perfect . . . strive to be human. Be warm, direct, friendly. Get angry occasionally . . . if this is the way you really feel. This is how real loyalty is developed and reinforced. Don't worry about being a saint; worry about being knowledgeable, respectful, prompt, and as courteous as possible without ever being supine.

• Be accessible. Recently, I had occasion to call a new bookstore in a vain attempt to make an appointment with its buyer. I heard every single conceivable excuse as to why he wasn't available. When at last I did connect, I discovered I had been in search of a kid . . . he couldn't have been more than 25. Just 25, yet he'd already discovered the joys of putting people off! You can imagine just what I think of him . . . and his store. I'll play their game, of course, because I must, but I don't have to like it . . . and I won't extend myself an inch for them, ever. You be different. Build the strongest possible case you can for all your info-products . . . and then let your customers get access to you, whenever they want to. Stop thinking that inaccessibility is a sign of power, authority and superiority. It isn't. It's a sign of insecurity, affectation, snobbery and bad manners. If you know your business . . . be accessible. And make sure that this accessibility shines out in all your direct response marketing.

If you follow what you've learned in this chapter and apply it in your business, I guarantee you something more than product sales . . . although these you'll surely have. I guarantee you that you'll sleep soundly every night and develop a legion of friends and admirers . . . people who need a person like you in their lives because they know that with you they aren't just getting products, no matter how valuable; they're getting a friend and confidant. When they feel that you are that to them, they'll buy again and again and again, tell their friends to buy and spread your fame far and wide. Won't that — and all the money — make you feel terrific!

Other Ways Of Selling Your Info-Products

I have devoted so much time to selling your products via direct response marketing because that subject is of supreme importance to your becoming an info-product mega-millionaire. Still, you must master other means of marketing your products, too. These include:

- selling through workshops & talk programs;
- selling through your own dealer network;
- selling to bookstores, selling to libraries;
- selling through trade shows, and
- selling foreign rights.

Let's look at each of these in turn.

Selling Through Workshops and Talk Programs

A little later this week, just about the time I finish this chapter, I'll be getting on a plane to Atlanta to give a workshop to a small professional association of consultants in the information services industry. They're paying me a nice professional fee for conducting the workshop . . . but I already know I'll be making far more from the sale of my books to participants. This is just as it should be: if you're running your info-empire properly, you'll *always* make more from product sales than from a speaking honorarium. What's more, you should already have sold some of your products *before* you utter the merest word from the platform. These are your objectives . . . let's see how you go about achieving them.

Finding Sponsors For Your Talks

America is the golden land of the association. There is scarcely a personal or professional interest that is not represented by at least one association, and most of these associations have annual meetings. True, as I write, the number of, and attendance at, these meetings is lower than last year; meeting attendance, like everything else in life, is cyclical. But even though the numbers are off this year, they'll come back. Still, despite the momentary decline, meetings are still happening and meetings remain a prime way for you to market your info-products . . . if you're willing to follow some common sense suggestions.

The first of these suggestions is not to begin in this business by sponsoring your own talks. As I made very clear in MONEY TALKS, my book on how to make money from talk programs, when you don't know the workshop business well, self-sponsoring is a good way to lose your shirt. One individual to whom I now consult *lost* $30,000 promoting a short series of self-sponsored programs. Now that he works with seminar promoters he characteristically *makes* over $20,000 *per* program . . . a very big difference.

But let's start at the beginning.

1. Consult the Gale *Encyclopedia of Associations*. As you already know, here you'll find over 25,000 of the nation's largest organizations. Virtually all have annual meetings; many have both regional affiliates and regional meetings, too. And every time they have a meeting, they need speakers! Identify the associations whose members have the problem you can solve. This is your targeted universe of prospects. Supplement this list by your reading of professional publications and by consulting such specialized periodicals as Dottie Walter's *Sharing Ideas* to which I've already directed you.

In addition, ask your buyers what professional associations they belong to and give them a reward for referring you to their group. You can include a post script at the end of your upgrade letter, for instance, letting your buyers know you're available for making presentations on a given subject of interest to them (stress benefits, not features!). Or you can create a separate insert flyer. Either way offer them something of value for their assistance. I provide a HUGH reward: 10% of my speaker honorarium and all the products I sell the day of the program. This can mount up fast to as much as $3,000 for the happy referrer.

Dear friend: this could be *you*. Call me with your speaking leads. Before you do so, however, find out if the organization uses paid speakers and about how much they pay. Find out if they are looking for speakers now. In short, come prepared! I'll then send out anything the decision maker needs to hire me — video tape, review copies of books, testimonials, references, *etc*. As soon as I get booked, I notify you. And as soon as I get paid — I sent you your whopping check.

2.   Begin to develop a relationship with the association. Instead of imme-diately writing and asking to be a speaker, become part of the association's family. Offer the newsletter editor your columns/Special Reports. Or ask to have appropriate products reviewed and featured. In short, get your name before both the membership and the powers that be before asking to be a speaker. When they know you, the chances are much better you'll get what you want.

3.   After even one of your articles runs . . . or one of your products is reviewed (it must be featured favorably, of course!), arrange with the editor to run more articles . . . and ask for a referral to the individual selecting speakers for the next meeting. Then write this individual a letter. In this letter:

   •   say that you have been referred by the publication editor. A known name is helpful to start with;

   •   mention the article by you or about your product that's just run in their publication and that other articles are coming out soon;

   •   say that you're a professional speaker who would be happy to help the membership in other ways;

   •   provide the names of one or two of your programs that you feel certain would be of interest to the members of this organization;

   •   say that if the theme of the next meeting permits, you'd like to be part of it, and

   •   indicate that you'll be calling within ten business days to discuss matters.

Note: if the organization hasn't run any of your articles or featured any of your products, the situation is obviously marginally less good for you. Don't worry, however. In this case, find out first what the theme of the next meeting is (a call to the meeting planner will get it), and then craft a letter in which you show just how your particular expertise fits in. If you can, mention the names of other associations you've spoken to recently and comparable talks you've given. If you don't have the benefit of the "family" association to draw on, you have to put more emphasis on your experience.

Before Calling The Meeting Planner

Before you call the meeting planner, you've got to know exactly what you want . . . and have a good idea what the planner can give you. The problem with most info-entrepreneurs is that they approach meetings as if the only important time was the moment they're at the platform. Doing things this way ensures that you've lost several significant opportunities both to sell products and build up your reputation. Instead, when making use of talk programs sponsored by organizations, you must think about the opportunities both before, during and after the actual presentation. Here's what you need to do beforehand:

- Develop client-centered program descriptions. I don't think I need to tell you now that most workshop descriptions are about the program itself . . . not about what the people get when they attend the program. Remember, your participants come for benefits . . . not merely the chance to listen to you, O Great One. Thus, before you do anything else, perfect your product (the program) to make sure it offers maximum benefits to participants. Then write a description that clearly describes these benefits. Keep in mind that when you're in the talk business, you have twin audiences to motivate: the meeting planner and the actual program participant. A client-centered program description works with both.

- Write at least two columns/Special Reports for the organization's publication. You want coverage before you speak. This helps turn you into a star. Since you want the coverage, and since everybody else is either busy on their own tasks or characteristically slothful, write your own. Make sure you have a captioned photo, too.

- Develop a list of what you want and when you want it. These are the things you want to present to the meeting planner and get agreement on as part of a package. This list should include:

  - articles you want printed and how long before your program they should begin to be published (at least two issues);

  - a product marketing agreement. Ideally, you want all participants in your program to be given your info-product the day of your program as part of the program fee. Make a distributor agreement (a simple letter will do) with the organization giving them a 50% discount. You'll get 50% plus shipping charges. Then use the full retail value of the book as a premium to induce early registration. Note: when you have more than one comparably priced info-product, give participants a choice of premium. People like this, and there's a very good sales reason to give them a choice, too. Different people in your audience will have different products and will thus become roving salespersons for what you've got available.

Note: make sure the sponsor organization agrees to run the product table at the meeting. You'll be far too busy to do so, and they'll have staff present. Organizations are much more cooperative to deal with when they know they're getting half the take. This is also more convenient for you . . . since you can simply send one invoice to the organization which is responsible for paying you (they're also responsible for any losses that occur when the books are displayed. Yes, theft occurs even in such august surroundings). There's yet another reason to have the sponsor get half the product take: often they'll make enough on the product sales alone to cover your fee and expenses. This makes you a very attractive speaker to book . . . and rebook, since you essentially cost nothing.

- your desire to have at least one of your products reviewed in the organization's publication before your talk;

- your fee. When you're just starting out in the business and are not well known, your fee will not be stellar. However, charging too little gives you too little leverage. What you charge should be a reflection of both your standing in the field and the value of your information to participants. Here are some current speaking rate guidelines:

  - if you are giving a one-day workshop in your local area, never charge less than $500;

  - if you are giving a one-day workshop outside your area, never charge less than $500 plus a 50% surcharge for travel time beyond a reasonable commuting distance. Note: do not tell the sponsor you are charging a surcharge, simply quote the combined fee;

  - if you are giving a one-hour talk in your area, charge at least 30% of your daily rate;

  - if you are giving a one-hour talk outside your area, charge either 50% of your daily rate (if the talk is relatively near your office) or 100% of your daily rate if significant travel is involved. In this case, what you may like to do to sweeten the pill for your sponsor is propose that in addition to your one-hour talk, you also do at least one 45-minute workshop. This is also in your interest, since you will have more time with a targeted group of prospects.

Remember, all customary expenses are additional, including air and ground transportation and accommodation.

- audio rights. You make money as an info-entrepreneur by becoming savvy about rights. Just because you're getting paid to talk doesn't mean the organization has the right to tape you and make additional money from the presentation . . . unless you benefit, too. Thus, ask the organization for an audio rights fee if they intend either to give a taped copy of your program to participants or to sell it both to participants and to non-attending members of the organization. How much should this fee be? In my view that depends on the number of people in the organization to whom the organization will try to sell the tape. Organizations of under 1000 members should pay at least $250 for the audio rights to any program; organizations of between 1000-2000 should pay twice as much, *etc.* This fee, like everything else I'm discussing, is clearly negotiable. Note: in addition to your audio rights fee, make sure you get follow-up information on each tape. Create a Resource Box so that everybody getting the tape can get direct access to you. Just because you're selling the audio rights, doesn't mean you don't get this benefit.

Should you always sell the audio rights? Not necessarily. If you are selling your own comparable cassette program, it may not be in your interest to sell the audio rights at all. Whether you are selling audio rights or not, however, you must make sure no one in the audience tapes your program. That is an extra benefit they simply haven't paid for. Still, if members of the audience are not allowed to tape the program themselves, one way or another there must be a tape of what you say. You'll need it when dealing with future meeting planners. They need to know what you sound like! For this purpose, self-taping on a simple cassette recorder will do nicely. If the organization does the taping, ask for six copies of the finished cassette(s).

Note: when you mention the matter of an audio rights fee to a program planner, he may tell you no one has ever raised this issue before. That's probably true. But you're scarcely responsible for the stupidity of other info-entrepreneurs. Feel free to render this sentiment in the politest possible way for the meeting planner.

- your information in the participants' conference packets. Of course, you can pass out your information, but it's more professional if your catalogs and information are in the participants' conference packets. Keep in mind, however, that if the organization is selling your products for their benefit they may not want your literature passed out at their meeting. Fair enough. So long as you have the names and addresses of conference participants, you can get your sales material to them promptly.

- a list of program participants. For your mailing list, you need to know just who attended.

Other Matters That Need Consideration

Before you discuss your program with any meeting planner, you've got to be clear on just what you want and just when you want it. You've also got to be prepared for the kinds of obstacles and characteristic problems that emerge in this business. Here are some tricks of the trade:

- "We can't pay you." One of the biggest obstacles a meeting planner will throw at you is this one. Is this a problem? That depends. So long as you know how much money you need to make as a result of this engagement and are willing to structure a mutually satisfactory plan with the meeting planner, it isn't. Thus, in addition to the above items (which you need with every presentation), in this situation you can also negotiate for the following:

  - free ads in the organization's publication. Okay, the organization can't pay you. But that doesn't mean you should do the presentation for free. You are not an eleemosynary institution — yet! Thus, ask for ad space worth twice your regular talk fee for this kind of program. Again, you'll be told no other speaker has ever asked for this kind of consideration. So what! You'll undercut your own standing as a professional and reduce the value of your information if you're not paid.

  - the organization's mailing list on cheshire labels or mag tape. It's very doubtful that all the members of an organization will be at any one meeting, particularly when the organization is national. Thus, get as much of the organization's mailing list as you can so you can promote your products to them as soon as possible.

  - all product revenues. If an organization isn't going to pay you, they don't deserve any of the revenues from product sales. But you do deserve their help in running the product table. Thus, you keep 100% of the revenues . . . they run the on-site product table.

Be creative! Does this organization have products and services that you want? Trade your speech for things that you can use . . . or sell. This will probably be on a retail dollar exchange basis, you charging the organization full price for your services, them charging you full price for theirs.

Again, I would like to stress just how different this approach is to both standard workshop remuneration and product sales. Too many speakers and info-entrepreneurs don't follow these steps because they (foolishly) believe the good will they engender and the publicity and any sales they make after their talk will fully compensate them for their presentation. I don't believe this. Why just the other day I gave a speech at a conference of business brokers, people buying and selling businesses for a living. I arranged to be the last speaker (better for selling products) and came in time to hear the tail-end of one speaker's presentation and a 50-minute presentation from my platform predecessor. Although both were older and at least one was a professional speaker, neither was being paid.

At the end of their talk, they passed out a few business cards and laid their brochures on a literature table. That was it. I doubt whether either received any business from the day, much less a speaker's fee. In other words, it was a complete waste.

As for me, I negotiated my regular fee for an hour's talk . . . and arranged to have one of my articles (complete with Resource Box, of course) sent to all members of the organization before I arrived (there was no organization newsletter). While no list of participants was available to anyone, I exchanged a free year's subscription to my Sure-Fire Business Success Catalog for a business card . . . and got virtually everyone's.

The man who spoke before me stayed for my talk and watched what I was doing with dismay. Why hadn't he thought of these things!!! Now, of course, it was too late.

The moral of the story? You're not in this business to give talks. You're in this business to sell info-products, as fast as possible. Sure, you want to sell them now. But you also want to sell to the people who aren't ready to buy right this minute. You've got to be prepared for both. You've also got to hit all the people in the organization who didn't come to your program . . . and the chances are there are many more of them.

It's too bad the organization can't pay you . . . but don't roll over and play dead because of it. Be creative! And remember what you are here to do.

- your introduction. If the organization is getting some of the proceeds from sale of your products the day of the program, make sure the person who introduces you says so. Find out if the organization has a useful charitable activity, like a youth camp or scholarship fund. Ask if the money raised from your products this day could go towards that objective, and if it can, make sure this is announced. Thus, "Jeffrey is generously donating half the proceeds from sale of his products to Camp Hiawatha . . . but only if you buy these products today!" This is a very clever — and socially constructive — marketing strategem, since it establishes you as a member of the organization's family and a damned fine person, too. Note: at the end of the day, have the organization tote up how much money they made from your product sales. Then make sure they give you whatever mark of respect and recognition they give to donors at this level. At the very least, make sure your gift is announced in their newsletter. You're entitled!

- autographed copy. Present an autographed copy of one of your products from the platform to either the person who introduced you, to the individual who arranged the meeting or to the chairperson or president of the organization. This is not only a gracious act, it's a smart one; after all, you want a testimonial from this individual after you speak. You also want to be perceived as a generous individual . . . and get at least one of your products into the audience where others can see it. If you're not going to be able to get a list of participants and don't have time to pass a paper around and get people to sign in, consider having a business card drawing. Ask everyone to throw a business card into a hat and select an individual to get a free copy of one of your products. It's a little hokey, but it does get you the names and addresses you need.

- "We've got to cancel the program." What happens if the program has to be cancelled? My own policy is not to charge people a cancellation fee . . . but to work out something mutually beneficial. Thus, instead of forcing them to pay me money for a program they didn't hear . . . I offer them a product distribution agreement and ask them to enclose a flyer at their expense about these products in their next publication . . . perhaps along with one of my articles. Thus, I say, despite the fact that people didn't get the program, at least they can get the info-products that will help them solve their problems. If I've been a good sport about the cancellation (I make sure I am), the organization is usually quite amenable to doing things this way. Moreover, the chance remains that I will be invited back in future . . . when they're better organized! Note: a few months ago I did charge an organization my full fee after they cancelled, but this was an exception. They had previously cancelled a date and when they rescheduled asked me to rearrange another speaking engagement. I told them that if they cancelled this time, they'd have to pay full price, and when they did . . . they did!

Making Contact With The Meeting Planner

Now that you know what you want, it's time to connect with the person who can give it to you . . . the meeting planner. But first a piece of advice: don't tell this person all you want instantly. Sell the benefits of the program first. Then get yourself accepted as a speaker. Finally, negotiate the terms.

This is not a resource about how to get booked as a speaker. I've already written that book, and it's called MONEY TALKS: THE COMPLETE GUIDE TO CREATING A PROFITABLE WORKSHOP OR SEMINAR IN ANY FIELD. I recommend it to you. However, I'd still like to give you a few tips on how to motivate and deal with meeting planners, because if you don't succeed in doing this, you'll miss out on a prime method of selling info-products. Thus, these suggestions:

- Whenever possible, call ahead to find out both the meeting planner's name and title and the theme of the next meeting. Remember, large organizations set their meeting places and often their themes years in advance, and it's not at all unusual to be working on meeting bookings 12-18 months ahead.

- Once you know the theme, consider how you can fit in. Remember, you're a problem solver with solutions expertise.

- Develop a letter which explains to the meeting planner just how what you do fits into the theme of the meeting . . . and will give the participants what they want. Again, focus on benefits. How will the participants be better off as a result of hearing you?

- Provide information on both your speaking skills and products. Include a flyer or promotional information from a recent presentation and a couple of testimonials, if you have them.

- Ask for the opportunity to discuss the meeting with the planner. You need to know just what this planner is looking for and what meeting slots are available.

Now call to follow up.

During your telephone conversation, act like the consummate speaking professional you are. Your ultimate objective, of course, is to sell products — and get a speaker's fee. But, for now, the less said about this the better. Now you need to find out what the meeting planner is attempting to accomplish, what meeting slots are open (keynote speaker, workshop presenter, lunch speaker, *etc.*) so you can make the appropriate suggestion about what you should do, and whether the planner needs any further information from you. You'll probably have to follow up this telephone call with yet another letter based on this conversation and confirming what you and the meeting planner have agreed.

Now keep in touch with the meeting planner. Depending on how many products you have and the size of the organization you're dealing with and the number of people attending your program, you'll make either several hundreds . . . or many *thousands* of dollars from the product sales at just one program. Indeed, I've personally seen top info-entrepreneurs make anywhere between $50,000-$150,000 in just a few *hours* from product sales . . . dwarfing their actual speaking fee. Thus, it pays to stay in touch with the meeting planner who can put you in a position to make this money.

What these people want from you is usually straightforward and reasonable. They want to know you're:

- a good speaker. Have you got something useful to say and will you say it in a way the participants will respond to and benefit from?

- easy to work with. Many speakers are prima donnas . . . a pain in the posterior. The meeting planner wants to make sure you're not one of them.

- understanding of the meeting planner's job . . . and can help him achieve it. Meeting planners are generally overworked and rather stressed, particularly as the meeting approaches. They have rigid deadlines and need the utmost cooperation. Let meeting planners know you understand their business and will give them what they want, when they want it.

By the same token, you want certain things from the meeting planner, including:

- a clear agreement about what each of you does and when you do it. Is it your responsibility to book your own hotel room or his? Are you going to have to arrange the product table or will he do it? This kind of clarity is essential to the organization of a good meeting . . . and to your ability to sell the most products you can as quickly as possible.

- his helpfulness and promptness in responding to your reasonable requests. Many meeting planners, employees of a particular organization, think of speakers, when they think of them at all, as bothersome disturbances. In just the last few months, for instance, I was keynote speaker at a national meeting where no one bothered to tell me about an evening of parties the organization had organized while another organization didn't bother to give me the information on how to get a room in the hotel where I was speaking until all the rooms were booked up. Participants stayed in the hotel . . . I cabbed in from miles away. In short, although speakers are crucial to the success of every meeting, they are often treated as distinctly second-class citizens. You've got to work hard to ensure this doesn't happen to you.

Final Tips On Selling Info-Products Through Talk Programs

Before I leave the subject of how to sell info-products through talk programs, I'd like to share a few techniques with you which you'll find helpful both at and after the meeting.

— At The Meeting

The worst thing you can do at a meeting is be perceived as a sales person. You are at the meeting as a problem solver, not a product seller — officially. Unofficially, of course, you've got to keep your eye on the main objective, selling your products. To achieve just the right balance takes practice, and the earlier you perfect the necessary techniques the better.

- Have the person introducing you, introduce your products. If the organization is benefitting from product sales the day of your talk, the announcer should say so.

- If you are giving a one-hour talk, spend just three minutes at the end talking about your products. Indicate what they are and where they are and (if you don't already have the audience's names and addresses) make sure you indicate what you need from them before they leave. At the end of your talk, don't stand around the podium. As soon as the applause dies, move to your product table. Stay there to answer questions and autograph your books.

- If you are giving a multi-hour workshop presentation, the chances are very good someone in the audience will ask you for further information about your products. Then you can present what you need to do as a service . . . not a sales pitch. Again, during breaks move to the product table and deal with people's questions at that location. By all means, point questioners in the direction of the products you've created that will help them get what they want. If no one asks any questions about your products, take five minutes at the end of the first hour . . . and at the end of the final hour . . . to describe what you've got and how your products help participants. Remember to stress any special inducement you've provided to motivate people to buy today.

Note: don't bring boxes and boxes of your products either with you or ship them ahead. Aim to run out. Here are some rules of thumb I use:

- If I'm part of a group of speakers addressing the same audience, I bring catalogs for everyone . . . but only sample copies of the products. Here my aim is to get information about my products into everyone's hands and get their names and addresses. The real selling will take place via direct response.

- If I'm the sole speaker before a large group of people, I bring catalogs for everyone and get the organization to run the product table. I also bring products enough for 10% of the audience. Here my offer often is that if the prospect buys by the end of the program, I'll give him free shipping. Thus, the organization charges only the retail price. If the organization cannot give me a list of the participants and their addresses, I pass out a flyer indicating that people can get a free one year's subscription to my catalog . . . but only if they return the paper to me *before* I leave. (Using this technique at a San Francisco meeting of dieticians attended by about 1500 people, I received about 1300 responses!)

- If I'm sole speaker before a smallish group of people (under 50), I can run the product table myself; again I bring products for about 10% of those present . . . always ensuring that I get my sales material into the hands of the rest and get their names and addresses, too.

- If I'm giving a workshop where participants already have at least one of my products, I bring sufficient copies of my products so that each person could buy at least one more thing.

And if you run out of products? Be glad! You won't have to lug any extra merchandise home (a real drag), and you can ship out the remainder of the purchases the next business day.

— *After The Meeting*

The purpose of one speaking engagement is to . . . sell more products to both members of the same organization and to get another speaking engagement where you can sell still more products. Here's how you meet these objectives:

- After the meeting, here's what you need to do with the meeting planner. Thank him for all he's done . . . even if what he's done has been mediocre and second-rate (as so often happens). You need this person! (By the way, if the meeting planner has been at all exceptional or helpful, write a testimonial about him to the organization's president. You are well positioned to do this good deed . . . so do it!) Then ask this person for both a written testimonial and a referral to at least one other meeting planner with whom he's good friends. The testimonial should stress how effective your presentation was, how easy you were to work with, and how much money the organization made from product sales. After all, keeping your cost down is one reason others will want you. I need hardly say that you should follow up the referral immediately.

- Begin working with the first meeting planner right away on regional programs . . . and the next annual meeting. If you were good and cost them little, it's very much in their interest to have you back. If they seem reluctant to have you back right away, indicate you would like to work with them again . . . and stay in touch. Often organizations will skip a year or two before inviting you back. Fair enough; your objective is to be part of their extended family.

- Now return to the organization's newsletter editor and suggest . . . more articles by you and more reviews, including a review of your speech or presentation. Ask this person, too, if she knows any other newsletter editors or association personnel. You've shown what you can do; now get referrals so you can do more of it.

Before leaving this section, I'd like to stress just how valuable meetings are for selling info-products and how inept most info-entrepreneurs are at using them. At all times keep your eye on the main chance: the fact that you're doing meetings to sell products (as well as make some money from the speaker's fee). Everything you do must be geared towards making the most product sales before, during and after you speak. Your actual presentation, in short, is merely an episode in the entire sales process. This does not mean, however, that the presentation itself is insignificant. No, indeed. From the platform you must project the exact things you must project in your products: knowledgeability, helpfulness, the ability to solve problems thoroughly, briskly, and well. You must do this in your products; you must do this from the podium. If you do, you'll produce a superior product . . . and be able to sell it from the platform.

Selling Through Your Own Dealer Network

One of the leitmotifs of this book is control . . . your ability to control your environment and profit accordingly. Think how different this is from the lives of most authors and most publishers. Consider the author who visited me the other day. He's written several books, all produced by major publishers. His wife is in a key position at a well-known national radio network. They are, in short, part of the communications establishment. But this author candidly told me that he never makes more than about $10,000 on a book . . . most of that on the advance. I'm dedicating this section to him . . . and to the tens of thousands like him who are at the mercy of other people and have not taken both info-product production and distribution into their own hands.

Once you've decided to assume responsibility for your own products . . . you'll necessarily move as rapidly as possible to the creation of your own dealer network. Why not? Not only should you be selling your own products . . . but you should enlist as many others as you possibly can to sell them, too. Like many other things in this book, you'll no doubt approach the creation and development of your dealer network in stages. That's fine. Just realize that if you're to become a mega-millionaire information impressario, you're going to need people selling your products and using *their* distribution channels to make money for you. As soon as you've come to this conclusion, you'll need to know how to set up such a network.

Keep in mind that a successful dealer program is based on five essential ingredients: useful products, sufficient discounts, creation of a process to identify potential dealers, developing the Dealer Sales Kit, and regular dealer contact and motivation. We have already discussed how you create useful products, so let's take a look at the other four essential ingredients of dealer network success.

Giving Sufficient Discounts

In creating a dealer network, there are essentially two kinds of distributors you must deal with — those who sell directly to customers and those who sell to other dealers who then sell to customers. You must be prepared for both.

— Dealers Who Sell Directly To Customers

To make your products attractive to other dealers, you must give them the discounts they need to market your products and make a profit. In practice, this means you must give dealers a minimum discount of 50% off the retail price. Consider the implications of this discount: 1) you must be able to make a profit at this level (so your product must be priced accordingly), and 2) when you offer this kind of discount, your products will be more attractive for sale by dealers than virtually all of the larger publishers. Their discounts range between 32-44% depending on the number of products purchased.

I regularly receive correspondence from independent publishers who don't understand the financial realities of attracting dealers. Thus, they pattern their discount pricing structures after the larger publishers, who (because of their restrictive and often ludicrous pricing and distribution policies) generally have few dealers selling their books. Offering a dealer a discount of 20% on a single order (as you could well do with a bookstore, for instance) makes no sense. That dealer simply cannot afford to sell your product.

Note: my policy is to give my dealers an even more substantial discount if they buy my products by the case (25 books). They must pay at the time of the order and the products are non-returnable. Here I offer a 60% discount. The dealer pays shipping.

— Wholesalers Who Sell To Dealers Who Then Sell To Customers

From time to time, you'll be in a position to sell a large quantity of books to a wholesaler who has his own dealers who then sell the products directly to the customer. In this chain there are thus four links: the customer, the dealer selling to the customer, the wholesaler selling to the dealer, and you. Except for the customer (who gets the product), each of the remaining links must make a profit. This means cutting the pie very finely indeed. In this case, the wholesaler will want a discount of between 75-80%; he probably gives individual dealers a discount of between 40-60%, depending on how much stock they order. For this kind of situation, you must price your product so that you can still make a profit with a discount of 80% . . . always remembering that the wholesaler may ask you to pay the freight costs, too. In this situation, see if you can still make a profit with a 75% discount off the retail price while paying freight. If you're a good negotiator, you can probably make this deal.

Note: keep in mind that the wholesaler will probably also want two kinds of sales materials from you . . . materials he can use to induce his dealers to buy and materials the dealer can use to get his prospects to buy. We'll be discussing these materials shortly. Always remember, however, just how much your sales case with a wholesaler will be helped if you have the two kinds of marketing materials he needs.

Resource

For many years now, I've done business with one of the best wholesalers in the business, Neal Michaels. Neal is a tough negotiator but fair. He pays cash with his order and runs a tight ship selling how-to info-products. At the very least, write for a copy of his catalog and see if you've got what he wants. Premier Publishers, Inc., P.O. Box 330309, Ft. Worth, TX 76163-0309 (817) 293-7030.

Creating The Process To Identify Potential Dealers

Over the course of the last decade, I've come to an important conclusion about the information product business. It is inhabited by essentially two different kinds of people: those who develop and sell info-products . . . and those who just sell them. It may be that all info-product sellers secretly harbor the desire to become product developers; they probably have instinctive knowledge that that is where the real profits are. Still, for whatever reason, they either can't or won't develop their own products . . . or develop too few of them (and those at the low-price end) to become serious product developers. They are dependent on people like you and me to develop what they want to sell. But, of course, you and I need them to sell it. The real question is: how do we connect?

In fact, there is a tremendous international network of independent info-product distributors. These are people who sell products largely by mail although many also use their workshop and talk programs. Tellingly, almost no major publisher is aware of these people; I don't know of a major publisher who makes any effort to identify them or do business with them. To these grandees, the little guys are just that — little — and as such not worthy of a second thought or glance. You and I just can't think this way. While an extra few hundred or even few thousand dollars a week may mean nothing to the McGraw-Hills of the world, I think you'd agree such sums could make a nice difference in your lifestyle. They are yours for the taking . . . but first you have to connect with the dealer prospects and persuade them to carry your products.

Connecting with these people is *not* difficult. There are literally scores of (particularly) mail order publications in existence read by dealers craving products. Some of these publications are periodicals; some are directories. Here are some leads to the best that exist. Get on their mailing lists, read their publications and use their services.

- Donald R. Blum, Editor, *Savannah Business Journal*, 2517 Abercorn St., Savannah, GA 31401-9172 (912) 236-6325

- Bill S. Booth, *Wisdom for Wealth*, Infopreneur Services, 3755 Avocado Blvd., Suite 110, La Mesa, CA 91941 (619) 561-8539 ext. 114

- Barbara Brabec, *National Home Business Report*, P.O. Box 2137, Naperville, IL 60567

- John Cali, Jr., President, *BottomLine Digest*, Great Western Pubishing Company, 778 Manor Ridge Road, Santa Paula, CA 93060-1651 (805) 933-2317

- Gery Carson, Publisher, *Mail Profits*, P.O. Box 4785, Lincoln, NE 68504 (402) 434-8480

- Jerry Cianciolo, Editor, *Contributions*, 634 Commonwealth Ave., Suite 201, Newton Centre, MA 02159 (617) 964-2688. The only publication on my list specializing in non-profit organizations.

- Bruce David, *Starting Smart*, 230 Clay St., Kane, PA 16735 (800) 837-6522

- Gary Davis, *Idea Digest*, GD Services, P.O. Box 80, Foyil, OK 74031

- Ted Estey, Publisher, and Denise Estey, Editor, *Emerald Coast News*, P.O. Box 190, Niceville, FL 32588-0190 (904) 729-7979

- Gary M. Haiser, *Personal Wealth News*, 8535 Bay Meadows Rd., Suite 25, Jacksonville, FL 32256

- Stan Holden, Editor, *Spare Time* Magazine, Box 1456, Evanston, IL 60204

- Russell R. Hunter, Niagara Promotions, Box 79515, Hamilton, Ontario, Canada L8T 5A2

- Keith Laggos, Publisher, *Money Maker's Monthly*, 643 Executive Dr., Willowbrook, IL 60521

- Phil Longenecker, President, *Cutting Edge Opportunities Magazine*, 1250 Ridge Road, Elizabethtown, PA 17022 (717) 361-9007

- Mrs. H.C. McGarity, Editor, *Working at Home*, P.O. Box 200504, Cartersville, GA 30120

- John K. Moreland, *The Dream Merchant*, 2309 Torrance Blvd., Suite 201, Torrance, CA 90501 (310) 328-1925

- Tom Muraso, TNT Books, P.O. Box 681519, Miami, FL 33168 (407) 686-8765

- Gary N G, Publisher, *Mail 'N Profits Magazine*, 39 Bowery St., Box 919, New York, NY 10002 (212) 406-8050, ext. 2

- Bob Riemke, Editor, *The Real Entrepreneur*, 806 King's Row, Cohutta, GA 30170 (706) 694-8441

- Anne Root, Publisher, *Home Biz*, 1508, 3600 Brenner Dr., N.W., Calgary, Alberta, Canada T2L 1Y2 (403) 282-0509

- Ed Simpson, *Home Business News*, 12221 Beaver Pike, Jackson, OH 45640

- Bob Teague, Teague Publishing Group, P.O. Box 14705, Dayton, OH 45414

- Joseph Vitale, Awareness Publications, P.O. Box 300792, Houston, TX 77230-0792 (713) 434-2845

- Annette Walker, Walker's Publications, 12 Westerville Sq., #147, Westerville, OH 43081

- Bruce Young, *Mail Order Messenger*, Route 1, Box 13, P.O. Box 358, Middleton, TN 38052 (901) 376-1570

These individuals (many of them publishing several periodicals) will:

- publish media releases and ads seeking dealers;
- give you the names and addresses of dealers seeking products; and/or
- provide an opportunity to publish your articles . . . with Resource Boxes.

Moreover, by carefully reading both the ads and news columns in these publications, you'll get leads to new publications and new dealers . . . and be able to take advantage of helpful articles by a wide variety of product promotion experts (including me!). Without them, you'll have a very difficult time establishing any kind of meaningful dealer network.

A Tribute

Over the course of many years, I've developed wonderful professional relationships with most of these people; they are a crucial part of the system that I'm describing to you in this book. They publish my articles; they feature my books and sell my products. I am proud to take this opportunity to salute them as honorable business people and grateful to call them my friends. I hope you seize this chance to know and work with them. They all have much to offer.

Note: I hope I need not say that you should also use your own catalog as a means of generating dealers. Take a look at the Sure-Fire Business Success Catalog in the back of this book. There's an item there I use to identify new dealers and, a secondary benefit, keep in touch with existing dealers. I advise you to use your catalog similarly.

Developing The Dealer Sales Kit

Identifying dealers is no good unless you can convince them to become *your* dealers. That's why you need a convincing Dealer Sales Kit. This kit has one purpose and one purpose only: persuading a dealer he absolutely must sell your products . . . NOW!

Like all sales materials, your kit needs to lead with benefits and follow with features. Now, while you may meet the odd information fanatic who sells info-products merely for the good they'll do the world (yes, such people do exist), on the whole most people are in this business for two reasons: they can make money and they can set their own hours. Thus, your dealer sales kit must stress each of these benefits . . . as specifically as possible.

Dealing with the latter point (flexible hours) really doesn't take much effort. Dealing with the former (the money) does. How do you know how much money anyone can make selling your products when you're just starting out?

Well, first you consider your own track record. Second, you can stay in close touch with your dealers to see how well they're doing. Why, just this week one of my dealers made over $10,000 selling some of my products at one of his workshops. Getting a testimonial from him shouldn't be too difficult . . .

There are other things dealer prospects want to know, too, including:

- descriptions of your products. Exactly what are they selling and why are these products better.

- media and user testimonials. Have both users and critics said good things about what your new dealers will be selling?

- promotion support you provide. Are you running ads or articles? Do you keep pestering media sources for reviews and feature stories and keep getting great press? Your dealers want to know.

- price and stock guarantees. Dealers dread the possibility you'll raise your prices without telling them (leaving them with outmoded sales material or less profit) . . . or inconvenience their customers by having long periods without stock. Thus, guarantee your prices through a certain date (a year ahead is a good idea), and let them know you keep your products in stock. (By the way, the big publishers are very bad on both these points which is a nagging source of inconvenience to anyone carrying their products. In fairness, some of the smaller publishers are not much better. I just heard from small one publisher the other day who raised the price on one of the items in my catalog after failing to respond to my questionnaire about whether he'd do just that. I pointed out how inconvenient this was . . . and he did get me a stay of execution until the next catalog comes out.)

- prompt shipping. Dealers fret that their orders aren't shipped promptly. Reassure them. When you open a regular UPS account, your packages will be picked up daily. This means no one in the nation has to wait more than five days for one of your products to arrive.

- your ability to handle their credit card orders. Mail order dealers around America generally find it very difficult to get a local bank to give them a MasterCard and VISA merchant account. If you can't accept credit card orders, however, it will cut your sales. Thus, if you can accept credit card orders for your dealers, this is a real plus. (Here's an interesting look at this problem. During the writing of this chapter, I decided to call my local Cambridge bank to see if they'd open an MC/VISA account for one of my New Jersey mail order clients who was having trouble getting a local merchant account, despite having annual sales approaching a half million dollars. My banker said ordinarily he wouldn't accept an out-of-state account but that since he knew me and since I vouched for the company, he would. And you know . . . after a year of fruitless search in New Jersey, my client was able to open a Cambridge account the very day I talked to my banker. Don't tell me networking doesn't help. If you're having trouble with your banker, try a little networking yourself.)

All these things are important to dealers. But there's another category of items that's probably even more important: the sales materials they need to convince their prospects to buy your products and guidelines on how to use them.

Developing The Dealer Sales Kit

Did you like syllogisms in college? Well, here's one for you. Most people are lousy marketers. Most dealers are people. Most dealers are lousy marketers. Whether you accept my syllogism as an apt representation of the art or not, at least accept my conclusion, for most dealers *are* lousy marketers. That's why you need to create all the sales materials *they* need . . . and use these materials as yet another lever persuading them to become dealers for you. These materials need to be in your Dealer Sales Kit. This kit should include:

- a cover letter from you to the dealer explaining your trade policies and discounts;

- several examples of classified and small space ads both soliciting inquiries and selling your merchandise direct;

- at least two illustrations of sales cover letters, one to be sent to someone who has inquired about the product(s) and the second to someone who has not;

- an upgrade letter to a customer who has bought one of your products but could buy other, related products.

Let's take a look at each of these items.

A Cover Letter To The Dealer Explaining Your Trade Policies And Discounts

For this category, you actually need two letters: one you'll be sending to a prospect attempting to motivate him to become a dealer, the second to someone who has in fact decided to become a dealer. Both letters are related and may contain much similar language. You should, however, be aware that you'll need two. In any event, include with this letter:

- complete descriptions of your info-products;

- details on your in-house promotional efforts that assist the dealer;

- a description of the dealer marketing materials you have available;

- your trade, purchase quantity and discount terms;

- how you handle credit card orders;

- how you handle shipping;

- how you handle dealer and customer returns.

It should go without saying that if you have an offer motivating the dealer to sign up faster (I use one of my sixty-minute audio cassettes if a dealer signs up within thirty days of my letter to him), display it prominently.

I think by now you're fairly familiar with most of these items, except, perhaps, for dealer and customer returns. You need a policy not only on whether dealers can return their stock to you . . . but also what happens if a customer returns a product to you that's been sold to him by a dealer. As far as returns are concerned, this has always been a very small problem for me. I'm either drop-shipping merchandise for dealers who send their check or credit card information or selling them merchandise by the case with a better discount but on a non-returnable basis. Hence, no problem. I advise you to handle your dealer business similarly . . . most info-producers do.

If a customer returns a product to me that he's bought from a dealer (this happens because my name and address appear in all the products), I write the customer and ask whom he purchased the product from and tell him I cannot refund his money until I know; after all, I say, he didn't buy the product from *me* but from a dealer. The customer will ordinarily respond to this letter! When he does, as a service to my dealer, I'm willing to refund the complete retail price (I don't refund shipping costs) and ask the dealer for the extra 50% I've just paid. There has never been a problem getting the dealer to pay up, either; after all, I control the merchandise!

It goes without saying that this letter . . . and the cover letter you send to your new dealer . . . should be available on your computer. But then you already know that!

Several Examples Of Classified And Small Space Ads Both Soliciting Inquiries And Selling Your Merchandise Direct

Dealers need both classified ad copy . . . and camera-ready space ads, and you've got to produce them. Complete details on how to create and use these ads lie outside the scope of this book; for these you need CASH COPY and MONEY MAKING MARKETING! Here, however, are a few guidelines:

- You should never try to sell a product direct from a classified ad. The purpose of a classified ad is to elicit an inquiry and to follow up with your sales materials.

- Classified ads should be as short as possible . . . not a word longer than you need to get the prospect to respond. Remember, you are paying by the word!

- Most publications have a minimum price for classified ads; this price is the equivalent of a ten-word ad. Thus, you should aim to produce all your ads in exactly ten words, including your address.

- Classified ads are composed of the following parts: audience identifier (who you're selling to) + benefit they get + offer that gets them to respond immediately.

- To write a classified ad, first write a sentence embodying these three parts. Thus: "Small business people — make money by getting a free subscription to Jeffrey Lant's 350+ item Sure-Fire Business Success Catalog. Request it by writing 50 Follen St., Suite 507, Cambridge, MA 02138." This is 32 words, over three times your space allocation. Now begin turning these 32 words into a tight ad that loses nothing in reduction.

- Work from end of the ad, the address, to the front. Thus: "JLA, 50 Follen, #507, Cambridge, MA 02138." This is either six or seven words (depending on whether the publication counts the state and zip as one or two words; different publications have different policies about this.)

- Add your offer: "free subscription";

- Add your benefit: "business success".

Note: in this case, there's no need to add an explicit audience identifier because it is implicit in the words "business success". Too, the kind of publication the ad runs in might explicitly limit the audience. Don't use (and pay for) words unless you must.

Put it all together: "Free business success subscription JLA/a, 50 Follen #507, Cambridge, MA 02138." 10 words, if the state and zip are counted as one word.

And what is the "/a" after the company name? It's a code indicating the month and publication in which this ad ran. You need to know this so you can decide if investing in this publication made sense.

Now write up several of these classifieds. There are a couple of reasons for this: 1) you want your dealers to have a choice; 2) you don't want several dealers to run the same ad in the same publication; 3) you need to see which ad draws best.

As far as space ads are concerned, they work similarly. Some things are different, however:

- with a space ad, you may be trying to sell direct, not just elicit an inquiry;
- the benefits to the purchaser must be crystal-clear;
- there must be an immediate reason for action now;
- space ads must be available in standard sizes and with camera-ready art.

Of these points, perhaps only the last needs additional comment. What your dealers are looking for from you is camera-ready art in standard sizes. These sizes include the following three widths: 2 1/4", 4 1/2", 7 1/2" and run in depth from 1 inch through 10 inches.

Obviously, the Lant rule of thumb is to use the smallest size ad (and cost) to accomplish the job. I suggest you create at least six different ads in three sizes. In each size have one space ad soliciting inquiries and one to make the immediate sale. This allows your dealer a wide range of choice. Try the following standard sizes:

- 1" x 2 1/4"
- 2" x 2 1/4"
- 2" x 4 1/2"

This will do for a start.

In addition to these smaller sizes, you're also going to need an 8 1/2" x 11" ad. While this gets used mostly as an insert piece, some dealers will also want to run it as a space ad from time to time. So at least make sure you tell them about it.

At Least Two Sales Cover Letters, One To Be Sent To Someone Who Has Inquired About The Products And The Second To Someone Who Has Not

There are two kinds of prospects in the world: people who have told you they're a prospect and those who haven't . . . but whom you've decided are. Your dealers are going to be dealing with both . . . so be prepared!

You need a cover letter your dealer can send to a prospect who has responded to an ad. This letter should include:

- include an offer for an immediate response;
- one benefit piled on another about the info-product;

- testimonials from both satisfied customers and reputable media sources;

- a post script reinforcing the immediate reason for action.

Obviously, this letter — as all sales materials — must use graphic devices designed to emphasize key points. One of the problems with much of the dealer material I see is not only that it's second-rate in content but visually mediocre and unappealing.

Note: along with this sales letter, you may like to design a single 8 1/2" x 11" flyer (one- or two-sided) detailing the contents of the product. This flyer is, of course, a sales piece, but, unlike the most hard-driving cover letter, it is designed to tell prospects just what the product contains. If your product sells for over $30, it's probably a good idea to develop this piece.

Frankly, the letter you send to someone who has answered your ad and the one you send to someone who hasn't are very similar. The real difference comes in the opening sentences. A person who has told you he wants the benefit is obviously a stronger prospect than the person you think wants it. Make sure you use this knowledge. Thus: "So, you want to learn how to cash in on Greater Washington, D.C. real estate!" would be a perfectly appropriate opening for someone having answered an ad. It's a tad too strong for someone whose interest is as yet unknown. This person needs this kind of opening: "Real estate in Greater Washington, D.C. appreciated 22% last year. If you didn't get this kind of return on your other investments, isn't it time to learn how you can profit from what's happening in your own back yard?"

An Upgrade Letter To A Customer Who Has Bought One Of Your Products But Could Buy Other, Related Products

One of the crazy things I've noticed about the literally hundreds of dealers I deal with is how retarded most are about making upgrade sales. They seem to think — like most "marketers" — that once you've sold a prospect a product that's the end of the transaction. Nothing could be further from the truth. Just as I was writing this section, in fact, I received a telephone call from one of my customers in Libertyville, Illinois. Only a few days ago I sent him his first order . . . with an upgrade letter. Within 72 hours he called back to buy something else, something else I told him could help him achieve what he wants to achieve. Are you doing this?

I think the reason most info-entrepreneurs aren't using the upgrade system is that they: 1) don't have enough related products and 2) don't have the computer capability so they can easily create the letters they need. What folly!

Whether you have to upgrade your customers with one or more of your info-products or with products produced by others, at least try to sell them more immediately. And make sure you help your dealers upgrade *their* customers, too. Thus develop a computer-generated letter that:

- thanks the customer for his first purchase;

- tells him he made a wise decision;

- reminds him what this purchase will help him accomplish;

- presents information about another product (or products) that will also assist him;

- makes him an offer about how to get them at a special price, and

- urges him to act immediately.

Your job is to position your customer's mind . . . to move him in the direction you want him to go . . . the direction which will also benefit him. What's more you must move your customer quickly, at the very time he is focusing on the problem you can help him solve. You want to make these upgrade sales . . . your dealer wants to make them, too . . . if only you show him how he can.

Note: you need to make a decision about whether you'll charge people to become dealers and get your materials . . . or whether you'll simply give your kits away free. Personally, I charge my dealers a one-time only fee of $75. This entitles them to represent my products, get all the materials discussed above, and purchase my products at dealer discounts. I set this fee for several reasons:

- many people say they're going to be dealers, but only want to get products at the discount prices without bothering to promote them to anyone. The fee discourages them;

- people who pay the fee are going to be more serious about my products and work harder to represent them . . . which is what I really want, and

- the monies generated from the fees pay for the time and trouble it takes me to create the dealer materials. In other words, dealer fees make this project self-supporting.

Has there been grumbling about the fee? Of course. You can't please all the people all the time. I'm sensitive, however, to dealers with an established track record who don't want to pay the fee . . . and to those who are just looking for a cheap way of getting my products. I therefore generally waive the $75 fee for well-established dealers and others who can convince me they are serious about selling my products and can sell them in volume. In general, however, I don't think the small fee I charge is too much to pay for what the dealers get. The bellyaching of a few would-be "dealers" hasn't changed my mind!

Regular Dealer Contact And Motivation

Once you've got a dealer, you make money by staying in regular touch with him . . . helping him sell more, encouraging and motivating him. This is part of your job. One way of staying in regular touch is through your catalog: have items of interest for your dealers; announce the availability of new sales materials and marketing aids. Too, send out regular mailings and marketing tip sheets to your dealers as materials become available. As for me, I'm constantly pushing, prodding, complimenting, urging my dealers in a series of short notes to them as their orders come in.

What you must communicate to your dealers, who too often have a "get rich quick" mentality, is that selling info-products is a good way of making money . . . if they follow a system, the system outlined in this book. This system must be worked daily. Those who expect instant oceans of money are bound to be disappointed. Those, however, who are willing to learn the business and use the tricks of the trade can make money. This is the message you must regularly communicate to your dealers along with the procedures and materials they need to implement it.

Remember, many dealers get easily discouraged, especially if they expected to be millionaires by next Thursday. Your job is to tell the truth, poke, prod and enthuse, while making sure they continue to bring your info-products to their markets. You're the wagon master now, and if you expect to get to the promised land, it's your job to keep these little dogies going. Ghee-up!

Selling To Bookstores, Selling To Libraries

Given the fact that most people think first about bookstores and libraries as obvious markets for books, when, then, have I stuck this section towards the end of a chapter towards the end of this book? There is, dear reader, a very good reason: this is the priority they deserve in your master plan.

As we start this section, let me make a couple of things perfectly plain:

1. You can find my books in both bookstores and libraries nationwide;

2. I count on a certain amount of revenue from bookstores and libraries, just as all smart publishers do;

3. I devote a certain amount of attention to both preserving and augmenting this income;

4. My info-business is in no way dependent on either bookstore or library sales . . . in other words, I would continue to prosper (if a little less quickly) if I never sold another product to a library or bookstore. Ever.

These sentiments represent both a positioning statement and a bias. I do not necessarily expect you to share either, but I hope you will understand both. The clear focus of this book is on developing an info-empire that you control . . . that places you in direct contact with your buyers and enables — indeed forces — you to do everything necessary to identify, motivate and serve those buyers. When you enter the murky depths of bookstore and library distribution, you lose this kind of control . . . because you will have to work with and through others, others who will not always share your business probity, efficiency and organization. In this world, you'll find many people who:

- won't pay you promptly . . . indeed, some who feel no obligation to pay you at all;

- keep your products for months on end . . . and then return them in deplorable condition;

- feel affronted when you ask for details on what they're doing to sell your books and don't want your advice about how to do things better;

- want you to stay small and dependent;

- are rude and ill-mannered, virtually as a matter of policy;

- never return a phone call or answer a letter . . . until they need stock;

- ask for steep discounts in return for laughable marketing efforts;

- are only too anxious to take over the accounts you've already developed . . . but seem helpless about establishing new accounts themselves.

And, as they say, much, much more.

Selling to bookstores and libraries is, therefore, not for the idealistic, the faint of heart, or the uninitiated. These people lose their shirts . . . or worse. What I want you to keep in mind, therefore, as you read this section is that I'm sharing these guidelines with you for a reason. If they seem defensive, it's because they are. They're designed to help you make maximum sales in the shortest period of time, giving up the least conceivable amount of discount, and exposing yourself to the least amount of bad debt. If you can succeed in achieving these objectives, your time selling to bookstores and libraries will be profitable and (relatively) painless. Having said this, let's begin with selling to bookstores.

Selling To Bookstores

There are several things to keep in mind when selling to bookstores and to the distributors that cater to bookstores:

1. A large percentage have significant cash-flow and financial problems.

2. While many are perfectly happy to sell your merchandise, rather fewer are equally happy to pay for it promptly and efficiently.

3. You'll be dealing with some perfectly wonderful people, bright, well-spoken, intelligent, whose business ethics constantly teeter on the brink of thievery.

Here are the steps to profit in this world.

Selling Direct Versus Selling Through Bookstore Distributors

There are essentially two ways to sell to bookstores . . . either you can represent your own products to them handling all business matters . . . or you can persuade a bookstore distributor to represent you within a territory (regional or national) in return for a percentage of gross sales. Let's take a look at the pros and cons of each.

— Representing Your Own Titles To Bookstores

To represent your titles to bookstores successfully, you must remember three major things: 1) it's very time-consuming; 2) it's a lot of work; 3) it can be very frustrating. Nonetheless, since getting a reputable distributor can be very difficult nowadays, this may be the road you're forced to take. Thus, you must understand what bookstores want from you and must learn the tricks of the trade to limit your exposure.

Bookstores want:

- a minimum discount of 40%;

- fast shipping by you;

- liberal credit terms (meaning they pay in 90 to 120 days or more);

- the right to return a book for cash within 11 months if they've paid for but haven't sold it;

- evidence that your books are good sellers in bookstores, and

- proof that you're promoting them feverishly.

This is what they *want!*

While you may be able to (and indeed should) bend these policies with smaller, independent bookstores, I warn you to expect no mercy with the chain stores (B Dalton and Waldenbooks) that control approximately half the retail book trade. These stores tell you exactly what they will and won't do . . . and the sad fact is that with only a book or two, you probably won't be able to sell your products to them . . . unless you work through a distributor.

For their purposes, your volume of business is just too low, and your ability to promote your products too meager. While this is undoubtedly disappointing news, keep two things in mind: you can easily become a mega-millionaire in the info-product business *without* the chain stores . . . and you *will* be able to get access to them as your own product line develops . . . or if you secure representation through a competent, aggressive distributor.

This doesn't mean that you should abandon the chain stores altogether. Call and ask for the name of the buyer handling books like yours, and get their current discount rates, policies and procedures. While all the chains are listed in *American Book Trade Directory* (see below), the two you must contact are:

- B Dalton Bookseller, One Corporate Center, 7505 Metro Blvd., Minneapolis, MN 55435 (612) 893-7000

- Waldenbooks, 201 High Ridge Rd., Stamford, CT 06905 (203) 352-2000

Note: if the chains are willing to buy your book, don't let them go overboard on the first order. Have them purchase a few hundred copies and see how fast they sell; if you can, advise them on the areas where you think your book will do best. The worst thing for you is to have the chains make a large, enthusiastic order for a book that doesn't sell. You can then count on having a mountain of damaged returns that you'll have trouble disposing of. It's better to go slow . . . but be sure. I know you think this won't happen to your baby . . . but it's happened to plenty of others, so please take note.

Given what I've said about the chain stores, this discussion must focus on independent bookstores and the distributors that serve them. To make money from these bookstores and distributors, here are the steps to take:

- get an ISBN and get yourself listed in *Books In Print;*

- give each book a bar code;

- determine your discount and returns policy;

- work out your payment terms;

- develop a list of bookstore and distributor prospects;

- create your marketing plan;

- develop your sales materials;

- implement your plan . . . integrate bookstore and distributor selling into your daily life;

- keep checking stock . . . and building relationships.

Let's look at each of these objectives.

Get An ISBN And Get Yourself Listed In *Books In Print*

The first thing to do to sell to bookstores and libraries is get a standard identification number for each of your books. Called an ISBN for International Standard Book Number, this is the unique identifier for each of your books . . . including each *new* edition. Remember, this number is as important — perhaps even more important — than your book's title to bookstores and distributors. You get both the number and helpful background information about ISBN from R.R. Bowker, ATTN International Standard Book Numbering, 245 W. 17th St., New York, NY 10011 (212) 337-6971.

Secondly, get yourself listed in *Books In Print*. Again, you'll be working with the folks at R. R. Bowker Co. This time you must fill out the Advance Book Information forms which you also get from the above address.

Determine Your Discount And Returns Policy

Bookstores and wholesale distributors make money from the difference on the retail price of your product and what you charge them for it. Your discount policy is therefore of the utmost interest to them. Too, in case they don't sell a book . . . or a customer who originally wanted it changes his mind . . . they also need to know under what circumstances they can return it to you. The numbers I'm about to give you are suggestive, not set in cement. But they work for me.

Number of Books Ordered	Discount
1-4	20%
4-10	30%
10-50	40%
50-75	42%
75-200	46%
200+	50%

Freight, of course, is additional.

As far as returns are concerned, I let both bookstores and wholesalers know that books are not returnable. They may be exchanged up to 11 months after the sale for other merchandise and a credit, if applicable. If, however, the book was defective or damaged in transit and the customer no longer wants it, I'll be happy to refund the money under these circumstances.

Note: the information I've supplied above is not, I repeat, not universal. Different publishers have different discount schedules. For instance, if your book is being used as a classroom textbook and the bookstore has to do nothing more than take the order, you're at perfect liberty to have what is called "short" discount rates; in this case, you might give the bookstore a discount of just 20% . . . no matter how many books they buy. After all, they didn't have to do much, did they?

Work Out Your Payment Terms

While there are many problems with bookstores and distributors (lackadaisical and uneducated personnel, disorganization and sloth), what galls most of us in the book business is just how cavalier so many of them are about payment . . . as if it were *noblesse oblige* to give us our money. Thus, if you want your money, you need to play a defensive game.

Therefore, if an independent bookstore or smaller regional distributor orders one or two copies of your books, by all means ask for payment in advance. Indeed, some publishers give a discount of 50% for books on a cash-in-advance, non-returnable basis. I like this system because it gets you the cash you need and avoids the hassles you don't. If you don't feel comfortable asking for payment in advance the first time (you'll get over that quick enough), then you may certainly extend credit. The usual terms are net 60, although they are more often honored in the breach. If you can't seem to get payment promptly (or at all!), then switch to a payment-in-advance system. Personally, I use all my options selectively. The publishing newsletters are fairly good about reporting which distributors are egregiously behind in their payments (and some are notorious for ripping off the uninitiated). With these distributors, it's strictly cash on the barrelhead . . . and no returns.

Note: many wholesalers and bookstores now have company credit cards. When they call in an order, see if they can pay for it immediately. Why should you have to extend credit, if you don't have to? Money in your hand today is always worth more than money in your hand tomorrow. Under no circumstances, assume that all the people who want to sell your books will pay for them. Extend small amounts of credit, and see if your good faith is abused. Personally, I have very few credit problems with bookstores and wholesalers because I monitor the situation closely and do not let these organizations, which are quite capable of abusing the situation, do so. Take heed!

Note: if you've been in business at least a year and have published at least three books, you'll want to be listed in the *ABA Book Buyers' Handbook*. Published annually by the American Booksellers Association, it has two purposes: 1) it lists participating publishers, wholesalers, and distributors giving their trade and discount policies, and 2) it enables booksellers to send you a STOP check along with their order. STOP is the "Single Title Order Plan". If you're a publisher listed in the handbook, a bookseller can check your discount policies and send you a check along with their order. This check will either be blank, allowing you to fill in the correct amount for a single purchase, or will give the bookseller's best estimate on your product's price with shipping. Either way, you get your money immediately and won't have to bother with invoicing and collections. It's therefore very much to your interest to participate in this program. Thus, no later than March in any year, write the ABA (Att: *ABA Book Buyers' Handbook*), 137 W. 25th St., New York, NY 10001 or call either (800) 637-0037 or (212) 463-8450. Ask for the necessary forms so you can be included. The book itself comes out in about November after which it's distributed to ABA members.

Develop A List Of Bookstore And Distributor Prospects

Before you can deal with bookstores and distributors, you've got to know where they are and develop a list of prospects. To do this for your local area, of course, you can use the Yellow Pages. Beyond your local area, you need the *American Book Trade Directory,* published by the R.R. Bowker Company, 245 W. 17th St., New York, NY 10011. This detailed volume lists retailers and antiquarians in the United States and Canada; wholesalers of books and magazines, and specialists in the book trade. Given that it has nearly 1800 pages in very small type, you can gauge just how thorough it is! In fact, I don't see how you could possibly market your own products to bookstores and wholesalers without using this volume . . . unless you planned to stay just in your own back yard. Of course, staying in your own back yard makes sense . . . at the beginning and until you learn the ropes.

One of the problems with new info-entrepreneurs is that they try to be McGraw-Hill immediately. Frankly, with all facets of this business, and uncertainty in your relations with bookstores and distributors, I urge you to start small and to learn the ins and outs. Then, by all means, expand. One of the worst things that can happen to a new info-entrepreneur is to expand too quickly . . . before he really understands the business. Disaster is usually just a step behind.

Thus, my advice to you is:

- Start familiarizing yourself with local bookstores. Visit every bookstore in your area and check its stock of how-to books. Using this method, you'll discover that certain bookstores are really not prospects for you. You'll also discover those which are.

- Call those bookstores you've decided are prospects and ask for the name of the buyer in your product area. You're developing a prospect list of individuals who could buy your books and with whom you need to develop a relationship.

- Log this information so you have it readily available. While it is certainly true that at many bookstores buyers change rapidly, you're always going to need to deal with the buyer. You might as well get your system together so you always have these names at your fingertips.

Create Your Marketing Plan

Your marketing plan is simply a statement of what you intend to do to get your products into bookstores and bring them to the attention of wholesalers, when you intend to do these things, and what marketing materials you'll need to accomplish these objectives. Given that you'll be marketing both locally and outside your local area, I think it makes perfect sense to divide your marketing plan into two parts: Local and Beyond.

After you secure the names of local prospects, here is what you must accomplish with them:

- send introductory letter and marketing materials;
- follow up with telephone call;
- schedule the sales presentation;
- make the sales presentation;
- follow-up the sales presentation appropriately.

Beyond your local area, you'll probably just:

- send an introductory letter with supporting marketing materials;
- follow up with a telephone call.

Develop Your Sales Materials

As soon as you've drafted your plan, you'll know just what kinds of marketing materials to develop. Remember, here as elsewhere, the objective is to create a plan, to integrate your computer into the efficient achievement of that plan, and to work the plan continually.

The sales materials you need include:

- a detailed description of each book;
- testimonial and media comments about each book;
- a sheet with information about your discount rates, payment due date, shipping, and returns, and
- an order form.

In addition, you need:

- a letter introducing yourself and your products and saying you'll be in touch shortly to schedule an appointment to present your products. (You'll use this with local buyers).
- a letter introducing your products to buyers you won't be meeting with personally but will be following up by phone;
- a letter to buyers you haven't been able to connect with personally;
- a stock-checking letter asking a buyer to see how many of your books are available and to reorder if necessary (this letter can double as an order form). All the buyer has to do is add how many books he wants and return to you immediately).

Note: it's also a good idea to develop a testimonial letter filled with user and media quotations about your book(s). This can be sent both to buyers who haven't yet stocked your books . . . and to those who have, along with a request to check their stock.

Another Note: if you intend to do media promotion in selected cities, you'll also want a letter advising bookstore buyers when you'll be in town, what media will be featuring you, and how to get books promptly.

Implement Your Plan . . . Integrate Bookstore Selling Into Your Daily Life

Remember, for your plan to be successful you not only need to know what to do . . . but have a precise idea of how many times daily you'll be doing it. I suggest you make some combination of at least five letter and/or telephone connections with prospects daily. This may seem like a small number to you when you're starting out . . . but I assure you that over the course of a year, it mounts up to a truly significant number. "Day in, day out" marketing is the only kind of marketing that makes sense!

Keep Checking Stock . . . And Building Relationships

The entire thrust of this book has been to create a product from which you can draw income for life by seizing an important problem-solving topic and developing a product from which you can profit both when it is first available and from its periodic updates. Think how powerful this is! Are you still making money from the work you did a decade ago? Or did you do the work, get the money, and spend it . . . forcing yourself into an endlessly repetitive cycle based on the sale of your labor? When you create info-products that truly meet people's needs and work hard to create the distribution channels that regularly bring your solutions (in product form) to their attention, you break this cycle . . . and profit accordingly. But to do this, you must build long-term relationships with people who will regularly buy . . . and sell . . . your products.

Obviously, it takes time, lots of time, to identify bookstores and distributors who could carry your products . . . and lots more time to get them to listen to you and stock your products. Thus, when you break through and get your products accepted, congratulate yourself. You've done something good.

Next, write a genuine and enthusiastic thank-you letter to the buyer who has taken your products . . . even if he's only been willing to do so on a straight commission basis. It's at least a start. Tell this person just how grateful you are . . . *and mean it!*

Then stay in touch . . . send periodic updates with user and media comments; call to check stock . . . ask what the buyer thinks will help him sell more of what you're offering. In short, develop a relationship. Over the course of many years, I've developed excellent relationships with many buyers . . . people I've never actually met but connect with regularly. Do the same. So long as your books sell reasonably well, they'll be happy to keep stocking them . . . and when your products only sell reasonably well, the relationship you have with the buyer may, in the final analysis, prove to be the pivotal reason why your products are retained on the shelf while others are sent back to their disappointed producers.

A Few Particular Words About Wholesalers

So far, the discussion has focused largely on bookstores. A few words about wholesalers are, however, in order. Unlike bookstores which sell direct to consumers, wholesalers sell largely to bookstores and libraries. Whatever they say to the contrary, most seem to be fairly passive about stimulating orders. That is, they are quite happy to fulfill orders when a bookstore or library requests materials . . . but they don't do a lot of what's necessary to stimulate the order. As a result, you should:

- send wholesalers information about your books so that they at least know what you've got available;

- include flyers and other marketing materials about your products in the packages you send them, and

- most importantly, cut your wholesaler discount.

While the first two points are obvious, the third isn't.

Although no wholesaler will appreciate what I'm about to say, say it I shall; after all, *you're* my client! Unless you secure evidence that wholesalers are promoting your books in a way that justifies giving them a better discount, only give them 20% off the retail price. I have never understand the logic that says I must give a dealer a 40% discount (or more) because *Booklist* has favorably reviewed one of my books and an individual library has decided to order through a wholesaler rather than from me directly. Keep this important point in mind as it could be worth literally tens of thousands of dollars to you as your business grows.

Note: while you'll be dealing with literally dozens of wholesalers and distributors, two are worth particular mention because of their size and importance in the industry. With these two, you must stay in close touch and do everything possible to maintain good relations. They are:

- Ingram Distribution Group, 1125 Heil Quaker Blvd., LaVergne, TN 77230-0792 (615) 793-5000

- the four regional locations of Baker & Taylor, including:

  — Eastern Div., 50 Kirby Ave., Somerville, NJ 08876 (908) 722-8000

  — Midwestern Div., 501 S. Gladiolus St., Momence, IL 60954 (815) 472-2444

  — Southern Div., Mount Olive Road, Commerce, GA 30599 (404) 335-5000

  — Western Div., 380 Edison Way, Reno, NV 89564 (702) 786-6700

A Personal Vignette

When I was just starting out in the book business, I knew nothing about the things I've just been sharing with you. I did, however, remember the stripper's advice from "Gypsy" and knew I had to have a gimmick.

About the time I needed to begin opening bookstore accounts, I made friends with a waiter who wanted to supplement his night job by earning a little money during the day. I asked if he wanted to sell some books to local bookstores, and he agreed. Neither of us knew what we were getting into . . .

Jim Bacchi, however, had an impressario's flair, and he came up with the idea of a T-shirt with a picture of my book THE CONSULTANT'S KIT and these immortal words: "This book is better than sex." His bold signature followed.

Bookstore buyers, no doubt bored by all the more staid and traditional salespeople they saw, liked the T-shirt . . . liked Jim . . . and took the book. Which has sold from that day to this. The moral of the story? When you're small, be creative. And, remember, your job is to make friends with the buyers and get your book in the stores. Never lose sight of this objective.

Selling To Libraries

The other day I read an article that said American libraries continue to be the largest single source of book purchases. Obviously, you want to get your share. Fortunately, you've got one big thing in your favor: librarians love the kinds of books you're creating . . . practical, informative, detailed.

In selling to libraries, however, you need to keep the following points in mind. Acquisitions librarians:

- are very concerned about credentials . . . the more credible you are as a source the better for your sales. Too, the more well known you are, the better for your sales. Obviously, librarians cater to local demand, and if people are likely to want your books, librarians will have to stock it.

- will buy both from you . . . and from the wholesalers. Thus, the wholesalers must have information about your books.

- take a *Booklist* review very seriously. In fact, if you do not succeed in getting a *Booklist* review, your library sales will be seriously reduced.

Of these three points, I think only the third calls for more information: *Booklist*. *Booklist* is a publication of the American Library Association. It only reviews about 1/5 of the books it receives . . . and each review is an outright purchase recommendation to subscribing libraries. Purchase price and address information accompany the article. Despite the fact that a *Booklist* review is always short, it is powerful. Such an article should be worth at least $10,000 in library sales to you and, depending on the nature of your book, possibly many times more. Thus, Rule 1 for successfully selling to libraries is to make sure you send a copy of your book the very minute it's available to the Adult Book Editor, *Booklist*, American Library Association, 50 E. Huron St., Chicago, IL 60611.

If your book is featured in *Booklist* (they are very good about sending an advance copy of the review), consider purchasing a few of the smallest sized ads. Remember, more is better than big. Cite the *Booklist* review comments and date in your ad.

What if your book isn't reviewed in *Booklist?* Should you simply give up? Not necessarily. My first three books were reviewed by *Booklist* (favorably, as all their reviews are) . . . but the next one wasn't. I didn't think much of this; even I don't expect 100%. Then something strange happened.

I sent MONEY MAKING MARKETING in for review and was very confident about the book. I knew the literature of small business marketing inside and out and knew this book to be a truly superior creation, eminently helpful. Pride, as they say, goeth before a fall! Within just a few days of when I sent the book to be reviewed, I received a note from a New York psychologist with the cover letter I had sent to *Booklist* about MONEY MAKING MARKETING. The book had been rejected for review . . . and sold, along with my cover letter, to a New York bookstore which sells review books for the benefit of the American Library Association. First, I was irked that a book they wouldn't review was being sold for their benefit . . . secondly, I knew that the book warranted being recommended. Obviously, an injustice had been committed. So, I called the editor.

Well-organized, the editor was able to tell me on what grounds the book had been rejected. The reviewer, he said, found it "disorganized" (I shall never forget the word). At that I launched a spirited defense of the book, for if there's one thing my books are not . . . it's disorganized! Perhaps the editor simply expected me to accept what he'd said, roll over and play dead. I didn't. And he, to his credit, listened while I delivered a truly blistering attack on the reviewer . . . and suggested another reviewer take a look. He said he'd do this, although he cautioned me that this was a *very* special favor. Happily, the new reviewer concurred with my estimation of the book . . . and the usual cornucopia of library sales resulted.

Moral? If you're confident about the value of your book . . . don't be supine. Defend it. There's a lot of money at stake . . . and, of course, your customers need the information you've got.

Other Ways To Generate Library Sales

Librarians live in a political universe. They buy books that they think local citizens want. You can take full advantage of this fact by sending every direct purchaser of your book(s) a recommendation letter they can send their local librarian. To make this system work, you need:

- the *American Library Directory*. Published by R.R. Bowker Co., this book lists all the libraries — and librarians — of the United States and Canada. Here are the relevant names and addresses you need.

- a letter from your customer to his local acquisitions librarian. Face it, your prospects are not going to take the time to write their own letter on your behalf to their local librarian. Therefore, you need to write it for them. This letter should recommend one of your books for purchase by the library and should give reasons why, including, if you have one, your *Booklist* review (provide the date it appeared).

- a computer. Your letter should be available on your computer. All you have to do is add the customer's name and address and the acquisition librarian's name and address and print. This letter should go out with every package.

Will people send it? Of course, they will. First, they've never seen a marketing gimmick as creative as this one. And second, you're going to give them a little present for being cooperative, aren't you? What about a Special Report . . . or a discount on their next purchase? Either way, all you need is a copy of the letter the customer sends . . . or just a note telling you he's sent it.

It goes without saying that the more orders you generate from customers and the more letters you're able to send, the more additional library orders you'll get.

Other Suggestions

Another idea I've found profitable is to turn the back covers of all my books into book menus . . . a list of what else I've got available. As every magazine advertiser knows, the back cover of a publication is a powerful marketing spot. Use it to feature information about all your products and why people should buy them. Librarians will see these covers when your books arrive . . . and so will their patrons. Patrons who know about books get librarians to purchase them. Take full advantage of this fact.

Finally, consider co-op mailings. The publishing newsletters list cooperative mailing opportunities to both libraries and bookstores. The main selling point about such mailings is that they are much less expensive than doing a direct mailing yourself. Unfortunately, you must also compete against a number of other offers. To make co-op mailings productive for you, therefore, do the following:

- design a marketing flyer that speaks to acquisitions librarians. Remember, they are interested in the value of your book for their patrons, why their patrons want the book now, and would very much like to see excepts from a *Booklist* review. If you have these details, provide them;

- use bright colored paper . . . like canary yellow . . . to attract attention;

- ask for a spot towards the front of the packet;

- give librarians a chance to get a free year's subscription to your catalog.

Don't just sell books direct . . . elicit inquiries that will enable you to send your information directly and have the whole show to yourself.

Resource

For information on some of the cooperative book selling programs that exist, both to libraries and elsewhere, get Dan Poynter's Special Report entitled "Cooperative Book Promotion." It's available from Para Publishing, P.O. Box 4232, Santa Barbara, CA 93140-4232. Like all Dan's Special Reports, this one is packed with information. I suggest you call and ask for his complete catalog, although I'll be recommending several items specifically. By the way, tell him I sent you!

Getting Bookstore And Library Distributors

So far, I've been talking about doing everything yourself. As you can see, it's lots of work. But I'll tell you something, whether you get a distributor or not, no one is ever going to be as interested in selling your books as you are. Ever. So, at least some of this work cannot be delegated. To a greater or lesser extent, when you're producing info-products, you're going to have to be involved with bookstores and libraries. The question is . . . how deep do you want to be?

My personal answer to that question, operating a one-man shop as I do, is that while I'm undoubtedly the most effective representative for my products, I also have the least amount of time to represent them. Thus, while it is important to retain a few bookstore accounts to handle personally (how else are you going to have a feel for the business and see what sells and how long it takes?), it is equally important to get a distributor. The problem is finding one you can work with, who's competent, and whom you can trust.

During the writing of this chapter, yet another disgruntled publisher called to ask for a recommendation about distributors. The one he was working with was ineffective in selling his books . . . and didn't pay him for what they did sell. It's an all too familiar refrain. If, therefore, what you're about to read depresses you, I'm sorry . . . but it cannot be helped. Still, because your time is limited, you must make the effort to find a suitable distributor. Here are my guidelines for doing so:

- Get a copy of *Literary Marketplace*. Published by R.R. Bowker (you can see how they built their info-empire), it gives the names and addresses of both the regional and national distributors.

- Write to each distributor to see if they are taking on new publishers. Give them an indication of the kinds of books you're producing.

- Call those who do not respond to this letter, but who seem appropriate to you. Expect to make this call; remember, there are more people who want distributors than distributors looking for products. If you can, during this phone call ascertain if your kind of products would be of interest to this company, get the name of the right buyer, and his address. If possible, chat with this buyer briefly.

- Now follow up. Remember, what the buyer wants to know is: can his company make money from your books. He wants to know how well your books are already doing in bookstores, the kinds of stores they do best in, and what kind of assistance (like generating on-going media coverage) you'll be providing to assist their sales. Too, he wants to see some user and media comments to get a sense of what others think about your products. In other words, he wants you to build a case not just about the value of your products but how easy they'll be to sell. If you can't provide this kind of information, you're sunk.

By the same token, there are things you need to know about the distributor. You want to know:

- his discount structure. How much are you going to have to pay for the privilege of having this company represent you?

- his distribution territories. Just where are they going to sell your books? I have worked with two distributors who claimed to be national but who seem not to know that the Eastern United States even exists. Make sure this doesn't happen to you! It's one thing to proclaim you're working in a given territory . . . quite another to work it effectively.

- how prompt he is about paying you. Of course, the distributor is going to put the best gloss he can on this question, so ask for three or four other publishers with whom you can check. They'll probably have something to add!

- what he'll be doing to market your books. Does the distributor have a catalog? A sales conference with its representatives you could attend and present your books to? Can he assist you with foreign rights sales and with representation at various trade shows? You need to know. The distributor should be proud to tell you what he's going to do for you. Make sure you get the specific details you need.

I say all this knowing full well circumstances favor the distributor. The sad fact is, most small publishers, whatever they're producing, will not get the distributor they deserve. They'll get the kinds of distributors that exist now. Recently, for instance, Publishers Group West, one of the larger distributors of independent publishers, raised its rates yet again. They're not providing any new services

. . . but they know they have their clients over a barrel. This raise in their rates was, therefore, predictable; so are future raises.

What can we say of this? That Lord Acton was right when he said "Power corrupts. Absolute power corrupts absolutely." But what's equally bad in this world of ever-increasing rates for never-increasing service is the bad attitudes so many distributors exhibit. Too many are not client-centered and are often arrogantly condescending. Publishers Group West is guilty of this kind of mindless condescension . . . so is the Talman Co. in New York. Yet no one dares say anything . . . because there are so few distributor choices. Thus, a few people, because of the service they provide, are allowed to get away not only with rapaciousness but persistently unprofessional and pernicious behavior. Their time will come . . .

But until it does, you must do what you can to accommodate yourself to them. This is nothing more than political reality. Find out exactly what the distributor wants . . . and give it to him. Find out how you can help him sell your books. And do it. Stay on the best possible terms you can, swallowing the little humiliations that so many of them have become so good at delivering. Your job is to focus on the main objective: deriving as much income as you can, while positioning your business so that you're never dependent on your distributor.

Note: when dealing with a distributor, keep close tabs on what he owes you and on getting paid promptly. Don't send additional books until your account is up-to-date and if the company starts getting farther and farther behind on paying you, cut your shipments in half . . . or more, so you can maintain some leverage. If I had it all to do over again with distributors, I'd send only half the initial allotment of books they ordered . . . and use my books more effectively as a lever to induce prompter payment. I don't like doing business this way . . . but in the book business there's a well-established tradition of exploiting publishers, letting bills slide or just overlooking them altogether. Don't be victimized by this . . . as so many others have been.

Getting Distributed To Libraries

I am pleased to say the situation is different with libraries. There are, to be sure, many fewer distributors. But the tone and prevailing business practices are better. In my opinion, this is largely due to one man and one company, Tom Drewes of Quality Books. Tom is no longer CEO of Quality Books; he's retired with his charming wife and former high school sweetheart to live the good life they earned for themselves. During his many years at the helm of Quality while he was building his business, Tom went out of his way to help smaller publishers like us. He understood the importance of smaller presses and was an endless promoter of their interests. I'm therefore most glad to be able to compliment him here.

Oh, he had his quirks, to be sure. One of his crazy ideas was that once a book starts getting "too much" publicity, it becomes too well known to be marketed by Quality. Having read this book, you can appreciate just why I think this a completely daft notion. For one thing, there's no such thing as "too much" publicity for a book; for another, the more publicity you get — the more marketing you do — the easier it is for Quality to market the book.

I've never asked Tom's successor Jim Hickey if he subscribes to Tom's little foible, but I can say that despite Tom's absence Quality Books continues to be the best library distributor for small presses in the nation — not least because they pay on time and are easy to work with. Thus, you'd be mad not to contact them for their book submission forms and copies of a few of their monthly newsletters. These contain helpful information about the best-selling books and videos in the library market and a useful occasional feature where they list the books librarians want to see written — so they can buy them! Contact Jim Hickey, President, Quality books, 918 Sherwood Dr., Lake Bluff, IL 60044-2204 (312) 295-2010. If you do talk to him, make sure to tell him all you're doing to promote your books... and make sure to say that it's impossible for any book to get too much publicity, just in case he shows any signs of adhering to the heresy of his predecessor!

Note: it goes without saying there are many other distributors to the library market. You'll find them in the *American Book Trade Directory*. Fortunately, these companies all work on a non-exclusive basis, which means you can be represented by all of them. Do so. You want as many people as possible selling your books.

Selling Through Trade Shows

Let me tell you why trade shows don't work for most people. Recently I was speaker at a business meeting in Boston. My co-presenter, another publisher, happened to have a booth in the exhibition area and asked me if I cared to pass out my catalogs from his stand. Of course, I was delighted. While I feverishly collared every passer-by, I watched his staffers from the corner of my eye. Not once in all the time I was available did any of the three of them take the initiative to approach a single individual. They just waited . . . and waited . . . and waited for someone to approach them. I passed out dozens of my catalogs; to my certain knowledge, they passed out just two in the same period. Later in the afternoon, I watched these staffers without their knowledge. They were simply talking to themselves . . . not marketing at all . . . but costing their boss money every single minute. For reasons which escape me, they seemed to think they deserved this subsidy and probably thought they were working hard.

This is what's wrong with trade shows. And if this is the way you intend to approach them, don't waste your money. If you want to make money from trade shows, here are a few suggestions:

- Try to avoid buying booth space. Booth space in a trade show exhibition area is expensive. It can easily cost you $500-1000 per day given the size of the show; travel and accommodation are additional. When you consider that you can easily buy 100,000 direct response post cards for $1200, you need to consider the cost-benefit ratio for this kind of marketing. Does it make sense? There are three ways of avoiding this expense:

  — Get to be a speaker. If you produce the kinds of books and solve the kinds of problems show participants are interested in, see if you can become a speaker. This way you get direct access to your market and, through the methods already discussed, get a chance to sell both to those attending the trade show and those who don't. By the way, if you do become a speaker, make sure to ask the sponsor for space on the exhibit floor where you can hand out your materials. Sponsors usually have booths from which you can operate.

  — Use a friend's booth. Over the course of the last several years, I have become very adept at asking people I know who get booths if I can appear for a couple of hours and pass out my materials. Because most of these people are not good marketers, I tell them I'll pass out their flyers, *etc.*, too if they help me. This works well.

  — Use the various exhibit services. Places like COSMEP and Publishers Marketing Association now maintain low-cost exhibit services. So do other companies which are both listed in *Literary Marketplace* and in the various publishing periodicals. I've never placed much reliance on these services, but they are a (relatively) low cost way of making sure your titles are displayed at the show. Whenever possible, see if you can get a list of the names and addresses of the people who dropped by the booth where your products were displayed, so you can follow up. I know, for instance, that COSMEP offers such a list from one or two of the shows it participates in.

If these techniques fail, pick your shots. Thousands of meetings take place annually; books are represented at many. Your real problem is knowing what meetings are taking place and deciding which ones to attend. Moreover, you must decide which ones to attend as an exhibitor and which ones merely as a participant.

— *When To Exhibit And What To Do*

There is only one reason for exhibiting, and that is to secure the names of prospects to whom you can subsequently sell your products. On the whole, people don't buy goods at trade shows. They come to look and to pick up materials. Your job, therefore, is two-fold: to get information into the hands of your prospects, and to get their names and addresses so you can follow up with the sales information that will persuade them to buy your info-products immediately.

Your tasks if you exhibit are simple: you must get your prospects to visit your booth . . . and you must get their names and addresses. Nothing else matters. While a discussion of the means of getting people to your booth lies outside this book, suffice it to say that you cannot be passive about this task. As in all other marketing activities, you must lead with benefit and follow with feature. Thus, instead of creating a sign for your booth that merely features your name (like every other booth holder in creation), lead with "SIGN UP HERE FOR YOUR FREE YEAR'S SUBSCRIPTION TO BUSINESS RESOURCES GUIDE . . . GET OVER 350 WAYS TO MAKE YOUR BUSINESS MORE PROFITABLE . . . FREE!" This is far more interesting than the name of your business, and will motivate people to come in . . . if you keep inviting them to do so.

Once they're in the booth, you have two objectives: 1) getting the prospect to provide his name and address so you can send the first issue of your catalog and 2) getting him to see some of the kinds of things you're selling (remember, this is part of the Rule of Seven). Having succeeded in these twin objectives, it's time to move on to the next person.

In short, when you have a booth, you need objectives. And since selling on the spot isn't likely to happen, use your time to get the names you need. This is a perfectly achievable trade show objective. Having it makes it perfectly clear which trade shows to participate in: you'll go to the places where your best prospects will be, and you'll work hard to get the information you need to develop a list of targeted prospects for immediate follow-up.

— *When You Don't Exhibit*

Trade shows still make sense if you don't exhibit, and you can still achieve some of the same objectives. But you have to be creative. Consider the following:

• target the convention workshops to be attended by your prospects. Bring your sales materials (particularly the ones featuring free offers like a year's subscription to your catalog) and either place them on the chairs in the lecture area, give a bunch to a participant and ask him to pass them around, or hand them out at the door . . . particularly when people are leaving. Don't ask anyone for permission. Just do it. Your objective, remember, is to secure the names and addresses of people attending. Get the information into their hands that will enable you to get what you want . . . by motivating them to get what they want.

- put your materials at places where participants are likely to be . . . at the telephones, in the lunch area, in the smoking areas. In short, don't think conventionally and don't put your materials where everybody else's are.

- read through the convention program and target the people you want to see. Some of these people are not likely to be available when you are. Thus, develop a computer-generated form that you can leave with attendants at the booth. It should read something like this: "I'm sorry I missed you. I am interested in □ carrying your books. Please call me to discuss a distribution agreement □ featuring your products at my workshops □ writing a story about (name of title)." In other words, take the initiative, not just to leave your business card, but give the person you've missed an idea of what you can do for him. It goes without saying, that you can also leave this exact paper with an individual you've talked to as reminder of who you are and what you want. It's much more effective than the standard business card!

The problem with most shows is that the people who go to them are too passive, have no objective, and no strategy for achieving their objective. This is a mistake. Before I leave for a trade show, whether I'm speaking (as is usually the case) or not, I remind myself why I'm going. I remind myself what I want to achieve and remind myself of the strategy I'll be using to achieve it. Then I program my mind and go on automatic pilot. Until I achieve my objective, I ignore everything. When I've achieved it, I can look for other opportunities. This is exactly how most people don't approach trade shows and why they're wasting their money by participating in them. Don't let this happen to you. You have too little money . . . and too many responsibilities. Use trade shows only if you're certain you'll be able to achieve your objectives.

Resource

Dan Poynter has written one of the best resources on trade shows for book people. It's called *Book Fairs,* and I recommend it to you.

A Personal Note

As you see I haven't suggested you necessarily attend the annual meeting of the American Booksellers Association. Personally, I haven't found it necessary to go for years. Still, having pooh-poohed this meeting to some extent, I do recommend you attend it at least once. If you love books and parties, this is the place to be. It just probably doesn't make a whole lot of sense as a marketing opportunity, however.

Selling Foreign Rights

Before I leave this over-long chapter, I'd like to say a few words about the sale of foreign rights. In considering foreign rights, you need to keep two things in mind:

1. do foreigners have the kind of problem your book will help them solve, and

2. are the methods of solution you are advocating and presenting available to foreigners, even if only selectively?

If you can answer both these questions affirmatively, then you should look into the sale of foreign rights for your books. Why? For two reasons, really: 1) because you want to help more people through the dissemination and application of the information you have available, and 2) because anything you make off a foreign rights sale is "found money."

Having said this, the real question is how do you find foreign publishers who might be interested in your products, and how do you approach them to make a deal? To answer these questions, I'd like to divide the world into two parts: Canadian and non-Canadian.

— *Selling To Canadian Publishers*

If your book meets the two criteria above, namely that it deals with a problem Canadians have and advances methods they can use to solve it, then you should see about getting a Canadian publisher. Here's how to do this:

• Look in *Literary Marketplace* for a list of Canadian publishers and their fields of interest. Write for their catalogs to see if they are offering books like yours.

• Once you've identified potential Canadian publishers, send a marketing letter full of the reasons why you think the book would both do well in Canada and why it would fit into the publisher's existing list. Call the publisher first to see who you should be sending your letter to for the kind of book you've got.

• Chances are if the publisher is interested in your book, he'll contact you, but don't be absolutely sure of this. Wait three weeks for a response, then call the person you wrote to.

• If the publisher rejects your project out of hand (this happens), ask why. It may simply be that his firm is the wrong place for your book. Thus, ask for referrals. If he feels the book is not appropriate for Canadians, ask why. At the very least, ask to be kept on their mailing list, so you can continue to get a sense of what they are doing. At some point, you may spot an opening.

- If the publisher accepts your project, he'll let you know. At this point, you should ask him if he feels it would be advantageous to have your project represented by a literary agent with Canadian interests. The publisher should be able to refer you to one. On the other hand, he may feel you both can go ahead without anyone else being involved. Of course, the real question is how do you know what to ask for. My rule of thumb is to get an advance equivalent to about 75% of the royalties the book will generate on its first printing. To know what this is, you have to know approximately how many copies the publisher will print at approximately what cover price. Until you know this information, you really won't know what to ask for.

Note: if your project is rejected by a publisher, and you can't talk to the person, write to ask for the information you need. This information is crucial in determining how to go ahead with this marketing project.

— Selling To Non-Canadian Publishers

I have separated Canadians from non-Canadians for one reason. It's easier to deal with Canadian publishers and to learn the foreign rights business from them. To be sure, you may not have a book that interests Canadians or in which you can interest a Canadian publisher. Then, you'll have to learn the foreign rights business by working with other publishers.

- To start with, look in *International Literary Marketplace* (again published by R.R. Bowker Co.). This awe-inspiring book contains information about publishers worldwide. Here you need to pick both your countries and your publishers.

- Follow the advice I've given above. Write for catalogs and send marketing letters. This time, however, to save your phone bill, simply write to the president of the firm. He'll know how to direct your inquiry. Of course, it would be helpful if you could write in the language of the country you're approaching, but don't worry about this too much. English is the world's international language. Again, give the best reasons you can think of why your book will do well in both the nation and with the publisher you're approaching.

- If you don't want to follow up with a phone call, fine. However, if you don't get a response within four weeks, send a copy of your original letter (you do have it on your computer, don't you?) and a request for an answer.

As above, if your book is rejected, find out why. It may simply be that a book about how to prepare and serve tacos would be a tad *de trop* in Mexico.

Other Strategies For Identifying Foreign Rights Buyers

Fortunately for you there are other ways you can identify foreign rights buyers:

- Read the publishing newsletters. Associations like Publishers Marketing Association participate in both U.S. and foreign trade shows. They can display your book, and get you the names of interested foreign publishers.

- If you have a U.S. bookstore distributor, see if they can represent your titles abroad. For instance, Slawson Communications, the firm representing my books, does.

- Use *Rights From USA Review*. Published by Hunter House Publishers, Box 847, Claremont, CA 91711, this is a periodical sent to foreign publishers and lists currently available American publishers' rights.

Finally, read Dan Poynter's Special Report on "Exports/Foreign Rights." He provides his usual solid information on how to export your books as well as how to sell foreign rights. A variety of contractual agreements is included, including the sale of translation rights. This report is available through Para Publishing.

Last Words

If you've now gotten the idea that there are lots of ways to sell books and lots of things you have to know about selling books, you're right. This isn't something you approach casually. It demands your full commitment. Before ending this chapter, I'd like to give you some final pointers about marketing your info-products:

- Work on your marketing every single day. Marketing products is always more important than producing products.

- Keep in mind that your primary sources of income are likely to be non-bookstore sources. Focus on these first and do what is necessary to maintain these streams of income.

- Don't try to look into every other source of marketing books at the same time. Make a preliminary decision about which marketing activities are likely to be the most profitable; do these first. Explore the others as you have time.

- Don't get overwhelmed. Selling info-products is a complicated business with dozens of facets. Always keep your basic strategy in mind: to get the income you need and hold that income source . . . while continuing to prospect for new distribution and marketing sources, understanding how they work, and drawing income from them. Don't think "Get rich quick," think "Get rich sure." Bit by bit understand and use all the marketing sources outlined in this book . . . and in the many recommended sources . . . to do just that. I guarantee you — this approach works!

13

Deciding The Form Of Your Information Empire And Managing It So You Reach Your Personal And Financial Objectives

In the previous twelve chapters, you've learned just what it takes to conceptualize, create and market info-products. When you follow these guidelines, here's what will happen:

To begin with, you'll make money *every single business day* . . . that's six days a week. Moreover, by creating a telephone sales center, you'll also make money most Sundays and holidays, too.

How much money? That depends on you . . . on the number of products you've created, your ability to identify markets and to create a coherent and relentless marketing program. But as you implement these steps, you'll make at least $500 virtually every day . . . $1000 most days . . . and really big money, $5000, even $10,000 or more, on many days. You'll have a very impressive cash flow.

Think what this will mean for your life! Think how few people in the world . . . a world where a sizable number of people go hungry every day . . . get anywhere near this stunning result. These people, even most info-entrepreneurs, never achieve this kind of success. Instead, they have to learn to make do, to scrimp, save, and deal with their corrosive anger.

You, on the other hand, will have success. And you'll have an entirely different set of problems . . . the problems that stem from or influence prosperity. It

497

is these problems that I'd like to address in this final chapter, and I see them in three distinct clusters involving:

- the form of your business;
- wealth maintenance and growth, and
- time management.

Let's look at each

The Form Of Your Business

A business exists for two major reasons: to create wealth for you and to protect you from personal liability as a result of claims stemming from business pursuits and problems. The objectives when you set up your business are clear. Your business must be in a form that:

- protects you personally from liability;

- minimizes your tax burden;

- provides you with necessary benefits, including health insurance and workman's compensation; and

- maximizes the profit you can take from the business.

To ensure you get these benefits, I suggest you do two things:

1. familiarize yourself with the legal forms a small business can take, and

2. hire a good accountant to assist you in creating the business form that makes most sense for you.

Small Business Start-Up Resources

Two excellent resources will assist you in becoming knowledgeable about the form your business should take so that you'll achieve the four objectives above. These are:

- *Starting Your Subchapter "S" Corporation: How To Build A Business The Right Way* by Arnold Goldstein, John Wiley & Sons.

- *Inc. Yourself: How To Profit By Setting Up Your Own Corporation* by Judith McQuown, MacMillan.

Finding An Accountant And Making Sure He's Good

The job of an accountant is to assist you in protecting yourself and developing strategies for minimizing taxes and maximixing retained earnings. It won't be difficult finding an accountant, but it will be difficult finding one who can help you do these things in the most timely and organized way.

The first problem, however, is finding an accountant. You can do so by:

- soliciting referrals. Ask other publishers and small business people in your area for a referral to their accountant. It's better if you have some idea about the strengths and weaknesses of an accountant before you see him.

- asking your bookkeeper. If you're already working with a bookkeeper, ask him for a referral. It's advantageous in any event for your bookkeeper and accountant to know each other and to have worked with each other. This probably means they're familiar with each other's operating procedures. Thus, you can use the (less expensive) bookkeeper to prepare materials for the (more expensive) accountant and probably save yourself some money.

- using the Yellow Pages. There's nothing wrong with calling an accounting firm to see about becoming a client. Remember, however: you want to do business with a firm that specializes in small businesses and has expertise in business start-up. Don't hesitate to ask about this expertise before scheduling an appointment.

The second problem is making sure the accountant you're thinking about is the right accountant for you. Here are some things to inquire into. Does the accountant:

- have a background in small business start-up?

- specialize in your industry?

- have a good reputation in the local business community?

- have contacts with local bankers so he can aid you with possible financing?

- have an alert system to notify you about impending changes in tax laws and regulations affecting you? The last thing you want is to be notified by your accountant just a few days before a new regulation takes place that costs you. My accountant did this to me this year, and I had no trouble whatsoever telling him what was wrong with his management system and how to improve it.

- understand what you are trying to accomplish and have ideas, strategies and procedures on how he can help you achieve it?

In short, does this individual understand what you want to do with your business . . . and can he help you achieve it, both now and later?

If you have the slightest doubt, find another accountant candidate.

My experience with accountants over the last decade has made it clear to me that they need to be regularly reminded about what one is trying to do with one's business . . . and urged to come up with suggestions on how to achieve this. This means you need regular conferences with your accountant (at least once a year) and must continually scrutinize what he's doing. Insist, for instance, that you receive bills that are scrupulously annotated so that you know exactly what was done and exactly how long it took. On one notorious occasion my accountant charged me $150 for photocopying my tax returns and sending them to my bank! I made sure that charge was rescinded fast . . .

First Session With Your New Accountant

As soon as possible, you need a working session with your new accountant. The purpose of this session is to establish procedures and areas of responsibility that will ensure your operation runs smoothly, your tax obligations are met, and the best individual (hopefully the least expensive individual) is responsible for the tasks that need to get done. Tasks that need to be accomplished at this meeting include setting up systems for:

- Social Security/FICA payments. How much will you pay? How will you make payments? Remember, as a self-employed individual, you'll be paying both your personal share and that ordinarily paid by the company, nearly doubling your FICA payment.

- federal income tax withholding. Will you make quarterly estimated payments or monthly payments? Who will fill out the forms? How much should they be for?

- state income tax withholding. Ditto.

- state workman's compensation. If your state requires payment of a workman's compensation insurance, you need to know when payment is due and how the relevant forms will be completed.

- state sales tax. If your state has sales tax, you must collect it for in-state sales of your products. You'll need a resale number from the state. Will you or your accountant get it? Once you receive the number, the state will (obligingly) send you the relevant forms and deposit coupons.

- product inventory tax. Your accountant should be able to advise you on whether your state has an inventory tax that would apply to the books in your warehouse. If so, it may be advantageous for you to warehouse your books in another state that does not have this tax and have them shipped to you on an as needed basis.

- corporate maintenance fee. Many states charge an annual fee to maintain a corporation. Along with the fee, this involves filing certain papers. Who will complete them?

- your pension. To lower your taxable corporate profits and provide for your future welfare, you need a pension plan. Your accountant should be able to advise you as to how to make maximum payments into a tax-deferred pension plan. It's then your responsibility to make sure you contribute the maximum amount!

- your other benefits. Your accountant should advise you on all the benefits you're entitled to take including health and disability insurance, general liability insurance, reimbursed business expenses, business use of an auto, life insurance, and certain business related travel expenses.

During this meeting, your accountant should also be able to advise you how to set up your cash disbursements journal so that, for year-end accounting, he has the material he needs in the most usable form.

Note: it makes sense to include your bookkeeper in this initial meeting with your accountant, particularly since areas of responsibility are being defined and allotted. For instance, while the accountant will probably be the one to advise on your pension plan, your bookkeeper is ordinarily qualified to handle all the FICA and tax withholding questions. Moreover, it is important for the bookkeeper and accountant to discuss what each needs and will do relative to your annual report. As far as the bookkeeper is concerned, these are the tasks he's most likely to do for you himself:

- properly expensing and balancing out cash disbursement journals to arrive at total expenses and total cash spent;

- preparation of cash receipt journals by income type and balanced to bank deposits made;

- reconciling of bank statements and recording of any adjustments required;

- recording of all payroll information to be ultimately used to prepare annual W-2 forms for employees;

- preparation of quarterly federal and state payroll tax returns;

- summarization of financial data accumulated from all journals for submission to accountant who will prepare annual income tax returns;

- preparation of annual 1099 forms that are required for payment of services rendered to a non-employee.

Dividing the tasks in this way means you use each professional in just the right way and don't pay extra.

Resources

Because of the importance of various kinds of insurance, I'd like to recommend two resources to you:

- *101 Ways To Cut Your Business Insurance Costs Without Sacrificing Protection* by McIntyre and Gibson, McGraw-Hill. This general book deals with many different forms of insurance including property, liability and worker's compensation.

- *The Complete Guide To Health Insurance: How To Beat The High Cost Of Being Sick* by Hugue, Jensen & Urban, Walker & Co. This encyclopedic work deals with health insurance policies, hospitalization, medical/ surgical coverage, self-insurance, health maintenance organizations, claims, coordination of benefits and special insurance needs like catastrophes and nursing homes.

Setting Up Your Corporation

It should be clear to you from the foregoing discussion that it probably makes the most sense for you to incorporate your business. The primary reason, to attempt to insulate you personally from any business/corporate liability. A secondary reason to incorporate can be certain tax benefits allowed at the corporate level.

A few more words about liability are in order. From time to time cases are reported in the trade press about book authors and publishers being sued by individuals who followed the published techniques and were injured. They then sue for damages and occasionally win them. As you'll remember, the standard publishing contract (previously discussed) renders the publisher (that's you!) free from liability due to author error. However, when you are the author and publisher, this isn't much help. Thus, you need to give yourself the (admittedly rather porous) protection a corporation affords.

If you want to incorporate yourself, you can follow one of the many pattern books that exist. Judith McQuown's is a good one. However, I recommend you also use a lawyer to assist you. He will help you with the:

- articles of incorporation
- corporate purposes statement
- corporate officers
- corporate by-laws.

I advise you to elect your lawyer as one of your officers; clerk (or secretary) will do nicely. In some situations, this is absolutely necessary. While I taught workshops at the University of Connecticut, for example, and wanted my checks made payable to my corporation (so I wouldn't have to take the income personally), they wouldn't permit me to sign the necessary paperwork both as president and secretary since this would mean I was witnessing my own signature. In this (admittedly rare) case, an outside corporate clerk was absolutely necessary, and my lawyer was perfectly suitable.

Your major area of corporate vulnerability is the advice you give individuals to do things that may injure them. While it is unlikely, it is not impossible that they would then take action against you. It is your lawyer's job to advise you on how to protect yourself against this possibility. He may need to:

- review sections of your info-products to determine your possible liability;

- supply you with language limiting your responsibility which you can print on the inside front cover, or

- actually represent you in the event of a suit.

Lest I alarm you, I wish to say that for most producers of how-to books, legal action against you is highly unlikely. Most of us, after all, are neither absolutely guaranteeing results (which might well give grounds for legal action if our client failed to achieve them) nor dealing in areas where life and limb are at risk. Moreover, most of us really are specialists in what we're talking about so that our methods work . . . not maim! Nonetheless, you need to be sure you can deliver what you say you can deliver . . . and use your lawyer to make sure you are not exposing yourself unnecessarily or rashly.

Wealth Maintenance And Growth

Besides an accountant, bookkeeper and lawyer, you're going to be working with other professionals, too . . . professionals who can assist you in maintaining and developing your wealth. That you'll have such wealth is not open to the slightest doubt . . . for two reasons:

First, because as you follow the guidelines in this book and continue to develop and sell new, precisely market-centered info-products, you will profit, and

Second, because you'll consistently be investing at least a portion of this profit in two kinds of investments, those producing both present and future income.

Here, then, is what you wish to achieve:

1. a constant flow of profit from your primary info-business;

2. an understanding of available taxable, tax-free and tax-deferred income alternatives and the use of those that make the most sense at any given moment, and

3. setting and working towards financial objectives which, year by year, bring you closer to your ultimate goal of financial autonomy and which continually lessen your dependence on the primary revenue stream generated by your business and products.

In other words, conceive of the situation like this: in the beginning of your business, unless you have private means or another job-related income, you must be entirely dependent on the proceeds from sale of your products. Given the inevitable vicissitudes and uncertainties of the market, this must be a relatively uncomfortable position to be in. Thus, you must create and begin to implement your Wealth Plan, the plan that will, over time, inevitably lessen your dependence on your info-business and increase your independent wealth and autonomy until such time as you are completely secure from market conditions.

Is this possible? *It most assuredly is.* That's why achieving this enviable situation must be one of your chief life goals. Let us then look at the necessary steps to doing so. You already know, of course, about how to create profit in your info-business. Each day you must work to do so.

But are you aware of the available taxable, tax-free and tax-deferred alternatives you should be using which will, over time, gradually decrease your dependence on your currently primary revenue source?

Remember, from the beginning of your info-business, you need to take into account *three* distinct revenue streams available to you:

1. profit from current sales;

2. income from personal investments the necessary capital for which you generate from the salary, bonuses and dividends from your primary business, and

3. future income from various long-term, tax-deferred vehicles to which you are allowed to contribute up to a certain amount annually, that amount changing as the regulating law changes.

Each of these streams is significant and must be used.

To use them properly, however, you must:

- consider your life as a whole, not just the present;
- set future income objectives;
- plan which part of your annual income objectives will be met by your different revenue streams;
- create your Wealth Plan and have it available on computer;
- make the necessary sacrifices so you can contribute the capital amounts that enable you, as your investments mature, to achieve these objectives;
- keep familiarizing yourself with both changing laws and regulations pertaining to your investments and the changing economic circumstances that dictate which investments make sense at any given time;
- find and work with dedicated professionals who can assist you in both understanding and benefitting from the present economic situation and in reaching your objective.

Let's look at each of these in turn.

Considering Your Life As A Whole, Not Just The Present

America is a presentist society . . . this means the future has virtually been obliterated in the service of the present. Only the present is important . . . the future be damned. Ronald Reagan built a presidency on this philosophy, and you need do nothing more than leaf through the pages of any publication to catch of a whiff of future abandonment, the importance of present satisfaction.

Of course, in the marketing chapters of this very book, I urged you to take advantage of this situation . . . to generate immediate enthusiasm in your prospects and get them to act NOW! This is the way you'll achieve your sales . . . by stressing benefits and getting customers to take instant action. You, however, must heighten your immunity to this situation . . . or you'll lose the money you need to build your personal security.

You must learn to look beyond the moment, to get beyond the present . . . to see yourself not only as you are now . . . but as you wish to be at age 50, 60, 75 and 90. Though the trend of our society is to focus on youth, you must remember that you are part of a society that is aging rapidly and where you stand an excellent change of living to a very ripe old age. You must ensure that that age is neither pinched nor impoverished. What I am talking about now will ensure that you use your info-empire to create the means you'll need then so you'll avoid the sad fate of most wage earners, who are forced to rely on inadequate savings and paltry pensions.

You must take the long view of your life. You must understand that *now* is the moment to prepare for every other moment of your life; that the earlier you begin to prepare for the rest of your life, the easier it must be to generate the kind of wealth that will sustain the lifestyle you want. Just the other day, I read an article by a far-sighted financial planner who said that the day to prepare for retirement is the day you are born . . . and that the most loving parents are those who take this view and act accordingly. How few such parents there are! Which is why you must become parent to yourself.

Set Future Income Objectives

Throughout this book, I have stressed setting numerical objectives . . . objectives which easily enable you to determine how much you have achieved, or how far you have to go. Now I recommend this again . . . in setting future income objectives.

You must set an income objective for the remaining years of your life. Of course, you don't know how many years you'll live, but you can make a good guess by looking at the average ages of either your (deceased) grandparents or parents or by asking your insurance agent to consult one of his charts. Personally, this means I had to plan on living to be at least 95, since I come from a long-lived stock. And I can tell you something: I'll want to live at least as well at 95 as I lived at 42. *Ergo*, as of this moment I have to deal with income objectives for a minimum of 53 years.

The future income objectives you set should enable you to maintain at least your present lifestyle and pay present expenses with a constant inflation rate of 8%. Thus, if you're 50 and need $40,000 to maintain your present lifestyle, you'll need over $86,000 to maintain it at the same level by age 60. If you plan on improving your lifestyle significantly, these changes must be factored into your income objectives, too.

It goes without saying that if you intend, at least in the early years of your business, to rely primarily on your business-generated income, you must write down precisely how many products, and precisely what volume of sales, you must do to achieve the income objective you've set.

Plan Which Part Of Your Annual Income Will Be Met By Your Different Revenue Streams

In the beginning of your business, your primary income will be generated by that business. Over time, however, as other investments mature, more and more of your income should come from these sources. Your task, however, is to determine how much of your income will come from the different sources

. . . current business income, current non-business income, long-term tax-deferred income sources.

Present Age	Income Goal	Income Needed From Business (Factoring In Current Investment Income)	Invested In Current Income Investment	Total In Current Income Investment Acct.
42	$50,000	$49,400	$6,000	$6,000
43	$54,000	$52,800	$6,000	$12,000
44	$58,320	$56,520	$6,000	$18,000
45	$62,895	$60,495	$6,000	$24,000
46	$68,024	$65,024	$6,000	$30,000
47	$73,466	$69,866	$6,000	$36,000
48	$79,343	$75,143	$6,000	$42,000
49	$85,691	$80,891	$6,000	$48,000
50	$92,546	$87,146	$6,000	$54,000
51	$99,950	$93,950	$6,000	$60,000
52	$107,946	$101,346	$6,000	$66,000

Present Age	Income from Current Income Investments	Invested in Tax-Deferred Investments	Total In Tax-Deferred Investment Accounts	Income From Tax-Deferred Investment
42	$600	$6,000	$6,600	No
43	$1,200	$6,000	$13,860	income
44	$1,800	$6,000	$21,846	may
45	$2,400	$6,000	$30,630	be
46	$3,000	$6,000	$40,293	taken
47	$3,600	$6,000	$50,923	until
48	$4,200	$6,000	$62,615	you're
49	$4,800	$6,000	$75,476	59.5 years old
50	$5,400	$6,000	$89,624	or
51	$6,000	$6,000	$105,187	disabled,
52	$6,600	$6,000	$122,305	etc.

Consider that you are age 42 and are making some income projections. To do projections, we must make some assumptions. Say that:

1. you need the constant dollar equivalent of $50,000 to maintain your present lifestyle;

2. inflation is a constant 8%;

3. you make investments of $12,000 yearly, investing $6,000 in long-term tax-deferred investments and $6,000 in investments paying immediate income;

4. your investments appreciate at a constant rate of 10%.

Note: you will understand, of course, that neither investment income nor inflation is constant and that you may want to (and legally can) invest more in your tax-deferred account as your income rises. Here, however, rather than give you a definite plan, I'm trying to make several points:

1. You must create a marketing plan that enables you to make sufficient income so that you have the excess capital you need to invest in both personal investments and in tax-deferred investments through your corporation;

2. You must continually strive to lessen your dependence on the primary income stream provided by that company;

3. You must start as early as possible making both kinds of investments so you achieve maximum appreciation;

4. You must be willing to put the maximum amount of capital away in tax-deferred accounts for the maximum period of time to achieve maximum appreciation.

Create Your Wealth Plan And Have It Available On Computer

Once you know what you need and where it's coming from, you need to write down your Wealth Plan and put it on your computer. This plan must consist of the following parts:

• annual income objective for each year of the rest of your life;

• certain income you can now project will be available in each year;

• deficiency still to be made up so that you reach the set objective for that year.

To show you what I mean, let's go back to the chart above.

At age 52, you have $122,305 in your tax-deferred investment accounts. Assuming constant contributions of $6,000 and an annual appreciation of 10%, by age 65 you'll have $584,079 in this account and (with a 10% return) an annual income of just over $58,000. Additional income will be available through your other investments, the ones you've been drawing annual income from. You are now in a position to determine if this is sufficient for your purposes or whether you need to make still more investments earlier . . . which means creating a more aggressive marketing campaign to sell more products, so you have the necessary investment capital . . . or live on less.

By the same token, if you're investing in long-term government bonds like FICO strips, CATs, or Zero Coupon bonds, you can determine which years you need bonds for . . . and which years now have sufficient projected income.

In any event, when you plot out your investments in this fashion, you know how much you have now, how much income each investment will provide in the future, and what deficiencies remain to be dealt with. You also have a sense of what you must do to sell the necessary products so you have the investment capital you need.

This plan, therefore, is crucial!

Make The Necessary Sacrifices So You Can Contribute The Capital Amounts That Enable You To Achieve These Objectives

Setting up a lifetime investment program isn't easy. Everything in this society, where we have the world's lowest savings rate among industrialized nations, works against it. There always seem to be "reasons" why investment should be deferred . . . you always "need" this or that and simply cannot put off acquiring it.

But I have news for you: you also can't put off old age, infirmity, or a lessening of the vitality that it takes to run a profitable info-empire. Every other creature in the universe has weakened. You must weaken, too. But, at least you can be prepared!

Thus, if you have decided you need to invest $1000 monthly for the rest of your life to achieve financial independence, you must invest:

- $230.77 *each* week;
- $38.46 *each* business day;
- $4.81 *each* hour of each 8-hour business day.

This may mean:

- giving up a couple of days of vacation each year;
- foregoing a new coat . . . so you can invest the money;
- eating leftovers instead of going out to dinner.

In short, it means deliberating and rearranging your habits, while all around you others are living by fatuous "Do it! Do it! Now! Now!" precepts.

You can't. You now have high standards. You know how hard money is to make. You know how difficult it is to build an info-empire from which you can generate, year after year, the income you want and the capital you need. You know how difficult it is to keep what you've made. You know both how important a self-sufficient autonomy is to you . . . and how vulnerable the run of mankind is because they don't have it. You have decided to avoid this vulnerability, to ensure your independence. And if this means making a series of sacrifices that are relatively trivial in the present to guarantee substantial comfort and security in the future, so be it. There is, you see, no other wise and certain way of getting what you want.

Familiarizing Yourself With Both Changing Laws And Regulations Pertaining To Your Investments And To Changing Economic Circumstances

One thing is certain. If you are a smaller investor (and by this I mean anyone with under $1,000,000 in investments other than your home), you are unlikely to secure the very best advice from investment advisors. Entrepreneurs themselves, they spend more time catering to their larger accounts. I accept this.

This means you must familiarize yourself with both the changing laws and regulations pertaining to your investments and be alert to changing economic circumstances and how they impact on the kinds of investments you've made. Literally thousands of books have been written on these topics, and it is decidedly outside the scope of this volume, which after all focuses on how to create and sell information products, to supply you with all the information you need in this area. However, let me recommend these steps:

- Take a basic investments course so that you are familiar with both investment terminology and investment cycles. Focus on learning about long-term investments which you can buy and forget about, like U.S. Treasury bonds or mutual funds. Unless you are a sophisticated investor, avoid individual stocks and things like commodities which fluctuate violently and where you can lose your money quickly. You want security, after all; this is achieved through the continuous and regular infusion of capital into safe investments that need time, not professional expertise and daily oversight, to turn a profit.

- Find out at any given moment (your accountant can be helpful here) just how much you can invest through your corporation and make sure you arrange matters so that you not only know what the maximum limit is but contribute as close to it as you possibly can. If you are falling far short of this maximum limit, see what you can do to improve your product marketing program to generate the additional investment capital you need.

* Ask your accountant to assist you in the creation of an investment and tax-minimization plan. Ask him precisely what you should do, given your situation, to minimize current federal and state tax . . . and maximize capital for further investment.

Here, as elsewhere, you cannot abdicate responsibility; no one, after all, will ever be as interested as you are in assisting you achieve financial security and autonomy. Nor can you expect them to be. This is not a problem, however. Given a reasonable amount of time and study, you can become proficient in the kinds of investments you need to know about: those that are low-risk and appreciate regularly.

As I write this chapter, another quarter is ending and a series of account summaries arriving from my various investments. One of my tax-deferred funds paid a dividend of $500 on my shares. This represented a 13% return . . . at a time when long-term U.S. Treasury bonds are paying about 8.5%. I haven't given this account three seconds' thought in the last year. However, because it's an investment I plan to rely on in my retirement, I did give it a great deal of thought before making it. This is precisely what you should do . . . so you can sleep well at night and spend all your days developing new products and selling the ones you've already got . . . not worrying about where you've put your money.

Finding and Working With Dedicated Professionals Who Can Assist You In Both Understanding And Benefitting From The Present Economic Situation

Recently, a host of books critical of financial professionals has been written. They point out how people like stock brokers, insurance agents and financial planners, to name the three perhaps most heavily criticized groups, bilk and mislead unsuspecting consumers. I must say these fragrant exposés haven't surprised me very much.

These individuals make their money by getting you to give them their money. They promise the moon . . . but their real desire is getting an immediate commission from you. They benefit only if you buy or trade. And they're usually long gone by the time the vehicle you've acquired is expected to pay off. Of course, the situation is ripe for the kind of misrepresentation and exploitation that thrives. Thus, expect it, plan accordingly . . . but nonetheless take advantage of the kind of information these kinds of professionals have.

Your job, remember, is creating info-products that meet the needs of targeted prospects . . . and creating an unrelenting sales program that brings these products to their attention and gets them to buy NOW. You must spend the bulk of your time on these necessary tasks. It is therefore doubtful, unless you are writing investment resources, that you'll ever become the complete investment professional. I, at least, have accepted this . . . and accepted the fact that I need investment assistance. But here, as elsewhere, I play a very defensive game. So should you. Hence, these suggestions:

• Interview several professionals before you invest any money.

• Never maintain just one investment account for one kind of investment. Have at least two.

• Before you invest any money, ascertain from each of your advisors how he'd invest it just now and why.

• If you don't understand what you're thinking of doing, don't do it.

• Review how your investment professionals stay in touch with you to see how badly they want to handle your business.

• Chastise poor service, but compliment good service.

• Meet each of your professional investment advisors for a once-a-year strategy meeting to see how your investments are coming along and what you should be doing.

Let's look at each of these suggestions.

Interview Several Professionals Before You Invest Any Money

Because of my marketing books, workshops and consultations, I have come to meet literally thousands of people who live by selling various kinds of investments. Most of them come with the regulation blue suit, red tie and tasseled loafers. But most are nothing more than glorified salesmen. That is, most are given products to sell by their companies and told to go out, get their own prospects and close deals. That's all. As the exposé books point out, many know little or nothing about how the products really work and are selected for their jobs less because of their interest in client welfare than their own piranha-like desire to be wealthy.

There's nothing much you can do about this situation . . . except be prepared for it. Thus, you need to interview your investment advisors . . . your stock and bond brokers, insurance agents and financial planners . . . as carefully as your accountant and your lawyer. These advisors are very important to you . . . influencing as they do not merely the disposition of your current money but the kind of lifestyle you'll have when you're older and past your work. The seriousness of what you want them for should dictate an equally serious search for the right people to represent you.

What you're looking for are people who:

- are understanding about what you're trying to achieve;
- are honest with you;
- aren't merely representing one product but can present you with the pros and cons of several;
- will call to alert you about changing economic situations so you can both take advantage of them and protect yourself from them;
- don't take your business for granted.

Never Maintain Just One Investment Account For One Kind Of Investment. Have At Least Two

One of the worst things you can do is become dependent on a single source of investment information. If you do, you're placing too many eggs in one basket. Part of any good investment strategy is dividing the risk, and part of this division is working with at least two investment advisors for *each* of the different investments you have. Thus, if you are investing in U.S. government bonds, work with two brokers in two different companies. The same is true with mutual funds; don't put all your money into one. Go with at least two funds at two different companies.

Before You Invest Any Money, Ascertain From Each Of Your Advisors How He'd Invest It Just Now And Why

There are several advantages to dealing with several different agents for each of your investments:

1. You keep them on their toes. Tell each of them that you do at least part of your business elsewhere. This makes them compete for your (perhaps now small) account. On one occasion, one of my bond brokers whom I'd called at 10 a.m. to make a purchase (I always say this in my messages) didn't return my call until 2 p.m. By then I'd made the purchase elsewhere, and when the original broker finally condescended to return my call, I told him just where I'd made the purchase and just how much it was for. I've noticed since then my calls get returned promptly.

2. You can easily switch over to a second account for the bulk of your business if your first investment advisor proves less than satisfactory.

3. You get to compare their advice.

As so often happens among specialists, different experts will disagree, often for the best of reasons. You need to know why each is pitching his particular line . . . and why another may be advocating something entirely different. These kinds of disagreements happen frequently. I recall one recent occasion when an advisor was advocating buying U.S. Treasury bonds long (that is, for the longest period of time one could), while another was saying to buy the same bonds for only three or four years. If you put yourself solely in the hands of only one advisor, you never get to understand the full range of possibilities. Nor will you feel in control if you've only heard one opinion.

Your job is to pick people who understand what you're trying to do, understand the kinds of (usually long-term) investments that make the most sense for you, and then weigh the often differing advice they give you on how to achieve what you want.

Remember: to make this program work for you, you must occasionally buy something from each of your investment advisors. No one is going to keep giving you advice on the off-chance that you'll finally get around to buying. If you must, buy something small . . . but to keep getting the information you need, buy something.

If You Don't Understand What You're Thinking Of Doing, Don't Do It

If this one piece of advice were implemented by the investing public, there would be an immediate drop in business by all investment personnel and, very quickly, much clearer explanations about potential investments.

I have sadly concluded that no investment advisor will ever spontaneously take the time to explain fully an investment to a client unless he is asked to do so, often several times.

Understand, therefore, that it is your responsibility to make sure you know precisely what your advisor is suggesting and precisely how it will either help you (or not help you!) achieve your objective. Don't feel abashed in the slightest about having to ask your adviser exactly what he's proposing and exactly how it'll affect you. I have become expert at saying "Whoa! I don't understand what you mean. Please slow down and explain this again . . . clearly." And I don't feel any less intelligent because I must do this . . . more so, in fact, because I'm at least smart enough to realize we're both playing with *my* money!

There are two good reasons for making your investment advisor be crystal clear with you:

1. you must know what you're doing before you invest your money, and

2. since you'll be talking with another investment advisor in the same area shortly, you need to understand just what you may be getting (or giving up) in buying one product over another.

Review How Your Investment Professionals Stay In Touch With You To See How Badly They Want Your Business

Like so many entrepreneurs, the investment personnel you'll be dealing with are mostly scalp counters. They want to put you in their sack . . . and rush on to the next prospect. Of course, they want you to stay loyal to them . . . but they're often woefully underdeveloped as client-centered marketers.

Gauge the seriousness of your advisors' interest in you by:

- how often they send you current information about the kinds of investments you've got. Remember, they should be getting this kind of information regularly and should pass it to you as often;

- whether they ask you for and schedule an annual meeting at which you can assess your investment strategy and make necessary changes;

- invitations they may send you to the kinds of social engagements and seminars they make available to their best customers.

In short, do your advisors act like they want you? Are they working to keep your business? Or do they just want you to keep buying without offering you necessary service in return?

Chastise Poor Service, Compliment Good Service

By this token, it's your responsibility to pipe up if you don't feel you're getting the service to which you're entitled. And my advice to you is: pipe up early.

Thus, if your broker returns your phone calls hours after you make them, draw his attention to this immediately. If you feel uncomfortable doing this on the phone, send a pointed, but polite, note . . . and keep a copy for your files.

If problems emerge in your statement and are not taken care of promptly, again complain. I've just gone through a curious interlude with Shearson, Lehman, Hutton concerning mysterious trades that took place in an account I had previously closed . . . trades that were not initiated by me! I wrote a couple of standard letters to my designated broker asking him to correct this matter. They received no action. Then I wrote a note saying that if the problem was not solved within thirty days, I'd turn it over to a securities investigator from the

Massachusetts Secretary of State's Office. This, too, failed to produce any response. But the investigator's phone call to them (for I did what I said I was going to do) produced *instantaneous* action!

Likewise, if you:

• don't get information pertaining to new economic circumstances that impact on your investments, complain.

• don't get invitations to special events, bring this to your broker's attention, and

• find yourself waiting for necessary paperwork and having to make several phone calls to get it, bring this up immediately.

As must no doubt be clear to you now, I no longer believe that so-called "professionals" will necessarily and inevitably behave in a professional manner and that if you are to secure the service to which you're entitled, you must make it clear what you expect . . . and work immediately to get it if, at the first opportunity, you fail to be properly handled. This is a sad fact of life in late twentieth century America, so accept it and act accordingly.

By the same token, if you receive the good service you have a right to expect, or even (imagine!) better service, write an immediate note of sincere thanks. One of Bill Clinton's nicest traits is his constant note writing to people who have done him some service. Literally thousands of people have received these notes from the president, a man who obviously understands that you cannot in good conscience criticize poor service if you are not willing to commend good service. Be advised!

Meet Each Of Your Professional Investment Advisors For A Once-A-Year Strategy Session

Money needs supervising. It needs your care, and it needs the care of the professional advising team you've assembled. True, many of the investment vehicles you select will not need constant oversight. But, because of the constant fluctuations in economic situations, both your strategy and particularly your tactics must be regularly reviewed.

Thus, make sure you schedule at least an annual meeting with your various investment advisors. You want to know:

• how things are coming along with your investments;

• whether there are investments that need to be changed or opportunities to be seized, and

- what kinds of things your advisor is currently recommending for both purchase and avoidance.

This is also a superb opportunity to renew the personal bonds which are so important in creating a strong investment team. Whatever charm you have, it pays to bring it to these meetings. You want your advisors to like you, to care about you, and to want to assist you reach your objectives. Furthermore, lest there be any doubt what your objectives are, take advantage of this meeting to reannounce and clarify them.

By following these steps, you will avoid the tragic problems that afflict so many Americans and so many careless info-entrepreneurs: the demeaning, debilitating trap of poverty. America is a damnable place to be poor in, and to be poor, elderly and infirm is the very definition of hell. Don't let this happen to you.

By studying this book closely and applying its guidelines, you will create many useful and profit-making info-products. Simultaneous with this strenuous creation, you must do all you can to keep this money, and to augment it through a careful and continuing investment program, a program that begins today . . . and continues through the rest of your life. This is truly how you spin your ideas and mold your products into gold . . . and how you ensure yourself of the most prosperous, most comfortable, most contented and amiable old age. Let this be yours!

Time Management

Perhaps you are now scratching your head wondering how you can do all the things that you must do to both create and market a line of info-products and to maintain and develop the wealth that will inevitably be yours if you follow all these suggestions. Admit it, you're wondering how you can do it all, aren't you? You're wondering if, given all your other responsibilities, you can find the time it takes to build this kind of glorious and remunerative empire, and whether you have the kind of unrelenting habits you must have to do all that needs to be done.

The truth is, to do the tasks outlined in this book and so achieve the desired results, you must master the art of setting priorities and so arranging your time and habits to achieve them. It is now time, therefore, to look at the vital subject of time management, because until you learn how to control time the empire outlined in these pages will be merely a mocking chimera, nothing more. Here, then, is what you must do:

- Consider the next year of your life. What do you want to achieve by its conclusion . . . be specific!

- Assign each task a completion date.

- Divide each task into sections and assign each a completion date.

- Now consider the structure of each of your days. What must be completed and when are the best times to do each of the necessary tasks.

- Create a "to do today" binder and use it daily.

- Arrange your work station for maximum efficiency.

- Learn how to handle office tasks in a time efficient and directed manner.

- Determine which tasks you don't need to do . . . and then stop doing them!

- Keep analyzing your tasks to see how each can be done more efficiently.

Let's look at each of these crucial areas.

Consider The Next Year Of Your Life. What Do You Want To Achieve By Its Conclusion?

The only way to achieve objectives is to set objectives and to arrange your life so that you accomplish them. This sounds easy, yet millions and millions of people in this nation who claim to want success cannot seem to understand this point or learn how to implement it. Fortunately, you're not one of them!

Whether you start your year on January 1st or the first day of your corporate fiscal year is not important. What is important is that you are specific about precisely what you mean to achieve in the next 365 days. I am talking here, of course, about your major projects, including:

- books
- booklets
- audio cassettes
- Special Reports

and the like.

Your job is to write down precisely how many of each of these you mean to produce (or commission and oversee) and precisely how long each will be. Thus:

- one 80,000 word book;
- two 10,000 word booklets;
- four 60-minute audio cassettes, and
- twenty-four 2,500 word Special Reports.

Of course, the first time you do this you may not be precisely sure of the exact length or time. Don't let this hold you back! Be as specific as you can. What you are setting now is your destination. If you don't know precisely where you're going, your year will be nothing so much as a futile exercise in aimless meandering. Which is the way it is for most people, including far too many info-entrepreneurs.

Assign Each Task A Completion Date

I am, as you now know, a firm believer in what I call Mind Channelling, that is the ability to lock the mind on a certain task and to so arrange one's entire life that, whether conscious or not, you are always moving in the direction to which you've committed yourself. Part of Mind Channelling is setting a fixed, firm, *absolute* completion date for each major task. The mind must know, you see, and the body must work towards this absolute date . . . every day!

Thus, take your product objectives and assign dates to them, so:

* one 80,000 word book. Completion date: July 4

* two 10,000 word booklets. One to be completed November 1, the second January 1.

* four 60-minute audio cassettes. One to be completed the first day of the month in February, March, April and May.

* twenty-four 2,500 word Special Reports. Six to be completed the beginning of January, April, July, and October.

Post these completion dates prominently where you can see them daily. If you are not creating these products yourself, send them to the people who are so they can post them.

Divide Each Task Into Sections And Assign Each A Completion Date

Once you have determined the completion dates for your major tasks, you must outline each project and assign completion dates for each major section. Again, it is a good idea to post your outline of these major sections and set completion dates.

Consider The Structure Of Each Of Your Days; Know What Must Be Completed And When Are The Best Times To Complete Each Of The Necessary Tasks

Your life as an info-entrepreneur is essentially composed of the following tasks:

- idea generation for new products;
- market research for new products;
- product outline;
- product data collection and research;
- product creation;
- product production;
- product marketing;
- product updating;
- order taking;
- product shipping;
- customer relations and problems to be solved.

Some of these things demand intellectual freshness and consummate vitality (like idea generation and product creation); some you can do by rote (product shipping comes to mind).

The important thing is to divide your day so that you do the most important and most demanding tasks when you are freshest. For most of us this is the morning. Your day, for instance, might look like this:

- 9 a.m.- noon. Research or write depending on present product stage.

- 12:30 - 2:30. Handle today's orders

- 2:45 - 4:00. Make telephone calls and handle letters relative to opening new markets, following up previous marketing correspondence and phone calls, *etc.*

- 4:15 - 5:00. Update mailing list, input new data, *etc.*

Create A "To Do Today" Binder And Use It Daily

Most people treat all tasks equally . . . a trip to the water cooler is as important as sending a marketing letter to a catalog asking them to sell your products. Be real! All tasks are not equally important. You need to determine which must be done today . . . and do them.

The purpose of a "to do today" binder is to:

- get you to think about which tasks are the most important;

- put more important tasks before less important;

- enable you to check off what you get done . . . and to see both progress and how much more needs to be done.

To make this system work, consider which tasks are truly important to your info-business. They are:

- product development and creation, and
- product marketing.

You can get along without many other things in your business, but you can't get along without these. Thus, these two general task groups must be prominently represented on each day's "to do" list.

These tasks must not only be represented, however, they must be *specifically* outlined, thus:

1. Write 500 words of Special Report.

2. Send five marketing letters to pending or new retail sources.

3. Contact three free publicity sources.

4. Contact Wholesaler A about buying 3 cases of my product.

The more specific you can be here, the better. Include: amounts of work to be done, numbers of people to be contacted, their names, and the *result* you want to achieve. The more general you are here, the less you have grasped how this system works and the farther you are from true time and task management.

Before leaving this page, put numbers before each task . . . with 1 being the most important to achieve today, 2 the second most important, *etc.* It is your job to complete these tasks . . . or make discernible progress . . . before the end of the day.

Note: it is perfectly acceptable for you to keep your "to do" lists in your computer. If you don't complete a task, simply move it over to the next new file you open. Try, however, to complete all your tasks before the end of the day.

After reviewing your "to do" list for today and making sure you've done all you could, complete your day by drawing up the "to do" list for tomorrow. Don't do this in the morning . . . do this before leaving your office. The reason is plain: you want your mind to have the maximum amount of time possible to think about these tasks, arrange them, consider the best way of handling them.

Arrange Your Work Station For Maximum Efficiency

When my readers visit me (as so many do these days), they always want to see the way I've arranged my work station. They're looking for the magic set-up that enables just one man working alone to achieve so much! In fact, there's nothing magic about it. The work station was set up for maximum efficiency to achieve the necessary tasks I must complete each day, especially the crucial product production and marketing tasks.

Personally, since I spend most of my time at a computer keyboard, the work station is centered on this essential machine. To handle the mass of papers I have to get through, I find it most convenient to have my computer on a standard card table. This allows for paper space . . . and for the telephone, which I must be able to reach without getting out of my chair. It's this configuration that enables me to pick up most telephone calls on the first ring, something which regularly astonishes people.

By the same token, I need to be able to reach my constantly-in-use printer without getting up as well as a host of necessary office tools and supplies such as the rolodex, calculator, order blanks, *etc.* The work station is so arranged for this necessary economy.

I also have a secondary work station made up of two distinct parts: 1) typewriter (for short notes and labels) and 2) a packing and shipping area. This secondary work station is composed of a long board resting on two two-drawer filing cabinets in which a series of regularly used "pending" files are easily at hand.

Elsewhere in my studio office are necessary office supplies, catalogs and other marketing devices, boxes, *etc.* There's even a refrigerator which, for health purposes only of course, I keep stocked with champagne. Winston Churchill taught me the necessity of drinking a pint of bubbly daily and while I confess I do not fully live up to this high standard, I find this cheering liquid near at hand a necessity of civilized existence. Since I only drink on the job, the champagne is owned by my company!

The point here is not to get you to emulate this set-up (though I commend it to you), but to get you to consider how you can arrange your necessary office machines so that, with a minimum of movement and inconvenience, you can do the maximum of work. This is the objective. Arrange your work station so you accomplish it.

Learn How To Handle Office Tasks In A Time Efficient And Directed Manner

You already know my feelings about running an efficient office. As you know from our discussion of how to integrate your computer into your info-empire, most people are nowhere near doing so. As you succeed in computer integration, however, you will be.

In addition, you must do what you can to handle the inevitable office tasks more expeditiously. Try the following:

- Don't take phone calls while you're creating your products. Phone calls inevitably disrupt your creative work flow. Thus, keep your answering machine on when you're writing. If you create in the mornings, by the way, you'll find this isn't a great problem, since you'll probably receive the bulk of your calls after lunch. And, of course, Friday-Sunday you get the fewest calls of all.

- When you do take calls, find out instantly what the caller wants. You'll find, especially as you get better known or after a good article has appeared on you and your products, many unfocused people will contact you. They are looking for a missionary; you don't have to oblige. Wait 30 seconds to see if the caller knows what he wants, then say "How can I help you?" If this question doesn't succeed in focusing the caller, ask it again. If this doesn't work, say "Your question is obviously an important one, but I'm in conference right now and cannot attend to it properly. I wonder if you'd be good enough to write me a short letter telling me exactly what you want? Do you have my address?" Serious people will follow up this invitation in a serious way; the unfocused will not . . . but you've placed the full onus of failure to act where it belongs: on them!

- Don't use the phone as a social vehicle during business hours. By all means be pleasant, but try to limit your phone calls to three minutes. My father made me do this when I was growing up and now that I'm an adult, I find that this amount of time is perfectly adequate for most business tasks — where you know what you're doing.

- Before you go to anybody else's office for a meeting, see if he'll come to yours. Traveling is disruptive, expensive and time consuming. Avoid it whenever possible. If a person is going to benefit from you, chances are he'll be perfectly agreeable to coming to see you if you are relatively conveniently located. In any event, it never hurts to ask.

- Before agreeing to see anyone at your office, find out precisely what he wants. If he's not sure, ask him to send you a letter. Indicate a willingness to meet with everyone . . . but only if a meeting makes mutual sense.

Remember, as your products circulate more and more generally, more and more people will want to see you. Don't let them waste your time; find out in advance just what they want. Note: yes, you will get requests from autograph seekers and people who just "happen to be in the neighborhood" who want to see you. I advise you to accommodate them . . . but for not more than 15 minutes each at the end of your day. I can assure you of this: I don't believe a single person has come to see me in this way who hasn't bought at least one more book or product. These visits, therefore, are not only productive of good will . . . but of cold cash, too. Tell such people in advance that you're terribly busy but anxious to see them. Should they be able to come by for just a quarter-hour (you name the time), you'll be happy to see them.

- If you do agree to a meeting (whether at your office or not), work out in advance exactly what you want to accomplish. Then ask yourself whether by meeting with this individual you can accomplish this. Make sure that the person you're meeting with understands why you're meeting ("I'm coming to see you, you know, to convince you of the benefits of your carrying my new book.") and make sure he can do what you want him to do ("I suppose if you like my book you could write out a purchase order right away, couldn't you?"). If he doesn't see the meeting as you do and cannot authorize what you want, this may be a meeting that really doesn't need to happen.

- Keep all meetings, whether at your office or not, to a specified amount of time. Most meetings go on far too long. I tell people before I meet with them precisely how much time I need/they get, and then I arrange matters accordingly. Do the same.

- Before the meeting is ended, state what has been accomplished, what needs to be done, and who will do it. Have you accomplished what you wanted to accomplish? If not, try again before ending the meeting to see if you can achieve your objective.

- Sort through all your mail immediately upon receipt. Put orders (and payments) in one pile; future orders (queries, requests for information) into another; "junk" mail and advertisements into a third, and personal mail into a fourth. The first pile ordinarily involves your sending something (or having something sent); the second involves information being sent; the third is possible purchases you may make, and the fourth can be dealt with after business hours.

- Know what you're going to do with each stack. Orders will be shipped promptly. Future orders either involve your sending information immediately or inputting the name into your computer so that appropriate sales literature can be sent. "Junk" mail and advertisements either get thrown out (if you're not immediately interested and do not need the information) or filed in an appropriate file folder for later reference. Personal letters you can keep for after-hours reading and response.

- Make it your goal to answer all your letters (and certainly send out all your orders) by the end of the day they're received. Mark Twain, among many other well-known folk, did this; I do this. So can you. Whenever possible develop a necessary form letter. Make it personal . . . make it warm . . . but make it a form . . . if you are going to have to deal with this particular matter more than once. (Also, keep your printer on draft mode: you'll be able to send more letters faster.) Too, write your responses on the bottom or back of letters whenever possible. The objective is quick and accurate communication, not a letter fit for the Tsar of All the Russias.

- Learn which tasks can be handled simultaneously. Sending out as much mail as I do, I have to keep cleaning my list . . . which means doing endless computer searches to find out which names are still current. I've discovered I can take care of this task while getting the day's orders out . . . or when I'm on the phone talking to clients, *etc.* Too, my printer enables me to work on one document while another document is being printed. Thus, I'm able to work on two documents simultaneously. You must find out what tasks you can do simultaneously, too . . . and do them!

- Hire a helper to bring books from your warehouse and do the time-consuming errands we all have to do. Yes, these things must be done . . . but you certainly don't have to do them!

Finally, and again, use your computer. It's the single most important aid in making you more efficient and helping you save time. Stop developing and sending original letters to people. Most business tasks are routine. Make sure you treat them that way!

Determine Which Tasks You Don't Need To Do . . . And Then Stop Doing Them!

Most of life is composed of tasks that are, however necessary, unutterably trivial and mundane. Once, in an outburst against the thrall of these tasks, my mother shouted, "I was not put on this earth to mop floors!" I took this message to heart in a way she could never have expected of the young boy I then was. I haven't washed a floor . . . or a window . . . or even my own clothes in many, many years. I don't vacuum or make the bed . . . I don't dust or even repot my plants. I don't, in short, use my very limited time for the things which others can and will do for me (admittedly for a price) . . . and I don't ever expect to do them. Instead, I focus on what I can best do and what, indeed, must be done: creating and marketing info-products. This is my métier and I pursue it, because, like my mother, I was not put on this earth to mop floors.

If you are to become an info-tycoon, neither were you!

Trivia are cancers that destroy the soul of life. They will, if you let them, destroy you, too, until you are left, at life's end, wondering at just what point you lost sight of your objective and allowed yourself (for you have the power of choice) to be so waylaid. Trivia are a constant and unrelenting enemy which is why you must constantly be on your guard against them. Against this enervating scourge, you must deploy constant vigilance and constant deliberation. You must continually ask yourself if what you are about to do will assist you in producing a superior info-product . . . or in selling that superior info-product to someone who needs it. If the action you are contemplating will not succeed in achieving these objectives, why then that action is highly likely to be trivial . . . and as such not worth doing.

Do you live your life this way? Probably not. Indeed, I'd wager not. You feel obliged to:

- cut your day in half to have lunch with someone . . . merely because he asked you to do so;

- attend a meeting where you are not sure of the outcome or how the meeting can benefit you;

- go miles out of your way to deliver a speech to a group whose organizers couldn't be bothered to do what was necessary to give you a crowd;

- take care of all the prosaic tasks of your life . . . because you're perfectly capable of doing them and they need to be done.

STOP! *Each thing you do either helps you achieve your objectives, or it keeps you from achieving your objectives.* Of course, you are fully capable of washing your own clothes (even I remain capable of doing so) . . . but is this the best use of your time?

I tell you this: you must banish all the time-wasting prosaic tasks from your life, every single one of them, unless you have decided that such a task is therapeutic for you helping you relax, unwind, regenerate. Personally, I actually like packing books. It's dull, brainless, undemanding work . . . exactly the opposite of the usual highly exacting tasks I must ordinarily do. You'll need such a task in your life, too, if you're organizing your time properly. But you only need one such task!

Thus, analyze your life. How many things are you doing now that are not focused on either the developing of superior info-products or their sale? Now start chopping these out of your life, root and branch. Of course, you may not have the money today to get rid of them all. But your inability to make a complete sweep of time-destroying tasks is hardly a reason for not jettisoning those you can. Do what you can now. Do the rest as soon as you can. And put the increasing amount of time you have available to the necessary tasks that you must accomplish if you are to build the lucrative info-empire you say you wish to create.

Before concluding this point, I wish to share an anecdote with you. Some time ago I met an fellow about my age who told me how much he wanted to be a writer. Visiting him at home one day, I found his subterreanean living room dominated by a framed copy of one of his articles. The date of the article was fully a decade before the date of our meeting. Clearly this article had a special significance . . . special and, so it proved, horrifying to me. This, you see, was the last article this "writer" had actually written, much less had published. Not a word in ten years!

Why? He had an endless list of "reasons", job, family, God, cosmos. I didn't find a single one convincing . . . and I still don't. Indeed, I was completely contemptuous of these reasons and of the man who presumed to think I'd be stupid (or polite) enough to accept them. I told him the truth: that he'd never be a writer and that he should either do what it takes to succeed . . . or stop talking about it altogether. Moreover, that he should take the article down from its honored place . . . and instead, put up another frame, this time empty except for a giant date: the date by which his next article would be published.

Of course, this sad individual didn't follow my directions and now, years later, he is still unpublished, still no doubt bemoaning his sad fate and the disdain of a cruel world. I have no time for such degrading excuses, such contemptible creatures. But I do have time for the crucial tasks of my work . . . because I don't do floors. And neither should you!

Keep Analyzing Your Tasks To See How Each Can Be Done More Efficiently

I am an essentially conservative man . . . except when it comes to saving time. Here I run in a revolutionary crowd. I want to know . . . as you must want to know . . . everything you can about how you can do what you must do ever more efficiently.

This means making you and your work the subject of a constant time and motion study. You must be conscious both of what you need to do daily and how you do it. You need to scrutinize your work as an efficiency expert would do. And you need to be constantly on the alert for how you can do more while spending less time.

Concentrate on one task at a time. Examine, for instance, how you pack your books. Are you having to run from one side of the shipping area to another for the materials you need to bundle and send a single package? This, then, needs your earnest consideration. Progress, you see, is possible here.

Or how about the steps you go through when someone calls to request information. Do you write these data down? Why not input them directly into the computer and save yourself a step?

You see, the secret to efficiency is to consider each task separately and to think, really think, about how to do what needs to be done in ever less time.

This is not, regrettably, how most of us work. Most of us developed habits for no particular reason and work accordingly. In such circumstances, work comes to be seen as an end in itself. But, dear reader, work is never an end in itself. Work in itself in not ennobling or commendable. What is ennobling for us info-entrepreneurs certainly is this: to work so that we create the most superior products imaginable, the most helpful, useful, utilitarian and up-to-date, and to do everything we can to bring these products to the attention of the people who need them . . . and then get these people to buy them immediately. *This* is ennobling, commendable . . . and deliciously profitable.

People constantly ask me nowadays how I, a single person working largely alone, can achieve all that I do, building an enterprise of useful products, stupendous reach and escalating profits. The answer is both simple and profound: I approach each day with the deliberation it deserves. I remind myself upon waking that all too soon the day which is before me will be gone, irrevocably gone. That a fraction of my life will be beyond recall. And that if there is to be some meaningful result from the few hours that are now to be mine, I must do what needs to be done to accomplish it. Full responsibility rests on me for the fulfillment of this day, as full responsibility rests upon you for the fulfillment of yours. Do I want this to be known as the day in which I wasted my possibilities, abused my potential, and deprived my prospects of the crucial information that I have and which they need? Or can I turn this day . . . this day, too! . . . into a time when I made inexorable progress towards both my immediate and grander goals . . . helping myself, helping others?

Each day demands you ask these questions, because each day represents the possibility for measurable advance, or despicable decline. Today the multitude of men will not advance. At day's end they will not be closer to achieving their substantial goals. They will spend their evening offering excuses, seeking scapegoats, pointing fingers, cunningly exonerating themselves of all responsibility for bringing forth from such a promising day so very little.

But you will be doing something different. As the sun sets, you will look over today's "to do" list and be rightly pleased with yourself because of all that you have done. Before you turn out the lights and take your well merited rest, you will draw up a list of what must be done tomorrow . . . so that then you can continue your relentless march to achievement.

You are now the master of time. Your substantial achievements will follow as a matter of course!

Resources

Two excellent resources will help you get organized and become more efficient doing the tasks that we all must do. They are:

Organize Yourself by Ronni Eisenberg with Kate Kelley, MacMillan Publishing. Use this for help with your desk, calendar, bookshelves, taxes, travel planning and packing, medical payments, bill paying, banking, health records, even closets.

Working Smart: How To Accomplish More In Half The Time by Michael LeBoeuf, McGraw-Hill. You get many tips including 10 ways to make the telephone work for you; 14 things you can do to make meetings useful; 6 ways to strengthen your ability to concentrate and complete tasks, 20 suggestions for effective delegation, *etc.*

CONCLUSION

Congratulations!

You have arrived at the conclusion of this course and are ready to proceed with the most exciting adventure of your life . . . an adventure that will put your ideas and techniques in tangible form, get them into the hands of multitudes of people, and change their lives for the better! It also happens to be an adventure that can make you rich.

Now you have just what you need to accomplish all these objectives. You know how to:

- conceive of both a useful and marketable information product;

- make sure the right number of prospects exist to make this product worth creating;

- create a product that enables your targeted prospects to achieve what they want;

- market this product in a variety of cost-effective ways that will motivate your prospects to buy NOW;

- develop a line of info-products including books, booklets, audio cassettes and Special Reports;

- use techniques that get your happy customers to buy many of your info-products;

- update all your products so you can sell them so long as the problem exists that these products were created to solve;

531

- get other people to create profit-making products for you;

- integrate your computer into your business so that you can do more faster.

You also know how to develop and implement a Wealth Plan so that, with the profits you'll continually be making, you can move towards an ample life free from the inevitable uncertainties of business.

Yes, all this can be yours . . . *will be* . . . so long as you follow the directions in this guide conscientiously.

Fortunately, for us both our journey together need not end here. I have been with you this far, and I wish to be with you as you craft and market your next information product. If you got this book from me, you'll be hearing from me regularly with additional suggestions about how I can help you. If you didn't get this book from me . . . picked it up in a library or bookstore . . . you have to take the initiative to get in touch. Do. It's very much in your interest . . . whether you simply want additional profit-making suggestions from me, or whether you want me to help you directly craft and market your info-products.

It goes without saying that if you've created something that fits in my Sure-Fire Business Success Catalog, I especially want to see it . . . and perhaps to sell it. Nothing would give me greater pleasure than to market to my audience a product which I may have been of some small assistance in creating.

But whether I can sell your info-product or not, tell me about it. Share your tips and helpful information about the new things you discovered that I need to know to make this book better. You see, my learning journey is not over nor my desire to discover all that I can to assist people like you create the most utilitarian, client-centered info-products. And nothing would please me more than to learn these new things from you, my new friend, the person who is now equipped both to create and market the next great how-to product, a product that will enrich you while enriching the many who conscientiously use it. I salute you and look forward to hearing from you soon!

Surrounded by a mountain of paper, an underused exercise machine and the incessant hum of his computer, Dr. Jeffrey Lant confronts each day with one insistent question: "How can I help even more people develop their business by helping them raise the money they need, by helping them sell more of their products and services?"

He's answered—and continues to answer—this question in a variety of ways. Over the last 14 years, he's created the 8 volume "Get Ahead" Series that presents the exact steps people need to sell any product or service. In addition, he's written the standard book on how nonprofit organizations can raise the money they need from corporations, foundations, and individuals. His other books include a volume he edited on Harvard College and a rollicking history of Queen Victoria's Court that was presented to Queen Elizabeth II on a blue silk pillow.

Jeffrey also created and regularly writes the Sure-Fire Business Success Column now reaching over 1.5 million people monthly in about 200 print and electronic information sources in many countries... puts out the quarterly Sure-Fire Business Success Catalog... his quarterly Sales & Marketing Success card-deck and nationwide Lead-Generator Program ... and is president of JLA Ventures, which develops and markets many different products and services. Further, he is a well-known speaker on many business development and fund raising topics, offering programs around America and in other countries.

Holder of four earned university degrees, including a Ph.D. from Harvard, Jeffrey and his work have been honored by many institutions, both public and private. In 1991, he was raised to the dignity of The Rt. Hon. The Count of Raban by His Beatitude Alexander II, Patriarch of Antioch, Syria. This title was originally held by one of Jeffrey's ancestors who traveled with King Richard I of England to the Third Crusade, 800 years ago. Through his mother, a peeress in her own right, he is also heir to both the Barony of Barlais and the Barony of Kezoun, Crusader titles 8 centuries old.

At some point, like millions of people around the world who first connected with Jeffrey through a workshop, media program, audio or video cassette, article or book, you'll want to be in closer touch with this man to see how he can help you better. No problem! Whenever you're ready, simply call (617) 547-6372 or write P.O. Box 38-2767, Cambridge, MA 02238 to request your free year's subscription to his quarterly catalog (a copy of which concludes this book). He's ready for you *now!*

Call (301) 946-4284 now for your FREE marketing consultation

JEFFREY LANT'S
NATIONAL
COPYWRITING CENTER...

Where we produce *your* Cash Copy!

Get all the new business you need... right now!
Face it. You don't have the time or inclination to create the kind of forceful, benefit-rich, client-centered copy that gets prospects to BUY NOW... and customers to BUY AGAIN FAST! *So, let us do it for you!*

Now, thanks to our National Copywriting Center, you get:

- sales letters
- ads of any kind
- post cards/deck cards
- audio/video scripts
- brochures
- newsletters
- direct mail packages
- news releases/media kits

... or *anything else* designed to get your prospects/customers to ACT!

Do you need graphic design, yellow pages ads, mailhouse production and strategic marketing and PR consultation?
We do that, too — and our work is FAST and SURPRISINGLY AFFORDABLE! Indeed, some of our competitors are charging 5 times our prices! If you paid that much for marketing help you'd be awfully sorry...

One call to (301) 946-4284 starts things off. Call Director Dan McComas today to find out how to improve all your marketing communications NOW!!! There's no charge for this consultation... Don't wait until poor results convince you your marketing communications aren't working. Find out today!

Our assertive, results-oriented cash copy writers will help you sell more of your products/services FASTER than you thought possible with "killer" ads, sales letters, flyers, brochures... and anything else you need to generate leads and new sales.

CASH COPY: HOW TO OFFER YOUR PRODUCTS AND SERVICES SO YOUR PROSPECTS BUY THEM... *NOW!*

#B6 Cash Copy
NEW REVISED EDITION!!!
JUST UPDATED!!!

Look at the marketing "communications" you're putting out... ads, flyers, post cards, cover letters, proposals... and all the rest.

Is the first thing you see... your name? Your company name? Your photograph? Your address? Your logo? THEN YOU'RE PRODUCING SELF-ISH, "ME-CENTERED" MARKETING DOCUMENTS... INSTEAD OF CASH COPY... and your sales are suffering!!!

> *"I just finished reading your book CASH COPY. I have gotten a lot of books on selling, and it is by far the BEST!!!"*
> Ken Romeo, Elizabethtown, PA

Over 98% of the marketing communications you're producing right this minute are ending up in the trash. They don't get anyone to act. They don't get anyone to buy. Yet because you're spending a pile on producing this junk you think you're "marketing". GET OVER IT!

The marketing communications you're using are failures unless they get people to ACT... unless they get people to BUY. There is never another reason for producing any kind of marketing communication — certainly massaging your ego isn't one!

That's why you need CASH COPY in your office... now! Learn:
- the 21 biggest copywriting mistakes you're making — and how to avoid them;
- directions for turning your copy around so it's about your prospects... and not about you;
- how to turn product/service features into the benefits that really get people to buy.

You'll learn how to:
- turn every word, every line, each paragraph and page into hooks that motivate your prospects to buy NOW;
- get and use client-centered testimonials;
- create offers that motivate buyers...

And much, much more.

> *"Jeffrey, it's embarrassing but true that reading CASH COPY has been an enlightening, near-religious experience for me, so much so that I've become keenly evangelical about prospect-centered, results-oriented marketing for my small-business clients... Jeffrey, CASH COPY is so good that I'll continue to reread it until your marketing philosophy and fundamental principles are indelibly etched on my brain."*
> J. Frederick Blais, Jr., Richmond, VA

Thousands of business of every kind all around the world are profiting from this book. It's time you did, too.

Over 15,000 in print!
480 pages. $38.50

> *"Thank you for your book CASH COPY — it should be made mandatory reading for all corporate communications people."*
> Gregg Siegel, Wilmington, DE

#T1

CASH COPY AUDIO CASSETTE PROGRAM

Do you learn better by hearing? Then get the cash copy message in 12 hard-hitting audio cassettes based on the book. You get 18 hours of focused, profit-making advice, exactly what you need so you stop wasting your marketing dollars producing selfish, me-centered marketing.

These tapes are for people who are truly committed to getting more prospects to respond to their marketing communications faster... doing everything that's necessary to reduce the waste in their marketing budgets and substantially increase the return.

If that's you, here is it. $125

> *"CASH COPY is a <u>fantastic</u> book! It gave me more real, useable information about copywriting than anything else that I've ever read."*
> Kevin Hayden, Tucson, AZ

#C1

CASH COPY AUDIO CASSETTE AND BOOK PACKAGE

Get the complete CASH COPY package, including 480 page book and 18 hours of audio tape. Just $140. Save $23.50. This is the most comprehensive package ever assembled for creating marketing communications that get people to respond fast. You know this is what you want. This is, therefore, what you need.

THE UNABASHED SELF-PROMOTER'S GUIDE
What Every Man, Woman, Child And Organization In America Needs To Know About Getting Ahead by Exploiting The Media

Thousands and thousands of people around the world are already profiting from this book. They range from people running small businesses to two sitting members of the United States Senate, from people with the most idealistic motives to those who have no other motive than simply wanting to get filthy rich. Members of state legislatures and celebrities with well-known names are using this book to build their stature and promote their interests... entrepreneurs swear by it because it promotes their products and services to targeted markets.

"When I first bought your book THE UNABASHED SELF-PROMOTER'S GUIDE, I had no idea that it would be so instrumental in furthering my career... Your books have taught me more than four years of business school. And that statement says a lot! All I can say is THANK YOU."
Paul Hodgdon, Sudbury, MA

You need this book if you're:

• running *any* kind of business entity;
• selling *any* product or service;
• running *any* charitable or nonprofit organization;
• a professional who's tired of laboring in obscurity!

"Thanks for your material. It is truly worth its weight in platinum!"
Ronald Cusson, San Jose, CA

You get 364 of Jeffrey's characteristically information-dense pages. Learn how to:

• create Quintessential American Success Images... and avoid Failure Images;
• produce the documents you need to deal with the media. It's all here from media advisory, standard media release, biographical documents, fact sheets, chronology, position papers, prepared statements, media schedule, clip sheet, announcements, etc. *Every* form you'll ever use when dealing with the media is

already done... and immediately available for you;
• create and maintain a media Self-Promotion Network;
• produce all the print articles you'll ever need... you get exact formats the print media use every day and how and when to use them;
• handle every kind of media interview... including hostile ones;
• get just the right photographs... and how to use them;
• constantly appear on radio and television programs... and know what to do to promote your products/ services when you get there;
• get "waves" of media... not just isolated, single-shot appearances;
• create and promote books through free media... yes, there isn't an author or publisher in the world who should be without this book!
• use negative media... to enhance your image.
And much, much more.

Over 20,000 copies in print!
Item #B2
365 pages. $39.50 postpaid!

IF YOU'RE NOT MAKING *AT LEAST* $100,000 EVERY YEAR AS A SUCCESSFUL CONSULTANT, CALL JEFFREY IMMEDIATELY TO ACQUIRE THESE TWO ESSENTIAL RESOURCES:

#B1
THE CONSULTANT'S KIT: ESTABLISHING AND OPERATING YOUR SUCCESSFUL CONSULTING BUSINESS

This is the *only* book on consulting recommended by the U.S. Small Business Admin. to people who want to get off to a fast start in consulting... and there's a real good reason why. Jeffrey doesn't fool around. If you have specialized or technical skills and want to build a profitable consulting career fast, start here. This is his essential book for beginners... people who have been in business under a year... or are having trouble getting their act together.

Here's the help you need to:
- define your speciality to make the most money
- develop a contact network and get business fast
- market and promote your expertise
- upgrade a lead into a contract
- write contracts that protect your interests (yes, you get the *exact* language you need for letters of intent, commission engagements and full contracts)
- set up shop
- incorporate
- handle bookkeeping, accounting and tax matters

and much, much more.

Over 26,000 people worldwide have used this crucial resource to launch their consulting businesses in every imaginable field. How good is it? IBM just bought a bunch of them to give to top execs taking early retirement. If it's good enough for Big Blue... it's precisely what you need, too!

208 pages. $38.50

"My consulting and public speaking business is growing rapidly and I attribute a great deal of my success to you and your books."
Greg Smith, San Antonio, TX

#B4
HOW TO MAKE AT LEAST $100,000 EVERY YEAR AS A SUCCESSFUL CONSULTANT IN YOUR OWN FIELD: THE COMPLETE GUIDE TO SUCCEEDING IN THE ADVICE BUSINESS

Once you've mastered the consulting basics, here's where you go. This is the book that'll give you exactly what you need to make at least $100,000 every year as a consultant.

"May I offer my congratulations on your book THE CONSULTANT'S KIT! I checked it out at my local library. It is concise, well written, and an enjoyable read as well since you always seem to inject just the right amount of humor into your material."
Michael Cooney, Glendale, CA

There has never been a resource this detailed about what it really takes to make a six-figure consulting income. You find out how to:
- raise your fees higher than your competitors — and still seem like a bargain;
- get the big retainer contracts that get you income every month,

whether you're working for the client or not;
- develop a national — or even international — consulting business — in person and by phone;
- get the best results for the client — so you can leverage these results to get more clients in the same field... fast;
- develop the "passive income" sources that enable you to make money every day whether you're otherwise working or not... we're talking about books, booklets, audio cassettes, special reports, and more.

You'll get the low-down on how to use your computer for maximum efficiency (and where to get state-of-the-art hardware and software for rock-bottom prices); how to get detailed problem-solving information fast. There's even ready-to-use information on time management, stress reduction, and traveling smart.

This book — like everything Jeffrey produces — is packed with detailed money-making follow-up information. You get the names, addresses and phone numbers of the experts who can help you make the big money now. And complete details on dozens of other resources you'll want to know about and use to your advantage.

315 pages. $39.50

#C8
Get a deal on a combined package including THE CONSULTANT'S KIT and HOW TO MAKE AT LEAST $100,000 EVERY YEAR AS A SUCCESSFUL CONSULTANT IN YOUR OWN FIELD.

Stop wondering how to launch your consulting practice and squeeze it for all the profit possible. The information you need is right here, right now.

Just $68. Save $10.

Warning: I'll be raising the price of Money Talks soon. If you want the book at this low price, you have to move NOW!!!

#B3
MONEY TALKS: THE COMPLETE GUIDE TO CREATING A PROFITABLE WORKSHOP OR SEMINAR IN ANY FIELD

"Your knowledge of the subject of marketing is mind-boggling!"
Richard Lawrence, Lowell, MA

These are the only reasons for giving talk programs:
- you make money from them directly;
- you can use them to sell your products and services to people who attend;
- you can generate heaps of favorable publicity from them and build your reputation and perceived value.

Is this happening to you every time you give a talk program? If not, you need The Rev. Second Edition of MONEY TALKS.

For years now, this has been widely recognized as the most complete resource ever written on what it really takes to make money from talk. And with this revision, everything in it is up to date!

You'll find out how to:
- get sponsors for your programs;
- make the best deals with people who hire you;
- write descriptions of your programs that make people want to attend;
- make big money from back-of-the-room sales... even when you don't have products of your own;
- develop the audio & video cassettes, booklets, special reports and books you need to make really big money. I'm talking about over $10,000 a day... and, if you assiduously follow the directions, a whole lot more;
- squeeze the most publicity from every engagement;
- develop a networking system that generates a steady stream of speaking leads.

And a whole lot more.
308 pages. $35.

"I ran across your book MONEY TALKS at the local library, and I thought it was an absolutely superb work! I also heard about your book HOW TO MAKE AT LEAST $100,000 EVERY YEAR AS A SUCCESSFUL CONSULTANT IN YOUR OWN FIELD from a colleague, who recommended it highly."
Rick Ott, Richmond, VA

Now you can earn up to $3,000 easy dollars for just a few minutes work... and you can earn this much over and over again.

Who isn't looking for some easy money these days? I'm sure YOU are. Now you can get it... all by recommending Dr. Jeffrey Lant as a speaker to:
- business and professional groups
- colleges and universities
- trade shows and conferences... and any one else who needs a profit-making speaker.

When your recommendation results in an assignment, you get 10% of Jeffrey's honorarium... and product sales the day of the program. This can add up fast — up to $3,000 for you!

Here are just some of Jeffrey's popular topics:
- How to sell another million dollars of your product or service... now;
- Ten marketing mistakes you'll never make again;
- How to create marketing communicationns that get people to respond fast... and what to do when they do;
- How to make big money from your home-based business;
- How to make at least $100,000 every year as a successful consultant in your field;

- How to raise money for your nonprofit organization from corporations, foundations and individuals...

and many more!

Meeting planners: Call now for complete details about how you can book Dr. Jeffrey Lant for *your* programs. Jeffrey is a knowledgeable, enthusiastic and often electrifying platform speaker with a client-centered marketing message that will not merely inform and entertain your audiences but transform their business and personal lives.

How do you get on this gravy train? Contact the groups you're a member of... the business and professional associations you belong to... and recommend Jeffrey to them. Make sure they can either pay his minimum daily fee ($5000) or are willing to work with him to create a deal that generates this much money from a combination of fee and product sales. Then call Jeffrey at (617) 547-6372, and he'll take it from there. He has the necessary audio & video cassettes, books, articles, testimonials and recommendations to close the deal! As soon as he gets paid... you get paid. And remember, you can do this over and over again... and keep getting paid!

"I would like to say again how much I really enjoyed your lecture at Jacksonville, FL recently... I have two masters and you're the 1st educated person that really had anything of importance to say about making money."
Mike Winslett, Jacksonville, FL

YOUR NONPROFIT OR CHARITABLE ORGANIZATION IS LOOKING FOR MONEY. HERE'S WHAT YOU NEED TO GET IT...

#B8 New Edition! Just Published!
DEVELOPMENT TODAY: A FUND RAISING GUIDE FOR NONPROFIT ORGANIZATIONS

"The best tool I have is your book DEVELOPMENT TODAY. It's written in language I can understand and it's like having a friend hold my hand every step of the way! I refer to it constantly."
Helaine Fogel, American Friends of Assaf Harofeh Medical Center, Beverly Hills, CA

Tens of thousands of nonprofit organizations around America have made this book by Jeffrey the premier fundraising resource of its kind. Why? Because by following its detailed step-by-step guidelines, you raise the money you need for your capital, program and operating needs... even when money is tight.
You'll learn how to:
• determine how much money you can realistically raise;
• create the plan that'll get it for you;
• get even recalcitrant Board members to assist;
• pick just the right corporations and foundations to solicit;
• write fund raising proposals that get results and...
• ... follow up proposals that get rejected... so you can turn a no into a yes;
• raise money from community residents and businesses;
• use direct mail effectively and raise more money faster;

• mount profit-making special events... year after year;
• do your own capital campaign needs assessment and save tens of thousands of dollars;
• find volunteers... and get them to do what needs to be done...
and much, much more — including one of Jeffrey's characteristically packed Samples Sections containing ready-to-use documents, letters, log forms, etc. 282 pages. $29.95

PG#2
THE COMPLETE GUIDE TO PLANNED GIVING: EVERYTHING YOU NEED TO KNOW TO COMPETE SUCCESSFULLY FOR MAJOR GIFTS.

Look who's recommending Debra Ashton's definitive planned giving book these days:
American Association of Museums
American Lung Association
CASE
Christian Management Association
National Catholic Stewardship Council
National Hospice Organization
National Easter Seals
National Society of Fund Raising Executives
Planned Parenthood
Public Broadcasting System
Society for Nonprofit Organizations
and many, many more.
Why? Because if you expect to raise money from major gifts, the experts agree you must have this book.

"This is the most complete, practical guide ever written on planned giving!"
Frank Minton, President, National Committee on Planned Giving

Awesomely detailed information on how to:
• start a pooled income fund and gift annuity program
• use life insurance to facilitate major gifts
• conduct screening sessions to identify prospects capable of making major gifts
• find & use planned giving software & consultants;
• build board support for planned giving;
• use planned gifts to solve major donor problems
• develop a 12-month plan ensuring success for your program!
Based on current tax laws, this is a book you cannot afford to be without. 400 pages. $54.

BOTH THESE BOOKS ARE RECOMMENDED BY THE AMERICAN LIBRARY ASSOCIATION. IF YOUR CASH IS TIGHT, YOUR LOCAL LIBRARY WILL EITHER HAVE THEM... OR GET THEM FOR YOU! ASK!!!

"I'm mid way through HOW TO MAKE A WHOLE LOT MORE THAN $1,000,000... and had to stop to order additional books from you. I've read such junk published by hucksters, I wanted to let you know how grateful I am for your book. Besides being incredibly informative, it's downright funny! Thanks."
Frances O'Brien, Westport, CT

HEY, BARGAIN HUNTERS... HERE ARE FOUR PACKAGES THAT'LL SAVE YOU MONEY AND GIVE YOU MORE DETAILED, PROFIT-MAKING INFORMATION THAN YOU'VE PROBABLY EVER SEEN IN ONE PLACE IN YOUR LIFE.

#C4

Combined offer for the future information millionaire...

Four fast-paced, densely detailed books by Jeffrey give you a fast start towards becoming a million dollar+ producer & seller of books, booklets, audio cassettes and Special Reports. Whatever your field! Get **HOW TO MAKE A WHOLE LOT MORE THAN $1,000,000 WRITING, COMMISSIONING, PUBLISHING AND SELLING "HOW-TO" INFORMATION; CASH COPY; THE UNABASHED SELF-PROMOTER'S GUIDE** and **MONEY TALKS.** Just $115. You save over $40!

#C6

Combined offer for the people who want to sell more of their products and services faster...

Now benefit from Jeffrey's step-by-step marketing advice and learn how to sell more of your products and services for the least possible cost. Get a deal on **THE UNABASHED SELF-PROMOTER'S GUIDE, MONEY MAKING MARKETING** and **CASH COPY.** $80 for all three. You save $23.45.

#C7

... when you want to master all the master's profit-making techniques.

Get all eight books in Jeffrey's "Get Ahead" Series, including **CASH COPY, THE CONSULTANT'S KIT, THE UNABASHED SELF-PROMOTER'S GUIDE, MONEY TALKS, HOW TO MAKE AT LEAST $100,000 EVERY YEAR AS A SUCCESSFUL CONSULTANT IN YOUR OWN FIELD, MONEY MAKING MARKETING, HOW TO MAKE A WHOLE LOT MORE THAN $1,000,000 WRITING,**

COMMISSIONING, PUBLISHING AND SELLING "HOW-TO" INFORMATION and **NO MORE COLD CALLS!** Well over 3,000 pages of detailed step-by-step guidelines on achieving success by creating and selling products and services. No other specialist — anywhere — has ever written such complete instructions on what it takes to make money — lots of money. We'll be flabbergasted if you don't make back the cost of this package many hundreds of time. Get all eight for just $240. Save over $60! You automatically qualify for a free 60-minute cassette with this order!!!

#C9

Combined offer for service sellers who won't rest content until they're millionaires...

Now get a deal on the four essential resources that'll turn your service business into a cash-generating process that'll make you a millionaire. Package includes **NO MORE COLD CALLS!; CASH COPY; MONEY MAKING MARKETING,** and **THE UNABASHED SELF-PROMOTER'S GUIDE.** Just $110. You save $47!

All prices include shipping!

Special Reports ▬▬▬▬▬▬▬▬▬

We've already sold tens of thousands of these quick and dirty profit-making reports (#R1 – #R98). They're densely written five-page, single-spaced computer print-outs personalized with your name so you know you're supposed to follow the good-for-you directions. Don't expect fancy packaging. Just solid, up-to-date information you can use right now. Each report is packed with use-it-now details so you can achieve what the title promises. No one else in the country offers this kind of instantly available, eminently practical information in this form or gets them to you this fast. Stock up on 'em.

Just 6 bucks each, 3 for $14. ▬▬▬▬▬▬▬▬▬

#R1

THE SECRET TO BECOMING A MILLIONAIRE SELLING "HOW-TO" INFORMATION: 10 STEPS FOR CREATING, COMMISSION-ING, PUBLISHING AND SELLING PROBLEM-SOLVING BOOKS, BOOKLETS, SPECIAL REPORTS AND AUDIO CASSETTES. In honor of his new book **HOW TO MAKE A WHOLE LOT MORE THAN $1,000,000 WRITING, COMMIS-SIONING, PUBLISHING AND SELLING "HOW-TO" INFORMA-TION,** Jeffrey lays down the rules for profitably selling problem-solving information. $6

#R2

SIX STEPS TO MORE SUCCESS-FUL NEWSLETTERS. If you're putting any money into producing either a free or subscription newslet-ter... or even thinking about it... don't do anything until you get Roger Parker's steps for designing the product so it accomplishes your objectives. Roger's one smart cookie, and he knows what it takes to get people to pay attention to your newsletter. Here he shares this vital information with you. $6

#R3

WHICH 2% WILL YOUR AUDI-ENCE SIT STILL FOR? In honor of the publication of her new book, Jeffrey interviews author Marian Woodall on how to find the focus that is appropriate for each audience. Too many speakers try to cram everything they know into their talk... and end up alienating their audience. Not you. Here you learn exactly what you've got to do to give the right talk to the people you're speaking to. $6

#R4

HOW TO ELIMINATE JOB STRESS AND INCREASE PROF-ITS AND PRODUCTIVITY THROUGH STRESS MANAGE-MENT. Jeffrey interviews author Dr. Andrew Goliszek about what you can do to cut stress in the office. Stress doesn't just debilitate and even kill you... it cuts your profits! Here's what you can do to help yourself and break your stress habit. $6

#R5

MEGATRAITS: 12 TRAITS OF SUCCESSFUL PEOPLE. Jeffrey interviews Doris Lee McCoy, author of a new book based on interviews with several hundred successful people, and identifies the crucial traits, the "megatraits", they possess in common that helped get them where they are. $6

#R6

HOW TO MAKE YOUR PR MAKE MONEY. For most businesses, public relations is a useless activity that is not tied to the profit picture. Now Jeffrey tells you how to turn your expensive public relations into a money-making activity that will sell your products and services faster. $6

#R8

OVERWORKED ENTREPRE-NEURS' GUIDE TO LUXURIOUS CRUISE DISCOUNTS. Jeffrey interviews Captain Bill Miller, author of the superb new book *Insider's Guide To Cruise Discounts*, and provides you with specific information on how you can take some of the world's best and most luxurious cruises for ridiculously low rates. $6

#R9

WHAT EVERY INVENTOR ABSO-LUTELY MUST DO BEFORE CONTACTING ANY MANUFAC-TURER. Jeffrey interviews consultant Arnold Winkelman, author of the new book *The Inventor's Guide To Market-ing*, about precisely what you've got to do before you show any manufacturer your creation so that your rights are fully protected. Must reading if you're an inventor! $6

#R10

EIGHT SELF-DEFEATING BE-HAVIORS PREVENTING YOU FROM BECOMING THE MILLION-AIRE YOU *SAY* YOU WANT TO BE... AND WHAT TO DO ABOUT THEM! Here Jeffrey lays out eight significant behaviors making it difficult, if not impossible, for people to become millionaires and indicates just what to do to overcome them. If you keep talking about wanting to be a millionaire but just can't seem to get started... or keep failing along the way... these behaviors are probably bedevilling you. Learn what they are... and how to get rid of them. $6

#R11

EVERYTHING YOU NEED TO KNOW TO PREPARE YOUR OWN WILL — WITHOUT THE EXPENSE OF A LAWYER! Eight out of ten people in America die without a will, throwing their accumulated posses-sions and savings into the hands of the court system which then allocates what's available. To stop this idiocy, Jeffrey interviews Attorney Daniel Sitarz, author of the new book *Prepare Your Own Will And Testament — Without A Lawyer*. Here's exactly what you need to do to prepare your own legal will without a lawyer, securing your estate and saving the lawyer's fees. $6

#R12

WHY MOST CONSULTANTS CAN NEVER MAKE AT LEAST $100,000 A YEAR... AND WHAT TO DO SO YOU WILL. Jeffrey shows you why most consultants fail to make at least $100,000 a year... and provides specific steps to follow so you will. $6

#R13

HOW TO GET FREE AND LOW-COST SOFTWARE FOR YOUR IBM AND IBM-COMPATIBLE COMPUTER. Jeffrey interviews John Gliedman, author of the new book *Tips And Techniques for Using Low-Cost And Public Domain Software*, on how to get your hands on some of the stupendous amount of free and low-cost software currently available for IBM and IBM-compatible personal computers. Gliedman provides the names, addresses and phone numbers of just where to go to save big money on your software and techniques on how to use it effectively. $6

#R14

HOW TO CREATE CLASSIFIED AND SMALL SPACE ADS THAT GET YOUR PROSPECTS TO RESPOND... AND WHAT TO DO WHEN THEY DO! Jeffrey gives you the low-down on how to create classified and small space ads that get people to respond... and how to create an effective, profit-making program so you can turn your new prospects into buyers... fast! $6

#R15

SETTING AND GETTING YOUR FEE. Jeffrey interviews author Kate Kelly upon the occasion of a new edition being published of her well-known book *How To Set Your Fees And Get Them*. People selling a service either run the risk of pricing themselves too low (and working for too little) or too high... and losing the business. Kate tells you just what you need to do so you price your services just right... for fast sale and maximum return. $6

#R16

HOW TO MAKE MONEY BUYING PRE-FORECLOSURE PROPER-TIES BEFORE THEY HIT THE COURTHOUSE STEPS. Jeffrey interviews property investment advisor Tom Lucier, author of the new book *How To Make Money Buying Pre-Foreclosure Properties Before They Hit The Courthouse Steps*, on just what it takes to make big money in pre-foreclosure properties. New workshops have sprung up recently charging as much as $6000 for a weekend providing this kind of advice. Why pay 6G's when specialist Tom Lucier provides the detailed steps right here? $6

#R17

HOW TO DEVELOP AND USE A CLIENT-CENTERED QUESTION-NAIRE THAT GETS YOUR PROS-PECTS TO TELL YOU WHAT

THEY WANT... SO YOU CAN SELL IT TO THEM. In this report, Jeffrey helps people who hate making cold calls... and can't figure out how to get their prospects to tell them what they want. If you can solve this problem, you can sell any product or service. Here are the guidelines you need to create this unique client-centered prospecting questionnaire... and how to use it. When you do, your prospects start telling you precisely what they want... all you have to do is give it to them. $6

#R18

HOW TO DO "HOW-TO" (BOOK-LETS AND BOOKS, THAT IS). Here Jeffrey tells you exactly how to produce a how-to booklet or book that really tells your readers how to do what your title promises. Most how-to products are dismal failures, because they don't provide the details your readers need to achieve what they want. Don't let this happen to you. Learn how to create a truly useful how-to. $6

#R19

HOW TO MAKE OVER $100,000 *EVERY* YEAR WITH YOUR OWN CATALOG SELLING PROBLEM-SOLVING INFORMATION PROD-UCTS. Most people in mail order try to make a big kill from a single problem-solving information product... or just a few. Here Jeffrey shows you why that's futile... and how to go about establishing a client-centered catalog selling how-to information products that will make you at least $100,000 every year... and maybe a whole lot more. $6

#R20

HOW TO USE JOB ADS TO LAND THE JOB YOU *REALLY* WANT. If you've ever tried to get a job using classified job ads you know how time consuming and frustrating it is. Here Jeffrey interviews jobs-finding specialist Kenton Elderkin, author of the new book *How To Get Interviews From Job Ads: Where To Look, What To Select, Who To Write, What To Say, When To Follow-Up, How To Save Time.* With these techniques answering job ads can lead to the interviews you need... and the good job you want. $6

#R21

YOUR WORST FEARS REALIZED, OR WHAT TO DO WHEN THE CORPORATION OR FOUNDA-TION DECLINES YOUR PRO-POSAL. The competition for corporate and foundation dollars for non-profit organizations has never been greater... and will get worse. You can count on getting turned down, often. What you do next determines whether your organization will ever get the money it needs from these sources. Here are Jeffrey's guidelines for turning a no into a yes, for doing what it takes to build a lucrative relationship with a funding source that has just turned you down. Since this will happen to you (if it isn't happening already), prepare for it now. $6

Ordering multiple products? If what you're ordering comes from different pro-ducers, it will not be delivered at the same time. So, if you've only received a partial order, don't worry. THE REST IS ON IT'S WAY!

#R22

IT ISN'T JUST SAYING THE RIGHT THING THAT MAKES A SUCCESSFUL PRESENTATION... OR WHAT YOU'VE REALLY GOT TO DO TO CONNECT WITH YOUR AUDIENCE AND PERSUADE THEM TO LISTEN TO YOU. This isn't a report about speech content... it's a report about how to deal with your audience so they like you and want to listen to what you have to say. Verbal presentations aren't just about imparting information; they're about persuading people to do things. Here's what you've got to do to achieve this crucial objective. $6

#R23

HOW TO CREATE A BROCHURE AND COVER LETTER YOUR PROSPECTS WILL RESPOND TO... NOW! In honor of the new second printing of his book CASH COPY: HOW TO OFFER YOUR PRODUCTS AND SERVICES SO YOUR PROSPECTS BUY THEM... NOW!, Jeffrey tells you how to solve one of the most basic marketing problems of any business: what it takes to create a brochure and cover letter that gets people to respond, instead of being tossed. $6

#R24

HOW TO RAISE MONEY FOR YOUR NON-PROFIT ORGANIZA-TION WITH AN ANNUAL PHON-A-THON. Jeffrey tells you what you've got to do to use telemarketing to raise money for your non-profit organiza-tion... when you've got to work with community volunteers and can't afford professional help. $6

#F7

Join Jeffrey & Watkins
Looking for a money-making MLM?

Join Watkins:
• Stock nothing.
• Top quality products everyone uses everyday.
• Proven sales materials.
• Well-known, stable com-pany.
• Steadily growing monthly checks.
• Easy to sell.

For free information, contact Jeffrey at (617) 547-6372 or write F7 on page 566.

#R25

HOW TO BRING ORDER TO DESK CHAOS, OR ESSENTIALS OF ORGANIZING YOURSELF. Jeffrey talks to organizational specialist Kate Kelly, author (along with Ronni Eisenberg) of the best-selling book *Organize Yourself!*, about what you've got to do to control clutter and get all those papers in your business life under control. $6

#R26

HOW TO AVOID DESKTOP DIS-APPOINTMENT, OR WHAT YOU'VE *REALLY* GOT TO KNOW TO MAKE DESKTOP PUBLISH-ING WORK FOR YOU. Jeffrey interviews desktop design specialist Roger Parker, author of *Looking Good In Print*, on what to do to avoid the pitfalls of desktop publishing and use design to create compelling marketing communications. $6

#R28

HOW TO CREATE A MARKETING PLAN THAT SELLS YOUR SER-VICE... WITHOUT COSTING YOU ALL YOUR MONEY. Most people selling a service are "winging it" with predictable results: their marketing is episodic, spasmodic... unproductive. Jeffrey tells you how to create a marketing plan that will sell a service for the least possible cost and greatest results. $6

#R29

TELESELLING: HOW TO GET THROUGH THE SCREEN THAT'S KEEPING YOU FROM YOUR PROSPECT. Jeffrey talks to Art Sobczak, editor of *Telephone Selling Report*, on what you've got to do to get through your prospects' screens... switchboard operators, secretaries... anybody who stands between you and your next sale. $6

#R30

HOW TO OPEN A TELEPHONE SALES CALL WITH EITHER A PROSPECT OR A CUSTOMER... SO YOU GET THE BUSINESS. Jeffrey again talks to Art Sobczak, editor of *Telephone Selling Report*, on what to say during those crucial opening moments with a telephone prospect... and how to build profitable relationships by phone with existing customers. $6

Take Jeffrey's easy quiz to find out your business I.Q.:

- Do you have a laser printer in your office? Are you getting between 4,000-5,000 sheets per cartridge? And are you pay-ing no more than $45 per cartridge? You're not intelligent if you're getting fewer sheets than this for a greater price. Get your toner from us... and get smart! (See page 3)

- Do you place any space or card deck ads without a guarantee of a specific number of responses? If so, you're dumb! Use our nationwide Lead-Generator Program and get at least 200 guaranteed leads — with phone numbers. And get the rest of your leads for just 75 cents each. (See pages 16 & 17)

- Are you running a service business but aren't a millionaire yet? If this is you... and you aren't using my new book NO MORE COLD CALLS... it's time for analysis! Just $44.95 can significantly boost your wealth and help you squeeze *more from your business.*

- Do you call to place an order from one of my catalogs that's three, four or even 8 years old and berate me because prices have gone up? In this case, there's no hope for you.

#R31

HOW TO CREATE A PROPOSAL THAT A CORPORATION OR FOUNDATION WILL FUND. Jeffrey tells you and your non-profit organiza-tion what it takes to create a proposal that a corporate or foundation funding source will give money to support. $6

#R32

WHAT YOU HAVE TO DO TO SELL YOUR PRODUCTS AND SERVICES THROUGH A FREE CLIENT NEWSLETTER. Jeffrey tells you how to produce free client newsletters that get your prospects to buy your products and services. $6

#R33

HOW TO CREATE INEXPENSIVE, EFFECTIVE AUDIO CASSETTES TO GET MORE OF YOUR PROS-PECTS TO RESPOND FASTER... AND MAKE EXTRA MONEY, TOO. Jeffrey tells you how to create inexpen-sive 60-minute audio cassettes in your home or office that you can use to induce more and faster sales... and sell profitably, too. $6

#R34

HOW TO PROFIT BY INVESTING IN USED AND BRUISED HOUSES. Jeffrey gets step-by-step advice from Florida author and investor Thomas Lucier on how to make money in real estate through affordable used and bruised houses, one of today's smart investments for people with a moder-ate amount to spend. $6

#R35

HOW TO USE WORKSHOPS AND OTHER TALK PROGRAMS TO GET CLIENTS. In honor of the publication of the new Second Edition of his well-known book MONEY TALKS: HOW TO CREATE A PROF-ITABLE WORKSHOP OR SEMINAR IN ANY FIELD, Jeffrey tells you how to use lectures and talk programs to get clients. $6

The list of Special Reports continues on page 552. First look at the Special Offers on pages 550-551!

GET *REALLY* RICH WITH JEFFREY LANT'S SALES & MARKETING SUCCESS CARD DECK

Are you selling nationwide? Are you offering a product/service that will increase another business' profitability? How about a health, travel or investment service? Or a business opportunity? Do you offer business equipment or products? Or have you got a way of making a business more efficient? Are you interested in getting AN UNLIMITED NUMBER of qualified leads for the least possible cost? Or selling direct? ━━━━━━━━

If you've said yes to *any* of these questions, and you're not already using my Card-Deck Lead-Generator Programs, IT'S TIME YOU DID!

#1 ▪▪▪▪▪▪▪▪▪▪▪▪▪▪▪▪
Make Money From Jeffrey Lant's Sales & Marketing SuccessDek

A) My deck offers 100,000 carefully targeted **card-deck responsive names**. Other decks offer inferior subscription or compiled names. Not me. 100% of the business decision makers we mail to have already responded to an offer in a business card deck... within the last 90 days! Therefore you are assured of getting to people who not only want offers that help them... but are willing to respond IMMEDIATELY.

B) **My prices.** No one in the entire industry offers you prices like mine. We've been the lowest since our first day of business; we're the lowest now. Just $650 for 50,000 two-color cards; $1199 for 100,000 two-color cards and $1350 for 100,000 four-color cards. **No one in the entire industry is remotely close to us in price.** (You could easily pay over $3,000 more for the same circulation if you go with someone else. Check

Standard Rate & Data and see for yourself.) If money is important to you, we're the right place for you. We can offer you the lowest cost — and hence the lowest per-lead and per-sales cost — in the whole card-deck industry WITHOUT EXCEPTION.

Why are my prices so low? First, we pre-pay our printing bill and pass on the savings to you. Second, we give no credit. Everyone pays for their card up front. This way, we don't have to bear the heavy cost of credit... and we pass all these savings on to you. Moreover, I participate in the deck myself... with up to 8 cards. So I make money just like you do — by selling my products/ services. No other publisher in the industry advertises as heavily in his own deck as I do. Other decks make their money the minute you buy their cards; they are principally card-deck publishers. We make money like you do — by selling our products and services through the deck. I hope you understand this difference — it's crucial to why our deck works so well and why it will pay off big for you.

C) **Free second color.** Other decks charge you for color. I don't. If you want a second color, you get it free. And if you need help deciding where to put this color, we provide it.

D) **Free copywriting assistance.** If you need **help** with your copy, you

get it — free. Other decks don't offer this service. We do. We know what's going to get you the best results (after all, we mail millions of cards yearly), and we're happy to work with you — at no charge — so you get them. If you want us to develop your card from scratch, we can help you there, too — but there is a charge for this service. Call our expert copywriter Dan McComas for this service at (301) 946-4284. He can create a card up to two days before our closing... but he'll be grateful if you don't wait so long until contacting him. **Note:** Dan can also help you create the response packages you're going to need for all your new business! Call him for a **FREE CONSULTATION** about what you're using now... or for ideas on what to use to increase your response.

E) **Top 10 & Top 20 Positions.** If you pay for your card 90 days before the issue mails, you'll get a TOP 10 position — assuming any remain. If you pay for your card 60 days prior to publication, you'll get a TOP 20 position, again if space is available. Other decks charge you extra for position. We don't. We run 88 cards per issue and if you want to be among the first cards recipients see, just pay early — NOT MORE. If you pay at closing, we put you where we want you!

GENERATE
UNLIMITED LEADS
THROUGH THE JLA
LEAD-GENERATOR PROGRAM

#2 • • • • • • • • • • • • • • • •

Profit from the JLA Lead-Generator Program.

With this simple, inexpensive program you can generate **UNLIMITED** leads from around the country for your product/service. How does it work? Easy: we buy space in many business card decks and run your ad along with others on a single card. You get access to hundreds of thousands of people at incredibly low prices!

Check out these benefits:

A) **Get as many leads as you want... without a long-term commitment.** If you want thousands of leads, we can accommodate you! If you want fewer, no problem! You can cancel whenever you want.

B) **Get leads in the format you want.** We offer names on labels, on computer diskette, and on laser print-out. With the last two you get phone numbers, too, (if respondents have supplied them.) Sorry, we do not supply phone numbers if you ask for output on labels.

C) **Get your leads FAST.** Once you sign up, it takes 6-7 weeks to start getting leads. As your leads start coming in, we ship them every two weeks COD. We pay the COD charge, not you!

D) **Low cost.** We're already famous for the low cost of our Sales & Marketing SuccessDek, described above. This program is no different. There's a one-time only sign up charge of $300 which covers typesetting your ad, copywriting assistance

Get in on the July mailings! At least 650,000 cards are going out. You can be part of this. Your space on the card is assigned when you pay. Deadline for July mailings is June 15th! If you miss this deadline, we will accommodate you for September mailings.

and *200 guaranteed leads*! Thereafter, the per name cost drops to just 75 cents per name, so long as you stay in the program. In other words, you can get unlimited names at 75 cents each... a big savings when you consider comparable programs charge up to $3 per name. And keep in mind that you never get any guarantee of leads from any space advertising program... or from any other card deck!!! **We'll keep running your ad until you get at least 200 people who say they're interested in what you've got!**

E) **Get Better Qualified Leads...** *people who really want to buy what you're selling right now!* Since we've been running lead-generating cards in our card deck for other companies for many years now, we know the tricks of this game. There are certain "freebie seekers" who send in such cards with every single

thing checked. The typical publisher knows who these people are (they respond to everything), but never deletes them from his list. He makes big bucks sending you junk names. We're different. We know who these "freebie seekers" are — and we ruthlessly purge them off our list. Also, if a person checks too many things, we just toss the inquiry card away. We want you to have success... and we don't want to waste our money, either, by mailing them our information. We all gain. Try to get this commitment from other lead-generator companies. **You can't!**

When you're ready to start making money from card-decks, generating unlimited leads and selling direct call Jeffrey at (617) 547-6372.

Space is severely limited for both programs... and we're looking for serious people only who want us to work with them to make them wealthy.

1993 Sales & Marketing SuccessDek CLOSING DATES

May 28 (mailing June 30)
August 25 (mailing October 4)
November 22 (mailing Jan 4, 1994)

The Special Reports listing continues here...
$6 each; 3 for $14

#R36
THINKING ON YOUR FEET, ANSWERING QUESTIONS WELL WHETHER YOU KNOW THE ANSWER — OR NOT. People who can't deal effectively with questions present a poor self-image and can harm a company Here Jeffrey interviews Marian Woodall, author of a popular book on the subject, about how people can master the crucial "thinking on your feet" strategies. $6

#R38
WHY YOU NEED SPECIAL REPORTS: HOW TO WRITE THEM, USE THEM TO GET PEOPLE TO BUY WHAT YOU'RE SELLING NOW, TO PUBLICIZE YOUR BUSINESS, AND MAKE MONEY! The secret to successful marketing is making people take action NOW to get what you're selling. Jeffrey shows you how to create inexpensive but powerful Special Reports and how to turn them into compelling marketing tools that get your prospects to respond NOW, and that you can also sell profitably. $6

#R39
COPY FLAWS THAT DOOM YOUR EXPENSIVE MARKETING DOCUMENTS TO LINE BIRDCAGES IN SAINT LOUIS. Jeffrey tells you just what you need to write marketing copy that gets people to buy. Key rules of profit-making copy. $6

#R40
YOUR GRAND OPENING: HOW TO START YOUR MARKETING DOCUMENTS SO PEOPLE *BUY* WHAT YOU'RE SELLING. If your marketing documents don't draw people in immediately, you — and your next sale — are lost. Jeffrey tells you precisely what to do to begin documents so your prospects read what you have to say — and buy what you have to sell. $6

#R41
COMPUTER-ASSISTED MARKETING: HOW TO INCREASE YOUR PRODUCTIVITY AND MAKE EVERY PROSPECT AND CUSTOMER FEEL YOU'RE DELIVERING *EXACTLY* WHAT HE WANTS. People have computers but aren't using them effectively. Now learn to turn the computer into your best marketing tool. You'll read things here you've never seen before and increase your marketing productivity astonishingly. $6

#R42
MONEY MAKING MAIL, OR HOW TO AVOID THE TEN BIGGEST MAIL ORDER MISTAKES. Every day I get deluged with mail order offers that make me weep for the trees that have died. What rubbish! There are rules to succeed in mail order. Here's what you should avoid — and what you should do. $6

#R43
HOW TO CREATE AND USE OFFERS YOUR PROSPECTS FIND IRRESISTIBLE. The trick to marketing is to create and sell offers — not products and services. Here's what you need to know about offers, how to create them and use them so that your prospects will buy. $6

#R44
KNOWING WHAT TO DO WHEN PEOPLE OWE YOU MONEY, OR HOW TO GET PAYMENT IN FULL. Don't give way to the rage and frustration of being owed money by deadbeats. Get what you're owed. Here's what you need to do in practical detail. $6

#R45
HOW AUTHORS AND THEIR PUBLISHERS MUST WORK TOGETHER TO SELL MORE BOOKS. Follow these precise steps to construct a profitable author-publisher partnership, so each of you makes money from the book. $6

#R46
YOUR IRA: WHY YOU *STILL* NEED IT, WHAT YOU NEED TO KNOW ABOUT INVESTING IT. If you've lost interest in the IRA, think again. Tax-free compounding of earning's no joke, and millions can still take their contribution off their taxes. Here's the low-down. (By the way, last year IRA contributions were substantially up. This report no doubt helped!) $6

#R47
TELESMARTS: EFFECTIVELY USING TELEMARKETING TO SELL YOUR PRODUCTS AND SERVICES. Most people are hideously ill-equipped to use the phone to sell anything. Here are the basics (and some advanced tips, too) on how you can turn the phone into a profitable business tool. Have I reached out and touched you? $6

#R48
HOW TO OVERCOME SALES OBJECTIONS, INCLUDING THE BIGGEST ONE OF ALL: "YOUR PRICE IS TOO HIGH!" If you're in sales (and if you're reading this, you are), you've got to learn how to deal with objections. Here's what you need to know so that you can. $6

#R49
HOW TO STOP BEING THE LOWLY ORDER-TAKER, BECOME THE CONSUMMATE MARKETER, AND GET MORE SALES FROM NEW BUYERS. The dumb marketer simply sells a prospect what that prospect wants to buy. The expert marketer learns the prospect's problem and persuades him to take an upgraded solution. Here's how to do that. $6

#R50
TESTIMONIALS FOR YOUR PRODUCT OR SERVICE: WHY YOU NEED THEM, HOW TO GET THEM, HOW TO USE THEM. If you aren't using testimonials now, you are missing a prime marketing device. If you are, make sure you're doing it right! $6

> *"I am enthralled by your book HOW TO MAKE A WHOLE LOT MORE THAN $1,000,000.... It is superb. I intend to get more of your books!"*
>
> Bob Bishop, Pearl, MS

#R51

UNDERSTANDING AND PROFITING FROM THE RULE OF SEVEN: CONNECTING WITH YOUR BUYERS AND CONNECTING WITH THEM AGAIN UNTIL THEY BUY WHAT YOU'RE SELLING. Most marketing gambits don't work. In part this is because you don't hit your prospects sufficiently often to interest them in what you're selling. Now learn how you can. The Rule of Seven is the prime rule of marketing. $6

#R52

MARKETING YOUR BOOK BEFORE IT'S PUBLISHED. Stupid authors and publishers wait to begin marketing and making money from their books until they are physically available. Don't you be one of them. Follow the detailed guidelines in this report and make money long before your book is even printed. $6

#R53

WHAT TO DO WHEN YOUR PROSPECT SAYS NO. We all get turned down. Now what? Tears? Rage? No! Use Jeffrey's step-by-step guidelines to get the sale after all — or do what it takes to get the next one! $6

#R54

ESSENTIALS OF MONEY MAKING MARKETING. Successful marketing is the key to business success. Now learn precisely what you have to do to improve your marketing. Follow these steps; sell more. $6

#R55

WHY YOU NEED A BUSINESS PLAN, WHY YOU RESIST CREATING ONE. Makes a clear case for why you must have a business plan to succeed, how to overcome your resistance to creating one, and what should go in it. A must, particularly for new and struggling entrepreneurs. $6

#R56

HOW TO GET THE LOWEST CARD-DECK ADVERTISING PRICES AND MAKE THE MOST MONEY FROM CARD-DECK ADVERTISING. Card-decks can get you maximum response for the least price. Now in honor of Jeffrey's Sales & Marketing SuccessDek, you can learn the secrets of how to get the lowest prices and biggest response. $6

#R57

TEN THINGS YOU CAN DO RIGHT NOW TO GET MORE MONEY FROM YOUR NEXT FUND RAISING LETTER. If you're running a non-profit organization and expect to raise money using fund-raising letters, read this report first. Jeffrey's been writing profit-making fund-raising letters for non-profits for over a decade. Here's what he's learned to make you more money. $6

#R58

HOW TO GET THE MOST BENEFIT WHEN WORKING WITH CONSULTANTS: THE 10 BIGGEST MISTAKES YOU'RE NOT GOING TO MAKE. All too often organizations hiring consultants don't get their money's worth. This won't happen to you if you follow the guidelines in this sensible report. $6

#R59

WHAT YOU THINK MAY BE A COPY PROBLEM MAY REALLY BE A STRATEGIC MARKETING PROBLEM ... HERE'S WHAT YOU CAN DO TO SOLVE IT. All too often what people think is a copy problem is actually a strategic marketing problem. Your marketing strategy has got to be right before you can create the most effective copy. For just $6 you learn how to create the strategy that gets people to buy what you're selling. (Then you can use CASH COPY to create the copy itself!)

#R60

HOW TO HAVE AN EFFECTIVE MEETING, OR WHAT YOU'VE REALLY GOT TO DO TO STOP WASTING YOUR TIME AT NON-PRODUCTIVE BUSINESS GET-TOGETHERS. Before you waste another senseless minute in a pointless meeting (or, God forbid, chair such a meeting) get this report and learn how to structure meetings so you get what you want — the only reason for having a meeting in the first place. $6

#R61

HOW TO TURN YOUR (PREVIOUSLY UNREAD) ANNUAL REPORT INTO AN ACTION ORIENTED MARKETING DOCUMENT THAT GETS PEOPLE TO DO WHAT YOU WANT THEM TO DO! For most organizations — profit and not-for-profit — annual reports are a complete waste of time and money. Who reads them? But properly created annual reports can become powerful marketing documents that get you new business. Here's what you need to know about creating them. $6

#R62

HOW TO GET YOUR CLIENTS TO GET BUSINESS FOR YOU. There are tricks for getting your existing (and past) customers to get new business for you. Here they are. When you have a customer you get not only current income but future business ... if you use these techniques. $6

"Everyone selling or marketing anything absolutely must have all of your books and tapes!!"
Dan Bodanis, Mississauga, Ont., Canada

#R63

HOW TO SET UP AN INDEPEN-DENT AGENT REFERRAL SYS-TEM AND GET HUNDREDS OF PEOPLE TO REFER YOU TO ORGANIZATIONS NEEDING PAID SPEAKERS. Talk programs remain a superb way to make money — often astonishingly large amounts of money. Problem is: booking agents don't want you until you're a celebrity and cold calling is an agony. The solution? Set up your own Independent Agent Referral System to generate a constant stream of program leads. Here Jeffrey — one of America's best-known speakers — explains just how to do it! $6

#R64

HOW YOU CAN MANAGE YOUR BUSINESS' CASH FLOW EFFEC-TIVELY. Prosperity in the 'nineties means getting your hands on money earlier and managing that money more effectively. Here Jeffrey gets tips from Les Masonson, author of a new book intriguingly titled *Cash, Cash, Cash*, about the secrets of better cash management. Details about how to work with your bank you've never seen before. $6

#R66

HOW TO WRITE A BUSINESS PROPOSAL THAT GETS YOU THE BUSINESS. If you have to write proposals to get contracts, learn Jeffrey's secrets for creating proposals that get you the business — instead of wasting your time and money. $6

#R68

MARKETING IN THE BAD TIMES: HOW TO SELL MORE OF YOUR PRODUCTS AND SERVICES EVEN IN A RECESSION! If you didn't read this in my syndicated column and are still in a part of the country (as I am) where the recession isn't over, here are detailed sugges-tions to keep selling your product/service — yes *more* of your product/service! — even when times are bad. $6

#R69

WHAT YOU'VE GOT TO DO BEFORE YOU WRITE ANY MAR-KETING COMMUNICATION — FLYER, PROPOSAL, AD, COVER LETTER, ETC., OR DOING THE HOMEWORK THAT PRODUCES THE MARKETING COMMUNICA-TION THAT GETS YOUR PROS-PECT TO BUY WHAT YOU'RE SELLING In honor of the publication of his well-known book MONEY MAK-ING MARKETING: FINDING THE PEOPLE WHO NEED WHAT YOU'RE SELLING AND MAKING SURE THEY BUY IT, Jeffrey tackles one of the most important marketing prob-lems: showing how lack of client-centered preparation makes it impos-sible to produce marketing communi-cations that get people to respond. Here are the steps you need to take so you'll regularly produce profit-making marketing documents. $6

#R70

FIVE CRUCIAL THINGS YOU NEED TO KNOW TO MAKE REAL MONEY IN YOUR HOME-BASED BUSINESS. Up to 22,000,000 Ameri-cans derive some or all of their income working from home. Yet the vast majority gross only about $15,000 yearly — peanuts! Here Jeffrey, who's run a home-based business for over 12 years and became a millionaire in the process, provides crucial information on how to create a business at home that will produce $100,000 a year — or more. $6

#R71

HOW YOU CAN OVERCOME WRITER'S ANXIETY AND PRO-DUCE EFFECTIVE LETTERS, MEMOS, REPORTS, PROPOSALS, ETC. Virtually everyone in American business is called upon to write something for the job. Yet the vast majority of people hate to write — and do it badly. Here Jeffrey interviews New York writing coach Jim Evers, author of *The Hate To Write But Have To Writer's Guide*, to get specific suggestions on how you can overcome your writer's anxiety and produce effective business writing. $6

#R72

HOW TO TALK SO MEN WILL LISTEN. Women regularly report that talking to men (bosses, colleagues,

Significant Others) is like talking to a brick wall. They talk, but does anyone really *hear* them? Now Oregon specialist Marian Woodall tackles one of civilization's oldest problems and, as usual, offers detailed suggestions on what women can do to get their points across — and what men should do to hear women. A perfect report for women who want to communicate more effectively with men... and men who really care about women! $6

#R73

HOW TO DETERMINE THE RIGHT COMPUTER OR PRINTER FOR YOUR BUSINESS AND WHERE TO BUY THEM FOR THE BEST PRICES. This report is for people who may be selecting their first computer and printer, or for seasoned veterans who want to make sure they get just the right kinds of machines for their needs — and don't overpay for them. Jeffrey interviews Maine computer expert Ted Stevens on how to determine how to get the right computer and printer for your situa-tion and where to get the best prices for them. $6

Order from this catalog by October 1, 1994 and you get these special free premiums:

1) Order anything, and keep getting this catalog. Don't miss out on Jeffrey's latest recommendations for improving your business.

2) Order at least $150 and get — *absolutely free* — your choice of any one of Jeffrey's three 60-minute audio cassettes (#T1,2,3). A $16 value, practical infor-mation you can put to work immediately.

3) Order at least $275 and get any one of Jeffrey's "Get Ahead" Books absolutely free... up to a $44.95 value. Select any title from #B1, B2, B3, B4, B5, B6, B7, B8 or B9 AND GET THE 60-MINUTE AUDIO CAS-SETTE OF YOUR CHOICE, TOO!!!

#R74

HOW TO MAKE MONEY WITH REAL ESTATE OPTIONS. Here Jeffrey interviews real estate expert Tom Lucier, author of the new book *How To Make Money With Real Estate Options*. Tom provides step-by-step details about how investors with limited funds can profit from real estate — without *owning* any real estate... thanks to real estate options. Shows you how to get the right properties, pay the lowest option fees, and create the right kind of option to purchase agreements. Crucial information so you can make money in real estate despite the current real estate market "melt-down." $6

#R75

THE TOP FIVE SALES-KILLING MISTAKES YOU'RE MAKING IN TELESALES... AND HOW TO AVOID THEM! Jeffrey interviews Art Sobczak, the super-smart publisher of *Telephone Selling Report* newsletter, about the five biggest mistakes telephone sales people make that kill sales — and how to avoid them. Must reading if you're trying to sell a product/service by phone. $6

#R76

HOW TO LOWER YOUR PROP-ERTY TAXES THIS YEAR — AND KEEP THEM DOWN YEAR AFTER YEAR! Jeffrey interviews Gary Whalen, author of the new book *Digging For Gold In Your Own Back Yard: The Complete Homeowners Guide To Lowering Your Real Estate Taxes*. Millions of Americans are paying too much property tax. This could be you. Here Jeffrey draws on Gary Whalen's experience to show you how to pay the lowest legal real estate tax. $6

#R77

CONSULTANTS: EIGHT CRUCIAL THINGS YOU MUST DO TO MAKE AT LEAST $100,000 EVERY YEAR. Smart consultants now have mid-six figure and even 7-figure incomes. But most consultants earn a tiny fraction of these high flyers. Why? Here Jeffrey lays out the reasons most consultants consistently fail to reach their income objectives and lays down specific rules you can follow so you'll make at least $100,000 every year from your practice. $6

#R78

THE TEN THINGS YOU MUST DO TO BECOME A MILLIONAIRE SELLING SERVICES. Millions of Americans sell services but most of them aren't anywhere close to being millionaires. This is because they don't understand how to use their service business as a lever to make themselves really rich. Here Jeffrey shows exactly what service sellers must do to become millionaires. Clear, easy-to-follow steps that could make you really rich, even in the deflationary 'nineties! $6

#R79

HOW TO GET RICH USING CARD-DECK ADVERTISING. Many more people than currently advertise in card-decks should be in them, Jeffrey asserts. They're a superb and cost effective way for generating a large volume of fast leads and making sales; a crucial part of a sensible marketing program. Here Jeffrey points out just what businesses must do to use card-decks effectively so they get the most leads and make the most sales from them. Getting rich from card-decks is possible for many businesses. Jeffrey's suggestions show you how to do it. $6

If you're serious about card-decks, you should be in Jeffrey's deck and nationwide lead-genera-tor program. They offer the lowest prices in the industry and always fill up. Call (617) 547-6372 for complete details.

#R80

HOW TO CREATE AND MAKE MONEY FROM AN INFORMA-TION PRODUCT... FOR LIFE! Tens of thousands of 'how-to' booklets, books, audio & video cassettes and Special Reports are produced annually — but most of their creators don't make much money, much less turn their creation into a life-time income. Here Jeffrey, the doyen of America's info-producers, lays out the necessary steps that ensure that *each* information product produces maximum income for life. $6

#R81

THE 10 THINGS YOUR (NON-PROFIT) MARKETING SHOULD NEVER BE! Are you working for a nonprofit organization? Then chances are your marketing is rudimentary and inefficient. Here is Jeffrey's hard-hitting look at the mistakes nonprofits make and precisely what to do to correct them. With virtually all nonprofit organizations facing tough budget times, it is immoral to fail to learn exactly how to use the limited dollars you've got for marketing more productively. Here's what you need! $6

#R82

MAXIMIZING MEMORY POWER: MAKING SURE YOU NEVER FORGET GOOD OL' WHAT'S HIS NAME. Jeffrey interviews Bob Burg, creator of the six-cassette tape album "On Your Way To Remembering Names & Faces", about how to solve the important business problem of remembering names and crucial information about the people you meet... people you want to remember and do business with. The perceptive Burg offers an easy-to-follow six-step method that gives you just what you need so you never forget crucial information about the people you're meeting. $6

#R83

HOW TO MOVE A WHOLE LOT MORE OF YOUR PRODUCTS AND SERVICES.... THANKS TO MOV-ING MESSAGE SIGNS! Jeffrey interviews moving message sign king Bill Reece about how to use these signs to move more products and services faster. These signs have been popping up everywhere... in airports, banks, school cafeterias, at trade shows... everywhere! Now learn how to select the right sign for your business and how to turn it into a fascinating client-centered marketing tool that gets your message out 24 hours a day for just the cost of the electricity. Whatever you're selling, Reece clearly shows why there's a moving message sign in your future. $6

#R84

HOW TO MAKE $100,000 EVERY YEAR FOR YOUR MLM OPPORTUNITY USING CARD-DECK ADVERTISING. Most people in MLM make pitiable amounts of money. The disaffected drop out of one program, latch on to another, hopeful all over again, only to find they're not making money in that either. Here, however, Jeffrey shows you how to use card-deck advertising to generate thousands of leads quickly at minimum cost and build a 6-figure MLM income. Up till now card-decks have been too expensive for most MLM people, many of whom run small organizations. Not any more! Indeed, Jeffrey even shows you how to get 100,000 cards for no direct cost... $6

#R85

THE INGENUE MARKETER'S GUIDE TO CERTAIN FAILURE... OR, IT WOULD BE A LOT FASTER AND EASIER SIMPLY TO THROW YOUR MONEY OUT THE WINDOW. This article is principally for non-profit organizations but the lessons are relevant to all ingenue marketers who need to be aware of the mistakes they're making so they can correct them and start running a marketing program that achieves substantial results. If that's your objective, you'll be certain to want to read this step-by-step report. $6

#R86

WHEN YOU CAN'T WRITE THE MARKETING COPY YOURSELF, OR HOW TO GET THE BEST

RESULTS FROM YOUR COPY WRITER. Most business people are terrible writers, and as a result they produce terrible marketing communications which don't get them the clients they need. Here Jeffrey interviews nationally known copywriter Dan McComas, director of the National Copywriting Center, on how to find the right copywriter and how to work with him/her to get the results you want. $6

Note:

Want to get started producing superior copy faster? Call Dan McComas directly at (301) 946-4284!

#R87

HOW TO GENERATE FAR MORE LEADS FOR SELLING YOUR PRODUCT AND SERVICE AND HOW TO DETERMINE WHICH OF THEM ARE WORTH YOUR TIME AND MONEY. Most business people get too few leads, too few good leads, and thus spend far too much time with both too few people and the kinds of people they shouldn't be trying to work with at all. Here Jeffrey, one of America's most aggressive lead generators, shows you how to generate all the leads you want... and how to decide which of them you should be spending your time with. $6

#R88

DO YOU *REALLY* WANT TO BE RICH? TAKE THIS REVEALING QUIZ AND FIND OUT... I've often wondered how many of those people talking about wanting to be rich actually will do what it takes to become rich. If you' re wondering about yourself, take my handy quiz and find out if you *really* have what it takes to get rich. $6

R89

FIVE MARKETING COMMUNICATIONS YOU CAN USE RIGHT NOW TO GET FAST NEW BUSINESS. Most business people are wasting their precious resources producing marketing communications that just get trashed. Here Jeffrey provides the detailed information they need to produce five key marketing communications in use in most offices, namely "the reason why" communica-

tion (providing reasons why prospects should buy what you're selling); the comparison document (showing that what you've got is superior to your competitors); the marketing document that sells your offer to induce faster prospect response; the quick follow-up document to prospects who haven't yet responded, and the "we thought you were dead" marketing communication that compels your prospects' attention and gets them to respond at last. $6

R90

HOW TO MAKE MONEY FROM THE PLATFORM: WHAT IT REALLY TAKES TO SELL THE MAXIMUM AMOUNT OF YOUR PRODUCT WHEN YOU'RE GIVING A SPEECH OR WORKSHOP. Jeffrey, one of America's most successful platform and workshop speakers, provides detailed guidelines on what it takes to make maximum money selling product at your workshops and other talk programs. Real money in the talk market is made by selling product, not by getting a speaker fee. Here's what you need to know to really cash in. $6

R91

EIGHT SELF-DEFEATING BEHAVIORS CRIPPLING YOUR MARKETING... AND HOW TO GET RID OF THEM AND MAKE MORE MONEY! After so many years monitoring the marketing programs of thousands of companies here and internationally, Jeffrey is firmly convinced that most "marketers" are continually shooting themselves in the foot. Here you learn the 8 key self-defeating behaviors that cripple profitable marketing and how to solve them so you can turn your marketing into a constant wealth-producing machine. $6

R92

EVERY SPEECH A SUCCESS: 12 THINGS YOU CAN DO RIGHT NOW TO MAKE SURE WHEN YOU SPEAK YOU'RE ALWAYS WELL RECEIVED. Every business day thousands of speeches and business presentations are made. Too many of them are failures. They don't persuade, don't motivate, and do not increase the reputation of the speaker. Don't let this be you. Every speech you ever give can and should be a success. Here Jeffrey provides just what you need so that it will be! $6

R93

DIM PROSPECTS: YOUR FATE IF YOU DON'T USE YOUR BUSINESS TO DEVELOP THE COMFORTABLE RETIREMENT INCOME YOU WANT. If you're lucky, you get old. But unless you plan, when you get old, you'll be like the vast majority of Americans who, having worked hard all their lives, retire to a significantly diminished income — with all the frustration and bitterness that entails. Here Jeffrey, an obsessive retirement planner, provides just what you need to turn your business into a certain means of producing the necessary pension capital and income you'll need for a substantial — not a pinched — retirement. Note: the younger you are, the more important it is for you to absorb this crucial report and follow the directions! $6

New! #R94

SIX SIMPLE THINGS YOU CAN DO RIGHT NOW TO MAKE MORE MONEY FROM YOUR MARKETING. Jeffrey provides you with six simple things you can do right now to make more money from your marketing. These are things that don't take any money (imagine!)... but are guaranteed to improve the return on your marketing investment. $6

New! #R95

HOW TO SELL YOUR PRODUCT TO CATALOGS AND CASH IN! Have you got a product and want to expand your market dramatically? Have you thought about selling through catalogs but weren't sure how to find sources and get your product accepted? Then you need this just-published report giving you precise instructions on how to sell to catalogs... and resources listing thousands of specialty catalogs. $6

New! #R96

HOW TO ARRANGE YOUR DAY FOR MAXIMUM MARKETING ADVANTAGE. One significant reason why so much of the marketing you do doesn't work... is because you aren't organized to work your marketing properly. Here Jeffrey lays down detailed suggestions on what you can do — every single day — to squeeze maximum advantage from the day and from all the marketing you do! $6

New! #R97

HOW TO MAKE A STEADY PROFIT FROM NATIONWIDE LEAD-GENERATOR CARDS. If you have a product or service you're selling nationwide, this special report is for you! It lays out, in Jeffrey's characteristically detailed style, everything you need to do to profit from lead-generator cards that run in card-decks nationwide. Note: whether you're a big advertiser or a small one with very limited resources, you need this special report if you're doing national advertising... or want to add it to your marketing mix. $6

New! #R98

WHY SALES CONTESTS WILL MOTIVATE YOUR TELEMARKETERS TO SELL MORE — AND 7 IDEAS TO HELP YOU RUN THEM THE RIGHT WAY. Jeffrey interviews telemarketing sales contest guru David L. Worman, author of the new book *"Motivating With Sales Contests: Motivating Your Telephone Professionals With Contests That Produce Record-Breaking Records."* Step-by-step guidelines for making your contests make you money! If you have more than 4 telemarketing reps in your office, then this report is for you. $6

... HERE'S WHAT YOU NEED IF YOU'VE GOT LESS THAN AN HOUR TO GET SMARTER...

Right between Special Reports (Jeffrey's unique contribution to get-ahead literature) and full-scale books, are Crisp publications. You've probably seen them. Thousands and thousands of businesses and professionals have made them best sellers. What's different about them is that they take less than one hour to read (Mike Crisp bills them as the 50-minute publications), have sensible, easy-to-follow information you can put to work immediately... and are good value. I've listed below as many as I could pack into this space. With Crisp, the title says it all... you don't need a lengthy description. (All Crisp item numbers begin with CR. Please make sure to include complete number on the order form on page 32.)

#CR1

LEADERSHIP SKILLS FOR WOMEN by Marilyn Manning, Ph.D. Provides details on the essential factors that help women become business leaders. 88 pages. $10.95

#CR2

DELEGATING FOR RESULTS by Robert Maddux. If you're overwhelmed, you need to delegate. Here are the key elements of successful delegation. 80 pages. $10.95

#CR3

INCREASING EMPLOYEE PRODUCTIVITY. Of course you want to get more benefit out of your employees. Lynn Tylczak shows you how. 100 pages. $10.95

#CR4

AN HONEST DAY'S WORK: MOTIVATING EMPLOYEES TO GIVE THEIR BEST. My friend Twyla Dell knows that if your employees aren't motivated, they can't produce. She shows you how to motivate your employees to increase their productivity. 80 pages. $10.95

#CR5

MANAGING FOR COMMITMENT: BUILDING LOYALTY WITHIN AN ORGANIZATION. This practical book by Dr. Carol Goman shows you how to build a level of commitment and loyalty with today's new, more independent workforce. 96 pages. $10.95.

#CR6

TRAINING METHODS THAT WORK by Dr. Lois Hart. Want to sharpen your training skills? In just 96 pages you'll learn how. $10.95.

#CR7

RECRUITING VOLUNTEERS: A GUIDE FOR NONPROFITS. Carl Liljenstolpe knows that your nonprofit needs extra volunteer help. Here's how you get it. 100 pages. $10.95

#CR8

STEPPING UP TO SUPERVISOR. Revised edition by Marion Haynes. If you want to become a supervisor or have just become one, here's what you need to make a success of your position. 280 pages. $17.95

#CR9

NO MORE MISTAKES. Twenty four techniques for doing things right the first time. 48 pages. $5.95 (I'm applying for a govt. grant to give every congressperson a copy!)

#CR10

PLAN YOUR WORK — WORK YOUR PLAN. James Sherman shows you how to plan and get what you want. 96 pages. $10.95

#CR11

DEVELOPING POSITIVE ASSERTIVENESS by Sam Lloyd. If you're the mouse who can't roar (or know one of these poor creatures), learn how to develop the positive assertiveness you need to get ahead on the job or in life. 80 pages. $10.95

#CR12

MANAGING ANGER by Dr. Rebecca Luhn. Here you get the methods you need to manage your emotions in a positive manner. 90 pages. $10.95

#CR13

GUIDE TO AFFIRMATIVE AC-TION. Pamela Conrad gives you guidelines supported by case studies to ensure that managers make correct decisions on affirmative action, equal employment opportunity, age and sex discrimination and sexual harassment. 96 pages. $10.95

#CR14

YOUR FIRST THIRTY DAYS: BUILDING A PROFESSIONAL IMAGE IN A NEW JOB. Elwood Chapman shows you how to adjust with greater confidence. If you're new, get off to the right start. 96 pages. $10.95

#CR15

QUALITY INTERVIEWING. Robert Maddux' best-selling book helps you master interviewing skills that will lead to sound hiring decisions. 72 pages $10.95

#CR16

PROFESSIONAL EXCELLENCE FOR SECRETARIES. Marilyn Manning provides the information a professional secretary needs so office work gets done promptly and right. 80 pages. $10.95

#CR17

GIVING AND RECEIVING CRITI-CISM by Patti Hathaway. There are right ways and wrong ways to give it... and to take it. Here they are. 96 pages $10.95

#CR18

WELLNESS IN THE WORKPLACE: HOW TO DEVELOP A COMPANY WELLNESS PROGRAM. Merlene Sherman provides the components of an effective health program with case studies, resources, diagrams, inventories, examples and strategies. 100 pages. $10.95

#CR19

BALANCING HOME AND CAREER: SKILLS FOR SUCCESSFUL LIFE MANAGEMENT. Pamela Conrad's revised edition is for busy people who have to juggle. Includes chapters on home, business, travel and relocation. Shows you how to put quality time where you want it. 80 pages. $10.95

#CR20

OVERCOMING ANXIETY by Lynn Fossum. Anxiety is one of the most common problems medical doctors encounter. Learn what anxiety is and is not and how to overcome it. 96 pages. $10.95

#CR21

PREVENTING JOB BURNOUT by Dr. Beverly Potter. Burnout is a terrifically common problem in all businesses these days. Here are 8 proven strategies to beat job burnout and help you deal with the pressures of your job. 80 pages. $10.95

#CR22

FIRST AID ESSENTIALS. Written by the National Safety Council, you get the latest information on how to deal with a wide variety of injuries and emergency situations. Quick emergency index so you'll know what to do when problems arise. Should be in every business — and home. 222 pages. $11.95

#CR23

MAKING HUMOR WORK. Dr. Terry Paulson shows you how to use humor in the workplace with problem-solving, defusing resistance to change, disarming anger, and improving memory. 108 pages. $10.95

#CR24
FORMATTING LETTERS AND MEMOS ON THE COMPUTER. Dr. Eleanor Davidson has written this for computer beginners. Offers tips and exercises for designing letters, reports and memos on the computer. 90 pages. $10.95

#CR25
BUSINESS REPORT WRITING by Susan Brock. A super quick guide for writing business reports and proposals. Teaches how to organize, research, develop and edit winning documents. 90 pages. $10.95

#CR26
SPEEDREADING IN BUSINESS by Joyce Turley. Of course, you have more to read. So, you either skip it (and stay uninformed)... or learn speedreading HERE! 96 pages $10.95

#CR27
EXHIBITING AT TRADESHOWS. Susan Friedman shows you how to gain a competitive edge at a tradeshow in a cost-effective manner. 90 pages. $10.95

#CR28
CALMING UPSET CUSTOMERS by Rebecca Morgan. You're going to have them, so let author Morgan show you how to deal with both a disturbed and an upset customer. (No, they're not the same!) 74 pages. $10.95

#CR29
STARTING YOUR NEW BUSINESS by Charles Martin. If you're just getting your toe in the water, get this. In addition to a thorough discussion of the basics, includes superb annotated bibliography pointing you to lots of other helpful materials. 110 pages. $10.95

#CR30
EFFECTIVE NETWORKING by Venda Raye-Johnson. Shows you how to use networking to share information, resources and support to build and maintain effective career and personal relationships. 96 pages. $10.95

#CR31
SUCCESSFUL NEGOTIATION by Robert Maddux. Learn the basics of "win-win" negotiations. Save money, time and achieve satisfaction by learning to negotiate profitably. 72 pages. $10.95

#CR32
TRAINING MANAGERS TO TRAIN by Brother Herman Zaccarelli. A key element of any manager's job is training. This practical 96 page book teaches how to prepare for, plan, present and follow up on training programs. $10.95

#CR33
PRACTICAL TIME MANAGEMENT by Marion E. Hayes. Tells you how to plan, delegate and analyze time utilization, both on the job and at home. 138 pages. $13.95

#CR34
STOP PROCRASTINATING by James R. Sherman. The title says it all. If you can't seem to either get started or get finished, get this 72 page book. If you're so far gone you can't order either, get a friend or co-worker to do it for you! $10.95

#CR35
CONCENTRATION!: HOW TO FOCUS FOR SUCCESS by Sam Horn. Concentration is one of the crucial keys of success. This book helps develop the necessary mental discipline to keep the mind from wandering... and keep you focused on what you've got to do. 96 pages. $10.95

#CR36
MANAGING ANGER by Rebecca Luhn, Ph.D. If you find yourself getting angry... or know someone in your home or office who does, get this handy 90 page book and get help correcting this corrosive problem. $10.95

#CR37
ATTACKING ABSENTEEISM by Lynn Tylczak. Owners and Managers, if absenteeism is bugging you, get this book now. $30 billion a year is lost to

American businesses through absenteeism. Here's practical advice to reduce it — and your problem! $10.95

#CR38

STOP IT NOW! by Ken Cooper, Ph.D. This best-selling book provides thoughtful ways for managers and targets to end sexual harassment. 223 pages. $12.95

#CR39

EMPLOYEE BENEFITS WITH COST CONTROL by Rebecca Luhn, Ph.D. One of the most critical issues organizations face today is deciding what benefits plan it can afford to offer its employees. Key topics in this 90 page book include life and health insurance plans, employee retirement plans and many other benefit plans. $10.95

#CR40

JOB PERFORMANCE AND CHEMICAL DEPENDENCY by Robert B. Maddux. Case studies and exercises help managers and supervisors learn about chemical dependency in the workplace and how to deal with it. How to recognize performance problems caused by chemical dependency, use performance appraisal to discuss these problems, find professional help and gain a worker's commitment to correct the problem. 96 pages. $10.95

#CR41

VISUAL AIDS IN BUSINESS by Claire Raines. 88 pages show you how to use visual communications in the board room, at a management conference, in a training session or as part of regular staff meetings. $10.95

#CR42

DESKTOP DESIGN by Laura Lamar. For individuals who already understand the basics of typography, printing and graphics, this book presents the fundamental concepts of desktop publishing as related to desktop design, including hardware, software and the "environment" of the desktop. Includes information on MacWrite, SuperPaint and Illustrator and a page layout program. Basics of printing for desktop and how to create color separations on a computer. 96 pages. $11.95

60 Money-Making Minutes with Jeffrey (on tape)

#T3

HOW TO GET FREE TIME ON RADIO AND T.V. AND USE IT TO GET YOUR PROSPECTS TO BUY WHAT YOU'RE SELLING. Listen as Jeffrey gives you the secrets of getting valuable free time on radio and television so you can sell your products and services without spending any of your money. Getting on *just one* program could return your investment dozens of times! $16

#T4

HOW TO CREATE MARKETING DOCUMENTS THAT GET YOUR PROSPECTS TO BUY WHAT YOU'RE SELLING ... NOW! Since you spend thousands of dollars on your marketing documents, don't you think you should know what will get

people to respond to them faster ... to buy what you're selling **NOW**? Here's just what you need to know. $16

#T5

ESSENTIALS OF MONEY MAKING MARKETING: WHAT YOU'VE REALLY GOT TO DO TO SELL YOUR PRODUCTS AND SERVICES, EVERY DAY! Jeffrey shares his secrets of successful marketing, what you've got to do, when and how you've got to do it to sell your products and services. $16

#C3

ALL THREE OF JEFFREY'S 60 MINUTE AUDIO CASSETTES (T3, T4, T5). Just $38. You save $10!

If any of these conditions apply to you... you need an electronic moving message display unit NOW!

- you've got cash registers;
- you've got a waiting room where your customers wait to see you;
- sidewalk traffic passes your establishment;
- you've got a streetside location;
- you go to trade shows
- you need to communicate messages to your employees (like safety messages to assembly line personnel);
- you've got windows potential customers see...

Moving signs have been the rage for years in Europe and Japan... and they're increasingly popular here. Been to Las Vegas lately? You know what I mean!!!

These are the kinds of places electronic moving message display units make sense.

You've already seen them... in airports, banks, malls, airports, in schools, industrial settings... why the restaurant down the street from me has been pulling in customers with its moving sign for years.

For assistance in getting you the right moving sign at the right price, call Bill Reece, Nat'l Sales Manager, at (617) 278-4344 or by fax at (617) 547-0061. He'll help you find the sign that's just right for you... including making recommendations on a custom sign.

Dealer Opportunity: We are now setting up dealers nationwide to represent these signs. Interested in adding these easy-to-sell moving signs to your line? Or selling them alone? This is the right time to get into this profitable business... before the field is oversaturated, as it surely will be. For complete, no obligation details, contact Bill Reece above.

Once you've got your moving sign, get Jeffrey's special report on how to use them most effectively to make money faster.

#R83

SPECIAL NOTE FROM JEFFREY:

I'M CONSTANTLY ON THE LOOK-OUT FOR SUPERB BOOKLETS, BOOKS AND AUDIO AND VIDEO CASSETTES THAT WILL HELP YOU IMPROVE YOUR BUSINESS PROFITABILITY AND LIFE. IF YOU'RE A PUBLISHER WITH SUCH MATERIALS, GET IN TOUCH ASAP. WE PAY CASH WITH OUR ORDERS, NO CREDIT AND ARE ALWAYS HAPPY TO BRING GOOD THINGS TO OUR READERS.

READERS: HERE'S THE BEST OF WHAT I'M CURRENTLY RECOMMENDING FROM OTHER PUBLISHERS. BUY THEM AND SUPPORT THIS FINE WORK!

Finding Facts Fast

#B29

All of us are dependent on information, knowing where to find it and where to find it fast is important. That's why you need **FINDING FACTS FAST**, the best little book ever written on quick, economical information gathering. $7.45

Collecting Your $$$

#B46

You've got uncollected and uncollectible invoices sitting in your drawer right now. Makes you sick, right? Well, if you used the techniques in **PAYMENT IN FULL: A GUIDE TO SUCCESSFUL BILL COLLECTING**, some of them wouldn't be there. If you'd use it now, you can still collect on some of them. $29.95 is also a pretty fair price to pay to cut the anger you feel about the deadbeats who are ripping you off.

Consultants: More $ For You Here!

New! #B163

THE CONSULTANT'S GUIDE TO HIDDEN PROFITS. If you're a consultant and want to squeeze more money from what you do, Herman Holtz' new 230-page book is must reading. Use it to create and sustain a demand for your consulting services; pinpoint and eliminate shortcomings in sales volume; find hidden profits in all your marketing; rethink your "product line" and serve new clients — and much, much more. A real investment at $32.95

Making Niche Marketing Work For You!

New! #B164

MAKING NICHE MARKETING WORK: HOW TO GROW BIGGER BY ACTING SMALLER. This new 260-page paperback by Linneman & Stanton, Jr. will really help you rethink

your marketing and make more money. I've been using niche marketing for years — in my Sales & Marketing SuccessDek, non-profit books, and more — and this kind of thinking pays BIG DIVIDENDS. Shows you how to get started in niche marketing, how to build a niche-marketing database, how to create new niches, how to differentiate yourself, how to make regional marketing work, how to test, and much more. Just $19.95

Presentation Smarts

New! #B165

PRESENTATIONS PLUS: DAVID PEOPLES' PROVEN TECHNIQUES. God, but most people are hideous presenters. That's why I feel obliged as a public service to keep recommending resources to help our tongue-tied and leaden fellow citizens. Peoples' 288-page paperback will help! Handles the usual stuff found in these books but in a way that makes good sense: how to avoid the 7 deadly presentation mistakes; what to do about the butterflies in your stomach; getting your presentation organized for maximum effect; how to get attention and keep it; how to handle questions; how to handle troublemakers; how to rehearse... and how to get rid of your bad habits. (Yes, Cicero, you have them!) $19.95

> *Are you from Missouri? Or just cash poor? To see Jeffrey's books before you buy, go to any public library. They all stock some or all of Jeffrey's books... librarians constantly complain they are some of their most-stolen resources, a flattering recommendation!*

Making Money As A Writer

New! #B166

HOW TO START & RUN A WRITING & EDITING BUSINESS. I've included this new 253-page book by Holtz (who ought, by the way, to be giving me more credit in *his* books for all the write-ups I do on him) because most writers don't make any money. But that just isn't necessary. I make a very hefty six-figure income... Holtz, I know, does well, too. And his techniques make sense for turning your writing talent into a steady income. Tells you what writing and editing services people want to buy; writing for government markets; writing needs of businesses & professionals; how to get individual clients... and much more. You can become a millionaire with your writing skills... but you can't do it writing first person narratives about your housepets. $19.95

Your Parent's Financial Security

New! #B167

YOUR PARENT'S FINANCIAL SECURITY. If you're a baby boomer like me, your parents are using their senior citizen cards to get into the movies. That's nice, of course, but you — and they — need some real help. That's where Barbara Weltman's new 262-page book comes in. Tells you what you need to know about trusts, living wills, annuities, home care and housing alternatives, medicare and medicaid — and lots more. If you really care about your parents, you'll learn what's in this guide. $15.95

Motivating With Sales Contests

New! #B168

MOTIVATING WITH SALES CONTESTS: THE COMPLETE GUIDE TO MOTIVATING YOUR TELEPHONE PROFESSIONALS WITH CONTESTS THAT PRO-DUCE RECORD-BREAKING RESULTS. The title says it all in this new 252-page resource by telemarketing contest guru David L. Worman. If you have a team of telemarketers in your office who need inspiring, you need this resource featuring lots of helpful advice and 79 contests you can run right now. $32.00

Profitable Print Advertising

#B160

GREAT PRINT ADVERTISING: CREATIVE APPROACHES, STRAT-EGIES AND TACTICS. I ran this new 288-page book by print maven Tony Antin in my winter catalog without much success. The book deserves to sell more copies than I've moved so far... so here it is again. Tells you *exactly* what to do to move products and services through your print advertising; how to use appealing propositional benefits; how to layout your ads for maximum advantage; how to write headlines; how to condense; the kind of typography you should use, and much more. If you're going to use space ads... you're going to want Antin. $34.95

Making Money With Your Own 900 Number!

New! #B169

900 KNOW-HOW: HOW TO SUC-CEED WITH YOUR OWN 900 NUMBER BUSINESS. There are now several books on this subject on the market, but this little 174-page paperback by Bob Mastin makes sense to me. Provides the pros & cons of getting into the business; how to get off to a fast start; how to do marketing and market research; how to select a service bureau; financial projections; measure-ment and testing; contests, games and sweepstakes and much more. Just $21.95 **Note:** Don't forget you can call me at 1-900-446-6075 EXT. 855 ($2.95/MINUTE) to get focused, straight

answers to all your marketing and business development problems!

Slash Your Mortgage In Half

New! #B173

SLASH YOUR MORTGAGE IN HALF. This short, inexpensive 93-page booklet by Dr. Tag Powell will show you how to save tens of thousands of dollars off your mortgage — or your money back! I'm following techniques like these and have sliced over $100,000 so far off my mortgage *interest* payments. I know they work and that's why I'm recommending them to you now. If you'd like to keep a good sized chunk of the money that's now going monthly to your bank, send me just $14.00 for this helpful little guide.

Making Exhibits Work For You

New! #B170

EXHIBIT MARKETING: A SUR-VIVAL GUIDE FOR MANAGERS. Author Edward Chapman, Jr. knows that a ton of money gets wasted in the exhibit business. But, frankly, you just can't afford that kind of mindless expense. That's why you need this 306-page resource that deals with the whole exhibit process — from start to finish! I can't tell you all the good stuff that's in it... there's just too much. But you get the low-down on planning, opera-tions before, during and after the show, preparing an annual exhibit plan, establishing reachable objectives, time, productivity and space, exhibit budget and company costs and much more. If

you exhibit, send me $30.95 for this resource!

Selecting The Right Franchise

New! #B171

FRANCHISE SELECTION: SEPA-RATING FACT FROM FICTION. This unpretentious 212-page paperback from franchise specialist and lawyer Raymond J. Munna has got what you want... if you're even thinking of buying a franchise. Provides detailed information on all franchise categories; how to own your own business; advan-tages and disadvantages of franchising; how to protect yourself; how to select all the professionals you need to work with; locating potential hot franchises; laws affecting franchising... and much more. Lots of helpful names and addresses you'll need. $22.95

Generating Breakthrough Products

New! #B172

THE NEW PRODUCTS WORK-SHOP: HANDS-ON TOOLS FOR DEVELOPING WINNERS. Nobody gets rich working for someone else. Take my word for it. That's why you need to develop and profit from your own product. For this, Barry Feig's new 241-page resource will help. Contains what you need to know to generate breakthrough ideas; position new products; revitalize existing products; test products; name new products; price products to sell and a whole lot more. $31.95

Millions Edition **Order Form** *Complete 30-Day Money-Back Guarantee!*

Photocopy or return this page to: Dr. Jeffrey Lant, Jeffrey Lant Associates
P.O. Box 38-2767, Cambridge, MA 02238

CLEARLY write down the item number(s) of what you order here. Each item number is composed of a letter and a number. Please make sure to give both!

—— , —— , —— , —— , —— , —— , —— , —— , —— , —— , —— , —— , —— , —— , —— , —— , —— , —— , —— , ——

Remember, if you're ordering my Special Reports (#R1 – #R98), you get **any three for $14**. Individual Reports are $6 each.

Total your order here $ _____ . Are you a Massachusetts resident? ❑ Yes ❑ No

If so, add 5% sales tax here $ _____ .   Total enclosed $ _____ .

| Your Day Telephone |
| ( )_____ |

Shipping. If you are ordering books, tapes and Special Reports by Dr. Jeffrey Lant, they are sent the day you order (unless you are using a post office box address that is not guaranteed by a MC/VISA/AMEX). Other books are sent to you direct from their publishers by fourth class/book rate shipping. Allow four-six weeks. If you want them faster, add $3 per item for first class or UPS shipping. Remember: to ship UPS, I must have a street address!

Canada and overseas. If you want your items shipped to Canada, add $1 for *each* item ordered and $1 to the total for our bank's fees, even if you pay in U.S. dollars. If you want shipment to any other country, you must pay by credit card. I'll charge your account surface or air shipping, as you like. Check ❑ surface ❑ air.

Premiums. If your order totals at least $150, you can select any one of my three 60 minute audio cassettes as my gift to you. The three titles are listed on page 560. Write down the one you want here # _____. If your order totals over $275, you get your free audio cassette and any one of my eight "Get Ahead" books (#B1 – #B7 & # B9) or **Development Today** (#B8). List the item number of the one you want here _____. Remember to get these free premiums, you must order from this catalog by 10/01/94.

Payment & Billing. Unless you are a government agency, college, library or other official public organization (in which case, include your Purchase Order # here _____), COMPLETE PAYMENT MUST ACCOMPANY YOUR ORDER. I cannot invoice individuals and private businesses. If paying by check, make it payable to Jeffrey Lant Associates, Inc. If you are using a post office box number for shipment, I require a Master Card/VISA/AMEX number and expiration date to guarantee your check, or else I wait for the check to clear. Sadly, several rip-off artists use post office boxes to defraud reputable merchants like me, so I have to inconvenience good people like you. You can also Fax your order to me at 617-547-0061.

If paying by credit card (or using a post office box for shipment):

✓ ❑ MasterCard   ❑ VISA   ❑ AMEX   #_____

Expiration date_____   Signature_____

For faster service, place your order by telephone twenty-four hours a day at (617) 547-6372. (Yes, I really do answer my own phone.) Before calling make sure your credit card is handy. The order tape doesn't last forever! **Speak clearly!**

Your books and materials will be sent to the address on the shipping label below, unless you indicate otherwise. Please be clear about where you want your items sent.

Send materials to:

Name _____

Organization _____

Street Address _____

City _____ State _____ Zip _____

Telephone (_____) _____

Millions
Edition **Order Form** *Complete 30-Day Money-Back Guarantee!*

Photocopy or return this page to: Dr. Jeffrey Lant, Jeffrey Lant Associates
P.O. Box 38-2767, Cambridge, MA 02238

CLEARLY write down the item number(s) of what you order here. Each item number is composed of a letter and a number. Please make sure to give both!

———, ———,

Remember, if you're ordering my Special Reports (#R1 – #R98), you get **any three for $14**. Individual Reports are $6 each.

Total your order here $ _____. Are you a Massachusetts resident? ❏ Yes ❏ No

If so, add 5% sales tax here $ _____.   Total enclosed $ _____.

Your Day Telephone
( )_____

Shipping. If you are ordering books, tapes and Special Reports by Dr. Jeffrey Lant, they are sent the day you order (unless you are using a post office box address that is not guaranteed by a MC/VISA/AMEX). Other books are sent to you direct from their publishers by fourth class/book rate shipping. Allow four-six weeks. If you want them faster, add $3 per item for first class or UPS shipping. Remember: to ship UPS, I must have a street address!

Canada and overseas. If you want your items shipped to Canada, add $1 for *each* item ordered and $1 to the total for our bank's fees, even if you pay in U.S. dollars. If you want shipment to any other country, you must pay by credit card. I'll charge your account surface or air shipping, as you like. Check ❏ surface ❏ air.

Premiums. If your order totals at least $150, you can select any one of my three 60 minute audio cassettes as my gift to you. The three titles are listed on page 560. Write down the one you want here # _____. If your order totals over $275, you get your free audio cassette and any one of my eight "Get Ahead" books (#B1 – #B7 & # B9) or **Development Today** (#B8). List the item number of the one you want here _____. Remember to get these free premiums, you must order from this catalog by 10/01/94.

Payment & Billing. Unless you are a government agency, college, library or other official public organization (in which case, include your Purchase Order # here _____), COMPLETE PAYMENT MUST ACCOMPANY YOUR ORDER. I cannot invoice individuals and private businesses. If paying by check, make it payable to Jeffrey Lant Associates, Inc. If you are using a post office box number for shipment, I require a Master Card/VISA/AMEX number and expiration date to guarantee your check, or else I wait for the check to clear. Sadly, several rip-off artists use post office boxes to defraud reputable merchants like me, so I have to inconvenience good people like you. You can also Fax your order to me at 617-547-0061.

If paying by credit card (or using a post office box for shipment):

✓ ❏ MasterCard   ❏ VISA   ❏ AMEX #_____

     Expiration date_____   Signature_____

For faster service, place your order by telephone twenty-four hours a day at (617) 547-6372. (Yes, I really do answer my own phone.) Before calling make sure your credit card is handy. The order tape doesn't last forever! **Speak clearly!**

Your books and materials will be sent to the address on the shipping label below, unless you indicate otherwise. Please be clear about where you want your items sent.

Send materials to:

Name _____

Organization _____

Street Address _____

City _____ State _____ Zip _____

Telephone ( )_____

mlib